Feminist Issues

RACE, CLASS, AND SEXUALITY

FIFTH EDITION

EDITED BY

Nancy Mandell

York University

Pearson Canada
Toronto

Library and Archives Canada Cataloguing in Publication

Feminist issues : race, class and sexuality / edited by Nancy Mandell. — 5th ed.

Includes index.
ISBN 978-0-13-514668-2

1. Feminism. 2. Women—Social conditions. I. Mandell, Nancy

HQ1206.F445 2010   305.4   C2008-905779-1

ISBN-13: 978-0-13-514668-2
ISBN-10: 0-13-514668-2

Vice President, Editorial Director: Gary Bennett
Editor-in-Chief: Ky Pruesse
Senior Acquisitions Editor: Laura Forbes
Marketing Manager: Arthur Gee
Associate Editor: Megan Burns
Production Editors: Susan Broadhurst, Kevin Leung
Copy Editor: Molly Wolf
Proofreader: Susan Broadhurst
Production Coordinator: Lynn O'Rourke
Composition: Laserwords
Art Director: Julia Hall
Cover Image: veer Inc.

7 8 9   14 13 12

Printed and bound in Canada.

Contents

Notes on Contributors *iv*
Preface *vii*
Acknowledgments *viii*
Introduction *ix*

PART 1   CHALLENGING BORDERS AND RESISTING BOUNDARIES

Chapter 1   Liberal, Socialist, and Radical Feminism: An Introduction to Three Theories about Women's Oppression and Social Change   1

Chapter 2   An Introduction to Feminist Poststructural Theorizing   40

Chapter 3   Third-Wave Feminisms   63

Chapter 4   Feminist Theorizing on Race and Racism   87

PART 2   WOMEN'S EXPERIENCES

Chapter 5   Strange Sisters in No Man's Land: Still Thinking Sex 26 Years Later   110

Chapter 6   Exacting Beauty: Exploring Women's Body Projects and Problems in the 21st Century   131

Chapter 7   Violence against Women   161

Chapter 8   From "Little Lady" to "Little Old Lady": Women and Aging   197

PART 3   RESTRUCTURING INSTITUTIONS

Chapter 9   Mothers' Maintenance of Families through Market and Family Care Relations   219

Chapter 10   Women and Education   247

Chapter 11   Underpinnings and Understandings of Girls' and Women's Health   272

Chapter 12   Women and Religion: Female Spirituality, Feminist Theology, and Feminist Goddess Worship   298

Weblinks *333*

Index *335*

Notes on Contributors

SHANA L. CALIXTE is a PhD candidate in the School of Women's Studies at York University in Toronto. She holds an MA in Women's Studies and a Bachelor of Journalism and Women's Studies from Carleton University in her home city, Ottawa. Her current academic work explores histories of Caribbean Girl Guide movements, focusing on the intersections of girlhood, sexuality, and empire-building within this colonial organization. She currently teaches in the Women's Studies Department at Thorneloe College, Laurentian University.

ANN DUFFY is Professor, Department of Sociology, Brock University, where she is also cross-appointed to the Labour Studies Program and is active in the Masters in Social Justice and Equity Studies Program. Her research interests include women and violence, gendered patterns of employment, and women and aging. Her published work includes *Canadian Society* (co-edited), *Good Jobs, Bad Jobs, No Jobs* (co-edited), *Family Violence: A Canadian Introduction,* and *Connection, Compromise and Control: Canadian Women Discuss Midlife* (co-authored). She is currently completing a co-edited collection on work in the "new economy."

AMBER GAZSO is Assistant Professor, Department of Sociology, York University. Her research interests include: feminist conceptualizations of the family; transformations in intimate relations; individualization and risk society theory; social citizenship, social policy and the welfare state; and the feminization and racialization of poverty. Her recent publications focus on transformations in mothers' and fathers' social citizenship rights to social assistance and subsequent changes in their market and family care relations. Her current research explores how diverse families manage poverty intergenerationally through networks of social support.

DIANA L. GUSTAFSON is Associate Professor, Faculty of Medicine, and affiliate faculty, Department of Women's Studies, Memorial University. These positions allow her pursue her commitment to health-related equity and social justice issues in teaching, research, and community life. Her concern for the health needs of marginalized populations has resulted in publications about newcomer women, Aboriginal and Labradorean peoples, people who inject drugs, and the elderly disabled. Her book, *Unbecoming Mothers: The Social Construction of Maternal Absence* (2005), explores how women negotiate their lives apart from their children and how they recreate their identities and family structures.

JENNIFER L. JOHNSON is a lecturer in Women's Studies, Thorneloe College, Laurentian University, and a PhD candidate at the School of Women's Studies at Toronto's York University. She holds degrees from Queen's University and the University of Oxford. Her research focuses on international trade relations between Canada and the English-speaking Caribbean, using feminist anti-imperialist critiques of globalization. She has worked at Canada's federal Department of Foreign Affairs and International Trade, assisting in research on the export activities of Canadian businesswomen. She acts as management counsel on gender equity in sound management practice at the Manitoba Institute of Management. Her publications include research on the impact of globalization on local communities and the history of women's education in Canada.

LARA KARAIAN is a PhD candidate in the School of Women's Studies at York University in Toronto. She holds an MA in Women's Studies (York) and an Honours Bachelor of Sociology and Criminology (University of Toronto). Her research interests include: feminist, postmodern, and queer legal theory; critical legal strategies; and anti-oppression activism through the use of the *Canadian Charter of Rights and Freedoms* and Canadian human rights law. Lara is a co-editor of *Turbo Chicks: Talking Young Feminisms* (Sumach, 2001) and was a member of the guest editorial board for *Canadian Woman Studies'* Young Women: Feminists, Activists, Grrrls issue (20–21[1], 2001).

NANCY MANDELL teaches in the Sociology and Women's Studies programs at York University. She has published on a variety of topics: midlife women's experiences of intimacy and family; gendered social capital; parental involvement in children's schoolwork; academic-community research partnerships; violence against women; and the feminization of poverty in Canada.

ALLYSON MITCHELL is an Assistant Professor in the School of Women's Studies at York University. Her research interests include body image and size activism, geographies of power, independent cultural production, and queer art and politics. Her writing is published in *Brazen Femme: Queering Femininity* (Arsenal, 2002), *Fat: The Anthropology of an Obsession* (Penguin, 2002), and the forthcoming *Extra/ordinary: Craft Culture and Contemporary Art* (Duke, 2008), as well as various independent publications. Allyson is an internationally exhibited visual artist and filmmaker. Her lesbian feminist sasquatch monsters can be seen on her website **www.allysonmitchell.com**, and her films can be previewed at **www.cfmdc.org**.

MAKI MOTAPANYANE is a PhD candidate in Women's Studies at York University. Her research interests include the history of feminist theory and practice in South Africa, women's movements of the global South, and the politics of transnational feminist coalitions. She has published academically on Canadian women in hip hop. Her poetry appears in a number of independent Canadian publications, audio recordings, and performances for Canadian Atlantic Jazz festivals and productions.

BOBBY NOBLE is an Assistant Professor in the Sexuality Studies program, housed in the School of Women's Studies at York University (Toronto). Bobby is the author of the recently published monograph *Sons of the Movement: FtMs Risking Incoherence in a Post-Queer Cultural Landscape* (Women's Press, 2006). He is also the author of the monograph *Masculinities Without Men?* (University of British Columbia Press, 2004), listed as a Choice Outstanding Title, 2004; and was co-editor of *The Drag King Anthology,* a 2004 Lambda Literary Finalist (Harrington Press, 2003).

RAIMUNDA REECE is currently a PhD candidate in the School of Women's Studies at York University. Her research focuses on exploring how Canadian capitalist regimes of incarceration and detention are mediated through a racialized and gendered lens in relation to federally sentenced Black women in Canada. She has coordinated projects and conducted workshops that focus on ethno-racial and culturally conscious approaches to eradicating violence against women and children. In addition, she works as the Women's Prison Worker for the Prisoners with HIV/AIDS Support Action Network. She is a member of the Prisoners' Justice Action Committee.

CARLA RICE is an Associate Professor in Women's Studies at Trent University where she lectures in culture, health, and psychology. A Canadian leader in the field of body image, she is a founding member and former director of innovative initiatives such as the National Eating Disorder Information Centre and the Body Image Project at Women's

College Hospital in Toronto. She has worked with school boards, teachers' organizations, public health departments, industry, and governments at all levels to develop ground-breaking body positive programs for children, adolescents, and adult women. Her award-winning research explores body image as not only a health but also an equity issue. Currently, she is working on *Envisioning New Meanings of Disability and Difference*, a photography and digital storytelling project designed to give women with disabilities and physical differences the opportunity through their words and images to depict difference in a bold new way. Upcoming projects include a book that explores women's diverse narratives of embodiment.

LISA ROSENBERG is Adjunct Professor in the School of Women's Studies at York University. She has recently taught courses entitled "Women's Lives Today: Issues and Experiences," "Introduction to Women's Studies," and "Male Violence against Women and Children," including an activist component. She has lectured, presented papers, and published in the area of male violence. Her chapter on male violence against women in the Jewish community will be published shortly by Woman's Press in an edited collection examining the impact of male violence on women in diverse communities in Canada.

SHARON ROSENBERG is Associate Professor in Theory/Culture, Department of Sociology at the University of Alberta. She primarily teaches courses in contemporary feminist and queer theorizing, critiques of modernity, and loss, trauma, and memorialization; she was recently named in *Maclean's* Guide to Canadian Universities as one of the University of Alberta's most popular instructors. Key publications include: *Between Hope and Despair: Pedagogy and the Remembrance of Historical Trauma*, with Roger I. Simon and Claudia Eppert, editors (Rowman and Littlefield, 2000) and *Troubling Women's Studies: Pasts, Presents and Possibilities*, co-authored with Ann Braithwaite, Susan Heald, and Susanne Luhmann (Sumach Press, 2004). She was guest editor of *torquere* (vol. 6, 2004/5) on "Memorializing queers/queering remembrances." Forthcoming work includes essays in *The Future of Memory* (Berghan Books) and *Democracy in Crisis* (University of Manchester Press).

JOHANNA H. STUCKEY is Professor Emerita in the Humanities Division and the Religious Studies Program, Faculty of Arts, and in the Graduate Program in Women's Studies at York University. Before retirement she taught many courses on Goddess worship and female spirituality at York University and at the School of Continuing Studies, University of Toronto. In 1998 she published a book entitled *Feminist Spirituality: An Introduction to Feminist Theology in Judaism, Christianity, Islam, and Feminist Goddess Worship* (Centre for Feminist Research, York University), which she is currently revising. She is also working on a new book on goddesses and "dying" gods.

MICHELLE WEBBER is an Associate Professor in Sociology at Brock University. She teaches courses on the sociology of education and the sociology of gender. Her research interests include higher education, the work of academics, and gender. Her current research (with Sandra Acker and Elizabeth Smyth, University of Toronto) explores the regulation of academic work and academic subjectivities through the tenure process in Ontario universities.

SUSANNAH WILSON is Professor in the School of Nutrition at Ryerson University where she teaches courses in research methods, professional practice, and nutrition communication. Her recent research has focused on women's health and well-being. Recent published work includes analyses of midlife women in Canada and caregiving through the life course with Nancy Mandell and Ann Duffy. A longitudinal qualitative project has explored the role of spirituality in breast cancer treatment and recovery.

Preface

This fifth edition provides an update on trends and recent developments in women's studies. Building on the strengths of the fourth edition, contributors have revised their original pieces, providing theoretical and substantive overviews of the most up-to-date material in their fields. Authors explore the range and diversity of contemporary feminist perspectives as seen through the lens of race, class, sexuality, disability, and poverty. Each chapter addresses questions and social problems that have received little attention in Canadian writing. The lives of previously forgotten and silenced women are brought to the forefront as their experiences of work, family, violence, sexuality, aging, health, religion, and education are examined. New to this edition, Weblinks for each topic are collected in an appendix at the end of the book for easy reference. The result is an innovative, challenging, and comprehensive survey of Canadian feminist issues today.

Undergraduate students should find this book particularly accessible because authors have been asked to present their arguments in as clear and compelling a fashion as possible. Our purpose is to answer a number of central questions: How is a particular topic a feminist issue? What has feminist research in health care and religion, for instance, discovered as systemic and persistent biases against women? How has feminism addressed the inequities revealed through feminist analyses? What sorts of personal and institutional responses have been taken to redress the mislabelling and misdirection of women, such as gender tracking in high schools? And, finally, what are the immediate and long-term consequences of feminist intervention and analysis? Has the discovery of the "double day" of wage and domestic labour, for which women are responsible, in fact lessened or redistributed women's load? Students, as members of groups usually ignored and as members of institutional settings in which they are often muffled, may find, for the first time, their lives, their experiences, their feelings, and their histories explored. Students may find in this text revelations that are unsettling, contentious, validating, and liberating—it is unlikely they will emerge untouched.

Putting this book together has been a profound privilege and pleasure. An excellent group of contributors has broadened previous feminist critiques by incorporating debates about race, class, sexuality, disability, poverty, and violence into everyday explanations of women's omission and oppression. Struggling with mainstream definitions and attempting to expand the boundaries of feminist understanding is challenging.

CourseSmart

CourseSmart is a new way for instructors and students to access textbooks online anytime from anywhere. With thousands of titles across hundreds of courses, CourseSmart helps instructors to choose the best textbook for their class and give their students a new option for buying the assigned textbook as a lower-cost eTextbook. For more information, visit **www.coursesmart.com**.

Acknowledgments

Numerous people have read and edited versions of these chapters, suggesting significant improvements. I extend, once again, a very special note of appreciation to Johanna Stuckey, my favourite women's studies teaching partner and the inspiration for this book. At Pearson we would like to thank Laura Forbes, Megan Burns, Kevin Leung, Susan Broadhurst, Molly Wolf, and Lynn O'Rourke. They have nurtured this book and intervened at important moments to ensure its successful completion. We are grateful to the following reviewers for their thoughtful comments and suggestions: Susan Driver, Didi Khayatt, and Andil Gosine, York University; Cheryl Gosselin, Bishop's University; Fiona MacGregor, University of Calgary; Margaret Hobbs, Trent University; Rhonda Semple, University of Northern British Columbia; Vivian Shalla, University of Guelph; Tonya Callaghan, University of Toronto; and Natalie Beausoleil, Memorial University of Newfoundland. My deepest gratitude to the feminist men in my life—Lionel, Jeremy, Ben, and Adam—and to the new feminist women who have joined our family, Marissa and Caroline. I cherish your continued love, humour, and good common sense.

Introduction

Most young Canadian women and men have grown up in a world in which feminism as a social and ideological movement is firmly established. Contemporary youth have lived with feminist mothers struggling to juggle work and family lives. They had high school and university teachers who integrated feminist perspectives in their courses. They have been exposed to countless songs and images on television and in magazines that gesture toward feminism and to an ample selection of non-traditional role models in all walks of life. Feminism has infiltrated our understanding of everyday life to such an extent that, as Mary Evans (1997) said, you would have had to have been living on Mars not to have been touched by feminism.

Yet how do young women feel about feminism, and how do they experience it in their everyday lives? Although Canadian evidence is scant, studies from abroad reveal interesting patterns. In her interviews with 33 young women aged 16–20, Budgeon (2001) shows that young women feel alienated from the second-wave feminist movement, even though their identities have been informed by its feminist ideals. Bulbeck (2001) tells us that in Australia, liberal or equality feminism has significant purchase as a structural way to identify women's subordination, including explanations of patriarchy and class, but that feminism has had less of an impact at the level of consciousness and policy. Letherby and Marchbank (2001) review feminist discourses female students hear from other women's studies students revealing a legacy of ambivalence, contradiction, backlash, and marketing. Volman and ten Dam (1998) in their study of high school students in the Netherlands, reveal that even though young women and men consider gender equity the norm, traditional and often contradictory discourses on masculinity and femininity remain intact.

All of these studies show that discourses of gender difference clash with emancipation or equality discourses. Although many young adults consider equity to have been achieved, they are unaware of the ways in which traditional discourses shape their expectations and experiences. Somehow it seems old-fashioned now to talk as though gender inequity existed. Liberal notions of individuals freely choosing their fates clash with feminist notions of structured inequality. As Volman and ten Dam's (1998) students put it, it's okay to explain history using discourses of feminism or inequality because "everyone knows" it was bad back then. But now that equality has been achieved, if men and women "choose" different fields, it is because they want to be in these areas or because their innate talents have led them down different family and career paths. However, when these same students come face to face with inexplicable conditions of inequality, contradiction, confusion, and ambivalence abound.

In this collection, we position women's issues at the forefront of Canadian concerns. In areas as diverse as romance, intimacy, law, education, work, beauty, spirituality, and violence, the role of women as equal participants is still uncertain. This is not to say that distinct achievements have not occurred. Women now outpace men in all areas of educational achievement. They get better grades and are more likely to achieve post-secondary education than are men. Paid work offers another glimpse into shifting gender patterns. Men, especially young men, are more likely to be unemployed and to work fewer hours than are their female counterparts (Statistics Canada, 2004). Structural changes in global economic patterns have precipitated a shift in Canadian workplace trends, but how do we account for the dramatic alteration in gendered patterns of education? And, why, given these spectacular shifts, have our ideological notions of women and men's roles in society not shifted as dramatically?

This fifth edition of *Feminist Issues* attempts to address contemporary changes in our ideas about equity. Although certainly not comprehensive, the 12 chapters in this book represent a wide range of concerns facing young Canadian women. The first section contains four chapters—three thoroughly revised and one new—by a range of young and exciting feminists who are theorizing social issues through the lens of modernism, postmodernism, and racism. The second section contains three entirely new chapters and one completely updated chapter that focus on women's experiences of exclusion and marginalization in areas of sexuality, beauty, aging, and violence. These chapters capture a range of women's experiences as they move through the life course. The final section contains two completely revised chapters and two new chapters that concentrate on the structural context within which women live, learn, work, worship, and receive health care.

It is important to understand the roots and diversity of women's concerns. Shana L. Calixte, Jennifer L. Johnson, and J. Maki Motapanyane begin the book by tracing the historical and social implications of the second-wave feminist thinking of liberal feminists, socialist feminists, and radical feminists. Chapter 1, "Liberal, Socialist, and Radical Feminism: An Introduction to Three Theories about Women's Oppression and Social Change," provides an accessible review of mainstream first- and second-wave feminist theories. Canadian feminism is now about 150 years old. Although "waves" overlap and distort, specific political issues arising in particular historical periods have mobilized women around a common set of concerns. First-wave feminism covers the time period from the mid-19th century to the end of the Second World War. It grew out of the enfranchisement movement as women began to recognize the limitations they faced without the vote. Second-wave feminism, covering the early 1950s to the early 1990s, grew out of the civil rights and anti-war movements. By showing the historical and social contexts within which feminist theories emerged, the authors examine how social, economic, and cultural arrangements shape our views of what causes women's subordination. Feminist theories are roadmaps through the complexity of structural and personal features contouring women's experiences. Theories provide ways to understand and criticize these understandings, thus ensuring that feminists continually sharpen and clarify their vision. Different political positions offer distinct ways of thinking about the causes of and solutions for women's oppression.

Theoretical approaches to feminist studies constantly shift. As feminist theorist Sharon Rosenberg tells us in Chapter 2, "An Introduction to Feminist Poststructural Theorizing," postmodernism has profoundly disrupted our thinking about gender and sexuality, moving us away from dichotomous depictions of gender as binary—two genders of male and female—and opened up possibilities of multiple and fluid genders. Transgendering now captures our thinking about the ways many individuals cross gender boundaries as they live their lives, enter relationships, and create intimate relationships. Gender is both more complex and more global than it appeared 10 years ago. Multiple discourses, contradictions, and active production of meaning on both an individual and social level together define possibilities for resistance and change. Gender is seen as a layered concept of symbolic constructions, social relations, and social organization. Rosenberg leads us slowly and carefully through postmodernism, showing us how to use recent theorizing about women in our everyday relationships.

Third-wave feminism began in the early 1990s and continues today. But what does it mean to claim third-wave identification? In Chapter 3, "Third-Wave Feminisms," Lara Karaian and Allyson Mitchell show how postmodern third-wavers embrace multiplicity and diversity in their enactment of feminism in their personal, political, and work lives. Just as there is not one feminism, there is not one feminist politic, social agenda, or economic objective. Rather, young women live, display, challenge, annoy, resist, disrupt, and support multiple feminisms and ways of being feminist. With their emphasis on pop feminism, Karaian and Mitchell detail multiple resistance tactics being undertaken by young feminists through alternative media representations in art, film, and zines. Personal narratives authored by young women explore the transformative ways women interrupt traditional stories of women's motives, means, and methods for living their lives. Turbo Chicks, Action Grrrls, and Pretty, Porky, and Pissed Off represent contemporary sites of cultural resistance. This chapter reveals the energy with which young women have revitalized and reshaped the women's movement, a process bound to enliven classroom discussions.

All nations and their practices have been affected by processes of economic, political, and cultural globalization. How has women's equality been advanced or retarded by these forces? In Chapter 4, "Feminist Theorizing on Race and Racism," Raimunda Reece "compares the experiences of First Nations and Black women in Canada to see how positionality and marginalization shape life chances. Beginning with a sociological understanding of race as a socially organized and socially organizing discourse, Reece looks at the economic, political, and social implications of race and racism in Canadian society. Historically, the formation of a Canadian empire required the genocidal colonization of First Nations women's bodies to conform to European ideas of domesticity and womanhood. Gendering the empire was essential in consolidating power over indigenous peoples (Reyes, 2002). Reece goes on to examine historic patterns of racialization as articulated in immigration laws, environmental racism, and violence against women. Domestic worker programs, educational and employment policies, citizenship rights, degradation of communities, and violence against women represent some of the key ways in which racism remains perpetuated (Brand, 1999; Ehrenreich and Hochschild, 2003). Reece's chapter provides a powerful critique of the ways in which discourses of domination collide with neo-liberal and neo-colonial forms of marginalization to ensure that white Anglos maintain privilege.

Chapter 5, "Strange Sisters in No Man's Land: Still Thinking Sex 26 Years Later" by Bobby Noble, discusses the dilemma between how one feels about sex and how one thinks a feminist ought to feel about sex. Situating sexuality as a social and political construction, Noble begins by taking readers through the "sex wars" debate of the second wave of the women's movement when feminists argued about what constituted "proper" feminist sexuality. With the emergence of postmodernist theory, debates about sexuality as essential or constructed dissolved as theorists began to envision multiple intersections between gender and sexuality resulting in multiple ways of being sexual and doing sex. Central to third-wave critiques is the concept of heteronormativity. Defined as both an ideological structure and a set of social and cultural practices, heteronormativity refers to a process in which certain norms, ideas, and ideals hold sway over embodied life, and provide coercive criteria for normal "men" and "women." Gendered and sexualized normativity also refers to the aims and aspirations that guide us, the precepts by which we are compelled to act or speak to one another, and the commonly held presuppositions by which we are oriented and which give direction to our actions (Butler, 2003). Female subjectivities are constituted in and through gendered practices of sexuality. Citing a wide range of diverse contemporary cultural practices, Noble deconstructs the multiple ways in which sexuality is embodied and displayed. The chapter provides a provocative call to third-wave feminists to rethink and reorient their theorizing of sexuality.

Chapter 6, "Exacting Beauty: Exploring Women's Body Projects and Problems in the 21st Century" by Carla Rice, takes us through the complex ways in which beauty standards are embodied, meaning the multiple ways in which women use their bodies to display their genders. Most women feel compelled to carve and starve their bodies into shapes that conform to North American standards of beauty. At all ages, women are fretting about how their bodies look because they know that society judges them by their appearance. Using her own original research, Rice focuses on weight, hair, breasts, and skin as embodying cultural meanings of difference and desirability. Image enhancement through continuous consumption means that women constantly work on themselves to achieve the best possible face, hair, and body that they can. Because beauty and aging remain gendered, raced, and abilist, evaluating themselves against cultural standards of beauty results in women always falling short of the ideal and feeling like social failures. Following Rice, we ask you to wonder why it is that, just as women have begun to achieve economic, social, and political power, are they being controlled, dominated, and ultimately diminished by impossibly exacting cultural standards of beauty?

As Lisa Rosenberg and Ann Duffy remind us in Chapter 7, "Violence against Women," fear of and exposure to violence binds all women together. Regardless of their class, race, sexual orientation, or education, all women are united in their vulnerability to victimization. On December 6, 1989, Canada experienced its first mass gendercide in the Montreal Massacre when 14 women were killed at the École Polytechnique, at the University of Montreal's School of Engineering. Rosenberg and Duffy document the global nature of violence, documenting how large numbers of girls and women worldwide are either exposed to or experience violence on a daily basis. Sexual violence, even against little girls, is not related to sexual needs. Victims are usually chosen because they are available and powerless—easy targets for male coercion and abuse. The greater women's social and individual powerlessness, the more likely they are to find themselves victimized. Native women face eight times the risk of family violence as non-Native women. Every day the newspapers report incidents of assault directed against women with disabilities, older women, and visible minority women. Despite advertising campaigns, shelters, violence hotlines, and police intervention, violence against women will only be ended when communities form broad political, economic, and social coalitions to end this horrifying national and international social problem.

Chapter 8, "From 'Little Lady' to 'Little Old Lady': Women and Aging" by Nancy Mandell, Ann Duffy, and Susannah Wilson, tackles the thorny issue of ageism in the women's movement. As Mandell notes, despite having four previous editions of this book, each of which has involved multiple authors and reviewers across the country, ageism has never been raised as a feminist issue that needs addressing. How do we account for this glaring omission? A pernicious ageism underlies the women's movement just as a pernicious sexism underlies theories of age. The combination of ageism and sexism result in the marginalization of older women. In this ground-breaking chapter, the authors begin with an overview of feminist age theories and outline their materialist and constructivist approach to understanding the intersection of age with gender, race, economics, disability, and sexuality. Looking at the material world of old women—their pensions, poverty, and economic insecurity—the authors discuss the economic implications of the impending age "tsunami."

Turning to caring as a form of labour, the authors then discuss the continuity of care work as a constant theme in women's lives. Despite myths of leisurely "golden years," many aging women spend the last years of their lives precisely as they have spent their middle years: caring for others (Calsanti, 2006). The chapter ends with a consideration of aging bodies. Wrinkles and lines and sagging bodies, are, by normative definitions of femininity, not shiny enough, not new enough, and certainly not slick enough to be considered beautiful. By ending with an analysis of aging bodies, the authors turn our attention to the ways bodies become sites for identity construction and control of women. We hope that this emphasis on the body will provide a bridge for younger and older women to unite against ageism and sexism.

Families and workplaces remain sites of intense feminist struggle. As places that offer warmth, security, and happiness, families initiate women into their most intense experiences of pain, oppression, and suffering. Gaining, sustaining, and working at intimacy has become, for many women, the central project of their lives. Yet women also need and want to be gainfully employed in order to obtain any measure of economic security; keeping a balance between intimacy and material security still cause women enormous difficulty (Hunsley, 2006; Pyper, 2006; Williams and Normand, 2003). In Chapter 9, "Mothers' Maintenance of Families through Market and Family Care Relations," Amber Gazso traces some of the ways feminists have theorized both work and family. Modern discourses of romance and intimacy continue to contour women's partnership dreams. While marriage is less popular statistically, same- and opposite-sex commitment remains strong. Cohabitation emerges as the new prelude to the marriage pattern taken up by most young people in their late 20s and early 30s. Canadians spend a lot of their lives trying to establish and maintain families. At the same time, women engage in paid labour their entire lives and increasingly are the primary wage earners in their families (Sussman and Bonnell, 2006). Rather than being an option, employment is a basic necessity for women, especially those who are responsible for children and relatives. Falling wages, increasing taxes, and economic restructuring have decreased the number of paid jobs available for men and increased those available for women, mostly in part-time, poorly paid service positions. Feminists have been central in deconstructing work as a site of emancipation for women. Racialized and immigrant women and those with disabilities face particular obstacles in finding employment. They do not have equitable access to training and education programs, and this restricts their access to the labour force. Moreover, sexual harassment and institutional racism keep groups of women marginalized, vulnerable, and literally shut out of certain workplaces and schools. By examining the gendered, raced, and sexualized nature of women's labour, Gazso reveals the complex ways in which work affects women's status.

Feminist analyses of schooling note an interesting dilemma: despite historically high rates of female academic achievement, women still earn less money than men in the labour force. Women's education seems to "buy" them less than that of men's. In Chapter 10, "Women and Education," Michelle Webber takes this dilemma as her starting point to investigate the ways in which traditional beliefs about women and men have been used as inappropriate and inequitable sorting and streaming mechanisms in education and employment. Beginning with primary school, Webber looks at how schools reproduce gender differences rather than diminishing them. Some kind of "gender tracking" (Mandell and Crysdale, 1993) appears to be at work, in which extensive gender segregation of domestic labour, schooling, and workplaces means that women and men live, work, and study in different areas. Exclusion from organized forms of knowledge remains a political battle. Its effects are revealed in the intersection of school and work, in the social reproduction processes by which gendered and raced subjects are prepared by schools to take up workplace positions.

In Chapter 11, "Underpinnings and Understandings of Girls' and Women's Health," health expert Diana Gustafson demonstrates that women's bodies remain contested terrain. Contrasting two approaches to women's health—the biomedical model and the population health model—Gustafson shows how both approaches to health and health care are socially constructed frameworks that reflect shifting understandings of what contributes to differences in health status between women and men and across groups of women. Eichler and Gustafson (1999) describe three main types of gender bias that exist in health research: androcentricity, gender insensitivity, and double standard. Gustafson uses these categories to illustrate how biomedical research constructs women as objects of health research. While the biomedical model locates disease causality in the individual, the population health approach, especially feminist versions thereof, is concerned with a wide range of factors that have an impact on the health of an entire population (Shields, 2004). As mediators of care, women translate broader cultural ideas and practices of health into the everyday personal performance of health in the home and the community. Gustafson provides a comprehensive, accessible, and thorough overview of women's health issues.

In Chapter 12, "Women and Religion: Female Spirituality, Feminist Theology, and Feminist Goddess Worship," feminist religious studies scholar Johanna Stuckey provides a detailed overview of women's insertion into traditional religions and their creation of female-centred worship. Focusing here on Christianity, Judaism, and Islam, Stuckey carefully outlines the principles and traditions of each religion. Using four categories of analysis—revisionist, reformist, revolutionary, and rejectionist—Stuckey evaluates women's attempts to feminize practice within each of these religions. Revisionist Christian theologians, for example, in recovering church history, have demonstrated that women were instrumental in establishing and spreading Christianity. Revisionist Jewish feminists have worked to effect change in *halakhah* Jewish law and *agunot* (women whose husbands refuse to give them a religious divorce or *get*). Muslim revisionist feminists re-interpret the Qur'an. They also examine the *hadiths*, the sayings of the Prophet Muhammad, which are often used to support and even justify *Sharia* (Muslim law) and sometimes question their authenticity. Others who work within traditional religions push the traditions to their limits, altering language and symbols of deity to include female imagery, sometimes importing language, imagery, and ritual from other traditions in their attempts to make their religion more inclusive. Still others reject the traditions, judging them to be irredeemably sexist, and set about creating new spiritual traditions. Stuckey ends her chapter with a review of the burgeoning interest in feminist Goddess worship. Beginning in the 1970s, Goddess worship circles ritualized sharing of experience, communal validation, and creation of safe and comfortable spaces for women. Myths, rituals, language, and practices began to emerge from this new religion or spiritual entity, created by women to empower and nurture women. Humans have always sought the spiritual to nourish their souls; Stuckey's overview reminds us that women continue to search for non-sexist ways to fulfill their spiritual needs.

CONCLUSION

Women's studies classrooms now comprise young women and men who assume gender equity is complete. Contemporary students represent a generation who have been raised by working mothers for whom the feminist movement has been a central force. Most Canadian women have or will experience the challenges of achieving equity in their personal and work lives. There is no going back to the post-war traditional thinking of "men's jobs" and "women's jobs." Indeed, current generations wouldn't even consider stepping backward. Those days are firmly in the past, but old ideologies die hard. Intimacy, sexuality, health and well-being, employment, and appearance are shaped by notions of gender, race, ability, and economics. Women are still held captive by norms and ideals of femininity. Women learn early in life that conforming to norms of femininity and being beautiful brings power and material rewards in the form of easier access to jobs and male wages. Accordingly, women starve, vomit, purge, and carve themselves up in order to become desirable sex objects at the same time as they wrap their lives around those of men in order to reap the benefits of access to male privilege.

This fifth edition brings together a lively and energetic series of debates about the nature of women's lives in a variety of contexts. Each chapter challenges traditional stereotypes as discursive constructions underscoring prevailing beliefs that often stray far from empirical reality. Socialization into gender is no longer seen as a linear process with fixed and well-defined outcomes, but a process full of contradictions and ambivalence (Marshall, 2006). Even though the gender revolution is far from complete (Cambell and Carroll, 2007), chapters in this book only begin to touch on some of the issues. Readers may find it unsettling to have their ideas challenged, but being uncomfortable is the first step toward initiating personal and political change. The dynamic quality of social life, responding as it does to material, historical, and cultural forces, presses against static concepts, urging us to engage in the creative remaking of old ideas. The journey to new thinking can be difficult. I hope that these chapters provide readers with sustenance, encouragement, and enjoyment as they make their way along the feminist path.

Bibliography

Boyd, Monica. 1992. Gender, visible minority and immigrant earning inequality: Reassessing an employment equity premise, in *Deconstructing a nation: Immigration, multiculturalism and racism in '90's Canada,* ed. Vic Satzewich. Saskatoon: Univ. of Saskatchewan Press.

Brand, Dionne. 1999. Black women and work: The impact of racially constructed gender roles on the sexual division of labour, in *Scratching the surface: Canadian anti-racist feminist thought,* eds. Enakshi Dua and Angela Robertson. Toronto: Women's Press.

Budgeon, Shelly. 2001. Emergent feminist (?) identities: Young women and the practice of micropolitics. *European Journal of Women's Studies* 8(1): 7–28.

Bulbeck, Chilla. 2001. Articulating structure and agency: How women's studies students express their relationships with feminism. *Women's Studies International Forum* 24(2): 141–156.

Butler, J. 2003. The question of social transformation, in *Women and Social Transformation,* eds. E. Beck-Gernsheim, J. Butler, and L. Pulgvert. New York: Peter Lang.

Calsanti, T. 2006. Gender and old age: Lessons from spousal care work, in *Age matters: Realigning feminist thinking,* eds. T. Calsanti and K. Slevin, 269–294. Routledge: London.

Campbell, L.D., and M.P. Carroll. 2007. The incomplete revolution: Theorizing gender when studying men who provide care to aging parents. *Men and Masculinities* 9(4): 491–508.

Carty, Linda. 1999. The discourse of empire and the social construction of gender, in *Scratching the surface: Canadian anti-racist feminist thought,* eds. Enakshi Dua and Angela Robertson. Toronto: Women's Press.

Clark, Beverley, and Jo-Anne Whitcomb. 1996. Women's spirituality, in *An introduction to women's studies,* eds. Beryl Madoc-Jones and Jennifer Coates, 250–270. Oxford: Blackwell.

Collins, Patricia Hill. 2000. *Black feminist thought: Knowledge, consciousness, and the politics of empowerment.* New York: Routledge.

Ehrenreich, B., and A. Hochschild. 2003. *Global woman: Nannies, maids, and sex workers in the new economy.* New York: Metropolitan.

Eichler, Margrit, and Diana L. Gustafson. 2000. Between hope and despair: Feminists working with/for the state. Paper presented at the BAITWorM Conference, Toronto.

Evans, Mary. 1997. *Introducing contemporary feminist thought.* New York: Polity Press.

Heisz, Andrew, and Sébastien LaRochelle-Coté. 2003. *Working hours in Canada and the United States.* Ottawa: Statistics Canada.

Hunsley, T. 2006. Work-life balance in an aging population. *Horizons* 8(3): 3–13.

Letherby, Gail, and Jen Marchbank. 2001. Why do women's studies? A cross England profile. *Women's Studies International Forum* 24(5): 587–603.

Mandell, Nancy, and Stewart Crysdale. 1993. Gender tracks: Male-female perceptions of home-school-work transitions, in *Transitions: Schooling and employment in Canada,* eds. Paul Anisef and Paul Axelrod, 21–24. Toronto: Thompson.

Marshall, K. 2006. Converging gender roles. *Perspectives* 7(7): 5–17. Statistics Canada, Catalogue no. 75-001-XIE, 5–17.

Pyper, Wendy. 2006. Balancing career and care. *Perspectives* 7(11): 5–15. Statistics Canada, Catalogue no. 75-001 XIE.

Reyes, A. 2002. I'm not mad, I'm postcolonial, a woman, and a mother: Introduction, in *Mothering across cultures: Postcolonial representations,* ed. Angela Reyes, 1–31. Minneapolis: Univ. of Minnesota Press.

Shields, M. 2004. Stress, health and the benefit of social support. *Health Reports* 15(1): 9–38.

Statistics Canada. 2004. *The time of our lives: Juggling work and leisure over the life cycle.* Catalogue no. 89-584-MIE. Ottawa: Ministry of Industry.

Sussman, D., and S. Bonnell. 2006. Wives as primary breadwinners, in *Perspectives.* Statistics Canada, Catalogue no. 75-001-XIE, 10–17. Ottawa: Ministry of Industry.

Volman, Monique, and Geert ten Dam. 1998. Equal but different: Contradictions in the development of gender identity in the 1990s. *British Journal of Sociology of Education* 19(4): 529–545.

Williams, C., and J. Normand. 2003. Stress at work. *Canadian Social Trends* 70 (Fall): 7–13.

CHAPTER 1

Liberal, Socialist, and Radical Feminism: An Introduction to Three Theories about Women's Oppression and Social Change

Shana L. Calixte, Jennifer L. Johnson, and J. Maki Motapanyane[1]

> Simply put, feminism is a movement to end sexism, sexist exploitation, and oppression.
>
> bell hooks (2000:1)

WHAT IS FEMINISM?

Although hooks's (2000) definition is very straightforward, feminism has come to mean many things to different people. There are a wide range of feminist ideas and practices that vary according to one's understanding of the source of women's oppression. But at its core, "[f]eminism begins with the premise that women's and men's positions in society are the result of social, not natural or biological, factors" (Andersen, 1997: 8). Feminism is a political way of being, thinking, and living in the world, the aim of which is to achieve gender equality in all spheres of life (social, political, economic, religious, and cultural). Feminism is also about seeing the connection between our day-to-day activities and experiences as women and larger social processes. These include institutions such as the political and legal systems, sociocultural institutions such as the family, the popular media (newspapers, television, radio, and internet), and even contemporary economic processes such as globalization.

Feminism: Theory and Practice

Feminist theory is a road map for understanding feminism. There are many different kinds of feminist theory, each with its own historical basis, theoretical predecessors, and methods of achieving social change. Theory provides a framework for explaining the complex connections between people's everyday lives and larger social, political, and economic forces. Feminist theories typically offer an analysis of systems of power in society and indicate how the unequal distribution of this power shapes the lives of men and women. An understanding of this unequal distribution can also expose other equally insidious oppressions based on factors such as race, sexuality, and class (Code, 1993: 20).

One of the main tensions between feminist theorists and activists is the idea that theorists sit back while the "woman in the street" does the work of social change. hooks (1994) argues that theory and practice are in fact inseparable and that it is pointless to engage in one without the other. She says that "by reinforcing the idea that there is a split between theory and practice, or by creating such a split, both groups deny the power of liberatory education for critical consciousness, thereby perpetuating conditions that reinforce our collective exploitation and repression" (hooks, 2000: 32). We would add that even activists doing frontline work in demonstrations, women's shelters, and courtrooms have a theory behind their actions, although it may not be articulated in an academic text. hooks' idea that theory and practice are meaningless without each other is therefore a really important one to keep in mind as you read about the theories behind the actions of liberal, socialist, and radical feminists.

1 The authors thank Nancy Mandell and Jon Maxfield and send a special thank-you to Johanna Stuckey and the anonymous reviewer who generously commented and offered advice on drafts of this chapter.

This chapter addresses liberal, socialist, and radical feminist perspectives as they have developed in a "Western" (European, American, and Canadian) context, outlining the core concepts and critical debates in each theory. The authors therefore urge readers to consider this presentation of the theories as culturally specific to Western society. At the same time, the actions of feminists in the West can be situated in a global context, a reality that we highlight throughout the chapter while still focusing on the ideas of three particular strands of feminist thought. We ask readers to take feminists' achievements as important and significant in their own right but also to recognize that different women have come to understand gender inequality and women's oppression differently.

Liberal, socialist, and radical feminist theory have in common a commitment to redefining the relationship of sex to gender and to making visible relations of power between women and men. Western society has embraced the idea of a dichotomous and hierarchical relationship between "male" and "female" or "masculinity" and "femininity." These dichotomies and hierarchies in turn shape the positions, opportunities, and levels of access of individuals to political, economic, and social spaces. And yet the questionable relationship between sex and gender is often invisible to us. A central understanding in each theory is that one's biological sex (male/female) should not necessarily determine one's gender identity (masculine/feminine) and the social status, behaviours, and opportunities ascribed to each gender. Part of feminist theorizing is seeing the world as gendered and challenging the ways in which different characteristics, roles, and behaviours are attributed to men and women. Therefore, feminist theory seeks to identify the source of women's oppression and develop effective methods for social change and, in some cases, for revolution. Although there is a diversity of feminist theoretical approaches, and ongoing debates within and between these, what remains fundamental to each of the theories presented here is a commitment to social change through the eradication of women's oppression.

LIBERAL FEMINISM

Defining Liberal Feminism: Principles and Goals

Liberal feminist theory is founded on a core set of principles originating in liberal philosophy. Liberal philosophy developed during a period of European social change called the "Enlightenment" or the "Age of Reason" in the 17th and 18th centuries. Major shifts in European understanding of the world came about in the fields of physics, biology, and geography. Scientists such as Newton and Galileo determined that, instead of relying on the traditions of folk wisdom or the decrees of kings, the natural world can be known through careful scientific experiment. Such ways of thinking were translated by philosophers and politicians and applied to human society.

First, liberals believe that all human beings are inherently rational and, as such, people should be considered equal to one another in their shared humanity. Second, liberals believe in meritocracy. People should be able to earn their status in society, such as by earning rewards for doing well at a job or in school. To merit something implies that a status cannot be passed on hereditarily or through personal favours. Third, liberals believe in the principle of equal opportunity. Everyone should have the chance to merit a status or reward. If people in a society do not have equal opportunity, as in a monarchy for example, where only the heirs of the royal family can become king or queen, liberals would strive to ensure that the head of state be elected in such a way that any person might ascend to this position. Last, all rational beings should have freedom of choice unless for some reason they are incapacitated (Bryson, 1992; MacIvor, 1996). Liberalism is however, a Western philosophy that has in great part been applied to relationships between men—and specifically, white propertied men. Women, slaves, minors, and various other groups have often been deliberately excluded or have existed outside the purview of legal and political systems that espouse a liberal point of view.

Liberal feminists take the core principles of liberalism and apply them to inequalities between men and women; they espouse the idea that women should be equally integrated into existing social, political, religious, and economic institutions and that they should enjoy the same benefits that accrue to men. First, liberal feminists, past and present, are concerned with establishing women's capacity for rational thought and thus their shared humanity with men. Second, liberal feminists endorse the concept of meritocracy. These first two principles have been particularly important in shaping the goal of achieving access to formal education for women, largely achieved in Western societies in the early 20th century. Third, liberal feminists are concerned with establishing equality of opportunity for women in all areas of social, economic, legal, and political life. This principle was critical in shaping liberal feminists' goal of women's suffrage, achieved in Canada at varying points throughout the 20th century. Fourth, freedom of choice is a principle of liberal feminism.

Liberal Feminism: A Historical Context

In a period when democracy threatened monarchy as form of government, liberal ideas upset European ways of thinking about social relations between the nobility and the peasant class. Liberalism especially questioned the hereditary rule of monarchies over the masses. Why should one man rule over another simply because he was born to it? The French in particular did not think so and undertook a bloody revolution in 1789 to overthrow the French monarchy. They fought on the principles of liberty, equality, and fraternity to establish a meritocracy in which, theoretically, any man could ascend to power and government. Liberalism was therefore a primary ideological goal of the French Revolution and its success gave credence to other major social reforms taking place in England, Europe, and parts of the Americas.

The Enlightenment was also the age of colonialism and the beginnings of industrial capitalism in the Western world. Colonialism was mainly the project of European states seeking to develop industrial capitalist economic practices through free trade. While European men fought and acquired more legal rights, the countries in whose name they fought were in effect squelching the rights of First Peoples on several continents. From 1492 onward, European nations actively undertook the conquest of many parts of the world for the riches these lands offered, including the Americas and the Caribbean, heralding the beginnings of modern globalization. Once indigenous populations had been subdued, eliminated, or enslaved, the Europeans found that not enough labour could be extracted from them and so began first the indentureship of poor and working-class whites from Europe and then the capture, transport, and enslavement of Africans in the Americas and the Caribbean. Given that European society was a class-based society of nobility, citizens, servants, and slaves, it is hard to understand liberal feminist thought without examining the hierarchical relationships between differently racialized and classed groups of women and men that emerged during this period of colonialism.

In Canada, a complex history of trade, resistance and turf warfare between the French, English, First Nations peoples, and other European interests developed most intensely from the 17th century on. Europeans may have determined that rational men shared a common humanity, but they applied this liberal rhetoric oppressively in the case of women, First Nations people, and enslaved Africans, arguing that these groups were not capable of rational thought.

The ideas of several liberal feminist thinkers are discussed here in order to explore the principles of liberal feminism: rationality, meritocracy, equality of opportunity, and freedom of choice.

Rational Thought and Human Worth

The ideas of Christine de Pizan (1365–1430), a widowed Frenchwoman, and Mary Astell (1666–1731), an Englishwoman, should be noted as early critical feminist works in Western thought. They challenged the dominant idea of the time that women are essentially weak-minded, frail, and irrational by nature, unlike men, who are naturally strong of body and mind, steadfast in opinion, and inherently rational beings. In contrast, de Pizan and Astell both proposed that women have a natural capacity for rational thought, just as men do. De Pizan argued that women's status in relation to men would be improved if society acknowledged women's capacity for rational thought. Much later, Astell (1694, 1697/1997) argued specifically for the equality of the sexes based on men and women's shared humanity. These women's ideas were viciously rejected by their societies and all but erased through the repression of women's historical significance in Western history.

Mary Wollstonecraft (1759–1797) is one of the first figures in Western history to articulate a basic framework for women's equality with men. In *A Vindication of the Rights of Woman* (1792) she challenges liberal thinkers to apply the concept of liberalism to relationships between men and women, not just to men. Wollstonecraft takes issue with Jean-Jacques Rousseau's depiction of children's ability to learn. His tract on education, *Émile*, demonstrates the propensity of boys from any social background to be educated. Girls, on the other hand, are seen to be fickle and feeble versions of their male counterparts (Bryson, 1992: 22). Instead of seeing women as inherently simple, irrational, and emotional, Wollstonecraft argues that these gender characteristics are not innate in the female sex but are the result of an environment that requires them to be so (Kramnick, 1982: 12). She argues that through formal education, women can develop their innate capabilities for intellectual thought and thus become better wives and mothers. Wollstonecraft's ideas scandalized her contemporaries for their appropriation of liberal ideology. And yet she was extremely forward thinking in her anticipation of the arguments put forward by women in later centuries.

Equality of Opportunity, Meritocracy, and Freedom of Choice

The principles of equality of opportunity and meritocracy emerge clearly in the works of Harriet Taylor Mill (1807–1858) and her long-time companion, the political philosopher John Stuart Mill (1806–1873). Harriet Taylor Mill argued radically for the desirability of women to earn and have control of their own property and money. In addition to shared humanity on the basis of their mutual capacity for rational thought, she proposed that the sexes might achieve equality through women's control over their own property. Only then would women have a chance at equality of opportunity with men in other spheres. John

Stuart Mill's work also reflects a deeply held belief that women should have control of their persons. In *The Subjection of Women* (1869) Mill argues that the legal subordination of women to men is in itself wrong and is actually a hindrance to human progress. Nothing less than legal equality, he believed, ought to replace this relationship of subordination (Hall, 1992).

Another way to think about what equality of opportunity, meritocracy, and freedom of choice means for women is to consider a diversity of women's experiences with these concepts. White women in Europe and the Americas might have seen hope in liberal ideas, but the status of Aboriginal and Inuit women within their own communities was particularly compromised by those acting on liberal democratic—but patriarchal and racist—ideas (Maracle, 2003: 74). First Peoples in Canada have suffered a diminished economic, political, and social status under the purview of the *Indian Act* (1876). A major intention of the act was for First Nations women and children to become subject to their husbands and fathers just as European women were. The Europeans viewed this as a path to "civilizing" First Nations people, while First Nations people found this to be an aggressive and nonsensical destruction of the diverse and strong family structures already in place throughout Aboriginal societies (Stevenson, 1999). Women who enjoyed meaningful political participation and high status in their society before the arrival of Europeans actually had their status reversed by the presence of European liberal democratic rule. The *Indian Act* initially determined who is and is not an Indian through patrilineage and marriage. If a woman was born a registered Indian but married a non-Status Indian, the law said that she was no longer an Indian. She would be removed from the register and denied the range of protections and rights set out by the Act. An Indian man on the other hand, could marry whomever he wished and that person could gain Indian status through marriage even if she was not of Aboriginal parentage (Stevenson, 1999).

In 1951 the Act became more exclusionary, removing Indian status from any woman who married out of her band. Simultaneously, women were accorded the right to vote in band council elections, providing a formal opportunity for women's open political participation. In the 1950s, Mary Two Axe Early (1911–1996) of Kahnawake was one of the first to speak publicly about the sexism of the *Indian Act*. Jeanette Lavall and Yvonne Bedard legally challenged the legislation in 1973, but the Supreme Court of Canada declared that the *Canadian Bill of Rights* did not apply to the *Indian Act*. Sandra Lovelace of the Tobique Reserve, New Brunswick, took this complaint to the United Nations Human Rights Committee in 1977. The committee found Canada to be in violation of international human rights laws on the basis of its sexual discrimination in 1981. In the meantime, frustrated by the lack of support from the National Indian Brotherhood (now the Assembly of First Nations), the Tobique Women's Group of New Brunswick marched from Oka, Quebec, to Parliament Hill in Ottawa to raise awareness of these issues (Gehl, 2000). In 1985 the federal government amended the *Indian Act* to reinstate Aboriginal peoples who had lost their Indian status either through marriage or enfranchisement (Dickason, 2002).[2] Women's experience of equality of opportunity, meritocracy, and freedom

---

2 First Nations people could be enfranchised after 1851 but were required to give up their Indian status and pass a battery of tests in order to receive the right to vote. Understandably, very few people deliberately took this opportunity (Dickason, 2002).

of choice is therefore heavily mediated by the ways in which their legal and political history are gendered and racialized.

Examples of liberal feminist theory in practice are given below, demonstrating the variety of methods feminists have taken up in order to achieve their primary goal of equality with men.

Women and Access to Formal Education

Early liberal feminists realized very quickly that without a formal education, women could not advance in social status or political participation. They also realized that it would be difficult to acquire other rights without an education on a par with that available to men. Through women's physical presence on campuses, and informal but highly effective networks of women graduates, education for women came to be thought of as an enhancement of the young middle-class woman's "natural" qualities (Garvie and Johnson, 1999). She would, after all, one day be a wife and mother in charge of the moral instruction of her children. As women entered the labour force in greater numbers after the Second World War the number of women seeking higher education again increased dramatically.

The suggestion that women have a formal education beyond elementary or high school was preposterous to most people. Women who wanted further education found themselves up against the view that educated women were strangely divorced from their natural roles as child bearers (Garvie and Johnson, 1999; Kromnick, 1982). White women who wanted an education, or a life beyond motherhood, were accused of "racial suicide" because the racial ideas of the time presumed the moral superiority of white people and women's obligation to reproduce that "race" (Valverde, 1992). Women of colour on the other hand, such as in the large Black communities in eastern Canada and southern Ontario, may have found more support for their education. Slavery in Canada was abolished in 1834, and as early as 1830 Black Canadians ran separate schools, which were an important form of resistance to the racism Black people experienced from white Canadians (Kelly, 1998; Sadlier, 1994).

In Canada West (now southwestern Ontario) and Upper and Lower Canada, female teachers proliferated throughout the 1850s, providing what little education was considered necessary for girls, such as writing, reading, and needlework (Prentice et al., 1996). In 1858, Canada's first female university students studied at Mount Allison University in New Brunswick. They studied a limited range of topics that typically included literature, languages, rhetoric, history, and home economics (developed specifically for female students' entry to post-secondary education). Typically, women students were segregated in all-female classrooms and required to sit apart from male students in adjoining rooms where they could hear the lecture but not be seen by the men (Garvie and Johnson, 1999). Women were rare in Canadian university programs in medicine, the sciences, and engineering until the 1940s, when Canada's participation in the Second World War necessitated more doctors. Although some female physicians did practice medicine in Canada before the Second World War, the number of female students began to approach the number of male students in the arts after that time. Only at the end of the 20th century did women's numbers creep up in the sciences. Women have worked their way slowly into universities and colleges and into traditionally male-dominated areas of study, such as the sciences and engineering, such that their numbers have begun to approach those of men. Access to education is one of the major accomplishments of liberal feminism.

The Vote, 1918[3]

Liberal feminist thought was both informed and developed through women's agitation for suffrage between 1850 and 1920.[4] National controversies over the Riel Rebellions, and the ongoing colonization of Aboriginal peoples existed alongside a burgeoning feminist movement. (Strong-Boag, 1998: 130). The state and the media had a new focus because these were the generations in which immigration posed tremendous challenges to existing social and political institutions. Social reformers and religious organizations such as the Women's Christian Temperance Union (WCTU) were concerned about the state of urban dwellers, reacting to the poverty and malnutrition of the masses that came with urbanization and industrialization. At a time when in Western Canada, for example, milk was more costly than alcohol, women began to make the connections between poverty, the availability of alcohol, and the violence of men toward women and children (McClung, 1915/1972). The fight for the vote was premised on women's capacity for reason as well as the suffragists' understanding of women's feminine morality. Maternal feminists in particular embraced and applied the principles of equal opportunity and meritocracy but felt that women had a superior moral and racial integrity, indicating white female suitability for political participation (Roome, 2001; Valverde, 1992). Maternal feminists and liberal feminists worked together along with socialist and conservative women toward the goals of social reform and ultimately, the vote (Roome, 2001).

Feminists lobbied the state, held demonstrations and staged mock parliamentary debates to ridicule the men who upheld women's political and legal inequality. Led by Dr. Emily Howard Stowe (1831–1903) the Toronto Women's Literary Club (established in 1876) reorganized as the Canadian Women's Suffrage Association in 1883 when some minor rights for women to vote in municipal elections were won (Prentice et al., 1996). In Quebec, women's organizing around suffrage and social problems such as poverty and health took place largely through women's Roman Catholic organizations, reflecting the appeal of Christian-based public service organizations such as the WCTU and the Young Women's Christian Association (YWCA). Their work centred on providing shelter and educational programs for young, single, and poor women. With the slight increase in women's access to formal education and legislation such as the 1884 *Married Women's Property Act* (allowing married women to hold property exclusive of their husbands' ownership), feminists built the capacity for their movement (Prentice et al., 1996). Other organizations such as the National Council of Women of Canada (NCWC) (established in 1893), a predominantly Protestant umbrella group, had strong links to both the American and British women's and social reform movements, demonstrating Canadian women's capacity for the development of a suffrage movement that had an international network of alliances (Valverde, 1992).

Suffragists used a variety of tactics to challenge the familiar dichotomy of "passive" femininity versus the "active" and political masculinity thought appropriate for political decision-making (Roome, 2001). Some felt that petitioning, letter-writing, and public speaking were the best tactics to achieve their goals. The work of maternal feminist and

---

3 Some white, propertied women were occasionally allowed to vote before 1849 but all women were banned from voting after that time (Status of Women Canada, 2003a).

4 It should be noted that most suffragists did not actually call themselves feminists until the early 20th century (Roome, 2001).

journalist Nellie McClung (1875–1951) in Manitoba is a good example of effective public speaking; she used wit to ridicule male politicians in the press. Maternal feminists' attachment to feminine virtues, however, limited the scope of their actions in contrast to more militant British feminists such as Emmeline Pankhurst (1858–1929) and her daughters Christabel (1880–1958) and Sylvia (1882–1960). Beginning in 1903, these suffragettes heckled politicians, chained themselves to the British Parliament's fences, broke shop windows, set fires, and even persisted in hunger strikes, enduring forced feedings for their cause (Bryson, 1992; Prentice et al., 1996).

Unfortunately, the efforts of liberal and maternal feminists were applied unevenly to the goal of integrating women into social and political institutions. The issues of moral and racial degeneration and women's suffrage were very much linked in the late 19th and early 20th centuries. Social Darwinism dictated the meanings given to the racial and class organization of Canadian society at this time, which influenced ideas about various groups' fitness for political participation. At the extreme end of the political spectrum, Aboriginal peoples, women, people of Chinese origin, and new immigrants from Eastern and Southern Europe were viewed as biologically inferior to white men of British origin and were denied the vote on that basis (Dickason, 2002; Valverde, 1992). Social reformers who considered themselves more moderate felt that these groups had to be properly assimilated into Britishness before they should be able to vote. Neither Canada's first prime minister, Sir John A. Macdonald, or Robert Borden, the prime minister who granted some women the federal vote in 1918, were ever personally in favour of extending universal suffrage (Roome, 2001; Valverde, 1992). The suffragists were aware of these views and distanced themselves from categories of "degeneracy" by asserting white women's moral superiority. Flora MacDonald Denison, a Canadian suffragist, was particularly critical of the morals of recent male immigrants (Prentice et al., 1996), while Emily Murphy wrote extensively on the threat of Chinese and Black men's corruptive tendencies to the moral purity of white women (Valverde, 1992). The white ribbons worn by WCTU activists signified white racial purity as much as it did the purity of milk over alcohol (Valverde, 1992). Despite the activities of Black women such as Harriet Tubman (1820–1913) in the suffrage movement and of other women of colour in organizations such as the WCTU, white suffragists and social reformers persisted in the belief that the "mother of the race" would be free if she could only vote (Sadlier, 1994; Valverde, 1992). Most women were granted a federal vote in 1918 but this still excluded Aboriginal people and people of Chinese origin (Cleverdon, 1974: 108). After 1918 the federal government divested itself of responsibility for granting the provincial franchise. Some Manitoban women could vote provincially in 1916, but, for example, their Québécoise counterparts had to mobilize to bring 14 separate bills in 13 years to the Quebec legislature—they enjoyed success in 1940. Status Indian women achieved the vote in 1960 when the universal right to vote was introduced.

The Persons Case, 1929

The Persons Case of 1929 is another early example of the ways in which feminists have used the legal system to achieve their goals of overcoming women's oppression, by ensuring that women were fully integrated as citizens in the democratic state. The "Famous Five"—Emily Murphy (1868–1933), Nellie McClung (1875–1951), Mary Irene Parlby (1868–1965), Henrietta Muir Edwards (1849–1931), and Louise McKinney (1868–1933)— challenged a provision in the *British North America Act* (1867) that excluded women from being considered "persons" in the matter of privileges and rights (Falardeau-Ramsay, 1999: 52). The success of the Persons Case did not mean that women were entirely equal to men under the law, particularly in terms of family law and property rights, but these "rights and privileges" did include eligibility to take up public offices such as appointment to the Senate of Canada (Cleverdon, 1974: 149).

The Royal Commission on the Status of Women, 1970 and Beyond

A new generation of liberal feminists in North America emerged in the 1960s and 1970s whose actions must be contextualized through a number of different social movements (Brown, 1989). During the Second World War, the federal government empowered women to join the workforce to a certain extent by investing in subsidized daycare and encouraging women to join the war effort in traditionally male forms of employment (Timpson, 2001). After the Second World War, women were encouraged by the media, religious institutions, and school systems to go back to the role of homemaking. The post-war welfare state did not include a national daycare programme, so many women stayed at home to fulfill their roles as mothers and wives. Women who had previously worked outside the home, and even those who had not, became increasingly frustrated with their lot as financial dependants of husbands and fathers.

During the same period, the Canadian federal government was again actively recruiting new waves of immigrants to take up jobs in Canada. Non-white immigrants created new activist networks when they encountered racism in employment and housing and were occupationally segregated in low-paying jobs (Brown, 1989; Calliste, 2001). Additionally, new challenges to the federal *Indian Act* raised by First Nations, Métis, and Inuit peoples accompanied the revitalization of Aboriginal women's leadership in their communities (Maracle, 2003: 71). These movements provided a new base of women dissatisfied with their relationship to the state and ready to do something about it.

The Royal Commission on the Status of Women, 1970 (RCSW), is a benchmark moment of Canadian women's rights. With great struggle, a select group of women were making inroads into the commanding structures of the federal government. Spearheaded by Laura Sabia, then president of the Canadian Federation of University Women (CFUW), and with the help of several non-governmental organizations, they convinced the government of the need for a royal commission. They correctly recognized that a human rights framework that had equal opportunity as its goal would be most palatable to the federal government (Timpson, 2001: 29). Headed by Florence Bird (1908–1998), the RCSW spent over a year touring the country receiving briefs and hearing presentations from individuals and groups that had something to say about the status of women in Canadian society. The entire process was televised so that the nation watched; feminists were hopeful that the public nature of the RCSW would help them hold the federal government to carrying out the recommendations.

Based on the input of more than 300 women's organizations across the country and many more individuals, the RCSW identified four major areas of importance for Canadian women: the right to choose homemaking or paid employment; the shared responsibility for child care among mothers, fathers, and society at large; the special treatment of women relating to their maternity; and the special treatment of women to help them overcome the adverse effects of discriminatory practices in Canadian society (Paltiel, 1997: 29). These recommendations supported the central liberal feminist principle of equality of opportunity for women. Liberal feminists understand women's concentration in the private sphere (the home) to be a contributor to women's oppression if women lack the choice to move between the home and the public sphere (paid work). Women are at a disadvantage if they cannot choose between paid or unpaid work because they may not be able to care financially for themselves or their dependants. Being defined through their work in the home as caregivers, mothers, and housekeepers also circumscribes women's influence in society at large. Homemaking as such is not necessarily at issue; rather the lack of choice to pursue other careers is the problem. As such, contemporary liberal feminism focuses on expanding the range of choices available to women and ensuring that the doors that have already been opened remain open, such as access to education and full political participation. The RCSW made 167 specific recommendations to the federal government as to how women's social, political, and economic status could be improved. Some were implemented but many more were not. For example, Canada still lacks a national daycare program that would allow more women equal participation in the labour force. Many liberal-feminist organizations, while recognizing that many more issues have been added to the agenda, still use the RCSW recommendations as a measuring stick for women's equality with men in Canada.

Global Dimensions of Liberal Feminist Thought

Liberal feminist ideas have certainly been developed in western contexts but have also been taken up in countries around the world, often independently of western feminist interests. The integration of gender issues into the main framework of organizations like the United Nations and into the national government systems of individual countries are vehicles through which liberal feminist ideas proliferate. When considering the achievement of women's relative equality to men in global context, the question to be asked is: equal by which standards? If the integration of women's human rights into mainstream society and equal opportunities for employment and education are the standard, then we can compare countries to one another. Perhaps surprisingly, Canada is a global leader in supporting women's equality in only some of these areas. For example, Canadian girls and women enjoy extremely high labour force participation rates when one considers that globally, women account for about 36 percent of the paid labour force (Seager, 1997: 66). Statistics Canada reports that the percentage of women 18 years old and over in the paid workforce increased dramatically from 70 percent in 1986 to 81 percent in 2005 and has narrowed with that of men, which was 91 percent in that same year (Statistics Canada, *The Daily*, 2006b). Women's relative earnings to men have even narrowed. In 2001 women's average hourly wage rate was about 84–89 percent of the men's average, an increase from 1997 when women earned on average 72.5 cents for every dollar earned by a man (Drolet, 2001: 14). In the area of girls' access to education worldwide, Canadian girls have enrolled in secondary education at rates similar to most other countries. In Canada, roughly 48 percent of high school students are girls, which is slightly lower or the same as the vast majority of nations surveyed by the United Nations in 2005. Those countries with extremely low rates of formal education for girls, such as Afghanistan (23 percent), Guinea (33 percent), and Mali (37 percent) are relatively few (United Nations, 2007a).

But in looking at the degree to which women have integrated in the upper echelons of legislation and management in mainstream governance, Canada's achievements are not very remarkable. In fact, at 36 percent, Canada is far surpassed by Uganda (50 percent), the Philippines (58 percent), Mongolia (50 percent), Lesotho (52 percent), Anguilla (52 percent), and a number of other less developed or developing nations that have all achieved gender parity or better in their public services (United Nations, 2007b). It is also quite remarkable that despite women's achievements in the labour force, Canada has not been able to elect equal numbers of men and women to the House of Commons. In 2007, Canada even lagged behind Afghanistan, a country torn by war and other conflicts in which only 23 percent of girls had access to secondary school in the same year. While only 21 percent of Canada's elected federal representatives are women, 27 percent of Afghanistan's newly elected representatives are female (United Nations, 2007c).

Contemporary Liberal Feminist Thought: Breaking the Glass Ceiling?

Since the RCSW submitted its findings, liberal feminist principles have become somewhat institutionalized. In particular, the legal integration of gender into the *Canadian Charter of Human Rights* in 1985 was a major accomplishment. Additionally, the establishment of the National Action Committee on the Status of Women in 1973 created a non-governmental popular organization through which diverse groups of women have lobbied for women's rights. To some degree, liberal feminist principles have also been assimilated into institutions such as the establishment of the federal Status of Women secretariat, led by Doris Anderson. Now called Status of Women Canada, this arm of the federal government has been the source of research and policy interventions on gender equality for the government at large.

Unfortunately, if standards for gender equality are taken to mean that governments should continuously protect and support such efforts, then Canada has recently been set on a very different path. The 1990s saw repeated cuts to social funding under a Liberal government and the eventual dissolution and nascent reformation of the National Action Committee on the Status of Women, Canada's only national feminist lobby group. With the election of a Conservative government in 2006, the basic achievements of Canadian women were threatened further. In 2006 Status of Women Canada had its operating budget reduced by 43 percent as a result of shifts in political priorities of the federal government. Ironically, the responsibility of announcing and carrying out the extraordinary cuts fell to a woman, Minister Bev Oda, responsible for Status of Women, who also announced the removal of the word "equality" from the agency's main goals (Public Service Alliance of Canada, 2006).

The initial goals of liberal feminists, to have access to education and political participation, would seem like fairly staid and reasonable objectives if we did not know the difficulty with which they were achieved and their precarious continued existence. For example, few of Canada's elected female members of Parliament would deny that they owe something to the achievements of liberal feminists, but only a minority would call themselves "feminists." This in itself is both a fortunate and unfortunate accomplishment in the legacy of liberal feminism.

Critiques of Liberal Feminism

A primary criticism of liberal feminist theory is its selectivity and privileging of the objectives of white middle- or upper-class women. In the past, women's equality with men has not always been the primary consideration of women whose social class was far removed from that of the average middle- or upper-class wife. If one is subject to legislation like the *Indian Act*, arguing for gender equality with men makes little difference without racial and class equality (Arneil, 2001: 54). Yet much of liberal feminist theory has not historically been written using an integrated approach to gender, race, or class. This short-sightedness played out in the way that some early Canadian feminists argued that only white women of Canadian birth should be allowed the vote (Prentice et al., 1996).

Liberal feminist understanding of women's oppression and methods of social change incorporate women's presence into existing political and economic institutions without necessarily transforming the relations of power between men and women within those organizations or even in society at large. This is so, some argue, because having meritocracy as a central principle takes for granted a level playing field between different groups of women. The following statistic is alarming at a time when the goals of liberal feminism, such as access to education and political participation, are taken as a given by many Canadian women. In 2003, women working full-time year-round made only 71 percent of their male counterparts' income (Statistics Canada, 2006a). It has long been established that women earn less not because male and female co-workers can be paid different wages, but because women are occupationally segregated into lower-paying jobs across the country (Nelson and Robinson, 2002). Unfortunately, the common reasoning presented in the media or by governments suggests that since women now have equal opportunity as far as the law goes, they must simply work harder to merit higher-paying jobs. Explaining away such inequities misappropriates liberal discourse and masks structural and systemic inequalities within and between different groups of men and women. Liberal feminists continue to argue that a remedy to this inequity is possible through women's promotion into better-paying jobs and the safeguarding of their work environments from sexual harassment and discrimination.

SOCIALIST FEMINISM

Defining Socialist Feminism

Socialist feminism originates in Marxist theory and uses class and gender as central categories of analysis in its explanation of women's oppression. Socialist feminism holds several key goals in its analyses and activism. First, socialist feminism relates the oppression experienced by women to their economic dependence on men. One of the goals of socialist feminism is therefore to advocate for social conditions that allow women's economic independence. In addition, socialist feminism provides a materialist analysis of gender inequality by identifying the relationship between systems of patriarchal oppression in which women are subordinated to men, and class relations in capitalist economic systems, in which working classes are subordinated to the upper classes. The gendered division of labour in the home and wage labour market (unpaid and paid work) and women's economically subordinate position in the paid labour force account for the unequal position of women in capitalist patriarchal societies. Therefore, a second goal of socialist feminism is to expose and challenge the devaluation of women's unpaid labour in the home. In doing so, socialist feminists advocate for the acknowledgement of the value of women's domestic work, a sharing of domestic responsibilities between men and women, and state involvement (financial and legislative) in creating a society that is equitable and just for everyone. A third, related goal of socialist feminism is to highlight and do away with the continuing pay inequities between men and women (which lead to female financial dependency on men and/or over-representation of women among the total number of poor) and the gendered division of labour within the wage labour market (responsible for the over-representation of women in service industries).

Socialist feminism seeks to redress gender and class inequalities through changes in the state and its policies, changes that would allow for adequate incomes, pay and employment equity, state-sponsored child care, and maternity and paternity leave for all (among other desired outcomes). Socialist feminism uses analyses of class to explain the ways in which social, economic, and political power is distributed in varying amounts to members of society, usually in relation to factors such as gender, race, and sexuality.

Historical Background: Marxism

Karl Marx (1818–1883) and Friedrich Engels (1820–1895) were influential in the development of socialist feminist thought. Their *Communist Manifesto* (1848) laid the foundations of Marxist theory, outlining the relationship of human beings to the ways in which we produce and reproduce for survival, as a central factor in understanding the socio-political characteristics of any particular historical period. This is distinct from bees or ants, for instance, which have biologically predetermined methods of sustaining themselves (set patterns of collecting food and creating shelter); as humans we consciously and socially manipulate our environments in particular ways in order to feed, clothe, and house ourselves (Tong, 1998).

Marxists place the characteristics of the production and reproduction for the conditions of life at the centre of their understanding of history, in an analytical method called *historical materialism*. They use a materialist analysis (an analysis that focuses on class) to explain inequality in society, particularly as it is experienced within the capitalist context. Capitalism is an economic system of production that relies on the exchange of one's labour for wages, which in turn produces profit for someone else. Thus, capitalist modes of production (as understood within Marxist theory), are characterized by a class of owners (bourgeoisie) and a class of workers (proletariat). The wealth of the bourgeoisie can only be extracted through the exploitation of the proletariat. Workers produce at a disproportionate rate to the wages they receive, resulting in market profits for owners. Capitalism is characterized by a form of mass production that alienates the proletariat from the products of their labour. In accordance with Marxist theory then, the components needed for the production and reproduction of social life (raw materials, tools, and workers) and the ways in which this production and reproduction is organized (a capitalist versus a communist economy, for example) are extremely influential on the dominant political, social, and legal ideas of any historic period (Tong, 1998).

In *The German Ideology* (1846), Marx and Engels advance an analysis of capitalist oppression that features the family as the original site of an inequitable division of labour, later to be reflected in the capitalist labour market. Marx and Engels argued that wives and children constituted a "first property" for men, to whom they provided labour, and men exerted control over the context, conditions, and environment in which this labour took place. Although gender and the oppression of women were not a focus for much of early Marxist thought, in *The Origin of the Family, Private Property and the State* (1884), Engels did venture an examination of the sources of women's inequality (Somerville, 2000). Engels linked the economic conditions of people to the ways in which the family is organized as a productive and reproductive unit. The change in modes of production, which saw men in charge of the domestication and breeding of animals, was, according to Engels, a major factor in the unequal shifting of power between men and women. With men predominantly in charge of this new symbol of wealth and power came a devaluation of the work and material contributions of women to the community. Communal work and property came to be replaced by individual households and private property, which in turn made inheritance an important issue for men (who constituted the majority of property owners).

It is the concern over inheritance, suggests Engels, which led to the patriarchal formalization of the nuclear family unit as a method of ensuring the passing down of private property and wealth from father to children of his own blood (Somerville, 2000). Economic wealth allowed the husband to assume control of the household, subjugating his wife and children within the home. Engels advanced this as simply a reflection of the inequalities perpetuated by the capitalist labour market, with the husband representing the "bourgeoisie" and the wife taking the role of the "proletariat." Therefore, the source of women's oppression, according to Engels, lay in the fact that they did not own or have control over private property. As such, the liberation of women could be ensured only by the eradication of capitalism and the reintroduction of women on an equal footing in the production process (Brenner, 2000).

Marxist Feminism

Marxist feminism theorizes women's oppression as rooted in capitalism. It is women's economic dependence on men within the capitalist system that leads to their exploitation and inequality. This exploitation is based on a capitalist system that equates the value of an individual to paid work and the amount of money one earns in the labour market. Moreover, this capitalist economic system works simultaneously with a patriarchal sociopolitical system to divide and relegate certain types of work, and, subsequently, certain levels of pay to individuals based on their gender. The result is a society in which men are over-represented in the highest-paying professional jobs, women's (unpaid) domestic contributions are not regarded as work, and women are over-represented in service-oriented jobs at lower pay. The factors listed above have implications for women's economic standing, health care, pension plans, child care and maternity leave options, and susceptibility to violence (among other factors).

Women's relationship to work, both in the home and within the labour market, is a key point of analysis for Marxist feminists. Theorists such as Margaret Benston (1989) point to the division of labour according to sex, a key feature of capitalism, as central to women's oppression. One of the central functions of capitalism is to take advantage of the labour of workers for profit. Marxist feminists view this as an indication of capitalism's need to create a division of labour between home and economy. This process suggests a false notion of a supposedly clear division between private (home) and public (economy) spheres, with women and men being relegated particular responsibilities within those spheres, based on the perceived gender attributes of each (Hewitt, 2000).

Marx's discussion of the process of industrialization and the concentration of the production of goods outside the home is used by Marxist feminists to expose a shift in the popular understanding of what constitutes productivity. Working in a factory producing goods is viewed by capitalist states as productive, but cooking, cleaning, doing laundry, and taking care of children are not (Waring, 1999). The determinant of productivity and the value of work within a capitalist society is the wage. Marxist feminists emphasize that the ineligibility of woman's work in the home to be turned into a product that can be sold does not make it a less valuable contribution to society (Tong, 1998). Furthermore, as Mariarosa Dalla Costa and Selma James (1975) have suggested, to argue for the equal inclusion of women within the labour force (as liberal feminists have done), without socializing or making a public responsibility of child care and housework, will only increase the oppressive conditions under which women live. The result is, as Juliet Mitchell (1971) has to some extent argued, that waking up in the morning to prepare breakfast and lunch for the kids and husband, going to the office, and returning home in the evening only to cook dinner, finish the laundry, and clean, means a double day of work for women. Women's equal numerical representation and pay in the labour market does not constitute liberation.

Marxist feminist analyses argue for the socialization of child care and housework, and the dissolution of the nuclear family as an economic unit. They emphasize the need for women's economic independence and well-being (which they see the state as having some responsibility for ensuring). Marxist feminists also link women's unequal conditions in the workforce to their exploited position in the nuclear family, calling for an end to capitalism and the oppressive policies and social, economic, and political conditions it creates and perpetuates through the state. However, if women's oppression is rooted in capitalism and its exploitative characteristics (such as the ownership of private property, the gendered division of labour in the home and economy, and the accumulation of profit), how do we explain the existence of women's oppression prior to the existence of the capitalist system and their subordination within past and present socialist/communist states?[5]

Socialist Feminism

Socialist feminists, like Marxist feminists, consider capitalism a significant factor in the oppression experienced by women. Additionally, however, they seek to explain the oppression of women beyond their role as workers, at the hands of patriarchy. Patriarchy is an analytic category and system of distributing power in society that hierarchically ascribes importance to all things male or masculine over all things female or feminine. Socialist feminists find Marxist feminism problematic in that it locates most aspects of women's oppression within the bourgeoisie/proletariat paradigm, neglecting the more complex aspects of relationships between women and men. Although Marxist feminism has been able to explain the gendered division of labour within the home and workplace and the role of capitalism in this process, it has not been able to explain why these gendered roles, responsibilities, and attributes were assigned to women and men in the first place (Tong, 1998).

---

5 For example, in 1934, Russian Communist revolutionary Vladimir Lenin accused colleague Clara Zetkin of weakening the Communist Party platform by encouraging discussions of gender oppression among female party members (Tong, 1998). Discussions of women's realities were viewed as divisive to the aims of a party fighting for economic justice "for all." Additionally, socialist feminists active in the Canadian Socialist Party and the Socialist Democratic Party of Canada during the early decades of the 20th century frequently had to find ways of negotiating their positions within and between socialist politics (under the mandate of male-dominated parties) and socialist politics that also incorporated and supported the leading concerns of women's activism. These concerns included women's suffrage (the right of white women to vote), prohibition (the problem of alcohol), and women's positions within and in relation to the labour force (Newton, 1992).

Alison Jaggar (1983) focuses on the Marxist notion of workers' alienation in a way that exposes the particular alienation experienced by women within patriarchal capitalist systems. While Marx's notion of alienation is primarily concerned with the angst experienced by workers because of their ultimate separation from the products of their labour (as can be seen in the context of mass production and factory work), Jaggar engages with the alienation experienced by women in the processes of manoeuvring their bodies (shaving/tweezing body hair, dieting) for the pleasure and capitalist consumption of men. Thus, the alienation of women from their own bodies, as reflected in the efforts invested to change the body before the critical gaze of men, as well as the alienation of women from their bodies during childbirth in hospitals (with much of the process under the authority of doctors and nurses), are examples of the ways in which socialist feminism expands traditional Marxist and Marxist feminist analyses of capitalist exploitation and its relationship to gender inequality.

Socialist feminism is concerned with how capitalism interacts with patriarchy to oppress women workers more than and differently from men. In addition to the gendered division of labour in the home and economy, and women's relationship to the wage labour market, socialist feminism examines the pay inequality between men and women (contributing to female economic dependency on men and the over-representation of women among the poor) as a way of understanding the barriers and disadvantages experienced by women. Socialist feminism seeks to redress these inequalities through changes in the state and its policies, which should allow for adequate income provisions, pay and employment equity, state-sponsored child care, and maternity and paternity leave for all (Morris, 2002a).

The Household: Paid and Unpaid Labour

Socialist feminist analysis has provided important insights into the fundamental contribution of housework done predominantly by women, in the unfolding of the daily activities of individuals. As housewives and workers in the home, women contribute to the profits of the capitalist economy by ensuring that present-day and future workers in the paid labour force, be they teenagers or adults, are cared for in the home in ways that prepare and support them in their positions within the paid labour force (Morris, 2000). Whether by doing family laundry, preparing meals, cleaning and maintaining organization in the home, or transporting household members to and from school, work, and play, women provide an important service—not only to their families, but also to the capitalist patriarchy that benefits from the present and future labour of these family members.

With this exposition of the intricate relationship between the home and labour market, socialist feminist theory illustrates that the oppressive power of dominant capitalist, patriarchal discourse lies not only in its perpetuation of the notion of men and women as dichotomous categories, but also in its depiction of the home and the economy as separate and relatively unrelated to each other in any significant social, political, or economic sense. The suggestion that the "private" workings of the home are isolated from the larger "public" workings of the capitalist patriarchal economic, social, and political system facilitates the acceptance of housework on the part of women as a "natural" result of their love for their family. This in turn works to legitimize the view of wage labour as "real" labour while devaluing the significant contributions of women in the home and masking the benefits and profit that capitalist and state institutions enjoy from these contributions (the reproduction of future workforce labourers, the maintenance of their physical, emotional, and mental health allowing them to continue to be productive). Despite an increase in male participation in unpaid domestic work over the last three decades, a 2005 Statistics Canada General Social Survey indicates that Canadian women continue to do the majority of household work and feel more time-stressed than their male counterparts (Statistics Canada, 2006b). These statistics are not unrelated to the current over-representation of women among Canada's total number of poor. (For more information on women's paid and unpaid work, please see Chapter 9 in this volume.)

The Feminization of Poverty

The *feminization of poverty* is a term used by socialist feminists to identify the dispropor-tionate majority of women who are poor, linking their poverty to patriarchal and capitalist sexist and profit-based initiatives that segregate the labour market. This segregation is car-ried out based on constructed notions of gender ("women's work vs. men's work"); by devaluing labour in the home; by not factoring home work into official national labour-based calculations such as the Gross Domestic Product (GDP)[6]; and by reinforcing notions of household labour as a "natural" consequence of a woman's love for her family. The most recent Statistics Canada figures for the year 2003 calculated 1.5 million adult women in Canada as living in poverty (Townson, 2005). Furthermore, the National Council of Wel-fare shows single-parent mothers as the family type with the highest poverty rate (48.9 per-cent) for this same year (National Council of Welfare, 2006).

Since women's responsibilities for and within the home are not recognized as "real" work, women are not compensated by the state for reducing their wage labour to part-time in order to take care of children, or for losing job training and seniority upon taking mater-nity leave from waged work. The relegation of women to lower-paying employment sec-tors, long accepted as more suited to women's "feminine" characteristics (teaching, nursing, cleaning, cooking, typing), has contributed to women's disproportionate poverty while also maintaining the wage gap between men and women. A Canadian Labour Con-gress (CLC) report on working women indicates that in 2005, Canadian women working full-time, year-round jobs earned 70.5 cents to the dollar earned by their male counterparts in comparable jobs (Canadian Labour Congress, 2008). Contributing factors here include the large burden borne by women in connection to recent economic turns toward privati-zation and private sector employment, shifts that reinforce a gendered division of labour in the paid labour force, thereby reinforcing rather than alleviating wage gaps between men and women.

Child care has also formed an important part of discussions supporting women's greater and more equitable participation in the paid labour force. In 2003, Canada had a total of 750 000 licensed daycare spaces (Statistics Canada, 2006a). The 2001 Census Canada statistics on the national labour force put the total number of Canadians in the work-force at that time at 15.6 million. The increased presence of women in the paid labour force and in post-secondary education, along with the increase in single-parent homes led by women (Statistics Canada, 2006a), highlight the complicated constraints working women con-tinue to negotiate outside of adequate state and social support. From a feminist perspective of women and work, the positive impact of child care has already been demonstrated in Quebec,

---

6   The GDP is a calculation of the total economic value of a country's yearly output of goods and services.

which introduced a universal affordable daycare program in the late 1990s. The Quebec Ministry of Social Welfare estimates that this policy has removed 37 percent of young mothers in Quebec from welfare (Walker, 2000). More recent studies indicate that the Quebec program increased overall female participation in the province's paid labour force, and married women's participation in particular, allowing a number of women to move from no work to full-time work (Baker, Gruber, and Milligan, 2005).

It remains important to note that an increase in women's wage labour participation is not an indication of equitable labour relations as a whole. A noteworthy example of this is the growing population of retired Canadian women living in poverty. The average incomes of women 65 years of age and older living alone in 2003 were reported as $2300 below the Canadian poverty line (Townson, 2005). Women's lower income earnings over a lifetime make it more difficult to accumulate retirement savings through registered retirement savings plans (RRSPs). In addition, the shifts between paid and unpaid work over a lifetime significantly decrease women's Canada Pension Plan (CPP) eligibility amounts. For example, average CPP payments to new female retirees in 2005 averaged $333.76 per month in comparison to those to newly retired men at $527.04 (Townson, 2005). For socialist feminists, eradicating poverty and the oppression of women involves not only the equal sharing of domestic responsibilities between men and women, but also state policies that "increase women's choice about when and how they go back to work" (Harman, 2000).

Although the statistics above are valuable in painting a picture of poverty and the economic realities of Canadian women, it is important to remember that poverty does not affect all women in the same way. Aboriginal women, non-white women, and women with disabilities are particularly vulnerable to poverty. Statistics Canada's most recent *Women in Canada Report* put Aboriginal women's median annual income for the year 2000 at $5000 below that of non-Aboriginal women, and their rate of unemployment in 2001 at twice the rate of unemployment among non-Aboriginal women in Canada (Statistics Canada, 2006a). The successful challenge made by Jeanette Lavell, Yvonne Bedard, and Sandra Lovelace in 1985 to the sexism of the 1876 *Indian Act* alleviated one way in which systemic racism and sexism work within a patriarchal capitalist economic system to disadvantage women of Aboriginal heritage. Unfortunately, the success of their challenge is only a fraction of the economic disadvantages upheld through legislation such as the *Indian Act* (Dickason, 2002).

The history of the Live-In Caregiver Program in Canada is also reflective of the ways in which women's experiences of oppression differ within the capitalist system. The interconnectedness of race and racism, gender, class, and sexuality—all in relation to labour—is visible in the disproportionately large number of immigrant and non-white women occupying low-wage, non-unionized jobs with no benefits. With limited child-care spaces and a general increase in the working hours and responsibilities of employees—a consequence of contemporary economic restructuring—resorting to domestic service becomes one way Canadian women manage the responsibilities of a household and employment in the labour market (Morris, 2002a).

The exploitation of and discrimination against foreign domestic workers, primarily from the Caribbean and Philippines, in Canada spans several decades. Foreign domestic workers in the early 1970s were under a number of oppressive legislative restrictions and policies. Although the status of foreign domestics as temporary visa holders prevented them from accessing benefits such as paid medicare, their pay was docked for the Canada

Pension Plan (CPP), Employment Insurance, and income tax. Today, employees under this program are still required to live in their employers' homes (meaning they are always on call) and failure to do so risks disqualification from the program. It is still the case that domestic workers under this program can only work for the employer listed on their Employment Authorization (EA) form, and cannot legally work in the country past the date listed on this form (Citizenship and Immigration Canada website, 2007). These conditions are relevant to feminist theorizing and activism in Canada in that, as Himani Bannerji points out, "organization by race (or racism) is a fundamental way of forming class in Canada and this formation of class is a fully gendered one" (Bannerji, 1995).

Contemporary Socialist Feminist Analyses

Contemporary socialist feminist analyses, produced by women of colour particularly, have expanded the boundaries of materialist deconstructions of gender-based oppression, by revealing the ways in which "race," racism, colonialism/neo-colonialism, class, gender, dis/ability and sexuality work simultaneously to differentiate the experiences of women with oppression. Globalization and the role of gender in transnationalism[7] have also found a place within the work of some contemporary socialist feminist theorists (Dua, 1999; Ault and Sandberg, 2001; Sparr, 1994). This stretching of the boundaries of early socialist feminist theory to more adequately reflect the complexities and shifts of gender relations in a global economy is extremely valuable. It illustrates an understanding of the connection between, for example, an unemployed inner-city youth of colour with $200 Nike sneakers and the employed but overworked and underpaid Indonesian woman who sews these sneakers, yet barely affords to feed herself (Human Rights Watch, 2002). Global economic re-structuring has led many Canadian and American companies to downsize their operations and make use of the inexpensive labour available in non-Western countries. This downsizing has resulted in increased layoffs, increased workloads for those still employed, and increased part-time, temporary, low-security, low-wage, no-benefits, non-unionized jobs, largely worked by immigrants, particularly women of colour (Morris, 2000). The process of economic globalization illustrates the ways in which capitalism adapts and expands to protect its interest in profit.

In a global economic order, where one country's legislative policies can directly and indirectly influence the lives of people continents away, it is important to have analyses of gender and class that point to the interconnectedness of these processes of racialization and neo-colonialism. Socialist feminism has made important gains in the past few decades, a number of which are reflected in Canadian government policies. The inclusion of questions on work in the household within the 1996 Canadian census for example, is an important step toward making the gendered division of labour and the economic realities of women part of a socio-political dialogue within Canadian politics and culture. Women's organized struggles for state and employer-sponsored child care (as illustrated by the efforts of women associated with the Canadian Auto Workers Union [CAW] in the 1980s) has been another useful example of socialist feminist practice that made the contemporary economic realities of women difficult for the state to ignore.

---

7   The idea of economic and socio-political policies whose influences reach beyond the borders of the nation in which they originate.

Additional Dilemmas: Socialist Feminism and Global Trends

Two overarching observations are made by contemporary feminist scholars of political economy in capitalist democracies of the global northwest. First, feminists have critically questioned current neo-liberal policies that advocate unconstrained market economics with claims that open market competition on a global scale is likely to improve living and labour conditions for marginalized groups (Cohen and Brodie, 2007). Socialist feminists have pointed to the failure of laissez-faire market economics in pressuring large-scale employers (through the principle of open competition) to value the labour of their employees through improved pay, working conditions, and benefits. Instead, an oppressive "global care chain" (Hochschild, 2000) thrives, shaped significantly by the negative consequences of the structural adjustment programs (SAPS) and lending conditions to which many developing nations find themselves tied. This global care chain is characterized by the migration of women from lesser economically developed regions of the world to the wealthiest countries. Canada, for example, remains dependent on female migrant labour for its agricultural, sex, and domestic service industries. A complicated set of dynamics, involving rigid immigration and labour rights restrictions, perpetuates and compounds the vulnerability of women in these domains.

Second, socialist feminists have highlighted the transformation of the industrial economy of the 20th century into service and information-oriented economics. Developments in technology and a shift toward information-based work has introduced greater flexibility into the labour market, leading to what some political economy feminists (Fudge and Owens, 2006) call "precarious work" (lack of income and job security, part-time employment, temporary work, home work, on-call work, low wages, few benefits, and absence of union representation). But it is not only technological development that is influencing labour trends and shifts. The historically feminine and domesticated work responsibilities of women have a sharply increased presence on the paid labour market. Indeed, political economy feminists have noted a new economy of women's work (in which working-class men are now also increasingly participating). Hence, the increase of service-oriented jobs, many of which are precarious in nature, is termed the *feminization of work* (Fudge and Owens, 2006). As socialist feminists indicate, responsibility for domestic work has not decreased as more women have entered the wage labour market. The burden of an increased number of obligations without (any, or in-) adequate state support in wealthy countries is negotiated at the expense of more vulnerable women (Thistle, 2006).

Susan Thistle notes that the act of shifting domestic and socio-reproductive work responsibilities onto more vulnerable women prolongs the inequitable division of labour rather than forcing a socio-political shift in the gendered approach to domestic work, and increasing collective social responsibility for such tasks (2006). Currently, women continue to earn less than men for work of equal value and with comparable credentials. Women occupying higher positions in corporate and public institutions continue to struggle with glass ceilings, and women continue to be at a greater risk of poverty than men (Fudge and Owens, 2006). Thus, a large constituting factor of current sexist oppression from a feminist political economy approach is the new "transnational business masculinity" (Connell, 2001) that has demonstrated the power to attune both domestic and international economic relations to its anti-social and inequitable interests.

Critiques of Socialist Feminism

Socialist feminism's use of a materialist analysis as the basis of its deconstruction of oppression leaves some questions unanswered. For example, should the equitable redistribution of power and wealth in society actually occur, and economic systems find themselves operating outside of capitalism, would, as Dooley asks, "men simply no longer harass, abuse, rape, belittle, insult and hate women?" (Dooley, 2001). The theoretical engagement of radical feminism with other social realities, such as family forms outside of the heterosexual, nuclear family model (queer-identified, non-white, immigrant, Aboriginal, and single-parent family models), has also provided legitimate critiques of socialist feminist texts and forms of activism that have used the "ideology of separate spheres for men and women" (Mandell and Elliot, 2001) as a key component of materialist analyses of oppression.

RADICAL FEMINISM

Defining Radical Feminism

Have you ever wondered when women started to "Take Back the Night," rallying for safer streets and demanding that violence against women be stopped? These demonstrations (along with demonstrations for abortion rights as well as anti-violence protests) spring from a section of the women's movement called radical feminism. Radical feminists have contributed much to feminist theory by concentrating on sexuality, control, and violence, and by making clear-cut analyses of how men's power over women can be seen in all areas of women's lives, such as violence against women, rape, and prostitution.

The development of radical feminism in the 1960s and 1970s coincided with other movements such as the civil rights, anti-war, and broader women's liberation movements. These movements challenged the status quo as they attempted to shake up traditional societal institutions. In Canada, the Royal Commission on the Status of Women (Bird et al., 1970) suggested many ways in which equality for women could be attained. There was a sense of hope, energy, and urgency during this time.

Many scholars attribute the rise of radical feminism to a New York setting, naming groups such as the Red Stockings, the Furies, and the Radicalesbians, yet Canadian-based radical feminist groups such as the New Feminists of Toronto are also important to the development of radical feminist action in Canada (Echols, 1989). Groups like these organized around many issues through consciousness-raising (CR) sessions where women came together to share stories of sexist oppression and gendered exploitation to discover that "the personal is political" (Crow, 2000: 6). The CR group or "rap session" appealed to many women. In these sessions women could hear and share accounts of oppression across class and race lines, link those accounts to a larger theoretical framework in order to build critical organizing skills, and publicly air their goals. Radical feminists active in the 1960s and 1970s also used manifestos as a revolutionary method to "speak bitterness" (Freeman, 1975, quoted in Crow, 2000: 6). Collectively, radical feminist activities formed the basis for a global sisterhood, spreading feminism internationally and building alliances around concrete concerns such as violence and pornography (Morgan, 1970).

Sites of Oppression: Patriarchy, the State, and the Family

Radical feminists argue that finding the grand theory of women's oppression is key to deconstructing it. They insist that, in order to locate the root of women's oppression, one must look past laws or economic and political critiques forwarded by liberal and socialist feminists. In the early stages of the development of radical feminist thought, sex oppression was the first and most fundamental oppression, and all other areas of repression sprang from it and were shaped by it (Crow, 2000: 2). By sex oppression, radical feminists mean that women's oppression is based on the relations of domination and subordination between the sexes, where women are seen as a sex class, whose sexuality is directly controlled by men. Radical feminists insist that, in order for women to understand their inferior roles in patriarchal society, they must look at how men have come to hold and wield power over women in all social relationships.

Radical feminists identify three main areas where women are most affected: the state, the family, and motherhood. Unlike liberal feminists, who focused on women's status in terms of individual rights and laws, radical feminists theorize from women's everyday lives. They believe that patriarchy, a "sexual system of power in which the male possesses superior power and economic privilege," is what shapes everyday life and what specifically affects women, for the benefit of men (Eisenstein, 1979: 17). Patriarchy, they argued, is constituted in and through various social structures and is reproduced and activated in everyday relations, having impacts on a global scale. It can be found in all aspects of society, including the state, the family, and other institutions, such as schools, the media, and religious institutions. In order to free themselves from the "Father Land" of patriarchy, an autonomous social, historical, and political force created by men for their own benefit, women must resist and undermine this system (Daly, 1978: 28; Donovan, 2000: 156).

Radical feminists argue that the state (which includes political institutions, the legal system, and elected representatives) is founded on and is emblematic of male interests. Therefore, radical feminists believe that entrusting women's liberation to the state will result in them being once again taken for granted by the patriarchal order, and, in essence, "raped." State authority is male authority as it "is coercive and ensures men's control over women's sexuality; thus although the state assumes objectivity as its norm, in practice, women are raped by the state just as they are raped by men" (Andersen, 1997: 359). Despite many state-sponsored centres that aim to combat violence against women in this country, violence against women has not diminished. Therefore, for radical feminists, engaging with the state is futile, as it is considered a site of male power and control.

Another area of male power and control is the family. Radical feminists voice the need to look critically at this institution and point to the family as yet another site of oppression for women. Socialist-feminists centre their analyses on the unpaid work done by women within traditional families and the negative implications of women's economic dependence on men. Building on these analyses, radical feminists identify the harms of social reproduction, describing the sexual energies women give to men in order to reproduce the family biologically and sustain it culturally. For radical feminists, ideologies of romance and love support traditional family structures. Hegemonic state apparatuses, such as marriage, as well as "opiates" such as romantic love, keep women drugged and under male control. Romantic love, beauty, dating, dieting, and other cultural practices are seen as tools used by patriarchy to uphold and support heteronormativity, keeping women reliant on men's sexual attention and affection and by making women promote and service the desires of men

(Firestone, 1970: 131, 146). Ti-Grace Atkinson (1970), an early radical feminist, stated that love, as an institution of male power and control, supports violence and also "promotes vulnerability, dependence, possessiveness, susceptibility to pain, and prevents the full development of a woman's potential" (117).

Traditional mothering ideology and practice also comes under radical feminist scrutiny. As Rich has argued, mothering under patriarchy is an exploitative responsibility (Rich, 1976). The seeming naturalness of motherhood and its institutionalization has become a duty for women in patriarchal society. Mothering is a role women need to play that restricts women's caring and nurturing energies to the family unit. In the 1960s and 1970s in particular, radical feminists pointed to the idea that women were supposed to be on the mothering job 24 hours a day, every day, with no outside contacts (Tong, 1998: 83). The patriarchal order dictates that women's ability to mother becomes conflated with their worthiness as women. Therefore, women's identity as women becomes linked to their ability to mother (i.e., if you are not a good mother, you are not a good woman) (Kreps, 1973: 236). In the past few years, radical feminist analyses of motherhood have been critiqued, especially by feminist theorists who have formulated mothering as an empowering feminist enterprise. Many feminists have reclaimed motherhood as an important step in the formation of their feminism. As Andrea O'Reilly states, "[t]hough I had identified myself as a feminist for a number of years; motherhood made feminism real for me and radically redefined it" (O'Reilly, 2000: 182–183).

Women's Bodies: Reproduction, Pornography, and Violence

Many early radical feminist theorists looked to women's reproductive roles to discover the root problem of women's oppression (Firestone, 1970): Biology separates the sexes, and that division relegates an enormous amount of reproductive labour to women. As women nurture and care for children, men are freed to participate in public life and social institutions, where they can acquire power, privilege, and property, all of which emboldens their superior social status (Hamilton, 1996: 20). This seemingly "natural" sexual division of labour (men in the public, women in the private) means that women are at the mercy of their biology; radical feminists declared a need for this to be addressed (Firestone, 1970). Within this sexual division of labour, women's bodies become an object, passed down from father to husband, placing the ownership of their sexuality squarely in the hands of men (Hamilton, 1996: 65). According to radical feminists, women clearly needed to divest themselves of these relationships.

In order to destroy patriarchy, radical feminists called for a re-evaluation of women's reproductive roles and an elimination of the traditional family. Women had little control over their reproductive functions, as abortion was illegal in Canada until 1988[8] and birth control was hard to acquire in the early phases of the women's movement in the 1960s and 1970s. Many, therefore, suggested that freeing women from the "tyranny of reproduction" and relying on technological advances would diminish clearly marked and oppressive gendered differences (Firestone, 1970). As a remedy, some radical feminists believed that in

---

8 Abortion was first decriminalized in 1969, yet access to it had to be granted by committees composed usually of men, and only if it was to preserve women's "health," a term that was often interpreted differently depending on the committee. Full access to abortion was granted in 1988.

vitro fertilization, artificial insemination, and eventually cloning would separate women from their wombs, therefore breaking the oppressive tie of women to biology. Others countered that although women would be liberated from reproduction through new reproductive technologies, it would only lead to male control; those who held ownership of these technologies were doctors and scientists who were usually men. Margaret Atwood's famous novel *The Handmaid's Tale* (1985) exemplifies the concerns of some radical feminists, as it recounts a dystopian future where women become uniquely defined and controlled by their reproductive roles.

Radical feminist theorists question the meaning of masculinity and femininity, arguing that masculinity is linked to dominance and that femininity is linked to subordination. Furthermore, these unequal relations of power are eroticized in traditional heterosexual relations where women are positioned as objects of male pleasure, constantly available, constantly ready, and constantly scrutinized. In the popular media and pornography, which has become widely available on the internet, the male gaze constructs women's sexuality and structures male and female sexual relations. As a result, many young people define their own ideas around sexuality and sexual relations through these sources, and these sources alone. Popular feminists such as Eve Ensler, author of *The Vagina Monologues*, argue that these relations of power can be linked to global violence against women, resulting in various crimes against women, such as incest, honour killings, and rape as a war crime (see VDay website in Weblinks section).

Annette Koedt, in her well-known 1970 article "The Myth of the Vaginal Orgasm," discussed how medical literature about women's bodies had created the false belief that women who could not achieve orgasm solely through penetration of the vagina, and who instead achieved orgasm through clitoral stimulation, were described as "frigid" by their male partners and the medical establishment. Koedt and others challenged this notion and revealed how men owned and defined women's sexuality. In such an unequal model, women's needs and desires are ignored (MacKinnon, 1989).

Male power is still evident in much pornography and in prostitution, a sensitive area of female exploitation and domination critiqued by radical feminists. "Female sexual slavery," radical feminists argue, and the graphic depictions of women as sexual objects are manifestations of the patriarchal domination of women by men and have the effect of shaping an acceptance of violent and coercive hatred against women (Dworkin, 1981; Barry, 1984). Some radical feminists think that male violence against women stems from an intake of violent pornography, making it acceptable to see women as purely objects of sexual gratification rather than as mutual players of love and intimacy (Tong, 1998: 66). Radical feminism still sees teenage males and females as growing up in a misogynist culture in which double standards persist. Women find themselves dieting at an early age, and the number of young women suffering from bulimia and anorexia grows daily. In a society that delivers such violent cultural messages about women and women's bodies, it is not surprising that young women starve themselves to fit their bodies into a sexist cultural ideal of beauty.

Radical feminist theorists have also spoken strongly against rape, seeing it as a crime resulting from, and maintaining, male power. If domination and subordination are the basis for unequal sexual relations between men and women, and if these unequal sexual relations are a maintained and constitutive of force, what is the difference between sex and rape? (Dworkin, 1974; Brownmiller, 1976; MacKinnon, 1989). If women and men are not equals in society, and if men wield power over women, then loving and sexual relationships between the two are always mediated by unequal power exchanges, where one person (man) controls the other (woman). Radical feminists conclude that women cannot experience their sexuality as pleasurable, because sexuality is male-coded and controlled. How then, they ask, do women construct their own sexuality? What would woman-defined sexuality look like?

Female Separation: Lesbian Feminism and Cultural Feminism

Radical feminists see our societies as violent and male-dominated, a world in which cultural representations of women include those of prostitution, pornography, and rape. Radical feminists argue that eliminating patriarchal society is the only viable solution to ending inequality. Patriarchy is sustained by men maintaining relationships with one another and thus ensuring that their power and privilege is maintained through interlocking systems of oppression such as racism, classism, and women's sexual oppression. Radical feminists, especially lesbian and cultural feminists, suggest that women divest themselves of patriarchy by strengthening bonds among women and by removing themselves from patriarchy's grip.

Lesbian feminism sprang from radical feminists' desire to discover and value women's contributions to society. Lesbian feminists shifted the debate from analyzing and reacting to male structures of power to focusing on how passionate bonds between women can foster a politics of emancipation. Lesbianism connotes sexual relations between women. But it also represents a political stance, a support system that allows women to turn to other women to escape from an oppressive male-dominated world. Lesbian feminists argued that every culture is infused with phallocentric social and cultural values forcing women to live lives geared toward men and heterosexual and monogamous pairings (Rich, 1980). In part, women are taught that self-worth comes from heterosexual marriage and mothering. The idea of compulsory heterosexuality—where women are seen to be naturally sexually oriented toward men—restricts women socially and economically. Alternatives to this model, such as lesbian sexuality, were not well received by mainstream society and cast aside as deviant (Rich, 1980: 4).

Lesbian feminism suggests that the main way women can resist male domination and power is to refrain from having sexual relations with men. Arising from this idea came the famous slogan, "feminism is the theory and lesbianism is the practice." Or, as Catherine MacKinnon said, "feminism is the epistemology of which lesbianism is ontology" (quoted in Heller, 1997: 22). Adrienne Rich, a well-known American lesbian feminist, advanced the idea of the lesbian continuum in order to operationalize that slogan. In order to separate lesbianism from being solely a sexual relation between women, Rich described a continuum, a position of compromise where all relations between women (friendships and caring relationships such as elder care) can be placed within the definition of lesbian and lesbian feminist politics (Rich, 1980). Not all feminists were comfortable with Rich's suggestion that lesbian be adopted as a political slogan. In Canada particularly, homophobic responses led to the ejection of many lesbians from feminist organizing groups, as some believed that the prominent presence of lesbians would undermine the movement (Grant, 1998; Ross, 1995).

Radical cultural feminists, successors of radical feminists, banded together and mobilized around what they saw as women's uniqueness: their femaleness. Cultural feminists espouse a "politics of disengagement," a breaking out of a male-dominated society by providing women-only cultural spaces (Adamson, Briskin, and McPhail, 1988: 192; Donovan, 2000: 255–256). By concentrating on the positive features of women-only cultural spaces—care, sympathy, and nurturance—women would be able to promote and celebrate them and make them the basis for relationships between women. Often seen as the "separatists" in the feminist movement, cultural feminists believe that valuing women demands a woman-centred culture, where goddesses are worshipped, and bookstores, co-ops, and centres—run by women for women—can counter the negative effects of a male-dominated society.

Contemporary Theoretical Ideas

Radical feminist theorizing has been influential in shaping contemporary understandings of sex and sexuality, power and dominance. Radical feminist critiques continue to investigate patriarchy as problematic for women. Many important vehicles of feminist political action exist today because of the ideas of radical feminism.

How we understand violence against women in contemporary society has been shaped by radical feminist theories and ideas. The Canadian Research Institute for the Advancement of Women (CRIAW) reports that half of Canadian women are survivors of at least one incident of physical or sexual violence (Morris, 2002b). And although Statistics Canada's Measuring Violence Against Women report states that the "number of spousal violence incidents against women has declined since 2000," the rates of "violence perpetrated by boyfriends has increased" and the number of men who are reported to police for spousal abuse has also increased (Johnson, 2006). Also, the rates of spousal violence against Aboriginal women are higher than for non-Aboriginal women (Johnson, 2006).

Women continue to "Take Back the Night" and demand safer streets and harsher rape laws for offenders. A network of government-funded shelters for women escaping abusive partners located across Canada exists because of the important theoretical insights that radical feminism has provided on violence against women. Radical feminist ideas have provided a theoretical framework for understanding women's everyday lives and continue to be relevant to contemporary theorizing.

Organizations such as Women Against Pornography and Always Causing Legal Unrest (ACLU) and journals such as *Off Our Backs* continue to uphold radical-feminist theoretical tenets and to thrive within mainstream feminist discourse. Taking up similar topics to those of 30 years ago, contemporary radical feminist theorists remain committed to providing an analytical framework around women's oppression as a result of patriarchal domination. Pornography and prostitution are still on the agenda, as is the interrogation and abolition of male privilege. Groups like the ACLU continue to demonstrate in front of sex stores, doing "zaps" as seen in the tactics of feminists working in the 1960s, where small groups of people carry out symbolic protests and demonstrations. Their motto speaks to this, as they state, "we tear into sexism" (see website for ACLU in the Weblinks section).

Canadian Obscenity Laws: The Butler Case and Radical Feminist Theory

Radical feminist theories have been successful in providing a framework for understanding what is and is not considered criminally obscene in Canada. In 1992, a landmark Supreme Court decision in *Butler v. the Queen* brought into debate the definition of what constitutes criminal obscenity (Donald Butler was arrested for selling hard-core pornographic videos in his Manitoba store). According to the 1992 decision, the goal of outlawing certain types of material and defining them as obscene was to protect people, most notably women, from harm. What is considered pornographic and what is considered obscene is decided through one simple test: whether or not images are degrading to women. Obscenity laws were no longer seen as a matter of public morality or decency, but were evaluated according to questions of harm, especially harm to women (Cossman et al., 1997).

Catherine MacKinnon and Andrea Dworkin (1946–2005), two very famous radical feminists from the United States, along with the Canadian organization Women's Legal Education and Action Fund (LEAF) were instrumental in shaping the Canadian obscenity law. These anti-pornography proponents used earlier radical feminist ideas that viewed pornography as essentially violent and degrading to women as a facet of the patriarchal order. LEAF submitted a legal brief with sections written with the assistance of MacKinnon, which influenced the court's decision. It found that any images that portrayed "degrading" sex, especially of women, could be criminalized (Cossman et al., 1997: 18). This was seen as a victory for many anti-pornography feminists, who insisted that these images were detrimental to women.

This 1992 judgment also affected gay and lesbian materials in unforeseen ways. What is considered "obscene" in a homophobic society, critics argue, often means demonizing images, ideas, and texts that transgress the normative bounds of heterosexual sex. Many gay and lesbian bookstores across Canada (for example, Little Sister's Book and Art Emporium in Vancouver and Glad Day Books in Toronto) maintained that Canadian customs officials were more heavily scrutinizing, seizing, and destroying shipments intended for their stores, searching for contraventions to the 1992 ruling. In 1994, Little Sister's Book and Art Emporium went to court to challenge the Butler ruling, stating that freedom of expression as well as equality (for gays and lesbians) were being violated contrary to the *Canadian Charter of Rights and Freedoms* (Cossman et al., 1997: 36). The court disagreed, ruling that "homosexual obscenity is proscribed because it is obscene, not because it is homosexual" (Cossman et al., 1997: 47). Although this ruling is clearly still a concern for many gay and lesbian businesses, a small victory occurred in 2000 when the courts agreed that customs officials were overwhelmingly heavy-handed in their appraisal of lesbian and gay materials. However, the BC bookstore has been back to court numerous times since, attempting to follow through on this decision and to fight systemic homophobia that continues to censor gay and lesbian materials. In 2007, the bookstore was denied funds to challenge Canadian customs on their ongoing seizures of materials, meaning that the original obscenity laws continue to be applied in uneven ways (McCann, 2007a).

Global Dimensions of Radical Feminist Thought

The sexual dominance of men over women has global reach, according to radical feminist theorists. The sex industry and sex tourism are where this exploitation is most visible, and the growing "industrialized and internationalized" as well as profitable industry is evidence that women and children are continuing to be left behind (Barry, 1995). Jeffreys notes that a 1998 report found that sex work[9] accounted for upwards of 14 percent of the

---

9   Sex worker, advocate, and organizer Carol Leigh of COYOTE (Call Off Your Old Tired Ethics) has been claimed as the creator of the term "sex worker" as opposed to prostitute, which has been seen to have "connotations of shame, unworthiness or wrongdoing" (Bernstein, 1999). In opposition to this, the term "sex worker" has been viewed by many feminist thinkers as a more useful term, as it forwards sex-positive politics, and also attempts to normalize those involved in the industry as simply "service workers and care-giving professionals" who require rights as workers (Bernstein, 1999).

economy in the four Asian countries of Thailand, Indonesia, Malaysia, and the Philippines (Jeffreys, 1999: 185). In Europe, specifically the Netherlands, Jeffreys states that an estimated 20 000 women, both foreign and locally born, are sex workers (1999: 188). And the numbers are growing; according to the UNESCO Trafficking Statistics Project and the International Organization for Migration (IOM), as many as 4 million people are trafficked annually. Of this number, it is estimated that 85 percent of them are women and girls (United Nations Development Fund for Women, 2007; Valenta, 2007). This illegal industry generates an estimated US$7–12 billion dollars per year. Due to an increase in the need for migratory labour in a more globalized economic system, as well as factors such as war and militarization, internet pornography, and growing demands from tourists for easily accessible sex for sale, sex work and the trafficking of women have become a larger part of the international capitalist system, thriving on sexist and racist ideas about women and sexuality.

In order to combat what Jeffreys states is more accurately called "prostitution tourism" and sex trafficking, radical feminists believe an international feminism is required. This global feminism would link the actions of women around the world, and challenge the patriarchal and sexual exploitation of women that defies state and national borders (Barry, 1995; Jeffreys, 1999). Kathleen Barry, who has been theorizing around female sexual slavery since the 1980s, argues that the global sexual trafficking of women was an area where radical feminist thought and action could be most useful (Barry, 1995). Barry states, "strategies to confront sexual exploitation should be as global as the economy is international and as the dimensions of women's subordination are universal [feminists must] unravel and expose sexual exploitation in all its global complexity" (Barry, 1995: 276, 277). Global sex tourism and trafficking are seen as commercial male sexual violence, and consequently they violate women's human rights (Jeffreys, 1999: 180).

Along with other groups such as SAGE (Standing Against Global Exploitation), WHISPER (Women Hurt in Systems of Prostitution Engaged in Revolt) and the CATW (Coalition Against Trafficking in Women), an international response was formed to this global phenomena of exploitation through a proposed Convention Against Sexual Exploitation. This convention, proposed jointly between CATW and the United Nation Educational, Scientific and Cultural Organization (UNESCO), would "outlaw all sexual exploitation including female infanticide, woman murder, woman battering, genital mutilation, rape, incest, pornography, prostitution and trafficking" (Sullivan, 2003: 70). Defined as a violation of women's human rights, any man involved in the sex trade industry, whether as a trafficker or as a consumer, would be penalized criminally (Barry, 1995: Appendix). This convention was eventually opposed by sex workers and their allies and was consequently unsuccessful (Sullivan, 2003: 71). However, in December 2000 more than 80 countries signed what is called the "Trafficking Protocol," which would "suppress, prevent and punish trafficking in persons specifically women and children" (Dozema, 2005: 62). Again, opposed by advocates of the rights of sex workers and many transnational feminists, the main debate was a larger discussion around the idea of consent and how one would define when and if a person was trafficked (Dozema, 2005: 62).

The position of radical feminists on sex work and the sex trade industry has been challenged consistently by those who advocate for a forced vs. free distinction in trafficking theory. Forced sex work would include any person who has been compelled to participate within the sex trade industry as a "slavery-like practice" (Dozema, 1998). In opposition, free sex work is seen as a "personal choice and a form of work" (Dozema, 1998). By placing their experiences within the realm of work, sex workers would rather concentrate efforts on improving working conditions including health, safety, and wages with an eventual decriminalization of prostitution (Sullivan, 2003: 70). There is also a concern among many transnational feminists with the language and policy implementation by governmental bodies around trafficking, wherein the discourse is seen as being "firmly linked in postindustrial areas of the world to the criminalization of migrant women from the global South and to greater policing and control of their mobility, bodies and sexuality" (Kempadoo, 2005).

Critiques of Radical Feminism

Radical feminism has strengths and weaknesses. Charges of essentialism haunt radical feminists as they are brought to task for generalizing about the fundamental nature of each sex. Theoretical writings by radical feminists often make the assumption that men are inherently violent and aggressive, while women are nurturing and caring. This, of course, presents concerns for many theorists, as it limits a further engagement with sex and gender, naturalizing these concepts to biological ideologies of women and men and not necessarily interrogating them further. If one's biology is the sole defining feature of a person, how does one break free from the stranglehold of biology as destiny?

Discourses of victimization also pervade radical feminist theory. Women are seen as trapped in essential roles with little hope or ability to resist. What do women do if all relations between women and men are exploitative and if there are no spaces for resistance?

Many postmodern feminists claim that radical feminist theory suffers not only from essentialism but also from romanticism, ethnocentrism, and historicism (Mandell and Elliot, 2001). They argue that definitions given by radical feminists of patriarchy and women are homogenizing and limiting and do not account for the diversities offered by class, race, sexuality, age, history, and other aspects of women's lives that make them unique and multiple. In contrast, other radical feminists insist that we need to have a category of "woman" to rally around, for if we do not, how do we then establish a basis for feminist action and organizing? (Thompson, 2001: 69).

Many theorists of colour openly criticize radical feminists for their inattention to race, forwarding a vision of "global sisterhood" that is often racist and exclusionary. Many women of colour challenge white radical feminists on their imperialist and universalizing notions of women, in which women of colour and Third-World women are often cast as "backwards" and in need of "saving." Other scholars, such as Black American feminist Angela Davis, have taken white radical feminists to task for writing about non-white communities as deviant, writing about Black men and rape, and naturalizing the myth of the Black rapist, so prevalent during and after slavery (Tong, 1998: 223). Others also argue that the radical feminist attacks on the family are Euro- and ethnocentric, and helped to undermine the importance of family for many non-white people. As Linda Carty states, "[f]or Black people and people of colour, the family served as protection against, and a central source of resistance to, racist oppression" (Carty, 1999: 42).

Another issue of concern and contention relates to radical and cultural feminist questions about the "dangers" of transgendered people in general and transsexual women in particular, invading women's spaces and bodies. Rather than broaden their ideas about gender, many radical feminists consider transsexual women to be committing violence: Janice Raymond says, "Rape ... is a masculinist violation of bodily integrity. All transsexuals rape women's bodies by reducing the female form to an artifact, appropriating this body for themselves... Rape, although it is usually done by force, can also be accomplished by deception" (1998: 308). Many of these ideas persist, viewing transsexual women as a medicalized creation, out to deceive and conceal their "true" identities. For instance, in 1995 the Vancouver Rape Relief and Women's Shelter refused to let Kimberly Nixon, a transsexual woman, become a rape crisis counsellor out of the conviction that being born a woman is the basic and primary definition of being a woman (Wente, 2000). Initially, Nixon was awarded $7500 by the BC Human Rights Tribunal on the basis that she had been discriminated against. Since then, the case has been appealed by both sides, and was finally taken to the Supreme Court of Canada in 2007, where it was refused a hearing (McCann, 2007b).

Transgender feminists assert that biology should not be the sole defining characteristic of gendered identity. In fact, they argue that gender becomes politically problematic when it is so defined (Stone, 1991). As radical feminists seek to unhook women from their biology, they question the rigid mapping of sex onto gender and vice versa. Transgender feminists demand a serious re-evaluation of ahistorical and essentialist theories in their attempts to destabilize the fixity of sex/gender categories. Instead, they analyze the "social structures which enforce sex/gender identity congruity and stability at every level" (MacDonald, 2000: 289).

CONCLUSION

This chapter provides an introduction to liberal, socialist, and radical feminist theoretical approaches to understanding women's oppression. The theories are examined in terms of their central principles, their methods of challenging women's oppression, their practical goals, and their achievements.

Liberal feminism is based on the principles of women's capacity for rationality, meritocracy, equal opportunity, and freedom of choice. From the application of liberal philosophy to inequalities between men and women, we learn that at the source of women's oppression is an inequitable integration of women into society's institutions such as schools and universities, government, professions, and economic organizations. Furthermore, the avenues of opportunity that exist for women to make inroads to full participation in society with men are insufficient. Liberal feminists have thus concentrated on achieving equal opportunity for women by ensuring that all the rights, benefits, and responsibilities that accrue to men also accrue to women.

Socialist feminists explain and advocate for women's liberation through a theoretical framework that places the interconnectedness of capitalism, patriarchy, and more recently, race, sexuality, and globalization, at the centre of its analyses of women's oppression. Socialist feminists challenge women's oppression through unions, advocating for equal pay for work of equal value, increased state investment in social services, and the eradication of poverty. The theoretical and activist contributions of socialist feminists have been instrumental in influencing the Canadian state to include, for the first time in the 1996 census, questions on unpaid labour. In addition, many workplaces have passed paternity-leave provisions (although women continue to take the majority of parental leaves).

Radical feminists investigate what they believe to be the root cause of women's oppression; that is, sex oppression of women by men. They argue that sex oppression in a patriarchal society can be found in social structures such as the state and the family. Radical feminists identify how women's sexuality is directly controlled by men, through an analysis of reproduction, pornography, and rape, but also through other institutions of social control in everyday relations such as heterosexual love, marriage, and motherhood. Women's places within these systems are all shaped by male domination, where men wield and hold power over women, for the men's sole benefit. Radical feminist theorists posit many avenues of resistance against this system of control. Lesbian and cultural feminists argue that women need to break free from patriarchal culture, through an endorsement of lesbian relationships and women-only cultural spaces. Globally, radical feminists used their critiques to challenge the trafficking of women in prostitution, calling on nations to penalize both traffickers and consumers of sex tourism. Although radical feminist theorizing has been influential, bringing to light issues such as rape, pornography, and violence against women in a misogynist society, it has been subject to criticisms from transgendered scholars and scholars of colour who ask that it re-evaluate its essentialist ideas of the category "woman."

Suggested Readings

Bannerji, Himani. 2000. *The dark side of the nation: Essays on multiculturalism, nationalism and gender*. Toronto: Scholars Press. This text of critical essays provides a feminist theoretical framework for understanding the key issues related to the experiences of women of colour within the neo-colonial Canadian nation. Bannerji addresses the relationship of feminism to Marxist thought, always within an anti-racist analytical context. This book is very useful in helping think through some of the gaps left by mainstream class-oriented social justice movements.

Crow, Barbara A., ed. 2000. *Radical feminism: A documentary reader*. New York: New York Univ. Press. This compilation of key texts details the contributions of radical feminist theorizing and activism to the second-wave women's movement. Containing primary sources, such as manifestos, meeting minutes, and other published and unpublished records from the time, it provides a wealth of information on pressing issues in radical feminism, such as sexuality, lesbian separatism, race, and class.

Dua, Enakshi, and Angela Robertson, eds. 1999. *Scratching the surface: Canadian anti-racist feminist thought*. Toronto: Women's Press. This book is an insightful and informative reflection on anti-racist feminist thought and activism in Canada. Included are discussions on the central role of racialization in the colonial settler process and the creation of the Canadian nation. Its articles provide crucial context for debates concerning class and gender.

Newton, Janice. 1992. The alchemy of politicisation: Socialist women and the early Canadian left, in *Gender conflicts: New essays in women's history*, ed. Franca Iacovetta and Mariana Valverde, 118–148. Toronto: Univ. of Toronto Press. Newton recovers the significant contributions of early socialist feminists to the Canadian prohibition and suffrage movements as well as to socialist and communist politics at the turn of the 20th century. The article also includes a discussion of socialist women's activism about women's position in the labour force.

Prentice, Alison, et al. 1996. *Canadian women: A history*. Toronto: Harcourt Brace and Company. Prentice et al. provide a substantial integrative text on Canadian women's history. Chapters are organized both thematically and chronologically, providing the reader with a helpful contextual analysis of women's history in Canada.

Rich, Adrienne. 1980. Compulsory heterosexuality and lesbian existence. *Signs: Journal of Women in Culture and Society* 5/4: 3–32. Adrienne Rich's classic discussion on the destabilizing of heterosexuality as a "natural" biological fact provides critical insight into the importance of lesbian existence and visibility in the feminist movement.

Roome, Patricia. 2001. Women's suffrage movement in Canada. Chinook Multimedia Inc. Retrieved February 12, 2004, from the World Wide Web **www.chinookmultimedia.com/poccd/registered**.

Roome's discussion of Canadian women's suffrage is an account of a pivotal political moment in the history of first-wave feminism. The article offers a detailed consideration of the role of women's religious organizations in achieving the vote.

Scott-Dixon, Krista, ed. 2006. *Trans/forming feminisms: Transfeminist voices speak out*. Toronto: Sumach Press. Contributors to this text advance a critical analysis of feminist ideas through a transfeminist politic. Essays include references to events in Canadian politics concerning discourses around inclusion, most specifically the case of Kimberly Nixon v. Vancouver Rape Relief and Women's Shelter.

Valverde, Mariana. 1992. "When the Mother of the Race Is Free": Race, reproduction and sexuality in first-wave feminism, in *Gender conflicts: New essays in women's history*, ed. Franca Iacovetta and Mariana Valverde, 3–28. Toronto: Univ. of Toronto Press. Valverde provides an in-depth examination of the ways in which discourses of race, racism, sexuality, and gender were key in shaping first-wave feminists' approach to achieving suffrage. The intersection of the Canadian eugenics and temperance movements are examined and linked to the persons and organizations that also fed the early suffrage movement.

Discussion Questions

1. Define each of the three theories (liberal, socialist, and radical feminism) in your own words. Which one do you most identify with?

2. Discuss how each theory defines the source of women's oppression and their approaches to social change.

3. Identify an accomplishment or goal of each group of feminists. How did theory inform their actions?

4. What are the main criticisms of each theory? Are they valid critiques? Why or why not?

5. Do you see evidence of these theories at work today? Give examples.

Bibliography

Adamson, Nancy, Linda Briskin, and Margaret McPhail. 1988. *Feminist organizing for change: The contemporary women's movement in Canada*. London: Oxford Univ. Press.

Andersen, Margaret L. 1997. *Thinking about women: Sociological perspectives on sex and gender*, 4th ed. Boston: Allyn and Bacon.

Arneil, Barbara. 2001. Women as wives, servants and slaves: Rethinking the public/private divide. *Canadian Journal of Political Science* 34(1): 29–54.

Astell, Mary. 1694, 1697/1997. *A serious proposal to the ladies parts I & II*. Reprinted with an introduction by Patricia Springborg, London, England: Pickering and Chatto.

Atkinson, Ti-Grace. 1970. The institution of sexual intercourse, in *Notes from the third year*, ed. Shulamith Firestone. New York: Random House.

Atwood, Margaret. 1985. *The handmaid's tale*. Toronto: McClelland and Stewart.

Ault, Amber, and Eve Sandberg. 2001. Our policies, their consequences: Zambian women's lives under structural adjustment, in *An introduction to women's studies: Gender in a transnational world*, ed. Inderpal Grewal and Caren Kaplan, 469–473. New York: McGraw-Hill.

Baker, Michael, Jonathan Gruber, and Kevin Milligan. 2005. Universal childcare, maternal labor supply and family well-being. **www.econ.ubc.ca/kevinmil/research/childcare.oct2005**. (July 2005)

Bannerji, Himani. 1995. *Thinking through: Essays on feminism, Marxism, and anti-racism*. Toronto: Women's Press.

Barry, Kathleen. 1984. *Female sexual slavery*. New York: New York Univ. Press.

Barry, Kathleen. 1995. *The prostitution of sexuality: The global exploitation of women*. New York: New York Univ. Press.

Benston, Margaret. 1989. The political economy of women's liberation. *Monthly Review* 41(7): 31–43.

Bernstein, Elizabeth. 1999. What's wrong with prostitution? What's right with sex work? Comparing markets in female sexual labor. *Hastings Women's Law Journal* 91: 91–117.

Bird, Florence, et al. 1970. Commissioners' list of recommendations, in *Report on the Royal Commission on the Status of Women in Canada*. Ottawa: Government of Canada.

Brenner, Johanna. 2000. *Women and politics of class*. New York: Monthly Review Press.

Brown, Rosemary. 1989. *Being Brown: A very public life*. Toronto: Random House.

Brownmiller, Susan. 1976. *Against our will: Men, women and rape*. Toronto: Bantam.

Bryson, Valerie. 1992. *Feminist political theory: An introduction*. London: MacMillan.

Calliste, Agnes. 2001. Immigration of Caribbean nurses and domestic workers to Canada, 1955–1967. Chinook Multimedia Inc. **www.chinookmultimedia.com/poccd/registered**. Retrieved February 12, 2004.

Canadian Labour Congress. 2008. Working women: Still a long way from equality... **www.canadianlabour.ca**. Retrieved March 6, 2008.

Carty, Linda. 1999. The discourse of empire and the social construction of gender, in *Scratching the surface: Canadian anti-racist feminist thought*, ed. Enakshi Dua and Angela Robertson, 35–48. Toronto: Women's Press.

Cho, Lily. 2002. Rereading Chinese head tax racism: Redress, stereotype and antiracist critical practice. *Essays on Canadian Writing* 75: 62–84.

Citizenship and Immigration Canada. 2007. Working temporarily in Canada: The live-in caregiver program. **www.cic.gc.ca?ENGLISH/work/caregiver/index,asp**. Retrieved March 31, 2007.

Cleverdon, Catherine. 1974. *The women suffrage movement in Canada*. Toronto: Univ. of Toronto Press.

Code, Lorraine. 1993. Feminist theory, in *Changing patterns: Women in Canada*, 2d ed., ed. Sandra Burt, 19–58. Toronto: McClelland and Stewart.

Cohen, Marjorie Griffin, and Janine Brodie, eds. 2007. *Remapping gender in the new global order*. London: Routledge.

Connell, R.W. 2001. Masculinity politics on a world scale, in *The masculinities reader*, ed. Stephen M. Whitehead and Frank J. Barrett. Cambridge, UK: Polity Press.

Cossman, Brenda, et al. 1997. *Bad attitude/s on trial: Pornography, feminism, and the Butler decision*. Toronto: Univ. of Toronto Press.

Crow, Barbara A., ed. 2000. *Radical feminism: A documentary reader.* New York: New York Univ. Press.

Dalla Costa, Mariarosa, and Selma James. 1975. *The power of women and the subversion of the community.* Bristol: Falling Wall.

Daly, Mary. 1978. *Gyn/ecology, the metaethics of radical feminism.* Boston: Beacon Press.

de Pizan, Christine. 1405/1982. *The book of the city of ladies.* Foreword by Marina Warner. New York: Persea Books.

Dickason, Olive. 2002. *Canada's First Nations: A history of founding peoples from earliest times.* Oxford: Oxford Univ. Press.

Donovan, Josephine. 2000. *Feminist theory: The intellectual traditions,* 3d ed. New York: Continuum Publishing.

Dooley, Chantelle. 2001. Socialist feminism: Is it really just a class issue? Suite 101.Com, Society and Culture Page. **www.suite101.com/article.cfm/13914/75231**. Retrieved December 5, 2003.

Dozema, Jo. 2002. Who gets to choose? Coercion, consent, and the UN trafficking protocol. *Gender and Development: Trafficking and Slavery* 10(1): 20–27.

Dozema, Jo. 2005. Now you see her, now you don't: Sex workers at the UN trafficking protocol negotiation. *Social Legal Studies* 14: 61–89.

Drolet, Marie. 2001. The persistent gap: New evidence on the Canadian gender wage gap. Business and Labour Market Analysis Division, No. 157. Ottawa: Statistics Canada.

Dua, Enakshi, and Angela Robertson, eds. 1999. *Scratching the surface: Canadian anti-racist feminist thought.* Toronto: Women's Press.

Dworkin, Andrea. 1974. *Woman hating.* New York: E.P. Dutton.

Dworkin, Andrea. 1981. *Pornography: Men possessing women.* New York: Perigee Books.

Echols, Alice. 1989. *Daring to be bad: Radical feminism in America 1967–1975.* Minneapolis: Univ. of Minnesota Press.

Eisenstein, Zillah R. 1979. *Capitalist patriarchy and the case for socialist feminism.* New York: Monthly Review Press.

Engels, Friederich. 1884/1972. *The origin of the family, private property and the state.* New York: Pathfinder.

Falardeau-Ramsay, Michelle. 1999. Gender equality and the law: From the "Famous Five" to the new millennium. *Canadian Woman Studies* 19(1–2): 52–56.

Fiamengo, Janice. 2002. Rediscovering our foremothers again: The racial ideas of Canada's early feminists, 1885–1945. *Essays on Canadian Writing* 75: 85–117.

Firestone, Shulamith. 1970. *The dialectic of sex: The case for feminist revolution.* New York: William Morrow.

Friedan, Betty. 1963. *The feminine mystique.* New York: Dell.

Fudge, Judy, and Rosemarie Owens, eds. 2006. *Precarious work: Women and the new economy.* Oxford: Hart.

Garvie, Maureen McCallum, and Jennifer L. Johnson. 1999. *Their leaven of influence: Deans of women at Queen's University, 1916–1996*. Kingston: Queen's Alumni Association Committee on Women's Affairs.

Gehl, Lynn. 2000. The Queen and I: Discrimination against women in the "Indian Act" continues. *Canadian Woman Studies* 20(2): 64–69.

Grant, Ali. 1998, UnWomanly acts: Struggling over sites of resistance, in *New frontiers of space, bodies and gender*, ed. Rosa Ainley. New York: Routledge.

Hall, Catherine. 1992. *White, male and middle class: Explorations in feminism and history*. New York: Routledge.

Hamilton, Roberta. 1996. *Gendering the vertical mosaic: Feminist perspectives on Canadian society*. Toronto: Copp Clark.

Hanson, Cindy, Lori Hanson, and Barbara Adams. 2001. *Who benefits: Women, unpaid work and social policy*. Ottawa: Canadian Research Institute for the Advancement of Women (CRIAW).

Harman, Harriet. 2000. An urgent case for modernization: Public policy on women's work, in *New gender agenda: Why women still want more*, ed. Anna Coote, 109–116. London: Biddles.

Heller, Dana A. 1997. *Cross-purposes: Lesbians, feminists, and the limits of alliance*. Bloomington: Indiana Univ. Press.

Hewitt, Patricia. 2000. Gender and the knowledge economy: Work, family and e-business, in *New gender agenda: Why women still want more*, ed. Anna Coote, 137–147. London: Biddles.

Hochschild, Arlie. 2000. The nanny chain. *American Prospect* II 4. **www.prospect.org**

hooks, bell. 1994. Theory as liberatory practice, in bell hooks, *Teaching to transgress: Education as the practice of freedom*. New York: Routledge.

hooks, bell. 2000. *Feminism is for everybody: Passionate politics*. Cambridge, MA: South End Press.

Human Rights Watch. 2002. Sex discrimination in the maquiladoras, in *An introduction to women's studies: Gender in a transnational world*, ed. Inderpal Grewal and Caren Kaplan, 467–468. New York: McGraw-Hill.

Jaggar, Alison M. 1983. *Feminist politics and human nature*. Totowa, NJ: Rowman and Allanheld.

Jaggar, Alison M., and Paula S. Rothenberg, eds. 1993. *Feminist frameworks: Alternative theoretical accounts of the relations between women and men*, 3d ed. New York: McGraw-Hill.

Jeffreys, Sheila. 1999. Globalizing sexual exploitation: Sex tourism and the traffic in women. *Leisure Studies* 18(3): 179–196.

Johnson, Holly. 2006. Measuring violence against women: Statistical trends 2006. Ottawa: Statistics Canada. **www.statcan.ca/english/research/85-570-XIE/85-570-XIE2006001.htm**. Retrieved August 1, 2008.

Kelly, Jennifer. 1998. *Under the gaze: Learning to be Black in white society*. Halifax: Fernwood.

Kempadoo, Kamala. 2005. Victims and agents of crime: The new crusade against trafficking, in *Global lockdown: Race, gender and the post-industrial complex*, ed. Julia Sudbury and Julia Chinyere Oparah, 35–56. New York and London: Routledge.

Koedt, Annette. 1970. The myth of the vaginal orgasm, in *Notes from the first year*. New York: New York Radical Women. **http://scriptorium.lib.duke.edu/wlm/notes/#myth**. Retrieved August 1, 2008.

Kramnick, Miriam Brody. 1982. Introduction, in Mary Wollstonecraft, *A vindication of the rights of woman*. Harmondsworth, UK: Penguin Books.

Kreps, Bonnie. 1973. Radical feminism 1, in *Radical feminism*, ed. Anne Koedt, Ellen Levine, and Anita Rapone, 234–239. New York: Quadrangle Books.

MacDonald, Eleanor. 2000. Critical identities: Rethinking feminism through transgender politics, in *Open boundaries: A Canadian women's studies reader*, 2d ed., ed. Barbara A. Crow and Lise Gotell, 381–389. Toronto: Prentice Hall.

MacIvor, Heather. 1996. *Women and politics in Canada*. Peterborough, ON: Broadview Press.

MacKinnon, Catherine. 1989. Sexuality, in Catherine MacKinnon, *Towards a feminist theory of the state*. Cambridge, MA: Harvard Univ. Press.

Mandell, Nancy, and Patricia Elliot. 2001. Feminist theories, in *Feminist issues: Race, class, and sexuality*, 3d ed., ed. Nancy Mandell. Toronto: Prentice Hall.

Maracle, Sylvia. 2003. The eagle has landed: Native women, leadership and community development, in *Strong women stories: Native vision and community survival*, ed. Kim Anderson and Bonita Lawrence. Toronto: Sumach Press.

Marx, Karl, and Friedrich Engels. 1848/1998. *The communist manifesto*, tr. Samuel Moore. Halifax: Fernwood Press.

Marx, Karl, and Friedrich Engels. 1932/1968. *The German ideology*, ed. S. Ryazanskaya. Moscow: Progress Publishers.

McCann, Marcus. 2007a. Little Sister's declares defeat in the wake of 7–2 Supreme Court ruling: With no money to fight censorship, bookstore says seizures will go unchecked. In Xtra.ca. January 19, 2007. **www.xtra.ca/public/ viewstory.aspx?SESSIONID= nzvhqtqryza2q145 zfb0lbic&STORY_ID=2583&PUB_TEMPLATE_ID=2**. Retrieved August 1, 2008.

McCann, Marcus. 2007b. Supreme Court of Canada won't hear Kimberly Nixon case: Case put trans discrimination on the map. In Xtra.ca. February 1, 2007. **www.xtra.ca/public/ viewstory.aspx?AFF_TYPE=2&STORY_ID=2632&PUB_TEMPLATE_ID=2**. Retrieved May 1, 2008.

McClung, Nellie. 1915/1972. *In times like these*. Intro. Veronica Strong-Boag. Toronto: Univ. of Toronto Press.

McKeen, Wendy. 2001. The shaping of political agency: Feminism and the national social policy debate, the 1970s and early 1980s. *Studies in Political Economy* 66: 37–58.

Mill, Harriet Taylor. 1998. *The complete works of Harriet Taylor Mill*. Intro. Jo Ellen Jacobs. Indiana: Indiana Univ. Press.

Mill, John Stuart. 1869/1974. *The subjection of women*. Intro. Wendell Robert Carr. Cambridge, MA: MIT Press.

Mitchell, Juliet. 1971. *Woman's estate*. New York: Pantheon Books.

Morgan, Robin. 1970. *Sisterhood is powerful: An anthology of writings from the women's liberation movement*. New York: Random House.

Morris, Marika. 2000. *Women, poverty and Canadian public policy in an era of globalization.* Ottawa: Canadian Research Institute for the Advancement of Women.

Morris, Marika. 2002a. *Women and poverty.* Factsheet. Ottawa: Canadian Research Institute for the Advancement of Women.

Morris, Marika. 2002b. *Violence against women and girls.* Factsheet. Ottawa: Canadian Research Institute for the Advancement of Women.

Morris, Marika. 2002c. *Women's experience of racism: How race and gender interact.* Factsheet. Ottawa: Canadian Research Institute for the Advancement of Women.

National Council of Welfare. 2006. Poverty facts 2003. **www.ncwcnbes.net**. Retrieved July 2006.

Nelson, Adie, and Barrie W. Robinson. 2002. *Gender in Canada.* Toronto: Pearson Education Canada.

Newton, Janice. 1992. The alchemy of politicisation: Socialist women and the early Canadian left, in *Gender conflicts: New essays in women's history*, ed. Franca Iacovetta and Mariana Valverde, 118–148. Toronto: Univ. of Toronto Press.

O'Reilly, Andrea. 2000. A mom and her son: Thoughts on feminist mothering. *Journal of the Association for Research on Mothering* 2(1): 179–193.

Painter, Nell Irvin. 1982. Introduction, in Sojourner Truth, *Narrative of Sojourner Truth.* Harmondsworth, UK: Penguin Books.

Paltiel, Frieda L. 1997. State initiatives: Impetus and effects, in *Women and the Canadian state/Les femmes et l'état canadien*, ed. Caroline Andrew and Sanda Rodgers. Montreal and Kingston: McGill-Queen's Univ. Press.

Prentice, Alison, et al. 1996. *Canadian women: A history.* Toronto: Harcourt Brace.

Public Service Alliance of Canada. 2006. Help us to fight back for women's equality. Ottawa: Public Service Alliance of Canada. **www.psac-afpc.org**. Retrieved January 1, 2008.

Raymond, Janice. 1998. Sappho by surgery: The transexually constructed lesbian-feminist, in *Sex/machine: Readings in culture, gender and technology,* ed. Patrick D. Hopkins. Bloomington: Indiana Univ. Press.

Rich, Adrienne. 1976. *Of woman born: Motherhood as experience and institution.* New York: W.W. Norton.

Rich, Adrienne. 1980. Compulsory heterosexuality and lesbian existence. *Signs: Journal of Women in Culture and Society* 5(4): 3–32.

Roome, Patricia. 2001. Women's suffrage movement in Canada, in *Canada, Confederation to the present.* Chinook Multimedia Inc. **www.chinookmultimedia.com/poccd/registered**. Retrieved February 12, 2004.

Ross, Becki. 1995. *The house that Jill built: A lesbian nation in formation.* Toronto: Univ. of Toronto Press.

Sadlier, Rosemary. 1994. *Leading the way: Black women in Canada.* Toronto: Umbrella Press.

Seager, Joni. 1997. *The state of women in the world atlas*, 2d ed. London: Penguin.

Sethna, Christabelle. 2001. A bitter pill: Second wave feminist critiques of oral contraception, in *Canada, Confederation to the Present.* Chinook Multimedia Inc. **www.chinookmultimedia.com/poccd/registered**. Retrieved February 12, 2004.

Sommerville, Jennifer. 2000. *Feminism and the family: Politics and society in the UK and USA.* London: MacMillan.

Sparr, Pamela, ed. 1994. *Mortgaging women's lives: Feminist critiques of structural adjustment.* London: Zed Books.

Statistics Canada. 2000. *Women in Canada 2000: A gender-based statistical report.* Ottawa: Statistics Canada.

Statistics Canada. 2006a. *Women in Canada: A gender-based statistical report*, 5th ed. Ottawa: Statistics Canada.

Statistics Canada. 2006b. General social survey: Paid and unpaid work. *The Daily*, Wednesday, July 19, 2006. **www.statcan.ca/Daily/English/060719/d060719b.htm**. Retrieved January 1, 2008.

Status of Women Canada. 2003a. What do you mean women couldn't vote? Women's history month in Canada. Factsheet. Ottawa: Status of Women Canada, 2003a.

Status of Women Canada. 2003b. Women and education and training—Canada and the United Nations Assembly: Beijing+5 Factsheets. Ottawa: Status of Women Canada.

Stevenson, Winona. 1999. Colonialism and First Nations women in Canada, in *Scratching the surface: Canadian anti-racist feminist thought*, ed. Enakshi Dua and Angela Robertson, 49–80. Toronto: Women's Press.

Stone, Sandy. 1991. The "empire" strikes back: A posttranssexual manifesto, in *Body guards: The cultural politics of gender ambiguity*, ed. Kristina Straub and Julia Epstein. New York: Routledge.

Strong-Boag, Veronica. 1998. "A red girl's reasoning": E. Pauline Johnson constructs the new nation, in *Painting the maple: Essays on race, gender, and the construction of Canada,* eds. Veronica Strong-Boag et al., 130–154. Vancouver: Univ. of British Columbia Press.

Sullivan, Barbara. 2003. Trafficking in women: Feminism and new international law. *International Feminist Journal of Politics* 5(1): 67–91.

Thistle, Susan. 2006. *From marriage to the market: The transformation of women's lives and work.* Berkeley: Univ. of California Press.

Thompson, Denise. 2001. *Radical feminism today.* London: Sage.

Timpson, Annis May. 2001. *Driven apart: Women's employment equality and child care in Canadian public policy.* Vancouver: Univ. of British Columbia Press.

Tong, Rosemarie Putnam. 1998. *Feminist thought: A more comprehensive introduction.* Boulder, CO: Westview.

Townson, Monica. 2005. Poverty issues for Canadian women. Statistics Canada 2005. **www.swccfc.sc.ca/resources/consultations/ges09-2005/poverty_e.html**

Truth, Sojourner. 1850/1998. *Narrative of Sojourner Truth.* Intro. Nell Irvin Painter. Harmondsworth, UK: Penguin Books.

United Nations. Statistics. 2007a. Statistics and indicators on women and men: Table 4c. Secondary education. December 2007. **http://unstats.un.org/unsd/demographic/products/indwm/tab4c.htm**. Retrieved January 1, 2008.

United Nations. Statistics. 2007b. Statistics and indicators on women and men: Table 5d. Women legislators and managers. December 2007. **http://unstats.un.org/unsd/demographic/ products/indwm/tab5d.htm**. Retrieved January 1, 2008.

United Nations. Statistics. 2007c. Statistics and indicators on women and men: Table 6a. Women in Parliament. December 2007. **http://unstats.un.org/unsd/demographic/products/indwm/ tab6a.htm**. Retrieved January 1, 2008.

United Nations Development Fund for Women (UNIFEM). 2007. Facts & figures on VAW. **www.unifem.org/gender_issues/violence_against_women/facts_figures.php**. Retrieved May 1, 2008.

Valenta, Marcela. Argentina: 2007. Recruiting celebs against trafficking in women. InterPress Service News Agency. **www.ipsnews.net/news.asp?idnews=36936**. Retrieved May 1, 2008.

Valverde, Mariana. 1992. "When the mother of the race is free": Race, reproduction and sexuality in first-wave feminism, in *Gender conflicts: New essays in women's history*, ed. Franca Iacovetta and Mariana Valverde, 3–28. Toronto: Univ. of Toronto Press.

Walker, R. 2000. Quebec's bargain day care a hit with parents, educators. *Christian Science Monitor,* May.

Waring, Marilyn. 1999. *Counting for nothing: What men value and what women are worth*, 2d ed. Toronto: Univ. of Toronto Press.

Wente, Margaret. 2000. Who gets to be a woman? *Globe and Mail*, December 14.

Wollstonecraft, Mary. 1792/1982. *A vindication of the rights of woman*. Hardmondsworth, UK: Penguin Books.

CHAPTER 2

An Introduction to Feminist Postructural Theorizing

Sharon Rosenberg

"Theory" is a highly contested term within feminist discourse. The number of questions raised about it indicates the importance of the debate: what qualifies as "theory"? Who is the author of "theory"? Is it singular? Is it defined in opposition to something which is atheoretical, pretheoretical or post-theoretical? Is "theory" distinct from politics?

> Judith Butler and Joan Scott,
> *Feminists Theorize the Political*, 1992

INTRODUCTION

As the opening citation to this chapter suggests, "theory" is not a settled term within feminism. As you will have seen from the previous chapter, there is no singular version of feminism, nor is there one way in which differing feminisms define their relation to something called theory. While some argue that such non-singularity is a problem, others see this as a vibrant and productive difference. This chapter begins from the latter position and with the proposition that attending to theoretical interrogations in and of themselves is vital to feminism's aliveness. What such a proposition suggests is that it can be important to provisionally suspend the idea that theory is only relevant to the extent that it can forecast change "now." This is not to imply that change is not important, nor that theory is of no use to making changes. Instead, it is to argue that theory can help us to think about the world differently and that the work of this thinking can be invaluable to putting into place and sustaining broader changes. Moreover, it is the argument underpinning the kind of theorizing being presented in this chapter that the categories and concepts that most usually organize our world are worth a careful look—not only as categories and concepts per se, but also for how they both produce and confine critical engagements and, hence, possibilities for change.

> Poststructuralism is not, strictly speaking, *a position* [or a theory], but rather a critical interrogation of the exclusionary operations by which "positions" are established. In this sense, a feminist poststructuralism does not designate a position from which one operates, a point of view or standpoint which might be usefully compared with other "positions" within the theoretical field. (Butler and Scott, 1992: xiv, emphasis in original)

The particular form of theorizing that this chapter will introduce is broadly categorized under the title of "postmodern" and will focus on poststructuralism. We will look in particular at how key concepts and ideas generated by poststructural feminist thinking not only challenge central assumptions underlying modernist feminisms (e.g., liberal, radical, socialist), but also, in doing so, create different openings for contemporary thought and politics. A particular challenge for this chapter is negotiating, on the one hand, expectations of summary chapters (i.e., that they follow a linear, orderly, and forward-oriented narrative structure), and, on the other, that the chapter be attentive to the arguments of poststructural theorizing, which encourage a deep suspicion of universal claims, singular readings as "Truth," and coherent narratives. Thus, this chapter is formed on a paradox: It is caught in the demands of style expectations that run counter to the insights of the theorizing that is its substantive concern. That said, poststructural feminisms encourage us, as writers and readers, to live with paradoxes, to endeavour to hold contradictions, and to learn from what we might not otherwise have thought. So, in that spirit, what follows is one introduction to some key ideas and authors that you might find interesting and that might invite your curiosity to further exploration.

Interruption #1: Notes from the "Author"[1]

I am writing the first draft of this chapter in Edmonton, Alberta, in the fall of 2003. It's a bright and cool autumn day and although I am sitting alone in my office, with only the companionship of books, I keep looking over the top of my computer screen, in anticipation of the faces of students who might be reading this newest edition of *Feminist Issues*. Having taught various versions of introductory courses in feminist thinking and in women's studies as an arena of inquiry for more than a decade, the classes that materialize in my head range from small rooms of 15–25 students to large lecture halls of close to 300. In some ways, writing is quite different from teaching—it's likely that I won't know who is reading this chapter at all; I only have my imagined sense of who might be reading and why. The difficulty is that I can't check to see what sense you are making, whether a particular phrasing is helpful, where one example over another would have been better. In other ways, writing this chapter is like preparing a lecture—I know that I am writing with an imagined audience in mind, that I must focus on a specific topic or issue, and that I have to put certain limits on the writing in order to make it through in the time we have together (whether this is measured by minutes and hours or by word and page counts). I have some sense of what chapters you will have encountered before this one and what will come after, and I can anticipate that this is one chapter of many others you may be reading in any particular week on topics as far ranging as micro-economic theory and the history of painting. The problem is that we can't really "see" each other, what we have in common is this text—the question is: What terms of commonality might that create?

POSTMODERNISM AND POSTSTRUCTURALISM

According to the *Penguin Dictionary of Sociology* (fourth edition), "postmodern" refers to "[a] movement in painting, literature, television, film and the arts generally" (Abercrombie, Hill, and Turner, 2000: 272). The key characteristics of this movement are summarized by the dictionary compilers as irony and play, a questioning of objective standards of truth, a crossing of boundaries between genres and forms, and an emphasis on the text rather than on the author's intent for establishing meaning (272). This dictionary entry is followed by another, "postmodernity," which is defined as follows: "[a] term, usually contrasted with MODERNITY, which designates a new condition which contemporary advanced industrial societies are alleged to have reached. A large number of features are said to characterize postmodernity and they may be placed in four groups—social, cultural, economic and political" (272). The entry for "poststructuralism" is separate and it reads, in part, "[t]he fundamental idea is that we cannot apprehend reality without the intervention of language. This prioritizes the study of language—or texts. Texts can be understood only in relation to other texts, not in relation to an external reality against which they can be tested and measured" (273).

In the *Encyclopedia of Feminist Theories* (2000), "poststructuralism / postmodernism" is given as one entry, written by Chris Weedon, whose major work, *Feminist Practice and Poststructuralist Theory* (first published in 1987), has been influential in bringing poststructural thinking to feminism. Weedon's entry is substantially longer than those in the *Penguin Dictionary*.

I will summarize here some of her key points. First, she notes that "[p]oststructuralism and postmodernism are two distinct but related terms." She goes on to explain that poststructural thinking has critiqued foundational ideas of structural theories of language (hence the "post") and, in so doing, has "challenged some of the fundamental assumptions about knowledge, subjectivity and power in western philosophy" (397). In regards to postmodern, she states: "[m]ost often, 'postmodernism' and the related term 'postmodernity' are used to describe either the style and form taken by particular cultural phenomena or the present period of global late capitalism.... Like poststructuralism, postmodernism questions some of the fundamental assumptions of the Enlightenment tradition in the west. These include the belief in rational human progress, universal standards and values, and singular truth" (397). Patti Lather, in her new book, *Getting Lost*, adds that "poststructuralism... particularly foregrounds the limits of ... the will to power inscribed in sense-making efforts that aspire to totalizing explanatory frameworks ..." (Lather, 2007: 5).

Writing and working with definitions is tricky. On the one hand, it's helpful to have definitions of terms, particularly for an area of inquiry that is unfamiliar. Without some shared meanings, we would find it difficult to communicate with each other at all—and you would likely come away from this chapter completely frustrated that you weren't even offered a basic explanation of terms. On the other hand, definitions, by virtue of the work that they do, which is to summarize and condense a complex body of thought into a short paragraph or even a few pages, are necessarily limiting and partial. In addition, we need to consider that I have chosen two particular dictionaries to draw from (and hence not others) and have further condensed the definitions into what I think are first a manageable size and, second, highlight what I'm particularly interested in drawing your attention to at this point in the chapter. Thus, I suggest that we take definitions such as those outlined above as useful starting points, an orientation toward a way of thinking, *and* as matters to regard with some distrust in the recognition that no definition can be fully explanatory. With these remarks in mind, it might be a good time to pause and take note of what you understand from the definitions and the discussion to this point and what you are finding confusing. As you read each section that follows, come back to the definitions and see if they make a bit more sense.

Interruption #2: More Notes from Me

At this point, I need to make some decisions as the writer of this chapter. As Weedon explains, postmodernism and poststructuralism are related but distinct terms and, therefore, refer to related but distinct ways of thinking. In a 25-or-so-page chapter (and, of course, there are fewer than that number of pages left now), I could choose to try to summarize for you some key aspects of both kinds of work—how they are similar and how they may be different from each other. Or, I could work from the position that the similarities of critique are most helpful for re-engaging different feminisms and write from there. In discussion with Nancy, the editor of this book, I have decided on the latter and to focus on what is generally referred to as "feminist poststructuralism," in part because this is the form of theorizing that I find most exciting and interesting and the kind that I do myself, and I am eager to introduce some of that to you. More than my own desires are at issue here, however. I also think there is a strong argument to make that poststructuralism has offered particularly profound critiques of—and rich concepts to—feminism. There is a wealth of work now from scholars in disciplines ranging from education to philosophy to women's studies to sociology, who have been informed by, are engaging with, and are developing a form of theorizing in which feminism is in relation to poststructuralism. Because poststructuralism and postmodernism can be so closely connected, others may see this approach as best understood as "postmodern feminism." I would like to suggest that we live with this ambiguity in naming for two reasons: (a) however we name it, these modes of inquiry (as the definitions above suggest) push for a certain suspicion in regard to categorizations that attempt to mark one approach as entirely distinct and different from another (e.g., "this versus that"); and (b) getting caught up in struggles over which approach "owns" what kinds of inquiry and critique is a squabble that drains energy, resources, insights, and so on, away from how these inquiries and critiques may help open up and change the world in which we live. Thus, what I want to propose to you by way of this "Interruption #2" is that there is more than one way this chapter could proceed, that a different way of proceeding would illuminate ideas differently and in ways I will not, and that there is no inherently better way to proceed with this chapter. In explaining to you some of my process as I write, I am trying to bring to the foreground the decisions I am making and why, rather than leaving them unstated. I am doing so, so that we (myself as writer and you as reader) are both prompted to remember that this text is itself a construct, an offering of certain explanations, concepts, and insights, but not a claim to a universal truth about feminist poststructuralism or the only story that could be told.

KEY CRITIQUES AND CONCEPTS
Critiques of Modernity's Knowledge-Making Practices

By this point in the chapter, I expect it will not come as a surprise when I tell you that one of the key contributions of poststructural theorizing is a particular interrogation and critique of the practices of producing and representing knowledge that are more usually taken for granted and taught as "the right way," for example, to conduct research, write an essay, or interpret a poem. I anticipate that you are familiar with many of these practices; you were probably taught early in your school years, for instance, that it is proper to write papers and essays without the use of "I," and so you learned constructs such as "one believes" and "this evidence shows that." This avoidance of the first person is one feature, among many others, of what we might think of as a "scientist model" (Seidman, 1996: 701) of knowledge-making practices, sometimes also known as "enlightenment thinking." Because most of us have been so immersed in these ways of thinking, not only in schools and universities but also more broadly in "Western" societies, it can be difficult to actually see them as ways of thinking—rather than as just "normal" or "the way everyone does things."[2]

One way to begin this process of beginning to see differently, if you like, is to look over the chapter to this point, to perhaps begin by identifying how it is not written, or cannot be easily read, on the terms that you would anticipate. If you do that, you might identify practices that stand out because they are unexpected, because they do not follow a conventional approach to representing knowledge—an approach in which the author is expected to take on an authoritative voice that is clear and distinct in his or her statements, does not draw attention to ambiguity or the limits of his or her own knowledge, and is written without engaging much with readers. (To return to an earlier point I was making, you might notice similarities here between this style of writing and a common style of lecturing.) So, if you knew there was something odd about the style of this chapter, this is an indicator that you already know something about social scientist practices and enlightenment thinking.

Although one of the contributions of modernist feminisms was a critique of enlightenment notions—such as objectivity, for how it implicitly privileged and assumed a masculine point of view as objective—these feminisms, poststructural critics would argue, have also been caught up in other forms of knowledge associated with modernity and the modern university. For example, whereas liberal, radical, and socialist feminisms all differ in their explanation of why women's lives are limited and hindered (see previous chapter), all implicitly accept the necessity for *the* explanation that will illuminate *the* conditions that need to be addressed in *specified* ways for *all* women to be free. Such framings of explanation are known as "metanarratives" (Lyotard, 1984), theories that endeavour to provide explanations of the social world that are universal (that is, they tell "the big story" or what Lather referred to earlier as totalizing explanatory frameworks).

This is an approach to practices of producing and representing knowledge that was taken on by modernist feminists, particularly as they encountered and endeavoured to establish legitimization in universities. In such contexts, not only was a focus on gender and asking questions about how a theory may and may not be applicable to women's experiences regarded as shocking enough, but also it was difficult to have feminism taken seriously without a reliance on the categories and argument structures that were already familiar and accepted (see Koldony, 2000). Moreover, as Marysia Zalewski writes, "[f]or modernist feminists often dismayed and disgusted by the centuries of false and nasty stories about women, the ideas that good and true knowledge about women was possible seemed like a dream come true.... One way to make that dream come true and ensure that innocent knowledge was collected was to have clear foundations for knowledge-building" (2000: 45–46). Such foundations came with the development of modernity, which has its roots in industrialization, imperialism, and scientific thinking (see Hamilton, 1992, for example). As Zalewski goes on to note, these beliefs have carried over to much modernist feminist work that depends on the belief that there is an objective reality governed by laws independent of human perspectives, that this reality is in principle accessible to human understanding and knowledge, and that the central means for developing and establishing the truth of this knowledge is reason, a capacity that is available to all human beings (2000: 46). One further and vitally important aspect of this approach is the belief that "knowledge [is] a *progressive* force. The more we know about something, the more we understand the truth of it and can do something about it" (Zalewski, 2000: 47, emphasis in original).

Feminists attached to varying politics and modes of theorizing have challenged such conventional claims to knowledge on different fronts. As you will see in Chapter 4, anti-racist feminists have been critical of the way in which the category of "women" has been deployed in modernist formulations, noting that the category is used as if it includes all women but in actuality references women with particular "race" and "class" experiences and expectations of privilege (see also Bannerji, 2000; Dua and Robertson, 1999; Hill Collins, 1990; hooks, 1984; Rothenberg, 2001). This has led, anti-racist feminist critics argue, not only to partial but also to distorted explanations that cannot account for how women may be caught in and perpetuate relations of racism and colonialism in their very attempts to address sexism "for all women."

> While many types of theory appeal to *truth value* as the guarantee of their adequacy, this is not the case with poststructuralist theories. Feminist appropriations of poststructuralism tend to focus on the basic assumptions, the degree of explanatory power, and the political implications which a particular type of analysis yields. It is with these criteria in mind that I would argue the appropriateness of poststructuralism to feminist concerns, not as the answer to *all* feminist questions but as a way of conceptualizing the relationship between language, social institutions and individual consciousness which focuses on how power is exercised and the possibilities of change. (Weedon, 1987: 19, emphases in original)

Feminists influenced by poststructural critiques approach difference differently (an issue to which I will return), but also offer deep critiques of the kinds of ideas that Zalewski outlines, questioning the notion of Theory as a universal explanation, questioning ideas of knowledge as "innocent" or outside of the workings of power, questioning rationality as a neutral and defining force of democracy, and questioning the assumed linear relation among knowledge, progress, and change (see, for example, Butler and Scott, 1992; Flax, 1992; Raby, 2000). Feminist poststructural critics would pose the following kinds of questions to each of these claims: Which women have to be forgotten or obscured for a single theory of women's lives to be articulated as The Theory? Whose interests does this theory serve and whose lives does it obfuscate or worsen for those interests to be served? If reason is the defining arbiter, how are we to understand the prevalence of hatred, fear, anxiety, indifference, and other such "non-rational" expressions that seem immune to, or defend against, (more) information and (more) facts? If knowledge equals progress equals change, how are we to reconcile the profusion of knowledge available, for example, on the extent and degree of violences women seem to be subject to in contemporary societies with the limited, circumscribed, and ever-struggled-over efforts for change?

From an interest in feminist poststructural inquiries, the point is not to endeavour to answer such questions definitively, but to work with them as openings into prevailing feminist explanations and political strategies, and to deliberate on how assumptions and concepts previously taken as foundational (meaning no longer open to inquiry) may be supporting not only productive but also limiting analyses and possibilities for change. I turn now to how some of this kind of critical engagement works through introducing particular concepts of feminist poststructural inquiry.

Language/Discourse

The *Penguin Dictionary* definition of poststructuralism noted earlier includes the statement that "we cannot apprehend reality without the intervention of language." And, in the previous boxed quote, Weedon suggests that poststructuralism has an interest in how power might be exercised through language. What both of these notations orient us toward is a key concern of feminist poststructural inquiry: namely, how language (and more precisely, discourses, a concept to which I will turn shortly) constitutes the world in which we live. To say that language *constitutes* the world is to say something quite distinct from, and, indeed, challenging to, prevailing ways of thinking about language. What is more familiar to many of us is the idea that language is a neutral medium through which reality passes; it has no shaping effect on that reality, but simply presents it in linguistic form. And, so, for example, from this perspective, I am sitting at a chair typing on my laptop (this is the reality) and we have the words available to describe this in English (sitting, chair, typing, laptop) that, when strung together in the grammatically correct sequence, allow me to communicate a reality to you that you, assumed to be a competent reader of English, can readily discern. To return to an earlier idea: it is a belief in the inherent neutrality of language that provides one of the supports for the notion of objective representations of reality.

Some modernist feminists, however, have been quite critical of this idea of language as neutral; in line with the critique that "objectivity" has really meant "from the perspective of privileged men taken to be no perspective at all," feminist critics of English have argued that we have inherited what Dale Spender, over 25 years ago, called he/man language (1980). This is not a neutral medium, but one that is socially constructed such that "he" and "man" *appear* to stand for "everyone," but, in fact, are not generic and inscribe masculinity as (if it were) neutral, requiring that women be constantly marked in language to be recognized as not-men.[3] On the basis of this kind of critique, there have been various feminist approaches to re-working the English language, ranging from arguments for a more neutral terminology that will properly represent reality (i.e., replacing chairman with chairperson), to arguments that women cannot be represented in patriarchal languages and need to develop their own form of writing "from the body" (see, for example, Brossard, 1998; Gould, 1990; Warland, 1990).

Those informed and engaged by poststructuralism introduce another layer of critique—arguing that there is no "reality," there are no "bodies," that pre-exist how these are constituted in and through language. Rather, it is in and through language itself that the sign(s) for reality are produced, contested, and struggled over. There are no inherent meanings; there is no necessary relationship, for example, between the unit c-a-t (known as the signifier) and the meaning (known as the signified) that the word "cat" conjures (e.g., of soft, furry, four-legged, meowing creatures that have been domesticated in "the West"). If even words like "cat" and "dog," words that we are taught in the very first books that are given to us as children, are not stable and do not have inherent meaning, then you can imagine that this argument that language is constitutive of reality (rather than a neutral medium through which reality passes) is highly charged and has far-reaching effects.

Interruption #3: Still Here, Shouldering the Weight of Words Not My Own

As you might expect, if you've been following this line of argument, I'm in quite a quandary here! Every sentence that I type is constituting "a reality" of feminist poststructuralism for you. But it is not as if there is a clearly demarcated and agreed-upon body of work designated as "feminist poststructuralism" that I could be said to simply be representing in condensed form. Moreover, the argument goes much further than this: In writing feminist poststructuralism in this chapter, I am partly constituting what counts as feminist poststructuralism (such constitutive effects will vary to the extent that this chapter is read and may be cited elsewhere with authority and/or derision). "My version" is not innocent, this chapter is not a neutral medium … meanings are made in the spaces between words as well as through the words themselves in relation to other words from which they are articulated as similar and different … all these double-quote marks all over the place: signal that no word can be taken for granted and no meaning is stable; deploying a term does not necessarily imply agreement with its prevailing meaning … versionisnotinnocentthischapterisnotaneutralmedium.

   …b r E A k i N g d O w n…co

                    |

                    |

                        apsing

While my "breakdown" at the end of Interruption #3 is one possible response to the swirl of notions tied to the argument that language is constitutive, it does not take into account an idea I slipped in above: Language is a site of social and political struggle. From this perspective, it is not a matter of either accepting this language as it is or having a breakdown in attempting to refuse it (thankfully!). Instead, what is brought to our attention is how the notion of language-as-constitutive is productive for constituting other "realities." This is where the notion of discourse comes in. As it is used in the context of this chapter, "discourse" is a notion developed through the work of Michel Foucault and others who have worked with his ideas. Foucault did not develop a metanarrative or general theory, but rather was interested in how power, knowledge, and truth were constituted through and in a variety of historically specific social practices and endeavours to produce and discipline subjects. He did not provide one singular definition of the term, but it is regarded by those who are informed by what became poststructuralism to be a pivotal idea.

Sara Mills offers some helpful orienting points for grasping some aspects of this idea. "One of the most productive ways of thinking about discourse is not as a group of signs..., but as 'practices that systemically form the objects of which they speak' (Foucault, 1972). In this sense, a discourse is something which produces something else (an utterance, a concept, an effect), rather than something which exists in and of itself and which can be analysed in isolation" (Mills, 1997: 17). What Mills helpfully points us to here is the idea that we cannot actually see or grasp discourses per se (in the way that we can see a person walking into a room, for example). Rather, we can read (for) discourses through their traces, through what they produce as "the real." Follow the example of someone walking into a room: By reading how they gender themselves through hairstyle, body language, clothing, the presence or absence of makeup, shoes, and so on, we are likely to read them as either a woman or a man (contextually). We might refer to these genderings as *effects of discourses* of femininity and masculinity, discourses that are not universal but are historically and culturally specific. From this perspective, people are not authors of their gender (gender is not inherent nor necessarily attached to a particular body), but gender regimes are produced through people's embodiment. Such gender regimes are discursive because they are bounded and repetitive (Butler, 1999).

As Mills goes on to observe: "[a] discursive structure can be detected because of the *systematicity* of the ideas, opinions, concepts, ways of thinking and behaving which are formed within a particular context, and because of the effects of those ways of thinking and behaving" (Mills, 1997: 17, emphasis mine). Because discourses are not singular and do not exist in isolation, there is no such thing as one discourse of femininity and one discourse of masculinity. We might speak of femininity and masculinity as sites of discursive constitution, negotiation, struggle, and resistance, as different discourses of femininities and masculinities play out on, and are played out by, people who gender themselves and are gendered by others in ways that are made contextually intelligible. Discourses of femininity and masculinity do not have equal weight in such play, however; some are institutionalized and others are produced as "alternative," but the boundaries between these are not fixed and static. How they play out and are played out is a matter of constant negotiation through which "the truth" of femininity and masculinity is produced and struggled over.

> Why, do you suppose, some cultural phenomena are permitted to be dynamic and mutable, and so transformative, while other cultural phenomena, including gender, are considered to be static? Do you think there exists the possibility of a transformative nature in gender? And if so, how can we tap into that? (Bornstein, 1998: 20)

Although one of the key ways to trace discourses is through language (e.g., through the kinds of linguistic practices noted earlier), as the above discussion indicates, discourses do not only take form in this manner. Discourses of femininities and masculinities in particular produce and are produced through a wide variety of effects of embodiment, constituting specifically gendered subjects into "woman" and "man." It is to these ideas that I turn next.

(Gendering) The Subject

It is likely that you rarely spend any time at all consciously trying to determine whether you or someone else is a boy or a girl. (If that's not true, my apologies; you are already ahead of me in this section of the chapter and I will try to catch up to you as quickly as possible.)

This is because the prevailing ideas about gender in contemporary Western social formations, such as Canada, direct us to understanding sex/gender as a given: It is what we are. Hence, once the question "is it a girl or a boy?" has been answered correctly by caregivers (by that, I mean, by a positive response to one category *or* the other), sex/gender is no longer considered a question by most. This does not mean that what it means to be a girl or a boy, or grow up into a woman or a man, is static and uniform (as noted in the previous section), but it does mean that the distinction between girl and boy is assumed to be obvious. Indeed, such obviousness is assumed to be based on physiological and chromosomal distinctions, such that we are assumed to be born either as male or female and our gender identities of masculine or feminine develop from those bases.[4] Thus, most of us understand ourselves and each other to have a coherent and stable gender identity, such that if we have a penis and testicles and develop facial hair, we are masculine, and if we have breasts and a vagina and begin to menstruate in puberty, we are feminine.

Although these are all commonsensical ideas, so much so that they are almost beyond question and rarely even considered a matter of curiosity past a young age, there are a few things going on in this previous paragraph that feminist poststructural interrogations would encourage us take a second look at. There are three key ideas that I would like to focus on: that our gender describes who we are (it is an essence of us with biological roots), that sex/gender is a stable dichotomy (boy *or* girl, no ambiguity assumed or permitted without risk), and that gender is, can, and should be always and simply mapped onto sex in a straightforward manner (and if it is not, the problem is with the individual, not the mapping).

In contrast to these ideas, feminist poststructural theorists would argue for a very different understanding of the gendering of subjects. First, the argument is that gender is not what we are, but what we do (Butler, 1999). That is, rather than an essence of being, based on sex as an underpinning of gender, be(com)ing a woman or a man is a matter of performative reiteration (Butler, 1999). This is a concept that suggests that in order to be an intelligible subject—in this case to recognize one's self and be recognized by others as a woman or a man—one must undertake a constant and consistent practice of *doing* the gender that is expected of them/us. To recall Mills's reference above: it is because of the expectation of a systematicity of gendering that we know how to do intelligible gender to ourselves and what to look for in the doing of others. The question is not, then, Are you a girl or a boy? Rather, are you doing femininity or masculinity?[5]

If gendering is something we do to ourselves and to others and that others do to us, and is not a fixed category of being, then we might wonder: How is it that gendering looks *pretty similar* in specific times and places? If gendering is "up to us" in a sense, then doesn't that mean gendering is a choice? It may be possible that gendering could be open-ended, but the actuality of gendered life as most of us live it is not. There may be many reasons for this; I think most depend on the production of a foundational dichotomy of gender. This is the second key point of argument. Dichotomies work on a set of principles: The world is divided into two (in this case, two genders, women and men); these two are understood to be clearly demarcated, and one side of the dichotomy is assigned more value than the other (in the case of gender, this tends to be masculinity over femininity; think for example of the words associated with each side, e.g., strong, independent, and virile versus weak, dependent, and nurturing); and, by virtue of the construct of a dichotomy, if people associated with one side "appear" like those associated with the other side, they are seen to be transgressing their "natural" role and may be at varying degrees of risk (from, for example, women being called "bitch" for being "too much like a man," or men being threatened for "appearing" feminine). One other thing about dichotomies: Because they assume to divide the world into two, there are no other (legitimated) options; there is nothing else possible.[6]

Given all of this, it is hardly surprising that gendering isn't open-ended, isn't actually a choice. That is, in order to move through the world in ways that allow us to be recognized (i.e., to be loved, to be thought desirable, to be hired for particular jobs, to imagine our futures, etc.), we need to gender ourselves in ways that are intelligible within the regime of a gender dichotomy. Moreover, for gendering to work really well, gendered subjects must occupy a particularly intense paradox: On the one hand, we are told that gender is just who we are, and on the other hand, we are told that gender is an (almost impossible) achievement that takes enormous effort, resources, and labour (our own as well as others').[7]

Interruption #4: "The Author" Writing Back to Herself

But what about the ways in which legibly gendering ourselves and each other is fun? Or, how transgressing the presumed linearity and stability among sex, gender, and sexuality can be exciting? What these kinds of questions point us to is an aspect of gendering that you have not brought up in the previous critique, but one that some modes of feminist post-structural inquiry would instruct us to attend to. Such modes might also point to playing or messing with gendering as one way to negotiate and contest regimes of reiteration—for gendering-as-doing is no mere imposition from the outside, but is a practice in which we participate and therefore can be understood as an expression of agency (a concept that I know you will be introducing in the next section). What if we were to teach students about gender as a site of discipline and play, as a regime but also a series of associated pleasures? Would that make them/you/us more interested in thinking about and playing with gender? Or less?

Power

The prevalence of dichotomous thinking that I spoke to in the previous section also underpins how we tend to think about "power." It is typical to hear, for example, that someone has power or does not have power, a phrasing that understands power as a possession that is wielded over those who do not have it. Thus, for example, radical feminists would speak of men having patriarchal power and women not, and Marxists might speak of the bourgeoisie having power associated with the ownership of and access to resources that the proletariat do not. In other situations, we may speak of a "perpetrator versus victim" dichotomy, in which the position of perpetrator is understood to be a position with power and the position of victim is understood to be a passive position without capacity for action. What is further commonly held across these understandings is the notion of power as a force that oppresses, that literally and symbolically holds down people who are subject to it. In this sense, power has negative connotations, is not regarded as desirable and instead as something to be cut out of visions for an equitable society.

A story (it could be true): A man breaks into a woman's bedroom and attempts to rape her. She, realizing she cannot stop this but fearing for pregnancy or disease, insists he wear a condom. He does and proceeds to rape her. At a later point, the man is caught and charged. In his defence, it is argued that the woman cannot be considered to be a victim, nor the man a perpetrator; instead, it is argued that they participated in a consensual act. The jury agrees and the man is freed. This is a good example of how limited the notion of power as a possession of have or have not actually is. For, within the terms of this framing, it is not possible to conceive of the man as a perpetrator of an act of rape *and* a woman as having expressed limited agency in that moment. She can only be regarded as a (true) victim if she had "allowed" the rape to happen without "interference" (see Marcus, 1992, to follow up on this idea).

Feminist poststructural theorizing, drawing on the work of Foucault, offers a different reckoning with notions of power, one that can help us grasp and work with the more complicated expressions noted in the story in the box. Chris Weedon provides a very helpful summary of Foucault's articulation of power (recall, Foucault did not develop a Theory of Power, but offered instead theorizings, analyses of how power works contextually and specifically). In my comments here, I draw heavily on Weedon's summary (1999: 119; I am working from this page unless noted otherwise; the examples are mine). She notes, first, that Foucault argued against the notion that power is only repressive (or what I spoke to above as a negative force). Instead, he argued for "an analytics of power" and proposed guiding principles to consider in efforts to identify what Weedon calls "the nature and workings of power in any area of social and cultural analysis." She identifies eight such principles, which I will summarize and condense here into five points.

First, contrary to the dominant understanding of power that I described in the earlier paragraph, power is not a thing (owned or seized), but a relationship. We can't actually see relationships of power per se; instead, they exist in and take the form of specific social relations (for example, gender relations, class relations, colonial relations). Such relations both pre-exist us (that is, we enter them through subject formation) and are produced by us (that is, we are not only entered but also enter, we are not only produced, but also produce ourselves as particular subjects). Thus, relations of power can be said to be expressed intentionally and unintentionally. For example, in the story noted in the box, there are at least three social relations being expressed: first, a gendered relation between the man who entered the woman's bedroom and the woman who negotiated with him to reduce the amount of harm his rape produces; second, a policing relation between the police personnel who apprehended the man accused of raping the woman, and the man as he was apprehended and entered into the social practices and forms of policing as the criminal subject of accused rapist; and, third, a judicial relation between the man as accused rapist, the woman as accused rape victim, the lawyers, witnesses, and evidence produced for each side, and the judge and jury assigned to assess the case. Relations of gender, policing, and law are all operative in this example; they pre-exist the individuals involved in the specific circumstance, yet are given particular expression when the individuals convey intent (depending on the subject: to rape, to reduce the harms of rape, to apprehend, to judge). Note that one expression of an intent provokes and puts into play the others, but this isn't necessarily guaranteed. The man may not have attempted to rape the woman, the woman may have responded differently, the man may never have been apprehended, the event of the rape may not have become a court case. Hence, we might argue that the workings of relations of power are complicated, uneven, and contextual.

Interruption #5: A Problem that Haunts Me and One I Can't Resolve

As I work through and with the story of a rape, I know that I am on difficult and highly contested ground. Many modes of modernist feminisms, especially those attached to radical feminist conceptualizations of patriarchy, have made compelling and striking arguments about the character, extent, and effects of men's violences against women (see relevant chapters in this volume). Feminists working from these perspectives and on these social issues are often highly suspect and deeply critical of the kinds of questions and problematics I am putting forward here, arguing that they deflect attention from the real practice of men's rape of women, of what it means to be a woman and live in a "rape culture" (Buchenwald, Fletcher, and Roth, 1993). For those who encounter on a regular basis the actual stories of the violences and horrors women are subject to as women, the conceptualization of power that I am articulating here may be read as abhorrent, an anti-feminist betrayal in the face of already so much struggle to have women's stories believed and taken seriously. As Ann Brooks puts it, "from the perspective of second wave feminism, postmodern and poststructuralism's effective denial of the status of all epistemologies [for example, of women's experience as authentic and true] renders feminism politically and epistemologically powerless" (Brooks, 1997: 46). In some ways, I am sympathetic to these critiques; in other ways, concerned by the assumptions and delimiters they keep in place. It would be an entirely other paper to grapple with these more directly.[8] What I have come to, in brief, is a sense that—however risky and challenging feminist poststructural interrogations may feel for those (of us)[9] who are concerned with trauma, violence, loss, and suffering—I continue to think these are risks and challenges worth encountering and working through. For all of the research, activism, scholarship, panels, and support programs that feminist work on violence has produced and supported, deep changes are barely apparent. To me, that must mean that there are hard(er) questions that haven't been faced and that demand our attention. You may be wondering, what am I supposed to do with this as an undergraduate student, taking (perhaps) my first women's studies course? I don't have a single answer to that, but I do wonder: What does it mean to pass on feminist theorizing from one generation to another if these large questions aren't at the centre of what we are teaching?[10]

Second, as a series of statements in the chapter so far have suggested, power is not only restrictive, but also productive. This is an extremely important insight, I will argue.

That is, if power works through relationships, then relationships are not only delimiting, but also generative of subjects and possibilities. Following the concerns I noted in Interruption #5, let me turn toward a different kind of example here that might make the potential of this conceptualization easier to grasp, separate from critique. We might say that students and professors are produced through relations of knowledge/power (a well-known Foucaultian couplet; see Foucault, 1980), and that the creation of these subjects ("student" and "professor") means that certain ways of living are closed down or restricted (for example, both students and professors need to abide by particular timetables for courses that take them away from other things they may like to do), *and* certain ways of living are opened up and made possible (that same timetable of courses at university may mean no early mornings, for example, so it makes sleeping in feasible). This is a rather trite example, and things certainly get much more complicated (as the rape story example and discussion illustrates), but hopefully this idea of restriction and possibility starts to make some sense.

Third, because power takes form through relationships (and forms relationships), power is not uniform, is not discharged from one central source, but comes from diverse sources and directions and takes different shapes. If we follow the example in the previous paragraph: Although professors and students are expected to abide by a schedule of courses, there are limited means to regulate this. Students can use their positioning in the relationship of power "from below" by skipping classes and will not likely receive direct punishment "from above" for doing so. Yet, in small classes, professors generally know who attends regularly and may use attendance and participation marks to both "reward" and "discipline" students. Thus, although power is not uniform in its expression, it must be exercised, through aims and objectives, in order to have effects.

This example points me in the direction of the fourth key principle: Relationships of power establish the terms of resistance specifically and agency more generally. Thus, as power is not a thing, neither is resistance or agency. Nor are agency and resistance understood on Foucauldian terms as a priori (existing outside of the workings of power somewhere). Rather, what resistance and agency look like (how they are both produced and delimited) will depend, to varying degrees, upon the specific relationship of power being negotiated.[11] If you, for example, as a student-subject, have questions about a grade on an assignment, you can speak to the TA or professor, then the department head, then the faculty office, and so on. This institutionalized set of procedures demarcates for you as a student the legitimated terms on which you can "resist" a grade. (You might fantasize about other terms, but these are not legitimated within the relations of knowledge/power at the university and thus resistance in such forms would itself be subject to further discipline through the evocation of other relations of power.) Thus, resistance is circumscribed by the workings of relationships of power that make possible a limited and provisional practice of resistance. It is within and across these that the terms of (y)our agency are made possible and delimited.

The last principle that Weedon points us to is a slight refashioning of the previous focus on the localization of the workings of power. That is, although power takes shape and shapes locally, relationships of power are not isolated and discrete but are part of broader patterns that are made manifest in institutions and social apparatuses, such as laws and policies. To follow the example of relations of knowledge/power: Individual expressions of power and resistance "locally" between a particular professor and a specific student do not exist in isolation, but are constituted by and constitutive of a broader web of university regulations and modes of appropriate practice. This web may have many dimensions, being put into play through the operation of departments and faculties, through university-wide policies, and in provincial and/or national regulations and laws.

Theorizing Difference Differently: Que(e)rying Sex/Gender/Sexuality

Throughout the chapter, I've been endeavouring not only to introduce a series of (re)conceptualizations, but also to show how they may be productive and helpful for thinking about and engaging in the social world differently. In this last section, I want to try to bring together the main points of critique, and the different modes of thinking offered by feminist poststructural inquiry, to consider their contribution to theorizing difference differently—particularly in regards to sex/gender/sexuality. Earlier in the chapter, I introduced the argument that dichotomization is a central organizing practice of late modern social formations. I spoke about this practice particularly in regard to gender, for how it constitutes gender on either/or terms (i.e., masculinity *or* femininity). Here I want to turn my attention particularly to the ways in which this practice works in regard to constituting (un)intelligible categories of sexualities. The categories that are probably most familiar to you are the ones that circulate and prevail in a variety of modes, through education, media, religion, and so on: "heterosexuality" and "homosexuality." You might also think of these as straight versus gay, or normal versus abnormal, or ordinary folk versus "those who flaunt it."

Here is where feminist poststructural critiques of knowledge-making practices can be helpful. Notice first the construct of X *versus* Y, a construct that constitutes X as meaningful by virtue of its opposition to Y, which is marked through this construct as the "other" (different, not desired, aberrant, etc.). This is a construct that has two main effects. First, it constitutes X and Y as singular and coherent identity categories, in which all Xs are presumed to be alike because they are Xs, all Ys are presumed to be alike because they are Ys, and, therefore, Xs and Ys are, at minimum, inherently dissimilar from each other, and, further, in opposition to each other (to be an X means one must categorically not be a Y). Second, Xs and Ys are not constituted as equal in this dichotomous construct; rather, the Xs are considered to be the norm/al and the Ys are considered to be the abnormal. Hence, a hierarchy is established between the two terms and one way in which the Xs are continually imagined as coherent is through the production of the Ys as some*thing* to be anxious about, feared, hated, or, at minimum, kept at a distance (e.g., "they're okay so long as they don't flaunt it or come near me"). Critics refer to this as a heteronormative construct. As Lauren Berlant and Michael Warner explain, "heternormativity is more than ideology, or prejudice, or phobia against gays and lesbians; it is produced in almost every aspect of the forms and arrangements of social life ... as well as in the conventions and affects of narrativity, romance, and other protected spaces in culture" (1993: 359).

One response, on the part of folks who identify as "Ys" (you might insert here, for example, lesbians, gay men, bisexuals, although I don't offer such categories lightly as I will go on to explicate) committed to social justice and recognition, has been to challenge such normative thinking by arguing that Ys are not inherently different from Xs and thus should not be considered deviant or abnormal. Rather than align with Y as a category of shame, folks have claimed Y as an identity category of pride and self-definition, attempting to change its meaning from derisive to affirmative. These are the characteristics of gay and lesbian liberation movements and writings, beginning in North America in the late 1960s, which have emphasized what Tom Warner identifies as the "imperatives of fostering positive identities, building community and asserting visibility" (2002: 305). Such efforts are oriented to legal and social equality for gays and lesbians; the latest manifestations of which, in Canada, as you are probably aware, have been struggles for the full and equal recognition of gay couples under marriage laws. Indeed, as of July 2005, gay marriage is now legal in this country. In Michelle Owen's phrasing, such equity-oriented practices evidence a desire to "normalize the queer" (Owen, 2001: 87); that is, to constitute gays and lesbians as *just as* committed to one another, family oriented, monogamous, etc., as heterosexual folk. (These characteristics are, of course, argued in opposition to heteronormative ideas that have designated homosexuals as promiscuous destroyers of "The Family.") Efforts to have the rights and obligations of marriage extended to gay and lesbian couples, then, have depended upon stretching the category of normal to include those who have been excluded. Such inclusion is made possible when gays and lesbians can be read as "normal"—not fundamentally different from straight folk—and thus when sexual orientation is marked as a fairly neutral (meaning minimal and insignificant) difference.

If we follow the arguments outlined in earlier sections of this chapter, in regard to discourse, power, and the production of subjects, however, we begin to see traces of an inquiry that pushes for a deeper layer of questioning. For, what is clear is that the arguments for gay marriage in Canada are far from secured and settled; even though there has been a legal change, there is no guarantee this will remain in place and, moreover, a change at the level of the law does simply erase broader heteronormative ideas and their associated effects. Indeed, at stake still is the question of what difference the difference of sexuality makes. Is it a neutral difference, as those arguing for gay marriage suggest? Is it an inherent difference of abnormality of being, as conservative, homophobic discourses articulate? Is it a marker of inquiry, an opening into deconstructing heteronormative systems of classification, the articulation of non- or anti-normative sexual identities or que(e)rying of sexual practices, as a way out of the "regimes of normal" (Warner in Hall, 2003: 15) that discipline us all? As you might have guessed, feminist poststructural interrogations lend themselves most readily to the latter line of questioning and hence have an affiliation with what is known as "queer theorizing."

This is a practice of critical inquiry that would propose a re-reading of the paragraph above on gay affirmative strategies for inclusion in heteronormative forms of legitimation (such as marriage). The structure of the argument would be that it will always be a failed strategy to claim Y as possible to affirm on the terms of X; Y is always and already second-class in relation to X, it can only ever be "like" X, "resemble" X, it is not valued on its own or any other terms, and, moreover, has no grounds on which to question X. Thus, such strategies of inclusion may confront heteronormativity but do so in a very circumscribed way; to stretch the norm is not to deeply challenge, trouble, or undermine its structure. To queer heteronormativity is a different difference altogether; as Donald Hall, puts it, queering "may not destroy such systems [of dichotomous classification] but it certainly presses upon them, torturing their lines of demarcation, pressuring their easy designations" (Hall, 2003: 14).

You might wonder why all this torturing and pressuring of categories is necessary, shouldn't gays and lesbians simply be happy to be included? The problem is with the terms of inclusion. For, folks who are demarcated as Ys and may do Y identities themselves, contrary to the premises and efforts at boundary maintenance of the X/Y dichotomy, are not a coherent and singular "group." Indeed, their identities are no more coherent and singular than Xs (but Xs aren't required to defend themselves "as" Xs, that is part of how normative privilege works—the burden of intelligible identification is carried by the others). What this means is that some argue for inclusion and equity, but others are more hesitant or deeply suspect of such strategies. As the brief critique above delineates, the strategy of inclusion and acceptance can only be provisional and is always at risk of being taken away. Moreover, if the boundaries between inside/outside, inclusion/exclusion, are stretched and not questioned per se as inherent in structures that both produce and delimit all of our lives (to recall a Foucauldian understanding of power as productive and limiting), then gay and lesbian inclusion can only be achieved at the cost of excluding "other queers" (e.g., gays and lesbians who don't do their identity on legitimated terms and those who queer (transgress, trouble, mess with...) identity categories rather than define themselves within the normative notions of sex/gender/sexuality).

Feminist poststructural arguments can be used to support a third position here, to help us resist putting in place yet another dichotomy—in this case, inclusion versus queering—that would carry with it all the same problems of hierarchy, boundary policing, and the production of absolute right and wrong that inheres in such structures. This is an argument that might proceed by contending that neither position in and of itself is fully explanatory or inherently better politically (that is, neither should be made a metanarrative, nor should be regarded as outside of the complex and contextual workings of power; this is an especially important point to note when we attend to the workings of heteronormativity globally and not just in Canada). Instead, both need to be examined for their assumptions, conceptualizations, and strategies. Both need to be considered as theorizings of sex/gender/sexuality per se *and* for their implications for intervening politically. Similar to the questions I posed earlier in the chapter regarding modernist feminist theories, questions need to be asked of gay affirmative theories, such as: Whose queer lives and what queering of identities, desires, and practices need to be forgotten or obscured for gay affirmative theories to be upheld? Whose interests does this serve? But also, questions need to be posed of queer theories, i.e., In the current political climate in Canada, is it strategic to argue for gay marriage rather than to argue against it on the terms of que(e)rying? Are there ways to work with the insights of queer and poststructural forms of inquiry to support multiple and diverse strategies of intervention, so that gay marriage isn't made the arbiter of what it means "to be" or, better, "to do" queer in Canada, but nor is it not made possible for those who desire and long for such recognition? I don't propose to answer such questions here, nor do definitive answers most interest me. I offer such questions to you, however, for further discussion.

NOT AN ENDING

It's January 2004, some three months after I began to develop this chapter. Edmonton is bitterly cold and the second semester of classes is underway. There have been some changes in my life over these past few months; some wonderful, some difficult. Larger social struggles continue in a post-9/11 era in which anxiety, terror, threat, warfare, and harm are spilling over and across all of our lives, albeit very differently. As a reader, you won't be able to trace these changes and struggles as I haven't marked them explicitly, but they simmer under the surface of the writing for me. Not because I think feminist poststructural theorizing has "the answers," but because it offers a mode of inquiry and questioning of the workings of knowledge/power/subjects/difference that I think is useful in attending to what passes as normal—and may be made otherwise.

In—among—against—beside all of this, different versions of feminist theorizing are being played out in universities, as scholars struggle to instill, negotiate, and/or refuse various feminist theories and their implications for, among other things, what will be made to count as appropriate knowledge to be passed on to the next generation of students. For some, this is not really a question—they are clear about what the key texts are, how the debates are best framed, and what it is you need to know. From this perspective, the world as I signalled it above, and as it receives texture in this edited collection, presses heavily on those of us in universities, to do something with what we've learned, with what our models of making sense tell us. Thus, on these terms, there is a limit to theorizing, a point at which it stops becoming useful and slips into something else (Play? Narcissism? Theory for theory's sake?). I take this concern seriously, as I think the work of others that I have endeavoured to translate and represent to you here does also. But to take seriously does not necessarily mean to agree. And, that is where a difference is marked.

For there are those of us for whom the questioning of knowledge, learning, teaching, discipline, politics, truth, theory, representation, the making and unmaking of subjects ... is not secondary, does not stop, but is crucial to why and how we find ourselves here—in these places of education. This is not to suggest that politics does not matter or is of secondary concern. Rather, to return to where I began this chapter, it is to put forward the position that it is absolutely vital to have, maintain, and struggle for spaces and places where the immediacy of the now can be suspended (provisionally, momentarily), so that we, individually and in collectivities of classrooms, reading groups, etc., can push beyond what is readily thinkable in terms of how the world *is*. This is not, I would argue, a turning away from the world, but a turning toward it differently, as we too may be different because of our encounter with ideas that shatter, unsettle, question, and press against ways of thinking that are taken as a given, in which, to varying degrees, we have all been, and continue to be, immersed. This is not a morally righteous stance. I am not proffering here a better politic that is innocent of its own investments and struggles. Rather, this is about being here, now, fully mired in the workings of power, reaching for the edges of possibility. Over to you...

Interruption #6: A New Note from the Author

So it is winter here yet again, three years after I last wrote. I have made some minor revisions to this chapter, but its content and structure are largely the same. While this is a necessary practice (in that the key conceptualizations outlined here have not changed in the intervening years), it is also a curious one. I am not the same "I" writing now as then (although I am not altogether different either). You are not the same you; the yous that were reading three years ago have likely graduated by now. The questions that press for thought that is difficult to think have been amplified and show no sign of waning. The stakes of the present and future of feminism remain fraught: just last year, for example, I was part of a debate in which poststructural conceptualizations and transgender critiques animated such public anxiety among my peers that I was left shaken by the extent of (what I read as) feminist border protection. So it seems to me there is still much work (relational, psychic, intellectual, pedagogical) to be done in feminisms, as we endeavour to approach what is hard differently. My particular theoretical preoccupation has become one of dwelling with thinking about relations between the living and those violently dead, whose bodies seem to be accumulating ever more quickly. Feminist poststructural interrogations continue to be valuable to these undertakings, although they are no panacea. I venture there is none to be had. And, so I leave you again—hopeful that the ideas articulated here may touch you in ways you find important and anxiously curious about where we go from here.

ACKNOWLEDGMENTS

For their support and engagement during the initial writing of this chapter, my thanks to Tara Goldstein, Susan Heald, Diane Naugler, Nancy Mandell, Jon Maxfield, and anonymous reviewers.

I am further appreciative of the dialogues with students that I have had over the years in courses at York University and at the University of Alberta, through which the ideas presented here have been animated. My deepest gratitude to Tanya Lewis and Jude Davidson, for their offerings of the care and sustenance necessary to writing.

Endnotes

1. One of the oft-cited claims of postmodernism is that "the author is dead." This shorthand phrasing refers to a critique of the modernist notion that the author's intentions circumscribe and define the meaning of "their" text. Thus, titling sections such as this one as "from the author" may be read as rather contradictory in a chapter that is working with and from poststructural and postmodern ideas. Rather than read this contradiction as a problem, I offer that it may be read as a productive indicator of how relations among author, authority, and meaning might be reconfigured in and by feminist poststructuralism. For, while I am not The Author of this text in the modernist sense, "I" am nonetheless its writer, situated in a particular time and place; this chapter did not simply drop from the sky and land on the right desk at Pearson Education Canada, but was brought into being and negotiated through a complexity of social relations and cultural practices of which "I," with others, am a part. My interruption notes are not offered as expressions of my intentions but are initiated as an endeavour to mark the text with some particular traces of my-self-as-its-writer: breakages into the expected conventions of this as an objective rendering.

2. You'll notice a rather heavy use of double quotation marks in this paragraph. Informed by an attention to the workings of knowledge/power/language that is being profiled in this chapter, I use such quotation marks as a signal that the term or phrase being marked in this way should be read as problematic. That is, the term or phrase needs to be used because it speaks to ideas that commonly circulate, but its prevailing meanings are open to inquiry. You might ask why every word would not then be signalled in such a way. This is a reasonable question and certainly does follow from a strict interpretation of the issues being raised here. The difficulty is that such a practice would make a text so unwieldy as to be unapproachable. Already, you may find, as did some reviewers before you, the use of such signalling a little heavy-handed at times. I have endeavoured here to strike some kind of "balance" (there I go again!) between explicitly problematizing terms and creating an approachable text. See the section on language/discourse for more on the issues at stake here.

3. One of my favourite "tests" of this position is to consider the English-language practices whereby we designate people according to the schema of Mr., Mrs., Miss, and Ms. Note that where there is one designation for men, there are three for women—all of which generate their meaning through a relation to men. Although "Ms." was introduced as a "neutral" companion to "Mr.," in practice it has come to designate divorced women and/or feminists—in and of itself a matter for curiosity.

4. Recent work on intersexuality has shown that the assumed biological basis of a sex dichotomy is actually a social construct and not a given. Critics and advocates working in this area express deep concern with how medicalization imposes this dichotomy on bodies that are deemed not to "fit" correctly. See, for example, Fausto-Sterling, 2000, and Preves, 2003.

5. This question too is up for further consideration. Note the use of the "or" and its implications (you might want to skip ahead to "Theorizing Difference Differently" or bring this issue forward when you are at that point in the chapter). One of the reviewers of an earlier version of this chapter suggested that bringing in some literature and contemporary theorizing in regard to transgendering would be helpful

and pertinent in regard to this point and for the last substantive section of the chapter. I haven't been able to take as much space on this as I would like, but I concur with the reviewer—the recent transgender work on troubling the assumed (and reiterated) linear relation among sex, gender, and sexuality is not only exciting on its own terms, but also suggests important although deeply unsettling work needs to be done in rethinking how gender is thought foundationally in much feminism. Some of these critiques dovetail with the critiques of medicalization of intersexuality noted above; others move in different directions. Key for both, however, is the argument that there is no necessary relationship among one's embodiment, one's sense of gendered self, and one's sexual desires, practices, or interests. Rather, these are highly complex configurations that are not fixed. I would argue that what is central about this theorizing is that it "queers" the dominant story of gender—not only bringing forth different stories of how people live their gendered lives, but also troubling the presumed neutrality and universality of that story for us all (on que[e]rying, see the last section; for relevant reading on transgendering, see especially Bornstein, 1998; Halberstam, 1998, 2005; Nestle, Howell, and Wilchins, 2002; Noble, 2006; and Noble's chapter in this collection).

6. There are numerous dichotomies that are foundational to modernity; gender is but one of them. And dichotomies intersect, so gender dichotomies, for example, may intersect in particular historical moments and geo-political locations with race dichotomies, class dichotomies, and so on. This complicates what an "intelligible" gender means on whose body.

7. Feminists have generally been particularly concerned with the expenditure of energy, resources, and labour that is required for legitimated femininity (see, for example, Bordo, 1993; Brumberg, 1997; Connell, 2002). However, poststructural feminisms in particular may push for a more nuanced consideration of how such expenditures are also required by legitimated modes of masculinity, but on quite different terms. R.W. Connell has done important work in this area; see, for example, 2000, 2005.

8. Some theorists have begun to do this important work. For a formative text in this area, see Sharon Marcus (1992); for a book-length grappling, see Mayrisia Zalewski (2000). Wendy Brown's work on injurious identities is also hugely important to these debates (see her 1996 essay). I have attempted to come at these issues from a different angle in other work; see, for example, my chapter in *Between Hope and Despair* (Rosenberg, 2000). I regard sustained and complex conversation between radical and poststructuralist modes of inquiry and conceptualization as an emerging area of urgently needed feminist attention.

9. In putting the "of us" in parenthesis here, I am endeavouring to, on the one hand, acknowledge that some may object to including my work in this category, and, on the other, to maintain a position that this is a category that needs to be opened to interrogation itself, to let in the difficulties that it is often bordered against.

10. These are larger questions that are currently being grappled with by a number of scholars located in (relation to) Women's Studies. See, for example, the recent debate in *Feminist Theory* 4/3, 2003, and Ann Braithwaite, Susanne Luhmann, Susan Heald, and Sharon Rosenberg, *Troubling Women's Studies: Pasts, Presents and Possibilities* (Sumach Press, 2004).

11. I say to varying degrees, because relationships of power, inhering as they do in other social relations, do not exist in isolation, but criss-cross each other in complicated and unending ways. Thus, resistance in the context of one relationship of power may be informed and shaped in part by other relations. The more institutionalized a relation of power is, the less likely this is the case.

Suggested Readings

In addition to the texts cited in the bibliography, I recommend the following:

Davies, Bronwyn. 2003. *Shards of glass: Children reading and writing beyond gendered identities.* Rev. ed. Cresskill, NJ: Hampton. Her writing is some of the most accessible and applied work in feminist poststructural theorizing and its implications for educative practices.

Heald, Susan. 1991. Pianos to pedagogy: Pursuing the educational subject, in *Unsettling relations: The university as a site of feminist struggles,* ed. H. Bannerji et al. Toronto: Women's Press.

Kelly, Ursula. 1997. *Schooling desire: Literacy, cultural politics and pedagogy.* New York and London: Routledge.

Lewis, Tanya. 1999. *Living beside: Performing normal after incest memories return.* Toronto: McGilligan. Heald, Kelly, and Lewis all write and work in feminist poststructural theorizing in Canada. Although much of the field, given the politics of knowledge transnationally, is being defined by scholars in the United States and Britain, it is important to complicate those politics and recognize local theorists. There are others, of course; these are some of the ones I know the best.

Richardson, Laurel. 2000. Writing: A method of inquiry, in *Handbook of qualitative research,* eds. N.K. Denizen and Y.S. Lincoln, 516–529. Thousand Oaks, CA: Sage. Richardson's work is an excellent example of working with feminist poststructural theorizing for methodology and scholarly representation. I have been particularly inspired in this essay by the kinds of questions and suggestions she puts forth.

Discussion Questions

You'll notice that I raise larger discussion questions throughout the chapter; here are a few others for your consideration:

1. Did this chapter get you thinking about how knowledge is represented? How? What difference did that make to your understanding of the ideas presented?

2. In what ways do you experience gendering yourself and others? What happens when you cannot readily read someone else's gender? How is gender produced differently across social spaces?

3. How do you read heteronormativity being kept in place and/or countered through the gay marriage issue in Canada? What is not being included in mainstream media discussions that might make a difference to what is considered to be at issue and for whom?

4. How do you understand the relationship between modernist and poststructural or postmodern modes of feminist theorizing?

Bibliography

Abercrombie, Nicholas, Stephen Hill, and Bryan S. Turner. 2000. *The Penguin dictionary of sociology,* 4th ed. Harmondsworth, UK: Penguin.

Bannerji, Himani. 2000. *The dark side of the nation.* Toronto: Canadian Scholars Press.

Berlant, Lauren, and Michael Warner. 1993. Sex in public, in *The cultural studies reader,* 2d ed., ed. Simon During, 354–367. London and New York: Routledge.

Bordo, Susan. 1993. *Unbearable weight: Feminism, western culture and the body.* Berkeley: Univ. of California Press.

Bornstein, Kate. 1998. *My gender workbook.* New York and London: Routledge.

Brooks, Ann. 1997. *Postfeminisms: Feminism, cultural theory and cultural forms.* London and New York: Routledge.

Brossard, Nicole. 1998. *She would be the first sentence of my next novel*, tr. Susanne de Lotbiniere-Harwood. Toronto: Mercury.

Brown, Wendy. 1996. Injury, identities, politics, in *Mapping multiculturalism*, eds. Avery F. Gordon and Christopher Newfield, 149–166. Minneapolis: Univ. of Minnesota Press.

Brumberg, Joan Jacobs. 1997. *The body project: An intimate history of American girls.* New York: Random House.

Buchenwald, Emilie, Pamela Fletcher, and Martha Roth. 1993. *Transforming a rape culture.* Minneapolis: Milkweed Editions.

Butler, Judith. 1999. *Gender trouble*, 10th anniversary ed. New York: Routledge.

Butler, Judith, and Joan W. Scott, eds. 1992. *Feminists theorize the political.* New York: Routledge..

Code, Lorraine, ed. 2000. *The encyclopedia of feminist theories.* London and New York: Routledge.

Connell, R.W. 2000. *The men and the boys.* Sydney: Allen and Unwin.

Connell, R.W. 2002. *Gender.* Cambridge: Polity.

Connell, R.W. 2005. *Masculinities*, 2d. ed. Cambridge: Polity.

Dua, Enakshi, and Angela Robertson, eds. 1999. *Scratching the surface: Canadian anti-racist feminist thought.* Toronto: Women's Press.

Fausto-Sterling, Anne. 2000. The five sexes, revisited. *The Sciences* 40(4): 18–23.

Flax, Jane. 1992. The end of innocence, in *Feminists theorize the political*, eds. Judith Butler and Joan Scott, 445–463. New York: Routledge.

Foucault, Michel. 1980. *Power/knowledge: Selected interviews and other writings 1972–1977*, ed. Colin Gordon. New York: Pantheon.

Gould, Karen. 1990. *Writing in the feminine: Feminism and experimental writing in Quebec.* Carbondale and Edwardsville, IL: Southern Illinois Press.

Halberstam, Judith. 1998. *Female masculinities.* Durham, NC: Duke Univ. Press.

Halberstam, Judith. 2005. *In a queer time and place.* New York: New York Univ. Press.

Hall, Donald E. 2003. *Queer theories.* New York: Palgrave MacMillan.

Hamilton, Peter. The Enlightenment and the birth of social science, in *Formations of modernity*, eds. Stuart Hall and Bram Gieben, 18–58. Cambridge: Polity Press and Open University.

Hill Collins, Patricia. 1990. *Black feminist thought.* Boston: Unwin Hyman.

hooks, bell. 1984. *Feminist theory: From margin to center.* Boston: South End Press.

Kolodny, Annette. 2000. "A sense of discovery, mixed with a sense of justice": Creating the first women's studies program in Canada. *NWSA Journal* 12(1): 143–164.

Lather, Patti. 2007. *Getting lost.* Albany, NY: State Univ. of New York Press.

Lyotard, Francois. 1984. *The postmodern condition*, tr. G. Bennington and B. Massumi. Minneapolis: Univ. of Minnesota Press.

Marcus, Sharon. 1992. Fighting bodies, fighting words: A theory and politics of rape prevention, in *Feminists theorize the political*, eds. Judith Butler and Joan Scott, 385–403. New York: Routledge.

Mills, Sara. 1997. *Discourse*. New York and London: Routledge.

Nestle, Joan, Claire Howell, and Riki Wilchins, eds. 2002. *GENDERqUEER: Voices from beyond the sexual binary*. Los Angeles: Alyson.

Noble, J. Bobby. 2006. *Sons of the movement*. Toronto: Women's Press.

Owen, Michelle K. 2001. "Family" as a site of contestation: Queering the normal or normalizing the queer?, in *A queer country: Gay and lesbian studies in the Canadian context*, ed. Terry Goldie, 86–102. Vancouver: Arsenal Pulp.

Preves, Sharon E. 2003. *Intersex and identity: The contested self*. New Brunswick, NJ, and London: Rutgers Univ. Press.

Raby, Rebecca. 2000. Reconfiguring Agnes: The telling of a transsexual's story. *Torquere* 2: 18–35.

Rosenberg, Sharon. 2000. Standing in a circle of stone: Rupturing the binds of emblematic memory, in *Between hope and despair: Pedagogy and the remembrance of historical trauma*, eds. Roger I. Simon, Sharon Rosenberg, and Claudia Eppert, 75–89. Lanham, MD: Rowman and Littlefield.

Rothenberg, Paula S., ed. 2001. *Race, class and gender in the United States*, 5th ed. New York: Worth.

St. Pierre, Elizabeth, and Wanda S. Pillow, eds. 2000. *Working the ruins: Feminist poststructural theory and methods in education*. New York and London: Routledge.

Seidman, Steven. 1996. The political unconscious of the human sciences. *Sociological Quarterly* 37(4): 699–719.

Spender, Dale. 1980. *Man made language*. London: Routledge and Kegan Paul.

Warland, Betsy. 1990. *Proper deafinitions*. Vancouver: Press Gang.

Warner, Tom. 2002. *Never going back: A history of queer activism in Canada*. Toronto: Univ. of Toronto Press.

Weedon, Chris. 1987. *Feminist practice and poststructuralist theory*. Oxford and Malden, MA: Blackwell.

Weedon, Chris. 1999. *Feminism, theory and the politics of difference*. Oxford: Blackwell.

Weedon, Chris. 2000. Poststructuralism/postmodernism. *Encyclopaedia of feminist theories*, ed. Lorraine Code. New York and London: Routledge.

Zalewksi, Marysia. 2000. *Feminism after postmodernism: Theorizing through practice*. London and New York: Routledge.

Third-Wave Feminisms

Lara Karaian and Allyson Mitchell

> For me, feminism is two parts definition and one part struggle—a constant processing of defining, redefining and struggling against existing definitions.
>
> Mariko Tamaki (2001: 2)

INTRODUCTION

The Third Wave(s)

What does a third-wave feminist in the West look like? Is she *Legally Blonde*'s lesbian law student with a PhD in women's studies? Or is she MTV's Tila Tequila—tightly clothed, media savvy, and sexually in-charge? Is she a figure like Juno MacGuff, empowered to make informed choices? Does she sing about skater boys and wear ties like Avril Lavigne or describe herself as "the kind of bitch that you want to get with" like Peaches? Does she look like Hailey Wickenheiser, the butchy, sporty gal who played for the Canadian Women's Hockey team?

Many of these images of third-wavers are provided to us by mainstream media, but third-wavers also comprise many young women whom the media doesn't show us, such as radical cheerleaders, spoken-word artists D'bi Young or Nolan Natasha, and many others who volunteer at rape crisis shelters, march (or squat) against poverty, or fight for any number of other causes. Third-wavers are the sexy media darlings, as well as the grassroots activists (whom some people would call even sexier, but for a different set of reasons altogether).

So our efforts to describe and problematize the diversity that exists among third-wave feminists today makes this chapter a bit of a juggling act. The complexities can be overwhelming but the end result is a more integrative feminism, one that is applicable and accessible to the lived lives of a greater spectrum of people. Third-wavers, we hope to show, are simultaneously shattering and opening up definitions of feminism. This has been heralded as the third wave's greatest strength—as well as its greatest potential weakness.

"The third wave" refers to a dynamic feminist movement with no definitive shape or form. One of the main characteristics of the third wave is an active resistance to the imposition of labels, closures, boundaries, and categories. Some conceptualize the third wave as an attempt to synthesize, build on, and extend what has been accomplished by the first and second waves of feminism, while attending to the particulars of our present moment in historical and feminist contexts. Others contend that third-wave feminism is the feminism "outside of" rather than "after" the second wave. As Emi Koyama (2002) writes, the third wave is "the feminism that starts from the realization that there are many power imbalances among women that are as serious and important as the power imbalance between women and men."

Whatever the definition, a central characteristic of the third wave is its tendency to push the boundaries of the second-wave mantra "the personal is political." Young feminists have learned through their experience as activists and their education in women's studies classes to ask: Whose politics? They have learned to assert that the personal is also theoretical. Our experiences can be used to educate, trouble, disrupt, challenge, and reinforce feminism. Third wave is here and now— *doing* feminism in a society that has been transformed by the feminisms that came before us.

The word "wave" is used as a metaphor to describe the ebbs and flows of feminism occurring over time and place. Although this descriptor has been useful, we must also critique or problematize it. Some feel that breaking up feminism into waves presents an inevitable oversimplification of feminist scholarship and activism, erasing histories and sweeping over complexity and nuance. For example, the written history of the second wave in North America has largely been the record of a white women's movement. Although the second wave was often organized around exclusionary notions of the category "woman," there was also a healthy anti-racist movement and women of colour were active feminists at the time (Dua and Robertson, 1999: 3). This reality demonstrates the limits and possible drawbacks of using the wave metaphor. However, there are aspects of the term "wave" that are useful in describing contemporary feminism. There are no clear boundaries between the various and multiple feminist movements just as there are no clear disconnects between waves in an ocean. Taking this into account, it may be a particularly apt description for this generation of feminists given their fluidity and their inability to be held or pinned down.

We are third-wave feminists. We defy labels, embrace contradictions, and call for complexity. From the outside we appear eclectic, fragmented, and even trite. We prefer to see ourselves as inclusive, open to change, creative, painfully conscious, funny, and really, really smart.

We distance ourselves from earlier feminisms while at the same time acknowledging that we are a generation that has grown up in a world changed by feminism and other social movements. Leslie Heywood and Jennifer Drake, authors of *Third Wave Agenda,* credit these movements with helping us develop "modes of thinking that can come to terms with the multiple, constantly shifting bases of oppression in relation to the multiple interpenetrating axes of identity" (1997: 3). They write, "We know that what oppresses me may not oppress you, that what oppresses you may be something I participate in, and that what oppresses me may be something you participate in" (1997: 3). This chapter is all about the third wave and our relationships with one another as we continue to struggle with feminism's impact on, and understanding of, oppression and privilege. In order to do this we will consider how the third wave came to be, the tactics and strategies that are utilized by young feminists, and how the third wave is the same as and different from feminisms that came before it.

ORIGIN STORIES

The exact origins of the third wave are still being debated. Many argue that third-wave feminism in the West has come about as a result of Black women's critiques of white Western feminism. Certainly, anti-racist critiques of the women's movement have altered feminism forever. As a result, third-wavers start from the belief that being critical of our positions in relation to power structures does not undermine the many struggles within feminism, meaning that it is not necessary to have what is considered to be a "common front" in order to affect social change. Others argue that the third wave is a response to dissatisfaction with what is perceived to be first- and second-wave moralizing, especially in the area of sexuality. And still others see the third wave as a reaction to the 1990s anti-feminist or post-feminist movement that proclaimed equality to be achieved and feminism to be therefore dead. Some regard the third wave as simply "different" from the second wave; they set up a false, and not particularly useful, distinction. Regardless of the third wave's origins, and assuming that it is a movement that has in part come about as a result of a generation divide, it is fair to say that the dialogue between second- and third-wave feminism is complicated and often fraught with tensions.

Feminists of the third wave are uneasy about claiming that identity and writing about young feminism. It is our fear that in trying to explain or define young feminisms we will leave things out or create a false history. Is it possible to talk about young feminists without, to some degree, constructing them? Are we constructing these waves out of convenience? In the introduction to *The Subcultures Reader,* Ken Gelder and Sarah Thorton (1997) discuss how "in the process of portraying social groups, scholars inevitably construct them" (5). The mere labelling "of a social formation is in part to frame, shape and delineate it" (5). We come to terms with this framing by recognizing how and where we are doing it. In fact, we do not lament but embrace it to the fullest, so that when we talk about "young feminism" or "the third wave" we are conscious that we are marking and defining the community and the history. We recognize that this chapter defines the subjects of the third wave through the kinds of young feminism we document and how we are positioned in the text. We struggle with the ethics of making such a map of the third wave. But at the same time, we don't see ourselves as gatekeepers; we simply wish to increase the visibility of young feminism, particularly in an academic textbook that will, we hope, get more young women excited about the project of feminism.

BEING A THIRD-WAVER

How Is the Third Wave the Same as or Different from the First and Second Waves?

Third-wavers further deconstruct (take apart or problematize) the category of "women." Along with this, they critique seemingly clear-cut notions of identity such as the belief that being a woman means the same thing for all women across time and space, or that being a lesbian means the same thing for all lesbians, or that all people experience their classed positions in the same way. A continuation of this is to question notions of authenticity such as those beliefs that there is a "real" way of being "woman," "Black," or "feminist." Some second-wavers fear that this kind of exploration will prevent women from uniting in a common fight—that feminism is threatened if it can't present a united front. The argument is that if we complicate feminism too much, it may no longer look like the feminism that has provided the grounds for rallying "women" together against patriarchy. Third-wavers respond by arguing that this need for commonality is too simplistic an idea to base a resistance movement upon. They call for a greater acceptance of, and emphasis on, complexities, ambiguities, hybridity, intersectionality, and fluidity, as well as a rejection of dichotomous thinking that posits women as good and men as bad. Third-wavers believe fragmentation to be feminism's greatest strength, not its biggest downfall.

This generation of young feminists must still consider many of the issues politicized by the second wave, such as violence against women, reproductive rights, job equity, poverty, militarism, and the rights of children. But third-wavers' cultural context is quite different: Postmodern, post-structural, post-colonial, queer, anti-racist, queer, and trans theories, along with post-feminism, global capitalism, corporate media, and technological advances, make this generation's context—and thus its methods of resistance—its very own. When we look at the ways in which young women are "doing" feminism we can see that they offer new frameworks for understanding social movements and social change, new ways of knowing and being that are necessary for our times. The following sections will look more specifically at what some young women are "doing" with feminism by considering examples of activism and theory such as personal narrative, cultural production, body and sexual politics, and redefining gender. These examples will show, simultaneously, the key aspects of Western third-wave feminism and its methods of resistance.

What the Third Wave(s) Is/Are

Third-wave feminist scholarship is dedicated to the project of locating ourselves as feminists, academics, teachers, students, and anti-oppression activists. This means being as clear as possible about where we are coming from. For the authors of this chapter, a bit of self-identification is in order. Allyson Mitchell is a teacher, academic, lesbian, middle-class, white, able-bodied artist and size/body image activist. Lara Karaian is a non-trans, Armenian-Canadian, queer, able-bodied, 35-year-old (ack!), middle-class, perpetual PhD student, teacher, and activist. We both experience a great deal of cultural capital, recognizing that we possess a knowledge of available middle-class resources—how to move through the world in a way that allows us access to privileges—even though we may not have its economic status. These positionings via race, class, sexuality, ability, location, and so on, have influenced and shaped this chapter and how it is constructed. Both of us are dedicated to various feminist activist projects and we teach women's studies to undergraduate students. Along with our gal pal Lisa Bryn Rundle, we edited *Turbo Chicks: Talking Young Feminism,* one of the first collections of writings on feminism by young women from across Canada.

The emphasis of this chapter is also in part dictated by the constraints of space and subject matter. We would have liked to have done a more in-depth analysis of the third wave's relationship to the second wave, as well as an outline of young feminists' involvement in the anti-globalization and anti-war movements. The chapter is also largely Western in its focus and limited in its discussion of young feminism outside of the North American context. This is not to say, however, that the third wave in the West is not interested in, or connected to, the feminist resistance occurring beyond our borders.

We think it's also important to outline what we mean by "youth" with regards to third-wave feminism. In this chapter we refuse to define "young" feminism by age. Does it start at 14? Does it end at 35? We try to maintain an ambiguous relationship to the membership of "young" or "third wave" so that it includes politics and aesthetics as much as it does generational positioning.

As we understand it, a simple transition from youth to adulthood does not exist in terms of movements from irrationality to rationality or from simplicity to complexity (Valentine, Skelton, and Chambers, 1998: 4). Youth is a culturally, historically, and personally relative identity. The experiences, socio-economic status, personality, and age of the physical body and/or the "social body" all contribute to whether an individual is considered to be a "youth" by society, and by him- or herself (James, 1986: 157). While feminism is old news, it is also "forever young." That is, young women have always been active in the practices of feminism. They have been at the centre of feminist organization in all of feminism's supposed waves and have been involved in fighting against slavery, in fighting for women's right to vote, in resisting forced sterilization practices, and in the demand for access to birth control. For young women, being a part of feminism is not a new phenomenon. But there have been some changes in feminist theory, organization, and cultural expression. The ambiguity of the term "youth" or "young" is illustrated in our own use (and avoidance) of it in this chapter. Simplifying contemporary feminism to youth makes it easier to talk about ... but then again the third wave is all about further complicating feminism.

Third-Wave Resistance: What Does Fighting the Good Fight Look Like?

Third-wave feminists ask: What constitutes resistance and activism? How effective are these kinds of resistances? Who does this resistance benefit? All of the examples that we will outline in the following sections discuss how young women are doing feminism, enacting theories of resistance, and engaging with the above questions. Resistances in the form of personal narrative, cultural production, body politics, and political organizing are some of the areas that we will develop more fully.

Young feminists recognize that activism can range from the very personal to the institutional, taking up and expanding upon the second-wave mantra, "the personal is political." Civil disobedience, letter writing, street protests, culture jamming, direct action, public speaking, and education are some of the more recognizable or traditional forms of resistance. The third wave participates in these forms of action in ways similar to the forms of action used by those feminists who came before us. It also questions many of these forms of action/resistance and adds to the list of possible tactics.

Third-wave feminists argue for a diversity of tactics, taking up Audre Lorde's inspirational sentiment that "the master's tools will never dismantle the master's house" (1984: 112). This means that they question some previous efforts that rely on "legitimate" strategies of resistance such as political lobbying or legal strategy. Third-wavers do not reject these strategies outright. Rather, they argue that second-wave feminists might reconsider the efficacy of these methods.

Law No one can deny that the law is an important tool for change. Nevertheless, reliance upon it is problematized by young feminists who argue that particular equality-seeking movements are being forced to restructure their demands to fit within a liberal legal framework rather than having the law change to accommodate the particular needs of their struggle. In the case of gay marriage for instance, they could argue that the use of the courts as a means of recognizing and legitimizing the union of two same-sex individuals has forced gays and lesbians to reproduce normative heterosexual relationships and to thus lose some of the transgressive and radical potential that gay identity has had when it comes to challenging notions of the family and ideas of monogamy and the nuclear family form. Many feminist activists reject marriage as the key issue around which to rally for change. A diversity-of-tactics approach to resistance de-centres the law, not only questioning the effectiveness of the law but also rejecting it as one of the most legitimate means with which to resist. Instead, the third wave may place a greater emphasis on activism that works outside of state apparatus and gets to the heart of the communities within which the women themselves live. Institutional forms of resistance are not abandoned; rather these forms of resistance may seek to subvert more actively from within. For example, Teens Educating and Challenging Homophobia (TEACH) is a group of youth educators that resists homophobia and heterosexual privilege, both in the school system and beyond. Another example is the Miss G project. This group of young feminists has had a great deal of success lobbying the Education Minister and as a result Ontario will be adding a Women and Gender Studies course to the high school curriculum.

The third wave also takes up and argues for actions such as the squats that have taken place in Toronto, Vancouver, Montreal, and Sudbury by anti-poverty activists. These actions, usually cracked down on by police, involve reclaiming abandoned housing by third-wave, anti-poverty activists and the homeless in an effort to publicize and meet the needs of those most impoverished in our cities. Given the fact that young women, single mothers, and elderly women make up the greatest number of the poor in Canada, these actions are one way in which third-wavers actively address the issue of the feminization of poverty, as identified by the second wave. They also insist that the third wave always advance an intersectional analysis to the issue of the feminization of poverty, one that moves beyond gender and centres factors such as the inherent racism in changing immigration laws and cuts to social spending on mental health and disability.

Sexual orientation, human rights issues, and struggles against poverty do not necessarily originate within feminism, but many feminists have joined these struggles, sometimes because of direct connections to gender, such as lesbians' and trans-women's rights and the feminization of poverty. At the same time, these social movements have incorporated some feminist strategies and values. It is not productive to define the ways in which these examples of resistance are feminist. It is more useful to see these struggles as examples of the complex identification embraced by third-wavers.

Pornography and Sex Work What is important to recognize when it comes to third-wave resistance is that some of its interventions are equally threatening not only to the state but also to other feminists. For example, the creation of alternative pornography is a form of activism taken up by third-wave feminists in response to dominant notions of femininity and sexuality imposed upon them by patriarchy ... and by some second-wave radical feminists. Sites such as **nofauxxx.com** and **abbywinters.com** offer a different kind of porn to combat mainstream representations meant solely for the male gaze. In doing so, these third-wavers meet with the resistance of some second-wave feminists who argue that any porn is harmful to women, ignoring third-wavers' belief that alternative porn and other means of resisting mainstream representations of women's raced, classed, and sized bodies can be more liberating than destructive. The activism that third-wavers enact in this area includes celebrations and validations of sexual subcultures through events like the Feminist Porn Awards in Toronto and The Vancouver International Burlesque Festival.

In addition to these celebratory actions, however, third-wave activism around broader issues of sex work also encompasses economic and political critiques. While third-wavers articulate a variety of opinions on the moral or ethical implications of sex work, there is a marked movement *away* from arguments that position all sex workers as disempowered victims of patriarchy. Instead, third-wave feminism addresses the social, political, and economic barriers faced by sex workers and works toward eliminating them. Part of this process involves recognizing that workers enter the sex industry for a variety of reasons—some voluntary and some not. Accordingly, third-wave activism around sex work concerns itself with destigmatizing sex work, improving labour conditions in the sex industry, and securing rights for sex workers so that all women have the opportunity to live as they choose.

Personal Choices Third-wave resistance can be as personal and as private as coming out to your parents, challenging friends when they make sexist or racist jokes, or taking Wen Do self-defence classes. Third-wave resistance may even include the refusal to shop! When Western leaders urge us to save our faltering economy by hitting the malls, claiming that consumption is good, third-wavers respond by endorsing and participating in "Buy Nothing Day." Celebrated in more than 50 countries, individuals opt not to spend any money for 23 hours, enjoying instead "pranks, parades, street parties, credit-card cutups." Young feminists, a key target market in our global economy, also actively resist the reality that there are more malls than high schools in the United States by recycling clothing, arranging clothing swaps, shopping at thrift stores, and refusing to support the unfair labour practices of chains like the Gap.

Theorizing Experience: Resisting through Personal Narrative A great deal of third-wave resistance takes place in the writings, particularly the personal narratives, of young feminists. A personal narrative can be told through autobiographical writing, manifesto, confession, ethnography, oral tradition, or testimonial. Third-wave feminist theory and activism are made up of a variety of these forms of writing and are found in edited collections, zines, and websites. The processes of self-exploration and sharing are transformative and proactive for both the writer and the audience, whose perceptions are likely to be expanded. If activism is about education, interruption, and ideological change, then these forms of writing constitute activism. Feminists of the third wave believe in the importance of their life experiences, and it has been argued that their individual stories collectively tell the tale of larger social phenomena (Siegel, 1997). One example of self-exploration and sharing can be found on the website "Transracial Abductees," (**www.transracialabductees.org**) a space devoted to personal narratives and discussion of transnational adoption/abduction. Both the "Abductees Speak!" and the "Abductees Forum" offer spaces for its members to write about the politics of international abduction/adoption and the issues that they have personally faced as abductees/adoptees. The resulting narratives foster information sharing, support and critical analysis on topics such as feminism, racism, globalization, and Western imperialism, as well as the relationship of these to one another.

Some have argued that the third wave in the West is actually birthed by a textual community (Siegel, 1997). For over a decade, collections of writings by young women have contributed largely to shaping a new generation of feminists. Some of these edited collections include *Listen Up: Voices from the Next Feminist Generation* (1995), *To Be Real: Telling the Truth and Changing the Face of Feminism* (1995), *Body Outlaws: Young Women Write about Body Image and Identity* (2000), *Turbo Chicks: Talking Young Feminisms* (2001), *Colonize This!: Young Women of Color on Today's Feminism* (2002), *Yentl's Revenge: Young Jewish Women Write about Today's Feminism* (2001), *Catching a Wave: Reclaiming Feminism for the 21st Century* (2003), *The Fire This Time: Young Activists and the New Feminism* (2004), and *We Don't Need Another Wave: Dispatches from the Next Generation of Feminists* (2006).

These are formally bound and legitimized accounts of young women talking about, theorizing, documenting, and archiving their experiences and struggles with feminism. In most every essay, poem, and illustration within these books, young women are insisting on positioning themselves within the texts, writing in the first person and not even pretending to be objective. This is a significant and influential body of work, in which young women look for connections and context to their feminism. These anthologies helped create the third wave at the same time as young women themselves were developing it. Through these accounts, young women have made connections between geographical locations, levels of academic experience, and positions of privilege and oppression. By actively seeking connections with the works of other feminists and social justice activists, third-wavers make links between their experiences and the social and institutional processes and trends that shape their lives. For example, the stories about family dynamics, hip-hop culture, and hybrid identity negotiations in *Colonize This!,* although rooted in the personal, extend to the public and the political. Stories bring these elements together to create a dialogue about the continuing effects of colonization, racism, and imperialism.

It could be argued that the third wave's use of personal narratives comes out of challenges posed by Black feminists such as bell hooks and Patricia Hill Collins in the 1980s and 1990s that critiqued the second wave for its inaccessible academic writing and style. The third wave's proliferation of autobiographical writing can be seen as a form of resistance to inaccessible writing. To some third-wavers it is a political tactic to write in a way that everyone can understand and be inspired or excited by. Black feminist thought, then, set the tone for new feminist theory, politics, and history (Dua and Robertson, 1999). Feminist subjectivity, as it informs personal and situated forms of writing, can be a very powerful tool to make feminism a movement that new generations and larger groups of people can relate to.

Although some may see the inclusion of personal narrative as a strength of young feminism, others see it as a weakness, regarding it as self-indulgent, unchallengeable, and theoretically weak. This is an unfair accusation if we consider how feminist academic theory has influenced young feminism. Ideas about standpoint theory, identity politics, and postmodernism have positively informed how third-wave feminists practice, process, and write their feminism. For example, many of the accounts in these collections are by women who talk about their experiences in women's studies classes in which feminist theory has been a major influence on them as feminists. Others reveal how postmodern feminism has encouraged them to be subjective and speak from experience to avoid universalizing and appropriating. They understand the significance of sharing and validating their experiences in order to comprehend the differences between women, rather than attempting to come to some false common ground. Postmodern feminist methodology insists on a reflexive theoretical practice. Young feminists use personal narratives to understand not only how the personal is political but also how the *personal* is *theoretical.* The result of this theorizing is what Gina Dent (1995) refers to in her essay "Missionary Position" in *To Be Real* as a "collective benefit." Deborah Siegel (1997), in her essay about third-wave theory, understands the anthologies listed above as "disclosures not of personal lives but the political violences inflicted on whole communities."

Zines and Zine Culture Another prominent place where we can find examples of young feminists writing personal narratives as a means to theorize their experiences is in zines. Zines began as photocopied pamphlets that were often diaristic accounts of daily lives. Zine culture is an important vehicle for feminists in the third wave to express themselves, disseminate their ideas, and create community. This accessible form of publishing uses fast and cheap photocopying. Authors avoid jumping through hoops to get their ideas published. As well, many young women are posting their zines on the web. You can read more about zines and their significance to young feminists in the section on cultural production below. It is sufficient to say here that zines, in their form and content, represent an important part of how young feminists use their lives in a kind of emergency storytelling to understand their politics, feminist or otherwise.

This returns us to one of the basic strengths of the third wave, which is to expand the idea that the personal is political. An excellent example of this type of theorizing experience can be found in the writing of Emmanuelle Pantin. Pantin tells how she used ideas in introductory political theory texts to better understand the traumas of her childhood. She talks about how silenced she felt, how angry she was, and how she applies her new understandings of her own experience to larger social corruptions such as homophobia, racism, nationalism, and classism. Pantin claims that understanding how these theories work in terms of lived lives represents how she came to understand the source of her pain—systemic power relations. Her experience changed from that of an isolated individual, as articulated within the form of her zine writing, to an understanding of her context and connections placed in hierarchical power relations. This is an example of how the third wave has learned from earlier feminist critiques of impersonal or falsely objective theories and made them more real and applicable by inserting, recognizing, and using their subjectivities and subsequently making the personal a part of feminist theory and action.

This part of young women's feminist theorizing and activism can be called synthesis. This defining characteristic of the third wave involves examining what works or doesn't work from pre-existing feminist thought and combining these elements with new theories and tactics. The use of narrative is a key tool for resisting, reclaiming, and engaging in dialogue with others, be they third-wavers and other generations of feminists.

Third-Wave Resistance through Cultural Production

Third-wave feminist cultural production goes beyond the written word, linking art and activism together in an effort to resist economic, cultural, racial, and gender-related inequalities. It is important to look at cultural "production" rather than cultural "consumption" when examining young feminisms. Carly Stasko discusses the importance of girls creating their own brand of feminist culture in "Action Grrrls in the Dream Machine" in the anthology *Turbo Chicks* (2001). Stasko uses pop culture material such as television and glossy magazines to make collages that illustrate the necessity for a re-evaluation of mass media. Her discussion of play as a necessary component of feminist cultural production is significant. Stasko stresses the importance of engaging with one's surroundings through cultural production rather than simply consuming it or reacting to it. With the co-optation of feminist ideologies by corporations via the Spice Girls reunion tours or television shows like *The L Word* or *Sex and the City,* Do It Yourself (DIY) anti-capitalist third-wave production is crucial.

Performing/Enacting Feminism Young women of the third wave enact their feminism through a variety of methods of cultural production. Zine-making, songwriting, painting, sculpture, graffiti, radio, music, sticker-making, guerilla theatre, film, blogging, video, dance, and comedy are some of the types of cultural participation in which young feminists engage.

DIY Feminism These kinds of resistance through cultural production often employ a DIY strategy. DIY politics, born out of a Riot Grrrl response to sexism in punk rock scenes, was used by girls to carve out a culture for themselves. An anti-masculinist punk rock girl-power movement that was active in North America in the 1990s, Riot Grrrls' "learn-by-doing" approach used the media as a tool to strategically grow their movement, but they also reinforced a politic that commands and conveys an urgency for people to create their own culture and not to rely on the mainstream to do it for them. One riot grrrl claims that "at the heart of Riot Grrrl is the empowerment that you can do it yourself—in fact, you have to." Another describes the movement in this way: "The gist of it is the strength of standing on your own and taking action."[1] DIY is about people creating their own culture, partly out of economic necessity and partly out of political positioning; we should tell our own stories by any means necessary—and before someone else does it for us. Making a zine that talks about how to report a rape, how to organize a women's self-defence collective, how to address white privilege, or how to use a sound board, are all direct actions that challenge the ideological environment we live in. All are done within a third-wave DIY politic.

---

1   Testimonies like these are found at the web archive "Experience Music Project." For a comprehensive history of DIY feminism that comes out of riot grrrl, including video interviews, articles, and chronologies, see "Riot Grrrl Retro Retrospective," **www.emplive.com/explore/riot_grrrrl/index.asp** (accessed February 2008)

Young feminists use DIY cultural production tactics as a way to open up spaces where we can learn and challenge the hegemonic ideologies within our society. The efforts of artists like Miranda July increase the accessibility of women to film and video. Her networking project called "The Big Miss Moviola Project" is an excellent example. For this, July created a type of zine chain letter of women- and girl-made movies. She sent out a call and asked people to submit their short works. In return, she compiled them on tapes containing 10 "lady-made" films and sent it back to the original contributors. July initiated this project in order to address what she saw as a lack of access to women-made films in the film department at her art school. The purpose was to disseminate the films to a larger audience—in this case, beyond the circle of friends that the films would have been shown to without formal distribution. The result was a space to share the ideas of liberatory cultural expressions for young women. The politics of Riot Grrrl and DIY informed July's practice as a cultural producer.

After almost a decade of action and resistance, Riot Grrrl has a herstory and elders whose cultural artifacts, such as zines and films, have been archived, legitimized, and even commodified. What exists is a transformed feminist community that has been shaken up by the women who were at the forefront of this movement. Riot Grrrl has since gone underground and evolved into other forms in order to slip from the hands of mainstream media. The cultural productions of the third wave have strong affiliations with the Riot Grrrl movement, a movement that encouraged girls to tell their stories, claim their space, and crack their jokes—even if this meant writing directly on their bodies. DIY cultural artifacts are one example of how individuals communicate and proliferate shared ideologies and thus influence others. Third-wave politics creates community; it is about relationships, never only about individuals. An individual's political act or cultural production invariably links groups of people in political affiliation.

Lesbian graffiti is one type of cultural expression from which a young feminist community emerges. Understanding graffiti in a manner that gives it the power to create community and record history shows us how individual women and communities of women resist their invisibility. This sort of understanding validates a form of cultural production that usually exists under the radar of everyday perception. That is, someone who doesn't affiliate with or claim membership to any of these communities may not notice or understand the significance of its markers or presence. The lesbian (and other feminist) graffiti we see in our neighbourhoods, on bus ads, and in bathroom stalls, are acts of resistance against poverty, unemployment, the processes of gentrification, racism, and sexual conformity. Its origins lie in a number of subcultures such as lesbian, feminist, punk rock, Riot Grrrl, and youth.

However, we can't attribute all of the cultural production of the third wave to Riot Grrrl. As Kearney suggests, we must look to "other politicized ideologies and forms of cultural practice which also influence ... radical female culture" (1997: 217). Because of what the mainstream and the media define as "cultural production" and what sells in stories of "cultural producers" or even "radical subcultures," queer, trans folk, women of colour, and dis(en)abled women are often erased. We hear about the "radical" subcultures of the indie filmmaking scene or largely white zine shows, but whole other groups of people exist outside of what media deems newsworthy or what art councils deem fundable or what academics deem definable. Despite these barriers, young feminists continue to grow their own cultural productions with or without these legitimizations.

The group Turtle Gals, for example, is a performance ensemble of three native woman, Michelle St. John, Monique Mojica, and Jani Lauzon. The trio blends song, dance, text, video, and comedy in order to address cultural genocide and racism, both historical and internalized. True to third-wave tactics, the Turtle Gals employ a sharp comedic style to uncover and highlight social injustices. The three actors reclaim vaudeville as an offshoot of Indian medicine shows. They use Marx Brothers shtick, cartoon characters, and media clichés from mainstream culture to illuminate their politics. Their combination of anger, guilt, comedy, pop culture references, and memory is striking and effective. Their work is an example of political synthesis: It integrates critiques of racism, sexism, homophobia, colonialism, and anti-Semitism. The result is empowering for them as performers as well as their audiences.

> Several years ago, we gathered to talk about race, colour and sexuality. We told stories and talked about what could lie beyond the popular culture's imagery of Native women, i.e. Disney's Pocahontas. Out of the conversation emerged a recurring theme: scrubbing. Either we, or someone we knew had at some point tried to scrub off or bleach out their colour. This realization, whet our appetite to explore the manifestations of the internalized racism we carry. Coupled with our common theatre vocabulary in creating original and ensemble work, we felt a shared urge to form our own performance collective. (**www.turtlegals.com**)

Another example is the Toronto-based break dance troupe She Bang! This group of young women dances to address sexism in hip hop and other youth cultures. They also have a mandate to teach and empower other young women how to break dance their way out of the margins.

We can look to cultural production as a way of seeing, hearing, and tangibly touching how young feminists are "doing" feminism that is exciting and vibrant and often confrontational. Third-wave cultural production is an active political undertaking because it first identifies a lack of feminist cultural production and then functions to create alternatives for and by young feminists. Young feminists then are resisting mainstream cultural production through a diversity of artistic tactics.

Rethinking Bodies

Our body and our embodiments are one of our most personal experiences. At the same time, our bodies, women's bodies in particular, are held up to hyper-scrutiny both at a micro or private level and at a macro or public level. On the micro level, we survey ourselves through processes such as careful weigh-ins, calorie counting, plucking, shaving, and hair straightening and dyeing. We worry about skin tone and shading and have insecurities about toe and nose lengths and sizes. We scowl self-critically into the mirror while simultaneously spewing feminist theory. We "diet talk" and dream about a carb-free, temptationless world while discussing union activism with our friends. While we competitively compare the size and tone of our butts, we critique some second-wave feminists for their lack of inclusivity. How we experience ourselves and how we experience the contradictions within our feminisms is through our complex bodies.

Women's bodies are also scrutinized at the macro or public level. One way that this happens is through media. The bodies that appear to us through the media are most often white, thin, able-bodied, non-trans, and heterosexualized. At the same time, women's bodies have been culturally constructed as a site of sin, corruption, and uncleanliness. There is an absence of the bodies of women of colour, poor bodies, bodies with disabilities, trans-bodies, and fat bodies. When we do see these "other" bodies it is often through stereotypes that reflect racism, sizeism, genderism, and profound misunderstandings about ability. Through the media, women's bodies become homogenized. That is, there seems only one (or very few) ways to be "beautiful," "normal," and "sexy," thus "acceptable," "loved," and "worthy." Women are expected (and expect themselves) to meet these criteria. As the media and social values dictate our bodies, women are preoccupied with trying to live up to impossible standards.

The body is not merely personal, it is a place where broader social phenomena are addressed in relation to power, autonomy, racism, misogyny, genderism, homophobia, and ableism. The body is always political. For many third-wave feminists, the body has been an entry point to feminist consciousness and action. Experiences of "freedoms and gains" made by the women's movement, and the lived realities that may contradict these supposed freedoms, politicize our bodies and our fluid and opposing experiences of them. The body is a place where young women connect feminist theory with practice. This is not a new phenomenon for feminism. However, it has been noted by Amelia Richards in her essay "Body Image: Third Wave Feminism's Issue?" (2000) that there is a change in the politics around the body from second-wave feminism to third-wave feminism. The focus has moved from an external to a more internal spotlight on issues around the body.

The second wave largely concerns itself with violence and abuses, access to jobs, and reproductive choices. Though these issues are still concerns in the third wave, there have been institutional gains in these specific areas through law, legislation, and policy. Although there have been achievements in the public sphere, women struggle continuously with their relationships to their bodies. Feminists such as Joan Jacobs Brumberg, in her study of young women and body image (2000), have noted that the more social and economic freedoms people experience, the greater the restrictions on their bodies. In addition, the more global economic and social forces make their mark, the more all cultures are expected to measure up to white North American standards of beauty and acceptance. Our standards of body size do not exist cross-culturally or even cross-racially. For example, in the Caribbean, larger bodies—butts and breasts in particular—are seen as desirable, valuable, and attractive. However, with the proliferation of North American culture there is evidence that the body standards in other places are conforming to North American "proportions." Brumberg exemplifies this by discussing how women's experiences of "gains" in the public sphere are reflected in fashion restrictions: We see how tighter jeans, plunging necklines, and higher heels have permeated all corners of the globe.

Although fashion can be a place to reclaim feminist power and play with sexuality, it can also be a call to arms against the "standards" that dictate desirable and acceptable femininity. This is particularly true when feminists working against globalization have shown us how the dieting, fashion, and beauty industries work to oppress people not only in North America but in the so-called Third World, linking the struggles of Western women's right to shop for clothing that doesn't only fit a size 6 to those of the exploitation and policing of the bodies that make clothing and diet foods. In numerous different ways, then, bodies have become sites of political struggle and the redefinition of meanings about what is normal and what is not.

Body Outlaws In her book, *Body Outlaws: Young Women Write about Body Image and Identity,* Ophira Edut (2000) argues that there is a great need to provide women with safe spaces to explore their own experiences and struggles with their bodies as a way of healing and empowerment. In her outline of body activism, she describes women who reject and disrupt discourses of beauty as "body outlaws." By "breaking the laws" of what is ascribed to our bodies, women contradict and challenge societal values and work against the interests of industries that capitalize on women's uncomfortable relationships with their bodies. Edut explains that women who resist do a kind of "shock therapy" when they openly reject the norm. By showing, through their bodies, how they exist in many shapes, sizes, colours, and abilities, young feminists articulate their politics. They are doing what Nomy Lamm (2001) describes in her essay "It's a Big Fat Revolution" in the anthology *Listen Up: Voices from the Next Feminist Generation,* as the process of using what is available (fashion, for example) in a way that subverts and challenges dominant values. Lamm's politics are informed by her subjectivity as a Jewish, queer, dis(en)abled, fat woman.

Pretty Porky and Pissed Off The fat body is a specific site where women are punished for exceeding the boundaries of femininity. The fat body disrupts these values and norms, while at the same time the individual remains influenced, prescribed, and implicated by these norms. Pretty Porky and Pissed Off (PPPO'd) is an example of how young women have used their bodies as a way to resist oppressive power structures. PPPO'd was a fat activist group that used cultural production in the form of performance art to educate and serve up their own brand of advocacy for size acceptance. This group publicly defied stereotypes of fat women as incapable of being fashionable, sexy, smart, or active. They chose performance-based activism and humour as a way to challenge notions about the body. Sometimes this meant embodying the very stereotypes they were resisting as a way of addressing and undressing them as the falsehoods they are. Rather than shrinking or hiding behind loosely fitting clothing, they performed their bodies as BIG. PPPO'd is no longer performing, but the group has inspired numerous other young women to follow in their footsteps, including the Toronto-based Fat Femme Mafia.

Another example of fat activism is evidenced in the creation of "Flesh Mobs." The term "Flesh Mob" is a play on the phrase "flash mob." A flash mob is an event in which a large group of people gather simultaneously in a public place for a brief period of time, and do something unexpected (like freeze for 10 minutes, or clap for 15 seconds) before dispersing. These gatherings appear random and unplanned but they are usually organized with the help of the internet or other digital communications networks. Flash Mobs apparently started as pointless stunts (to make fun of hipsters and our culture's emphasis on conformity and of wanting to be an insider or part of "the next big thing") but later developed as a way to make people aware of a particular social agenda or address a certain form of oppression. The Flesh Mob is a Flash Mob made up of fat people, for fat people and fat activists. It's a fun, creative, and spontaneous way to reclaim public space for fat people as well as give power to fat visibility.

These collectives and actions are excellent examples of third-wave activists using the body. They look at the intersections of oppression and privilege in terms of sized bodies. They make the connections between obesity and poverty, a sizeist medical establishment, globalization and junk food, and low self-esteem and the capitalist placement of guilt on the fat body in a sort of millennial moral tale. Women concerned with issues pertaining to their bodies and their experiences as sexualized, raced, classed, gendered, (dis)enabled, and fat are central to third-wave theorizing as well as organizing.

Rethinking Gender

Third-wave feminism actively resists the idea that there are "good" feminists and "bad" feminists.

Referring back to our discussion about authenticity, there is no "correct" way to be a third-wave feminist. And, as young feminists have played with, there is no correct or "real" way to be female, feminine, or a "woman."

Sandra Lee Bartky describes femininity as "an artifice, an achievement" and agrees with Judith Butler's claim that femininity is performative, that it is "a mode of enacting and reenacting received gender norms which surface as so many styles of the flesh" (1990/1997: 95). But, for Bartky, normative femininity can only ever be seen as gender conformity. The disciplinary project of femininity, as she sees it, is a process by which the ideal body of femininity is constructed and one that nearly every woman fails to reproduce to some degree or another (100). Many third-wave feminists, including women with disabilities, women of colour, fat women, and trans women, trouble the ideal and narrowly defined feminine body while at the same time recognizing the need to complicate the conclusion that femininity is solely imposed upon women by disciplinary structures. They argue that Bartky's analysis is lacking in any conception of female self-determination and agency since, according to Bartky, there is no way for female femininity to be rendered a political or disruptive performance.

Third-wave feminism wrestles with the very dilemma of simultaneously destroying and reclaiming traditional notions of femininity, arguing that we can reinsert agency and self-determination by recoding, reclaiming, misappropriating, and re-appropriating femininity for ourselves. Young feminists reject the idea that if you wear makeup, shave your legs/pits/'stache, wear heels/minis/tight-tittie-Ts, then you're a dupe of patriarchy, and definitely not a good feminist. Leah Rumack, in her article "Lipstick" in *Turbo Chicks* (2001), recalls how in certain feminist communities she had to defend herself for simultaneously owning an eyelash comb and calling herself a feminist. Like her, third-wavers argue that any standard of beauty that is defined by others is oppressive and that includes judgments made by other feminists about what a good feminist looks like. Now she writes "with the growing cross-breeding of feminist thought into a wider arena of gender studies, with all its trannies and drag queens, the new message seems to be that it's okay to be fabulous, as long as you're ironic about it (at least a little), and that beauty is okay as long as there's a wider, more active definition of what it is" (Rumack, 2001: 97).

This idea of being ironic and widening the notion of femininity has been taken up by third-wavers drawing on Judith Butler's theory of gender as performative. "To say that gender is a performative act is to say that it does not need a material referent to be meaningful, is directed at others in an attempt to communicate, is not subject to falsification or verification, and is accomplished by 'doing' something rather than 'being' something" (Stryker and Whittle, 2006: 10). Butler (1990) seeks to subvert any notion of a "true" gender identity. Using drag queens as her example (problematically, according to some), Butler argues that, "In imitating gender, drag implicitly reveals the imitative structure of gender itself— as well as its contingency" (120). Butler goes on to claim that, "[j]ust as bodily surfaces are enacted as the natural, so these surfaces can become the site of dissonant and denaturalized performance that reveals the performative status of the natural itself" (126). Butler thus concludes that "gender parody reveals that the original identity after which gender fashions itself is an imitation without an origin" (120).

In addition to this, there is also the movement within the third wave to articulate "femme" as a gender experience that is not tied to biological sex. Chloe Brushwood Rose and Anna Camilleri, the editors of *Brazen Femme: Queering Femininity* (2002), explore this issue and ask, What makes femme different from femininity? What would it mean to be a femme and not a woman? What would it mean to be a femme outside of a lesbian framework? What is it that femmes have in common? Although they offer the following inroad to what femme might be, they do so without claiming this as a closed definition of what a femme is or locating femme in one place, in one time, or in one tidy package (2002: 12). They write, "femme might be described as 'femininity gone wrong'—bitch, slut, nag, whore, cougar, dyke, or brazen hussy. Femme is the trappings of femininity gone awry, gone to town, gone to the dogs. Femininity is a demand placed on female bodies and femme is the danger of a body read female or inappropriately feminine. We are not good girls—perhaps we are not girls at all" (13). Femme is complicated by maleness, by racist queers and racism, by transsexuality, by politics of fat, by class, by age, and by institutionalization. It transcends the binaries of male/female and gay/straight (13).

Femininity as complicated by race is taken up by Joan Morgan, the author of *When Chickenheads Come Home to Roost: A Hip Hop Feminist Breaks It Down* (2000). She writes about imposed prejudices experienced through stereotyped roles for women such as the "SOUTHERNBELL" and the "STRONGBLACKWOMAN." Both of these identities are based on what she calls the prejudices of the oppressor and the complex amalgamation of myths that surround white and Black female identity. These are myths that she rejects for their historically racist underpinnings. She takes up and celebrates those ideas of femininity that she feels she has been denied. She resists those aspects of femininity that have been forced upon her, the myth of the Black woman as superhuman, for example. She considers this myth to be both empowering and harmful in that it leads Black women to wrongly believe that they can carry the weight of the world (2000: 103–104). Her turn to vulnerability is an argument for the transgressive power of femininity. She claims that it's time Black women grant themselves humanity and not impose upon themselves super-power status.

Masculine Femininities In the end, the third wave strives for less restrictive gender roles and gender presentations, allowing for the recognition of the transgressive potential of female femininity but also alternative masculinities such as female masculinities and masculine femininities. It is with this understanding that third-wave feminism posits the question, Where does masculinity fit into the feminist movement? Third-wave feminism recognizes that masculinity extends beyond the male body and is constructed by female as well as male bodies. Judith Halberstam (1998) argues that masculinity is multiple: "Far from just being about men, the idea of masculinity engages, inflects and shapes everyone" (14). Like Halberstam, many third-wavers take up the belief that masculinity is produced by, for, and within women (15). This gender variance then can be used to question the dominance/submission power relations between men and women as presumed by patriarchy as well as some feminists. Taking up the project of alternative masculinities helps the third wave further "think through the messy identifications that make up contemporary power relations around gender, race and class" (18). Alternative masculinity re-presents masculinity as not always signifying power. In fact, it may undermine masculine authority by drawing attention to its performative nature and its ability to exist separately from misogyny.

Ana Marie Cox, Freya Johnson, Analee Newitz, and Jillian Sandell write in "Masculinity without Men: Women Reconciling Feminism and Male Identification" (1997) that, "our relationship to gender—both our masculinity and our femininity—is … inflected by our understanding that such identities are socially constructed and, by implication, subject to change" (199). They argue that "Whereas second wave feminism taught us to dissociate femininity from disempowerment, perhaps third wave feminism can promote the idea of masculinity without oppression."

Transgender Politics and/Is Third-Wave Feminism

> Can feminism see more than two genders? Can I? If I already know that there are boys with cunts and chicks with dicks ... and people with both.... If I already know that man and woman are impossible to define ... then how can I draw strength in a movement that relies on the existence of, and difference between, boys and girls? (Cat Pyne, 1997: 112)

First- and second-wave feminist thought has very much relied on a unified category of "woman"—one whose boundaries are not fluid and whose identity is therefore stable. Postmodernism and its deconstruction of the category "woman" has therefore been perceived by some feminists as posing a threat to women by leaving them defenceless—that they are no longer able to use this identity as a solid base from which to have their voices heard. And, as Riki Anne Wilchins (Nestle, Howell, and Wilchins, 2002) says, "some feminists want to know what's in your pants and how long it has been there. Everyone's gender is subject to change in their lifetime ... just like everything else about them. This scares patriarchs and feminists alike."

Third-wave feminisms further complicate the category "woman" by recognizing that it isn't a unified or "victimized" category and that power relations exist between women, including between non-trans and trans women in the West. According to the *Guide to Intersex and Trans Terminologies* published by Emi Koyama and the Survivor Project (n.d.b.), Trans is a broad umbrella term for "people [who] break away from one or more of the society's expectations around sex and gender. These expectations include that everyone is either a man or a woman, that one's gender is fixed, that gender is rooted in their physiological sex, and that our behaviours are linked to our gender" (**www.survivorproject.org**). Trans persons may have a disruptive potential with regards to the categorical imperatives of the male/female binary as well as the "dominant binary sex/gender ideology of Eurocentric modernity" (Stryker and Whittle, 2006: 3). Trans politics has also further revealed not only the privileging of some men over some women, but some women over other women and some women over other men. This is not a "fictionalized hierarchy" as some anti–trans women would contend (Croson, 2001). Rather, it is a necessary confrontation of the understanding of power that says patriarchy and sexual norms are constitutive of women's oppression.

Within both the third wave and the trans movement, there is a diverse group of people striving for self-definition. The boundaries between boys and girls, men and women, have to this point acted as the basis of identity-based feminist movements, so one can see how troubling it can be when third-wave and trans feminists question these often exclusionary boundaries by continuing to ask, Who is a woman? Who is a feminist? Who gets to decide? At whose expense? With these questions the third wave and trans movement seek to address the ongoing debates and intersections between women's studies and trans studies.

Unfortunately, the relationship between feminism and the trans peoples has been fraught with tensions. "Feminists have denounced transgendered people as dangerous to feminism, depoliticized the experiences of transgendered people, or celebrated the transgendered identity as emblematic of the subversive character of feminist postmodern theory" (MacDonald, 1998: 3). Transgendered women have often been portrayed as threats to women-only "safe spaces" such as music festivals and rape crisis centres, while transgendered men are treated as dupes of patriarchy and as traitors to their sex (3). Many third-wavers however celebrate the challenges that trans individuals force feminism to acknowledge.

Emi Koyama, 27, self-describes as a "multi issue, social-justice, slut" who synthesizes "feminist, Asian, survivor, dyke, queer, sex-worker, slut intersex, genderqueer, and crip politics" (Koyama, n.d.a.). Emi takes on the arguments of those who defend women-only spaces and not women-born-women-only spaces:

> I take some knowledge and wisdom from Latina feminism and theories about the politics of borders. Any time we try to draw a clear boundary around gender we end up cutting somebody's flesh. It's not that they are in the borderlands, it's that the borders are arbitrarily drawn on top of their bodies. I am not one of those people who want to get rid of women-only space, but I think any attempt to draw a clear boundary and legitimize that boundary as the official one would be problematic. I may not feel comfortable with somebody who has a penis; I may not feel comfortable with somebody who has white skin, but I don't have the entitlement to eliminate whatever makes me feel uncomfortable. (Koyama, 2002)

The issue of safety that comes up in debates about the exclusion or inclusion of transgendered folk into feminism is problematized by third-wavers like Emi who argue that the emphasis on safety can become threatening to a third-waver who embraces her multiple identities. The third wave thus struggles with this need to move beyond "essentialists and polemical definitions of gender" (Fireweed Collective, 2000: 7).

Third-wave feminism, then, is grappling with the exclusions within it with regard to the trans community in much the same way that second-wave feminism actively excluded women of colour or lesbians from its movement. But many trans and feminist activists also argue for expanding our questions and activism beyond those of identity and inclusion. Eleanor MacDonald (1998) challenges feminism to "move beyond identity as the basis of social movement politics and into new exploration of the ethical bases of alliances and formation of communities" (10). Viviane Namaste (2005: x) asserts that rather than continue with a focus on questions of identity and debates about who is and who is not a woman and whom to include or exclude, feminists should engage in a broader analysis of transsexual lives. In addition, third-wave and trans feminists seek to offer new ways of knowing. That is, their critical interventions seek to (de)subjugate "whole series of knowledges that have been disqualified as nonconceptual knowledges, as insufficiently elaborated knowledges, naïve knowledges, hierarchically inferior knowledges, knowledges that are below the required level of erudition or scientificity." (Foucault, quoted in Stryker and Whittle, 2006: 13).

Moving away from defining feminism as solely an identity-based political movement means that the third wave is making connections and working though the lived complexities of a variety of women's lives, including those of trans folk. This entails a recognition that power dynamics are complex across and within gender categories and relations. In the end, many third-wavers adopt the position advanced by trans activist Patrick Califia (2003) who writes, "If we really want to be free, women must realize that at the end of that struggle, we will not be women anymore. Or at least we will not be women the way we understand that term today" (90).

Grasping Sexual Power

Third-wave feminism is in part a response to the anti-sex or sex-negative feminism that has come before it. Hanne Blank (2002) in her article "Faster, Harder, Smarter, More: Finding a Political Future for Sex-Positive Smut" argues that third-wave feminists started "using explicit words and images to create a feminist, pro-sex response to the heteropatriarchal norm that discourages women's active sexuality, as well as to the anti-sex feminism that hoped to distance women from sexual oppression by distancing them from much of sex" (55). She thanks some second-wave feminists for asserting that women are allowed to experience sexual desire and sexual pleasure, but says that the third wave takes it further. "No longer asking whether consensual, beneficial, pleasurable sexuality is possible, sex positive ideologies work to improve people's access to an empowering and inclusive culture of sexuality" (57). But, she warns, the third wave must address that the production of smut and activism in this area is unbearably white and "caters . . . to the fantasies of people who want to believe that people of different racial or ethnic backgrounds have primary differences in their sexuality" (57).

Understandings of racism within this struggle for sexual empowerment are also complicated by the third wave's relationship with queer theory, hence its struggle not only with homophobia but also with heterophobia as it is experienced by bisexual or queer folk. Ruby Rowan (2001) writes in "Sleeping with the Enemy and Liking It" in *Turbo Chicks* that we're also still trying to reconcile those heterosexual parts of our relationships with our feminist frameworks (242). The third wave needs to make sure that women are not rejected by the feminist and queer community for heterosexuality any more than our heterosexual community rejects us for our love of women (243). Third-wave feminism runs with the critique of compulsory heterosexuality as identified by Adrienne Rich in her 1980 essay "Compulsory Heterosexuality and Lesbian Existence." She argues that heterosexuality is just that, compulsory, and that by breaking from the norm we may experience physical, economic, and emotional sanctions. Third-wavers actively queer heterosexuality; they recognize that a linear relationship among sex, gender, and sexuality is a construct that has been imposed upon us. It may not sound very revolutionary anymore, but sex can be for pleasure alone no matter what the right wing tells us. So you can be born a girl but identify as a femmie boy who loves butchy girls. You can be a lesbian who screws men and still be a lesbian, not bisexual or a "hasbian" (a lesbian that has gone straight). The combinations are endless!

The third wave also struggles with *how* it is that we love the women we love. Sarah Smith (2002) in her article, "A Cock of One's Own: Getting a Firm Grip of Feminist Sexual Power," explains how to have feminist sex with a dildo, penetration, objectification, and domination (300). She argues that when she penetrates her consenting lesbian partner with a dildo she's not an agent of heteropatriarchy or a "double-agent dyke." She also writes that when she's being penetrated and enjoying it she's not actually suffering from false consciousness about her own sexual desires and responses. She recognizes that a completely power-free society does not exist and neither does power-free sex and that this is not necessarily a bad thing (301)! She says the second-wave binary of dominance/submission as a model of power does not take into account all the complexities involved in sexual relations (303). She argues that sex-positive feminism speaks to more women as opposed to the anti-dildo feminism that seemed to thrive in the mainstream. She and other young feminists are making their sexual desires primary to a third-wave agenda in order to create models of female sexual agency and make feminism more relevant to women's lives (302).

Also, in *Jane Sexes It Up,* third-waver Caitlin Fisher (2002) takes on second-wave assumptions and erasures about young girls' sexuality. Fisher writes, "As I enter my thirties, I find it difficult to claim a theoretical space for the girlhood I remember as sexually empowered and erotically complicated in ways that the feminism I grew up with didn't help explain" (54). She argues that few public narratives have been generated by feminism about sexually desiring girls. She asks, "Why do they play such a small part in the stories we tell ourselves as feminists? And what might be the consequences of the feminist theories we are building?" (54). These are two key questions for the third wave, a wave that reclaims female/feminine sexuality and questions some second-wave assumptions that female sexuality is all about disempowerment and vulnerability. This is not to say that the third wave doesn't recognize the systemic, public, and very private dangers that we may experience because of our female sexuality. Rather, it points to how some young feminists are strategizing by refusing to let the fear come first, to have their sexual role predefined before they can set out to experience it themselves. With a vibrator in hand, the third wave seeks out the sex workshops at Good For Her in Toronto or Venus Envy in Halifax, and then picks up its feminist porn at Little Sister's Book Store in Vancouver. Hell, we make our own porn and put it on our websites!

The pro-sex-work position of most third-wave feminists disrupts the notion that we don't own our own bodies. Through this lens, sex can be seen as a choice women make for themselves rather than something that is forced upon them. Third-wave feminists take charge of their own sexual lives and put agency and desire back where it belongs: in the hearts, minds, and cunts of women. And the third wave is doing this well. Kristina Sheryl Wong is a third-waver who topples expectations about Asian women's sexuality. On Wong's webpage "Big Fat Chinese Mama," a porn/mail-order-bride spoof site, she lures her "oppressors" with promises of "demure lotus blossoms, geishas, and oriental sluts" and then presents them with text and images that are brash and meant to "subvert the expectations of a nasty guy in search of petite naked Asian bodies" (2002). In her FUQ section (Frequently Unasked Questions) she responds with subversive answers. For example:

> **Question:** Will my bride make an easy adjustment from her Asian Culture to the liberal American lifestyle?

> **Answer:** You may be able to buy yourself a nice little Asian porno, a Buddhist bracelet, or some other object that your capitalistic lifestyle Orientalize[s]—but you cannot buy these women. They are not for sale.

This is an example of our earlier discussion about the ways in which third-wave feminists create their own representations rather than solely responding or critiquing those that already exist. But what may be the most third-wave element about Wong's intervention is that she addresses her anger about the objectification and consumption of Asian bodies without arguing that all porn or sex is bad!

Apart from reclaiming porn, many third-wavers reclaim language. Terms such as "slut" and "whore" are emptied of their value judgments and their policing of women's bodies. Judith Butler argues in *Excitable Speech* (1997) that censoring certain words, keeping them unsaid and unsayable, works to preserve their power to injure. This, she says, may hinder "the possibility of a reworking that might shift their context and purpose" (38). Third-wave feminists have asked then whether her theory regarding the decontextualizing and recontextualizing of hate speech through "radical acts of public misappropriation" can hold for ideas of normative femininity. There's a great deal of debate about how successful we can be when it comes to reclaiming and re-appropriating images and words that have been traditionally used against women—but that isn't stopping the third wave from trying! The problem with reclaiming sex and sexuality is what Leah Rumack (2001) warns us about in her article "Lipstick." She writes that making feminism sexy may be used by mass media to take the edge off of this feminist politic. A sexually charged feminism is easily consumable; other feminist struggles that may not be as sexy aren't so readily taken up and are even ignored altogether. Rumack writes "the problem with sexual empowerment of what I call 'vibrator feminism' is this. While it's important for a young woman to feel entitled to a full, hot and self-directed sexuality, it also paradoxically makes it easier for the mainstream culture and media to eat her out, if you'll excuse the pun" (99). This brings us to our next summary that engages with pop feminism and asks the question, What happens when feminism goes mainstream?

IMPLICATIONS/CONCLUSIONS

When feminism reaches the general populace, it is called pop feminism. This returns us to our introduction and our questions about what a young feminist looks like. Is Avril Lavigne a feminist just because she wears ties, rocks out, and hangs with the boys? The irony, some would argue, is that once feminism becomes popular, it can no longer be called feminism because the politics have been removed or co-opted and commodified. That is, feminism is depoliticized and divorced from its political origins by mainstream culture and then made into a product that can be sold back to us. In the process of commodification, feminist ideas are turned into consumable objects like "pussy power" underwear or "Man Hater" baby-size tight T-shirts. Combat boots once worn by punk rockers and Riot Grrrls now adorn mannequin feet at Le Chateau. The accoutrements are no longer accessible to those who created the style, which now has a completely different politic around it. The co-optation, the ideological absorption of the ideas of a movement, means that the Gap can use revolutionary slogans such as "freedom to the people" on its store windows to sell clothing produced by folks working under unfair labour conditions. Similarly, youth culture is relabelled and redefined by dominant culture in a way that demonizes or exoticizes it. A contemporary example of this can be found in rave culture. A movement that espoused dance, community, and alternative expressions of sexuality was morphed into a dangerous drug, sex, and weapons culture that threatened to corrupt young, innocent children. The original meaning has been changed or lost. Feminism is popular as long as it's kind of "sexy" and non-threatening like *The L Word* or strip aerobics.

Any woman who is outspoken and powerful is labelled a feminist by the mainstream. This can be frustrating if the ideals and values expressed by some of these women represent classism, racism, or capitalism. Someone with a big mouth, holding a big microphone, is not necessarily a feminist. Therefore, one of the critiques of pop feminism is that it is ambiguous—that the politics are too vague and vulnerable to interpretation and may be taken the wrong way. This is the catch with pop feminism. On one hand there is the amazing opportunity to expose larger groups of people to a feminist discourse, and on the other the only things that seem to become popular are those that are easily digestible and can turn a profit. Does making feminism saleable to, or consumable by, mass culture necessarily mean dumbing or watering down its politics? Isn't the payoff that feminism's message (even if it is diluted) reaches farther and to more remote places than was ever believed possible by a small group of women meeting weekly to discuss how to overthrow patriarchy? Feminists who work in underground ways are troubled and frustrated by these questions.

It is difficult to measure whether pop feminism actively challenges stereotypes and normative assumptions about women. What may be more effective is attaining a balance between making culture and consuming it or between owning it and sharing it. Is being co-opted by the mainstream a privilege? Most certainly, and many within feminist circles, such as women of colour and trans folk, may never experience this kind of visibility. After all, the mainstream does have its limits. Kristina Gray (2002), in her article "I Sold My Soul for Rock and Roll" in *Colonize This!*, talks about how her love for mainstream music seemed a betrayal to her race because she wasn't listening to the "right" Black music and her feminist beliefs were a contradiction to her working-class background. Third-wave feminism, because of its potential co-optation and commodification by mainstream culture, must ask some crucial questions: What is the cost of popularizing feminism? Where does the third wave go from here?

Suggested Readings

Berger, Melody, ed. 2006. *We don't need another wave: Dispatches from the next generation of feminists.* Berkeley: Seal Press.

Dicker, Rory, and Alison Piepmeier, eds. 2003. *Catching a wave: Reclaiming feminism for the 21st century.* Boston: Northeastern Univ. Press.

Edut, Opheria, ed. 2000. *Body outlaws: Young women write about body image and identity.* New York: Seal Press.

Feminist Knowledge Network. 2001. Young women: Feminists, activists, grrrls. *Canadian Woman Studies/Les cahiers de la femme* 20(4)/21(1).

Findlen, Barbara, ed. 1995. *Listen up: Voices from the next feminist generation.* Seattle: Seal Press.

Fireweed. especially these issues: Fat issue, 67 (Fall 1999); Revolution girl style issue, 59/60 (Fall/Winter 1997); Sex work issue, 65 (Spring 1999); trans/scribes issue, 69 (Summer 2000).

Hernandez, Daisy, ed. 2002. *Colonize this! Young women of color on today's feminism.* New York: Seal Press.

Heywood, Leslie, and Jennifer Drake, eds. 1997. *Third wave agenda: Being feminist, doing feminism.* Minneapolis: Univ. of Minnesota Press.

Jervis, Lisa, and Andi Zeisler. 2006. *Bitchfest.* New York: Farrar, Strauss and Giroux.

Johnson, Lisa Merri, ed. 2002. *Jane sexes it up: True confessions of feminist desire.* New York: Four Walls Eight Windows.

Labaton, Vivien, and Dawn Lundy Martin, eds. 2004. *The fire this time: Young activists and the new feminism.* New York: Anchor Books.

Mitchell, Allyson, Lisa Bryn Rundle, and Lara Karaian, eds. 2001. *Turbo chicks: Talking young feminisms.* Toronto: Sumach Press.

Rowe-Finkbeiner, Kristin. 2004. *The F word: Feminism in jeopardy—women, politics and the future.* New York: Seal Press.

Seely, Megan. 2007. *Fight like a girl: How to be a fearless feminist.* New York: New York Univ. Press.

Discussion Questions

1. What does a third-wave feminist look like?

2. Third-wavers argue that personal narratives can help us navigate the world and understand oppressions and our relationships with feminism and activism. Discuss.

3. What are some of the ways third-wave feminists organize and resist? Do you think that all these methods constitute activism? Why or why not?

4. How have third-wavers troubled ideas about the body? Make sure to keep in mind their resistance not only to patriarchy but also to some of the feminist thought of the second wave.

5. How does the third wave interrupt "feminist" ideas about how a feminist is supposed to behave as well as interrupt the definitions of femininity and masculinity that have been put forward and enforced by patriarchy?

6. What are the sexual politics of the third wave? What are the benefits and downfalls of feminism being brought into the mainstream?

Bibliography

Baines, A., and Avi Lewis. 1998. *Spice girls: Girl power or Diet Pepsi?* On Too Much for Much. City TV. Much Music, Toronto. April 9.

Bartky, Sandra Lee. 1990/1997. Foucault, femininity, and the modernization of patriarchal power, in *Feminist social thought: A reader,* ed. D. Meyers, 95. New York: Routledge.

Baumgardner, Jennifer, and Amy Richards. 2000. *Manifesta: Young women, feminism, and the future.* New York: Farrar, Straus and Giroux.

Bitch Magazine. 2002. A fest in distress. Panel discussion. *Bitch Magazine* 17 (Summer): 71.

Blank, Hanna. 2002. Faster, harder, smarter, more: Finding a political future for sex-positive smut. *Bitch Magazine* 18: 55.

Brown, Wendy. 1991. Feminist hesitations, postmodern exposures. *Differences* 3 (Spring).

Brumberg, Joan Jacobs. 2000. *Fasting girls: The history of anorexia nervosa.* New York: Vintage.

Brushwood Rose, Chloe, and Anna Camilleri, eds. 2002. *Brazen femme: Queering femininity.* Vancouver: Arsenal Pulp Press.

Butler, Judith. 1990. *Gender trouble: Feminism and the subversion of identity.* New York: Routledge.

Butler, Judith. 1997. *Excitable speech: A politics of the performative.* New York: Routledge.

Califia, Patrick. 2003. The backlash: Transphobia in feminism. *Sex changes: The politics of transgenderism.* San Francisco: Cleis Press.

Cox, Anna Marie, et al. 1997. Masculinity without men: Women reconciling feminism and male-identification, in *Third wave agenda,* eds. Leslie Heywood and Jennifer Drake, 178–199. Minneapolis: Univ. of Minnesota Press.

Crosbie, Lynn, ed. 1997. *Click! Becoming feminists.* Toronto: McFarland Walter and Ross.

Croson, Charlotte. 2001. Sex, lies and feminism. *Off Our Backs* (June).

Culture Jammers Network. 2001. Fighting the good fight. <**jammers@lists.adbusters.org**> October 18.

Dent, Gina. 1995. Missionary position, in *To be real: Telling the truth and changing the face of feminism,* ed. Rebecca Walker. New York: Anchor Books.

Detloff, Madelyn. 1997. Mean spirits: The politics of contempt between feminist generations. *Hypatia* 12(3).

Dua, Enakshi, and Angela Robertson, eds. 1999. *Canadian anti-racist feminist thought: Scratching the surface of racism.* Toronto: Women's Press.

Edut, Ophira, ed. 2000. *Body outlaws: Young women write about body image and identity.* Seattle: Seal Press.

Feminist Knowledge Network. 2001. Young women: Feminists, activists, grrrls. *Canadian Woman Studies/Les cahiers de la femme* 20(4)/21(1).

Fireweed Collective. 2000. Are you a boy or a girl? An introduction. *Fireweed* trans/scribes 69 (Summer): 7.

Fisher, Caitlin. 2002. The sexual girl within: Breaking the feminist silence on desiring girlhoods, in *Jane sexes it up: True confessions of feminist desire,* ed. Lisa Merri Johnson. New York: Four Walls Eight Windows.

Gelder, Ken, and Sarah Thornton, eds. 1997. *The subcultures reader.* New York: Routledge.

Giese, R. 1998. 13-year-old girls rule the world. *Toronto Star,* February 14: N1.

Gray, Kristina. 2002. I sold my soul for rock and roll, in *Colonize this! Young women of color on today's feminism,* eds. Daisy Hernandez and Bushra Rehman. Seattle: Seal Press.

Grosz, Elizabeth. 1994. *Volatile bodies: Toward a corporeal feminism.* Bloomington, IN: Indiana Univ. Press.

Halberstam, Judith. 1998. *Female masculinity.* London: Duke Univ. Press.

Hernandez, Daisy, and Bushra Rehman, eds. 2002. *Colonize this! Young women of color on today's feminism.* Seattle: Seal Press.

Heywood, Leslie, and Jennifer Drake, eds. 1997. *Third wave agenda: Being feminist, doing feminism.* Minneapolis: Univ. Minnesota Press.

James, A. 1986. Learning to belong: The boundaries of adolescence, in *Symbolizing boundaries: Identity and diversity in British cultures,* ed. A.P. Cohen. Manchester: Manchester Univ. Press.

Karaian, Lara, Allyson Mitchell, and Lisa Bryn Rundle, eds. 2001. *Turbo chicks: Talking young feminists.* Freemont, MI: Sumac Press.

Koyama, Emi, n.d.a. **www.eminism.org/faqbasic.html**.

Koyama, Emi. n.d.b. Guide to intersex and trans terminologies. **www.survivorproject.org**. (Accessed August 6, 2008.)

Koyama, Emi. 2002. MI Way or the highway. *Bitch Magazine* 17 (Summer).

Lamm, Nomy. 1995. It's a big fat revolution, in *Listen up: Voices from the next feminist generation,* ed. Barbara Findlen. Seattle: Seal Press.

Leonard, M. 1988. Paper planes: Traveling the new grrrl geographies, in *Cool places: Geographies of youth cultures,* eds. Tracey Skelton and Gill Valentine, 101–120. London: Routledge.

Lorde, Audre. 1984. The master's tools will never dismantle the master's house. *Sister outsider: Essays and speeches by Audre Lorde.* Freedom, CA: Crossing Press.

MacDonald, Eleanor. 1998. Critical identities: Rethinking feminism through transgendered politics. *Atlantis* 23/1: 3.

Morgan, Joan. 2000. *When chickenheads come home to roost: A hip hop feminist breaks it down.* New York: Simon and Schuster.

Namaste, Viviane. 2005. *Sex change, social change: Reflections on identity, institutions, and imperialism.* Toronto: Women's Press.

Nestle, Joan, Clare Howell, and Riki Wilchins, eds. 2002. *GenderQueer: Voices from beyond the sexual binary.* Los Angeles: Alyson Books.

Pyne, Cat. 2001. A question for feminism, in *Turbo chicks: Talking young feminists,* eds. Lara Karaian, Allyson Mitchell, and Lisa Bryn Rundle. Freemont, MI: Sumac Press.

Rich, Adrienne. 1980. Compulsory heterosexuality and lesbian existence. *Signs: Journal of Women in Culture and Society* 5 (Summer): 630–660.

Richards, Amelia. 2000. Body image: Third wave feminism's issue? in *Body outlaws: Young women write about body image and identity,* ed. Ophira Edut. Seattle: Seal Press.

Rowan, Ruby. 2001. Sleeping with the enemy and liking it, in *Turbo chicks: talking young feminists,* eds. Lara Karaian, Allyson Mitchell, and Lisa Bryn Rundle. Freemont, MI: Sumac Press.

Rumack, Leah. 2001. Lipstick, in *Turbo chicks: Talking young feminists,* eds. Lara Karaian, Allyson Mitchell, and Lisa Bryn Rundle. Freemont, MI: Sumac Press.

Ruttenberg, Danya, and Susannah Heschel, eds. 2001. *Yentl's revenge: The next wave of Jewish feminism.* Seattle: Seal Press.

Smith, Sarah. 2002. A cock of one's own, in *Jane sexes it up: True confessions of feminist desire,* ed. Lisa Merri Johnson. New York: Four Walls Eight Windows.

Stasko, Carly. 2001. Action grrrls in the dream machine, in *Turbo chicks: Talking young feminisms,* eds. Allyson Mitchell, Lisa Bryn Rundle, and Lara Karaian. Toronto: Sumach Press.

Tamaki, Mariko. 2001. Robin and me, in *Turbo chicks: Talking young feminisms,* eds. Allyson Mitchell, Lisa Bryn Rundle, and Lara Karaian. Toronto: Sumach Press.

Turtle Gals. n.d. **www.turtlegals.com**.

Valentine, G., T. Skelton, and D. Chambers. 1998. *Cool places: Geographies of youth cultures.* London: Routledge.

Walker, Rebecca, ed. 1995. *To be real: Telling the truth and changing the face of feminism.* New York: Anchor Books.

Wong, Kristina Sheryl. n.d. **www.bigfatchinesemama.com**.

Wong, Kristina Sheryl. 2002. Dis-Orient express. *Bitch Magazine* 18 (Fall).

CHAPTER 4

Feminist Theorizing on Race and Racism

Raimunda Reece[1]

> The master's tools will never dismantle the master's house. They may allow us temporarily to beat him at his own game, but they will never enable us to bring about genuine change.
>
> Audre Lorde, 1984

INTRODUCTION

The purpose of this chapter is to provide a context for understanding some of the contemporary issues that abound in feminist theory as connected to studies in race and racism. Much of the discussion in this chapter focuses on the experiences of First Nations and Black women. The historical treatment of these two groups of women draws parallels that have seldom been analyzed and provides an opportunity to explore how the social location and marginal status of racialized women in general, and First Nations and Black women in particular, warrant further discussion in contemporary women's studies. For students, the challenge lies in using material on race and racism as a starting point for exploring new epistemological and actual ways of learning. Central to this analysis is a critique of the institutional and systemic denial of racism in Canada.

RE-READING DOMINANT DISCOURSE: ANALYZING "RACE"

Race is socially constructed and an organizing feature of society. It is more than simply an ideological construct, since race discursively demarcates "difference." To speak of race as a discourse is to explore the myriad ways in which individuals classify themselves (or are classified) according to physical characteristics and attribute meaning to those characteristics. According to Kenan Malik, "the

discourse of race emerged as a means of reconciling the conflict between the ideology of equality and the reality of the persistence of inequality" (Malik, 1998: np). Thus the idea of race is socially grounded in political, capitalist, and social unequal relations among different groups of people and is maintained by dominant elites.

Ideologically, the concept of race has no biological basis; it does not exist outside of social meaning. Since racism and racial ideology are inter-constituted, the tragic enigma of racism derives from an understanding of what race is and what it represents. Contemporary writers agree that there is no universal definition of race. Albert Memmi (1982) has argued that "[p]ure races ... are artificially designated varieties that humans deploy to accomplish certain tasks" (6). He examines how discourses of racism structure personal and social experiences, themselves embedded within the project of nation building. Similarly, Robert Miles (1993/2000) argues that we should do away with the concept of race and focus our attention on processes of racism, a more useful analytical category in which to explain unequal social relations. Racism can be defined as:

> A system in which one group of people exercises power over another on the basis of skin colour; an implicit or explicit set of beliefs, erroneous assumptions, and actions based on an ideology of the inherent superiority of one racial group over another, and evident in organizational or institutional structures and programs as well as in individual thought or behaviour patterns (Henry and Tator, 2006: 352).

For various purposes, individuals and groups give meaning to race as a way to inferiorize racialized people. Structurally, ideas about race and racism are embedded in our society via various social, political, cultural, and economic institutions and mediums. Thus the idea of race is used as a fixed signifier to ideologically mark spaces and bodies, effectively treating racialized groups differently and relegating them to marginal status in society. Taken together—discursively, ideologically, and structurally—we can see that race is an organizing feature of society.

Racial discourse operates in tandem with a host of other relational social systems (i.e., the criminal justice system, social welfare, globalization). Racism is institutionalized in Canada, embedded in our criminal justice, education, employment, social welfare, political, and economic systems. But Canada's "face" of racism is polite and covert, and maintaining racist policies and practices in Canadian institutions reinforces the concept of democratic racism.[2] Racist ideologies help us understand racist behaviours and attitudes of individuals and groups, especially as these ideas of race and racial systems change over time. Through global challenges and local struggles, race as a social constellation is constantly being transformed by shifting politics, economics, and culture. A move toward exploring how racism structures people's lives illuminates the many ways in which indices of power are irretrievably woven into racist discourse and how institutional and organizational racist ideologies are not immune from social processes.

Historically, the concept of race first appeared in the English language in the 17th century at the height of colonialism. Dividing human beings based on their skin colour justified exploitation, subjugation, and invasion of Indigenous lands. Capitalism and imperialism, married with social differentiation based on race, created a labouring class, grounded in the idea of racial superiority and inferiority. Discourses of inferiority target others, and seeing some races as superior to others allows for exploitation to be justified because "they are born" inferior. However, rather than examining inadequate social welfare systems or indices of power, and privilege that detrimentally affect the lives of people of colour, people deny racism, as they do not want to implicate themselves in processes that have been detrimental to other human beings, especially if they have benefited from them.

In Canada we tend to believe more in multiculturalism and diversity, and we talk less about race and racism. Many people feel that Canada is a country grounded in fairness and equality. We often see racism as something more common in the United States. Racialization of particular groups and racism as a practice may work differently here, but one need only look around to see that racism very much exists in Canada. The economic marginalization of visible minorities, racial profiling, and racist policing and security practices are just a few examples that illustrate how racism is, in fact, present in Canada. Some of our own university faculties do not reflect student populations, nor do our legislatures.

Why is there is such silence around issues of race and racism in public discourse and in classrooms? Why are anti-racist and equity-seeking initiatives often resisted? One way in which to enter into these discussions is to ask people to examine their own belief systems and their own positions of power and privilege. This is not an easy task because of the ways in which race functions as an organizing feature of society.

Canada is a colonial nation founded on white supremacy, meaning injustices will never cease until a clear anti-racism policy is articulated (Philip, 1992: 185). A clear anti-racism policy would examine racist institutional practices and policies that contribute to the problem of racism in contemporary society. Further, anti-racism policy should examine the ways in which systems of inequality exist, and how policy-making decisions and social programs are implemented (Henry and Tator, 2006). In Canada, a reliance on multiculturalism discourse rather than anti-racism policy and practice means that power relations and systems of power that keep racialized groups disenfranchised and marginalized are negated. Social equality is seen as embedded in multiculturalism discourse, reducing racism to an individual problem rather than a social one. Multiculturalism presumes that race does not matter because Canada is a nation suspended in a belief system that supports meritocracy.[3] Multiculturalism will not disappear because it serves political, economic, and social purposes. In order to move forward the Canadian government needs to sustain the fallacy of multiculturalism discourse. But rather than seeing multiculturalism and anti-racism as interchangeable, we need instead to focus on anti-racism, especially the interconnection of race and power.

The production of racist knowledge through language and social practices calls for an examination into, among other things, the ways in which race and racism affect how we teach and learn about feminism. Feminist writings on race have taken up much of the aforementioned discussion. In particular, historical underpinnings of the ideological tenets of racial discourse and ideology have influenced feminist theorizing about women who have been racialized. In order to explore some of these issues, we begin with a look at historical relations between the state, bodies, and race.

HISTORY OF THE CANADIAN STATE

In the 17th and 18th centuries, a period called "the Enlightenment" in England, ideas about the "rational man," reason, liberalism, and religious and traditional authority took shape. Theorists such as John Locke, Jean-Jacques Rousseau, and (later) John Stuart Mill were instrumental in shaping liberal ideas. Their values of individualism, independence, and equality of opportunity (Eisenstein, 1981) were instrumental in the development of Western feminist theory. Early feminist texts such as Mary Wollstonecraft's *A Vindication of the Rights of Woman* (1792) challenged and positioned women as rational autonomous individuals.

Wollstonecraft's ideas took shape within the new bourgeois order, which understood education as a way for women to obtain legal and political rights, but at the same time saw women's continued economic dependency on men. Wollstonecraft's arguments for the importance of "autonomy of the individual" were shaped by the economic and social position of 18th- and 19th-century heterosexual middle-class white women, usually married. Her arguments were underscored by reasoning that sought to position white middle-class women in the public sphere and free them from the "cult of domesticity." Liberation for women of colour during this time was not actualized in the minds of white women struggling for autonomy.

Historically, the early inception of liberal feminism coincided with the social location of white middle-class women during the first wave of feminism (mid-1800s to World War II). Structurally, these early tenets of liberal feminism emphasized individualism, freedom, equality, and material progress. In particular, ideas relating to "maternal politics" originated in the 17th and 18th centuries and subsequently informed liberal, radical, and socialist feminism in the 20th century (Eisenstein, 1981; Davis, 1981; Collins, 1990). Liberal feminists argued that women were denied political, individual, and economic liberty and freedom to develop themselves as fully self-autonomous human beings because they were denied equality of opportunity and civil rights. Furthermore, since women's autonomy was weakened by lack of education, they were economically dependent on men.

In addition, colonial and imperialist imperatives that were embedded in the political and cultural milieu of the time served to disenfranchise[4] First Nations women and women of colour. One such example was the 1929 Persons Case in which women fought for the right to be declared persons and be therefore eligible for appointment to the Canadian Senate (Elliot and Mandel, 2001). While this was a formidable gain for liberal feminists, it was mainly white women who benefited from this advance. Women of colour and Native women were not considered in the application, and thus intersectional issues such as race were ignored. In this way, the role of white women in colonialism was racially gendered. White women were seen in many different ways: they were the voice of normalcy, the reasons behind protecting the private sphere, the embodiment of chaste womanhood, and the protectors of a nation state. After all, they were more than responsible for the re-articulation of native *"truths"*; they were the creators and sustainers of a racial ideology that tied together "the 'pride of womanhood' and the 'pride of race' to the colonial project" (Sinha, 1992).

During the second wave of feminism (1970s–1990s), liberal feminists worked within existing patriarchal social structures to bring about legal equality and educational opportunities for women. These struggles resulted in changing married women's property and child custody rights, liberalizing divorce laws, providing better jobs and professions, and providing access to higher education (Elliot and Mandell, 2001: 27). At the same time, we also see the emergence of theoretical discussions that challenged race-blind and heterosexism-as-primary hierarchies that constituted much of the early feminist theorizing. In other words, women began to question why discussions of racism and normative heterosexuality were excluded from feminist thinking.

What began to materialize during this second wave was the challenge to white women to examine the social location they occupied in relation to how First Nations women and women of colour continued to be marginalized. Building coalitions across and within differences called for theoretical and practical analyses exploring race, class, gender, sexuality, and dis/ability as intersectional. Furthermore, essentialist critiques revealed the absence of heterogeneity among women.

Historical Movements: Race Is a Story of the Body—First Nations Women

European conquest and discovery shaped the lives of First Nations people in Canada. History presented stereotypes of Aboriginal peoples as savage, bestial, and uncivilized. Since history is written by the powerful, discursive racial characterizations of categories such as "Indian" and "Other" were constructed to disenfranchise and inferiorize First Nations people. These categories lay the foundation in which to construct Canada as a nation of "moral" and "civilized" persons. Native Canadians were positioned as contravening the tenets of morality and therefore as inappropriate bodies to take part in the building of Canada as a sovereign, white, "moral" nation (McCalla and Satzewich, 2002).

From the beginning of colonial exploitation, colonial agents represented Aboriginal peoples in racist ways (Stevenson, 1999: 49); Aboriginal women have frequently been referred to as "squaws" and Aboriginal men were viewed as pathologically violent (see Smith and Ross, 2004; Churchill, 1998). The French and the English appropriated Aboriginal lands for economic trade and marketability, resulting in the decimation of Native economies and cultural genocide, in which much of this devastation was caused by

European diseases such as smallpox and measles. This myth of occupation supports western philosophies that Canadian lands were unoccupied and in need of settlement. Missionaries sought to subvert and curtail the sexuality of Native women and in doing so labelled them as sexually promiscuous, and their children "accidents," and the colonization of First Nations women's bodies furthered their continual exploitation. Traditionally matrilineal societies, which flourished prior to European conquest, saw a decline in the social status and autonomy of women. With the establishment of residential schools, the fracturing of family life took hold. Residential schools were seen as a "solution" to the problem of educating and disciplining First Nations children, ridding them of their "immorality." Native women were deemed bad mothers and the solution was a civilizing mission where missionaries were to *convert* and *clean* First Nations mothers who resisted the ideals of Victorian womanhood (Stevenson, 1999).

In order to provide the ideological rationale for colonial conquest, it was imperative for missionaries to represent Native women as powerless, savage, and degraded (Stevenson, 1999); the gendering of the empire was necessary for Europe (the West) to subjugate "the rest." Colonial states operate through racialization and sexualization morality processes. In this system, the legal, economic, political, and social control of women's bodies is a form of state-sanctioned patriarchy that legitimizes the use of state violence as a way to regulate morality. Moral regulation processes enacted by the state ensure a ways for bodies of colour to be seen as "unfit" for the making of nation.

By all accounts much of the discussion concerning European conquests acknowledges the sexualized nature of the conquests. Sexual division of labour was a central defining feature of many colonial projects. Subsequently, sexual relations between European men and women, and indigenous populations were seen as unnatural and thus prohibited. By extension, then, Native women were not considered presentable icons for the image of Canada as "White Man's Country." In order for Canada to remain a white settler society, sexual relations between Native women and European men were discouraged and Native women could not participate in the project of nation-building. This exclusion was also extended to Métis women, who although active in the resistance movement, were gendered as wives and mothers (Dua, 1999). Gender-specific permutations interconnected with racial and sexual ideology to produce discourses of difference about First Nations communities, which undermined every aspect of their government, familial, economic, social, and cultural value systems.

By contrast, the establishment of the colonial states in many ways constructed European women as those who could maintain colonial domination. According to Adele Perry (1997), in Canada "a new appreciation for wives" was thought to prevent isolated men in the colonies from fornicating with Native women. European women were thought to be pure, chaste, and decent and therefore worthy purveyors of family, and thus family prestige could only be attained through marriage between European men and women. Racial mixing through marriage was discouraged and propaganda campaigns were launched to attract European women as domestic and marriageable partners. Therefore the construction of Canada as a white settler nation was intrinsically tied to the construction and categorization of "woman."

The continued subordination of First Nations women in Canadian society is deeply connected to First Nations' struggles for sovereignty and citizenship rights today. Works by Winona Stevenson (1999), Bonita Lawrence (2002), and Patricia Monture-Agnes (1995) investigate how colonization has been normalized at the expense of indigenous communities. Therefore it is important to explore how the sexualized, racialized, and gendered nature of colonial conquest reveals the interconnectedness of patriarchy, colonialism, and imperialism. It is critical that a contemporary re-reading of Native history be told from the perspective of Native Canadians, not through neo-colonial discourse, in order to de-mystify stereotypical imagery and ideologies about First Nations communities.

THEORIZING RACE AND FEMINISM

Anti-racist Feminist Approaches in Canada

The emergence of third-wave feminism and anti-racist feminism (1990s–present) recognizes the intersectionality of race, class, gender, dis/ability, and sexuality. In Canada, anti-racist scholars took note of the lack of inclusivity in feminist theory and pedagogical practice (see Dua, 1999). The respective environments that women of colour negotiated every day as racialized women were not evident within the canons of feminist discipline. Either the experiences of women of colour were completely negated, or perfunctory tributes in the form "special topics of interest" compartmentalized their narratives. In order to evaluate the social construction of exclusion facing many women of colour who were academics and activists, it was critical for Canadian anti-racist feminists to examine "the ways in which Canadian academia constructed knowledge about race" (Dua, 1999: 17). Feminists would play an important part in unpacking how political, social, economic, and cultural discourses of the Canadian state figured in the writings and teachings of feminism. In order to make differences and similarities visual and heard, an analysis of race was necessary.

Anti-racist feminists focus on deconstructing race and gender in an effort to focus on historic patterns of racialization in Canada (Dua, 1999). By examining immigration policies, environmental racism, and violence against women, anti-racist feminists explore how racism is manifested in state institutions and organizations. Other Canadian writers (see Brand, 1993, 1999; Philip, 1992; Henry and Tator, 2006; Calliste and Dei, 2000) have examined anti-racism theory and practice as political action ideologies. They have pointed to issues that challenge the relationship between the dominant elites (those who have decision-making power) and those who are adversely affected by such decisions. Thus, the individuals who make policy reinforce the power to re-represent their ruling ideas and allow these ideas to remain intact.

One area in which institutional racism can be examined is our immigration policies and the racialized pattern of immigration connected to citizenship and belonging in Canadian society. Specifically, racist immigration policies curtail the movement of women of colour entering this country; there are barriers to immigration and settlement for migrant domestic workers that marginalize these women as "others." Between the years 1955 and 1967, a domestic worker scheme was enacted in Canada. In her 1983 landmark work *Silenced*, Makeda Silvera explains how Canada's Domestic Worker Program annually brought hundreds of women from Trinidad, Jamaica, and Barbados to work as domestics. The conditions under which many of these women had to work were horrendous and stressful. Many experienced sexual harassment and in some cases physical and psychological violence. Like First Nations women, whose bodies were subjugated and sexually surveyed, the Canadian state saw Black women's labour as expendable for capitalist imperatives. Thus, Black women were also not seen as formidable players in the process of Canadian nation-building. Early immigration laws only allowed Black women entry into

Canada if they were "single" and "unattached." The message ideologically disseminated by the Canadian state was that Black women were no more than prongs on the capitalist wheel of profit making, seen as temporary workers rather than candidates for Canadian citizenship. Furthermore, the regulation of Black women's bodies was controlled by white men who served as their employers and monitored very intimate details of their sexual lives. These racist immigration laws allowed for the maintenance of a surplus of imported cheap labour.

The domestic worker scheme provides evidence to support historical racist notions of inferiority. Black women were seen as "naturally fit" to do domestic work and to "other-mother" white women's children. Today, although there have been some changes in domestic worker policy[5], the same racist sentiments still prevail. Currently, Black women coming into Canada are issued temporary work visas, so that under domestic worker employment conditions, they receive no employment insurance, Canada Pension Plan, vacation pay, or overtime pay. Furthermore, they can only apply for permanent residence after two years of living without any form of social security (Das Gupta, 2000).

Canada's approach to immigration and definition of "family" also requires a more fluid understanding, especially in reference to immigrant and refugee women. Many women working as domestic workers in Canada are, by force of economic status, engaged in "transnational motherhood" (Arat-Koc, 2001). Capitalism has structured women's lives in such a way that many women mother increasingly from locations in the world other than their home countries. Mothering from abroad is connected to a legacy of the Canadian state admitting women with temporary visas without recognizing family rights (Hontagneu-Sotelo and Avila, 2000, cited in Arat-Koc, 2001). As noted in Sedef Arat-Koc's 2001 study,

> ... one of the major problems with Immigration's approach to family reunification has been the fact that the conception of "family" as defined by Immigration Canada involves an imposition of a narrow, western and heterosexist definition of the nuclear family and fails to resonate with definitions in immigrants' society, culture or individual life (Arat-Koc, 2001: 23).

This example highlights the importance of anti-racist feminist theorizing in order to underscore how the tight net of racism interweaves race, class, and gender discussions.

Anti-racist approaches, then, call for institutions, individuals, activists, educators, and society to challenge racism (Henry and Tator, 2006). Anti-racism is "an educational political action-oriented strategy for institutional and systemic change to address racism and the interlocking systems of social oppression" (Dei, 1996: 25, quoted in Henry and Tator, 2006). In Canada anti-racism imperatives have been catapulted to the forefront of many discussions concerning race relations. Traditionally, much of the discourse revolved around ethnicity.[6] More specifically, anti-racist feminist approaches, in examining the current social positions of Black women in Canadian society, can aid us in contextualizing the marginal occupational status to which Black women have been relegated. For example, a 2005 study cites the following:

> The average annual income of Black women in 2000 was $20,029 where the average annual income of all Canadians was $29,769; Black women earn an average wage of 79% of what Black men earn and only 57% of what all Canadian men earn. In terms of poverty rates, over 34.5% of Black women in families are poor and over 52.7% of unattached Black women are poor. This compares to 13.7% of all women in families and 41.9% of all unattached women. (Canadian Association of Social Workers, 2005)

Dionne Brand (1993) analyzed how the Canadian state structures Black women's lives through the construction of their sexuality. As heads of households[7], numerous Black women work a double-day. Many work in low-paying jobs and their private workday continues as they maintain their households. Brand outlines that the current economic positions that Black women occupy can be attributed to socialization processes that direct young Black girls into service industry jobs (domestic work, nursing, factory jobs). The exploitation of Black women's labour is maintained through historical ideologies and images of Black women as "chattel" and "mammies"—representations that have generationally carried over and informed commonsensical racist, modern-day notions of the kind of work for which Black women are best suited.

This situation is not only relegated to Black women. Racism, sexism, and dis/ability has played and still plays a role in the types of jobs that women of colour acquire. A 2000 Manitoba study found that nearly 43 percent of Aboriginal women living off reserve were poor, compared to 35 percent of Aboriginal men, 20.3 percent of non-Aboriginal women, and 16.4 percent of non-Aboriginal men. Recent immigrant women had particularly low incomes; their average income in 1995 was only $12 000, about 62 percent of the amount earned by Canadian-born women that year. Women with disabilities also faced a higher risk of poverty; in 1997, 27 percent of women with disabilities, aged 16 to 64, lived in poverty. Almost two-thirds of those lived more than 25 percent below the low income cut-off (Donner, Busch, and Fontaine, 2002).

The making of Canada involved systemic exclusion and discrimination of certain groups of people. Today, non-European "others" are welcomed to Canada through an apparently non-discriminatory immigration policy, but notions of the white man's country are maintained through an immigration points system that serves to discriminatorily weed out "undesirables." As indicated above, women of colour particularly bear the brunt of institutional racist policies.

Anti-racist Feminist Approaches within the Context of Democratic Racism

The Canadian state has been complicit in the production and maintenance of racism, as the ways in which we have been taught about who belongs in Canada is a process of negotiation between dominant elites, those who hold socio-economic power, and persons who reside on the margins of society. The promise of meritocracy and equality occupies much rhetoric within the canons of public consciousness. Many in Canada espouse liberal values, believing in the promise of justice and egalitarian values. Yet the ideology of democracy operating in an impartial space conflicts with attitudes and behaviours that demonstrate negativity toward people of colour and results in the discrimination and differential treatment against them (Henry and Tator, 2006). As a result, in Canada what we have is a society grounded in liberal values of democracy, while simultaneously enacting institutional and systemic racism against persons of colour. Here, we turn our attention to some contemporary issues that can aid in our understanding of the functionality of democratic racism.

Environmental Racism Ideologies about raced bodies are tied to the spaces they inhabit, and "spaces are manufactured in ways that dictate what sorts of activities can and will take place in them" (Nelson, 2002: 218–219). The following story of Africville is thus an example of what we call "environmental racism."

Blacks who had arrived during the American Revolution or via the Underground Railroad resettled in parts of Nova Scotia and Southwestern Ontario, expecting that as "free" Black loyalists they would receive land promised to them by the British government. Instead, the Black settlement in Nova Scotia, which came to be known as Africville, was isolated from the rest of the nearby city of Halifax. A population of approximately 400 Blacks became surrounded by industrial factories, a prison, disposal pits, a city dump, and an infectious disease hospital. Over the years the city of Halifax refused to install proper sewage and sanitation systems or water drainage systems, or to maintain roads. This blatant denial of basic living necessities turned the community into a slum. Tax-paying citizens, once promised land under colonial criteria, were now viewed as scavengers. The Nova Scotian government effectively set up Africville to become a town outside of a city (Nelson, 2002), whose residents were described as "dirty," "slum residents," and "indolent." These were considered as inherent biological traits. In later years, without community consultation, families were displaced and relocated to slum housing via city dump trucks. In the mid-1960s, Africville was demolished to make way for a new cross-harbour bridge.

Anti-racist feminist approaches to this type of racism examines how white dominance aids in the maintenance of the status quo. Since "the state represents the interests of the most privileged class, it cannot at the same time work for the benefit of the working class because there are substantive differences in the interests of both classes and the two are always in conflict" (Carty and Brand, 1993: 173).

Another example of environmental racism in Canada is "transit equity." Public transit travel is one of the more affordable and eco-friendly modes of transportation available, which is nonetheless also viewed as a non-luxurious form of commuting. Owning a vehicle opens up discussions about class.[8] Issues of environmental racism abound when public transit commuters are socially positioned and classed as lower-income people undeserving of tax reform or affordable bus passes from their employers. In addition, as stated by Gord Perks, a campaigner for the Toronto Environmental Alliance, the move toward subsidizing transit passes should promote "discussion around environmental racism, [and] racism on public transit, both in terms of service levels provided to different communities and also in terms of the treatment that people of colour get from transit operators" (cited in Byckalo-Khan and Gosine, 2003).

Environmental justice initiatives can also be seen as an anti-racist feminist approach. Punam Khosla's 2003 study "If Low Income Women of Colour Counted in Toronto" argues that racism is a main determinant of poverty, and many immigrant women of colour do not have an income or qualify for social assistance. According to Khosla (2003) "[t]ransit costs are out of reach for low-income women … [t]hose who travel the TTC overwhelmingly report discrimination and abusive behaviour by operators towards poor and racialized women" (12). Because many women of colour work in the hospitality industry and wages in this sector are generally low, responsible employers should adhere to basic fundamental human rights whereby a subsidy for transit passes is seen as a way to promote better working conditions, as well as being better for the environment.

Since "going green" has become the 21st-century slogan for bringing awareness to the state of our local and global environment, environmental concerns have prompted individuals and organizations to rethink their roles in contributing to the destruction of the planet. Seldom discussed however, is the controversy surrounding environmental racism within the context of the green movement. There is a pervasive myth that the environmental movement is a white-dominated space. Andil Gosine (2003) argues that people of colour are indeed culturally, politically, and socially invested in the environmental issues, but that there is delegitimization and marginalization of people of colour within the movement.

Moreover, class imperatives need to be examined within environmental organizations as well. Activists championing environmental causes are not immune from racism. And it stands to reason that since human beings make up a large part of our environments, and women are the primary consumers for households, a move toward a more sustainable green environment should also be a move toward reasonably priced or geared-to-income "green" products, affordable housing, adequate medical care, an eradication of violence against women and children, and any other form of social injustice that affects the lives of those who are most vulnerable in our society.

Violence against Women Societal taboos about violence against women permeate our cultural landscape. Historically, women who experienced abuse have felt ashamed and were manipulated into keeping quiet about so-called "private" family matters. Women who experience any form of abuse (physical, verbal, psychological, financial, cultural) have been socialized to "not air their dirty laundry." The Canadian state has also been complicit in this form of thinking, dating from the 1767 English Common Law "rule of thumb," which allowed a husband to beat his wife, as long as the stick he hit her with was no thicker than his thumb. Feminists have long been arguing for issues about family violence and women abuse to be brought into the public sphere—to acknowledge that violence against women is connected to patriarchy and sex-gender role discrimination. Radical feminists have argued that since women are oppressed by patriarchy, control over women's sexuality is a key corollary in women's oppression, and therefore violence against women is simply one other way of controlling women.

The discourse of domination reasons that any analysis of domestic violence and woman abuse intrinsically involves discussions of colonialism and imperialism. In retrospect, the legacy of patriarchy is explicitly connected, but not limited to, colonial and imperial views and understandings of race, gender, class, dis/ability, and sexuality. By specifically exploring the divergent tenets of colonialism and imperialism, it is evident that patriarchy cannot exist separate and apart from these narratives. While there was and still continues to be no one single colonial process, nor one single axis from which to explore oppression, violence against women of colour is one area of analysis that warrants further discussion.

Canada's colonial history of nation-building and citizenship is predicated on the separation of women during these formative times. Colonial processes, which involved the destruction of old social, economic, and political systems and the development of new ones, maintain the ideology that women are inferior to men. Patriarchy, the idea of male domination, thus combined with racism as a part of the "civilizing mission" and of abusive conquest. First Nations women and Black women were not deemed beneficial to creating and maintaining Canada's loyalty to the British Empire. Therefore, women of colour were seen as detrimental to long-term capitalistic goals, and as such were treated in highly abusive manners.

Historical state violence perpetrated against Native Canadian women was often manifested through sexism. Native women were often defined in relation to European men—either as "noble princesses" or "savage squaws." Native women faced a "peculiar kind of sexism, grounded in the pernicious and ever-present ideologies of racism" (Albers, 1983, cited in Stevenson, 1999: 57). Definitions of violence against Native Canadian women identify other aspects of state violence that are expansive and connected to the historical treatment of First Nations communities: "Some Aboriginal women, for example, have argued that, for them the terms 'domestic violence' and 'culture of violence' do not simply mean violence against women by men, but that it often conjures up images of the violence of the Canadian state against the First Nations" (Arat-Koc, 2001: 10).

Furthermore, when missionaries arrived, the discourse of racism was made more apparent through travel writing, autobiographical texts, ethnographies, journals, and reports (Stevenson, 1999). The resultant stereotypical images and representations have traversed time and space, resulting in contemporary First Nations women representing one of the most disenfranchised groups in society. Interestingly, Yasmin Jiwani (2002) notes that cultural talk is absent when discussions about the supplanting of First Nations land claims and sovereignty come up.

Neo-colonial forms of violence against women manifested in a number of different ways. Racism plays a critical factor in societal responses to violence against women of colour. Often, in racialized communities, domestic violence is attributed to culture, and is used to explain away male violence and affirm white supremacy (Razack, 1998). In responding to domestic violence calls in racialized communities, the police either are slow in responding or fail to respond at all (Flynn and Crawford, 1998; Jiwani and Buhagiar, 1997, cited in Jiwani, 2002). Furthermore, for many Black women having historically been denied rights to marriage, race solidarity with Black men often means negotiating gender roles within a patriarchal sphere. Black women, who have witnessed the criminalization of Black men, are sometimes reluctant to call the police when confronted by abusive situations and may stay in abusive relationships for fear of being seen as race traitors (Flynn and Crawford, 1998, cited in Jiwani, 2002).

First Nations women have fared no better in state responses to domestic violence because cultural representations of First Nations communities have also often normalized violence against women. Stereotypical representations of First Nations men as primitive and savage affect judicial responses to eradicating violence against First Nations women, as stakeholders such as lawyers, judges, and police officers are not immune to racism. Due to stereotypes of First Nations communities, violence is seen as culturally "normal" and First Nations women are not provided with adequate social and legal protection. There is also an understandable mistrust of authorities due to historical acts of pain, mistreatment, and violence that many First Nations women and men have experienced by officials of the state.

A movement toward a more effective coordinated community response to domestic violence for First Nations women and women of colour should implicitly include effective programming that addresses the needs of diverse communities. These communities include, but are not limited to, communities of colour, women with disabilities, and same-sex communities. Women from communities of colour ought to be approached without judgment or reservation as to what they feel would best suit them in terms of developing a dialogue around domestic violence and safety. Often times a Eurocentric approach to providing service is used as the model template for *all* women. This kind of homogenization of women's voice and experience negates the very real components of racism and sexism that affect women's lives. It is also worth noting that although many domestic violence agencies and organizations have incorporated same-sex service delivery in their programming, seldom is same-sex racial/ethno-specific programming or programming for persons with disabilities delivered or even acknowledged. In addition to not asking women what their needs are, service providers fail to examine how colonialism, and specifically the tactics of the abuser, have shaped the lives of the colonized and the colonizer, and how patriarchy is implicitly interconnected in such processes.

Women in Prison The policing of women's bodies by the Canadian state has a long history. In 1897, *The Female Refuges Act* allowed women between the ages of 16 and 35 who were deemed "unmanageable and incorrigible" to be sentenced to reform schools for women (Sangster, 2002). By the 20th century, raced incarceration and the legal construction of race was evident in judicial dispositions. Emily Murphy's 1922 book *The Black Candle* exemplifies early racist discourse characteristic of Canadian criminal legislation. Murphy argues for legislation to curtail the "threat" of Chinese men and other men of colour who she sees as luring white women into opium smoking and unsavoury lifestyles.

Contemporary writers such as Luana Ross (1998), Colleen Anne Dell (2002), and Karlene Faith (1993) examine the confinement of Native American, Native Canadian, and Black women's bodies. They have explored how racialized and criminalized ideologies lead to state-sanctioned gendered incarceration, referring to women's incarceration based on historical sex-gender stereotypes that attempt to reinforce paternalist ideals in an effort to reform "bad" woman. Labelling and incarcerating women seen as criminal "lunatics," "temptresses," and "procurers" pathologized and criminalized them (Reece, 2005: 237).

In Canada, as of March 2006 there are approximately 909 women prisoners in the federal prison system. Of the women, 401 (44 percent) are incarcerated and 508 (56 percent) are on conditional release, serving the remainder of their sentences in the community (Correctional Service of Canada, 2006). Furthermore, approximately 19.1 percent of all incarcerated women are serving sentences for murder, many for killing an abusive spouse (Canadian Association of Elizabeth Fry Societies, 2001). Although the number of incarcerated women as compared to men may be low (there are about 12 494 men in the federal prison system), the majority of women serving federal sentences (2 years or more) are incarcerated for non-violent offences (Bell, 2004). There are also disproportionate numbers of First Nations women in prison; in 2003, Native women made up 29 percent of the federally sentenced women's population, while only accounting for 3 percent of Canada's population, and from 1997 to 2002 the number of Native women in federal custody increased by 36.7 percent (Canadian Association of Elizabeth Fry Societies, 2001). Women prisoners in general, and First Nations women in particular, tend to be overclassified as maximum security risks, making their movement within prisons under constant surveillance.

Patricia Monture-Angus (1995) has examined the politics of incarceration and the racialization of First Nations women within the Canadian criminal justice system. Her work shows that racism perpetuated against First Nations women is historically based. Systemic institutionalized racism is part of our Canadian legal system and First Nations women are thus under-represented in the criminal justice system. Monture-Angus calls for "Aboriginal justice systems" (Monture-Angus, 1995: 238), comprised of Aboriginal lawyers, judges, and social workers who would legitimize Native understandings of punishment and healing.

When it comes to Black women, many being housed in federal and provincial institutions have been sentenced for drug trafficking offences (Faith, 2003; Sudbury, 2005). At the Vanier Correctional Centre for Women, admissions of Black women increased 630 percent over the six years between 1986/87 and 1992/93. The comparable figure for white women was 59 percent (CAEFS, 2003). According to Sinclair and Boe (2002), between the years 1981 and 2002 the number of Black women incarcerated increased from 1 percent to 6 percent,[9] with the greatest consecutive increase occurring between 1989 (10 women) and 1990 (25 women). Black women often receive harsher sentences than their white counterparts (Reece, 2007) and, once released, Black women seem reluctant to utilize community services. Having returned to their home communities, many avoid disclosing their "time away" due to the stigma associated with mainstream notions of "criminality," which dictate that formerly incarcerated persons are deviant and social outcasts. These stereotypes are reinforced by popular media depictions of "criminal behaviour" and also by cultural discrimination that women face in their communities. According to a study conducted by Margaret Shaw (1994), 71 percent of institutionalized women surveyed had children and 80 percent were lone parents for some or all of the time (Shaw, 1994, cited in CEFSO, 2003). Black women's usual main concern is the welfare of their children and attaining employment—the latter made all the more difficult with a criminal record, regardless of the charge. For every woman housed in segregated conditions in a federal prison, it costs approximately $175 000–$250 000 per year (Council of Elizabeth Fry Societies of Ontario, 2008). For the fiscal year of 2004–2005, the Correctional Service of Canada's expenditures totalled $2.8 billion. That is an enormous amount of money spent on punishment. Considering that most women incarcerated in federal and provincial institutions are there for non-violent crimes, it might make more sense to divert these funds toward adequate housing, medical care, and access to employment programs. Alternatively, the costs of community-based options, such as bail, community supervision, and probation range from $5 to $25 per day (prisonjustice.ca, 2007). Many of the offences that women of colour are charged with are a direct result of impoverishment, since poverty often limits women's choices. A move toward working with women in contact with the law requires preventative social programs grounded in the material reality of women's lives.

By exploring the dynamics of environmental racism, violence against women, and incarcerated First Nations and Black women, this section has highlighted some anti-racist feminist approaches to issues affecting these two groups of women. Anti-racist feminist standpoints require an analysis of the internal and external power relations present within and outside of racialized communities. Racialized women are not a homogenous group. Class relations and sex-gender roles are areas where First Nations and Black women negotiate their shifting identities.

MAINSTREAMING BLACK FEMINIST THOUGHT

Introducing Black Feminist Thought: A Political Action Standpoint Theory

In terms of self-reflexivity, agency, and empowerment, hooks (1984) explains that "white feminists act as if Black women did not know sexist oppression existed until they voiced feminist sentiment" (11). During the early 1980s, women of colour began to challenge the gender-as-primary-oppression stance that the first and second waves of the feminist movement had taken up. Black women had always been keenly aware of the intersecting nature of oppression, but these ideas were de-legitimized and excluded from early feminist writing. Black women writers have long been making waves about the importance of centring Black women's experiences in theory and practice. For example, Barbara Smith (1983) and Audre Lorde (1984) wrote about the interlocking nature of Black women's sexual oppression as connected to systems of oppression such as class, gender, and race. They both acknowledged that anti-lesbian sentiments paralyze feminist theory and the women's movement. bell hooks (1984) explored the separation between margin and centre and/or the "outside" and "inside" politics of feminist theory. She pointed to the fact that separation and exclusion in feminist theory support paternalist ideology and practice. Angela Y. Davis (1981) argued that the legacy of slavery and the rape of Black women's bodies is connected to economic, class, and racial oppression.

Black feminist thought is both a social political theory and an activist program. Its purpose lies in critically centring Black women's experiences as connected to the political and economic exploitation of labour and cultural modes of production. Social arrangements—work, family, schooling, justice systems—maintain capitalist imperatives that subjugate Black women's lives. Black feminist thought thus calls attention to local and global systems of oppression that reinforce Black women's marginal social positions.

One of the most engaging and pivotal texts regarding a fluid and complete discussion of Black feminist thought comes from Patricia Hill Collins (1990). Not only does her work investigate the intersectionality of race, class, gender, and sexuality, but these discussions are tied to nation-state formations, empowerment, and resistance. Highlighting the need for multiple Black feminist standpoint theories, Collins argues that if Black feminist thought is intellectualized only by Black women in the academy, then it pays little tribute to foremothers who were not formally named feminists, but who struggled in the name of Black women's liberation.

How then is Black feminist thought articulated across cultures and continents? In North America, Black women experience racial, class, and gender oppression. Cross-continentally, in many African countries where the majority of people are Black, women's primary oppression may be sexism and/or classism. However, this does not mean that Black African women do not experience racism since we need only look at the historical legacy of apartheid for evidence that it exists. Moreover, Black women are a heterogeneous group and contextualize the oppression they face differently. Social locations in regard to class positions are mitigating factors in the racing and gendering of Black women's bodies.

Nevertheless, identifying as a Black feminist and/or employing Black feminist thought does not necessarily mean that those ideas are warranted as Black feminist consciousness. Black feminist thought involves a level of consciousness that articulates some aspects of the Black experience but avoids idealism and essentialism. It incorporates multiple theoretical and methodological perspectives and lived experience, and by extension embraces empowerment rather than victimization analysis. As such, Black feminist thought includes variants of Black and/or feminist knowledge and understanding (Collins, 1990). Consequently, Collins argues that "[d]efinitions claiming that anyone can produce and develop Black feminist thought risk obscuring the special angle of vision that Black women bring to the knowledge production process" (Collins, 1990: 13). And what about white women who seek to employ a Black consciousness? Sexism oppresses them, but racism enables them to exploit women of colour (Collins, 1990: hooks, 1984). Widening the conceptual framework of who "qualifies" as a Black feminist would allow grandmothers, mothers, daughters, and those who may not be formally educated, to particulate in the project of Black feminist thought.

In the Classroom: Examining Black Feminist Thought as a Feminist Political Pedagogy

Centring Black feminist thought in women's studies classrooms is important precisely because Black women have been and continue to be marginalized. We can use their social status (employment, political, economic, and class status) in relation to wider globalization processes as important starting points for empowerment, resistance, and activist pedagogies. Patricia Hill Collins argues that "maintaining the invisibility of Black women has been critical in maintaining social inequalities" (Collins, 1990: 3). Conversely, teaching and learning for transformative social change means envisioning new and different philosophical staring points. Canadian texts including, but not limited to, *Scratching the Surface*; *Thinking Through: Essays on Feminism, Marxism, and Anti-Racism*; *Returning the Gaze: Essay on Racism, Feminism, and Politic*; *Back to the Drawing Board: African Canadian Feminisms*; *And Still We Rise: Political Mobilizing in Contemporary Canada*; and the recent *Theorizing Empowerment: Canadian Perspectives on Black Feminist Thought* are examples of academic and activist forays into transformative education for social change. These texts challenge readers to question the making of social problems as interconnected to race, gender, class, and dis/ability. Students are provided with political as well as personal accounts of feminist theorizing from multiple standpoints.

The writings and teachings of Black women play an important role in research and activist praxis within classrooms. Local and global structural systems of oppression are maintained by white privilege, the "matrix of domination" (Collins, 1990: 18). As a political pedagogy, Black feminist thought focuses our attention on the lives of women of colour as connected to social justice imperatives. Social justice movements build links between organizations for First Nations women and women of colour and allow students to become engaged in building coalitions, resistance movements, and activist platforms. Social justice movements become sites of resistance where women who occupy marginal statuses come together in solidarity across difference. In Canada, organizations such as No One is Illegal, Kairos Canada, Justicia for Migrant Workers, the Don't Ask Don't Tell Coalition, and the Coalition to Support Indigenous Sovereignty advocate to raise awareness about the ways in which the Canadian state hegemonically structures labour relations in the public and private sphere, especially that of women of colour. Social justice imperatives create spaces not only for challenging white dominance, but also for empowering women of colour to play key roles in decision-making processes that affect their lives.

INTRODUCING THEORIES OF WHITENESS

Lack of attention to theories of whiteness in feminist theory has been profound. Third-wave feminists and anti-racist feminists challenged the ways in which whiteness has been coded in literature, pedagogy, and activism. Both white women and women of colour experience sexism, and understand racism as the work of white male patriarchy, but white women often perpetuate the ideals of racism, ignoring their own complicity in oppression. Thus the social privilege of the white middle-class woman has been applied universally to the notion of "women" without an inclusive analysis of race, class, or sexuality (Spelman, 1988: 186).

White-middle-class feminist ideas became dominant because white women were able to control their dissemination. Engaging in critical theories of whiteness means "revis[ing] the traditional focus of research on race relations by concentrating attention upon the socially constructed nature of white identity and the impact of whiteness upon intergroup relations" (Doane, 2003: 3). Whiteness theorists seldom draw connections to other systems of oppression outside of racism, and what results is a body of literature that explores whiteness and "race" and racism excluding the interconnectivity of whiteness, race, gender, class, dis/ability, and sexuality.

However, white is a racialized category that cannot be seen apart from centuries of colonial association and domination (Ware, 1992). Socio-political organization in Canada has been ideologically formed along racial lines whereby the history of Canada as a white settler society informs how discussions about racism take place. As such, an interrogation of whiteness is not an optional standpoint for whites. Racism shapes white people's lives and identities in a way that is inseparable from other facets of daily life (Frankenberg, 1993/2000: 451).

The Canadian rhetoric of multiculturalism is an example of how white privilege obscures past racist treatment of Native Canadians and more contemporary treatment of immigrants and refugees of colour. And the subsequent denial of systemic racism in Canada has allowed for discriminatory policies and procedures to be maintained by the status quo. Post 9/11, we have witnessed the political frenzy surrounding the proliferation of racist discourse directed at Muslim Canadians. Media representations of Muslims as terrorists, coupled with political propaganda, have justified detention and detainment without due process of those whom the Canadian government suspects of being involved with terrorism. In addition, re-colonization processes are currently taking place whereby women in the North and the South work in factories and multinational corporations located within the borders of free trade zones, and these neo-capitalist spaces do not protect women against forms of abuse, violation of labour laws, or pre-emptive dismissal. This political climate reasons that whiteness is a normative process and practice evident in law.

In the Classroom: Examining Whiteness as a Feminist Political Pedagogy

Whiteness in academic spaces and the ways in which whiteness structures women's lives outside of the academy is seldom examined by feminists. Whiteness scholars claim to situate their work in an analysis of privilege, however they hardly ever mention white racism, and/or global capitalism (Anderson, 2003). The result is that all of the "mechanisms of and sites of racial domination and subordination disappear from view" (Anderson, 2003: 28). Moreover, there is an absence of class dynamics in whiteness studies. As Dionne Brand says:

> I don't think it is up to black people to change white sensibilities. I think it is up to white people to do that. I think that racism is not our problem. I think it's a white problem. I think we can fight

against it. I think it's our job to fight for good laws, to fight for equality, but in terms of doing things like changing white attitudes, white people have to do that work (Brand, 1990, quoted in Levine-Rasky, 2002: 1).

Frankenberg avoids this trap by looking at whiteness as a set of cultural practices, and examines the intersectionality of whiteness, "race," class, and gender—the "material and discursive dimensions of whiteness" (1993/2000: 448). She argues that in colonial struggles "continual processes of slippage, condensation, and displacement among the constructs of 'race,' 'nation,' and 'culture' continue to 'unmark' white people while consistently marking and racializing others" (1993/2000: 6). Native Canadian women and Black women are continually seen as "others" in society when institutional racism creates barriers for access to social mobility.

Recognizing that whiteness is always about naming and locating dominance, a critique of whiteness is interstitially part of the politics of positionality. In feminist classrooms, white women's relationship to privilege and power has socially benefited them historically and contemporarily. Their dominance as "Imperial Mothers" or "chaste colonial benefactors" has played a central role in their whiteness not being named or seen. These roles were not *formally* named as part of the construction of whiteness, yet were *implicit*. The importance of this concept cannot be understated:

> To speak of the "construction of whiteness" asserts that there are locations, discourses, and material relations to which the term "whiteness" applies.... Naming "whiteness" displaces it from unmarked, unnamed status that is itself an effect of its dominance. Among the effects on white people both of race privilege and of the dominance of whiteness are their seeming normativity, their structured invisibility.... To speak of whiteness is ... to emphasize that dealing with racism is not merely an option for white people—that rather racism shapes white people's lives and identities in a way that is inseparable from other facets of daily life (Frankenberg, 1993/2000: 451).

According to Alison Bailey, white women who face the *"dilemma of white privilege awareness* [are] trapped in the awkward position of knowing that it is both impossible to dispose of [white] privilege and impossible to take advantage of it without perpetuating the systems of domination we wish to demolish" (Bailey, 1999: 86).

White women writing white are also re/writing themselves. Locating and naming whiteness in academic spaces is important in terms of how we theorize feminist locations both inside and outside the academy. Race matters within Canadian feminist classrooms; one can simply look at the under-representation of women of colour and First Nations women in universities as an example.

White women experience gender oppression *and* race privilege at the same time. In some instances, "white" and "woman" become synonymous with power and prestige. In other instances, "woman" is seen as the second sex. In contrast, First Nations women and women of colour always negotiate the confluence of multiple oppressions as racialized women. Class and social status allow middle-class white women to challenge gendered representations of themselves, and to carve out an identity for themselves that "in writing universal human characteristics—hard work, piousness, civility, cognitive ability, physical beauty—[are] associated with one racial group" (Babb, 1998: 87). By contrast, First Nations women, immigrant and refugee women, and women of colour continue to be located in marginal and shifting social positions.

CONCLUSION

Why are multiple feminist frameworks important for developing women's studies curricula and why is it important to address women's social inequality within and outside the classroom? Answering these questions becomes the responsibility of feminist academics, students, activists, and artists. The purpose of this chapter has been to underscore the importance of feminist theorizing on race and racism through an examination of specific issues relating to First Nations and Black women. We have examined how the historical treatment of these groups of racialized women has placed First Nations and Black women "outside" the perimeters of nationalist projects, while simultaneously placing them "inside" these very same projects as unfit biological, cultural, and political racialized bodies. Furthermore, we have shown how this historical treatment of First Nations and Black women as marginal persons without citizenship or fundamental human rights has contemporary resonance. Their continual marginalization means that students, activists, and teachers must theorize feminism at both the local and the global levels in order to build feminist coalition across differences.

Women's lives are heterogeneous and multi-vocal, meaning that class, race, gender, sexuality, and dis/ability shape our social environments, and that women speak from various social locations. We have, therefore, seen how feminist theorizing in the classroom about theories of whiteness and Black feminist thought underscore this importance. Historically, First Nations women and Black women have been the primary caregivers for their families and have engaged in acts of resistance when faced with losing their autonomy and when family "social-cultural cohesion" has been threatened by the state (Stevenson, 1999). When patriarchy threatened the livelihood of Black women in their communities they participated in feminist groups, civil rights organizing, labour unions, and revolts (Collins, 1990).

Finally, an important part of this chapter has been to examine how the activeness of racism demarcates political, social, and cultural boundaries using historically racist notions attached to the bodies of racialized women. Since nationalism involves the notion of unification and conformity, as well as the institutionalization of power and hegemony, the historical racializing of First Nations and Black women asks us to question the operation of race relations in a post-modern and post-colonial sphere. In sum, all feminist analysis needs to begin from critical race studies.

Endnotes

1. The author thanks Nancy Mandell and Andil Gosine for generously commenting and providing advice on this chapter.

2. Democratic racism as defined by Henry and Tator (2006) refers to "an ideology that permits and sustains people's ability to maintain two apparently conflicting sets of values. One set consists of a commitment to a liberal, democratic society motivated by egalitarian values of fairness, justice, and equality. Conflicting with these values are attitudes and behaviours that include negative feelings about people of colour and that result in differential treatment of them or discrimination against them."

3. Multiculturalism actually erases and ignores the numerous diverse cultures/ethnicities in Canada and masks specific acts of oppression. Specific examples outlined in Nourbese M. Phillip's 1992 work include Canada's past and present genocide of First Nations people; past treatment of Black loyalists

who fled to the Maritimes; racist immigration policies (treatment of Chinese and Indian immigrants); the treatment of Japanese and Jewish people in WWII; and the present treatment of Asian refugees.

4. Asian Canadians and First Nations people did not have the vote until well into the 1940s and 1960s, respectively.

5. Makeda Silvera notes that domestic workers "can now register complaints with the Ministry of Labour to claim for overtime wages ... [but] for many domestic workers, this entitlement is seen as bureaucratic jargon, the reality remains the same as it was in 1983, and that is, individual women remain afraid and intimidated, and complaints of any kind are rarely registered" (1993: 211).

6. As outlined by Henry and Tator (2006), discourses on ethnicity have been central to debates around social class. Scholars have argued that the focus on ethnicity may actually negate processes of racialization and the prevalence of racism that people of colour face on a daily basis. Overemphasis on ethnic relations obscures systemic racism and the social structural factors that marginalize people of colour.

7. Regarding gender roles and the gendered division of labour, Black women, like white women, experience male domination and the expectation that they will carry the weight of domestic responsibilities within the home (Calliste, 1996, cited in Das Gupta, 2000).

8. Clearly, working-class, middle-class, and upper-class people own vehicles. The point is that because transit commuters are socially classed as lower-income, there are stereotypical and racialized representational meanings associated with that categorization.

9. Sinclair and Boe's analysis states that there was an increase in Black women being incarcerated from 1981 (1 percent) to 1989 (4 percent), increasing in 1990 (8 percent), and remaining relatively stable to 1995 (7 percent). From 1996 there was a significant increase to 12 percent, followed by a decrease to 6 percent in 2002.

Suggested Readings

Andersen, Margaret. 2003. Whitewashing race: A critical perspective on whiteness, in *White out: The continuing significance of racism*, eds. Ashley W. Doane and Eduardo Bonilla-Silva, 21–34. New York and London: Routledge. This article uses whiteness studies as theoretical terrain for analyzing race relations. Margaret Anderson argues that whiteness studies ought to be grounded in the social situational positioning of race relations and not the dissolution of white identity politics. The author further interrogates whiteness studies in connection with the working of white privilege in academia.

Bannerji, Himani, ed. 1993. *Returning the gaze: Essays on racism, feminism and politics*. Toronto: Sister Vision Press. This collection of essays is an important contribution to the landscape of feminist theorizing from women of colour in Canada. The authors share anti-racist and anti-imperialist perspectives on social locations of women in relation to the material production of the political economy of the Canadian nation-state.

Collins, Patricia Hill. 1990. *Black feminist thought: Knowledge, consciousness, and the politics of empowerment*. New York: Routledge. This is one of the most seminal texts in the formation of Black feminist theorizing. The author argues that Black feminist thought is formulated on distinctive heterogeneous Black feminist intellectual traditions embedded in an intersectional analysis of oppression as constituted through social, cultural, economic, and political lived experiences of Black women's lives.

Dua, Enakshi, and Angela Robertson, eds. 1999. *Scratching the surface: Canadian anti-racist feminist thought*. Toronto: Women's Press. This book examines how race, gender, class, and sexuality are mitigated through an anti-racist feminist lens. The authors in the book present various arguments that investigate the social inequity of women's lives in relation to the making of "Canadianness."

Wing, Adrien Katherine, ed. 2003. *Critical race feminism: A reader,* 2d ed. New York and London: New York Univ. Press. This book offers readers a critical look at the readings of Latina, Black, Asian, and Aboriginal women, emphasizing how race and gender are embedded in historical and contemporary legal discourse as overtly articulated in legal discourse and judicial systems.

Discussion Questions

1. Racism and racialization processes are irretrievably connected to power. Define racism and provide five examples in relation to the treatment of First Nations and Black women in Canada.

2. How has the making of Canada as a "white settler society" affected First Nations and Black women politically, economically, and socially? Why is this analysis important for how we understand Canada as a multicultural nation?

3. Make a list of historical and contemporary examples of environmental racism. How is environmental racism connected to ideologies about "space" and raced bodies?

4. Historically, many nationalist projects took place during periods of colonialism. Using discourses of "morality" versus "deviance," women's bodies were surveyed, raced, and gendered in specific ways. How can feminist perspectives on race and racism inform our analysis concerning women's incarceration? How might social justice and activist imperatives aid in our understanding of this issue?

5. Black feminist thought informs anti-racist research, theory, and practice. Provide a definition of Black feminist thought and explain why an analysis of race, gender, class, sexuality, and dis/ability is important in terms of how we understand race and racism.

Bibliography

Andersen, Margaret. 2003. Whitewashing race: A critical perspective on whiteness, in *White out: The continuing significance of racism*, eds. Ashley W. Doane and Eduardo Bonilla-Silva, 21–34. New York and London: Routledge.

Arat-Koc, Sedef. 2001. *Caregivers break the silence: A participatory action research on the abuse and violence, including the impact of family separation, experienced by women in the live-in caregiver program.* Toronto: Intercede.

Babb, Valerie. 1998. *Whiteness visible: The meaning of whiteness in American literature and culture.* New York: New York Univ. Press.

Bailey, Allison. 1999. Despising an identity they taught me to claim, in *Whiteness: Feminist philosophical reflections*, eds. Chris J. Cuomo and Kim Q. Hall, 85–104. Lanham, MD: Rowman and Littlefield.

Bell, Amey. 2004. Women with violent offence histories: A comparison. *Forum on Corrections Research: Women offenders.* **www.csc-scc.gc.ca/text/pblct/forum/Vol16No1/forum-v16n1e .pdf**. Accessed February 23, 2008.

Brand, Dionne. 1993. A working paper on Black women in Toronto: Gender, race and class, in *Returning the gaze: Essays on racism, feminism and politics*, ed. Himani Bannerji, 220–243. Toronto: Sister Vision Press.

Brand, Dionne. 1999. Black women and work: The impact of racially constructed gender roles on the sexual division of labour, in *Scratching the surface: Canadian anti-racist feminist thought*, eds. Enakshi Dua and Angela Robertson, 83–96. Toronto: Women's Press.

Byckalo-Khan, Farrah, and Andil Gosine. 2003. Transit equity. *Alternatives Journal* 29(1) (Winter): 30.

Calliste, A., and G. Dei, eds. 2000. *Anti-racist feminism: Critical race and gender studies*. Halifax, NS: Fernwood Books.

Canadian Association of Elizabeth Fry Societies of Ontario (CAEFS). (2001). Women in prison—CAEFS fact sheets. **http://dawn.thot.net/election2004/issues32.htm**. Accessed January 15, 2005.

Canadian Association of Social Workers (CASW). 2005. Income of Black women in Canada, 2005. **www.casw-acts.ca/advocacy/Blackwomen_e.pdf**. Accessed February 12, 2008.

Carty, Linda, and Dionne Brand. 1993. "Visible minority" women: A creation of the Canadian state, in *Returning the gaze: Essays on racism, feminism and politics*, ed. Himani Bannerji, 169–254. Toronto: Sister Vision Press.

Churchill, Ward. 1998. *Fantasies of the master race: Literature, cinema and colonization of American Indians*. San Francisco: City Lights Books.

Collins, Patricia Hill. 1990. *Black feminist thought: Knowledge, consciousness, and the politics of empowerment*. New York: Routledge.

Correctional Service of Canada. 2006. Ten-year status report on women's corrections, 1996–2006. (April 2006). **www.csc-scc.gc.ca/text/pblcsbjct-eng.shtml#women**. Accessed June 18, 2008.

Council of Elizabeth Fry Societies of Ontario (CEFSO). 2003. Facts & figures: Profile of provincially sentenced women in Ontario. **www.cefso.ca/facts&figures.html**. Accessed August 12, 2008.

Council of Elizabeth Fry Societies of Ontario (CEFSO). 2008. Human and fiscal costs of prison, 2008. **www.elizabethfry.ca/facts1_e.htm**. Accessed April 24, 2008.

Das Gupta, Tania. 2000. Families of Native people, immigrants, and people of colour, in *Canadian families: Diversity, conflict and change*, 2d ed., eds. Nancy Mandell and Ann Duffy, 146–187. Toronto: Harcourt, Brace.

Davis, Angela Y. 1981. *Women, race and class*. New York: Vintage Books.

Dell, Colleen Anne. 2002. The criminalization of Aboriginal women: Commentary by a community activist, in *Crimes of colour: Racialization and the criminal justice system in Canada,* eds. Wendy Chan and Kiran Mirchandani, 127–138. Peterborough, ON: Broadview.

Doane, Ashley Woody. 2003. Rethinking whiteness studies, in *White out: The continuing significance of racism*, eds. Ashley W. Doane and Eduardo Bonilla-Silva, 3–20. New York and London: Routledge.

Donner, Lissa, Angela Busch, and Nahanni Fontaine. 2002. Women, income and health in Manitoba: An overview and ideas for action. Prepared for the Women's Health Clinic, Winnipeg. **www.womenshealthclinic.org/resources/wih/wih.html**. Accessed August 11, 2008.

Dua, Enakshi. 1999. Canadian anti-racist feminist thought: Scratching the surface of racism, in *Scratching the surface: Canadian anti-racist feminist thought*, eds. Enakshi Dua and Angela Robertson, 7–31. Toronto: Women's Press.

Eisenstein, Zillah R. 1981. *The radical future of liberal feminism*. New York and London: Longman.

Elliot, Patricia, and Nancy Mandell. 2001. Feminist theories, in *Feminist issues: Race, class, and sexuality*, 3d ed., ed. Nancy Mandell, 23-48. Toronto: Prentice Hall.

Faith, Karlene. 1993. *Unruly women: The politics of confinement and resistance*. Vancouver: Press Gang.

Flynn, Karen, and Charmaine Crawford. 1998. Committing race treason: Caribbean women and domestic violence in Toronto, in *Unsettling truths: Battered women, policy, politics, and contemporary research in Canada*, eds. George S. Rigakos and Kevin Bonnycastle. Vancouver: Collective Press.

Frankenberg, Ruth. 1993/2000. White women, race matters: The social construction of whiteness, in *Theories of race and racism: A reader*, eds. Les Black and John Solomos, 447–461. London: Routledge.

Gosine, Andil. 2003. Myths of diversity: Canadian environmentalists don't want to talk about racism—but too often that means the uncritical acceptance of popular diversity myths. *Alternatives Journal* 29(1): 12–18.

Henry, Frances, and Carol Tator. 2006. *The colour of democracy: Racism in Canadian society*. Scarborough, ON: Thomson Nelson.

hooks, bell. 1984. *Feminist theory: From margin to center*. Boston: South End Press.

Jiwani, Yasmin. 2002. The criminalization of race/The racialization of crime, in *Erasing connections*, eds. W. Chan and K. Mirchandana, 67–86. Toronto: Broadview.

Khosla, Punam. 2003. If low income women of colour counted in Toronto. Published by the Community Social Planning Council of Toronto. **www.socialplanningtoronto.org**. Accessed February 12, 2008.

Lawrence, Bonita. 2002. Rewriting histories of the land, in *Race, space and the law: Unmapping a white settler society*, ed. Sherene Razack, 22–46. Toronto: Between the Lines.

Levine-Rasky, Cynthia, ed. 2002. *Working through whiteness: International perspectives*. Albany: State Univ. of New York Press.

Lorde, Audre. 1984. *Sister outsider*. Freedom, CA: Crossing Press.

Malik, Kenan. 1998. Race, pluralism and the meaning of difference. **www.kenanmalik .com/papers/new_formations.html**. Retrieved February 22, 2008.

McCalla, Andrea, and Vic Satzewich. 2002. Settler capitalism and the construction of immigrants and "Indians" as racialized others, in *Crimes of colour: Racialization and the criminal justice system in Canada*, eds. Wendy Chan and Kiran Mirchandani, 25–44. Peterborough, ON: Broadview Press.

Memmi, Albert. 1982/2000. *Racism*. Minneapolis: Univ. of Minnesota Press.

Miles, Robert. 1993/2000. Apropos the idea of "race" … again, in *Theories of race and racism: A reader*, eds. Les Black and John Solomos, 125–143. London: Routledge.

Monture-Angus, Patricia.1995. *Thunder in my soul: A Mohawk woman speaks*. Halifax, NS: Fernwood.

Murphy, Emily F. 1922. *The black candle*. Toronto: Thomas Allen.

Nelson, Jennifer. 2002. The space of Africville: Creating, regulating, and re-membering the urban "slum," in *Race, space and the law: Unmapping a white settler society*, ed. Sherene Razack, 211–232. Toronto: Between the Lines.

Perry, Adele. 1997. *Gender, race, and the making of colonial society: British Columbia, 1858–1871*. PhD thesis, York University.

Philip, Nourbese M. 1992. *Frontiers: Selected essays and writings on racism and culture, 1984–1992*. Toronto: Mercury Press.

Prisonjustice. 2007. Statistics for 2004/2005. **www.prisonjustice.ca**. Accessed February 23, 2008.

Razack, Sherene. 1998. *Looking white people in the eye: Gender, race, and culture in courtrooms and classrooms*. Toronto: Univ. of Toronto Press.

Reece, Rai. 2005. Outside women inside: Defining deviance, incarcerating "race" and sexuality, in *Law and criminal justice: A critical inquiry*, ed. Livy A. Visano, 231–248. Toronto: APF Press.

Reece, Rai. 2007. Canadian Black feminist thought and scholar-activist praxis, in *Theorizing empowerment: Canadian perspectives on Black feminist thought*, eds. Njoki N. Wane and Notisha Massaquoi, 266–284. Toronto: Inanna.

Ross, Luana. 1998. *Inventing the savage: The social construction of Native American criminality*. Austin, TX: Univ. of Texas Press.

Sangster, Joan. 2002. Defining sexual promiscuity: "Race," gender, and class in the operation of Ontario's Female Refuges Act, 1930–1960, in *Crimes of colour: Racialization and the criminal justice system in Canada*, eds. Wendy Chan and Kiran Mirchandani, 45–63. Peterborough, ON: Broadview.

Shaw, M. 1994. Ontario Women in Conflict with the Law subsidiary report: Children and parenting, in Council of Elizabeth Fry Societies of Ontario (CEFSO). 2003. *Facts & figures: Profile of provincially sentenced women in Ontario*. **www.cefso.ca/facts&figures.html**. Accessed August 12, 2008.

Silvera, Makeda. 1983. *Silenced*. Toronto: Williams-Wallace.

Sinha, Mrinalini. 1992. Chathams, Pitts, and Gladstones in petticoats: The politics of gender and race in the Ilbert Bill controversy, 1883–1884, in *Western women and imperialism: Complicity and resistance*, eds. Nupur Chaudhuri and Margaret Strobel, 98–118. Bloomington: Indiana Univ. Press.

Sinclair, Roberta Lynn, and Roger Boe. 2002. *Canadian federal women offender profiles: Trends from 1981 to 2002 (Revised)*. Ottawa: CSC Research Branch.

Smith, Andrea, and Luana Ross. 2004. Introduction: Native women and state violence. *Social Justice* 31(4): 1–7.

Smith, Barbara. 1983. *Home girls: A Black feminist anthology* New York: Kitchen Table: Women of Colour Press.

Spelman, Elizabeth. 1988. *Inessential woman: Problems of exclusion in feminist thought*. Boston: Beacon Press.

Stevenson, Winona. 1999. Colonialism and First Nations women in Canada, in *Scratching the surface: Canadian anti-racist feminist thought*, eds. Enakshi Dua and Angela Robertson, 49–80. Toronto: Women's Press.

Sudbury, Julia. 2005. "Mules," "yardies" and other folk devils: Mapping cross-border imprisonment in Britain, in *Global lockdown: Race, gender and the prison industrial complex*, ed. Julia Sudbury, 173–189. London: Routledge.

Ware, Vron. 1992. *Beyond the pale: White women, racism and history*. London: Verso.

Wollstonecraft, Mary. 1792/1975. *A vindication of the rights of woman*, ed. Miriam Kramnick. London: Penguin Books.

CHAPTER 5

Strange Sisters in No Man's Land: Still Thinking Sex 26 Years Later

Bobby Noble

I cringe as I write that word, *boyfriend*, in this context—the qualifier "heterosexual" is, at best, an embarrassing adjunct to "feminist"; at worst, it seems like a contradiction in terms. Feminists are strong, independent women. Boyfriends are people whose class rings you wear around your neck—er, on a chain around your neck. Feminists don't have boyfriends—do they?

> Lisa Johnson, "Fuck You and Your Untouchable Face: Third Wave Feminism and the Problem of Romance," in *Jane Sexes It Up: True Confessions of Feminist Desire*, 14.

SEXUALITY AS CONTESTED FEMINIST TERRAIN

In an effort to reclaim the feminist and female body, North American, mid-20th-century second-wave feminism began to focus on issues of sexuality as one place where the influence of culture and patriarchy desperately needed to be challenged. Given that one of the first premises of feminism is that the *personal is political*, a great deal of work came to focus on the nature of "female" sexual practice and expression. Some 50 years later, Lisa Johnson published her extremely important collection of essays on sexuality, *Jane Sexes It Up* (2002). In the introduction, Johnson characterizes second-wave feminist thought as a kind of eccentric aging auntie who dispenses unhelpful quips to the younger generation, who are trying to make sense of both feminism and sexuality in an altogether different historical moment. Johnson writes: "My eccentric Aunt Feminism ... [is] always reminding us how smart we are," but never moves beyond telling them to "go get something pierced" at the moment the conversation comes to how exactly one might resolve conflicts between "my feelings or experiences" about sex and what a "feminist

should feel" or experience around sex (Johnson, 2002:14–15, 39). What happened to feminist thinking about sex to produce such an interesting characterization? And what do we make of the generational metaphors at stake in the excerpt from Johnson with which this chapter opens? Is there such a thing as "proper feminist sexual practice"? Is the nature of "proper" feminist sexuality in 2008 the same as it might have been in 1982? Are feminists even the same? Is feminist sexual expression the same? Should it be? Does gender have a history? Can sex have a history too?

This chapter will map out some ways of thinking about the relationships between sexuality, gender, power, culture, politics, and sexual representation as they have tangled together over the past 30 years in a North American context. Given that the personal is political, sexuality needs to be recontextualized in order to understand it as interlocking sets of sociocultural arrangements. That is, we might begin to hypothesize here that another premise of feminism, which informs this chapter, is that sexuality is not the possession of individuals or individual bodies, but rather a meeting point of the political, social, economic, historical, personal, and experiential. That these domains intersect does not at all mean that they are each the same as or identical to each other. But what it does mean is that sexuality, like other facets of identity, is a complex social construction.

Sex as Experience

Admittedly, it is a tricky argument to suggest that sexuality is fully a product of culture or that it is "socially constructed." Sexuality, like gender for many people, is experienced through the full force of the "natural" and as part of our own personal developmental histories. That experience overlaps with particular beliefs about sexuality told to us in and through our culture. Our popular understandings of sexuality hold that sex is a biological function; that it is a core set of truths about who we are, or who we are not; that this core essence or identity emerges in adolescence, is intimately linked to our gender and to the gender of our erotic object choice (the person to whom we find ourselves attracted); and that each stay the same throughout one's lifetime. But if we begin to think about the places where that "naturalized" feeling or experience meets culture, it becomes harder to sidestep the relationship between them. As Joan Scott (1992) has argued, experience is and has always been an important barometer of women's realities. But Scott also maintains that understanding social power alone, just through one's experience of it, may not be enough. Scott argues

> the evidence of experience ... takes meaning as transparent, reproduces rather than contests given ideological systems ... it is not individuals that have experience but subjects who are constituted through experience. Experience in this definition then becomes not the origin of our explanation, not the authoritative (because seen or felt) evidence that grounds what is known, but rather that which we seek to explain (Scott, 1992: 25–26).

In other words, Scott is suggesting that experience should not be understood as a measure of absolute truth but as a set of practices produced as the effect of ideas, power, social formations, and regulations.

Certainly, one's experience of sexuality is important, but those experiences cannot fully be accounted for without locating them within the domains of history and power. For example, despite a feeling that feminism has provided important conceptual tools for thinking about sex, the epigraph from Johnson that opens this chapter indicates that something is missing for young women. At the very least, Johnson is signalling to us that feminist theory about sexuality might need to generate more complex ways of thinking about pleasure. It is the assertion of this chapter that returning to the work of one early and important feminist, Gayle Rubin, and her extremely important "Thinking Sex: Notes for a Radical Theory of the Politics of Sexuality" (1984), might help move forward with questions like these: What 20th-century feminist conceptual frameworks, histories, and processes occurred to make Johnson's project necessary in the first place? What are the dominant ways of thinking about sex with which feminist contributors are taking issue? How have those processes positioned individuals and produced their experiences? Providing some new and complex feminist conceptual frameworks for thinking sex (not just experiencing it) is precisely what this chapter aims to accomplish.

HOW DO WE THINK SEX?

Before we move forward into our work of thinking sex, it might be useful to provide some definitions of the terms this chapter will use. One of the most significant essays that elaborated a complex set of working terms for thinking about sexuality was the Gayle Rubin essay mentioned in the introduction. First presented at the 1982 conference, "The Scholar and the Feminist: Toward a Politics of Sexuality," held at Barnard College in New York, Rubin's extremely important essay has become a foundational text in sexuality studies. This conference was an attempt to bring together many second-wave feminist activist, political, and community organizations and groups working in the areas of feminist sexuality. There was a desire to return to questions of female pleasure. The resulting book,

Pleasure and Danger: Exploring Female Sexuality (1984), documents the historical importance of this conference. What occurred after the 1982 conference lasted almost throughout the 1980s and has been dubbed the *sex wars*. These were nasty and very heated debates over what counts as "proper" feminist sexuality. These debates tended to focus on what theorist (and editor of *Pleasure and Danger*) Carole Vance calls the "big three": lesbian sadomasochism, butch-femme roles, and the relationship between violence against women, pornography, and the imagined remedy of censorship.

While some might suggest that the sex wars ended in a kind of truce, others suggest that these battles continue in books such as *Jane Sexes It Up*. It might also be suggested that the predominant questions shaping the sex wars changed with the publication of Judith Butler's book *Gender Trouble: Feminism and the Subversion of Identity* (1990). Butler's is a complicated text, however. As the subtitle suggests, one of the central premises of her work is that it might well prove impossible to establish as the ground of a political movement, within social constructionist frameworks, what counts as the categorical truth of "woman." Given Butler's argument, what might count as "feminist" will be equally elusive. At the very least, in an American context, *Gender Trouble* changed the terms of the debate by generating something of a paradigm shift. We can say that for the most part (and not all feminists may agree with this) the sex wars ended with a shared recognition that this war was actually a kind of moral panic, a situation that occurs when deep-rooted and difficult-to-resolve social anxieties become focused on symbolic agents that can be easily targeted (Rubin, 1984: 297).

Rubin's essay gestures toward many of these same questions. Her argument is amazingly simple, even though it sets the stage for important paradigm shifts not only in conceptualizing feminist sexuality but also for the arrival of queer theory. Rubin argues that sexuality, throughout the middle to end of the 20th century, has been subject to intensive regulation. She details this through various historical moments when sexuality and sexual regulation were—and continue to be—particularly incendiary, including the period of the 1950s and 1960s and the HIV/AIDS pandemic of the early 1980s. Drawing upon the work of Michel Foucault's *History of Sexuality* (1978), Rubin suggests that such regulatory practices have functioned to bring sexuality into the central operations of power. Rather than arguing that sexuality is peripheral to the workings of regulatory power, Rubin suggests that, as the thinking about sexuality goes, so too do shifts either toward the left or the right of political undercurrents.

Rubin's "Pervasive Assumptions"

In addition to mapping the interconnectedness of these domains, Rubin also builds what we can describe as an identification of the ideological supports for the regulation of sexual practice and cultures. Using a highly original framework for theorizing sex, Rubin identifies six ideological beliefs that structure thinking about sexuality. These she describes as beliefs, but also as "persistent features of thought" or "pervasive assumptions" that are rarely questioned or even noticed (Rubin, 1984: 278). These are:

1. Gender essentialism: the belief that both sex and gender exist prior to social life, that these are determinative and causal essences in nature and so in the body and, therefore, are unchanging and transhistorical.

2. Sex negativity: the belief that sex is a destructive, dangerous force that must be controlled by laws, morals, religion, etc.

3. The fallacy of misplaced scale: small differences in sex value or behaviour are experienced as cosmic threats.

4. The hierarchical valuation of sex acts: the belief in a hierarchy or "erotic pyramid" where married reproductive heterosexuals are at the top, and the "most despised sexual practices" are at the bottom.

5. The domino theory of sexual peril: the belief that a thin line stands between sexual order and chaos; and that, once crossed, return from demise is impossible.

6. The lack of a concept of benign sexual variation: "sexuality is supposed to conform to a single standard. One of the most tenacious ideas about sex is that there is one best way to do it and that everyone should do it that way" (Rubin, 1984: 283).

What Rubin builds by mapping these interrelated beliefs is a complex and layered conceptual framework for discerning the constructions of sexuality.

Rubin raises two further questions. First, what are the constructed articulations between sexual and gender essentialism? One could define essentialism in a simple way, by beginning with the term "essence." An essentialist belief about gender, sexuality, or race would tell us that these identities each have an essence—a biological or naturally occurring entity—that is the foundation or cause of the identities that follow. Doctrines of biological determinism or essentialism suggest that such fundamental essences pre-exist social formations and give the body as a kind of material object its inner shape. Proponents of sexual/gender essentialism believe that sex and gender are natural forces that exist prior to social life and are eternally unchanging, asocial, and transhistorical. That is, sexuality is gender is sexuality is the body. The constructionist approach, exemplified by questions at the beginning of this chapter, clearly stands in opposition to such beliefs. A constructionist approach counters with the argument that sexuality is a human product, an effect of social life and institutions. At its most conservative, the ideologies and the discourses of the sex/gender system (naturalism and essentialism) all suggest and, in fact, insist, that the most "natural" subjects in our culture are those who therefore must refuse to conceptualize distinctions between "sex" and "gender" at all.

Rubin posits that essentialism deeply shapes our beliefs about sexuality and gender through systems of language. She flags their epistemological (that is, how we know what we know) interconnectedness when she goes on to write

> in the English language, the word sex has two very different meanings. It means gender and gender identity, as in the female sex or the male sex. But sex also refers to sexual activity ... as in *to have sex*. This semantic merging reflects a cultural assumption that sexuality is reducible to sexual intercourse and that it is a function of the relations between women and men (Rubin, 1984: 307).

The question then becomes both politically and epistemologically reshaped under Rubin's work: these ideas about sex, gender, and sexuality construct how we see bodies. As such, how might we begin to understand all three of these (that is, sex, sexuality, and gender) conceptual and discursive social constructs when they themselves constitute the very ground we put our feet on in the first place? The shared proximity of these terms in language is, in other words, one of the first places essentialism links them together, suggesting that, as a result, heterosexuality, its genders, and its sexes (the naturalized bodies of its sexes) can be the only "natural" sexual arrangement. Rubin is clear: "It is this definitional fusion that I want to challenge" (Rubin, 1984: 308). This linkage, then, and its questioning under Rubin's scrutiny, sets up not only feminist work on sexuality but also the work of queer theory and the field of transgender activisms of the later 20th century: Is heterosexuality really the only natural sexual arrangement? Are all genders inherently heterosexualized? Indeed, are there really only just two sexes?

Finally, Rubin's essay concludes with a section called "The Limits of Feminism," which asks her second question: What are the limits of feminist theory in disarticulating or disaggregating that linkage? In this section, she suggests that if the social organization of sexuality is much more complex than what essentialism might tell us, to a certain extent, our conceptual frameworks must similarly be more complicated. Questioning how sophisticated our frameworks have been inside the context of second-wave feminism, she writes:

> Feminist conceptual tools were developed to detect and analyze gender-based hierarchies. To the extent that these overlap with erotic stratifications, feminist theory has some explanatory power. But as issues become less those of gender and more those of sexuality, feminist analysis becomes misleading and often irrelevant. Feminist thought simply lacks angles of vision which can fully encompass the social organization of sexuality. The criteria of relevance in feminist thought do not allow it to see or assess critical power relations in the area of sexuality (Rubin, 1984: 309).

In this passage, then, Rubin posits an analytical separation of gender and sexuality, a separation that has proven to be remarkably productive for shifting how we think about sex. Rubin does not abandon a feminist analysis of gender: "In the long run, feminism's critique of gender hierarchy must be incorporated into a radical theory of sex, and the critique of sexual oppression should enrich feminism," (Rubin, 1984: 309) but she certainly identifies the way that, at least in the early 1980s in North America, feminist conceptual frameworks subsumed sexuality under gender. That is, Rubin suggests that feminist thought could not see the way that sexuality was constructed separate from gender. Separating these by articulating them as two distinct systems of power is precisely what Rubin's new language seeks to explore. When these additional questions are added to the six beliefs outlined above, what emerges is a model for analyzing sexuality that has tremendous analytical precision.

THE NEW LANGUAGES OF SEX: THINKING THE HETERONORMATIVE

The concept of heteronormativity is useful to illustrate Rubin's analytical separation of sexuality and gender. The word "heteronormativity" refers to a belief and a set of cultural-institutional practices that enforce heterosexuality as the dominant, essential, and "natural" norm. Heteronormativity assumes heterosexuality in and through all social structures: institutions, family structures, legal systems, media, educational and knowledge structures and, like other systems that naturalize norms, it enforces this norm sometimes with good will (granting, for example, same-sex marriage to monogamous couples), and other times with violent hostility. The concept of compulsory heterosexuality circulated through the second wave of feminism in works such as Adrienne Rich's essay "Compulsory Heterosexuality and Lesbian Existence" (1983) and previously in the manifesto written by the Radicalesbian Collective, "Woman-Identified Woman" (1972). In these two examples, the notion of compulsory heterosexuality developed, in part as a response to homophobia within the feminist movement. Challenging the homophobic assumption inside of feminism that women have a "natural" orientation toward men, Rich, like her predecessors from the Radicalesbian Collective, used the notion of lesbian existence as a kind of desexualized subject position that was the ground zero of committed feminist practice. In particular, Rich posited that feminism might do well to understand that a wide range of experiences between women might be found across a lesbian continuum, all the more so given that in this continuum, "lesbian" is not reduced to nor defined by sexual (i.e., genital) contact between women. In fact, as a result of these desexualizations of "lesbian," expressions circulated within feminism celebrating the belief that "feminism is the theory, lesbianism is the practice."

Such an ironic "success" story is complex. On the one hand, that early second-wave feminist cultures addressed structural homophobia marked its continued commitments to the kind of internal self-reflection and examination flagged by the premise of *the personal is political*. But on the other hand, one might read such reconstructions of a long tradition of explicitly sexual relations between women as evidence not only of Judith Butler's argument that conceptual and definitional stability is somewhat of a myth, but also of Rubin's argument that "most systems of sexual judgment ... attempt to determine on which side of the line a particular acts falls [and that] only sex acts on the good side of the line are accorded moral complexity" (Rubin, 1984: 282). Clearly, within these early conceptualizations—those that actually pre-date the heated sex wars of the 1980s—no sex act was a good sex act. "Lesbian" served politics, not sexual desire, and as such was accorded a space higher up on the top of feminism's own "erotic pyramid" (Rubin, 1984: 279). By this account, Lisa Johnson's earlier measure of the contemporary pulse of sex in feminism has a long history.

Heterosexual vs. Heteronormative

Christine Overall, on the other hand, maps a slightly different deployment of the concept of heteronormativity. In her essay "Heterosexuality and Feminist Theory" Overall details how the emergence of the term "heteronormative" after Rubin's work signals a turn toward queer conceptual frameworks within not only feminist, but also gay and lesbian studies (Overall, 2005). Overall locates modern sexualities within what she argues are contradictory premises. Like many of the theorists discussed here, she is not particularly interested in resolving those contradictions, nor does she suggest that such resolution is possible. But she does suggest that what we understand to be self-evident categories of sexual subjects are instead, like any other taxonomy or categorical project, knowledge systems, the effects of institutionalized ways of knowing (medical, legal, literary, psychological, and so on). This essentializing taxonomy she's referencing—that we think we are constituted as sexual subjects with a gay essence or a straight essence—is instead power attempting to establish itself by articulating, or speaking through, and constructing knowable sexual subjects. She agrees with Rubin that sexuality is and remains one of the most meaning-intensive of all human and epistemological practices, whether or not we are conscious of these meanings. But like theorists Rubin, Foucault, and Jeffrey Weeks, Overall is suggesting that even though we think that sexuality is the most private aspect of our "selves," in fact, it is one of the most public and the most regulated socially, historically, and politically. For example, consider many of these questions that flag spaces of regulation around marriage: Who can marry? How many spouses can you have? Who are the "correct" objects of desire by what type of gendered subjects? Why are there laws and social implications regarding what we are supposed to do with which parts of our bodies and for what purposes? Can you legally trade those activities for money or services, should you choose to, in the same way you can choose to sell other types of labour in other parts of the economy?

Overall offers an interesting account of heteronormativity. She shares with the earlier work of Rich and the Radicalesbians an argument that within heteronormativity, heterosexuality is both compulsory and heavily regulated. There are, however, two paradoxes of heterosexuality that she teases out. First, like whiteness inside of white supremacies, heterosexuality is so pervasive that it is invisible in itself as a system and socially constructed structure. It is, she suggests, transparent (like plastic wrap) and present but all encompassing. Second, she notes the coexistence of both privilege and a constant process of self-policing. That is, while heterosexuality is constructed as a norm, it also requires constant hypervigilance to maintain that "norm." More often than not, such vigilance bespeaks a form of anxiety which, like that of whiteness, is obvious from an external gaze but isn't always obvious from inside the space of heteronormative identity itself.

However, such a structural unknowingness for practising heterosexuals can be crucial to working experiences of heterosexuality against systems of heteronormativity. It is in this very possibility of working the weakness inside the norm where Overall's work is quite different from the generation of feminists before her. Overall reminds us that categorically, heterosexuality is different from heteronormativity, which functions systemically as an institution. That is, she draws distinctions between heterosexuality and heteronormativity, arguing that for heteronormativity to work as effectively as it does, it must be embedded within systems of gender essentialism at the same time. In other words, gender essentialisms (the belief in a binary, essentialized sex) animates heteronormativity (the belief that heterosexuality is the natural sexuality). Unlike her predecessors, Overall makes distinctions between feminist critical practice and lesbian sexual practice so that she can ask a question similar to that posed by Lisa Johnson. Overall's primary question is: To what degree is feminist heterosexuality possible and what does it look like? By asking this question, she begins to generate for us a template of the answer to the "what to do?" question some of you might well be asking by now. Her answer: "To start to understand the institution of heterosexuality and the ideologies of heterosexism, is already to start to leave standard heterosexuality behind" (Overall, 2005: 369). The key word here is "standard." Overall continues, "For what is customarily meant by the ascription of heterosexuality is its unconscious 'perfectly natural' character" (Overall, 2005: 369). Resistance to compulsory heteronormativity, then, is not measured by assuming a subject position along a lesbian continuum. Instead, resistance is calibrated as disaffiliation with the institutionalization, regulation, and enforcement of heterosexuality as a naturalized norm, but also through its attendant articulations as dominant gender norms.

QUEERING HETERONORMATIVITIES, QUEERING GENDERS

As Rubin has already made clear, sexuality can be a difficult concept to define since it overlaps with the term "sex," which is another way of talking about the body or anatomy. But sexuality isn't reducible to, or definable as, anatomy, is it? Instead, it may well be helpful to define sexuality as the historical organization and regulation of desire and sexual practices into social identities that are constructed as if they emerge from nature; that is, as if they are natural. Within the terms of heteronormativity, sexuality (the way a culture organizes the exchange of desire and pleasure) is supposed to map onto gender (how one finds subjectivity in discourses of either masculinity or femininity), which then maps onto sex (whether one has a penis or vagina), all of which govern what one is supposed to do or be in those moments of sexual experience with another person. Those ideologies also tell us that sexuality and gender are supposed to be the same thing (that biological boys will desire biological girls, and the nature of their desires will be the same, for penetrative sex where the boy is on top and the girl is on the bottom) and that as far as gender is concerned, masculinity and femininity are also supposed to be at opposite ends of the same scale or continuum.

New ways of conceptualizing sexuality have been heavily influenced by Michel Foucault's *History of Sexuality* (1978). Foucault's text examines, in part, the increasing association of sexuality with a "real" self. He argues that this association is uniquely modern and Western and is the effect of scientific discourses of sex that allow and encourage scientists frenetically to gather more and more information about desire and "deviant" desire especially. In other words, he argues that the function of an increasing preoccupation with identifying deviance (code for non-reproductive sexuality) is imperative to establish a norm (usually bound to reproduction) so that norms are always relational, constructed, and dependent upon their other.

The Lived Messiness of Moral Panics: Kiss & Tell's *Drawing the Line*

Carole Vance, the editor of the volume of essays collected from the Barnard College conference, argues that for many women, sexuality and sexual experience has been characterized by the duality of pleasure and danger (hence the title of her collection of essays). In her introduction, she suggests that the overemphasis on danger can have the effect of impeding speech about sexual pleasure (Vance, 1983). Despite Vance's justifiable nervousness about the effect of an overvictimizing feminist discourse on the possibilities of sexual pleasure, the link for women between sexuality and danger must be seen as a real one. Sexual danger has been both psychological and physical for women. The extent to which both female children and adolescent girls have to repel male sexual invasions is considerable. Such an experience of sexuality as an uninvited intrusion influences social and psychological development as well as sexual development. The discussions around feminist sexuality in 1980s American second-wave feminism attempted to break the silence about the fact that an overwhelming number of women, from birth to death, have to constantly battle unwelcome sexual aggression. While these conversations about danger were important—both then and now—they nevertheless frequently employed a rhetoric of danger, and sidestepped the complex questions of how women, particularly heterosexual women, were to negotiate pleasure itself. This is not at all to suggest that same-sex desire is "easy" to negotiate; certainly lesbian culture flourished among and despite a hostile and homophobic culture, which also existed inside feminism. However, third-wave American feminism brought attention to the idea that the identity category of heterosexual feminist was uncertain about how to negotiate and articulate sexual pleasure.

The sex wars ended in a kind of truce and with a shared recognition that this war was actually a kind of moral panic, characterized by deep-rooted and difficult-to-resolve social anxieties about where to draw feminist lines around "appropriate" sexual practice, with what kinds of authority, and for whom. The sex wars in Canada emerged later than in the USA, although these debates resonated in Canadian feminist discourse. There are now discernable trends in Canada, centred in Toronto and Vancouver, associated with a very popular lesbian photography exhibition titled *Drawing the Line* by the collaborative artists who make up the Canadian performance troupe Kiss & Tell (Lizard Jones, Persimmon Blackridge, and Susan Stewart). What begins to transform these debates from private conversations into public countercultures was the artistic reworking of these conversations, as this group of artists responded with what has to be one of the most conceptually sophisticated art installations in Canadian queer and lesbian art history.

Drawing the Line was an interactive photography show that represented lesbian sex practices. Touring across Canada, the United States, and Australia, the exhibition involved two distinct elements. First, *Drawing the Line* was a collection of between 75 to 100 photographs arranged in a linear fashion upon the walls of the viewing space, usually a public art gallery. The first photograph shows two women sitting in a restaurant holding hands while the final image in the installation shows two women engaged in very graphic scenes of S/M sex play. Second, viewers were invited to literally draw lines and comment directly about the wall on their own limitations in terms of where they would personally draw lines on "appropriate" sexual practice. Invariably, viewers would comment not only on the images but also about other viewer's comments. The result was a collaborative restaging of the sex wars as an interactive art exhibition and public "conversation," not at all unlike graffiti on the walls of public bathrooms.

The photographs in the initial installations, as well as in the subsequent postcard book (1991), focus on sites of contestation and controversy. The same two white models are used in the photographs so that the focus is on what they are doing rather than on their identities. The images code for a very precise viewing audience. Historically specific signifiers that mark contested lesbian sex and identities are manipulated as props by the photographer to be deliberately provocative. For example, images in the beginning of the postcard book play with the imagery of butch-femme, a lesbian sexual system that is signified through gender-specific clothing, motorcycles, leather jackets, black stockings, and high-heels. Other images explore different types of sexual play: sex play with food, two women having sex in nature, women holding each other, and models ripping at clothing with obvious aggression. A selection of images are designed to be explicitly provocative: Some depict sex among Christian iconography, some look as though women paint each other with what could be menstrual blood, and others take place in public places like bathroom stalls. These are many of the same issues that were under intense debate throughout the sex wars of the 1980s and early 1990s and those debates are referred to and elaborated upon on the back of each postcard in the book. Comments from the many locations where the exhibition toured are included on the back of particular images and range from a celebration of each image to a critique of its premises.

What's particularly interesting about this interactive process, though, is that the photographs themselves are similarly transformed. That is, not only do the photographs produce a particular version of reality, but they also become inscribed by and, in turn, document competing and contradictory versions of reality in that archive. The artists describe this process in their artist statement:

> Reading the reactions to our photographs has been amazing. Not only do people see them as reality, but they seem to see their own reactions as the only reality. One woman wrote that she loved the tenderness in the photos, and another woman asked why there was no tenderness in any of them. And what brings up the most feelings for someone begins to overtake the rest of the show. One woman interviewer asked us why half the pictures were of sadomasochism, when ten out of the seventy-five pictures had s/m content (Kiss & Tell, 1991).

What this suggests is that photographs do not merely "represent" an objective reality that is presumed to exist "out there"; instead, the meanings attributed to the photographs are produced when the image is consumed by the viewer. *Drawing the Line* staged this crisis around the self-evidence of truth at a time when battles were being waged over the authenticity and veracity of such truths inside of feminism.

Perhaps no other set of images generates a fiercer response than those generated by images of penetration and sadomasochism. Sadomasochism is, as Vance acknowledged in her introduction to *Pleasure and Danger* (1984), one of the "big three" issues of the American sex wars, along with pornography and butch-femme sexualities. Many of the photographs deliberately provoked the viewer by depicting these three precise practices. Roped models, scenes of aggression, chains, whips, leather paraphernalia, bondage: these are put on public display through the photographs and the response to these images mirrors the kinds of debates occurring across communities both in public and in private. Particularly interesting are the depictions of penetration that are featured in many of the images of sadomasochism. One photograph shows a latex gloved hand inside the vagina of a woman on her back, depicting the sexual practice known as "fisting," which was fiercely contested and debated as a sexual practice. One comment from San Francisco is relevant: "I don't want to get sucked in by our increasingly violent and emotionally separated society. I want the opposite and I think that photos like this confirm male society's vision of the world." A year earlier, the Vancouver lesbian magazine *Diversity* used as its cover a pencil drawing of a similarly latex-gloved hand, and this generated the same fierce debate (Vol. 3[1], 1990). The cover advertised an article by Patrick Califia called "Fisting: The Ins and Outs," especially commissioned for *Diversity*. From the vantage point of the 21st century, it is tempting to dismiss such contestations, but they are tellingly indicative of the way that sexual practice—in this case, penetration and its connotations—remains an historically constructed measure of conservative moral panics inside lesbian contexts.

It is no surprise that lesbian artists like Kiss & Tell responded to that moral panic with a tenacious refusal of its frame of reference and through strategies of defiance. By wielding the camera for a very specific audience and debate, Kiss & Tell troubled the imagined realism and self-evidence of bodies, desires, and genders. Even though their photographs were staged with the same two white models and regardless of how well known that fact may be, the images staged and then put into crisis a tradition of realism associated with the photograph. The 1990 artist talk by Kiss & Tell detailed the power of contesting realism as a representational form:

> A photo is seen as "fact," as objective reality. No matter how many times we are reminded that photos can be set up, that the photographer manipulates the camera and the film, that where the photo is cropped can change its entire meaning, when we look at the photographs we react to the content of them as though the photographer wasn't there. The camera becomes a so-called objective window on "reality" ... an image can effect reality, but it is not reality, or even a picture of reality at the time it was taken. These photos are deliberately constructed, with particular aims in mind (Kiss & Tell, 1990).

As a result of problematizing that realism, the second part of the exhibition became all the more significant, where audience members were asked to draw lines directly on the walls marking the limits around their own comfort with the images and were then invited to leave comments around the photographs themselves. As a result, the end product of the show looked radically different than it did on opening night. It became an archive of not only public sexual discourse, but also of the queered public scenes of supposedly "private" sexual fantasy (Cvetkovich, 2003). This refusal of privacy was key and suggested that crises in definitions, as well as a refusal of normative sexual discourse, mark the formation of queer cultures through activist as well as artistic responses to heteronormativity. The end product of the installation, as epitomized in the final postcard in the book, certainly visualized that unusual archive. In the photograph, a woman kneels below a set of images arranged along a long wall, surrounded literally by the debates, voices in conversation with each other in a very public and defiant way.

What this artistic response to a feminist moral panic accomplished was the politicization of individual sexual practices. The sex wars revealed that the ground upon which feminist social movements had been built—in this case, assumptions about a shared set of sexual practices and values referenced by the category "Woman" and "feminist"—were extremely problematic and nowhere near obvious. As the quote from Lisa Johnson at the beginning of this chapter notes, one of the longer-lasting effects of the sex wars was the pitting of sexual pleasure against sexual danger. The result has been yet another set of contradictions and silences about sexuality that have been taken up by the next generation of feminists.

QUEERING NO MAN'S LAND: GENDERS NOT GENITALS?

Queering Gender

If "drawing the line" became a metaphor and touchstone for acrimony around sexuality, then the tensions and contradictions taken up by the next generation can similarly be summed up by another very successful collaborative artistic collective. Taste This is made up of four young queer and transgender artists, poets, musicians and performance artists: Anna Camilleri, Ivan E. Coyote, Zoë Eakle, and Lyndell Montgomery. Their book *Boys Like Her: Transfictions* (1998), was published to remarkable success in Canada and the US, and the contradictions of its title and authors tell us much about the legacies of the sex wars in the latter half of the 20th century. Like the photographs from *Drawing the Line*, the spoken-word, narrative, performance, and photographic texts that make up the collection *Boys Like Her* depict a complexly gendered landscape that includes a wide range of genders, from (but not limited to) gay, lesbian, butch, femme, and everything in between. That is, each of the identities and performance pieces forces us to address a set of ignorances about women, men, and sexuality, and about the many links that linger between and among them. These texts will defamiliarize or dissemble gender (making it something we become ignorant about) only to re-produce or re-distribute it on bodies where we least expect to see it, so that perhaps we can learn to see sex and gender quite differently.

This material is aimed precisely at the contradiction flagged for us by the central premises of feminist theory, that sex and gender are not the same thing. "Sex," in terms of the raw material of bodies, is not necessarily sexuality. Feminism posited the notion of the *sex/gender system*, where *sex* is supposedly the raw materials of the body and *gender* is the cultural role or script for that body, and that the sex/gender system itself was the set of socio-cultural and political arrangements whereby sex was transformed into gender. Taste This and other recent rethinkings of gender, sex, and sexuality call this into question, asking if this is true. Why must particular body types always line up neatly with the correct role or script for that body? In other words, if identification really is one of the key mechanisms that produces identity, why couldn't girl bodies identify with masculinity and sexual aggression and boy bodies identify with feminine subject positions?

The "trans fictions" of *Boys Like Her*, through performance, photography, and spoken word, depict the complications of gender working against heteronormativity in thoroughly, well, *queer* ways. One of the most interesting theoretical moments to emerge after the sex wars and through the work of early queer theorists like Judith Butler, Eve Kosofsky Sedgwick, Teresa de Lauretis, Michael Warner, and Diana Fuss was the emergence and possibilities of queer identifications. Deliberately troubling a relationship with the identity politics signalled by "gay and lesbian," the emergence of queer theory had as part of its original deployment a wilful separation from what was being described as a kind of assimilationalist politics. The feminist sex wars described earlier were waged over the kinds of beliefs associated with a conservative gay and lesbian identity politic: That all feminists will share a sexual practice; that all lesbians will practise the same kind of sexual activities; that, on the level of human rights, all gay and lesbian folks have the same kind of monogamous relationships as heterosexual folks and so should be able to get married. These kinds of assumptions about sexual practice, about gender norms, or about the importance of state recognition of same-sex marriage were deeply embroiled in debate inside gay and lesbian communities. So too were the politics of racism, of bisexuality, of cross-dressing, of butch-femme erotic systems, and of gay bathhouses and other public sex activities, as Rubin quite clearly indicates in her essay. The term "queer" emerges in the late 1980s to contest those gay and lesbian politics that were built upon assimilating value systems seen as antagonistic to radical sexual communities.

But as an anti-assimilationist banner, the term "queer" also emerges side by side with its function as an insult or homophobic slur. As Judith Butler (1997) indicates, the reclamation of the word "queer" as a name of self-identification opens up the possibility for a counter-speech, a way of talking back to the space and intention of the insult to deflect its force. She writes, "The revaluation of terms such as 'queer' suggests that speech can be 'returned' to its speaker in a different form, that it can be cited against its originary purposes, and perform a reversal of effects" (Butler, 1997: 14). The reversal around the word "queer" was significant for two reasons. First, as Butler suggests, it forces an interruption of the linkage between words, harms, and social space. By mapping a different space—one aggressively fighting against heteronormativity—it redefines the word "queer" as a space of defiance, of tenacity, of resistance. But second, it also refuses the shaming of particular practices *inside* gay and lesbian communities, suggesting that queer communities include those not so neatly mapped onto assimilationist, monogamous, or non-BDSM (bondage, domination, and sadomasochism) gay and lesbian identities. The emergence of "queer," then, is already in conversation both with heteronormativity and with what we might think of as homonormativity, those politics focused within gay and lesbian movements and cultures on the family and reproduction as the means by which citizenship and rights are secured (Murphy, Ruiz, and Serlin, 2008). Even though the term "queer" is relatively recent as a term marking something as outside the range of "normal" in terms of sexuality, it does have a complex gay and lesbian history that is worth detailing.

Queer is evocative of strangeness; but it also has functioned as an insult, a tool of shaming inside heteronormativity. In queer contexts—as in Queer Theory—the term is not at all meant to be synonymous with "gay, lesbian, bisexual, transgender." De Lauretis elaborates on this in the infamous *Differences* issue where she launched a deployment of queer in the early 1990s:

> the term "Queer Theory" was arrived at in the effort to avoid all of these fine distinctions in our discursive protocols, not to adhere to any one of the given terms, not to assume their ideological liabilities, but instead to both transgress and transcend them—or at the very least problematize them (1991: v).

Yet the term still resonates as synonymous with gay and lesbian spaces, adheres to its currency as a noun, a thing, and as a space decidedly gay rather than as a space of difference, oddity, or strangeness. For instance, in the final seasons of Showcase's infamous television series *Queer as Folk*, the main character, Brian, has a face-to-face debate about gay marriage with his friend Michael during their bike trip to Canada, where gay marriage has been legalized. Michael, who ends up marrying his boyfriend Ben while in Canada, argues for the right to step into gay marriage while Brian argues vehemently against it, claiming "we're queers; we don't get married." In this sense, the term is being used in opposition to all things normative (as seen in the folk expression from which the title of the show originates—"ain't nothing queer as folk") or, as a particular behaviour just attributable to the unpredictable strangeness of people (interview with the cast of *Queer as Folk*). This usage is very much in keeping with what De Lauretis (1991) has mapped, in which the term is not necessarily reducible only to gay identities, but to strangeness and difference in general.

But while queer is supposed to function in excess of the equation "gayandlesbian" and its ideological liabilities, the spaces it marks have just as often been subject to lesbian and feminist critiques at the same time (De Lauretis, 1991). For instance, Ruth Goldman suggests that many lesbian feminists have resisted the term because of the degree to which it erases gender and, by doing so, risks reducing an analysis of gender-based oppression to one of sexuality instead (Goldman, 1996: 171). Curiously, though, not all feminist theorists resist the term and this is where the waters become productively murky. Transnational feminist theorist Gloria Anzaldúa, for example, embraced the political anti-racist space marked by "queer" in a way decidedly unmarked by "lesbian": the latter, she argues, marks distinct Anglo-European roots and associations while the former appears as a positioning in many cultures even if the word does not (Anzaldúa, 1991). Still, though, Anzaldúa herself was cautious about any word that functions as a monolithic imperative: "Queer is used as a false unifying umbrella which all 'queers' of all races, ethnicities and classes are shoved under. At times we need this umbrella to solidify our ranks against outsiders. But even when we seek shelter under it we must not forget that it homogenizes, erase our differences" (Anzaldúa, 1991: 251).

Third-wave theorist Astrid Henry marks a potential new deployment of the term queer. In her book, *Not My Mother's Sister: Generational Conflict and Third-Wave Feminism*, Henry argues that the use of the term queer in feminist contexts marks a shift from second- to third-wave feminism. In a chapter provocatively called "Neither My Mother Nor My Lover," Henry engages in a critique of the book *Jane Sexes It Up*, writing: "While 'queer' is not always deployed to mark a generational changing of the guard in the manner intended by the third wave, many self-described queer writers have used the term precisely in order to mark a generational shift that identifies them as distinct from the lesbians and gay men who came of age in the 1970s and 1980s" (Henry, 2004: 116).

While there is often a great deal of productive debate and disagreement around the term "queer"—does it map neatly onto gay and lesbian spaces or does it mark anti-normative spaces outside of those contexts?—these tensions remind us that a word like "queer" itself embodies a multiplicity of meanings and traces of its past usages. For example, queer theorist Calvin Thomas (2000) works to queer heterosexuality, suggesting further strategic uses of the term queer beyond gay and lesbian. Thomas argues that one of the productive things about detaching "queer" from an exclusive gay and lesbian subject position is that it can also mark spaces inside of heteronormativity that resist what he calls the regimes of the normal, so heterosexuality itself can, in fact, be queered. Such queerings can be part of anti-heteronormative practices among heterosexual practices, realizing Overall's vision that was out of the reach of Rich and the Radicalesbians: a radical instability inside of heteronormativity. Working the weaknesses of the hetero-normative system makes queering heterosexuality part of a culture of resistance. Deploying feminist resistance against heteronormative structures doesn't mean collaps-ing all sexual resistances into a lesbian continuum; it means, among other things, queering normative gender essentialisms themselves.

This "troubling" of normative gender essentialisms is precisely what the performance troupe Taste This accomplishes in both their book and their performances. *Boys Like Her* is itself a multi-generic text. Working with first-person narratives, performance pieces, auto-biographical narrative, story-telling, and (most importantly) realist photography, the book works against the rules of genre in the same way it works against the rules of gender essen-tialism. Two of the performers, Ivan and Lyndell, identify as transgender, which means they identify with gender identities outside of those that are supposed to map onto their bio-logical bodies. Taking up identities of boy, female masculinity, butch, and female-to-male trans boy all at the same time creates a permanent rupture between our beliefs that one's genitals cause one's gender, creating what we might begin to think of as a kind of "no man's land" between sexes and genders, and also between sexualities. Ivan, for instance, muses in one piece about his memories of himself as a young girl refusing to wear a bathing suit top as "girls" were supposed to (Taste This, 1998: 20–24). The photographs that accompany the text are especially compelling. One photograph, for example, depicts Ivan from the waist up, without his shirt, his face chiseled, lean, and masculine looking, while two black and white photographs that follow show Ivan with breasts in one frame and with his hands covering his breasts in the next frame. The incongruity between the nar-rative, the masculinity, and the breasts visually depicts the gender incoherence that the use of the pronoun "he" performs. There is, in other words, a profound tension between a dis-cernable gender in the photographs (masculine) and the body that this gender appears on (female), despite the presence of breasts. Again, Taste This and its photographers are using the same tradition of realist photography that Kiss & Tell used, only where the latter used realism to stage sexual scenarios, the former use the photograph to stage gender incoherence. What category can we put Ivan into? Which pronoun would we use? If we can stabilize nei-ther a sex nor a gender pronoun or identification, how might we possibly stabilize or secure what we might call a sexual orientation? Don't most of our available sexual orientations—gay and lesbian as well as heteronormative systems—depend upon a categorical coherence around sex? Are we not also seeing in this photograph, as well as in the accompanying text, an example of Rubin's rupture between sexuality and gender? Certainly, sex, sexuality, and gender flourish quite beautifully throughout *Boys Like Her*; but neither can be fully reduced to the other as a way to secure meanings.

In fact, the very title of this book itself plays on these indeterminacies. We can read the title suggesting either that "boys look like her" or "boys desire her," where the "her" is the central figure of the cover image, queer femme writer and performance artist Anna Camilleri, who presents as female. In this sense, gender is part of desire in a heterogendered sense (where gender difference constitutes part of the erotic practice) but not necessarily in a heteronormative way. That is, heterosexuality is neither assumed nor practised even though a queer form of gender difference exists. But the title also wants us to see *boys that look like her*, that is, *they look like they might be female* (the photograph of Ivan), *may well not be female at all*. How might such a contradiction exist if the economies of gender essentialism (that one's genitals correlate to or are productive of one's gender) are true? The contradiction is telling us that there are more than two sexes and genders. To a large degree, then, *Boys Like Her* and its creators, queer or trouble that which heteronormative structures depend upon for their stability: a binary sex system.

Queering Femininity

A new development in rethinking feminist sex in the 21st century is the concept of queer femininity. The work of Toronto-based feminist performance artist Anna Camilleri takes centre stage in *Boys Like Her* as she depicts and performs the struggles of queer femininity, rendered invisible inside both lesbian communities, marked by female masculinity, and heteronormativity, in which all femininity is presumed to be signalling an attraction to masculinity. In particular, one of her pieces from the collection, "Super Hero," generates a fair bit of controversy whenever it is read or performed on university campuses, in theatres, or in performance spaces. "Super Hero" is a short, fantasy-based narrative that explores a late-night fantasy created by a young woman who is unable to sleep. In her fantasy, the main character recalls a moment walking home from work, quite late at night. She is followed by a van and then approached by a man named Dick. In her fantasy, she refuses Dick's attention, but when he persists, she changes her mind and invites him home. While he is expecting sex from her, she catches him in a vulnerable moment, hog-ties him, threatens him, removes his clothes, eventually unties him, tapes his keys to his back, and sends him out into the cold dark night to fend for himself.

The controversial questions raised by this story about both sex and aggression spur a great deal of debate. This piece brings to the foreground particular strategies of resisting heteronormativity and also raises questions about the role of representation and feminist cultural production. If representation plays a crucial role in constructing sex and gender, then can it play an equally crucial role in de-constructing them as well? If so, what happens if women in feminist and queer cultures respond to actual violence and aggression in their daily lives with symbolic violence in and through representation?

A good example of symbolic violence is evident in the work of feminist film theorist Laura Mulvey on the female gaze (1988). Mulvey posits that active looking is masculine while passive receipt of the male gaze is feminine, which is to say, the male active gaze is directed at the feminine spectacle, denying an active gaze to the female. The male gaze, or what we could think of as *looking,* can be regarded in two ways: first, as one of the ways that power works in our culture; and second, as a primary site through which gender is constructed. The gaze, or something as simple as just looking, already does a kind of act of violence to women. Many women can attest to how it might feel objectifying and somehow violent to be aggressively stared at by men, and people of colour will tell exactly the same thing about being looked at by white people. There is power in looking, especially when those looks reveal larger power and privilege structures. This begins to formulate a significant question: How is it possible for women and women's cultural work to resist this controlling aspect of the gaze if women are always already rendered object by that same gaze? Keeping these looking relations in mind, what can happen when those who are accustomed to being watched control what is being consumed from inside a position of being looked at? In other words, if women are burdened with the knowledge of always being looked at, then can women respond to that gaze with aggression to force it to look away? This is the question that a story like "Super Hero" is attempting to answer.

Women are caught in representational binds, especially when it comes to something as controversial as sexual aggression. When women are overly sexual, we shudder in horror; when they are virginal, they are reinforcing the conservative belief that good girls aren't sexual. If women are victims, then feminism certainly has agitated for a political response to cultures of rape, domestic violence, and aggression. If women respond to their victimization with what might be perceived as violent rage, however, it is regarded as inappropriate. Why might rage be seen as an inappropriate response to male and/or racist violence? This question and subsequent argument does not advocate "actual" violence in any simple sense, but it does seek to theorize a space of "imagined" violence, a violence or rage that is a political space opened up by representation in art, poetry, narrative, film, and television shows, an unsanctioned symbolic violence committed by subordinate groups upon those deemed more powerful by our culture's distribution of power. It's my argument here that works like "Super Hero" find their representational power in showing "in/appropriate" third-wave feminist subjects, women who step into behaviours and fantasies that are dubbed inappropriate, that is, not authorized by either feminism or mainstream cultures.

Female violence and female sexual aggression have the effect of transforming the symbolic function of the feminine within popular culture. They challenge the linking of power and force with masculinity, and victimization and passivity with femininity. These pieces are not advocating actual violent responses, but certainly they allow imagining the possibilities of fighting violence with violence. Women and men equally have much to gain from new and different configurations of violence, terror, and fantasy. Of course, the big question here for feminism is what happens when we make imagined violence or violent fantasy? One answer might be that these texts create a great deal of anxiety, in men and women alike, about women and power—anxiety that can be redirected toward challenging constructions of women as victims through aggression and hyperbolic manipulation or habitation of the terms used to insult women, such as bitch, slut, etc.

Mainstream popular culture has been preoccupied with female aggression for some time now. The 1991 film *Thelma and Louise*, directed by Ridley Scott, created an unprecedented wave of discussion around the issue of female revenge fantasy and the unusual role reversal involving female avengers. One scene in *Thelma and Louise* is worth looking at in some detail. After being annoyed by the trucker who makes obscene gestures to them on the road, the two main characters lure him off the road for a confrontation. Once off the road, and with the trucker thinking he's about to have sex with both of them, Thelma and Louise tell him his behaviour has been offensive and insist that he apologize. When he refuses, Louise takes her gun and shoots out the tires on his truck. Of course, this aggravates the trucker and the situation until Thelma and Louise fire their guns at his truck until it explodes. They then drive circles around the trucker, whose hat comes off while he is calling them "bitches from hell." During one of those circles, Thelma reaches down, picks up his hat, and they drive off with their trophy.

This preoccupation in pop culture with women as aggressive might be something that we understand as a figure of the female warrior or, to return to Taste This's Anna Camilleri, the female superhero. There is no shortage of examples of what we could call "girls with guns." In recent memory: Jodie Foster's *Panic Room*; Ashley Judd in *High Crimes*; Angelina Jolie in the *Lara Croft* series; Sandra Bullock in *Murder by Numbers*; *Charlie's Angels*; Jennifer Lopez's *Enough*; all of the *Alien* films; Linda Hamilton in *Terminator*; Uma Thurman in *Kill Bill*, and characters on television shows such as Scully in *X-Files*, Jennifer Garner in *Alias*; *Nikita*; *Buffy*—the list goes on. Hollywood's depictions of women seem to be shifting. At the very least, audiences seem far more sophisticated at the beginning of the 21st century, in large part due to the successes of feminism.

If that is the case, however, how can a music video network like the American MTV think audiences aren't up for the supposed violence in Madonna's video "What It Feels Like for a Girl"? This highly stylized video, produced by the singer's husband, Guy Ritchie, features Madonna as a polished-looking rebel in a black, skin-tight bodysuit and high heels, sporting a variety of identification cards, weapons, and so forth. Her character is set up as a kind of "spin" on the quintessential James Bond character. As the video opens, she is seen taking a very old woman out of a nursing home called "Ole Kuntz," and leaving in a hyped-up Camero. From there the two women drive around and eat at fast food drive-through windows. While driving, Madonna's character engages in a number of activities considered violent; she robs a businessman at an ATM using a stun gun, drives the car at a group of young men playing hockey, engages in a high-speed chase with two police officers after pointing and firing a water pistol at them, and lures a group of young men in a car into a chase that ends with their crashing. In the final scene, the car is driven in slow-motion violently into a pole. Since the video is the visualization of the song, "What It Feels Like for a Girl," the irony is that, according to the video, to be a girl means to move through that world of pleasure and danger with a cold, stylized, and indifferent aggressivity.

Madonna's video was banned on MTV in the USA and Canada's MUCH MUSIC followed suit. Eventually, MUCH MUSIC started airing the video quite late at night and ensured that it was followed by panels on violence, spots for a distress line, and interviews with academics about violence in the media. The ironic thing about this media event is that there is not one single image of blood, no depictions of actual violence in the video, but rather, the suggestion of violence. The camera, for instance, follows Madonna's character as she approaches a man at the bank machine; then in the next scene, she is walking away while the man is in a heap on the ground behind her. We do not see what happens between these two shots where, presumably, she attacks him with her weapon.

Why, then, was this censored by MTV and MUCH MUSIC? Revenge fantasies involving women have evolved since the time of *Thelma and Louise*, where the revenge occurs directly against men who have committed assaults against women. In Madonna's video, the revenge takes place against random groups of men—businessmen, guys playing hockey, the police. What is it that these men might have in common? Given that Madonna's character rescues an aging woman from a nursing home named with a differently spelled version of the phrase "old cunts," could it be that part of the very cold rage here is directed at anonymous groups of men for the way that girls and women are rendered no longer valuable if they age or become, by cultural standards, "unattractive"? "What It Feels Like for a

Girl" is a very stylized depiction of female aggression, in which the main character shows absolutely no emotion about what she is doing. There is neither joy nor recognizable rage, merely calculated indifference. It is conceivable that this video is a response to an earlier wave of Hollywood movies like *Thelma and Louise*, arguing that acts of female violence do not need to be crimes of passion in which women defend themselves from places of rage. What might it feel like to be a girl of whatever age in the third wave? Ironic indifference but active revenge seems to be Madonna's answer.

If a woman did identify with aggression and fantasies of revenge, why is it increasingly difficult in our culture to couple femininity and toughness? Popular culture theorist Sherrie Innes argues that unlike toughness for men, toughness for this new woman breaks down into four parts: first, toughness in body (the buffed body); second, attitude (displaying little or no fear, or if she does, it does not prevent her from getting the job done and showing appropriate amounts of anger); third, action (which is intelligent action, picking the right moment); and finally, having authority (acting with power) (Innes, 1998). The new tough woman, Innes argues, is somewhat of a paradox; she contests gender norms but she also has the ability to confirm and reaffirm them. Our question should always be, then: Does the development of this new tough woman offer women an image of power and strength or does she work to support and uphold the gender status quo?

Again, to return to the collection *Boys Like Her*, Anna Camilleri's "Super Hero" is an important depiction of the new tough woman. The Anna character ups the stakes on these earlier depictions of aggression in her fantasy. If gender is a social identification, as the work of social constructionism makes clear, then what we see in contemporary instances of engendering is a series of code crossing, or mixing, or queering. In "Super Hero," the figure of the "ball-busting bitch" is queered, twisted, transformed. Again, using the term "queer" in this context does not suggest that it functions as another way to say "gay and/or lesbian." Instead, it means to talk about that which is odd, different, set apart from the norm. Using it as a verb brings to the foreground its tactics as a strategy that batters against the normative gender essentialisms. The character Anna in the story is quite different from her transgendered counterparts in the group Taste This. Seemingly "normal" in her gender, she responds to "normalized" gender expectations with something of a sucker punch; that is, she occupies "normality abnormally" (Duggan and McHugh, 2002: 108). This is another way of describing queering strategies—to occupy the space of "normal" quite queerly so as to work that norm against the outcomes it hopes to achieve. These are women who are not shamed by controlling terms like "slut" or "bitch" but inhabit them to turn them against the way they are used to contain women in the same way that the word "queer" is reclaimed to refuse heteronormative enforcements of sexuality.

It is precisely that kind of refusal that "Super Hero" takes up. It not only situates a line of continuity between women who might find themselves travelling alone at night, but also attempts to reflect a male, heteronormative gaze back upon itself with dramatic narrative and symbolically violent effects. That is, the story is very ambiguous in its sexual categories but also in its desires; it is, after all, a fantasy even, perhaps, a sexual fantasy. The femme subject of "Super Hero" deliberately plays on the spaces between categories; she is neither lesbian nor heterosexual. Establishing the narrative frame in the opening, she reminds us that the entire scene that is about to unfold is a fantasy. "She" cannot be known and hence cannot be contained in either heteronormative or gender essentialist categories. "Her" articulations exist in narrative levels and in both sexual subjectivities (that is, both lesbian femme and heterosexual femme fatale simultaneously). It is precisely her control of what is intelligible or knowable for the male character known as Dick that allows the narrative to unfold the way it does. In other words, to be like these examples of violent femmes and queer feminists in "Super Hero" is to be both inside hegemonic systems (scripts of femininity) but re-articulating their heteronormativities against themselves.

To a certain degree, "Super Hero" brings us back to the questions raised by the quotation at the beginning of this chapter. What is the ground of knowledge that we think we have about gender? And how do we practise and measure resistance to these structures? The texts under consideration here, both mainstream and counter-cultural, all gesture toward one strategy that can exist among many others: resistance through the queering of gender norms as strategy of opposition. These have been just one small series of examples where we see something that we might dub genders without genitals (Jones, 2003).

CONCLUSION

Based on this cursory glance at pop culture, coupled with a number of the significant writings from third-wave feminism and from feminist, queer, and trans cultural production, it is clear that sexuality does not easily relinquish its erotic, imaginary, and/or symbolic ties to gender. Nor do we expect it to. Sexuality theorist Gayle Rubin shows that we need to think outside of causal explanatory models for relating sexuality to gender. Lisa Johnson takes up where Rubin left off and shows that even though women have far more sexual possibility now than ever before, we still live in a rape culture and as such we continue to need a feminist critique and a social justice, anti-racist politic. Even though sexualized women are still stigmatized (as much by internalized shame as by external sex-negative forces), we continue to need a strong, anti-essentialist critique with which to battle homophobia and transphobia. Even though we might agree that eroticizing different images is important (even if we have no idea how to get there), feminism's sexual politic has generated two related things: A grinding impasse given feminism's conflicts with itself around sexual politics; and a profound need for much more complex conceptual frameworks to theorize such impasses and the lived, sometimes contradictory messiness they generate (Johnson, 2002: 314). If we cannot shake the articulation of sexuality and gender, and if the sex wars produced an impasse over the nature of feminist sexual practice, then perhaps the nature of the questions themselves need to be rearticulated. Our feminisms badly need answers to the questions: What is female? What is the nature of female sexuality? What does a real feminist do in bed? We may realize that our questions themselves need to be rethought in order to find different answers.

Discussion Questions

1. By what means did you come to understand that you were a gender? What roles did your family, culture, community, or education play in helping you produce your gender identity? Why do we continue to assume that we can tell what another person's sexual orientation is by how they perform their gender identities?

2. At what point should artists and their work be censored for "inappropriate" content? Who should decide what "inappropriate" might mean? How might very diverse communities agree on such definitions?

3. What role does the state or Canadian government play in setting the limits of what any community might establish as "appropriate" sexual representation?

Bibliography

Anzaldúa, Gloria. 1991. To(o) queer the writer: Loca, escrita y chicana, in *InVersions: Writings by dykes, queers and lesbians,* ed. Betsy Warland, 249–263. Vancouver: Press Gang.

Butler, Judith. 1990. *Gender trouble: Feminism and the subversion of identity.* New York and London: Routledge, Chapman and Hall.

Butler, Judith. 1993. *Bodies that matter: On the discursive limits of "sex."* New York and London: Routledge.

Butler, Judith, 1997. *Excitable speech: A politics of the performative.* New York: Routledge.

Butler, Judith. 2004. *Undoing gender.* New York and London: Routledge.

Camilleri, Anna. 1998. Super hero, in *Boys like her: Transfictions,* ed. Taste This (Anna Camilleri, Ivan E. Coyote, Zoë Eakle, and Lyndell Montgomery), 130–135. Vancouver: Press Gang.

Cvetkovich, Ann. 2003. *An archive of feelings: Trauma, sexuality and lesbian public cultures.* Durham, NC: Duke Univ. Press.

De Lauretis, Teresa. 1991. Queer theory: Lesbian and gay sexualities. An introduction. *Differences: A Journal of Feminist Cultural Studies* 3(2): iii–xviii.

Duggan, Lisa, and Kathleen McHugh. 2002. A fem(me)inist manifesto, in *Brazen femme: Queering femininity,* eds. Chloë Brushwood Rose and Anna Camilleri, 165–170. Vancouver: Arsenal Pulp Press.

Foucault, Michel. 1978. *The history of sexuality. Volume 1: An introduction,* tr. Robert Hurley. New York: Random House.

Fuss, Diana, ed. 1991. *Inside/out: Lesbian theories, gay theories.* New York and London: Routledge.

Goldman, Ruth. 1996. Who is that *queer* queer? Exploring norms around sexuality, race, and class in queer theory, in *Queer studies: A lesbian, gay, bisexual and transgender anthology,* eds. Brett Beemyn and Mickey Eliason, 169–182. New York: New York Univ. Press.

Henry, Astrid. 2004. *Not my mother's sister: Generational conflict and third wave feminism.* Indianapolis: Indiana Univ. Press.

Innes, Sherrie. 1998. *Tough girls: Women warriors and wonder women in popular culture.* Philadelphia: Univ. of Pennsylvania Press.

Johnson, Merri Lisa, ed. 2002. *Jane sexes it up: True confessions of feminist desire.* New York: Four Walls Eight Windows.

Jones, Jordy. 2003. Hedwig's six inches: Gender without genitals. Other: Pop culture and politics for the new outcasts. June. **www.othermag.org/content/hedwig.php**. Accessed March 17, 2007.

Kiss & Tell. (Lizard Jones, Persimmon Blackridge, and Susan Stewart). 1990. Artist statement. *Diversity* 3(3/4).

Kiss & Tell. (Lizard Jones, Persimmon Blackridge, and Susan Stewart). 1991. *Drawing the line: Lesbian sexual politics on the wall.* Vancouver: Press Gang.

Kiss & Tell. (Lizard Jones, Persimmon Blackridge, and Susan Stewart). 1994. *Her tongue on my theory: Images, essays and fantasies*. Vancouver: Press Gang.

Mulvey, Laura. 1988. Visual pleasure and narrative cinema, in *Visual and Other Pleasures*. Bloomington: Indiana Univ. Press.

Murphy, Kevin P., Jason Ruiz, and David Serlin. 2008. Editors' introduction. Special issue: Queer futures. *Radical History Review*. Issue 100 (Winter): 1–9.

Overall, Christine. 2005. Heterosexuality and feminist theory, in *Open boundaries. A Canadian women's studies reader,* 2d ed., eds. Barbara A. Crow and Lise Gotell, 365–371. Toronto: Pearson.

Radicalesbians. 1972. Woman-identified woman, in *Out of the closets: Voices of gay liberation,* eds. Karla Jay and Allen Young, 172–177. New York: Douglas.

Rich, Adrienne. 1983. Compulsory heterosexuality and lesbian existence, in *The signs reader: Women, gender, and scholarship*, eds. Elizabeth Abel and Emily K. Abel, 139–168. Chicago: Univ. of Chicago Press.

Rubin, Gayle. 1984. Thinking sex: Notes for a radical theory of the politics of sexuality, in *Pleasure and danger: Exploring female sexuality,* ed. Carole S. Vance, 267–319. Boston: Routledge and K. Paul.

Scott, Joan. 1992. Experience, in *Feminists theorize the political,* eds. Judith Butler and Joan W. Scott, 22–40. New York and London: Routledge.

Sedgwick, Eve Kosofsky. 1990. *Epistemology of the closet*. Berkeley and Los Angeles: Univ. of California Press.

Taste This (Anna Camilleri, Ivan E. Coyote, Zoë Eakle, and Lyndell Montgomery). 1998. *Boys like her: Transfictions*. Vancouver: Press Gang.

Thomas, Calvin, ed. 2000. *Straight with a twist: Queer theory and the subject of heterosexuality*. Urbana and Chicago: Univ. of Illinois Press.

Vance, Carole S. 1984. Pleasure and danger: Toward a politics of sexuality, in *Pleasure and danger: Exploring female sexuality*, ed. Carole S. Vance, xvi–xxxix. Boston: Routledge and K. Paul.

Warner, Michael. 1993. Introduction, in *Fear of a queer planet: Queer politics and social theory*, ed. Michael Warner. Minneapolis: Univ. of Minnesota Press.

Weeks, Jeffrey. 1995. *Invented moralities: Sexual values in an age of uncertainty*. New York: Columbia Univ. Press.

Filmography

Interview with the cast of *Queer as Folk*. "CNN. Larry King Live." April 24, 2002—21:00 ET. **http://transcripts.cnn.com/TRANSCRIPTS/0204/24/lkl.00.html**. Accessed March 21, 2007.

Madonna and Guy Ritchie, dir. 2001. What it feels like for a girl. DNA, Inc.

Scott, Ridley, dir. 1991. *Thelma and Louise*. Culver City, CA: MGM/UA Home Video.

CHAPTER 6

Exacting Beauty: Exploring Women's Body Projects and Problems in the 21st Century

Carla Rice

Mostly my body image is negative. I bet that's true for many women: our chief relationship with our bodies is what we don't like …

> Jillian, 39, Jewish, white Canadian

Beauty ideals are racist … [But] most of what I read is only a white woman's point of view. They exclude the minority.

> Rose, 24, Korean born, Canadian raised

Not only do women with disabilities have to conform to some idiotic notion of the "ideal" but they can't even be seen as "normal" women.

> Frances, 42, white Canadian,
> born with a mobility disability

I want my point made public … I'm a fantastic person, but nobody could see past the fat. It angers me more than it hurts me. But it hurts.

> Leila, 34, born with a disability,
> size difference from childhood

INTRODUCTION

For girls coming of age in consumerist, individualist, and media-driven cultures, the body has become an important identity project. While the body has come to be a key medium of self-making, many girls and women also experience it as a significant obstacle and a source of distress. Studies conducted in many wealthy nations show how girls as young as six already express dissatisfaction with their bodies (Gardner, Friedman, and Jackson, 1999; Irving, 2000; Ricciardelli and McCabe, 2001; Shapiro, Newcomb, and Burns Loebl, 1997). More and more adolescents in the Western world suffer from eating problems. This includes a shocking 27 percent of Canadian middle school girls, who report disordered eating practices (Jones et al., 2001). Sixty percent of those in grades 7 and 8 have tried dieting to lose weight (McVey et al., 2002). Worldwide, millions of women worry about their image, believing that appearance shapes their self-esteem, social status, and life chances (Etcoff et al., 2004). This has come to the point that 15 percent of women in one study said they would sacrifice five years of their life to achieve their weight goal (Garner, 1997). A psychologically sophisticated, highly profitable, globalizing beauty/dieting industry has colonized and capitalized on women's most intimate worries and wishes about their bodies to sell a dizzying array of products to expanding consumer markets. As a result, millions are affected by a growing global trade in harmful skin-lightening products and by mounting fears about a global obesity epidemic that is said to threaten public health.

In this chapter, I will explore how the female body has become both a site of constraint and possibility for girls and women living in the West and (increasingly) around the world. I use the material culture of beauty and body histories of close to 100 Canadian women to show how women's new freedom to play with appearance during the 20th century has been accompanied by ever more exacting beauty standards at the beginning of the 21st. Drawing on cultural representations and women's personal experiences, I explore the ways in which pressure to control the body has intensified and diversified for girls growing up today in a contemporary Canadian context. I expand this analysis beyond the borders of Canada and the confines of adolescence to show how a transnational and intergenerational multi-billion-dollar beauty business has tapped into, and taken advantage of, expanding markets of female consumers—from "tweens" to seniors, from women living in the global north to those in the global south. I examine how, in the opening years of the 21st century, girls and women have come to see different body sites—including weight, skin, hair, and breasts—as significant body projects and problems.

To show how beauty culture shapes women's body images, I draw on two primary sources: first, the material culture of beauty; and second, body histories of close to 100 Canadian women from diverse backgrounds. By the "material culture of beauty," I mean cultural objects such as mirrors, cosmetics, fashion magazines, photographs, and film that illuminate changing ideologies of beauty and show how women have perceived their bodies in the past and the present. Detailing developments in the material culture of beauty over the 20th century demonstrates how our visual and commercial culture has encouraged women's discovery of their images and display of their bodies (Brumberg, 1998). Drawing from my own research on adult women's body histories, I use narratives by ordinary women of varying body sizes and ethnic and racial backgrounds, with and without disabilities and physical differences, to reveal the ways in which cultural images have shaped their body image and identity formation (Rice, 2003). By combining the material culture of beauty with individuals' narratives of embodiment, I hope to explain contemporary body projects and problems from the vantage points of diverse women.

HISTORY OF BEAUTY CULTURE AND WOMEN'S BODY PROJECTS

In Western culture, women are identified socially with our bodies (Odette, 1994). How the culture values or devalues our physical features, sizes, and capacities has a significant impact on our sense of body and self. Yet how do girls and women internalize cultural images? How do they use these images to shape their identities and sense of themselves? Why have feminists come to see cultural representations as a site of struggle for girls and women? To answer these questions, I briefly outline feminist theory on cultural representations, and I offer a feminist account of the history of beauty culture. I then examine, from a psychological and social perspective, individual women's stories of influential experiences that have shaped their bodily self-images.

In explaining why the body is so important to women's identity, French feminist Simone de Beauvoir famously wrote that, "one is not born, but becomes a woman" (de Beauvoir, 1974: 249). She argued that women's bodies are central to this process; through media, schools, medical systems, and beauty culture we learn how to fashion our bodies to "create" our gender. Teresa de Lauretis (1987), a contemporary feminist theorist, has called everyday objects such as high heels, makeup, and push-up bras "technologies of gender" because we use these devices and methods in our daily lives to construct and convey our gender. Feminist critics have long been interested in cultural representations of female bodies, because women looking at these often have had a hard time recognizing themselves (Hearne, 2007). When they looked at images, women quickly came to see that they were "objects" of men's gaze. As cultural critic John Berger (1980) said of the ways that women have been depicted in Western art and advertising: "women are to-be-looked-at" and men do the looking. Observing that women have been the principal, recurring subjects of Western imagery, he further notes: "Men look at women. Women watch themselves being looked at. This determines not only most relations between men and women but also the relation of women to themselves ... Thus she turns herself into an object—and most particularly an object of vision: a sight." (Berger, 1980: 47).

It can be difficult to develop a critical perspective on the gendered looking relations that Berger describes because we live inside them. Values and assumptions that are "naturalized" in art, advertising, and popular culture can be hard to question. Immersed as we are in these conventions, they simply appear as "normal." If you have doubts about Berger's feminist analysis, try the following experiment: choose an image of a nude from a traditional European painting and then change the white woman into a white man or a man or woman of colour in your mind's eye or in your drawing of a reproduction. What does this do to your assumptions and judgments about the figure in the picture?

By remaking classical nudes in this way, modern-day Japanese "appropriation" artist Yasumasa Morimura invites us to think about the complexity of the relationship between the viewer and the visual text (Morimura, 2008). He alters his face and body features through makeup, costume, props, and digital image manipulation to insert himself in place of the idealized female figures in some of the most famous European paintings such as Da Vinci's "Mona Lisa" and Manet's "Olympia." By putting himself, as a Japanese man, in place of iconic beauty "ideals," he draws our attention to gendered and racialized looking relations, challenging Western conventions of seeing female bodies as objects "to be looked at" and especially of seeing *white* women's bodies as desirable objects. These looking relations that are pervasive throughout the history of Western art continue in contemporary commercial culture. When women look at media, we learn to identify with actual or imagined spectators looking at the ideal woman depicted in the image. In this way, we become conscious of potential or actual others looking at us. As feminists have noted, these looking relations are not only inequitable; in teaching us to value certain bodies and traits and devalue others, they also are highly evaluative.

For most of us, mirrors are the oldest and most ubiquitous image-making technologies in our day-to-day lives. When reflecting surfaces became a staple of stores and homes from the late 19th century on, images of their bodies became more assessable to women and girls (Brumberg, 1998). As cultural historians have shown, prior to the Victorian period only the wealthy could afford mirrors. In the 16th century, for example, a small glass mirror framed in precious metals and jewels cost the equivalent of a luxury car in today's currency (Melchior-Bonnet, 2001). Technological advancements in the 19th century saw massive increases in mirror production and their installation in public and private spaces. The new department stores, such as Eaton's, in Canada and Macy's in the United States, used reflecting surfaces to inundate interiors with light (O'Brien and Szeman, 2004). Retailers hoped this would incite consumer desire and encourage spending. Urban dwelling women of all classes now regularly faced their reflections as they indulged a new pastime: window shopping.

At the same time, mirrors became permanent fixtures of middle-class homes, especially in bathrooms and bedrooms, as well as portable accessories for many girls and women. We know that a woman gazing at herself in the mirror is a common theme in art, advertising, and popular culture. While "being looked at" has been coded as female throughout Western cultural history (Hearne, 2007), a majority of Western women began to subject their bodies' features to greater scrutiny only with the introduction of affordable image technologies—first mirrors, then photography and film. From its status as precious item to commonplace object, the mirror has come to occupy an important place in our imaginations. Amplifying our awareness of our bodies as images, mirrors and other image technologies have made sight, not touch, a primary sense through which we experience our physical selves (Rice, 2003).

Within contemporary image culture, appearance is portrayed as paramount to women. Yet in the 19th century, beauty was believed to derive from inner qualities such as character, morality, and spirituality. A moral aesthetic governing beauty associated the use of makeup with "painted ladies," a Victorian euphemism for prostitutes (Peiss, 1998). Women who paid too much attention to image ran the risk of being perceived as shallow and vain and (more alarming still) as sexually impure. To overcome these associations and orient female buyers toward consumption of cosmetics, advertisers invited them to see body beautification as an acceptable moral lapse, an innocent sin. Marketers also heightened women's image consciousness by reminding them of the critical gaze of others. For example, one ad warns women "Strangers' eyes, keen and critical—can you meet them proudly, confidently, without fear?" Another claims, "Your husband's eyes ... more searching than your mirror."[1] Positioned as objects of an outsider's gaze, female viewers of commercial culture were, for the first time, invited to see themselves as recipients of evaluative looks.

Historically, skin became women's first body project as they learned the power of complexion to advance or undermine their social inclusion. From ancient times, pallor was associated with high social status; women at work outdoors were tanned and aged faster, whereas women of high social status were not obliged to work in the fields but stayed indoors and were pale-skinned. To be fair (in the sense of colour of skin and hair) was to be fair (in the sense of beauty)—and beauty of person was strongly associated with beauty of soul. During the 17th, 18th, and (especially) the 19th century, this superiority of white over dark was scientifically proclaimed, as white Europeans needed a convincing justification for slavery and colonization. Their oppression of persons of colour contradicted emerging political theories grounded in principles of human rights (Schiebinger, 1993). Scientists constructed a hierarchy of races based on physical traits such as skin colour and bone structure to rationalize the continued disenfranchisement of racialized peoples.

As a result, women of every hue attempted to improve their social standing through skin whitening, the most popular cosmetic of the 19th century (Brumberg, 1998). In period advertisements, skin whiteners for white women promised to enhance their complexion while products for Black women pledged to remove their dark skin. For instance, one "face bleach" ad claims to "turn the skin of a black or brown person four or five shades lighter, and a mulatto person perfectly white" (*St. Louis Palladium*, 1901, cited in Rooks, 1996). According to Black feminist scholar Noliwe Rooks (1996), these ads persuaded African-American women to purchase products by presenting dark skin as an ugly imperfection and by suggesting that skin lightening would promote women's class mobility and social acceptance in colourist, white supremacist society.

Surprisingly, while large corporations today control cosmetics markets, ordinary women were industry innovators. Canadian working-class farm girl Elizabeth Arden, poor Jewish immigrant Helena Rubinstein, and African-American domestic servant and daughter of slaves Madame C.J. Walker became successful entrepreneurs (Peiss, 1998). Feminist social historian Kathy Peiss suggests that these socially marginalized women built their businesses by attracting other women to act as sales agents, and by using stories of their own struggles to attract customers (Peiss, 1998). Early entrepreneurs brought to advertising the idea that women could improve their social situation through personal transformation. Madame C.J. Walker, who is credited with popularizing the "hot" comb for straightening hair, sold such products as Black women's "passport to prosperity" (Rooks, 1996: 65). She saw Black women's beauty in a political light—as a "vindication of black womanhood"

---

1   Unless otherwise noted in a citation, all historical advertisements discussed in this chapter were retrieved from Ad*Access On-Line Project, Duke University, at **http://scriptorium.lib.duke.edu/ adaccess**.

demeaned by slavery and as a pathway to prosperity and respectability denied by white society (Peiss, 1998; Rooks, 1996). Many Black feminist and critical race scholars have debated whether Madame C.J. Walker preyed on African-American women's feelings of inferiority or promoted pro-Black beauty through dignifying their beauty practices (Byrd and Tharps, 2001; Rooks, 1996; Russell, Wilson, and Hall, 1992). Yet in her advertisements, personal letters, and public talks, Walker clearly did not seek to embody white ideals. Instead, beauty was a way to challenge widespread stereotypes of Black women as unfeminine and unattractive, and in so doing, to raise Black women's self-confidence and contribute to their collective advancement.

By the 1920s, the beauty business mushroomed into a mass market overtaken by male manufacturers (Peiss, 1998). Possessing more capital to supply retailers and to advertise products than the early female entrepreneurs who had innovated "pyramid" style marketing, new manufacturing firms soon dominated markets (Peiss, 1998). Male owners authorized their involvement in women's appearance work by representing themselves as "experts" in the "science of beauty." One ad from the 1920s featuring a stylish woman with the caption "Man Made Beauty" states: "I give credit to men in large part for my beauty and my youth. To the scientists in France and elsewhere who gave their best to me." Drawing from the social permissiveness of the period, advertisers connected women's cosmetic use with greater individuality, mobility, and modernity. The caption of another ad exclaims "The Lovely Rebel Who fought for Youth and Won!" and a third reads "Be as MODERN as you like—for you can still be lovely." While marketers sold makeup as a means for women to assert autonomy and resist outmoded gender expectations, by the end of the 1930s, messages increasingly equated beauty with a woman's "true femininity." For example, in one ad entitled "Beauty Lost—Beauty Regained," readers are told how a "lovely lady who goes to pieces" recovers her mental health by "regaining her lost youth." Beauty ads now encouraged women's investment in appearance in the name of their emotional well-being and psychological health. When image became intertwined with a woman's identity, personality, and psychology in this way, modifying the body became, for many, a principal method of caring for the self. In this way, a woman's appearance came to be read as a prime measure of her self-esteem, feminine essence, and mental health.

Throughout the 1930s and 1940s, medical professionals and marketers encouraged middle-class mothers to invest energy in their own and their daughters' appearance in the name of physical and emotional health (Brumberg, 1998). In one period ad, mothers are told that keeping their daughters' complexion clear is "a mother's duty" and in another, that girls "are never too young" to begin their beauty routines. During World War II, beauty became a means for women to support the war effort, with ad copy announcing that "beauty is a duty," that "fit" bodies increased women's productivity while "lovely" faces enhanced troop morale. In another Canadian ad, women are told that time-saving beauty routines would allow them to "work for victory and stay lovely."

It was not until the 1950s that cosmetics companies first targeted teenage girls—who had started to hold part-time jobs and had their own disposable income—with ads designed to appeal to their sense of generational distinctiveness and romantic desires. With copy encouraging readers to get "The 'natural' look men look for," ads for Seventeen Cosmetics spoke to girls' romantic desires to fit with prevailing heterosexual scripts by reinforcing their wish to attract an admiring male gaze.

In today's media, explicit reference to an evaluative other is no longer necessary. Take a look at a recent *Cosmo, Vogue,* or other fashion magazine. Let's explore the looking relations surrounding the image of the model on the cover. As you study the cover photo, ask yourself the following questions: *Who is the woman on the cover looking at? Who does she think is looking at her?* As discussed earlier, feminists have long argued that women within Western art and advertising have been positioned as recipients of an implicit male gaze. Yet as you explore looking relations surrounding the picture, your analysis might suggest that the cover image operates not only as an object of vision for *male* but also for *female* audiences. As viewers, we might imagine ourselves to be a male or female spectator looking at the model with envy or desire. Alternately, we might imagine ourselves to be the beautiful, sexy model looking back with confidence, desire, or the conviction of our own desirability at the male and female spectators who are looking at us. In either case, through this complex relay of looks, the model becomes an object of desire for imagined spectators *who want her* and for those *who want to be like her*.

WOMEN'S BODY HISTORIES

To gain insight into women's body image formation, I undertook a research project investigating diverse women's experiences of their bodies in the timeframe from early childhood to late adolescence. The women, from all walks of life and living in Canada, who participated in this study are among the first generation to come of age in a world replete with image technologies of mirrors, cameras, TV, and computers. As I talked with them, I found that rather than telling many disparate stories, their narratives became a chorus of harmonized voices. Each woman spoke of how she gained awareness of her appearance and difference through symbolic meanings conveyed in social interactions, and how messages about her body significantly shaped her sense of identity and self (Rice, 2003). Yet when recalling their earliest memories, most of these women describe experiences of their bodies that were not image-based. Instead, most remember how bodies were fun, playful vehicles for their active exploration of the world. This was true whether or not they were born with a disability or physical difference.

> I would get out of my wheelchair, and in this "crazy car" I would be just like the [kids without disabilities]. I was pretty fast and I was pretty proud that I was able to do this.... What comes to mind is how much freedom there was with that. (Eva, 39, white Canadian, born with a mobility disability)

> One of my favourite things that my mom did was to make roads on my face. She would take her finger and trace along. It was her way of saying "your face is still lovable and I accept you the way you are ..." (Elizabeth, 40, white Canadian, born with a facial difference)

As you read these quotes, you may want to reflect on your own body history. Ask yourself the following questions: What are your early memories of your body? Was there a time when you can remember experiencing your body mainly as a medium for exploring your environment? What do you remember about your response to adult women's bodies? How did you see your mother's or other caretakers' bodies? If women thought about bodies at all, many perceived their mothers' bodies in terms of capacity for comfort and love rather than according to visual attributes like fat or thin.

> I would put my head on my mother's tummy ... I would say "It's time for tummy talk." Because she is full bodied she would laugh and her whole body would vibrate and I just thought that was wonderful. (Zoë, 29, West Indian Canadian)

For participants in this study, the power of image was imposed early. Many ponder ways in which the presence of mirrors and other image technologies has shaped how they perceive their bodies. Growing up in a world of mirrors, women suggest that *sight* eclipsed other experiences of bodies—especially touch and movement—which were the bases for their first tangible reality (Rice, 2003). Yet, with one exception, none can say how images overshadowed other body perceptions. Because she spent her early years on a farm in rural Jamaica, one woman, Shirley, had no consciousness of her body as an image until she moved to the city:

> Moving from rural to urban was huge. I remember shopping because for the first time I could choose what looked flattering. I began to think: "You can look nice in clothes." I liked that. Before I became conscious of what I looked like, my grandmother would make my clothes. There was no concept of shopping and looking at your self in the mirror. All that despairing, it didn't enter my mind. (Shirley, 31, Jamaican Canadian, immigrant)

All women recall the pleasure of gazing on their girl bodies and imagining their future female selves. Yet many recollect how the new consciousness of image also instilled a vulnerability to others' evaluative looks. Living in a world of reflecting surfaces and observing eyes, women tell how they came to experience their bodies as sources of self-identity and as objects of others' and their own scrutiny (Rice, 2003).

Women in my research acquired consciousness of appearance through the many cultural images in their daily lives. Photographs taught many to perceive their bodies along cultural binaries of thin/fat, light/dark, and tall/short. For most, comparisons and comments became early sources of knowledge about their bodies. Family members first imparted the significance of physical traits through comparisons with sisters, cousins, and female friends (significantly, 70 percent of those with sisters were compared to each other). As a result of such comparisons, a majority of women interviewed learned unequal values given to differences in size (58 percent), facial features (40 percent), hair (20 percent), and hue (28 percent).

> My sister is chubbier. I was "la flaca" [the thin one] and she was "la gorda" [the fat one]. Together, we make the perfect ten. It was terrible. They're lavishing on me and disregarding her... (Aurora, 26, Ecuadorian Canadian, with scoliosis from adolescence)

> I was always told "Oh you have such good hair" because it is relatively straight. While my sister who has kinky hair used to straighten it.... I don't remember my grandmother with much fondness. When she had Alzheimer's, she used to call me "the little servant girl" because I was darker skinned. (Zoë, 29, West Indian Canadian)

Gendered power relations operating in encounters with fathers, brothers, and other boys also opened up women-as-girls' bodies to a particularly critical gaze. In my research, 58 percent recall brothers and 50 percent recall fathers making critical comments about their appearance. Through greater power given to their harsh and harassing comments, boys and men often dictated attitudes that informed women's body and self-perceptions.

> My brother started to give me the nickname Moose or Cow. But I wasn't aware of it and it wasn't negative until people started to comment. (Catherine, 37, white Canadian, size difference from childhood)

> I remember my dad telling me that I am average looking. I think that still eats away at me today. It's amazing how one comment can scar, especially when it's from parents. It's like a really deep judgment. (Kasha, 24, white Ukranian Canadian, immigrant)

Messages about the significance of appearance to women's sense of identity and possibility reverberate throughout the narratives. Entering peer groups, participants keenly felt the social consequences of physical appearances, discovering which differences were distinguished and devalued in interactions. Because most had little access to alternative frameworks, they were especially susceptible to incorporating others' attributions into their developing body images. Most racialized women in this research did not remember learning about racist ideals of beauty through popular culture. Instead, most first encountered offensive cultural stereotypes about racialized bodies as out of the ordinary, unclean, unattractive, and not desirable in white-dominated spaces of communities and schools.

> Kids would ask me if I took a shower would the colour come off. (Maya, 22, Jamaican Canadian, disability from late childhood)

> Somebody said, "You're pretty for a black girl." Such a profound statement, suggesting that generally we are not pretty. (Nicole, 25, Jamaican Canadian)

> I remember the Judy Blume book, "Otherwise Known as Sheila the Great." In one part, the characters play a game. You pass around a sheet of paper with questions, "What we like about you. What should be changed." We decided to play that game and the comments we wrote were not nice. The darker girl got black. I got hairy. Someone else got fat. That was a big mistake because it hurts when you are taught at a young age that it is not good to be hairy or fatter or darker. (Sheila, 22, South Asian Canadian, chronic illness)

One location that women suggested was more generative of identity than other social spaces was school, a place where perceptions of appearance and difference shaped their belonging and standing (Rice, 2007). In account after account, they tell how body standards and stereotypes were communicated *everywhere* at school. These were conveyed through furniture and dress codes, playground interactions, seating arrangements, student placement in class pictures, and most of all, in gym classes. While a majority of women enjoyed physical education, once "big girls" were identified as "fat girls," others' critical comments undermined their physical abilities. When teachers and students rooted assessments of fat girls' abilities in stereotypes about their size—if you are fat you must be unfit—almost all stopped engaging in physical activity.

> Once I was a fat kid, there's limitations on your abilities. You're unfit ... NO, I lost confidence in that. I didn't like sports or gym. Not because I couldn't actually perform the sports. It's because I didn't like being taunted. (Iris, 32, English Canadian, immigrant, size difference from childhood)

> My teacher commented on how I was gaining weight. He said I had poor eating habits. When we had to run in the gym, he said I had problems running ... I felt upset in front of everybody. (Isobel, 32, Bermudian Canadian, size difference from childhood)

> My body became a source of torment. This is why I HATE my grade 5 teacher: he had the practice of letting kids divide up teams for sports. My best friend and I were always picked last. (Gayle, 29, English and Métis Canadian, size difference from childhood)

Unlike other participants, a majority of women born with physical disabilities attended schools for kids with "special" needs and many spent significant time throughout childhood in health care institutions. They recall early experiences of institutional interventions in medical and segregated school systems marked with a lack of privacy and respect, where physical differences were the main focus and other aspects of women's identities and physical or intellectual development were not acknowledged (Rice, 2008a). For many women with disabilities, schools imposed body norms in physiotherapy classes (such as by trying to teach students how to move their bodies like someone without a disability) rather than helping them explore physical abilities and possibilities unique to different bodies. Many further tell of intrusive, disrespectful treatment in health care institutions, where their bodies were handled roughly, or looked at or touched without warning or permission. When differences were the main focus and the whole person was not acknowledged, many women felt objectified.

> I remember going to therapy classes. You had to strive to be normal and mobile and the ultimate was to walk. If you didn't walk, then there was a hierarchy of disability. They emphasized the physical as opposed to other parts of your development. (Gina, 36, white Estonian Canadian, born with a mobility disability)

> The medical establishment does treat you differently because you have a disability. Several times I've had "medical photographs" taken where they strip and take pictures of you. Somewhere there are photographs of me when I was 13. I look mature, totally stark naked. (Frances, 42, white Canadian, mobility disability at birth)

Contributors recall how looking relations at home, on the street, and in school and medical settings reinforced restrictive body standards. For most, messages received through popular culture only gained meaning and significance in face-to-face interactions. When messages repeated across situations, they had important implications for women's developing sense of body and self. Those who desired or aspired to attractiveness to escape devalued differences also were galvanized by deeper drives: to seek in others' approval of their body a sense of belonging and affirmation for their unique being.

> There was a girl who was blond, blue-eyed, attractive to the popular boys.... I wasn't blond or blue eyed so they didn't pay any mind to me. So what I did was I cut out a picture of a blond woman in a bathing suit to give them as a present. I don't know if I was thinking they would associate the picture with me, then like me. I remember carrying the picture then thinking, "This is stupid." I threw it away. (Vera, 28, Asian Canadian)

Many women moved through adolescence with a deep sense of difference when they grasped how their changing bodies diverged from a culturally normal body (which was male) *and* failed to fit an acceptable female form (shaped by media ideals and medical norms). A majority saw themselves as an early developer or a late bloomer, and many saw their breasts as too big or too small, but rarely quite right. Almost all viewed their weight as exceeding or lagging behind some imagined norm. All felt like they had to "qualify as a woman," and hoped for cultural acceptance.

> Growing up was getting away from what I was used to. It was easier to be treated equally as a kid than as a female.... Suddenly, I was different and that bothered me. I wanted to be normal. (Hasina, 26, Muslim, South Asian Canadian)

> I remember how scared and clumsy I felt. I was this little girl but I started getting breasts and hips. People would comment: "Rossetta is starting to bloom." I had to deal with having a woman's body with a kid's mind. (Rossetta, 33, African Canadian, blind from birth)

> My body didn't become really womanly, I didn't suddenly have big breasts, a little tiny waist, and hips. I got one bite of the cookie and somebody else got the rest, the girl sitting next to me in class. (Charmaine, 39, Bermudian Canadian)

Body dissatisfaction increased dramatically between ages 9 to 16 when all encountered mounting pressures to appear desirable. Participants describe confronting the "predicament of puberty"—the growing gap between their changing bodies and the idealized images promoted in our culture—when others commented on their physical development and differences. Coming of age in consumerist, image-oriented society, women dealt with the disparity between their differences and ideals of desirability by imagining their "best possible" body and "best possible" self.

> I never had an image of me that wasn't in the chair. But I would create images of me looking different in the sense that I would be much prettier, slimmer, more popular. The most attractive image I could imagine becoming: my best possible image of myself. (Frances, 42, white Canadian, mobility disability from birth)

All tried to navigate the "predicament of puberty" by envisioning or adopting diverse body alteration practices—from dieting, hair relaxing, and eating disorders to cosmetic surgery, concealing clothing, makeup, and changing their body movements to "pass" as someone without a visible difference.

TODAY'S BODY PROJECTS

Messages in today's magazines echo efforts of women in my study to close the gap between their body differences and desirable ideals. Fashion magazines are vehicles for delivering messages of the beauty business to female consumers; a primary purpose is to enlist readers into image enhancement through continuous consumption. Copy encourages women to partake in perpetual body improvement, aspiring to their best hair, face, and body. Rather than advocating one ideal, magazines try to democratize beauty by convincing readers that they can achieve their "best bodies." This message enables girls' and women's expression of individuality and celebration of difference. Yet it also portrays body modification as critical to self-expression. In addition, it pulls diverse audiences into preoccupation with perpetual body improvement and purchase of products.

In many ways, trendy TV shows like *America's Next Top Model*, *Search for the Next Pussy Cat Doll,* and *Girlicious* likewise instruct girls and young women that they can bridge the gap between their bodily difference and images of desirability by re-visioning their differences as desirable. Yet such shows frequently reinforce the idea that the greatest power a young woman can wield is her sexual sway over men. They thus present beauty makeovers as the ticket to success. Despite purporting to represent diversity, such shows still promote a narrow notion of beauty and encourage constant body modification through consumption to achieve the desirable look.

Interestingly, *Top Model*, *Gossip Girl*, and *Girlicious* are all owned by one company, The CW Network (**www.cwtv.com**). Formed in 2006, the network's primary aim is to reach a lucrative youth market (Fitzgerald, 2007; Seid, 2006). This is why, for example, The CW Network is happy to have Cover Girl Cosmetics sponsor *America's Next Top Model* (**www.covergirl.com/antm/cycle10**): Cover Girl contributes big advertising revenues to the company and, in return, the cosmetics giant can prime viewers to purchase their products. It is also why Disney, the largest children's entertainment corporation in the world, developed *High School Musical*, *Hannah Montana*, and *That's So Raven*—to move into the lucretive "tween" market (8 to 12 year olds) in order to sell a vast array of spinoff products (Disney Corporation, 2007). And tweens have become a huge market; in North

America alone, they spend about $50 billion a year, while family members spend another $200 billion on them (Clehane, 2007). Disney's global retail sales for its tween business in 2007 reached $400 million (Disney Corporation, 2007). Companies target tween and teen markets hoping to build brand loyalties that will last a lifetime.

Beauty pageants in which contestants are women with disabilities are yet another example of the idea of re-visioning differences as desirable, within narrow confines. *Miss Ability* is a reality TV beauty contest from the Netherlands that started in 2006; contestants have to display a "handicap visible to the eye." It is promoted this way: "Ever whistled at a woman in a wheelchair? Checked out the boobs of a blind babe? If the answer's 'no,' this barrier-breaking show will put an end to that" (Eye2Eye Media, 2008). The winner of the first pageant, crowned by the Dutch prime minister, was a young woman named Roos who wears a cervical collar due to an acquired disability affecting her neck. The cervical collar is the only indication she has any physical disability or difference and is not an average model. Roos manages her disability by using the cervical collar sometimes and lying prone sometimes, yet images often depict her as very desirable and sexual. While it can't be ignored that she is disabled, the nature of her disability is socially acceptable—no dribbling, sudden movements, speech impairments, or any deviance from social protocols that make people uncomfortable. Thus, the winner is someone the non-disabled population can relate to in fundamental ways. She can look "normal," albeit for very brief periods; she is seen as sexually desirable; and she meets expectations of what is feminine. Even in a forum where it's supposedly "celebrated," disability must remain invisible (Rice, Lenooy, and Odette, 2007). It is interesting to note that due to the show's surprisingly high ratings in the Netherlands, broadcasters have snapped up the rights to remake *Miss Ability* in Britain, France, Germany, and the US (Sherwin, 2006).

As a result of these cultural meanings given to notions of difference and desirability, many girls and women come to relate to their bodies as self-making projects (Beausoleil, 1994, 1999). Girls and women have come to see different body sites—weight, skin, hair, and breasts—as personal problems. For example, 90 percent of women interviewed in my study saw themselves as over- or underweight; close to 80 percent believed their breasts were too big or small; 31 percent believed their skin was too dark; and 27 percent disliked their hair colour and texture (Rice, 2003). This suggests that, despite celebrations of difference currently popular throughout image culture, pressure to control and re-shape the body is intensifying and diversifying for contemporary young women coming of age in "body-centric" culture. I now turn to explore each of these body projects in greater detail.

The Weight Project

In contemporary Western culture, we learn to value a certain size as part of the body beautiful. For example, the thin female body is associated with health, wealth, sexiness, self-discipline, and success. Despite growing dialogue about body acceptance, fat is seen as unattractive, not physically or emotionally healthy, downwardly mobile, and lacking in body- and self-control. In addition, today's magazines seem to criticize women's bodies whatever their weight. Headlines such as "Battle of the Bones," "Celebrities' Secret Weight Loss Surgery," and "Stars' Worst and Best Beach Bodies" regularly invite readers' critical evaluation of famous female bodies and encourage widespread comparison and competition based on looks and size. The main message appears to be that no body is acceptable or safe. Every woman's body is vulnerable to critical assessment and amenable to alteration and improvement. Recently, the Spanish government banned too-thin models from fashion shows in Madrid in response to public fears that ultra-thinness glamourized anorexic bodies and galvanized young women to adopt anorexic behaviours (Yeoman, Asome, and Keeley, 2006). While many praised the Spanish government's proactive response to a critical feminist concern, this move also raises important questions about solutions to restrictive ideals that involve increased regulation and surveillance of women's sizes. We can ask ourselves: *What is the effect of regulating individuals' weights rather than changing our beauty ideals or the gendered looking relations that position women as objects of our gaze? To what degree does this move unintentionally contribute to the problem of ideals by intensifying social surveillance of women's bodies, and enforcing narrow weight norms that make no size feel safe? Do you think the ban was a good move? What should be done about skinny models?*

While celebration and stigmatization of fat have fluctuated in different times among different cultures, concerns about medical and moral risks of being overweight have intensified over the last century (Stearns, 1997). In North America today, two competing frames shape dialogue on obesity. Is it an "epidemic" or is it a "myth" (Campos, 2004; Lawrence, 2004; Rice, 2007)? The first frame—the epidemic of obesity—dominates public discussion and debate. Global and national public health institutions have fuelled fear of fat by interpreting obesity as an escalating epidemic that threatens the health and fitness of populations and nations (Raine, 2004; World Health Organization, 2000, 2003). As a result, concerns about rising rates of obesity within Canada make headlines daily. For example, we are told that obesity rates have doubled in the last 20 years (Tremblay, Katzmarzyk, and Willms, 2002); that 60 percent of adult men and 50 percent of adult women are overweight; and that 25 percent of Canadian children weigh too much (Lau et al., 2007). Beyond health problems, an increasing number of social problems are being blamed on fat, from global warming (Jacobsen and McLay, 2006) to America's vulnerability to terrorist attacks (Associated Press, 2006).

Despite the ubiquity of such moralistic medical messages, there is considerable uncertainty and controversy within obesity research about the causes, health consequences, measures, and treatment of obesity (Cogan and Ernsberger, 1999; Jutel, 2006). In response to these critical questions, concerned scientists and social scientists recently have developed an alternative perspective on the "obesity epidemic" that shifts our attention away from stemming the epidemic of fat folk to examining the emergence of an idea—obesity as a dangerous disease—that has captured our cultural imagination (Campos, 2004; Gard and Wright, 2005; Sobal and Maurer, 1999). This view does not dismiss health concerns raised by doctors, governments, or others but instead invites us to question obesity researchers' assumptions and interests, and to explore why our society has become so alarmed about fat (Oliver, 2006).

For instance, some critics argue that framing fat as a dangerous disease not only denies and distorts empirical uncertainty within obesity research but also masks deeper cultural anxieties at work in this message (Gard and Wright, 2005; Jutel, 2006). Epidemiologists now suggest that rising weights in our society may be related to people's biology combined with obesity-causing environments (Brownell and Horgen, 2004; Raine, 2004). In addition, we simply do not know the health consequences of obesity. We know that the relationship between health and weight is a U-shaped curve, meaning that health risks increase at extreme under- and overweight (Ross, 2005). While high weight is associated with hypertension and heart disease, this association does not mean causal relationship—in other words, there is no evidence that being fat in itself causes these health problems (Cogan and Ernsberger, 1999). To date, there are no safe, proven treatments for excess weight (Ernsberger and Koletsky, 1999). The most common treatments such as dieting, pills, and surgery all have health risks and consequences (Bennett and Gurin, 1983).

Finally, weight measures such as Body Mass Index, or BMI (weight in kilos divided by the square of height in metres) have also been called into question. While BMI was originally meant as a screening tool (to tell if someone is at risk for developing a health problem), it is now widely misused as a diagnostic tool (to tell if someone needs to lose weight) (Ikeda, Crawford, and Woodward-Lopez, 2006; Jutel, 2006). BMI categories have been applied inappropriately to people of all ages, ethnicities, genders, and athletic abilities (Fairburn and Brownell, 2002; Ikeda, Crawford, and Woodward-Lopez, 2006). Kate Harding (2008) developed the *BMI Illustrated Categories Slide Show* to demonstrate the body sizes that fit BMI categories and to get us to think critically about them. Watch the slide show to judge for yourself whether you think these categories are skewed (**http://kateharding.net/bmi-illustrated/**).

Some scholars have written about "the obesity epidemic" as a moral panic, arguing that misplaced morality and ideological assumptions underlie our "war on fat" (Gard and Wright, 2005; Oliver, 2006). They argue that, despite serious debate among obesity experts about the culpability of bad habits such as overeating or inactivity in causing obesity, the causes of and solutions for obesity invariably come back to people's health practices. Not only does this view ignore empirical uncertainty about causes of weight gain, but it blames individuals by ignoring contexts such as poverty or weight prejudice that constrain their options for eating or activity.

Recent history shows that obesity epidemic discourses have emerged today as dominant partly because they dovetailed with earlier state-sponsored efforts designed to improve the health, fitness, and competitiveness of nations. From the late 1960s onwards, many Western governments, including Canada, initiated public education campaigns that advocated greater physical activity to prevent fatness and promote fitness in citizens (Bauman et al., 2004; MacNeill, 1999). In response to growing concerns about excessive consumption and the sedentary lifestyles of Canadians, Prime Minister Pierre Elliott Trudeau launched the ParticipACTION Campaign in the early 1970s (Rootman and Edwards, 2004). It famously compared the fitness levels of a 30-year-old Canadian with a 60-year-old Swede. (To see this ad, see the ParticipACTION Archive Project.) Many of these ads (see Figures 6.1 and 6.2) imagined the ideal Canadian citizen as a thin, fit, white, able-bodied male. They further raised the spectre of the unfit, feminized, underdeveloped, and Third-World "other," who threatened Canada's competitiveness on the global economic stage. Signifying the future health and prosperity of nations, children were targeted as a group needing special attention.

However, the effectiveness of interventions that link fatness prevention to fitness promotion has never been established. Studies show that fat kids are less likely to be physically active and more likely to have eating problems. *Yet research has not revealed whether overeating and under-exercising increases overweight or whether being fat increases their susceptibility to problem eating and inactivity* (Boutelle et al., 2002). Some women in my research suggest that ParticipACTION ads disseminated throughout the 1970s and 1980s heightened their fear of fat and instilled the belief that their big bodies were "bad." By linking thinness with fitness and positioning fat as opposite to fit, ParticipACTION's popular "FitFat" ad conveyed that fatness and fitness could *not* coincide in the same body (see Figure 6.3).

FIGURE 6.1

FIGURE 6.2

FIGURE 6.3

FIT FAT
August 1979

Those perceived as fat in childhood describe how the demanding physical education programs introduced into schools during this period often dissuaded them from participating in physical activity altogether. Adults' enforcement of restrictive diets in an attempt to regulate their weights also resulted in long-term struggles with food, including compulsive, binge, and secretive eating (Rice, 2007, 2008a). In other words, fatness prevention efforts contributed to producing the very behaviours and bodies that proponents were attempting to prevent!

> I remember this feeling of dread when the ["FitFat"] ad came on TV. Once my father and I were watching, I remember a man's voice saying, "This year fat's not where it's at." This made me so self-conscious ... (Maude, 27, white Canadian, blind from adolescence)

> I wasn't doing very well in ParticipACTION or Canada Fitness. I hated gym class. I didn't like being tested in front of everybody ... (Yolanda, 23, Dutch-Indonesian Canadian)

> My doctor said, "You should lose weight. Don't you want to go to your high school prom? Boys don't go out with fat girls." My mother brought me to him to help me lose weight. ... That was when I started to hide the food. (Sharon, 31, West Indian Canadian, immigrant from England)

Although ParticipACTION ended in 2001, the Canadian federal government recently re-launched the campaign to stem rising levels of obesity, once again focusing on kids as a high-risk group (Canadian Press, 2007). With a renewed focus on fatness prevention through fitness promotion, efforts to stem today's obesity epidemic may be leading a new cohort of large kids to adopt problem eating and inactivity, possibility contributing to their future problems with weight. This raises some critical questions for developing feminist-informed health and physical education policies and programs: *What do you think a fat-friendly and girl-friendly physical education curriculum would look like? What about a physical education program that affirmed the capacities of kids with different bodies, including those with physical differences or disabilities? If you had the task of designing a feminist health promotion campaign, what messages would you want to convey in order to promote girls' and young women's health?*

Framing fatness as undesirable and diseased implies that fat has become "abject." Adopted from the work of philosopher Julia Kristeva, the concept of "the abject" refers to body parts or processes associated in our culture with incapacity, vulnerability, uncleanliness, unattractiveness, and undesirability (Kristeva, 1982, 1991). The abject is feared and rejected because it resists our drive to master and control our bodies. Treating physical features or functions as abject reminds people of our connections with nature, vulnerability to disease, and inevitable death. One way to understand the abject is to see it as opposite to the ideal—the young, sexy, self-contained, hard body. Media images continually play on our fears of abjection and desire to embody ideals by showing us "rejected" "before" and "perfected" "after" pictures of women who undergo body makeovers (Covino, 2004). On pro-anorexia and pro-bulimia websites, for example, young women utterly reject the abject fat body and imbue idealized thinness with values of purity, perfection, and power. Significantly, the content of pro-ana and pro-mia sites mimics messages about the ideal and the abject body endemic in media, including "rejected" "before" and "idealized" "after" pictures of those who engage in commercialized body modification methods. While pro-ana and pro-mia sites send deeply problematic messages, girls also use them to create alternative accounts of disordered eating. They correctly frame eating disorders as logical outcomes of living in a culture that is committed to privileging fit, flawless, ultra-feminine bodies while punishing those deemed as unfit.

Women I interviewed likewise described beginning demanding dieting and disordered eating as a way of amending the abject fat body. Whether they started secretive eating in childhood to resist adult imposition of restrictive diets, or later adopted "disordered" eating to amend size differences, it is noteworthy that *all* participants perceived as fat eventually took up problem eating practices.

> At least I felt normal enough and desirable enough [when bulimic] that I could actually contemplate a sexual relationship. I could actually let go of protecting myself and enter into a relationship. (Gayle, 29, English and Métis Canadian, size difference from childhood)

> The times I have felt love are times my body has been the most socially acceptable [through starving and purging]. It makes me profoundly sad that the only ways of accessing those feelings are through having a conventional body. (Sylvie, 36, Italian-Scottish Canadian, size difference from childhood)

Other women talked of taking up "disordered" eating during adolescence once they encountered increased pressures to appear desirable. When women perceived as too fat, plain, unattractive, or ethnically different were positioned as "other than female" in the passage to womanhood, these women adopted problem eating to escape their labelling as deviant.

While weight restriction became a way of life for many I interviewed, research offers contradictory evidence about the race and class of those with disordered eating and dieting concerns. Many racialized women indicate that images of an attractive body spanned a broader range of sizes in their communities than in mainstream contexts. Yet those I interviewed grew up during a time when communities of colour comprised less than 5 percent of the Canadian population. For this reason, most recall being one of only a few children within their communities and schools identified as an ethnoracial "minority." Subjected to racial "othering" and to isolation within social and cultural landscapes of childhood, many lacked a cultural or community context in which to develop a critical consciousness about racist beauty ideals or to imagine an alternative body aesthetic (Poran, 2002). In addition, with stereotypical images of starving African bodies circulating in Western media throughout the 1970s (especially through children's charity commercials), thinness also became abject, especially for racialized women bearing the trait. As a result, many were caught between stigmatizing stereotypes of starving racialized bodies in the mainstream media and sexist pressures to conform to conflicting beauty ideals within the dominant culture and their own cultural communities.

> A girl at school said I looked like starving kids in the World Vision commercial. That was the most hurtful thing anybody ever said to me. I thought, "I should be bigger and more normal because I look like those poster kids." (Rhonda, 32, West Indian Canadian)

The Skin Project

As a result of Western colonization and widespread sexism, many cultures associate light skin with beauty, and this fuels and is fuelled by a profitable business in skin-whitening products. While some feminists have suggested that skin whitening is a practice relegated to our racist past (Brumberg, 1998; Peiss, 1998), they are missing the rapidly growing global trade in skin-lightening products. Feminist critical race scholar Amina Mire (2005) has called this phenomenon "the globalization of white western beauty ideals." (If you doubt Mire's claim, do an internet search for "skin lightening." It will yield over a million links!) In the West, many cosmetics companies market skin lightening to aging white women by associating light skin with youth and beauty. The aging process in ads frequently is framed as a pathological condition that can be mitigated through measures such as bleaching out "age spots." Globally, cosmetics companies also sell skin whitening products to women of colour, often covertly via the internet in order to avoid public scrutiny or state regulation of their commodities and campaigns (Mire, 2005). This is partially because many products contain unsafe chemicals such as hydroquinone and mercury, which inhibit the skin's melanin formation and which are toxic. The dangers of mercury poisoning due to skin lighteners—neurological, kidney, and psychiatric damage—are well known. However, the hazards of hydroquinone, which has been shown to be disfiguring in high doses and to cause cancer in laboratory studies, are less well documented. Press reports suggest that while governments have globally banned the most dangerous skin lighteners, in many countries, these are smuggled into domestic markets (Barnett and Smith, 2005; Counter, 2003; Van Marsh, 2007).

In Africa and other regions of the global south, skin-whitening is traditionally associated with white colonial oppression, when waves of European conquerors instituted economic, political, and cultural hierarchies based on language and skin colour. Because women who practise skin-lightening were and are harshly judged as suffering from an "inferiority complex" due to colonization, many engage in the practice covertly (Mire, 2005). Companies thus rely on covert advertising to mitigate women's secret shame about their perceived physical deficiencies, as well as their need to conceal such practices in order to avoid condemnation. Companies selling covertly also avoid scrutiny of injurious stereotypes used in product campaigns. In some campaigns, explicitly racist advertisements associate dark skin with "diseases" and "deformities" such as "hyperpigmentation," "melasma," and other "pigmentation pathologies." In contrast, they typically associate light skin with youth, beauty, and empowerment. In its internet ads, L'Oreal, a leading manufacturer and marketer of skin-whiteners such as *Bi-White* and *White Perfect*, references the inferiority of dark skin and the superiority of light complexions. *Bi-White* features an Asian woman unzipping her darker skin. (See the ad at **www.vichy.com/gb/biwhite**). Directed mainly to Asian women consumers, the ad uses medical language to suggest that Asian bodies produce too much melanin, which *Bi-White* will block. As Mire (2005) writes, darkness is associated with falseness, dirtiness, ugliness, and disease. Lightness is seen as true, clean, healthy, and beautiful.

There is a growing trend for many Western-owned cosmetics corporations to rely less on covert internet marketing and more on splashy TV and print campaigns to reach customers in Asia (Timmons, 2007). Since 1978, Hindustan Lever Limited, a subsidiary of the Western corporation Unilever, has sold its skin-whitening products to millions of women around the world (Melwani, 2007). *Fair & Lovely*, one of Hindustan Lever's best-known beauty brands, is marketed in over 38 countries and currently monopolizes a majority share of the skin-lightening market in India (Leistikow, 2003). One industry spokesperson recently stated that fairness creams are half of the skin-care market in India and that 60 to 65 percent of Indian women use these products on a daily basis (Timmons, 2007). Ads for *Fair & Lovely* frequently feature depressed young women with few prospects who gain brighter futures by attaining their dream job or desired boyfriend after becoming much fairer (Hossain, n.d.). Other commercials show shy young women who take charge of their lives and transform themselves into "modern" independent beauties. Appealing to women's dual aspirations for desirability and economic equality, ads feature taglines such as *Fair & Lovely: The power of beauty* and *Fair & Lovely: For complete fairness* (Timmons, 2007). (See ads at **www.youtube.com/watch?v=KIUQ5hbRHXk&NR=1**). Significantly, the success of *Fair & Lovely* has prompted several cosmetics corporations such as Avon, Ponds, and the Body Shop to market skin-lightening creams in Asia that women would not find on the shelves in Canada. Instead, other than the internet, such products tend to be sold in "ethnic-oriented" stores and beauty salons.

Globally, racialized women are fed a persuasive beauty myth: that fairness is glamorous and that lighter skin is the ticket to getting ahead in life. Of course, cosmetics corporations deny that the promise of fairness has anything to do with colonial and gender relations or with the idealization of white Western looks (Melwani, 2007; Timmons, 2007). Ironically, Western psychologists and psychiatrists have framed skin-whitening and other risky body modification practices as signs of mental illness, unconnected to colonial or other oppressive histories and legacies. Historically, in response to these discourses, feminists have spoken about women who adopt extreme body modification practices as "victims" of a powerful beauty system. They have analyzed how sexist, racist, and consumerist interests push women into appearance alteration to cure distresses and dissatisfactions created by oppressive forces (Bordo, 1993; Morgan, 1991). More recently, other feminist writers have contended that women are not cultural dupes of the beauty system but "secret agents" who rightly reject body otherness and strategically alter their appearance in their own best interests (Davis, 1995). Consideration of women's accounts about body modification suggests to me that appearance alteration encapsulates both feminist positions—that women's attempts at bodily transformation signify their capitulation to oppressive ideals *and* opposition to harmful abjection (Rice, 2008b). Within a social world intolerant of sexual ambiguity, ethnic variation, and physical difference, "amending the abject" may be one of our few chances for economic mobility, social acceptance, and emotional health (Covino, 2004).

Seen in this light, skin modification may be one of few options for racialized women who feel caught between the colonizing effects of white supremacy and their desires for feminine beauty and social acceptance. In the narratives of women I interviewed, as with fat women, some racialized women aspired to a light ideal to escape being seen as "other." Many spoke of avoiding sunlight, wearing light concealer, and using skin lightening in an effort to evade demeaning racist and sexist comments and/or to create a more desirable image.

> I saw neither beach nor bathing suit in high school! I was already black and with people who weren't black. (Marcia, 37, African, First Nations, Scottish Canadian)

> We have a family friend who is a lot darker than we are. She bought *Fair & Lovely* and when everyone found out, they used to say "Oh, she uses *Fair & Lovely.*" The fact that we talked about it is mean. The fact that she feels she has to use it is terrible. (Preeta, 29, South Asian Canadian)

Any exploration of skin lightening among racialized women raises important questions about the skin-altering practices of white women, especially those engaged in the current trend of tanning. Many white women are well aware of the cultural associations of dark skin with devalued status. Yet in a cultural context, where race is read off multiple body sites (skin colour, facial features, hair texture, etc.), tanned skin may be viewed as a temporary, detachable adornment rather than an essential feature that signifies someone's racial status (Ahmed, 1998).

Ironically, white women often see skin *darkening* as a beauty project. After World War I, tanning became a statement about high social status; a tan proclaimed the leisure to lie out in the sun and the money to go to tropical beaches in mid-winter. White women who tan can thus connect their bronzed skin to health, wealth, status, and attractiveness, secure in the knowledge that they still are seen as white and regardless of the health implications (increased risk of skin cancers, premature skin aging). Yet exploration of tanning too generates more interesting questions: *Why is there a greater emphasis placed on white women's attainment of a sun-kissed, sexy glow while racialized women feel pressured to aspire to the glow of fairness? Is bronzed skin a sign of a white woman's class status, suggesting her access to leisure time and vacation money? Is the obsession with fairness simply a bad case of a "colonial hangover," or is it an example of a Western cultural imperialism that uses global media to spread white beauty ideals? What are other possible roots of, and reasons for, women's differing skin projects?*

Colour may only be pigmentation, but by creating standards in complexion that differ depending on the perceived race of the woman bearing the trait, cultures attach a special cachet to women's hues, perpetuating belief in the magical power of body modification to transform our lives.

The Hair Project

Within a racial hierarchy of beauty, Black women encounter complex messages about hair due to deeply entrenched associations of long, flowing hair with social mobility and idealized femininity (Byrd and Tharps, 2001). An estimated 80 percent of African-American women in the US straighten their hair (Swee, Klontz, and Lambert, 2000). In

1993, the World Rio Corporation marketed a hair-straightening product on its late-night infomercials that targeted these women. In these ads, "good" hair was equated with a straightened hair and "bad" hair with curly locks. Once again, ads used the familiar format of abject "before" and ideal "after" shots featuring women who had been given a complete makeover. As Black feminist scholar Noliwe Rooks (1996) notes, women in the "before" shots were without makeup, jewellery, or other accessories. They looked unhappy and their hair was wild, un-styled, and unkempt, almost made to look "primitive." The "after" shots featured women who'd had a complete beauty makeover, including designer clothes, makeup, and a fashionable hairstyle. While manufacturers claimed Rio had low levels of acid, it actually contained harsh chemicals. Many women (and some men) who used it experienced hair loss, burns, blisters, and sores on their scalps. Of 340 000 people who purchased the product, over 3000 filed complaints, the largest number ever received in the United States for a cosmetic product (Swee, Klontz, and Lambert, 2000).

In the infomericals, women were repeatedly told that Rio would deliver them from the "bondage of chemically treated hair." Rio sold itself as a product that would enhance Black women's self-worth, freedom, and social mobility. It sent the message that they could escape sexist and racist oppression through relaxing their hair. Marketers used this message because it resonates with consumers. Many Black women in my study explained how they used hair relaxers, not because they desired whiteness, but because they wanted to avoid racial "other"ing, as well as aspiring to desirability, acceptability, and an enhanced sense of self.

> In high school, people would say, "What are you?" I realized if I blow dry my hair to get it straight I might not identify as anything separate.... The less I try to visually look like some stereotypes from the media or their beliefs, the less I am singled out. (Ada, 27, Trinidadian, Canadian, African, and Chinese)

> I had bad hair ... My younger sister, she had good hair. It was thinner, more manageable. When my mother started relaxing my hair, it became easier ... They always said the longer it was, the better. (Maya, 22, Jamaican Canadian, disability from childhood)

In case you think stigmatization of natural hair is a thing of the past, consider this: in October 2007, *Glamour* magazine developed a presentation called "The dos and don'ts of corporate fashion" that showed an African-American woman sporting an Afro with a caption reading "Say no to the 'fro" (Dorning, 2007). The presenter told a women's luncheon at a Wall Street law firm that Black female attorneys should avoid wearing "political" hairstyles like dreadlocks or Afros, because these styles were seen as unattractive and unprofessional. (To read *Glamour* magazine's account of the event, go to: **www.glamour.com/news/articles/2007/10/leive_letter**). Members of the audience were justifiably upset with the replay of negative stereotypes about "natural" hair as overly political, unfeminine, and unprofessional. Not only do these attitudes have an impact on Black girls' and women's beauty perceptions and practices, but they also are linked to blocked educational and economic opportunities. Like the other racialized women in my study, African-Canadian girls report witnessing or experiencing racial harassment in schools due to others' perceptions of their hair. In addition, some school boards in the US have suspended African-American students for wearing braids, beads, cornrows, dreadlocks, and other "extreme" hairstyles seen as making an overly strong political or cultural statement (Rooks, 2001). Black women have even been fired from jobs in major corporations for styling their hair in dreadlocks and braids. Because of the ways in which Black women's hair may be seen as connoting disruptive or oppositional identities, those with offending styles are banished, thus undermining their rights to represent themselves in preferred ways in public spaces (Rooks, 2001).

The Breast Project

I want to turn to breasts as a final site of modification. It is difficult to get an accurate read on how many Canadian women seek breast augmentation or reduction every year because the Canadian government does not keep track of cosmetic surgery procedures (Canadian Broadcasting Corporation News, 2008). Nor do many women, especially young women, have easy access to unbiased information about the negative health consequences of breast implants. However, it is estimated that 100 000 to 200 000 Canadian women have implants, and that most have or will have complications requiring additional surgery and/or implant removal (Tweed, 2003), due to rupture, deflation, and leakage that occurs in three-quarters of recipients (Brown et al., 2000). In addition, anywhere from 25 percent to 100 percent of women with implants suffer from capsular contracture, where scar tissue forms around the implant (because it is a foreign body), causing implanted breasts to become hard, painful, misshapen, or lopsided (Tweed, 2003). In a recent study into the long-term health risks of implants, researchers have found that, compared to other recipients of plastic surgery, women with breast implants are twice as likely to die from brain cancer, three times as likely to die from lung cancer, and four times as likely to kill themselves (Brinton et al., 2001). There may also be a link between silicone gel implants and autoimmune diseases such as fibromyalgia (Brown, 2001).

In our makeover culture, the mainstream media increasingly promotes cosmetic surgery as a preferred solution to girls' body image problems. Given the health risks associated with implants, it is particularly distressing that breast augmentation and other cosmetic surgeries are advocated as reasonable solutions to young women's body dissatisfaction resulting from harassment. For example, an article in *The Globe and Mail* (MacDonald, 2001) presents cosmetic breast and eye surgeries as the only viable responses for young women to the emotional effects of racist and sexist body-related comments. By promoting individualized responses like cosmetic surgery to others' rejection, the article ignores possible systemic solutions to body image concerns—for example, stopping the harassment (Larkin and Rice, 2005):

> A few years ago [Dr. Claudio De Lorenzi] operated on a 15-year-old girl to give her a B cup … her doctor wrote me a letter saying this girl's emotional problems stem mainly from her appearance. She doesn't have the ability to withstand the teasing. She came into my office with her head bowed, her bangs covering her whole face … I remember when she came back, she had her hair up, she was a totally different person … the amazing difference was in her self-confidence. It made me think sometimes it is justifiable. (MacDonald, 2001, p. R25)

In the absence of institutional policies addressing harassment, or of the political will to enforce polices where they exist, the drive for young women to seek out individualized solutions such as altering their perceived defects through surgery begins to make sense. As feminist cultural theorist Susan Bordo (1999) has noted, consumer culture depends on the continual creation and proliferation of female "defects." By making us feel bad about our bodies while pumping us with our own sense of choice, freedom, and agency, we are primed to purchase solutions offered by the beauty and cosmetic medical industries.

Women in my own study sought breast augmentation and reduction surgeries to avert harassing looks and hurtful comments, and to free themselves from stressful efforts to conceal their breast size and shape.

> I got messages that I was provocative. I remember doing trampoline. A group of guys who I thought were waiting for their turn, came to watch me. That hurt. Later, I had a breast reduction. I didn't want to buy into some patriarchal racist notion of what my breasts were supposed to look like. But I felt so restricted. (Marcia, 37, African and First Nations Canadian)

> [Before my implants] I felt so uncomfortable hiding my breasts. I used to take off my bra, get under the covers, make sure it was dark so you couldn't see. I wouldn't let him touch the smaller one. If he did touch it, then he'd be "How come one's smaller?" (Maya, 22, Jamaican Canadian, disability from late childhood)

In general, cultural meanings given to girls' and women's bodies that circulate in their everyday social lives play a primary role in constructing their bodies (including weight, skin, hair and breasts) as problem sites that need to be corrected. Women respond to these messages through diverse body modification projects that range from dieting and disordered eating to skin lightening and cosmetic surgery. Moving beyond these individual solutions, I take up a few examples of feminist responses to oppressive beauty ideals in the context of my concluding comments.

CONCLUSION

Women report two responses to beauty standards: changing their bodies, which can lead to harmful body image problems and risky body alteration practices; or changing their situations, which can lead to improved body self-images. Of course, most of us navigate between both solutions; we try changing certain aspects of our bodies to fit into our environments and altering aspects of our environments to enhance our sense of "fit" and belonging. In my research, many women learned to redirect their energy into creating life circumstances where self-worth was based on things other than appearance. Significantly, a woman's capacity to alter her environment emerged in each narrative as key to her greater control and ownership of image.

Beyond individuals' improvisational efforts to affirm their bodies and identities, other critical ways that women might change their situations is through changing their institutional and image environments. For instance, feminist-informed health and social policy might better serve girls and women (and boys and men) by shifting focus from changing people's bodies to altering aspects of social and cultural worlds that impede their options for eating, activity, and other aspects of embodiment. A "body equity" approach in schools, health care settings, and other institutional sites that would advocate the acceptance of diverse bodies could work to stop stereotyping and stigma based on size, disability, or other physical differences (Rice and Russell, 2002). The primary objective of a feminist "body ethics" would be to move away from current cultural practices of enforcing body norms and toward more creative endeavours of exploring physical abilities and possibilities unique to different bodies.

Of course, feminists committed to changing our image environments have developed and continue to offer critical analyses of cultural messages and to create counter-images that challenge conventional views. For many activists and artists, this has meant creating representations that celebrate bodily differences or that dare to depict the abject. In various times and across diverse spaces, feminist cultural production (in books, plays, and visual arts) has worked to disrupt dominant ways of portraying bodies. One example is the development of "fat drag," live performances that poke fun at our cultural stereotypes about fat. Another is theatre that explores Black women's relationship to beauty. A third is art activism that uncovers and critiques the under- and misrepresentation of women in the art world. Feminists have shown how limitations of resources, space, and opportunity, rather than lack of courage or creativity, have constrained women artists and activists from imagining new possibilities for representations.

In closing, women do not modify their bodies because they are mindless dupes of sexist, racist, and classist media culture. Rather, they respond to oppressive ideals and evaluative others by seeking a "best possible" body and self. I see women's greater focus on appearance as signs neither of their victimization nor of their emancipation in consumer culture, but as their best attempts to navigate an image system in which bodies have become critical markers of identity and value. Yet our solutions to the hegemonic image system have come at a high cost, intensifying and diversifying our body projects and problems into the 21st century.

Suggested Readings

Bordo, S. 1993. *Unbearable weight: Feminism, Western culture and the body*. Los Angeles: Univ. of California Press. A scholarly yet accessible feminist classic that examines the cultural and historical roots of Western women's obsession with appearance and their struggles to control food and hunger.

Covino, D. 2004. *Amending the abject body: Aesthetic makeovers in medicine and culture*. Albany: State Univ. of New York Press. An important study of makeover culture, including an analysis of cosmetic surgery procedures, reality TV shows, magazines aimed at aging audiences, and Oprah Winfrey's *O Magazine*.

Gard, M., and J. Wright. 2005. *Obesity epidemic: Science, morality and ideology*. New York: Taylor and Francis. A much-needed critical antidote to the alarmist debate about weight and health that shows how social meanings of fat are shaped by moral and ideological agendas masking as objective science.

Hobson, J. 2005. *Venus in the dark: Blackness and beauty in popular culture*. New York: Routledge. An important cultural history of Black female beauty that examines Western culture's fascination with Black women's bodies throughout the history of slavery and colonial conquest using the enduring figure of the "Hottentot Venus."

Malson, H. and M. Burns, eds. 2008. *Critical feminist perspectives on eating dis/orders*. London: Psychology Press. This forthcoming edited collection features writing and research by many well-known and newly emerging feminist scholars in the fields of eating disorders, dieting, and obesity.

Mire, A. 2005. Pigmentation and empire: The emerging skin-whitening industry. *Counterpunch Magazine*, July 28. **www.counterpunch.org/mire07282005.html**. An excellent, widely-cited, classic article that analyzes the emerging and expanding global market for skin-lightening products.

Rooks, N. 1996. *Hair raising: Beauty, culture, and African-American women*. New Brunswick, NJ: Rutgers Univ. Press. An insightful and engaging exploration of the history and politics of hair and beauty culture in African-American communities from the 19th century to the 1990s.

Discussion Questions

1. Discuss how dominant beauty ideals have changed since the 19th century. How were these ideals shaped by particular assumptions about class, race, and physical ability? Consider the implications of these ideals for racialized women, poor women, fat women, and women with disabilities.

2. List the image-based technologies you use (e.g., mirrors, cameras, computers, TV) and the image-based media you and your friends and family consume in your everyday lives (e.g., movies, TV, videos). Spend a few minutes reflecting on the prevalence of visual images everywhere in people's environments because of these technologies. How have technological developments increased the pressures and opportunities for body- and self-scrutiny in the 20th century? Using feminist theory introduced in this chapter, explain why the proliferation of visual technologies and images in our everyday lives has a particular significance for girls and women.

3. Discuss the various "body projects" that engage girls and women in response to pressures and messages they receive about their bodies. In what ways has the body become "an important identity project"? Reflect on your own consumption patterns and the beauty products that you and your peers purchase. What are you buying when you buy clothes, cosmetics, beauty products, women's magazines, and other image-enhancing items? How do you construct and distinguish your identities through these purchases?

4. Debate the effects of makeover shows such as *The Swan*, *Extreme Makeover*, *What Not to Wear*, *Skin Deep*, and *Say Yes to the Dress*, or the use of skin-lightening products such as *Fair & Lovely* and *Bi-White*. Does body modification (cosmetic surgeries, hair, face, and wardrobe makeovers, skin-lightening creams, tanning salons) work primarily to enhance the self-esteem of girls and women who seek them out? Or do they conscript young and adult women into prescribed roles in a patriarchal, racist, and classist world? What are the possible effects of makeover shows and ads for body modification products on diverse female audiences?

5. Discuss and debate the origins and implications of the "obesity epidemic" and the "epidemic" of disordered eating within Western and global contexts. Why have Western populations become so concerned about weight? Are poor countries really facing an "epidemic" of obesity? What are the possible effects on the public of frightening messages linking over- or underweight with people's health? How can people evaluate such information about weight in order to do what's best for themselves, their families, and communities?

6. What do you think girls and women really need to break free of the image system? How should we be advocating for a change to restrictive ideals? Is shutting down pro-ana and pro-mia websites the answer? Will banning super-thin models from fashion shows change our ideals? Should all skin-lightening, hair relaxing, and other beauty advertisements and products be banned? Are *Miss Ability* beauty contests the answer? What other changes would you like to see? What do you think "real" autonomy and liberation might look like for girls and women?

Bibliography

Ahmed, S. 1998. Animated borders: Skin, colour and tanning, in *Vital signs: Feminist reconfigurations of the bio/logical body,* eds. M. Shildrick and J. Price, 45–65. Edinburgh: Edinburgh Univ. Press.

Associated Press. 2006. Surgeon General: Obesity epidemic will dwarf terrorism threat. *LiveScience.com*, March 2. **www.livescience.com/health/ap_060302_obesity.html.** Retrieved April 15, 2008.

Barnett, A., and Z. Smith. 2005. Toxic creams for sale as thousands seek whiter skin. *The Observer,* October 16. **www.guardian.co.uk/uk/2005/oct/16/health.healthandwellbeing.** Retrieved April 18, 2008.

Bauman, A., et al. 2004. ParticipACTION: This mouse roared, but did it get the cheese? *Canadian Journal of Public Health* 95(S2): S14–S19.

Beausoleil, N. 1994. Makeup in everyday life: An inquiry into the practices of urban American women of diverse backgrounds, in *Many mirrors: Body image and social relations*, ed. N Sault, 33–57. New Brunswick, NJ: Rutgers Univ. Press.

Beausoleil, N. 1999. Afterword, in *That body image thing: Young women speak out*, ed. S. Torres, 106–110. Ottawa: CRIAW/ICREF.

Bennett, W., and J. Gurin. 1983. *The dieter's dilemma: Eating less and weighing more.* New York: Basic Books.

Berger, J. 1980. *Ways of seeing.* Harmondsworth, UK: Penguin Books.

Bordo, S. 1993. *Unbearable weight: Feminism, Western culture and the body.* Los Angeles: Univ. of California Press.

Bordo, S. 1999. *Twilight zones: The hidden life of cultural images from Plato to O.J.* Berkeley: Univ. of California Press.

Boutelle, K., et al. 2002. Weight control behaviors among obese, overweight, and non-overweight adolescents. *Journal of Pediatric Psychology* 27(6): 531–540.

Brinton, L., et al. 2001. Mortality among augmentation mammoplasty patients. *Epidemiology* 12: 321–326.

Brown, L. 2001. Silicone gel breast implant rupture, extracapsular silicone and health status in a population of women, *Journal of Rheumatology* 28: 996–1103.

Brown, L., et al. 2000. Prevalence of rupture of silicone gel breast implants in a population of women in Birmingham, Alabama. *American Journal of Roentgenology* 175: 1–8.

Brownell, K., and K. Horgen. 2004. *Food fight.* New York: Contemporary Books.

Brumberg, J. 1998. *The body project: An intimate history of American girls.* New York: Vintage Books.

Byrd, A., and L. Tharps. 2001. *Hair story: Untangling the roots of black hair in America.* New York: St. Martin's Griffen.

Campos, P. 2004. *The obesity myth.* New York: Gotham Books.

Canadian Broadcasting Corporation. 2008. Cosmetic surgery: Balancing risk. *CBC News In Depth: Health*, April 10. **www.cbc.ca/news/background/health/cosmetic-surgery.html.** Retrieved April 19, 2008.

Canadian Press. 2007. $5M to bring back ParticipACTION exercise program. *CBCnews.ca*, February 19. **www.cbc.ca/health/story/2007/02/19/participaction.html.** Retrieved April 17, 2008.

Clehane, D. 2007. Lines drawn for tween market: Celebrity designers tap into spending power. *Variety Magazine Online*, March 29. **www.variety.com/article/VR1117962097.html?categoryid=2529&cs=1**. Retrieved April 17, 2008.

Cogan, J., and P. Ernsberger. 1999. Dieting, weight, and health: Reconceptualizing research and policy. *Journal of Social Issues* 55(2): 187–205.

Counter, A. 2003. Whitening skin can be deadly. *The Boston Globe, Boston.com News*, December 16. **www.boston.com/news/globe/health_science/articles/2003/12/16/whitening_skin_can_be_deadly/**. Retrieved April 18, 2008.

Covino, D. 2004. *Amending the abject body: Aesthetic makeovers in medicine and culture*. Albany: State Univ. of New York Press.

Davis, K. 1995. *Reshaping the female body: The dilemma of cosmetic surgery*. New York: Routledge.

de Beauvoir, S. 1974. *The second sex*, 2d ed., tr. H. M. Parshley. New York: Vintage Books.

de Lauretis, T. 1987. *Technologies of gender: Essays on theory, film, and fiction*. Indianapolis: Indiana Univ. Press.

Disney Corporation. 2007. Disney consumer products continue strong growth at retail. Disney Corporation Press Release, June 19. **https://licensing.disney.com/Home**. Retrieved April 12, 2008.

Dorning, A. 2007. Black hair dos and don'ts: *Glamour Magazine* can't shake fallout from bad hair advice. *ABC News Online*, October 10. **http://abcnews.go.com/US/story?id=3710971&page=1**. Retrieved April 19, 2008.

Etcoff, N., et al. 2004. The real truth about beauty: Findings of the global study on women, beauty and well-being. Unpublished report commissioned by Dove, Unilever Corporation, London, September.

Ernsberger, P., and R. Koletsky. 1999. Biomedical rationale for a wellness approach to obesity: An alternative to a focus on weight loss. *Journal of Social Issues* 55(2): 221–259.

Eye2Eye Media. 2008. *Miss Ability*. **www.eye2eyemedia.nl/engels/index.htm.** Retrieved April 12, 2008.

Fairburn, C., and K. Brownell, eds. 2002. *Eating disorders and obesity: A comprehensive handbook*, 2d ed. New York: Guilford Press.

Fitzgerald, T. 2007. With teens at least, "Gossip Girl" is hot! It's the top-rated new show among 12–17-year-olds. *Media Life Magazine*, October 5. **www.medialifemagazine.com/artman2/publish/Younger_viewers_49/With_teens_at_least_Gossip_Girl_is_hot.asp.** Retrieved April 17, 2008.

Gard, M., and J. Wright. 2005. *Obesity epidemic: Science, morality and ideology*. New York: Taylor and Francis.

Gardner, R., B. Friedman, and N. Jackson. 1999. Body size estimations, body dissatisfaction, and ideal size preferences in children six through sixteen. *Journal of Youth and Adolescence* 28: 603–618.

Garner, D. 1997. The 1997 body image survey results. *Psychology Today* 30: 30–64.

Harding, K. 2008. BMI illustrated categories project. **http://kateharding.net/bmi-illustrated/**. Retrieved April 14, 2008.

Hearne, A. 2007. Shake yo' tail feathers: Watching and performing gender. Lecture, January 11, Women's Studies 100, An Introduction to Women's Studies. Trent University, Peterborough, ON.

Hossain, A. n.d. The color complex: Is the fixation really fair? *Sapna Magazine*. **www. sapnamagazine.com/index.php?option=com_content&task=view&id=121&Itemid=30**. Retrieved April 18, 2008.

Hurst, N. 1996. Lactation after augmentation mammoplasty. *Obstetrics & Gynecology* 87: 30–34.

Ikeda, J., P. Crawford, and G. Woodward-Lopez. 2006. BMI screening in schools: Helpful or harmful. *Health Education Research* 21(6): 761–769.

Irving, L. 2000. Promoting size acceptance in elementary school children: The EDAP puppet program. *Eating Disorders* 8: 221–232.

Jacobson, S., and L. McLay. 2006. The economic impact of obesity on automobile fuel consumption, *The Engineering Economist* 51(4): 307–323.

Jones, J., et al. 2001. Disordered eating attitudes and behaviours in teenaged girls: A school-based study. *Canadian Medical Association Journal* 165(50): 547–552.

Jutel, A. 2006. The emergence of overweight as a disease entity: Measuring up normality. *Social Science and Medicine* 63: 2268–2276.

Kristeva, J. 1982. *Powers of horror: An essay on abjection*, tr. L. Roudiez. New York: Columbia Univ. Press.

Kristeva, J. 1991. *Strangers to ourselves*, tr. L. Roudiez. New York: Columbia Univ. Press.

Larkin, J., and C. Rice. 2005. Beyond "healthy eating" and "healthy weights": Harassment and the health curriculum in middle schools. *Body Image* 2: 219–232.

Lau, D., et al. 2007. 2006 Canadian clinical practice guidelines on the management and prevention of obesity in adults and children. *Canadian Medical Association Journal* 176(8): 118.

Lawrence, R. 2004. Reframing obesity: The evolution of news discourse on a public health issue. *Harvard International Journal of Press-Politics* 9(3): 56–75.

Leistikow N. 2003. Indian women criticize "Fair and Lovely" ideal. *Women's E-News*, April 28. **www.womensenews.org/article.cfm/dyn/aid/1308/context/archive.** Retrieved April 18, 2008.

MacDonald, G. 2001. Girls under the knife. *The Globe and Mail*, January 15, R1, R25.

MacNeill, M. 1999. Social marketing, gender, and the science of fitness: A case study of ParticipACTION campaigns, in *Sport and gender in Canada*, eds. P. White and K. Young, 215–231. Toronto: Oxford Univ. Press.

McVey, G., et al. 2002. Risk and protective factors associated with disordered eating during early adolescence. *Journal of Early Adolescence* 22: 76–96.

Melchior-Bonnet, S. 2001. *The mirror: A history*, tr. K. Jewett. New York: Routledge.

Melwani, L. 2007. The white complex: What's behind the Indian prejudice for fair skin? *Little India*, August 18. **www.littleindia.com/news/134/ARTICLE/1828/2007-08-18.html.** Retrieved April 18, 2008.

Mire, A. 2005. Pigmentation and empire: The emerging skin-whitening industry. *Counterpunch Magazine Online,* July 28. **www.counterpunch.org/mire07282005.html**. Retrieved April 18, 2008.

Morgan, M. 1991. Women and the knife: Cosmetic surgery and the colonization of women's bodies. *Hypatia* 6: 25–53.

Morimura, Yasumasa. 2008. "Self-portrait as art history." **www.assemblylanguage.com/images/ Morimura.html**. Retrieved June 26, 2008.

Neifert, M., et al. 1990. The influence of breast surgery, breast appearance, and pregnancy-induced breast changes on lactation sufficiency as measured by infant weight gain. *Birth* 17: 31–38.

O'Brien, S., and I. Szeman. 2004. *Popular culture: A user's guide.* Toronto: Nelson Education.

Odette, F. 1994. Body beautiful/Body perfect: Where do women with disabilities fit in? *Canadian Woman Studies/Les cahiers de la femme* 14(3): 41–43.

Oliver, E. 2006. *Fat politics: The real story behind America's obesity epidemic.* New York: Oxford Univ. Press.

ParticipACTION Archive Project. **www.usask.ca/archives/participaction/english/home.html**. Retrieved June 26, 2008.

Peiss, K. 1998. *Hope in a jar: The making of America's beauty culture.* New York: Henry Holt.

Poran, M. 2002. Denying diversity: Perceptions of beauty and social comparison processes among Latino, Black and white women. *Sex Roles* 47(1/2): 65–81.

Raine, K. 2004. *Overweight and obesity in Canada: A population health perspective.* Ottawa: Canadian Institute for Health Information.

Ricciardelli, L., and M. McCabe. 2001. Children's body image concerns and eating disturbances: A review of the literature. *Clinical Psychology Review* 21: 325–344.

Rice, C. 2003. *Becoming women: Body image, identity, and difference in the passage to womanhood.* Unpublished Women's Studies PhD dissertation, York University, Toronto.

Rice, C. 2007. Becoming "the fat girl": Acquisition of an unfit identity. *Women's Studies International Forum* 30(2): 158–174.

Rice, C. 2008a (forthcoming). Imagining the other? Ethical challenges of researching and writing women's embodied lives. *Feminism & Psychology.*

Rice, C. 2008b (forthcoming). How big girls become fat girls: The cultural production of problem eating and physical inactivity, in *Critical feminist perspectives on eating disorders: An international reader*, eds. H. Malson and M. Burns. London: Psychology Press.

Rice, C., et al. 2005. Envisioning new meanings of disability and difference. *International Journal of Narrative Counselling and Community Work* 3/4: 119–130.

Rice, C., L. Lenooy, and F. Odette. 2007. Talking about body image, identity, and difference. Envisioning New Meanings of Disability and Difference Project Workshop, November 26, Women's College Research Institute, Toronto.

Rice, C., and V. Russell. 2002. *Embodying equity: Body image as an equity issue.* Toronto: Green Dragon Press.

Rooks, N. 1996. *Hair raising: Beauty, culture, and African-American women.* New Brunswick, NJ: Rutgers Univ. Press.

Rooks, N. 2001. Wearing your race wrong: Hair, drama and the politics of representation for African American women at play on a battlefield, in *Recovering the black female body: Self representations by African American women*, eds. M. Bennett and V. Dickerson, 279–295. New Brunswick, NJ: Rutgers Univ. Press.

Rootman, I., and P. Edwards. 2004. The best laid schemes of mice and men … ParticipACTION's legacy and the future of physical activity promotion in Canada. *Canadian Journal of Public Health* 95(S2): S37–S44.

Ross, B. 2005. Fat or fiction: Weighing the obesity epidemic, in *Obesity epidemic: Science, morality and ideology*, eds. M. Gard and J. Wright, 86–106. New York: Taylor and Francis.

Russell, K., M. Wilson, and R. Hall. 1992. *The color complex: The politics of skin color among African Americans*. New York: Anchor Books.

Schwartz, H. 1986. *Never satisfied: A cultural history of diets, fantasies, and fat*. New York: Free Press.

Schiebinger, L. 1993. *Nature's body: Gender and the making of modern science*. Boston: Beacon Press.

Seid, J. 2006. CW Network to combine WB, UPN in CBS-Warner venture beginning in September. *CNNMoney.com*, January 24. **http://money.cnn.com/2006/01/24/news/companies/cbs_warner/index.htm.** Retrieved April 17, 2008.

Shapiro, S., M. Newcomb, and T. Burns Loeb. 1997. Fear of fat, disregulated-restrained eating, and body-esteem: Prevalence and gender differences among eight- to ten-year-old children. *Journal of Clinical Child Psychology* 26: 358–365.

Sherwin, A. 2006. Reality TV puts disabled women in beauty show. *The Times Online*, December 27. **www.timesonline.co.uk/tol/news/world/europe/article1068730.ece.** Retrieved April 12, 2008.

Sobal, J., and D. Maurer, eds. 1999. *Interpreting weight: The social management of fatness and thinness*. New York: Walter de Gruyter.

Stearns, P. 1997. *Fat history: Bodies and beauty in the modern West*. New York: New York Univ. Press.

Swee, W., K. Klontz, and L. Lambert. 2000. A nationwide outbreak of alopecia associated with the use of hair-relaxing formulation. *Archives of Dermatology* 136: 1104–1108.

Timmons, H. 2007. Telling India's modern women they have power. *New York Times Online*, May 30. **www.nytimes.com/2007/05/30/business/media/30adco.html?ex=1181620800&en=201bcdec 2fbde98d&ei=5070&emc=eta1.** Retrieved April 19, 2008.

Tjepkema, M. 2005. *Measured obesity. Adult obesity in Canada: Measured height and weight*. Ottawa: Statistics Canada.

Tremblay, M., P. Katzmarzyk, and J. Willms. 2002. Temporal trends in overweight and obesity in Canada, 1981–1996. *International Journal of Obesity* 26: 538–543.

Tweed, A. 2003. *Health care utilization among women who have undergone breast implant surgery*. Vancouver, BC: British Columbia Centre of Excellence for Women's Health.

Van Marsh, A. 2007. UK's skin bleaching trade exposed. CNN International.com/Health. **http://edition.cnn.com/2007/HEALTH/11/26/vanmarsh.skinbleaching/index.html.** Retrieved April 18, 2008.

World Health Organization. 2000. *Obesity: Preventing and managing the global epidemic*. Geneva, Switzerland.

World Health Organization. 2003. *Controlling the global obesity epidemic*. Geneva, Switzerland. **www.who.int/nutrition/topics/obesity/en/index.html.** Retrieved April 30, 2006.

Yeoman, F., C. Asome, and G. Keeley. 2006. Skinniest models are banned from catwalk. *The Times Online*, September 9. **www.timesonline.co.uk/tol/news/world/europe/article633568.ece**. Retrieved April 17, 2008.

CHAPTER 7

Violence against Women

Lisa Rosenberg and Ann Duffy

Without an understanding of male supremacy and
female oppression, it is impossible to explain why
the vast majority of incest perpetrators ... are male
and why the majority of victims ... are female.
> Herman and Hirschman (1993: 47)

The question of why men batter women can on one
level be answered quite simply. Men batter women
because they can.
> Freedman (1985: 41)

Gender violence, in all of its varied manifestations,
is not random and it is not about sex.
> UNICEF Report, as cited in Handelman (1997: A16)

INTRODUCTION

One of the experiential cements that binds together
the experiences of women is the fear and fact of
male violence. All women, regardless of class,
colour, race/ethnicity, religion, ability, age, or sexual orientation, are subject to male violence. Not
only waitresses but also female medical students
are subject to attack and abuse (Priest, 1994: A3).
The wives of prime ministers, sports celebrities,
doctors, lawyers, and corporate chieftains have
been subject to wife battery. Daughters of executives, religious ministers, and university professors
have been victims of incest and rape. A former
prime minister of Japan was publicly accused by
his wife of being physically abusive. In 1996, trial
documents revealed that the chairman of the board
of Canadian Tire and Gulf Canada Resources Limited had emotionally and physically abused his
wife (Andrews, 1999). In the 1980s, an ex–Miss
America claimed that for years she had been the
victim of incest by her corporate-executive father.
Women surgeons, senior government officials, corporate executives, and Crown attorneys have come
forward to lay complaints of sexual harassment and
assault. No amount of economic, racial, sexual, or
class-based privilege can absolutely protect women
from violence in a patriarchal[1] society. Most
women recognize their vulnerability to victimization. At home, in the workplace, in the throes of
giving birth, or in the last gasps of life, women
have been abused and violated. The 25-year-old
female college student in Mississauga, the 90-year-
old housewife in Somalia, and the 45-year-old
woman religious worker in Guatemala have in common their vulnerability and their wariness. Violence and the fear of violence frame many women's
lives and sculpt their identities.

The second wave of feminism was instrumental in exposing the dimensions and complexities of
violence against women, especially in the more
affluent and industrialized countries of the world.
From sexual harassment, date rape, and incest to
woman abuse in the home and in war crimes, feminists pulled away the hegemonic blinders and
revealed the devastation. Third-wave feminisms
have developed a more complex and nuanced
understanding of male violence and have honed an
expanded critique of the universalizing tendencies
of Western feminists who tended to overlook the
cultural particularities of women's victimization.
Today, feminists are drawing more attention to the
global and historical parameters of the violence:
the interconnections with colonialism, globalization, imperialism, heterosexism, ableism, and
racism. As a result, there is growing documentation of the global toll on women's lives. However,
as feminist scrutiny has expanded from a more
Western preoccupation, it has become clear that
violence against women must be understood in
terms of localities of history, culture, and power. In
short, the violence is being revealed as much
more complexly interwoven with local, national,
and international axes of power, privilege, and
oppression.

STICKS AND STONES: THE TOLL OF MALE VIOLENCE AGAINST WOMEN

Violence against women encompasses an enormous range of actions, actors, and social locations. Many researchers today define the concept to include psychological and emotional violence as well as economic/financial abuse and spiritual coercion (Rosenberg, 2005). Non-physical forms of male violence, such as financial, psychological, and emotional abuse, should not be trivialized or ignored, since they are extremely significant and prevalent. Indeed, survivors of wife assault frequently report that the emotional violence is much harder to endure and transcend than the physical blows and injuries (Statistics Canada, 2006a). Further, it is often, of course, impossible to fully separate emotional and physical violence. Physical and sexual attacks on women are frequently accompanied by vicious verbal tirades and persistent efforts to humiliate and dominate the victim.

Here the focus is on feminist research (particularly in Canada), which documents the nature and extent of the violence, especially physical violence, perpetrated against women. Although it is not possible to do justice to the global literature, it is clear from this overview that violence against women in multiple forms is a common and persistent reality in most women's lives.

GROWING UP FEMALE: VIOLENCE IN THE FAMILY

Historically and cross-culturally, there is considerable evidence that, particularly in the family, women have been targeted for victimization (Coomaraswamy, 2006; Mooney, 2000).[2] Indeed, many commentators have made the point that, for many women and girls, the family is the most dangerous and violent institution in society. Historically, of course, many girls did not even experience the family because they were the victims of infanticide. As unwanted or insupportable burdens on family resources they were smothered or abandoned. This practice persists in several countries to this day. Indeed, analysts are expressing alarm at the increasingly skewed ratio of boys to girls in India and China. In North America, women compose approximately 51 percent of the population; in India between 1991 and 2001 the number of girls (six and under) dropped from 945 to 927 per 1000 boys. In some states of India it is a mere 770. Female infanticide, along with ultrasound-aided selective abortion of female fetuses, has meant fewer girls growing up in families (Sen, 2006; Sharma, 2003).

Sexual Abuse

Infanticide and selective abortion are not common for girls in Canadian families, but there are many other grave concerns. Given the pervasive patriarchal tradition of controlling and directing the sexuality of young girls, it is not surprising that much of the violence against girls and young women has been in the form of sexual abuse within the family.

The extent of the abuse was first revealed in the 1980s. Robin Bagley's groundbreaking national survey of child sexual abuse in Canada found that one in two females and one in three males had been victims of sexual offences (Bagley, 1984: 193). Diana Russell's (1986) breakthrough research using a probability sample of 930 San Francisco women focused more specifically on the issue of incest. She found that 16 percent of the women had been incestuously abused. Based on a review of this and other research data, Bagley and King concluded that serious sexual abuse in childhood (much of it unreported) occurs in at least 15 percent of the female Canadian population and 5 percent of the male population (Bagley and King, 1990: 70).

The recent Statistics Canada report, "Measuring Violence against Women: Statistical Trends 2006," corroborates this gendered pattern (Statistics Canada, 2006a). Overwhelmingly, it is girls who are victimized in reported family-related sexual assaults. Even as girls mature, they remain the primary targets for both the enactment of power and the frustration of powerlessness (Au Coin, 2003: 34, 35). Among girls, certain groups are particularly at risk. Considerable research shows, for example, that Aboriginal girls have been and continue to be subject to high rates of victimization (Olsen Harper, 2009; Bourassa et al., 2006; Ursel and Gorkoff, 2001).

The global patterns similarly bear testimony to the extent of abuse. From the research available regarding the percentage of adults who report having been sexually abused as children, statistics suggest that victimization is common. In Barbados, Costa Rica, Nicaragua, Switzerland, Spain, the United States, and Australia from one in five to more than one in four women indicate they were abused. Further, where data exist, they are clearly gendered, with girls consistently more likely to be victimized than boys (Jiwani, 2005; Seager, 2003: 58–59; Kendall-Tackett, 2001).

In addition, there are global patterns of sexual violence toward girls that are specific to certain locales. In particular, feminist activists have identified female genital mutilation as an important issue in a number of African, Middle Eastern, and South American countries. Although practices vary among cultural groups, typically in this ritual all or part of the girl's clitoris is removed when she is between 6 and 12 years of age. The practice is justified in terms of religious obligation and tradition, as a means to ensure virginity until marriage, to ensure marriage itself, to enhance male sexual pleasure, to bring honour to the family, and to control women's and girls' sexual activities. Although the practice is banned in many countries (for example, in Kenya under the 2002 *Children's Act*), activists estimate that millions of girls have been and continue to be subject to this practice and many have, as a result, suffered serious infections, difficulties in childbirth, or even death (Fiorillo, 2008; Wood, 2005; Munala, 2003).

Historically, girls were a form of property within the traditional patriarchal family. As evident from the Talmud and Bible, the sexual misuse of children is embedded in Western traditions—traditions later exported with colonialism. For example, according to Florence Rush, Talmudic law allows for the betrothal of a female child of "three years and one day ... by sexual intercourse" (1980: 18). From biblical times and until the late Middle Ages, child marriage[3] (when the girl was about age 12) was the norm and was generally seen as a property transaction between the father and the husband. Similarly, in biblical terms, child rape was a property crime against the father; the rapist, if unmarried, was required to marry his victim and pay a fine to her father. Within this historical tradition, with its implicit sexualization of female children and normalization of adult–child sexuality, it is not surprising that violence against many female children often takes the form of sexual abuse. In this context, it is not surprising that fundamentalist Mormon sects, such as those in Bountiful, British Columbia, would still be engaging in marriages with child brides (Bramham, 2008).

Although a law specifically prohibiting incest was introduced into the Canadian criminal law in 1890, child sexual abuse has only been acknowledged as a pervasive social problem in most Western countries since the 1970s, and, as a result, the research base has been relatively limited until recently (Sangster, 2001). There is some evidence that incest, predominantly the sexual assault of girls by older male relatives, has been a documented social problem since before the turn of the 20th century (Gordon, 1986). However, the interesting findings presented by Freud, Kinsey, and others were dismissed by a society intent on blaming the victim, ignoring the issue, and upholding patriarchal rights. Only with the advent of the second wave of the women's movement and its explorations of violence against women were incest survivors empowered to come forward. In the late 1970s and 1980s, landmark memoirs such as Katherine Brady's *Father's Days: A True Story of Incest* (1979), Charlotte Vale Allen's *Daddy's Girl: A Very Personal Memoir* (1980), and Elly Danica's *Don't Is a Woman's Word* (1988) established incest as a central feminist issue. Shirley Turcotte also raised awareness about incest in her 1987 National Film Board of Canada documentary, *To a Safer Place*, which details her father's abuse, the impact this abuse has on her as an adult, and her quest to survive the abuse and lead a healthy, good life (Turcotte, 1987).

The horrifying magnitude of sexual abuse experiences, as well as the poor institutional response, continues to be frequently reported in the media. In a recent incest case, the judge harshly criticized Ontario's child-protection system for failing to protect five Ottawa-area sisters who were sexually abused by their father for years. As children, the five sisters slept in the same room. Each night their father would come to their bedroom and pick one of them to join him in his bedroom for sexual intercourse. Two of the daughters became pregnant by their father. Another one was taken out of Canada at gunpoint to another country, where she was isolated and served as a sex slave for more than a year. One daughter managed to run away but was returned home by the police, who did not take her complaints seriously. Once back home, her father beat her and threatened her with a gun, saying that he would kill her if she ran away again. All five sisters, two brothers, and their mother were viciously beaten, terrorized, and threatened on a regular basis. It took more than 25 years to charge this father with different criminal offences. Eventually he was found too ill to stand a criminal trial and died during a civil suit (Vincent, 1999).

Rape

The second wave of the women's movement was instrumental in naming, documenting, and analyzing rape. Theorists and activists documented the large-scale nature of rape, showed how rape negatively affects women, opened rape crisis centres, revealed damaging societal attitudes toward women, and took on the legal system's inadequate treatment of rape victims and leniency toward rapists. Groundbreaking analyses by Susan Brownmiller, in *Against Our Will: Men, Women and Rape* (1975), and by Lorene Clark and Debra Lewis, in *Rape: The Price of Coercive Sexuality* (1977), helped to move society's minimalization and trivialization of rape toward an understanding that rape was a serious offence, with serious consequences, and could happen to any woman. A woman could be raped by a stranger, a family member, a date, or an acquaintance. A very important part of this new understanding of rape was putting forth the demand that, regardless of a woman's situation or her appearance, she had the right to say "No" to unwanted sexual demands.

As feminist analysts have subsequently and repeatedly pointed out, this pattern of sexual violence and abuse cannot be dismissed as a natural or evolutionary feature of the human race. Rather, anthropological analysis reveals that non- or low-rape cultures are well documented. In cultures where sexual equality is the norm, the sexes are seen as complementary, and women are understood to make a significant contribution to social continuity. They typically display socialization practices and gender dynamics that are not premised on gendered control and authority (Watson-Franke, 2002; Sanday, 2002).

In contrast, more patriarchal societies tend to endorse beliefs and attitudes that are "rape-prone." Researchers have repeatedly reported that young men in such societies embrace notions of coercive sexuality. For example, in one study, more than half of male high school students said they believed it was acceptable for a boy to hold a girl down and force her into intercourse when, for example, she had made him sexually excited (Malamuth, 1981: 152). Similarly, Neil Malamuth, Scott Haber, and Seymour Feschbach found that 51 percent of a sample of college males said there was "some likelihood" they would rape a woman in a dating situation if they were assured they would not be punished (1980: 130).

These coercive and rape-prone attitudes appear to be more than theoretical. Mary Koss and Cheryl Oros (1982: 456) found that one in five men in a representative survey of 3862 American university students recalled "being in a situation in which they became so aroused that they could not stop themselves from having sexual intercourse even though the woman didn't want to." Approximately one in three of the women in this sample reported "being in a situation where a man became so sexually aroused that they felt it was useless to stop him even though the woman did not want to have intercourse." Similarly, over the past two decades "rape prevalence" research with US college students has consistently reported that one in seven female respondents was the victim of a completed rape (Rozee and Koss, 2001: 296). Other research indicates that many men do not subscribe to the "no means no" script and will continue to press sexual advances after a woman has explicitly refused (Wood, 2005) or will interpret relatively innocuous behaviour as an invitation to sexual contact (Anderson et al., 2004). Mark Totten's interviews with male youth in Ottawa support the view that many young men are socialized to engage in the sexual objectification and abuse of their girlfriends while embracing attitudes that define their behaviour as morally right (Totten, 2000: 132, 139).

As pointed out by numerous feminist activists, dominant ideologies perpetuate this coercive behaviour. In particular, a variety of popular rape myths legitimate male aggression and blame women for their own victimization. These rape myths, which remain remarkably resistant to change, are as follows: Women who are raped are really asking to be attacked; a woman is asking for rape by being out late at night, by the clothes she wears, the way she walks, her gestures, the way she makes eye contact, and so on; a woman can actually prevent herself from being raped if she really wants to do so; a woman often says "no" when she really means "yes" so that she doesn't seem "too easy"; only young, beautiful women are raped (or only "bad" girls are raped); rape only happens in cities, in bad areas of town, and/or only at night; "real" rape only happens with strangers (a woman cannot be raped by a boyfriend or husband); women are raped because men are too impulsive or too passionate to stop; and women very often cry rape because they are angry or jealous (Women's Support Network of York Region, 2004).

Research indicates that these erroneous beliefs and attitudes frequently result in actual rapes. The landmark[4] Canadian Violence Against Women (CVAW) survey found that rape is an alarmingly common phenomenon. Researchers estimate that 39 percent of Canadian women have experienced at least one incident of sexual assault (Statistics Canada, 2006a: 26). Male violence during dating relationships is also very common. In the past decade, the popularization of date rape drugs such as Rohypnol have created a new danger for women and a strategy for rapists. Added to a drink, the potent sedative is colourless, odourless, tasteless, and easily dissolves. When the drugged woman wakes up, she typically has only a foggy recollection of the night before. Not only does the woman have to be concerned about having her drink tampered with by men at bars, but there have been instances of bartenders drugging women's drinks on behalf of their male patrons (National Women's Health Information Centre, 2006).

It is estimated that fewer than 10 percent of women victims report being raped to the police (Statistics Canada, 2006a). Whether their fears are unfounded or not, women who have been victimized indicate that they fear not being believed by the police, not being taken seriously or treated respectfully by the legal system, and not being able to maintain their personal privacy around their past sexual history. The introduction of Bill C-127 in 1983, which amended the *Criminal Code*, transformed the offence of rape into a series of sexual assault offences (level 1, 2, or 3 depending on the severity of physical violence employed in the attack). It included provisions called the "Rape Shield Law," which set out very strict guidelines regarding the judicial relevance of a woman's past sexual history (McIntyre, 2005). Section 276 limited questioning of victims in sexual assault trials about past sexual history, and Section 277 stated sexual reputation cannot be admitted if used to challenge the credibility of the victim. However, protections afforded by this law were weakened by court challenges, such as the Seaboyer case, heard by the Supreme Court of Canada in 1991. Seaboyer argued that his right to a fair trial was impeded by Sections 276 and 277. The Supreme Court agreed and struck down Section 276 (McIntyre, 2005). In 1992 further reforms to the "Rape Shield Law" resulted in judges following eight guidelines in deciding whether a woman's past sexual history could be used in a specific case. Research suggests that judges are frequently using this judicial discretion to admit past women's sexual history in rape cases (Doe, 2007; McIntyre, 2005).

One woman who did report her rape and then went on to make legal history in Canada is "Jane Doe" (the anonymous designation given to female victims of violent crime). Jane Doe was the fifth victim of the "Balcony Rapist," a serial rapist who operated in a certain area of Toronto in the summer of 1986 (Doe, 2003). After a neighbour recognized the man and he was arrested, Jane Doe decided she would be best represented at trial by her own lawyer, whereupon she became the first raped woman in Ontario to obtain her own legal representation. This helped her to secure the right to sit in on the trial, instead of leaving after her own testimony, as was the custom for raped women (Doe, 2003). What she learned from the trial itself and from police officers soon after her rape was that she had been used as bait by police to try to catch this rapist. Rather than being afforded the protection she could reasonably expect as a citizen, she was an unwitting pawn in the investigation. In light of this information, Jane Doe sued the Metropolitan Toronto Police Force for their negligence in the investigation of her rape. She cited the systemic sexism embedded in police practices and argued that her *Charter* rights had been violated. In 1991 the Ontario Supreme Court ruled that her case could go to trial—a landmark victory since this was the first time in Ontario that police were held accountable in court for their actions while on the job. In 1997 the highly publicized trial began. The next year, she won and was awarded $220 000 (Doe, 2003). This was a personal victory for her and a symbolic one for women in Ontario. Following the court ruling, the Toronto City Council ordered an audit, called the Jane Doe social audit, to investigate and hopefully rectify the systemic sexist practices in the police force. This report was completed in 1999. However, since then, according to Jane Doe, the audit recommendations have not been implemented (Doe, 2007).

Rape, like incest, is a global phenomenon. In the late 1990s, approximately 40 000 Chinese, 90 000 US, 7000 German, 2000 Polish, 3000 Pakistani, and 15 000 Indian women each year reported that they had been raped (Seager, 2003: 58–59). Once again the reported rates vastly under-represent the actual incidence, which is estimated to be (very conservatively) ten times what was reported. South Africa, beset by a bitter history of colonialism and apartheid, reported the highest rape rate in the world with an estimated 4100 women a day raped (52 000 a year) (Nolen, 2007; Kaliehman, 2005; Seager, 2003: 58–59).

Social upheaval and military conflict both contribute to high rates of rape victimization. For centuries, rape has been employed as a strategy of war—a means of systematically humiliating and demoralizing the enemy population. Predictably, in recent years an enormous number of women have been raped in the course of armed conflicts or wars in countries such as Bosnia, Sierra Leone, the Sudan, and the Democratic Republic of Congo (Sesay, 2008; Ofoma, 2008). Despite the Rome Statute enacted in 2002, which established the International Criminal Court (in The Hague) and which identified gender-based crimes (rape, sexual slavery, forced pregnancy, and human trafficking) as war crimes as well as crimes against humanity, very little progress has been made toward punishing those who use rape as a weapon of war (Kielburger and Kielburger, 2008).

This worldwide litany of victimization is significant not only in terms of the millions of individual victims but also in terms of the women, never personally victimized, who grow up in a rape culture. The majority of Canadian women are not themselves direct casualties of dating violence or date rape, yet this potential for violence is a significant feature of their sexual and social socialization, as well as that of girls and young women around the globe (Cameron, 2008; Gordon, 2008; Stymest, 2008; Yonak, 2008). If not personally involved, they are likely to know someone who has been subjected to physical or sexual violence. Concerns about victimization, often reinforced by parents, teachers, the media, and peers, colour the experience of forming cross-gender relationships. Young women learn, for example, to anticipate their vulnerability walking at night, travelling on their own, and so on. They grow up in the shadow of interpersonal violence, a shadow that routinely distorts the formation of their most intimate relationships. Patterns of violence are reflected in a more generalized dating culture of coercion in which young women and men often act out traditional gender roles. According to this gender dating script, men are to demand, pressure, harass, and joke while women are to avoid, give in, blame themselves, and feel guilty (Littleton and Axsom, 2003).

OUT OF THE FRYING PAN AND INTO A RELATIONSHIP

Woman Abuse

For the overwhelming majority of Canadian young women, dating leads to a more-or-less permanent relationship and to common-law or legal marriage. Unfortunately, for far too many women, love and marriage lead to abuse and violence. According to the General Social Survey of Statistics Canada, 7 percent of women (and 6 percent of men) living in a common-law or marital relationship in 2004 reported that they had been sexually or physically assaulted during the previous 5 years (Statistics Canada, 2006a: 16). Despite the almost equivalent reporting rates for men and women,[5] research indicates that the more severe forms of violence are directed toward women. Research indicates that women are 2.5 times more likely than men to report the most severe forms of violence (being beaten, choked, threatened with a gun or knife, sexual assault). Over a five-year period, more than 250 000 women (compared with 89 000 men) experienced these types of severe assault (Statistics Canada, 2006a: 20).

Predictably, only one-third of abused women (37 percent) report spousal abuse incidents to the police (Statistics Canada, 2006a: 20–21). The rates of reported spousal violence have increased in recent years and presumably reflect a growing willingness to report these crimes (Patterson, 2003). Policies that require police to lay charges in spousal violence cases, regardless of the victim's wishes, and that require charges when the assailants counter-charge their victims ("she hit me too") may also be responsible for these increased rates of reported incidents. Victimization surveys (which sample the general population about their experience with domestic violence) suggest that there has, in fact, been a decline in the rates of spousal abuse in the past five years (Statistics Canada, 2006a: 18). It remains to be seen whether this indicates a long-term trend.

Within these overall patterns of woman abuse, victimization cuts across social class, immigrant status, age, sexual orientation, disability, and racial/ethnic divisions (Statistics Canada, 2006a: 14, 41); there appear to be no safe zones for women. However, some women are more vulnerable than others. Age is the biggest correlate for abuse, with young women having the highest rates (Statistics Canada, 2006a: 14, 36). Low occupational status and low family income are also commonly cited as strong correlates of abuse. Women who are living in low-income homes, and women whose spouses are unemployed, were twice as likely to be assaulted (Statistics Canada, 2006a: 40). Also, women living in common-law relationships experience higher rates of violence (Statistics Canada, 2006a: 14, 38; Brownridge and Halli, 2001). Being pregnant is now also seen as a dangerous time for women, as studies have shown 40 percent of women report that male violence began with their first pregnancy (Tyyskä, 2006).

Aboriginal women have notably higher rates of woman abuse and are more likely to report severe abuse such as being beaten, choked, or threatened with a knife or gun. Three times as many Aboriginal women report victimization. Similarly, spousal homicide rates are eight times higher for Aboriginal women than non-Aboriginal women (and 18 times higher for Aboriginal men than non-Aboriginal men) (Statistics Canada, 2006a: 64–69). In contrast, the rate of spousal abuse among the immigrant population (6 percent of women, 4 percent of men) and among the visible minority population (7 percent of women, 4 percent of men) is slightly lower than the Canadian average. Analysts argue that factors such as systemic discrimination against Aboriginal people, economic and social deprivation, alcohol and substance abuse, intergenerational violence, and the colonial legacy (as reflected in outcomes of residential schooling) generally result in increased violence (Razack, forthcoming; Baskin, 2003; Federal-Provincial-Territorial Ministers Responsible for the Status of Women, 2002: 14, 15, 18). Women who are disabled, elderly women, refugee women, and women who are sex-trade workers are also at a higher risk for male violence (Statistics Canada, 2006a).

So why do women not leave abusive situations? This is the question frequently posed by the Canadian public when faced with intimate partner abuse. One important answer has been provided by Lenore Walker, who maintains that most women in an abusive relationship go through a cycle called the "Walker Cycle of Abuse." In this cycle, tension builds up in the abuser, the violent act occurs, and the abuser apologizes and says it will never happen again. A honeymoon period follows, but then the tension builds up again and the cycle repeats (Walker, 1979). Walker's work was groundbreaking, not only because it recognized the cyclical pattern typical of many abusive relationships, but also because it identified the pattern of "learned helplessness" that often resulted from this pattern. Women who spent years trapped in abusive relationships lost their ability to accurately understand and respond to their situation (Boyle, 1990). Partially because of Walker's work, the justices in the 1987 Supreme Court of Canada case *Lavallee v. R* accepted the "Battered Woman Syndrome" defence for the first time. They found that Lavallee was not criminally responsible for killing her long-term abuser because decades of abuse had led to an inability to fully appreciate and understand the nature of her actions against her abuser (Boyle, 1990).

Although "Battered Woman Syndrome" can now be used as a legal defence by abused women who respond violently to their long-time abusers, the strategy is problematic. First, translating male violence against women into a syndrome means that the onus is taken off the abuser, and women have to fit into this psychologized and medicalized model, which stresses women's emotionality and vulnerability. Secondly, "learned helplessness" is a problematic term, in that it delimits women's agency. Certainly, the concept highlights the complexity and confusion that can accompany an abusive situation and underscores that the decision to leave may be emotionally loaded and unclear. After all, the abuse is often intermittent, the abuser may be remorseful, and the relationship between abuser and abused may have been based at one time in love and romance. However, an abused woman's decisions to stay may also be a rational and careful evaluation of her life situation and that of her children: Will she be able to support herself and her family? What will the impact be on her children? Does she have someone to stay with, or have years of abuse left her isolated from family and friends?

One important reason to postpone leaving is financial. Women in Canada still face great inequities in the labour market; even women who are employed on a full-time, year-round basis earn only 71 percent of comparable male wages. Recent years have seen very little real improvement in this pattern (Statistics Canada, 2006b: 139). Married women employed full-time, year-round earn about 65 percent of the earnings of comparable men, and women aged 45 to 54 working full-time, year-round earn under 70 percent of comparable men's wages (Statistics Canada, 2006b: 139–140). Against this backdrop, it is not surprising that many abused women struggle with issues surrounding financial autonomy.

While going to a shelter is an option, it may not seem accessible for rural women, women living on reserves, or women who speak neither English nor French. Often, a shelter is seen as a last resort (Statistics Canada, 2006a: 55). For a mother with children, fleeing to a shelter means uprooting her family, with few possessions, while the abuser often stays in the family home. Many shelters in Canada have also been criticized for not being culturally sensitive or linguistically equipped to service women's diverse needs, although many are attending to this or have changed their service provision (Miedema and Wachholz, 1998). Finally, access to a shelter bed may ultimately be problematic because of inadequate funding as a result of ongoing governmental funding cuts (Brodie, 2005). In sum, the struggle to break free of an abusive relationship may involve a complex morass of personal, familial, and practical issues. Perhaps, given the terror and threats, the question should be how do so many of them find the courage and strength to escape the violence?

Globally, evidence of woman abuse in intimate relationships is found almost everywhere. In the United States, Britain, New Zealand, Nigeria, Pakistan, India, Australia, Zimbabwe, South Korea, Egypt, and Barbados, research indicates that upwards of one-third of women indicate they have experienced physical abuse at the hands of a male intimate. In some countries the figures are even higher, such as Pakistan (80 percent), Ethiopia (45 percent), Poland (50 percent), Portugal (53 percent), Japan (59 percent), Bolivia (62 percent), and Guatemala (49 percent) (Seager, 2003: 26–27; Shallat, 2000; Saeed, 2000). Not surprisingly, there are also important diversities in women's experiences of battering. In some instances, woman abuse escalates during periods of social turmoil. In this respect, it is not surprising that in the past five years, rates of domestic abuse have risen dramatically in war-torn Iraq (MacKinnon, 2008). In troubled Uganda, the problem of domestic violence interweaves with high rates of HIV infection; in this strictly male-dominated society, wives report that they and their children are exposed to infection by abusive HIV-positive husbands who refuse to use condoms (Karanja, 2003).

In many settings, this pattern of woman abuse is the enactment of a centuries-old tradition of patriarchal violence against women in intimate relations. In numerous countries, women's subordination in marriage was and is often enshrined in law. In Britain and North America, the common-law tradition ensured women's familial vulnerability. According to Sir William Blackstone's influential treatise, "The common law gave a husband almost unlimited power to control his wife's property; he was, in fact, the titled owner of all her property. He also controlled her person, and had the right to discipline her. ... the husband ... might give his wife moderate correction just as he is allowed to correct his apprentices or children" (cited in Dranoff, 1977). And historical research suggests that these rights were far from theoretical. Nancy Tomes's examination of trial accounts in the *London Times* between 1841 and 1875 found that working-class women were subject to a "torrent of abuse" and that violent wife-beating was so common that middle-class reformers introduced the *Wife Beaters Act* (1882), which gave magistrates the power to flog and publicly pillory men who battered their wives (Tomes, 1978: 340).

In Canada (as elsewhere), European colonialists transported patriarchal traditions and imposed them on indigenous peoples. Under English common-law tradition, upon marriage a women's legal identity was submerged into that of her husband. This meant that any notion of husbands injuring wives was unthinkable; one cannot assault "oneself." When wives were given some property rights in the 1870s, they became able to sue their husbands for damage to their property but were still unable to take legal action against damage to themselves. If a husband broke his wife's nose and in the process shattered her glasses, she could sue only to recover the cost of the glasses. In 1975, Ontario became the first province to permit a wife to sue for personal injury compensation. The Napoleonic Code, which dominated Quebec customs and laws, also assumed the complete legal and social subordination of women to their husbands (Dranoff, 1977: 23, 12).

Within this social context, woman abuse was for generations simply experienced as part of everyday life. Just as many contemporary Canadians endorse spanking children, people saw violence between husbands and wives as, at worst, an unfortunate, shameful, and very private aspect of married life.[6] As Carolyn Strange points out, "the civil and the criminal law upheld the deeply patriarchal character of marriage, both by granting husbands enormous latitude in exercising their power, and by severely limiting married women's ability to extricate themselves from violent partners" (Strange, 1995: 296). It was not until the 1960s, with the second wave of feminism, that wife battering was "named" and conceptualized as a serious social problem. In 1974, the publication of British feminist Erin Pizzey's *Scream Quietly or the Neighbours Will Hear* firmly established wife (woman) battering as a central feminist issue (Walker, 1990). The 1980 publication of Linda MacLeod's *Wife Battering in Canada: The Vicious Circle* signalled to Canadian policymakers and the public at large that violence against wives was a social issue that was not going to go away. However, as the statistics show, progress toward eliminating the victimization of women has been slow and uneven.

Sexual Assault in Intimate Relationships

The discussion and examination of woman abuse in turn generated new areas of concern. In particular, marital rape was identified as an important dimension of the violence against women in intimate relationships. Given the common-law tradition that women belonged "lock, stock, and barrel" to their husbands, it is not surprising that the notion of raping one's own wife was initially considered an oxymoron. Women and men assumed that a wife owed her husband sexual access. Throughout Canada and the United States, the law defined rape as an act committed by a man on a female "not his wife." Just as a man could not rob from himself, he could not take by force that which already belonged to him[7] (Finkelhor and Yllo, 1985; Dranoff, 1977).

By the mid-1970s, marital rape was identified as an important part of the mosaic (Brownmiller, 1975). Diana Russell's survey of a random representative sample of 930 women in San Francisco revealed that 14 percent of women who had ever been married had been raped by a husband or ex-husband (Russell, 1982: 2). By the late 1970s, feminists in Canada and the United States were demanding the removal of the marital rape exemption from the law. In 1983, under Bill C-127, Canadian law was reformed, and it became possible for wives to lay charges of sexual assault against their husbands[8] (Cote, 1984). Although few legal cases[9] have been pursued after this change in the legislation, the research continues to suggest that sexual assault is a significant element in woman abuse in relationships. The CVAW survey found that 16 percent of never-married women 18 years and over had been sexually assaulted by a current or previous partner (Statistics Canada, 2006a:19).

Once again, this victimization of women is a global phenomenon. In the late 1990s research documented that large numbers of women around the world reported that they had been subjected to sexual assault or attempted sexual assault by an intimate male partner. The rates range from slightly more than one in ten in Switzerland, to one in seven in Canada, Germany, and the United States, to roughly one in four in the United Kingdom, Zimbabwe, and India (Seager, 2003: 59). Recent research in rural Uganda reports that one in four women reports having experienced coercive sex with their current male partner (Koenig et al., 2004).

Criminal Harassment and Intimate Femicide

Through the 1980s and 1990s more and more media accounts appeared documenting the stalking and sometimes the murder of women seeking to escape their abusive partners. In 1993, the Canadian federal government responded to public concerns by passing a law that afforded stalked women some protection by creating the new offence of criminal harassment (Canadian Panel on Violence Against Women, 1993). Although the legislation was not gender specific, it provided women with better legal recourse when they were followed, watched, and/or threatened by their ex-spouses and boyfriends. In order to lay charges of criminal harassment, victims must reasonably fear for their safety or the safety of someone close to them and harassers must know of, or be reckless toward, their victims' fear (Beattie, 2003).

Not surprisingly, most victims of criminal harassment are women and most stalkers are men (Statistics Canada, 2006a: 27–30). Although women are stalked by neighbours, colleagues, and acquaintances, many women are criminally harassed by partners, since violence by an intimate partner does not necessarily end when the relationship ends. Of women reporting being stalked, 21 percent indicated that they were being stalked by a current or former partner (Statistics Canada, 2006a: 28). The evidence documents that when women are stalked by intimate partners, they are at considerable risk for violence, including sexual assault, homicide, and attempted homicide. For women, being separated from a spouse is an especially dangerous time, as 26 percent of women who are murdered by a spouse are separated at the time of the homicide (Statistics Canada, 2006a: 30, 38).

It remains to be seen whether this legislative initiative will assist women in responding to violence. The increased rates of charges since 1995 may indicate that victims are increasingly willing to involve the police and lay charges. However, incidents of women being stalked and killed by their estranged partners continue to appear in the popular media. On March 1996, Arlene May, a 39-year-old mother of five, was shot through the head in her Collingwood, Ontario, home by her estranged boyfriend, Randy Iles. One of the most tragic aspects of this murder was the fact that Iles had a long history of assaulting May and was out on bail with instructions to stay away from her. He did not follow the instructions but was granted bail again. He took this opportunity to track down May and kill her. Between 2001 and 2007, when a total of 101 Canadian police officers and soldiers were killed, more than 500 Canadian women were shot, stabbed, strangled, or beaten to death by their intimate partners (Vallee, 2007).

Intimate femicide is not, of course, peculiar to Canada. Between 2001 and 2007, while 4588 US solders and police officers were killed by hostile action or accidents, more than 8000 US women were murdered by their male partners (Vallee, 2007). Other countries, particularly those with very strong patriarchal traditions, reveal more intense patterns of wife murder. In India in the past three decades, "dowry murder" has emerged as a significant expression of violence against women, so much so that death by domestic violence rates are comparable to Western countries such as the United States (Rudd, 2001: 514). When a groom's family believes that the bride's family has short-changed them in terms of the bride's dowry, they may resort to the practice of bride burning: The unacceptable bride is doused with kerosene and set afire by her in-laws. The groom is, as a result, free to marry again and obtain a new dowry.

Attention from the Western media and the growth of women's liberation organizations in India and Pakistan have not stemmed the tide of killings. Although the dowry system was banned in 1961, the practice persists (Corrales, 2008). Analysts fear that as many as 11 000 young brides were killed or forced to commit suicide between 1988 and 1991 (Gargan, 1994). The official number of dowry deaths increased from 6758 in 1996 to 7543 in 1997, but estimates state that 25 000 women are killed annually in this manner (Samuel, 2002; Seager, 2003: 29). Dowry-related killings have also increased in other countries; in Bangladesh, for example, 25 out of 48 femicide cases in 1993 were related to disputes over dowry (Zaman, 1999).

Honour killings also put women at risk. The term refers to "legally or socially sanctioned revenge exercised within a family against a woman" who is seen to have damaged the family's honour, typically through sexual behaviour that is defined as inappropriate (Seager, 2003). In a number of patriarchal countries (for example, Ecuador, Brazil, Morocco, Turkey, Italy, Albania, Yugoslavia, Bangladesh, Egypt, Jordan, Iraq, and Afghanistan) men and women subscribe to the view that the women of the family embody the family's honour (Taherzadeh, 2008; Pervizat, 2003). If women are seen to misbehave, by disobeying their husbands or fathers, by engaging in premarital or extramarital sexual relations, by wearing Western-style clothing, by putting on makeup, by venturing in public without a male family member, and so on, they may be subject to stabbing, shooting, or stoning for dishonouring the family and shaming its male members. This practice has extended to various Western countries in the context of migration. In several incidents, immigrant parents have resorted to honour killing to punish their Westernized daughters who were seen to be acting in inappropriate ways (Akpinar, 2003). In a recent incident in Toronto, a 16-year-old girl was allegedly killed by her father because she adamantly refused to wear a hijab, the traditional Muslim head scarf, when out in public. While leaders in the Islamic community rejected any notion that their religion condones this behaviour, the trial, now pending, will likely intensify concern about the rights of women in immigrant communities (Stuffco, 2007).

In sum, for women around the world, love and marriage do not provide protection from violence. Indeed, the research repeatedly indicates that women are in greater peril in their home and in their close personal relationships than they are in the public domain. However, despite the perils of their private lives, most women are acutely aware that they must also confront violence in the public domain.

PUBLIC PERILS AND STRANGER ATTACKS

Despite women's and girls' vulnerability in their homes, it is in public areas that Canadian women most frequently worry about their personal safety—and, often, with good reason. This sense of vulnerability often makes women feel afraid, whether or not they are attacked. For example, 58 percent of women reported that they were concerned about their safety after dark or when using public transit (Statistics Canada, 2006a: 32). Because of this fear, women are susceptible to the prevalent belief in Canadian society that women should be responsible for their own safety, instead of placing the emphasis where it belongs: on the perpetrators.

Focusing so much on women's safety may translate into support for rape myths. If a woman does not "protect" herself and goes out alone after dark, or was wearing a short skirt, what did she expect? Numerous safety pamphlets encourage women to do everything from carrying their keys a certain way to looking under their car and in the backseat before driving. One pamphleteer pointedly spoofs these safety pamphlets with the following advice: In the home: "If you live alone, or with other women, get extra locks, buy a big dog, take karate lessons and carry a can of mace. If you live with a man, take the dog and the mace to bed with you." Public transportation: "Avoid all areas in which sexual assault usually takes place: bars, restaurants, parks, streets, offices, corridors, elevators, cars, lobbies, apartments, homes. Avoid people who commonly commit assaults: strangers, relatives, friends, spouses." If attacked: "scream and struggle unless your attacker is the type who will kill you for it. If you cooperate, make sure that he wouldn't have let you go if you had struggled. Talk kindly to him, but don't say anything that will sound bad in court. Protect yourself from injury, but make sure that you get some bruises to count as evidence. Glance at your watch occasionally so that you can make a coherent police report. Don't stay too calm though: if you weren't hysterical you probably enjoyed it" (Thunder Bay Neighbourhood Watch, n.d.).

As a result of this strong emphasis on women's responsibilities to secure their own safety, much of women's time and energy is directed toward staying safe from male violence. Gill Valentine (1989) calls this the "geography of women's fear" and maintains that women often make a mental map, either consciously or unconsciously, to try to keep safe. This map means that their energy is directed toward traversing this mental geography as they go about their everyday acts. This vigilance, arguably, does not keep many women safe, especially since most rapes are not, statistically speaking, stranger rapes. And if women do not often veer off their safety map, this actually translates into the routine containment of women's lives.

SEXUAL HARASSMENT AND GENDER HARASSMENT

One of the important accomplishments of the second wave of the women's movement was to name sexual and gender harassment and to document it as a very pervasive feature of women's public lives. Prior to feminist activism in the 1960s, sexual and other forms of public harassment of women were persistently trivialized as harmless, flattering, or an inevitable feature of "office politics" or "guys being guys." Even today, situation comedies on television continue to use gender harassment as material for humour (Montemurro, 2003). Despite the ongoing struggle, feminists have made great strides toward "naming" public harassment of women as a serious offence and identifying the costs to women.

According to the Supreme Court of Canada, sexual harassment ranges from coerced intercourse to persistent propositions to insults and taunting. The net result is a "negative psychological and emotional work environment." Of course, the harassment is not restricted to the work context. As researchers point out, sexual harassment may also occur in streets, transit systems, malls, sports, and the military (Quinn, 2004). Gender harassment is closely related to (and in some instances considered a sub-category of) sexual harassment. It involves generalized sexist comments or behaviour that insults, degrades, or embarrasses women. For example, gender harassment might involve co-workers routinely mocking a female worker who wears pants, rather than more feminine attire, to work. The resultant "chilly" climate may have damaging consequences in terms of women's education, employment, and other public activities, and may have long-standing effects in terms of anger, frustration, depression, shame, fearfulness, and guilt (Ontario Women's Justice Network, 2008; Quinn, 2004; LeMoncheck and Sterba, 2001).

Globally, the stories sound familiar. A US study indicates that at least 40 percent, and perhaps as much as 85 percent, of American women have experienced sexual harassment on the job (Lichtman, 1993: 13A). A Madrid survey found that 80 percent of employed women reported sexual harassment, and 4 percent indicated they were subject to violent sexual harassment. In Holland, 58 percent of employed women indicated that they had been physically or verbally harassed in the workplace. In a Tokyo survey of 6500 women, 70 percent of employed women said they had been harassed while working, and 90 percent said they had been molested during commuting; about 3 percent reported they were forced to have sexual relations at work (*Toronto Star*, Febuary 7, 1992: F1). Similarly, researchers report that 85 percent of women in Hong Kong and 73 percent of women in Britain report experiencing sexual harassment in the workplace (Burn, 2000). The International Labour Organization (ILO) survey of industrialized countries found that 15 percent to 30 percent of employed women reported frequent, serious sexual harassment such as unwanted touching, pinching, offensive remarks, and requests for sexual favours (Burn, 2000). A recent examination of sexual harassment in Kenyan schools and educational institutions also documents the seriousness of violence directed against girls and women (Omale, 2000).

Predictably, certain kinds of workplaces are especially hazardous for women. Cultural norms surrounding service occupations may, for example, serve to set women up for sexual harassment (Folgero and Fjelstad, 1995). Often, a certain level of attractiveness and sexuality are expected in women holding occupations such as waitress, flight attendant, and sales "girl." Finally, although poorly documented in the research literature, women who work in explicitly sexual occupations (prostitution, pornography, and so forth) have long been subject to the most overtly physical and violent forms of harassment by both customers and managers/pimps (Miles, 2003; Canadian Panel on Violence Against Women, 1993).

In short, an extensive and growing body of research literature demonstrates that for many women there are real dangers in the public domain, including their workplace. Regardless of the form the violence takes, it has a dramatic impact on its targets and may lead to severe anxiety, loss of employment, intense depression, and even attempted suicide.

UNDERSTANDING THE VIOLENCE: FEMINIST THEORIZING

Power, Control, and Patriarchy

Second-wave feminists made an immense contribution through simply starting to identify and document the extent of violence against women. Prior to the 1970s, domestic violence, incest, sexual harassment, dowry burning, female genital mutilation, and other forms of violence against women were not on the public agenda. Rape was considered extremely uncommon and was defined almost exclusively in terms of stranger violence (Chasteen, 2001). Incest was virtually ignored in most studies of the family, as was domestic violence, while sexual harassment had only recently been named (Nelson and Robinson, 2002: 316). To unearth the violence and demand that it be addressed as a societal rather than a private issue was an enormous accomplishment. That the third wave also provided important theoretical perspectives from which to address the violence speaks to the vitality of the emergent movement.

In particular, second-wave feminists located the violence in terms of patriarchal relations of power and control. Rape and incest, for example, were not about sexuality. The men involved often had access to sexual partners. Rather, the violence was about power. Men commit violence against women because their power in society allows them to do so. Their historical property rights over women and children, along with their contemporary position in the social order—as heads of households, as fathers, as husbands, as brothers, as employers, as professors, and so on—provide them with the power to oppress and violate women. In this sense, violence is a reflection of male power and privilege in society. Men, regardless of their class, race, ability, or other defining characteristics, will be able to identify women to whom they are superior and whom they are able to control and abuse. Rejecting more psychoanalytic explanations of the rapist or wife-beater, radical feminists pointed out that violence against women was endemic in Western societies: "rape—the all-American crime—and societal institutions such as the criminal justice system, religion, and the military both tacitly accepted and openly endorsed the control and abuse of women" (Griffin, 1971: 31).

Not surprisingly, this identification of violence against women within patriarchal societies led to a close examination of prevailing beliefs, values, and attitudes. As a result, considerable attention focused on (for example) rape-prone beliefs and attitudes. Patriarchy was understood to be embodied in the beliefs that some women were responsible for their own victimization. Radical feminists targeted these beliefs with "no means no" campaigns.

For Marxist and socialist feminists, it was not so much prevailing beliefs and values but the material conditions of women's lives—that is, their role in the family and their marginalized role in paid employment—that resulted in their relative dependence and powerlessness in the social order (Luxton, 1980). Women and their children were likely to be trapped in violence if they lacked alternative ways to survive economically. Rather than leave an abusive relationship and risk impoverishment for their children, women would stay in the family and, possibly, poorly paid and marginal female employment. Of course women's work in the home—the daily and generational reproduction of the labour force—as well as their resultant role as marginal or reserve labour force, were both vital to the interests of the capitalist economy. In this manner, capitalism and patriarchy could be understood to be complexly intertwined.

Patterns of male violence also were understood to sustain the existing patterns of male dominance and female subordination. In the past and present, violence served/serves not only as a male privilege, but also to sustain male power and control in the family and in society in general. For centuries, in groups and as individuals, as soldiers and civilians, ordinary men have used rape to humiliate and subordinate women and to proclaim their masculine superiority and dominance. Similarly, the control and abuse of girls in the family could be seen as part of socialization into male control. Witnessing the abuse of mothers similarly confirmed that men were in every sense the head of the household. Public violence completed the domination by encouraging a "protection racket" in which women would embrace personal relationships with individual men in the interests of gaining protection. Women would accept any private oppression rather than risk becoming "open territory" women—prostitutes, sluts—who were denied male (gentlemanly) protection from exploitation and abuse (Griffin, 1971). On a daily and life-long basis, gender and sexual harassment served to remind women that there were places, at work, in school, and in public domains, where they must tread carefully, and others where they were "inviting" male abuse and violence. In short, these various forms of violence and, perhaps more importantly, the fear of violence, perform an invaluable social control function for men and patriarchal traditions by encouraging women to tread lightly in the public domain, to restrict their activities, to accept whatever sanctuary marriage may offer, and to avoid challenging male preserves, such as male-dominated jobs and social situations (Kader, 1982).

Of course, the articulation of a power and control model necessitated questioning and dismantling opposing theoretical explanations. Considerable attention, for example, was directed against evolutionary and "human nature" explanations of male violence. Numerous analysts had argued (and continue to) that "male behaviour"—competitive, aggressive, unemotional, and so on—is the result of behaviours that bestowed evolutionary advantages on their owners and, as a result, that contemporary men are genetically wired to act in this manner (Boyd, 2000). Feminist efforts in biological, anthropological, and historical research challenged this perspective by pointing out the variability both in male behaviour and in societal structures (Sanday, 1981; Watson-Franke, 2002). For example, Kersti Yllo found that the rate of wife abuse reported in a random US survey varied from one state to another (Yllo, 1984). Specifically, in states where women enjoy relatively high social status in terms of participation in professional and technical occupations, enrolment in post-secondary education, and representation in political office, women are particularly at risk for severe physical violence from their husbands when they live in a husband-dominated family. Also, wife beating is more common in states where women are accorded a low social status and the wife dominates in the family. In other words, Yllo's research suggests that when women's power in society at large is high, men have to resort to greater use of force in the family to remain dominant. In addition, when women's power in society at large is low, men respond violently to what is regarded as women's illegitimate use of power in the family (Yllo, 1984). As explored in greater detail below, this body of research clearly suggests that the construction of masculinity varies according to cultural and historical context; human social structure is not inevitably or uniformly patriarchal.

As second-wave feminists mobilized their ideas in terms of shelters, rape crisis centres, and other anti-violence activism, they also made important advances in the theoretical conceptualization of patriarchal power and control. Domestic violence, for example, was not simply a matter of men hitting their wives. The violence could take many forms, including threats, intimidation, economic control, using children and other loved ones, and isolation. This increasingly complex understanding of violence is evident, for example, in the power and control model developed in the domestic violence movement—a model that identified not only physical but also sexual, economic, and psychological dimensions of woman abuse (Sev'er, 2002: 57). Over the years, the model has become increasing multifaceted as analysts have incorporated an ever-greater array of violent behaviours and strategies.

This more sophisticated model of power and control was, in turn, reflected in a more nuanced understanding of the processes of violence. Concepts such as "learned helplessness" and "the battered woman syndrome" emphasized that the violence was not simply an external threat but rather could be internalized into women's sense of self. Similarly, explorations of the popular attitudes and beliefs surrounding violence against women, such as rape-supportive beliefs, led to explanations that focused on the ideological structures of society. The prevailing beliefs and attitudes under patriarchy encouraged women to blame themselves and other women for their victimization. Issues of power and control were understood to permeate the individual as well as the societal levels of analysis.

As feminist theorizing progressed, analysts emphasized that the issue was not individual men (rapists, abusers), nor was it men in general, but rather a social order (patriarchy) in which men, in general, enjoyed more power and privilege than women and in which the institutional structures (family, religion, military, media, economy, education, the state) were structured to support male privilege. Rape, for example, was in part sustained by media that endorsed the sexual objectification of women in pornography as well as the popular media, by a criminal justice system that ignored or replicated the abuse of women, by religious institutions that enshrined female subordination, and so on. In short, theorizing violence was integral to a deconstruction of the patriarchal order.

Intersectionalities/Inclusiveness

It is, of course, impossible to draw a clear line between second- and third-wave feminisms. Certainly, the popularization of postmodernism and its application to feminist issues was a key milestone, but there is as much continuity as discontinuity in much feminist writings. Postmodernist feminism, however, encouraged a re-examination of the most fundamental and taken-for-granted concepts in feminist analysis. Even the conception of the woman who was the victim of violence was recast (Meintjes, Pillay, and Turshen, 2001). As Ann Cahill comments, "Where modernism emphasized the subject predicated on the autonomy and superiority of the mind, postmodern theories drew a portrait of a being who was radically divided from itself, whose identity, rather than being a static thing, was an ongoing process, affected by historical and cultural forces and undergoing constant change" (Cahill, 2002: 65). Not surprisingly, the resultant approach to violence against women was cast in profoundly different terms: "By understanding rape as an embodied experience, as an attack on an embodied subject that directly involves and invokes the sexuality of both the assailant and the victim, we can perceive the phenomenon as a threat to the possibility of embodied subjectivity, a threat to the victim's (sexually specific) personhood and inter-subjectivity" (Cahill, 2002: 138).

This desire for a much more nuanced and complex understanding of subjectivity and victimization is also highlighted in two central themes of third-wave feminism: inclusivity and anti-essentialism (Diaz, 2004). Hewing out a new theoretical position, these analysts argued that second-wave feminists had theorized in ways that focused exclusively on middle-class white Western women and tended to posit some unitary female sex-class or feminine "essence" (Hautzinger, 2002). This is, of course, not entirely true since lesbians, Aboriginal women, visible minority women, and poor and working-class women had long been active in the women's movement, and feminist analysts had long been cognizant of classism, heterosexism, ethnocentrism, and so on.

There is no doubt, however, that positivist feminist accounts (such as those reviewed earlier) that present "women" as simple and undifferentiated obscure the diversity of women's experiences. In recent years analysts have devoted considerable effort to unpacking the obscured patterns of privilege and oppression that intersect in this category, including genderism (butch/femme), racism, Eurocentrism (European orientation), heterosexism, ableism (able-bodied/other-abled), educationalism (educated/illiterate), ageism (young/old), the politics of appearance, class bias, language bias (English/ESL), colourism (light/dark), anti-Semitism, rural/urban, and pro-natalism (fertile/infertile, mother/non-mother). In addition, these differences intersect with one another—elderly lesbians, upper-class Europeans—resulting in a myriad of distinctive experiences and issues. Indeed, considerable research has focused on excavating the particularities of women's experiences (Collins, 2000) and challenging any analyses that tend to universalize white middle-class Western women's lives.

This "difference feminism" perspective is reflected in a variety of recent research. Family violence, for example, was complexly interwoven with issues of class and poverty. The CVAW survey reported, for example, that unemployed men and men living in families with incomes of less than $15 000 had rates of violence twice as high as employed men and men in affluent families (Johnson, 1996: 154). It would seem that when men cannot assert their dominance over the family through economic clout, they are much more likely to resort to the most direct and blunt expression of power: physical force and violence (Smith, 1990). Women trapped in violent relationships are often (although not always) unemployed or low-wage earners—women who lack the economic power to fend for themselves and their children (MacLeod, 1986: 20–21). Homeless women and other women who have been pushed to the economic perimeters of society are completely vulnerable to sexual and physical violence. The Toronto Street Health Report of 1992 found that 43.3 percent of homeless women reported sexual assaults or harassment in the previous year, and half had experienced attacks five times or more (cited in Layton, 2008).

As noted above, Aboriginal women in Canada are not only at heightened risk of violence and abuse but also confront a criminal justice and social welfare system that often compounds their victimization. The sexual abuse of Aboriginal children has been extensively documented and, although boys and girls are both violated, it appears girls once again bear the brunt of the violence (Razack, forthcoming). Similarly, immigrant women, particularly when their cultural background is more patriarchal and/or when they do not speak English or French, may be at dramatically increased threat of domestic violence (Yelaja, 2006).

The powerlessness and vulnerability of women with disabilities have long been ignored and obscured. Women with disabilities have been rendered invisible by the use of gender-neutral terms, such as "people with disabilities" or "the disabled." The relatively scant research does suggest that women with disabilities are particularly vulnerable to violence (Howe, 2000). A survey of 30 women who attended the 1988 *Action femmes handicapées* conference found that 37 percent said they had been abused by their parents, 17 percent by medical personnel, 17 percent by their spouses, and 17 percent by caregivers. Similarly, 40 percent of the women who responded to the 1989 Disabled Women's Network survey reported they had been abused or assaulted (Barile, 1992/1993: 40–41; see also McPherson, 1991). In recent years, feminist activists have sought to replace the invisibility of women with disabilities with a new principle of inclusion (Stevens, 1995).

Lesbians also are subject to heightened rates of institutional and interpersonal violence. Though little has been documented in Canada in terms of "lesbian bashing," research suggests this is a common occurrence (Faulkner, 2001). A study of 1000 lesbians in Quebec found that 10 percent indicated they were victims of socio-economic, psychological, and professional abuse because of their sexual orientation. Further, popular ideology has long legitimated the sexual assault of lesbians ("all she needs is a good lay") (Canadian Panel on Violence Against Women, 1993). Alarmingly, data suggest that the violence is increasing (Berrill, 1992). Further, as in other "marginalized" groups, living in a pervasively hierarchical and homophobic society may translate into violence and abuse within lesbian relationships (Ristock, 2006; Renzetti, 1992). The CVAW survey found that same-sex intimate violence occurred in 2.5 percent of couples, of which 28 percent were female couples (Statistics Canada, 2006a: 39).

Age similarly affects women's experiences of violence. Older women, for example, are acknowledged to be at greater risk. Research into elder abuse, a relatively new field in family violence literature, tends to suggest that, in terms of abuse in domestic settings and by informal caregivers, elderly women are more likely to be physically abused than are elderly men, and that the abuse is more severe when directed against women (Vinton, 2001; McDonald et al., 1991: 11; see also the Canadian Panel on Violence Against Women, 1993). This intensified vulnerability likely reflects a complex interplay between their economic plight, increased physical frailty, "ageist" attitudes in society, and the institutionalization and/or social isolation of many elderly women.

Pursuing this theoretical thread has led to greater attention being paid to the diversities of women's lives and the complex interconnections between axes of oppression and subordination. For example, attention has focused on the victimization of immigrant women who confront not only issues of domestic abuse but also economic, social, linguistic, and cultural marginalization (MacLeod and Shin, 1990; MacLeod et al., 1993). Other research has focused on the particular issues faced by abused women living in isolated rural communities and those who live in Canadian military communities (Hornosty, 1995; Harrison, 2002). Outside the Canadian context, a wealth of research has documented the diversity and complexity of women's experiences of violence (Romito, 2008).

Even the attitudes, beliefs, and values that have been identified as underlying and supporting the victimization of women are found to be much more complex and differentiated. For example, attributions of blame to rape victims vary in terms of whether the victim was potentially attracted to the perpetrator (as a result, lesbians received less blame if victimized by heterosexual males) and in terms of homophobic attitudes (gay men, regardless of the orientation of their attacker, were more likely to be blamed) (Wakelin and Long, 2003). A growing body of international research underscores the complexities. For example, in a study of Turkish university students, males and females were fairly similar in their attitudes toward stranger rape but women were less likely than men to blame the victim in date rape and more likely to view the assault as a crime (Golge, 2003). A recent cross-national study of attitudes toward violence against women reported that in the four countries—India, Japan, Kuwait, and the United States—important national differences (within the general pattern of men being more likely to blame the victim of spousal and sexual assault) were, predictably, identified. More surprisingly, it appears that socio-cultural factors may in some instances be more influential than gender factors. Specifically, in Kuwait, there were negligible differences between men and women in terms of their tendency to blame the victims of woman abuse (Nayak et al., 2003).

These explorations are not only the outgrowth of a theoretical sensitivity to the ways axes of power and subordination intersect in women's lives; the research in turn has contributed to a more nuanced and open-ended understanding of central concepts including women and violence. Violence, for example, is increasingly understood as a much more encompassing process made up of relationships rather than a series of acts. For example, in a recent examination of women in a variety of national contexts who are living in post-conflict societies, the authors use the third-wave concern with diversity and anti-essentialism to point out not only the diversity of subjects included in the construct "woman," but also the important differences in the ways violence—rape in war and peace—is constructed and experienced (Sideris, 2001).

In the North American context, third-wave feminists have also pushed for a much more broadly framed understanding of violence against women. This perspective includes, for example, corporate and medical violence against women—the Dalkon Shield, DES, and defective breast implants—as elements integral to "ordinary violence" against women (Stewart, 2002). The feminization of poverty and the inadequacies of the social welfare system can be understood as an expression of "everyday assaults" on women. The outcomes of domestic violence—women fleeing their homes and becoming single parents dependent on inadequate social welfare support—cannot be theoretically amputated from the physical violence that may have triggered these results. The violence must be understood as extending into the impoverishment and vulnerability of the single mother. Similarly, the torture of women in countries around the world—as victims of agents of the state, such as soldiers, prison guards, and police officers—cannot be hived off from the global struggle against violence and for women's equal rights (Youngs, 2003). Of course, this broadening perspective inevitably has lead to a more global framework.

Global/Localities and Postcolonial Feminism

Postmodern feminist theorizing has not been uniformly embraced by feminist theorists. Indeed, in recent years the criticisms have become increasingly heated. For example, Carine Mardorossian takes postmodernist feminists to task for failing to advance theorizing on violence against women and for engaging in psychologizing and victim-blaming. In short, she argues, they have endorsed a conservative approach while also leaving the theoretical field open to conservatives such as Katie Roiphe, Camille Paglia, and Christina Sommers—conservatives who downplay the severity of anti-woman violence and accuse feminists of encouraging a victim mentality in women (Mardorossian, 2002: 748–749). Similarly, Angela Diaz argues that in its desire to capture the differences and specificities within women's experiences postmodernist (third-wave) feminists have tended to "focus on unique personal experiences, circumstances and contexts ... [They] deliberately turn their gaze inward to the Self and focus on ways by which the Self is produced and reproduced via lived experiences within a particular milieu" (Diaz, 2004: 15). In the process, Mardorossian suggests, the political has been reduced to the personal and the important issues such as the relations between gender and patriarchal capitalism and "between rape and 'the systematic working of wage labor and capital and the way that such a system needs the superexploitation of women'" have been relentlessly obscured. As a result, she argues much postmodernist feminist activism and theorizing is increasingly irrelevant to the victims of rape and the struggle for change (Mardorossian, 2002: 772).

Other analysts have taken issue with postmodern feminists' preoccupation with anti-essentialism and diversity. The feminist project, as articulated in second-wave analyses, appears to rest on some acknowledgment of commonalities among women, despite differences of class, race, ability, and so on. An emphasis on diversity tends to promote a segmentation of women's experience that does not lend itself to social action or social change. For example, Sarah Hautzinger (2002) explores the notion of anti-essentialism in her study of Brazil's creation of all-female police stations as a response to violent crimes against women. As she points out, as important as it has been to acknowledge "difference" among women, anti-essentialism remains a tension in feminist theorizing; it is not clear where to draw the line between essentialism and, as bell hooks describes it, "the authority of experience" that women share with one another (hooks, 2003). As Hautzinger points out, it is precisely some belief in essentialism—in our shared experience as women across boundaries—that often animates the "imagined communities" that enable women's collective struggle (Hautzinger, 2002: 249).

Perhaps feminisms informed by globalization and postcolonialism may provide the much-needed antidote to the extremes of postmodernism. As feminist analysis has been established around the globe and has focused on an increasing diversity of women's experiences, much feminist theorizing has moved toward an examination of local-global intersections in specific national contexts. Working from a feminist postcolonialist perspective, these theorists often focus on the lives of women in the aftermath of colonialism. They specifically reject Eurocentric approaches to reality, for example, the principles of binary oppositions such as civilization/barbarism and us/them that have created a "monolithic" image of Third-World women as passive, powerless, backward, uneducated, and so on. Here, the emphasis is on locating women's experiences in a specific set of historical and material conditions. The localities of women's experience in a specific time and place is understood as an intersection between local and global realities—realities in which the local must be understood as shaped by, for instance, historical and contemporary imperialism (Diaz, 2004).

Diaz (2004) provides a provocative example of this approach in her examination of Filipino women's identities and experiences. She explores the historical construction of social institutions—notably, economic, religious, and educational—that establish the boundaries of Filipino women's day-to-day and overall lives. She also explicitly rejects traditional third-wave approaches to feminism on the grounds that they tend to be oblivious to the implications of the intersections of local and global realities for Third-World women. For instance, she points out, she lives a daily life in which she cannot help but be complexly aware of the Philippine-American neocolonial connection as it is embodied in the valuation of local currency, the price of gasoline, the presence of US military in the

Philippines, the presence of American media on Philippine radio, television, and film, and so on. Diaz argues that it is precisely this exploration of the interconnections between the global and the local and an understanding of the personal and cultural implications of these connections that is not reflected in third-wave feminism.

It is very much this perspective that seems also to animate several recent feminist analyses of domestic violence and dowry murder in India. Here, the analysis locates the violence against individual women in the context not simply of marriage, tradition, and culture but also in terms of social class, the response of the state, and the global division of labour. Dowry murder, it is argued, must be seen as a recent phenomenon that owes much to shifts in the economy, increased middle-class consumerism, and changes in the status of women. In this way, researchers make connections between the individual victimization of women and the suspension of US aid to India, the arrival of millions of refugees in India as a result of the India–Pakistan conflict, the decrease in agricultural production, and OPEC's oil pricing. The economic stagnation that resulted from these events has meant that many families were in increased need of cash and in this particular time and place the result was an escalation in dowry deaths. In short, the theoretical approach not only acknowledges the "differences" of Indian women's lives but also their interconnectedness with global as well as local events. Importantly, in light of criticism of postmodern feminism, it is also pointedly concerned with social change and is unwilling to be drawn into collaborations with the state (Rudd, 2001; Samuel, 2002). Similarly, Pande's (2002) examination of domestic violence in India is located in the context of development policies, patterns of literacy, and popular campaigns for social change. The personal and political are understood as woven together, and the analysis seeks to explore the complex connection between structure and personal issues. Most important, in terms of critiques of postmodernist feminist perspectives, the analysis is embedded in issues of social change and women's empowerment.

Gender Studies and Hegemonic Masculinities

Although increasingly complex and global understandings are emerging in feminist literature, so too is a provocative examination of the ways in which masculinities are socially constructed, deployed, and supported. Drawing from the anti-essentialist positions of postmodern feminism, analysts working from this perspective consider the ways in which certain scripts for "being a man" are valued, especially in Western countries, while others are stigmatized (Messerschmidt, 1993; Kimmel, 1987; Kaufman, 1993). Although this line of analysis has deep roots in elements of the contemporary men's movement and second-wave "power and patriarchy" feminism, it has expanded into a dynamic resource for contemporary feminist theorizing with important applications to violence against women.

The research and analysis coming out of gender studies has revealed the diverse ways—historically and cross-culturally—in which growing up male is experienced and understood and in which specific conceptions of masculinity are socially valued and legitimated over others. As with much feminist discussion, this has entailed in-depth examinations of the ways in which diverse men—those with disabilities, racial minorities, gay men, immigrants, working-class men, young men—both confront and construct masculinities (hooks, 2003; Murtadha-Watts, 2003; Gerschick and Miller, 2000; Sampath, 2001). Furthermore, these diversities are conceptualized as embedded in specific institutional arrangements. Considerable work has been done on the roles played by education, the military, the media, the economic order, sports, and so on, in reinforcing particular understandings and enactments of masculinities (Messner, 2003; Thorne, 2003; Connell, 2002; Gardiner, 2003; Williams, 2003; Jensen, 2003).

Most recently, this literature has increasingly focused on the global positioning of masculinities and the interweaving of gender with material interests and practices (production/reproduction; wage work/housework) (Connell, 2000a, 2000b). Viewed from this perspective, economic and cultural globalization can be seen as gendered. For example, colonialism and imperialism (past and present) are gendered processes in which indigenous gender orders are disrupted and new gender divisions of labour and gender ideologies are imposed (Connell, 2000a, 2000b; see, for example, Diaz, 2004). This approach provides support for a vital feminist approach to the "new world order."

Not surprisingly, this attention to gender and to masculinities, in particular, has been a powerful stimulus in the analysis of violence against women. What would cause a man to abuse a woman he loves, or to harass and attack women who are strangers to him? Some of the core issues can be approached in terms of how he sees "being a real man," how men and women relate in historically, culturally, socially, and economically constructed ways, and how specific dominant institutions construct and reinforce certain expressions of masculinity. For example, in their recent (2006) film, *A Killer's Paradise*, filmmakers Silva Basmajian and Karen O'Connor explore the construction of anti-woman violence in Guatemala as an expression of a history marked by militarism and US imperialist intervention. This vantage point addresses not only interpersonal violence but also the organized violence that often targets women and girls as victims (Connell, 2000a, 2000b; Totten, 2000). Finally, and importantly, the critical exploration of masculinities has lent itself to fresh initiatives in opposing violence against women. The White Ribbon Campaign was launched in Canada in response to the 1989 massacre of 14 women engineering students at the University of Montreal, who were singled out and murdered because they were studying in a non-traditional field for women and because, in the words of their murderer, they were "a bunch of feminists" (Rosenberg, 1999/2005). Since the Montreal Massacre, the White Ribbon Campaign has become an important instrument for mobilizing men who want to actively oppose the victimization of women.

CONCLUSION

An understanding of male violence against women and children is not complete without pondering the following: Since the advent of the second wave of the women's movement in Canada, male violence has been named, has been understood in all of its manifestations, and has been extensively theorized. The Canadian women's movement has also created a strong infrastructure of educational services, counselling services, help lines, battered women shelters, and rape crisis centres and has pushed the state to redress male violence through changes to the legal system. The Canadian government has also provided education about male violence, has funded women's services (however paltry some of that funding might be) and has indeed changed the *Criminal Code* and other statutes to try to address and mitigate male violence. Yet with all of the time that has passed, with all of the effort and money that has gone into trying to ameliorate male violence, the astounding question remains: Why, with this great push forward, is male violence still so shockingly prevalent? As long as men's power, embedded in so many people's conceptions and in institutions in society, remains enshrined and as long as male privilege is ensconced in the way that male violence is often normalized, tolerated, and perpetuated, the problem will remain. This means that women's formal equality in Canada, enshrined in the *Charter* and various laws, does not translate into women having substantive equality, for the reality of lived experiences remains one of fear of or the actuality of male violence.

This conclusion is not, however, without hope. Clearly, the work on violence against women is very much "in progress" as, year after year, the documentary evidence of violence against women is being compiled and expanded. In the course of these investigations there is a growing appreciation of the complexity and diversity of women's experiences of violence. Understanding and theorizing the violence has similarly evolved, albeit somewhat unevenly. Admittedly, these developments have been matched by continuing opposition and backlash as even the statistical documentation of violence is challenged (Doob, 2002), as feminists are castigated for propagating a victim mentality in women and as analysts argue for a mutuality of violence (men as victims of female violence and women as violent aggressors) (Straton, 2000).

And yet, despite the continuing struggle over the most basic aspects, there is a place for cautious optimism. In less than a lifetime, violence against women has been dragged into the light and extensively documented and theorized. Recent developments in theorizing anti-woman violence are promising, particularly in light of the growing wealth of transglobal perspectives and increased attention to both the material relations and the international and the institutional arrangements that frame violence against women. Finally, and most importantly, the dream of a world in which women and girls could "walk free" remains very much alive.

Endnotes

1. Patriarchy is here used to loosely define societies that are male-dominated; that is, societies in which men tend to occupy the positions of power and authority, and rewards and privileges tend to accrue to men. It is acknowledged that this understanding of patriarchy suggests a lengthy continuum, ranging from societies that overtly and harshly repress women to societies in which male dominance is less obvious and more contested. Although patriarchal societies do not necessarily render women powerless or lacking in "rights, influence, and resources," women, as a group, tend always to have "less" than men. Within this social context, men's violence against women is explicitly or tacitly legitimated and/or tolerated. Even though in Canada the family patriarch has been steadily replaced by the patriarchal state, the gender inequality between men and women has persisted (Canadian Panel on Violence Against Women, 1993: 14).

2. Both boys and girls are abused in families. However, it appears that boys are consistently abused at a younger age while the victimization persists for girls. One explanation is that in a patriarchal society, as boys become more adult they are seen as increasingly unacceptable subjects for victimization while girls continue to be seen as suitable. Or, given the contradiction between male adult status and being a victim, boys may be increasingly unwilling to identify themselves as a victim.

3. Child marriage was banned in 1950 in India (Rush, 1980). However, there is some evidence that girls continue to be "married off" while very young. For example, in Kebbi state in Nigeria the

average age of first marriage for girls was 11 (Seager, 2003: 22). Child bride marriage has also come to light in Mormon fundamentalist communities in western Canada and the United States (Bramham, 2008).

4. Based on a random representative sample of women in Canada, this telephone survey using an in-depth interview format provided a wealth of data pertaining to violence against women.

5. Considerable research indicates that women are not necessarily passive victims in wife-abuse situations. For example, a national US survey found that wives and husbands were equally likely to report that they hit, shoved, and threw things in relationship disputes. In other words, both partners acted violently. Research, however, consistently indicates that women are much more likely than men to report that they had been injured in these conflicts (Brush, 1993). Even when both husband and wife are injured, the wife's injuries are usually three times as severe as her husband's (Kurz, 1993: 258; Duffy and Momirov, 1997). Considerable media attention has focused on the issue of men as victims of domestic violence.

6. Traditionally, wife abuse has been the subject of humour. An example is the ditty: "A woman, a horse, and a hickory tree / The more you beat them the better they be." As many will recall, the serious introduction of the issue of wife abuse into the Canadian House of Commons was met with peals of laughter. There have been persistent efforts in the academic and scientific literature to muddy the issue by referring to the "battered-husband syndrome" and "spousal abuse," with the implication that the violence is mutual and the consequences shared.

7. It is interesting to note that the first wave of feminism (the so-called suffrage movement) had identified coerced sex in marriage (and, as a consequence, coerced childbearing) as an important feminist concern in the late nineteenth century (Finkelhor and Yllo, 1985: 3–4).

8. Change came somewhat more slowly in the United States. As late as January 1985, 27 American states still allowed marital exemption for husbands accused of raping a wife with whom they were currently living (Finkelhor and Yllo, 1985: 140).

9. In 1991, British courts imprisoned a man for raping his wife. This was the first conviction in which the assailant was living with his wife at the time of the offence.

Suggested Readings and Resources

Basmajian, Silva, and Karen O'Connor (producers). 2006. *A killer's paradise.* A BBC and National Film Board of Canada co-production. A deeply insightful examination of the patterns of routine violence (notably murder) almost routinely perpetrated against women in Guatemala. The filmmakers clearly make connections between the devastating public and private violence perpetrated against women and a cultural tradition rooted in generations of societal turmoil, militarism, and US imperialism.

Fong, Josephine, ed. 2008. *Out of the shadows: Woman abuse in ethnic, Aboriginal and refugee communities.* Toronto: Canadian Scholars Press. A very up-to-date collection of research findings as well as more anecdotal material that reveals the complexities of abuse against women in intimate relationships.

Romito, Patrizia. 2008. *A deafening silence: Hidden violence against women and children,* tr. Janet Eastwood. London: Policy Press. Italian social and community psychologist Patrizia Romito provides a provocative examination of the ongoing violence against women and children. She argues that despite the progress in anti-violence campaigns, the dimensions and devastation of anti-woman and anti-child violence continues to be covered up around the globe.

Vallee, Brian. 2007. *The war on women: Elly Armour, Jane Hurshman and criminal violence in Canadian homes*. Toronto: Key Porter Books. A distinctly Canadian examination of domestic violence against women. Animated by Canadian examples, Vallee documents the ongoing toll taken on women by domestic violence—violence that too frequently turns lethal. He concludes with concrete recommendations for action.

Discussion Questions

1. Discussions of violence against women tend to discuss "women" as a category. What important differences among women are obscured by these discussions and what are the implications of ignoring these differences?

2. In what ways do specific social institutions—the military, media, religion—contribute to patterns of violence? How would these patterns vary in other parts of the world?

3. The prevailing beliefs and values in a society serve to support (or challenge) patterns of violence against women. What beliefs and values in Canada and elsewhere have been instrumental in perpetuating the abuse of women?

4. How would second- and third-wave feminists differ in their approach to domestic violence in Canada? What contributions would be provided by paying attention to the interplay between global and local contexts?

Bibliography

Akpinar, Aylin. 2003. The honour/shame complex revisited: Violence against women in the migration context. *Women's Studies International Forum* 26 (September/October): 425–442.

Allen, Charlotte Vale. 1980. *Daddy's girl: A very personal memoir.* New York: Wyndham Books.

Anderson, Karen. 1987. A gendered world: Women, men, and the political economy of the seventeenth-century Huron, in *Feminism and political economy: Women's work, women's struggles,* eds. Heath Jon Maroney and Meg Luxton. Toronto: Methuen.

Anderson, Veanne N., et al. 2004. Gender, age, and rape-supportive rules. *Sex Roles* 50 (January): 77–90.

Andrews, Audrey. 1999. *Be good, sweet maid: The trials of Dorothy Joudrie*. Waterloo, ON: Sir Wilfrid Laurier University Press.

Au Coin, Kathy. 2003. Violence and abuse against children and youth by family members, in *Family violence in Canada: A statistical profile, 2003,* eds. H. Johnson and K. Au Coin, 33–45. Ottawa: Ministry of Industry.

Bagley, Christopher, and Kathleen King. 1990. *Child sexual abuse: The search for healing.* London: Tavistock/Routledge.

Bagley, Robin. 1984. *Sexual offences against Canadian children,* Vol. 1. Ottawa: Minister of Supply and Services.

Barile, Maria. 1992/1993. Validation as prevention for women with disabilities. *Women's education des femmes* 10 (Winter): 40–41.

Baskin, Cyndy. 2003. From victims to leaders: Activism against violence towards women, in *Strong stories: Native vision and community survival,* eds. K. Anderson and B. Lawrence, 213–227. Vancouver: Sumach Press.

Beattie, S. 2003. Criminal harassment, in *Family violence in Canada: A statistical profile, 2003*, eds. H. Johnson and K. Au Coin, 8–11. Ottawa: Ministry of Industry.

Berrill, Kevin T. 1992. Anti-gay violence and victimization in the United States: An overview, in *Hate crimes: Confronting violence against lesbians and gay men*, eds. G. Herek and K. Berrill. Newbury Park, CA: Sage.

Bourassa, Carrie, et al. 2006. Racism, sexism and colonialism: The impact on the health of Aboriginal women in Canada, in *Canadian woman studies: An introductory reader*, 2d ed., eds. Andrea Medovarski and Brenda Cranney. Toronto: Innana.

Boyd, N. 2000. *The beast within: Why men are violent*. Vancouver: Greystone Books.

Boyle, Christine. 1990. The battered wife syndrome and self-defense: *Lavallee v. R. Canadian Journal of Family Law* 9: 171–179.

Brady, Katherine. 1979. *Father's days: A true story of incest*. New York: Seaview Press.

Bramham, D. 2008. *The secret lives of saints: Child brides and lost boys in Canada's polygamous Mormon sect*. Toronto: Random House.

Brodie, Janine. 2005. The great undoing: State formation, gender politics, and social policy in Canada, in *Open boundaries: A Canadian women's studies reader,* 2d ed., eds. Barbara Crow and Lise Gotell. Toronto: Pearson Prentice Hall.

Brownmiller, Susan. 1975. *Against our will: Men, women and rape*. New York: Bantam Books.

Brownridge, Douglas A., and Shiva S. Halli. 2001. *Explaining violence against women in Canada*. Lanham, MD: Lexington Books.

Brush, Lisa D. 1993. Violent acts and injurious outcomes in married couples: Methodological issues in the national survey of families and households, in *Violence against women: The bloody footprints,* eds. Pauline B. Bart and Eileen Geil Moran, 240–251. Newbury Park, CA: Sage.

Burn, Shawn M. 2000. *Women across cultures: A global perspective*. London: Mayfield.

Cahill, Ann J. 2002. *Rethinking rape*. Ithaca, NY: Cornell University Press.

Cameron, Shannon. 2008. Violence against women in Ciudad Juarez, Mexico. Research essay for Women's Studies 4502, Male violence against women. Toronto: York University.

Canadian Panel on Violence Against Women. 1993. *Changing the landscape: Ending violence—achieving equality—executive summary*. Ottawa: Minister of Supply and Services Canada.

Chasteen, Amy L. 2001. Constructing rape: Feminism, change and women's everyday understandings of sexual assault. *Sociological Spectrum* 21 (April): 101–140.

Clark, Loreene, and Debra Lewis. 1977. *Rape: The price of coercive sexuality*. Toronto: The Women's Press.

Collins, Patricia Hill. 1993. The sexual politics of Black womanhood, in *Violence against women: The bloody footprints,* eds. Pauline B. Bart and Eileen Geil Moran, 85–104. Newbury Park, CA: Sage Publications.

Collins, Patricia Hill. 2000. *Black feminist thought: Knowledge, consciousness and the politics of empowerment.* New York: Routledge.

Connell, R.W. 2002. *Gender.* Cambridge, UK: Polity.

Connell, R.W. 2000a. *Masculinities.* Cambridge, UK: Polity.

Connell, R.W. 2000b. *The men and the boys.* Cambridge, UK: Polity.

Coomaraswamy, Radhika. 2006. Some reflections on violence against women, in *Canadian woman studies: An introductory reader*, 2d ed., eds. Andrea Medovarski and Brenda Cranney. Toronto: INANNA Publications.

Corrales, Miriam. 2008. Dowry deaths and bride burning in India. Research essay for Women's Studies 4502, Male violence against women. Toronto: York University.

Cote, Andree. 1984. The new rape legislation: An overview. *Status of Women News* (November): 8–12.

Crawford, Maria, and Rosemary Gartner. 1992. *Woman killing: Intimate femicide in Ontario, 1974–1990.* Women We Honour Committee.

Crocker, Diane, and Valery Kalemba. 1999. The incidence and impact of women's experiences of sexual harassment in Canadian workplaces. *Canadian Review of Sociology and Anthropology* 36(4): 541–558.

Curry, Don. 1997. Indian women face battle against violence. *Toronto Star*, April 3, D1, D7.

Danica, Elly. 1988. *Don't is a woman's word.* Charlottetown, PEI.: Cynergy.

DeKeseredy, Walter S., and Ronald Hinch. 1991. *Woman abuse: Sociological perspectives.* Toronto: Thompson Educational.

Diaz, Angeli R. 2004. Postcolonial theory and the third wave agenda. *Women and Language* 26 (January): 10–17.

Doe, Jane. 2003. *The story of Jane Doe.* Toronto: Vintage Canada.

Doe, Jane. 2007. Lecture, York University. Unpublished.

Doob, A. 2002. Understanding the attacks on Statistics Canada's violence against women survey, in *Violence against women: New Canadian perspectives*, eds. K. McKenna and J. Larkin, 55–62. Toronto: Inanna Publications/Education, Inc.

Dranoff, Linda Silver. 1977. *Women in Canadian life: Law.* Toronto: Fitzhenry and Whiteside.

Dranoff, Linda Silver. 1997. *Everyone's guide to the law.* Toronto: HarperCollins.

Duffy, Ann. 1983. Women, youth culture and coercive sexuality. Paper presented at the Family Life Conference, York University, Toronto, April.

Duffy, Ann, and Julianne Momirov. 1997. *Family violence: A Canadian introduction.* Toronto: Lorimer.

Faulkner, M. Ellen. 2001. Empowering victim advocates: Organizing against anti-gay/lesbian violence in Canada. *Critical Criminology* 1: 1–16.

Federal-Provincial-Territorial Ministers Responsible for the Status of Women. 2002. *Assessing violence against women: A statistical profile.* Ottawa: Status of Women Canada.

Fine, Sean. 1990. Study of Native women says 80 percent have suffered abuse. *The Globe and Mail*, January 19, A13.

Finkelhor, David, and Kersti Yllo. 1985. *License to rape: Sexual abuse of wives*. New York: Free Press.

Fiorillo, Isabella. 2008. Female genital mutilation in Africa. Research paper for Women's Studies 4502, Male violence against women. Toronto: York University.

Folgero, I.S., and I.H. Fjelstad. 1995. On duty–Off guard: Cultural norms and sexual harassment in service organizations. *Organization Studies* 16(2): 299–314.

Freedman, Lisa. 1985. Wife assault, in *No safe place: Violence against women and children*, eds. Connie Guberman and Margie Wolfe, 41–60. Toronto: The Women's Press.

Gardiner, J.K. 2003. South Park, blue men, anality and market masculinity, in *Masculinities: Interdisciplinary readings*, ed. M. Hussey, 100–115. Upper Saddle River, NJ: Prentice Hall.

Gargan, Edward. 1994. Dowry disputes bring murder to middle-class homes. *The Globe and Mail*, January 1, A1, A7.

Gerschick, T.J., and A.S. Miller. 2000. Gender identities at the crossroads of masculinity and physical disability. *Masculinities* 2: 34–55.

Golge, Z. Belma, et al. 2003. Turkish university students' attitudes toward rape. *Sex Roles* (December): 653–661.

Gordon, Linda. 1986. Incest and resistance: Patterns of father-daughter incest, 1880–1930. *Social Problems* 33: 253–267.

Gordon, Stephanie. 2008. Sexual violence against women and HIV infection in South Africa. Research essay for Women's Studies 4502, Male violence against women and children. Toronto: York University.

Gorkoff, Kelly, et al. 1999. *Violence prevention and the girl child: Final report*. The Alliance of Five Centres on Violence. **www.unbf.ca/arts/CFVR/documents/Girl-child-phase-1-report.pdf**. Accessed August 18, 2008.

Griffin, Susan. 1971. Rape: The all-American crime. *Ramparts* 10 (September).

Gurr, Jane, et al. 1996. *Breaking the links between poverty and violence against women*. Ottawa: Ministry of Supply and Services Canada.

Hadley, Gillian. 2005. And we still ain't satisfied: Gender inequality in Canada: A status report for 2001 (executive summary), in *Open boundaries: A Canadian women's studies reader*, 2d ed., eds. Barbara Crow and Lise Gotell. Toronto: Pearson Prentice Hall.

Handelman, Stephen. 1997. Violence killing millions of women: UNICEF. *Toronto Star*, July 22, A1, A16.

Harrison, Deborah. 2002. *The first casualty: Violence against women in Canadian military communities*. Toronto: James Lorimer.

Hautzinger, Sarah. 2002. Criminalising male violence in Brazil's women's police stations: From flawed essentialism to imagined communities. *Journal of Gender Studies* 11: 243–251.

Herman, Judith, and Lisa Hirschman. 1993. Father-daughter incest, in *Violence against women: The bloody footprints*, eds. Pauline B. Bart and Eileen Geil Moran, 47–56. Newbury Park, CA: Sage.

hooks, bell. 2003. Reconstructing Black masculinity, in *Masculinities: Interdisciplinary readings*, ed. M. Hussey, 298–316. Upper Saddle River, NJ: Prentice Hall.

Hornosty, Jennie. 1995. Wife abuse in rural regions: Structural problems in leaving abusive relationships (a case study in Canada), in *With a rural focus,* ed. F. Vanclay, 21–34. Australia: Charles Sturt University.

Howe, Keran. 2000. Violence against women with disabilities: An overview of the literature. **www.wwda.org.au/keran.htm.** Accessed August 18, 2008.

Howry, A.L., and J.T. Wood. 2001. Something old, something new, something borrowed: Themes in the voices of a new generation of feminists. *Southern Communication Journal* 66: 323–336.

Jensen, R. 2003. Using pornography, in *Masculinities: Interdisciplinary readings*, ed. M. Hussey, 262–270. Upper Saddle River, NJ: Prentice Hall.

Jiwani, Yasmin. 2005. The 1999 general social survey on spousal violence: An analysis, in *Open boundaries: A Canadian women's studies reader,* 2d ed., eds. Barbara Crow and Lise Gotell. Toronto: Pearson Prentice Hall.

Johnson, Holly. 1996. *Dangerous domains: Violence against women in Canada.* Toronto: Nelson.

Kadar, Marlene. 1982. Sexual harassment as a form of social control, in *Still ain't satisfied: Canadian feminism today*, eds. Maureen Fitzgerald et al., 169–180. Toronto: The Women's Press.

Kaliehman, Seth C., et al. 2005. Gender attitudes, sexual violence and HIV/AIDS risks among men and women in Cape Town, South Africa. *Journal of Sex Research* 42(4): 299–305.

Karanja, Lisa W. 2003. Domestic violence and HIV infection in Uganda. *Human Rights Dialogue* 10 (Fall): 10–11.

Kaufman, M. 1993. *Cracking the armour: Power, pain and the lives of men.* Toronto: Viking.

Kendall-Tackett, Kathleen A. 2001. Victimization of female children, in *Sourcebook on violence against women*, eds. C.M. Renzetti, J.L. Edleson, and R.K. Bergen, 101–116. Thousand Oaks, CA: Sage.

Kielburger, C., and M. Kielburger. 2008. Justice slow for female war victims. *Toronto Star*, March 3, AA2.

Kimmel, M.S. 1987. Rethinking "masculinity": New directions in research, in *Changing men: New directions in research on men and masculinity*, ed. M. Kimmel, 1–22. Newbury Park, CA: Sage.

Koenig, Michael, et al. 2004. Coercive sex in rural Uganda: Prevalence and associated risk factors. *Social Science and Medicine* 58(4): 787–798.

Koss, Mary P., and Cheryl J. Oros. 1982. Sexual experiences survey: A research instrument for investigating sexual aggression and victimization. *Journal of Consulting and Clinical Psychology* 50 (June): 455–457.

Kurz, Demie. 1993. Social science perspectives on wife abuse: Current debates and future directions, in *Violence against women: The bloody footprints*, eds. Pauline B. Bart and Eileen Geil Mora, 252–269. Newbury Park, CA: Sage, 1993.

Layton, J. 2008. *Homelessness: How to end the national crisis*, rev. ed. Toronto: Penguin.

LeMoncheck, Linda, and James P. Sterba, eds. 2001. *Sexual harassment: Issues and answers*. New York: Oxford Univ. Press.

Lenton, Rhonda, et al. 1999. Sexual harassment in public places: Experiences of Canadian women. *Canadian Review of Sociology and Anthropology* 36 (November): 517–555.

Lichtman, Judith L. 1993. How can we fight harassment? *USA Today*, October 14, 13A.

Littleton, Heather L., and Danny Axsom. 2003. Rape and seduction scripts of university students: Implications for rape attributions and unacknowledged rape. *Sex Roles* 49 (November): 465–475.

Lundberg-Love, Paula, and Robert Geffner. 1989. Date rape: Prevalence, risk factors, and a proposed model, in *Violence in dating relationships: Emerging social issues*, eds. Maureen A. Pirog-Good and Jan E. Stets, 169–184. New York: Praeger.

Luxton, Meg. 1980. *More than a labour of love.* Toronto: Women's Press.

MacKinnnon, M. 2008. Women: Iraq's persecuted majority. *The Globe and Mail,* March 18, A14.

MacLeod, Linda. 1980. *Wife battering in Canada: The vicious circle.* Ottawa: Supply and Services Canada.

MacLeod, Linda. 1986. *Battered but not beaten: Preventing wife battering in Canada.* Ottawa: Canadian Advisory Council on the Status of Women.

MacLeod, Linda, and M. Shin. 1990. *Isolated, afraid and forgotten: The service delivery needs and realities of immigrant and refugee women who are battered.* Ottawa: National Clearing House on Family Violence.

MacLeod, Linda, et al. 1993. *Like a wingless bird: A tribute to the survival and courage of women who are abused and who speak neither English nor French.* Ottawa: National Clearinghouse on Family Violence.

Malamuth, Neil M. 1981. Rape proclivity among males. *Journal of Social Issues* (Fall): 138–157.

Malamuth, Neil M., Scott Haber, and Seymour Feschbach. 1980. Testing hypotheses regarding rape: Exposure to sexual violence, sex differences and the "normality" of rapists. *Journal of Research in Personality* 14 (March): 121–137.

Mardorossian, Carine M. 2002. Towards a new feminist theory of rape. *Signs: Journal of Women in Culture and Society* 27: 743–775.

McCloskey, Laura Ann, et al. 2002. A comparative study of battered women and their children in Italy and the United States. *Journal of Family Violence* 17 (March): 53–74.

McDonald, P. Lynn, et al. 1991. *Elder abuse and neglect in Canada.* Toronto: Butterworths.

McEvoy, Maureen, and Judith Daniluk. 1995. Wounds to the soul: The experiences of Aboriginal women survivors of sexual abuse. *Canadian Psychology* 36(3): 221–235.

McIntyre, Sheila. 2005. Tracking and resisting backlash against equality: Gains in sexual offense law, in *Open boundaries: A Canadian women's studies reader,* 2d ed., eds. Barbara Crow and Lise Gotell. Toronto: Pearson Prentice Hall.

McPherson, Cathy. 1991. Tackling violence against women with disabilities. *Canadian Woman Studies* 12 (Fall): 63–65.

Meintjes, S., A. Pillay, and M. Turshen. 2001. There is no aftermath for women, in *The aftermath: Women in post-conflict transformation,* eds. S. Meintjes, A. Pillay, and M. Turshen, 1–18. London: Zed Books.

Messerschmidt, J.W. 1993. *Masculinities and crime: Critique and reconceptualization of theory.* Lanham, MD: Rowman and Littlefield.

Messner, M. 2003. Boyhood, organized sports, and the construction of masculinities, in *Masculinities: Interdisciplinary readings*, ed. M. Hussey, 140–152. Upper Saddle River, NJ: Prentice Hall.

Miedema, Baukje, and Sandra Wachholz. 1998. *A complex web: Access to justice for abused immigrant women in New Brunswick.* Report to Status of Women Canada. Ottawa: Status of Women Canada.

Miles, Angela. 2003. Prostitution, trafficking and the global sex industry: A conversation with Janice Raymond. *Canadian Woman Studies* 22(3/4): 26–37.

Montemurro, Beth. 2003. Not a laughing matter: Sexual harassment as "material" on workplace-based situation comedies. *Sex Roles* 48 (May): 433–445.

Mooney, Jayne. 2000. *Gender, violence and the social order.* New York: Palgrave.

Muehlenhard, C.L., et al. 1996. Beyond "just saying no": Dealing with men's unwanted sexual advances in heterosexual dating contexts, in *Sexual coercion in dating relationships*, eds. E.S. Byers and L.F. O'Sullivan, 141–168. New York: Haworth Press.

Munala, June. 2003. Combating FGM in Kenya's refugee camps. *Human Rights Dialogue* 10 (Fall): 17–18.

Murtadha-Watts, K. 2003. Theorists on constructions of black masculinities: Identity, consumerism, and agency, in *Masculinities: Interdisciplinary readings*, ed. M. Hussey, 323–330. Upper Saddle River, NJ: Prentice Hall.

National Women's Health Information Center (US). 2004. Fact sheet: Date rape drugs. **www.womenshealth.gov**

Nayak, Madhabika B., et al. 2003. Attitudes toward violence against women: A cross-nation study. *Sex Roles* 49 (October): 333–342.

Nelson, Adie, and Barrie W. Robinson. 2002. *Gender in Canada.* Toronto: Prentice-Hall.

Nolen, S. 2007. Violent crime strangling hope in South Africa. *The Globe and Mail*, March 31, A19.

Ofoma, Onyinye. 2008. War, rape and Congolese women. Research paper for Women's Studies 4502, Male violence against women. Toronto: York University.

Olsen Harper, Anita (forthcoming). Is Canada peaceful and safe for Aboriginal women?, in *Open boundaries: A Canadian women's studies reader*, 3d ed., eds. Barbara Crow and Lise Gotell. Toronto: Pearson Prentice Hall.

Omale, Juliana. 2000. Tested to their limit: Sexual harassment in schools and educational institutions in Kenya, in *No paradise yet: The world's women face the new century*, eds. J. Mirsky and M. Radlett, 19–38. London: Panos.

Pande, Rekha. 2002. The public face of a private domestic violence. *International Feminist Journal of Politics* 4 (December): 342–367.

Patterson, J. 2003. Spousal violence, in *Family violence in Canada: A statistical profile, 2003*, eds. H. Johnson and K. Au Coin, 4–20. Ottawa: Ministry of Industry.

Pervizat, Leyla. 2003. In the name of honor. *Human Rights Dialogue* 10 (Fall): 30–31.

Pizzey, Erin. 1974. *Scream quietly or the neighbours will hear*. London: Penguin.

Priest, Lisa. 1994. Medical students at U of T report harassment. *Toronto Star*, February 1, A3.

Quinn, Beth. 2004. Sexual harassment and masculinity: The power and meaning of "girl watching." in *The kaleidoscope of gender: Prisms, patterns and possibilities*, eds. Joan Z. Spade and Catherine G. Valentine. Belmont, CA: Thompson/Wadsworth.

Razack, Sherene (forthcoming). Gendered radical violence and spacialized justice: The murder of Pamela George, in *Open boundaries: A Canadian women's studies reader*, 3d ed., eds. Barbara Crow and Lise Gotell. Toronto: Pearson Prentice Hall.

Renzetti, C.M. 1992. *Violent betrayal: Partner abuse in lesbian relationships*. Newbury Park, CA: Sage.

Ristock, Janice L. 2002. Responding to lesbian relationship violence: An ethical challenge, in *Reclaiming self: Issues and resources for women abused by intimate partners*, eds. L. Tutty and C. Goard, 98–116. Halifax: Firewood/RESOLVE.

Romito, Patrizia. 2008. *A deafening silence: Hidden violence against women and children*, tr. Janet Eastwood. London: Policy.

Rosenberg, Sharon. 1999/2005. Neither forgotten nor fully remembered: Tracing an ambivalent public memory on the 10th anniversary of the Montreal massacre, in *Open boundaries: A Canadian women's studies reader*, 2d ed., eds. Barbara Crow and Lise Gotell. Toronto: Pearson Prentice Hall.

Rozee, Patricia D., and Mary P. Koss. 2001. Rape: A century of resistance. *Psychology of Women Quarterly* 25: 295–311.

Rudd, Jane. 2001. Dowry-murder: An example of violence against women. *Women's Studies International Forum* 24: 513–522.

Rush, Florence. 1980. *The best kept secret: Sexual abuse of children*. Englewood Cliffs, NJ: Prentice Hall.

Russell, Diana E.H. 1982. *Rape in marriage*. New York: MacMillan.

Russell, Diana E.H. 1986. *The secret trauma: Incest in the lives of girls and women*. New York: Basic Books.

Saeed, Rahal. 2000. File under "Hurt": Domestic violence in Sri Lanka, in *No paradise yet: The world's women face the new century*, eds. J. Mirsky and M. Radlett, 157–174. London: Panos.

Sampath, Niels. 2001. "Crabs in a bucket": Reforming male identities in Trinidad, in *The masculinities reader*, eds. S. Whitehead and F. Barrett, 330–340. Cambridge, UK: Polity.

Samuel, Edith. 2002. Dowry and dowry harassment in India: An assessment based on modified capitalist patriarchy. *African and Asian Studies* 1: 187–229.

Sanday, Peggy. 1981. The socio-cultural context of rape: A cross-cultural study. *Journal of Social Issues* 37: 5–27.

Sanday, Peggy. 2002. *Women at the center: Life in a modern matriarchy*. Ithaca, NY: Cornell University Press.

Sangster, Joan. 2001. *Regulating girls and women: Sexuality, family, and the law in Ontario, 1920–1960*. Toronto: Oxford Univ. Press.

Schmidt, K. Louise. 1995. *Transforming abuse: Nonviolent resistance and recovery*. Gabriola Island, BC: New Society Publishers.

Seager, Joni. 2003. *The Penguin atlas of women in the world*. New York: Penguin.

Sen, Amartya. 2006. *The argumentative Indian: Writings on Indian culture, history and identity*. Harmondsworth, UK: Penguin.

Sesay, Nabieu Musa. 2008. War: Another source of violence against women, The Sierra Leonean experience. Research essay for Women's Studies 4502, Male violence against women. Toronto: York University.

Sev'er, Aysan. 1999. Sexual harassment: Where we were, where we are and prospects for the new millenium. *Canadian Review of Sociology and Anthropology* 36 (November): 469–497.

Sev'er, Aysan. 2002. *Fleeing the house of horrors: Women who have left their abusive partners*. Toronto: Univ. of Toronto Press.

Shallat, Lezak. 2000. Democracy in the nation but not in the home: Domestic violence and women's reproductive health in Chile, in *No paradise yet: The world's women face the new century*, eds. J. Mirsky and M. Radlett, 137–156. London: Panos.

Sharma, Dinesh C. 2003. Widespread concern over India's missing girls. *Lancet* 362: 1553.

Sideris, Tina. 2001. Rape in war and peace: Social context, gender, power and identity, in *The aftermath: Women in post-conflict transformation*, eds. S. Meintjes, A. Pillay and M. Turshen, 142–158. London: Zed Books.

Smith, Michael D. 1990. Sociodemographic risk factors in wife abuse: Results from a survey of Toronto women. *Canadian Journal of Sociology* 15: 39–58.

Statistics Canada. 1990. *Women in Canada: A statistical report*. Ottawa: Minister of Supply and Services.

Statistics Canada. 1993. *Canadian violence against women survey*. Ottawa: Ministry of Industry.

Statistics Canada. 2003a. Homicide. *The Daily*, October 1.

Statistics Canada. 2003b. Sexual assaults. *The Daily*, July 25.

Statistics Canada. 2006a. *Family violence in Canada: A statistical profile*. Ottawa: Canadian Centre for Justice Statistics.

Statistics Canada. 2006b. *Women in Canada: A gender-based statistical report*, 5th ed. Ottawa: Statistics Canada.

Stevens, Kathy. 1995. Stopping violence against women with disabilities, in *Listening to the thunder: Advocates talk about the battered women's movement*, ed. L. Timmins, 223–234. Vancouver: Women's Research Centre.

Stewart, Mary White. 2002. *Ordinary violence: Everyday assaults against women*. Westport, CT: Bergin and Garvey:

Strange, Carolyn. 1995. Historical perspectives on wife assault, in *Wife assault and the Canadian criminal justice system*, eds. M. Valverde, L. MacLeod, and K. Johnson, 293–304. Toronto: University of Toronto Centre of Criminology.

Straton, J.C. 2000. The myth of the "battered husband syndrome," in *Gender through the prism of difference*, 2d ed., eds. M. Zinn et al., 126–128. Boston: Allyn and Bacon.

Stuffco, J. 2007. Islam not a factor in girl's death. Welland (ON) *Tribune*, December 14, A12.

Stymest, Kim. 2008. The war on women's bodies in the Democratic Republic of the Congo. Research essay for Women's Studies 4502, Male violence against women. Toronto: York University.

Taherzadeh, Leila. 2008. The hidden half: A research paper on the situation of women in Afghanistan. Research paper for Women's Studies 4502, Male violence against women. Toronto: York University.

Thorne, Barrie. 2003. Girls and boys together... but mostly apart: Gender arrangements in elementary school, in *Masculinities: Interdisciplinary readings,* ed. M. Hussey, 79–91. Upper Saddle River, NJ: Prentice Hall.

Thunder Bay Neighbourhood Watch, n.d. Women alone. Fact sheet.

Tomes, Nancy. 1978. A "torrent of abuse": Crimes of violence between working-class men and women in London, 1840–1875. *Journal of Social History* 11 (Spring): 328–345.

Toronto Star. 1992. Sexual harassment: Issue in Japan. February 7, F1.

Totten, Mark D. 2000. *Guys, gangs and girlfriend abuse.* Peterborough, ON: Broadview Press.

Turcotte, Shirley. 1987. *To a safer place.* National Film Board of Canada.

Tyyskä, V. 2006. Incidence of violence against intimate partners, in *Action and analysis: Readings in the sociology of gender*, ed. V. Tyyskä, 341–349. Toronto: Thomas Nelson.

Ursel, Jane, and Kelly Gorkoff. 2001. Court proceedings of child sexual abuse cases, in *Pieces of a puzzle: Perspectives on child sexual abuse*, eds. D. Hiebert-Murphy and L. Burnside, 79–94. Halifax: Fernwood/RESOLVE.

Valentine, Gill. 1989. The geography of women's fear. *Area* 21(4): 285–390.

Vallee, B. 2007. *The war on women: Elly Armour, Jane Hurshman, and criminal violence in Canadian homes*. Toronto: Key Porter.

Vincent, Donovan. 1999. System failed abused sisters. *Toronto Star*, September 23, A5.

Vinton, Linda. 2001. Violence against older women, in *Sourcebook on violence against women,* eds. C.M. Renzetti, J.L. Edleson, and R.K. Bergen, 179–192. Thousand Oaks, CA: Sage.

Wakelin, Anna, and Karen M. Long. 2003. Effects of victim gender and sexuality on attributions of blame to rape victims. *Sex Roles* 49 (November): 477–487.

Walker, Gillian. 1990. The conceptual politics of struggle: Wife battering, the women's movement, and the state. *Studies in Political Economy* 33 (Autumn): 63–90.

Walker, Leonore. 1979. *The battered woman.* New York: Colophon.

Watson-Franke, Maria-Barbara. 2002. A world in which women move freely without fear of men. *Women's Studies International Forum* 25 (November/December): 599–606.

Williams, C.L. 2003. The glass escalator: Hidden advantages for men in the "female" professions, in *Masculinities: Interdisciplinary readings*, ed. M. Hussey, 231–247. Upper Saddle River, NJ: Prentice Hall.

Women's Support Network of York Region. 2004. Myths and facts about sexual assault. Fact sheet. **www.womenssupportnetwork.ca**

Wood, Julia T. 2005. *Gendered lives: Communication, gender and culture*, 6th ed. Belmont, CA: Wadsworth/Thompson Learning.

Yelaja, P. 2006. Tough talk about wife abuse. *Toronto Star*, November 5, A3.

Yllo, Kersti. 1984. The status of women, marital equality, and violence against wives. *Journal of Family Issues* 5 (September): 307–320.

Youngs, Gillian. 2003. Private pain/public peace: Women's rights as human rights and Amnesty International's report on violence against women. *Signs: Journal of Women in Culture and Society* 28: 1209–1229.

Yonak, Yudum. 2008. Domestic violence in Turkey. Research essay for Women's Studies 4502, Male Violence against Women. Toronto: York University.

Zaman, Habiba. 1999. Violence against women in Bangladesh: Issue and responses. *Women's Studies International Forum* 22(1): 37–48.

CHAPTER 8

From "Little Lady" to "Little Old Lady": Women and Aging

Nancy Mandell, Ann Duffy, and Susannah Wilson

FEMINISM AND AGEISM

You are reading the fifth edition of *Feminist Issues*, which contains, for the first time, a chapter on women and aging. How is it possible that a book dedicated to exploring the changing nature of feminism in Canadian society failed to consider older women as a topic worthy of study until now? Not only did it not occur to me as the editor to include a chapter on aging women, but also it did not occur to the many reviewers who have read the last four editions. My own ageism blinded me to the topic just as the ageism that permeates women's studies blinded the reviewers. Invisible, ignored and disregarded, the subject of aging women and feminism remains our discipline's dirty little secret.

Coined in 1975 by Robert Butler, ageism refers to:

> a process of systematic stereotyping and discrimination against older people because they are old, just as racism and sexism accomplish this with skin colour and gender. Old people are categorized as senile, rigid in thought and manner, old fashioned in morality and skills . . . Ageism allows the younger generation to see old people as different from themselves, thus they subtly cease to identify with their elders as human beings (Butler, 1975: 12).

Ageism is insidious, invasive, and pervasive. It shapes our ideas of work, retirement, productivity, intimacy, friendship, health, body image, community involvement, and politics. Ageism underscores our ideas of appropriate behaviour for life stages—imagine club hopping at 40! Age gets attached to the display of certain emotions—is anger outlawed in the old? Ageism invades our ideas of appropriate dress—grandmothers in tank tops? Ageism is culturally represented in fashion, television, videos, and movies—Madonna turns 50!

Barbara Macdonald, an American radical feminist of the second wave, first identified the problem of ageism in feminism. During a "Take Back the Night" march to end violence against women, one of the young feminist activists organizing the event asked Macdonald if she would be able to keep up with the other marchers. Enraged, Macdonald later reflected on her anger and concluded that for years she had put up with discrimination because she was a woman, only to find herself putting up with discrimination from other women because she was old (Macdonald and Rich, 1991). The personal had indeed become political.

How does feminism perpetuate ageism? It begins with our feelings of revulsion, shame, and disgust toward the elderly. We shun their aging bodies. We turn away from their infirmities. We discount their opinions, calling them "old hags" behind their backs. Old feminists are just as likely to participate in ageism as young feminists are because all women understand how "unremitting" is the pervasive negativity facing the elderly (Gibson, 1996: 434) and will do almost anything to avoid it.

Feminists contribute to ageism by perpetuating a false dichotomy between the young and the aging and by attaching stereotypical characteristics to both. Prepare a list of characteristics that describe a 20-year-old woman and a 60-year-old woman. The young are imbued with all of society's positive traits—energy, vitality, strength—while the aging receive the opposite persona—fatigue, feebleness, fragility—qualities that denote powerlessness. Who wants to be known as puny and pathetic?

Given that the normative or ideal age in our society is now the decade between 25 and 35, women approaching 40 begin to feel the first twinges of anxiety as they drift away from the centre. Young women feel estranged from old women because their power lies in their youth. It is no wonder young women dread becoming old because young women's power is measured by the distance they keep from older women. As Macdonald tells us, "the older woman is who the younger women are better than—who they are more powerful than and who is compelled to serve them ... men are not the servants of youth; older women are" (Macdonald and Rich, 1991: 39).

Macdonald goes on to point out that "young" gets its meaning from what it is not, namely "old." By seeing young/old as binary opposites, we imbue youth with power. "Today the evidence is all around us that youth is bonded with the patriarchy in the enslavement of the older woman. There would, in fact, be no youth culture without the powerless, older woman" (Macdonald and Rich, 1991: 39).

The second wave of the Women's Movement reified this young/old division by focusing on the concerns of younger women: Moving married women into the labour force; breaking occupational segregation; sharing domestic labour; achieving equal pay for work of equal value; asserting legal equity; legalizing same-sex families; ending sexual exploitation; and averting the "male gaze" (Arber and Ginn, 1991). As a mostly white, middle-class, and young movement, the second wave was preoccupied with issues of production and reproduction—sexual, social, and economic—largely excluding the concerns of older women. In its rush to recruit young women to the movement, it failed to consider how age crosscuts gender in ways that create both similar and different challenges and opportunities for women and men. Nor did it encourage aging women to be activists and spokespersons (Connidis, 2006: 125).

If ageism is indeed propped up by young women, their attempts to avoid ageism are futile. American sociologist Jessie Bernard (1981) explains that a woman's relationship with a male protector provides only temporary immunity from the consequences of power-lessness; being female, at any age, means being subjected to constant degradation. As Shulamit Reinharz tells us, a general disrespect for women, and especially for feminists, is captured in the socially approved belittling term "little" (Reinharz, 1997: 84). Young or old, the mandate for women is to remain small and dominitable. From their earliest age as "little" girls until the day they die as "little old ladies," women are told to behave in gender-appropriate ways, being polite, deferential, well mannered, and refined.

In this chapter, we look at how ageism structures women's embodiment, care work, and paid work. The goal of feminism is to increase women's involvement in decision-making and social action, empower women, recognize their intrinsic value, increase their self-esteem, and protect their right to equal treatment. Ageism has made it difficult for all women to achieve these goals. Women can begin to confront ageism by unlearning their own biases and by using this self-reflection as a starting point for addressing the absence of age in feminist analysis (Ray, 2006).

Theorizing Age/Theorizing Feminism

Feminists have neglected age relations just as gerontologists have neglected feminism. If feminism is a political orientation designed to "intervene in and transform" power inequities between men and women (Hollows, 2000), then feminist age studies are a form of research and activism that aims to intervene in and transform the unequal power relations between age groups as influenced by gender. As Ruth Ray (2006) notes, feminist gerontologists study what aging looks like through a gender lens that is sensitive to power relations in order to advance knowledge and to promote social justice in the material world.

For feminists, age is a form of diversity that remains interconnected to, constitutive of, and implicated in all other forms of inequality. Using intersectionality theory (McCall, 2005), feminists pay attention to the complex relationships among social differences that socially, economically, and politically marginalize women. As Kathleen Woodward (1999) says, differences are produced by discursive formations, social practices, and material conditions. Focusing on intersections allows us to see the conjunction of old and young women's issues as articulated in material conditions such as wages, housing, and incarceration rates (L. Marshall, 2006).

A feminist political economy perspective—our feminist "standpoint"[1] (Harding, 1991)—focuses on how the material and social conditions of aging people are shaped by their positions in the social structure. This means that age, like race and gender and other primary markers of social difference, is socially and materially constructed. Major inequalities in the distribution of power, income, and property affect people's access to resources in later life, including health and body maintenance, income, assets, and access to informal and formal care (Arber and Ginn, 1991). A feminist political economy of aging describes the role of the economy and the state in establishing interlocking systems of domination that privilege some groups over others by structuring their access to material resources. Calasanti and Zajicek (1993) substitute the term "paradigm of domination" for the term "patriarchy" to reflect the interlocking system of oppression formed by race, class, and gender in particular. Inequality in later life originates in the multiple inequalities experienced early in life.

The state, through its social policies and ideological statements, props up ageism. For example, pension and retirement income systems, as well as social service benefits and entitlements, reflect the structure and culture of advantage/disadvantage as enacted through class, race/ethnicity, gender, and age relations. The state promotes and reproduces the dominant institutions that render older women vulnerable and dependent throughout their life course (Estes, 2003). An added crisis ideology—the notion that "greedy geezers" are going to "bankrupt" the Canadian economy—perpetuates ageism (McMullin, 2000), as do economic globalization and neo-liberal ideology, which frame the actions of the state in relation to the family and the market (Estes, 2003). In addition, the cultural norm of individual responsibility—the belief that individuals are wholly responsible for their fate—ignores the role of the economic realm in explaining how individuals become attached to the social structure.

According to feminist political economists, there are three central processes—production, reproduction and distribution—that shape individual life experiences. For example, the paid work one does, the amount of money one is paid, the security or insecurity of the position, and the ability to save for retirement, are all features of an individual's relationship to the economy, which shapes one's current and future life. Canadian feminists (Luxton and Corman, 2002; Baines, Evans, and Neysmith, 1991) expanded definitions of productive work to include unpaid economic activity such as care work, volunteerism, and domestic labour, but paid labour continues to be the most valued form of labour and the standard against which all other productive activity is evaluated (Calasanti, 2003). Reproduction refers to the ways in which life is maintained both daily and intergenerationally, including how children are socialized, how partners and the elderly are cared for, how the household is looked after, and how sex takes place. Reproduction includes then both the day-to-day social reproduction of dependents (children, parents, partners, friends, relatives) and the biological reproduction of children. It includes the work of producing Canadians as educated, healthy, knowledgeable, and productive citizens (Estes, 2003). Distribution refers to how services are generated and rendered: Who does what for whom?

Feminists have long argued that much of women's social reproductive work (care work, domestic labour, elder care) is unpaid and unacknowledged even though it consumes a large portion of women's daily lives and cuts into the time they can spend earning money and pursuing leisure. Often those not in the paid workforce are considered to be dependent because paid workers are the norm of productivity. Those under 19 and over 65 are considered to be "dependents" and thus "burdens." Interestingly, children are "light" burdens while the elderly feel "heavy," descriptions that reveal how dependence is socially constructed.

Feminists have also argued that the privileging of paid, productive work over unpaid, reproductive work spills over into cultural ideologies and personal relationships. For example, we tend to treat social reproductive work as private matters of the household even though we recognize that it is essential to making families work. Finding caregivers for dependent seniors is seen as a private affair. As theorists remind us, it is not the mere existence of reproduction and production that inevitably lead to social inequality, but rather the ways in which they are arranged (McMullin, 2000). Feminists have much to offer in terms of understanding how older people can be productive, as well as the value of labour and the social construction of the term "dependent" (Calasanti and Slevin, 2001). In the sections on paid labour and care work, we examine how age, gender, and ethnicity interlock to shape women's senior experiences.

AGING AND POVERTY

Women's economic experience of aging has changed profoundly in the last 50 years. In the not-so-distant past, aging was often a decidedly negative prospect. A societal reality that stereotyped women's aging in terms of loss of physical and sexual attractiveness, declining health, economic marginalization, and social stigmatization (as meddlesome mothers-in-law, pathetic widows or spinsters, or, at best, matronly grandmothers) was hardly an inviting prospect. Particularly alarming was the prospect of women having to spend their old age impoverished.

In 1980, more than one-quarter (26.7 percent) of women 65 and older (in contrast to one in seven, or 14.5 percent, of comparable men) were living in poverty (Statistics Canada, 2006a: 280). Today, it is still the case that poverty in old age remains very much a women's problem since poor seniors are typically female (Barnett, 2005: 25). Even in Sweden, with its strong social security system, older women, as a result of their domestic roles and labour market position earlier in life, are more likely than older men to be poor (Gunnarsson, 2002). However, perhaps the coming generation of senior women—the boomers whose youth was configured by the modern women's movement and the dramatic expansion of full-time, life-long employment among wives and mothers—faces better prospects both in aging and retirement.

As boomer women move into their 60s, it will become much clearer whether current generations of aging women will benefit from their dramatically increased educational qualifications and more continuous, full-time employment (Statistics Canada, 2006a: 274). Unfortunately, it may be the case that other recent social changes, notably in terms of the "new economy," changes in pension provisions, and increased social class polarization will imperil the economic progress many older women rightfully expect.

Short-term evidence does suggest that women of the boomer generation are benefiting from their increased participation in paid employment and resultant increases in their contributions to Canada and Quebec pension plans, RRSPs, and employer pension schemes.

In 1997, women born between 1935 and 1939 were retiring with higher average incomes than women their age ever had. From 1971 to 1997 their retirement income grew 10 times faster than men's; while men of the same age cohort saw their retirement incomes increase by only 6 percent in this period, the average after-tax income for this age cohort of women grew by 60 percent (Statistics Canada, 2000). These dramatic advances in senior women's incomes suggest that women's increased paid labour force participation has already paid off.

However, the improvement in older women's financial well-being is decidedly relative. In 2003, senior women 65 and older (born in 1938 or earlier) were receiving an average income from all sources of just over $20 000—more than $10 000 less on average than senior men. Over half (55 percent) of all senior women's income in 2003 depended on government transfer payments—Old Age Security (OAS) and the Guaranteed Income Supplement (GIS), spousal allowances, and the Canada and Quebec pension plans—and only 26.3 percent of their income came from private retirement pensions. In contrast, senior men's incomes were derived almost equally from government transfer payments (41.4 percent) and private retirement pensions (40.5 percent). In short, reflecting their traditional absences from the paid labour force, women are finding themselves much more reliant on government transfer payments. Even if they receive spousal benefits from their husband's pension when he dies, this income is typically significantly reduced (often by 50 percent) upon the death of the primary beneficiary. As a consequence, for almost 10 percent of widows, this loss of income means falling into poverty over the course of the first five years of widowhood (Statistics Canada, 2006b).

Poverty remains a stubborn, significant, and enduring problem for senior women. Senior women are still twice as likely as senior men to live below the Statistics Canada low income cut-off. In 2003, almost one in ten (8.7 percent) woman 65 and older was poor, in contrast to one in twenty (4.4 percent) men (Statistics Canada, 2006a: 289). Even though an extensive overhaul of Canadian government pension policies has significantly improved the financial status of both senior men and women, three significant gender issues remain: First, older women are still much more likely than comparable men to be poor in old age; second, as the size of the senior female population grows, the actual numbers of women affected by poverty has grown considerably; and third, as women continue to outlive men, they are likely to spend a longer period of their lives in poverty than senior males.

Women's Paths to Economic Insecurity

Women born prior to the post-war baby boom were more likely to lead traditional full-time homemaker lives. They might, as their children matured and left home, take on some form of paid employment, but the bulk of their lives and energies were often devoted to the home. Later-in-life efforts to regain paid employment rarely included returning to a well-paid career. In 2004, almost one in five women aged 65 and over (17 percent) had *never* been part of the paid workforce, compared to 2 percent of comparable males (Statistics Canada, 2006a: 276).

Older women are still not valued. Women typically do not enjoy "the premium of experience" enjoyed by their successful male counterparts. Men may attain stature, wisdom, and respect as they age and be sought out as leaders and mentors. Older women, despite their successes and experience, often find themselves stereotyped as old-fashioned and behind the times (Barnett, 2005: 26).

This pattern of sexist ageism may be one explanation of the ongoing under-representation of women in the paid labour force as they age. Certainly, there have been dramatic advances in the participation of all women, including midlife and older women, in paid work over the past three decades. In 1976 only 46 percent of women aged 45 to 54 and 30 percent of women aged 55 to 64 held paid jobs. In 2004, 76 percent of 45- to 54-year-old women and 46 percent of 55- to 64-year-old women held paid employment (Statistics Canada, 2006a: 104–105). However, this is not quite the stunning advance it might first appear to be.

Significantly, one-fifth of women aged 45 to 54 and 30 percent of women aged 55 to 64 are employed on a part-time basis while only 5 percent of men aged 45 to 54 and 11 percent of those aged 55 to 64 held part-time work (Statistics Canada, 2006a: 109–111). Part-time work, as extensively documented, often means low-paid, poorly benefited, dead-end forms of employment. In this regard and in others—such as temporary employment and multiple jobholding—midlife and older women are more likely than comparable males to find themselves in precarious or marginalized forms of employment. Their advances into paid employment must be evaluated in terms of this crucial reality.

Further, it is still the case that as women age, they are more likely than men to be diverted from paid employment. In 2005, 51 percent of women aged 55 to 64 had paid work (up from 41 percent 6 years earlier); however, 68 percent of comparable men were employed (up from 59 percent 6 years earlier). The greater likelihood of senior men holding paid work carries on with increasing age. Women aged 65 to 74 devoted less than half an hour a day to paid work, while comparable men averaged an hour a day. Necessarily, men's greater paid employment implies increased financial resources (Statistics Canada, 2006a).

Meanwhile, in each age group, women are devoting more of their time than men to unpaid work (caregiving) and less time than men to leisure. In 2005, women aged 55 to 74 devoted 4.8 hours a day to unpaid work while men spent considerably less time (men aged 55 to 64 devoted 3.1 hours and aged 65 to 74 devoted 3.9 hours per day to unpaid work).[2] Currently, even in senior years the traditional domestic division of labour appears to persist with men spending more time working for pay (and in leisure) and women spending more time on unpaid work (Statistics Canada, 2006c).

Finally, the senior labour force itself retains a traditional gender script. Although the numbers of Canadians 65 and older who are employed is increasing in recent years, the overwhelming majority of these workers are male (68.5 percent in 1996 and 67.9 in 2001) and the occupations filled mainly by senior men—doctors, judges, ministers of religion—are more likely to be well-paid and prestigious than those filled by senior women—secretaries and babysitters (Statistics Canada, 2004). This tendency for senior women to be occupationally ghettoized is also reflected by the fact that, in 2004, 50 percent of employed senior women were employed in clerical, sales, or service occupations, compared to only 25 percent of senior men (Statistics Canada, 2006a: 276). Although increased numbers of senior employed women are anticipated in the coming years, it remains to be seen to what degree their presence in the labour force challenges embedded patterns of gender inequality.

Problems for "De-tached" Women

Not surprisingly, women who opt for more traditional lives (marriage and motherhood) are at greater risk of economic marginalization as they age. Specifically, if they become "de-tached" from the marital relationship they are more at risk. For example, if they are widowed (which remains highly likely given older male/younger female marriage patterns and female patterns of longevity) or if they are divorced (as became increasingly the case from 1968 onwards) they are especially vulnerable to living on a low income or in poverty. Recent research indicates that older widows experience a steady decline in their median family income in the five years after the loss of their husband (more than 15 percent lower). Men, ironically, experience a higher median family income in the five years after their wives' deaths (5.8 percent higher). Significantly, higher economic class did not completely protect women from this impact. The richest widows experienced an 8.6 per-cent decline and the poorest a 9.8 percent drop. The pattern is also reflected in the fact that unattached senior women continue to have the lowest income, assets, and net worth of all senior family types (Williams, 2003). It seems that this is a fairly typical pattern through-out Western countries; women who are partnered are materially advantaged.

However, when women who have been partnered and who have limited their employ-ment participation because of caring obligations become single (through divorce or widowhood), their material well-being is likely to decline. Of course, the longer a woman lives the more likely she is to find herself in this situation. The overwhelming majority of once-married women who live into old age will find themselves on their own at some point. By their late 60s more than 20 percent of women are widowed and by age 75 widows outnumber married women (Giles et al., 2004).

Historically, never-married women tended to share this fate. Given the dearth of high-paying, secure employment for single women and the absence of single women in many professions, such women often found themselves trapped in dead-end, poorly paid occupa-tions such as service or secretarial workers. Today, interestingly, never-married women appear to be entering a new reality. More women are not marrying and are spending their entire adult lives in the paid labour force (Cooper, 2008: 45). Not surprisingly, these women tend to be better off materially than previous cohorts of single women. In a recent British study, never-married women were found to have longer occupational careers and their own pension rights and were more likely than married women to own a car (Arber, 2004). As marriage rates decline and more men and women spend all or a significant part of their adult lives as unattached individuals, it is likely that it will become clearer that it is not never-married women but rather women who become "de-tached" after making considerable investments in a marital-type relationship (investments that typically include some time away from the paid labour force) who are at dramatically increased risk for low income as they age.

Aging and the Pressures to Keep "Working"

One way in which workers can seek to avoid post-retirement impoverishment is by return-ing to the labour force. However, given women's caregiving responsibilities along with an unreceptive labour market, it appears that this is not a viable alternative for many women. Not only do women tend to retire earlier than men (often in response to a spouse's retire-ment), but they are also unlikely to return to paid employment post-retirement (Statistics Canada, 2005). Predictably, the combined impact of early retirement and lack of post-retirement employment tends to reduce the economic well-being of aging women.

Not surprisingly, as early retirement peaked in the mid-1990s workforce, increasing numbers of young retirees ended up returning to work, albeit in a dramatically reduced fashion, after they retired (Wannell, 2007). As analysts have pointed out, this move back into paid employment is triggered by a constellation of factors including ongoing good health, opportunities to move into part-time and contract employment (often in their previous sphere of employment), and financial needs. Predictably, given current ageist/sexist employment patterns, post-retirement men were more likely than comparable women to return to work. Reflecting social-class factors, retirees from professional occupations, followed by managers and technicians, were most likely to return to work. In short, post-retirement employees who had previous jobs offering "good pay, interesting work, and few physical demands" appeared more likely to return to paid work.

Given the gendered structure of the labour force, the majority of these employees were male (Statistics Canada, 2005). In 2004, 11 percent of senior men (65 and older) held paying jobs but only 4 percent of comparable women (Statistics Canada, 2006a: 275). Predictably, following other patterns of women's wage work in low-income, service work, more employed senior women (63 percent) held part-time jobs than comparable senior men (37 percent) (Statistics Canada, 2006a: 276).

The implications of the above statistics for all but the wealthiest employees and professionals are problematic; they are particularly troublesome for women. Because women tend to be occupationally segregated in less well-paid sectors of the economy, are likely to exit the paid labour force for some period in order to provide care for children or aging relatives (and as a result lose out on pension accumulations), and are likely to retire earlier and more permanently than men from paid work, they are clearly not well served by current retirement practices.

In recent years, the issue of post-retirement employment has moved increasingly away from a personal strategy to address financial shortfalls to a public response to an aging labour force. As a result of a wide variety of factors, the Canadian labour market is in the midst of dramatic change. The very nature of paid work is in transition and in this context society is facing a dramatic shift in its age profile. The baby boomers (born between 1946 and 1966) are now entering their retirement years. Predictably, media accounts speak with alarm about the potential shortage of employees as boomers retire and of the state's financial burden in trying to support the aging population. Not surprisingly, one popular solution to a variety of these issues is to encourage boomers to remain in the paid labour force past retirement.

Indeed, many Western countries are developing policies to encourage older male and female workers to remain in the paid labour force (Ginn and Arber, 2005). Research examining Canada, Australia, Germany, the Netherlands, the United Kingdom, and the United States suggests that current efforts to increase the labour force participation of older workers may in fact put these workers at greater risk of low-income work (Cooke, 2006). For example, efforts to retain older workers confront the desire of employers to keep wages low. Current employment trends toward part-time, temporary/contract, and generally precarious employment do keep the costs of work down, but are often not experienced as desirable employment options by workers. If lower stock market values reduce private pension holdings, older workers may indeed feel pushed into retaining or finding this less than desirable paid employment.

This scenario is likely to be particularly problematic for older women workers who have tended to be ghettoized in poorly paid and/or part-time service sector employment and who are more financially vulnerable that their male counterparts.

The problems of being "encouraged" to remain in or return to the paid labour force are not limited to undesirable jobs; the workplace itself may be less than welcoming. Despite anti-discrimination laws, it seems that perceptions of older workers as being less capable and more expensive persist. If more vulnerable senior workers do return to paid employment, the net result may be increased inequality among older Canadians—with the minority of seniors who are affluent being able to afford the option of a well-financed retirement while the majority struggle with pressures to manage on inadequate pension incomes and undesirable employment alternatives (Cooke, 2006). Once again, given that women, particularly widows and divorced women, are economically vulnerable in old age, any push to "encourage" post-retirement employment may have strongly negative gendered implications.

Precarious Pensions

The "new economy" has new realities in the realm of pensions. Many of these changes will affect both men and women; but given the larger numbers of female elderly, more women will be affected and for a longer period of time. One hundred years ago, relatively few Canadians lived into old age and many of those individuals were forced to rely on their families or private charities to provide them with food and shelter. With the emergence of the welfare state, there was increased provision for senior citizens, but frequently these provisions left many older Canadians in or near poverty. In 1980, for example, 27.3 percent of men and 38.4 percent of women aged 65 or older were poor (National Council of Welfare, 1994: 72). Public protests resulted in dramatic improvements in government provisions for the elderly, notably the Guaranteed Income Supplement and Old Age Supplement. As a result, markedly fewer seniors, including women, found themselves living at or near poverty.

However, in recent years there have been new challenges for pension provisions. In the wealthier countries, including Canada, there has been increasing pressure to shift the responsibility for economic support of the elderly from social insurance to private investments (Folbre, Shaw, and Stark, 2005; Townson, 2000). This is evidenced in Canada, for example, by diverse efforts to encourage Canadians to assume primary responsibility for their retirement income by investing in RRSPs. Ironically, part of the rationale for this shift has been the assumed ability of contemporary married women to earn pensions in their own names as they pursue paid employment (Townson, 2000: 3). This assumption, of course, ignores the realities of many married women's paid employment, which is often relatively low-wage "women's work." Women tend to be employed in part-time and non-standard jobs (temporary, contract, self-employment, or multiple job-holding) in an effort to manage competing work/family demands or, increasingly, because these jobs are the only ones being generated by the economy. Often these jobs by their very nature are not only poorly paid but insecure and lacking in benefits, including pension plans. The net effect is not likely to be a well-financed pension fund.

Some analysts also argue that there is a generational problem brewing in terms of pensions for boomers. The boomer generation has tended to be a consumer generation and they have tended to accumulate less in the way of savings and more in the way of debts.[3] As a result of economic conditions, home equity is a principal source of wealth for many boomers. However, as the housing market levels off or declines, much of this equity may be depleted or difficult to actualize. The overall aging of the population is likely to stimulate the market for condominiums while reducing the demand for family homes. Further, efforts to access home equity, such as reverse mortgages, have limited appeal, since homeowners may only borrow 10 to 40 percent of the appraised value of their home and the fees of costs of such loans are higher than on regular mortgages. In mid-2007 the five-year fixed reverse mortgage rate was 9.3 percent (Cooper, 2008; *Pension Benefits*, 2006). Once again, the impact of inadequate retirement equity is most likely to be felt by longer-lived woman.

Although perhaps less apparent, there is also an ongoing shift in pension provision away from employers. This pattern has taken a number of forms. As increasing numbers of employees are contract, short-term, and/or self-employed they do not qualify for employer pension benefits. In this regard, it is not surprising that employer retirement pension coverage is on the decline among younger cohorts of workers. These workers tend to typically earn less and accumulate less RRSP wealth and have, not surprisingly, longer working careers (Wannell, 2007). Currently, 38.5 percent of Canadian workers do not have workplace pensions and almost one-third have no retirement savings (Canadian Labour Congress, 2007: 1). Given women's typical location in the labour force, they are more likely to be disadvantaged by declines in "good" jobs.

Equally significant, employers have moved away from defined benefits retirement plans toward defined contributions plans. Defined benefit plans, as their name suggests, assure retirees of a specific retirement income, one that typically would be topped up by regular cost of living increases. These plans, which now are increasingly scarce and almost entirely the province of public service employees, are incredibly valuable to retirees in terms of their income security. In contrast, defined contributions plans are becoming the new norm and numerous employers are arguing this is the only form of pension plan they can afford. While touted by some supporters as a more flexible alternative to workers in an economy where they are more likely to move from one job to another, defined contributions plans mean that the employer is only responsible to make specified contributions. The successful management of these funds in retirement are in the hands of the retired employees (or their investment companies). Downturns in the market, catastrophic losses to pension funds (e.g., Enron) and the day-to-day costs of investment are burdens shouldered exclusively by the retiree—employers are, quite happily, off the hook (Cooper, 2008). Once again, the impact is, at the least, heightened financial insecurity for aging Canadians—most of whom are women.

If these trends toward pension "reform" are eventually coupled with efforts to privatize state-funded pensions, as is the case in the United States, the consequences would be dire for women, minorities, and lower-income men—all of whom tend to be located in either low-wage or no-wage work for some portion of their adult lives. In this process, a major source of power (and cash) would be transferred from the state to private corporate capital. The net result would be interplay between capital and the sex and gender system that would leave older women more vulnerable and dependent (Estes, 2004). Whether such an approach will be advanced in Canada remains to be seen. Currently, Canada is among the most progressive of Western countries in terms of the provision of state-funded pensions and financial supports to older Canadians and has, as indicated, an admirable record of dramatically reducing the numbers of impoverished seniors. However, there is considerable pressure on governments throughout the West to respond to the needs of capital under the pretext of maintaining global competitiveness.

Most women, with very few exceptions, are likely to be affected by these changes in pension arrangements. Since they live longer and since they frequently live out their lives on their own, any insecurity or reduction in pension benefits has a disproportionate impact on them. Further, specific groups of women are particularly vulnerable. Women who are members of any group that is likely to be marginalized in the labour force or relegated to low-wage, insecure, and poorly benefited work are in jeopardy. For example, visible minority women, disabled women, women who are recent immigrants and women who are poor and/or poorly educated face significant obstacles in seeking any economic security as they age.

Aging and Exceptional Women

In this discussion it is important continuously to acknowledge the diversity of women's experience of aging. Not only are some women, as previously noted, particularly at risk as they grow older, but others are likely to be particularly advantaged. It is likely that specific populations of aging women—professional women, female academics—may be particularly well-situated to benefit from increases in the numbers of employed older women. Certainly, there appears to be a direct correlation between level of education and labour force participation. In 2004, among high school graduates only 47.6 percent of women but 61.7 percent of men 45 and older were employed; however, among university graduates 82.1 percent of women and 89.0 percent of men in this age cohort were employed (Statistics Canada 2006a: 120). In other words, higher levels of education for women appear to result in increased labour force participation even at midlife.

Furthermore, recent policy changes appear likely to have positive impacts on the labour force participation of aging, well-educated women. The recent elimination of mandatory retirement in much of Canada has meant that many professional women who delayed or interrupted their careers for child-rearing or other reasons would now be in a position to extend their working lives and enhance both their careers and post-retirement finances (Tweedie, 2005). Finally, there is the small contingent of women in the Canadian corporate and political elite who have benefited from golden parachutes and gold-plated pensions (Canadian Labour Congress, 2007: 9–10).

AGING AND CARE WORK

Despite the media myths of old women as unproductive, empirical data reveal that neither the demands for care work nor women's feelings of obligation to perform care work are diminished with age. In fact, women's caregiving actually increases as they age, peaking at age 55 to 64 (K. Marshall, 2006). A feminist political economy perspective understands care work as an experience of moral obligation, structured by the gender-based division of labour. On average, women spend 35 years of their lives devoted to caring for children, grandchildren, and older people (Calasanti and Slevin, 2006). Some women begin the caring process in adolescence while others do not actively begin until the birth of their first child. Regardless of when it begins, cultural scripts of femininity assume that women will take responsibility for others, care for others, and put the needs of others before their own, even if this means sacrificing employment and leisure opportunities.

Care work involves both instrumental and affective dimensions. Instrumental duties include those taking place within the home such as preparing meals, doing housework, financial management, and personal care (bathing, dressing, toileting) as well as tasks that take place outside the home including yard work, house repairs, transportation, and financial maintenance. Emotional duties include the performance or supervision of concrete tasks as well as the assumption of psychological responsibility for others by checking up on them, visiting or telephoning them, and providing emotional support such as keeping up their spirits and offering reassurance and encouragement (Cranswick, 1997; Hooyman and Gonyea, 1999: 151).

Care work is shaped by social structures and is subject to the social and material conditions within which it occurs. Personal and social identities are embedded in social relationships. By accepting the cultural mandate of responsibility for care work and engaging in it, women construct their social identities as gendered, classed, and raced subjects (Twigg, 2004). By engaging in care work—mothering, grandmothering, and elder care—women produce their identities as females as well as reproduce the very structures that shape their lives.

But herein lies the dilemma. A significant investment in family care work means a lowered investment in the labour market, which results in women's reduced economic security in old age. Over-engagement in care work renders women poor in old age, but society then blames them for their own poverty (Holstein and Minkler, 2003). Yet to ignore the responsibilities associated with caring for others leaves women open to social censure and ostracism—women are "bad women" if they do not put the needs of others before their own. Discourses of love commingle with discourses of obligation, leaving many women feeling conflicted and trapped, unable to ignore care work even though the work itself remains socially undervalued and largely unrewarded.

Care work is gendered. Women provide 70 to 80 percent of in-home care to family members at every stage of the life course (K. Marshall, 2006). Caregiving increases with age, peaking between the ages of 55 and 64. Despite high levels of female labour force participation, many Canadians believe that home and children take precedence over working for pay in women's lives. Expectations remain for women, even when employed, to maintain primary responsibility for home and family. In 1995, 46 percent of both men and women agreed or strongly agreed that "while a job is all right, what most women really want is a home and family" (Ghalam, 1997). In the past decade, women have increased the time they spend in paid employment without a significant corresponding decrease in the time they spend on domestic labour and child care. In 1997, of all women in two-parent families, 62 percent of women with children under the age of 16 were employed (Hunsley, 2006). In 1998, employed mothers with children under the age of 5 spent double the amount of time on personal child-care activities than men: 91 minutes per day for mothers compared to 47 minutes per day for fathers (Hunsley, 2006).

Men are more likely than women to support aging family members financially and women are more likely to support them emotionally and in daily tasks such as household chores, shopping, and basic hygiene (Chisholm, 1999). Women take on the direct hands-on personal care duties while men generally assist in tasks such as home maintenance and financial management (Habtu and Popovic, 2006). Male and female subjectivities are thus constituted in and through gendered practices of caring (Twigg, 2004).

Care work is classed. Money disrupts the balance of power within households. High personal income, for either sex, is associated with spending more time at a job and less on housework. When wives have an income of $100 000 or more, the division of paid labour and housework between partners is more likely to be split equally. The higher a wife's education, the higher is her husband's share of housework. Partners with relatively high education and income have more power to get out of doing housework by buying domestic help. In addition, there has been a fairly recent rise in the number of wives who earn more than their husbands. In 2003, about 1.4 million couples or 1 in 4 dual-earner couples had wives as the primary breadwinner (Sussman and Bonnell, 2006). Primary-earner wives are slightly older and more educated than secondary-earner wives and primary-earner husbands. They are more likely to be employed in managerial and professional occupations (40 percent versus 26 percent), to work more hours per week, and to have had more years of experience than their secondary-earner counterparts (Sussman and Bonnell, 2006).

Care work is raced, but it is also diverse within each community. Racialized women are more likely to be involved in paid care work; Asian men perform almost as much care work as Asian women; more highly educated women perform less care work; higher-earning men perform very little care work; and many minority groups have more sources of care support available than do white groups. This diversity reveals the intersectional nature of care work and the power of social location. Racial, classed, and gendered advantages and disadvantages accrue through the life course leaving some marginalized individuals and groups with limited care work options (Hooyman and Gonyea, 1999: 152). The exploitation of women in the context of care work reinforces a system of coerced care. By caring for younger generations, older women and other mothers may ensure the survival of racial ethnic communities, but by taking up these caring subject positions, they simultaneously reproduce interlocking systems of marginality (Zajicek et al., 2006).

Within Canada, there exists a racial division of mothering with women of colour doing the hard "mother" work for women of privilege. White middle-class and upper-class mothers' employment is often made possible by the labour of women of colour who provide necessary child-care and domestic services (Arendell, 2000). Because they lack choices in life, they may have to put aside their responsibilities of caring for their own children while caring for the children of others (Bryceson and Vuorela, 2002). Nannies and au pairs "manufacture motherhood" through their care work (Macdonald, 1998), leaving unchallenged both the gender-stratified order in which women have primary responsibility for children and home and racialized systems of labour (Collins, 1994; Glenn, 1994).

Prioritizing child-care work over employment is neither possible nor wanted by many Canadian women. Traditional discourses of intensive mothering have always been primarily white, economically secure, ableist ones that have never matched the realities of working-class, dis/abled, or ethnic racial women. Economically insecure and racial ethnic mothers have always worked longer hours at lower-paying jobs than white mothers overall (Arendell, 2000). Providing economically for children is more commonly understood among some minority groups to be an intrinsic aspect of a woman's mothering role (Bryceson and Vuorela, 2002; Collins, 1994; Glenn, 1994).

Struggling to ensure economic survival involves racial ethnic mothers in what Reyes (2002) calls "postcolonial mothering," namely allowing other mothers close and far—grandmothers, aunts, sisters, neighbourhood women—to fulfill the mothering role. "Other mothering" practices including patterns of circular migration (sending their children off to extended family members in the home country for a period of time and then bringing them back to Canada), co-residing with their own mothers who can then perform the care work, using community members as mothers, and "mothering from afar" (leaving their children in their home countries for most of their childhood) (Arendell, 2000; Farrar and Gyant, 1998). In the latter case, mothers are often separated from children for long periods of time but see themselves as successful because they are economic providers for children and sometimes entire families; their labour improves their families' living standards.

Care work is affected by global economic shifts. Globalization has not brought the economic prosperity expected by middle-aged generations who increasingly rely on their families to help out. Half of contemporary three-generation households are headed by immigrants or Aboriginal families (Che-Alford and Hamm, 1999; Milan and Hamm, 2003). Parents born in Asia and Central and South America are far more likely to live with their adult children than those in some other ethnic groups (Turcotte, 2006).

Care work is shaped by state policies. Ideologies that see reproductive work as private and primarily the domain of women are used to justify minimal state involvement in long-term care and to draw old women into caring for family members (Estes, 2003). Old people, not always by choice, continue to work as unpaid caregivers in the home looking after grandchildren, spouses, and relatives (King, 2006). Grandmothers may be called upon to perform care work so that younger women can be "free" to engage in paid labour. Some 40 percent of American adult children with children under the age of 5 receive babysitting help from parents (Spitze and Logan, 1992). In Canada, in 1996, about 54 percent of grandparents in three-generation households helped out with household finances (Che-Alford and Hamm, 1999). Gender ideologies are also used to justify transferring care work from the formal sector of hospitals and state-run nursing homes to the informal sector of the home.

Care work is associated with quality of life. Caregivers experience both objective burdens (the actual demands they experience as caregivers) and subjective burdens (feelings of worry, sadness, resentment, anger, or guilt) (Hooeyman and Gonyea, 1999). Caring obligations are thought to account in part for the poorer health and higher levels of physical disability experienced by older women, as well as their limited financial resources.

But, when asked to evaluate their experiences in the 2002 Canadian General Social Survey, both middle-aged caregivers and senior caregivers rate their elder care positively. Between 80 and 90 percent feel that helping others strengthens their relationships with the care receivers and repays some of what they themselves have received from others and from life (Stobert and Cranswick, 2004). In fact, 20.6 percent of men and 22.2 percent of women felt they should be doing more (Habtu and Popovic, 2006). Feelings of love and duty intersect across the life course.

AGING AND EMBODIMENT

Our examination of paid work and care work highlights the importance of the material in structuring the lives of old women. But age is more than the sum total of material conditions. Age arises from the recursive interaction between structure, culture, and agency. In this view, age is less a biological prescription—years lived—than it is a social and cultural inscription. Aging is not a "natural" process but occurs within culture. It is through our involvement in culture that we give age meaning. Media images, representations, symbols, and metaphors offer important cultural descriptions from which women construct identities of aging.

Age is a key way in which women perform or accomplish gender. Like gender, age is not a property of individuals but rather a socially prescribed relationship, a process and a social construction (Ray, 1996). Both aged and gender identities are created and maintained through the social constructs by which we give them historical, material, and cultural meaning. We all tend to become who we are addressed as being. Gender and age identities represent ways of being in the world that take their meaning from our shared language, history, and culture (Ray, 1996).

Gender, like age, is too often presented dichotomously—male versus female; young versus old. Gender and age come together in the culture's "double standard," which pits young women against old women and aging men against aging women. Defined by Sontag (1972: 102) as a process by which women suffer scorn and exclusion as they grow old—a "humiliating process of gradual sexual disqualification"—the double standard of aging represents a form of double marginality. Racialized women experience a "triple jeopardy" as negative stereotypes of ethnicity intersect with negative stereotypes of women and the old.

Ironically, while young women are preoccupied with sexual exploitation, aging women are concerned about being sexual cast-offs. In fact, young women benefit from the negative sexual portrayal of old women as it enhances their social value and their opportunities with privileged men (Calasanti, 2003). Along with racism and ableism, sexual disqualification creates painful situations for all women by setting limits on how they can imagine and experience themselves. Of course, many aging women see themselves as healthily sexual and as having passed beyond the strictures of narrow sexual definitions of attractiveness.

Bodies are discursive, meaning they are shaped, represented, and constructed both materially and socially. James Paul Gee (2001) describes discourses as "ways of being in the world; they are forms of life which integrate words, acts, values, beliefs, attitudes and social identities as well as gestures, glances, body postures and clothes." Gee refers to discourses as "identity kits" because they come with complete "instructions on how to act, talk and often write, so as to take on a particular role that others will recognize."

Because bodies represent continuing sites of identity construction, age and gender are identities accrued over time by adhering to and performing body norms. In fact, bodies are so centrally implicated in the process of gender identity construction that Kontos (1999), following Butler, argues that bodies have no signifiable existence without the mark of gender. There are age and gender-based standards by which people manage their identity kits and this management is directed toward the body. Women of all ages, races, genders, classes, and ability types mould, pressure, push, and cajole their bodies into becoming public representations of how they want to be viewed.

What is the ideal body in our society? First, the ideal body is similar to every other type of body. The cultural norm says that every body should be the same, with similar abilities and energies, and certainly no impairments. Disability and visible age signify failure, particularly troubling norms because they reinforce cultural fears of bodily suffering and infirmity.

Second, a successful old body is an active body. Productive activity—economic, physical, and social—becomes the norm against which everyone is judged. "Staying active" becomes a type of moral obligation for the elderly, promoted as a way to avoid decline and dependency. Illness becomes a transgression of cultural rules because it prevents activity. Entire groups become marginalized when our societal vision of aging is staying economically engaged, socially active, and physically vigorous.

Third, the ideal body is an ageless body. Ultimately, the agenda of successful aging is not to age at all—to avoid becoming old altogether. But if a body has to age, then the ideal old body is a young body, which is projected into old age as the norm of successful aging (Holstein and Minkler, 2003). It is only by managing the surface of the body that one is able to perform an ageless identity (Wray, 2007).

If bodies are public presentations of our identities, then we need identity kits or body practices to maintain the ideal. Wendell (1996: 88) calls these body practices "disciplines of normality." "Keeping up"—being active—and "passing for normal"—dressing, talking and acting like someone who is younger—reduce the likelihood of being the target of ageist or ableist prejudice. Aging people are subject to what Katz (1996) calls a discipline of activity. Those who are less active are considered less attractive and thus less valuable.[4] This emphasis on youth and vitality subjects old people to a type of cultural imperialism; successful aging by not appearing old becomes a lifelong project that requires increasing levels of work as we age.

Adhering to disciplinary norms means we all participate in the social conspiracy of pretending there are no impaired or aged people. Cultural representations that advocate youthfulness and agelessness push women into participating in the anti-aging industry. Disciplining bodies to fight aging requires consumption. Buying cosmetic surgery or other consumer goods, joining a gym, and dieting are marketed as gendered body practices that will enable women to fight aging.

Aging experts are now available to tell the old how to age successfully. The "new gerontology" promoted by the experts tells people that to age successfully requires maintenance of activities popular among the privileged middle class with money and leisure time. And it seems to be working. Staying fit is highly valued social capital. American data show that those aged 64 to 75 spend more on consumer items than those aged 25 to 34. Imagined landscapes of consumption are marked by tanned golfers, tidy lawns, retirement communities, and hybrid cars. It is estimated that the new field of "longevity medicine" grosses between $27 billion and $43 billion a year with the expectation that it will rise to $64 billion by 2007 (US Special Senate Committee on Aging, 2008).

CONCLUSION

In this chapter, we have looked at the material and social effects of the double standard of aging and the ways in which ageism is embodied. Why is it that men are "allowed" to age naturally without social penalties but the aging female body arouses revulsion? As Reinharz (1986: 38) reminds us, the double standard is more than a matter of aesthetics; it is the beginning of a whole set of oppressive structures that keep women in their place. And as women age, the gap widens.

The development of feminism and ageism owes a huge debt of gratitude to disability studies (Overall, 2006). Disability, like age, is socially and materially constructed. This does not deny the reality of the aging body, but says that how we define it is socially constructed. Positive definitions of aging seem to have disappeared historically just at a time when women gained the possibility of achieving social capital by way of their own personal and professional development. The energy women could have used to affect their lower status and dependency has been re-channelled into worries about aging—worries for which the consumer economy offered resources such as makeup, surgery, and fashion literature (L. Marshall, 2006). Ultimately, ridding the body of visible signs of aging requires spending large sums of money.

In 1921, women aged 65 and older made up a scant 5 percent of Canadian women; in 2004 they were 15 percent and by 2031 one in four Canadian women will be a senior. It is possible that this demographic presence will translate into increased input for aging women into social policy. However, in the short run it appears that boomer women would be well advised not only to care for their physical health but also their financial well-being. Successful aging is, of course, in large measure dependent on being healthy enough to enjoy the benefits of retirement or reduced workload, but this is complexly intertwined with financial security (Schellenberg, Turcotte, and Ram, 2005).

Women who lack adequate financial resources have reduced opportunities to enjoy retirement (for example, travel, involvement in community activities, further education, and artistic endeavours) and increased pressure to take on poorly paid, marginalized employment. While public health campaigns concerning breast cancer and heart disease have drawn boomer women's attention to potential health threats, there has been less information for aging women about their financial security. Given persistent ageist and sexist patterns in the labour force, continuing pressure on aging women to assume care work, and their likelihood of becoming "de-tached," it is essential that older women be alerted to the financial problems of aging. However, a lifetime of caring for others leaves women financially insecure in old age. Intermittent or part-time employment, combined with low-wage jobs, means far too many women face poverty in old age, with racialized women particularly vulnerable.

We end by reminding our readers that feminist discourses are liberating discourses that offer new ways to reconstitute ourselves. As feminist Shulamit Reinharz reminds us, "Feminists, along with everyone else, have been socialized into our ... geronto-phobic culture" (1986: 507). As contemporary feminists, we need to begin to eliminate ageism by confronting our own fears and misgivings. Understanding the social and material construction of ageism offers a way to begin this journey.

Endnotes

1. Sandra Harding defined "feminist standpoint theories" as political forms of inquiry that seek to redress imbalances by researching and writing from an overtly political point of view. As Ray (1996) notes, this includes socialist feminists who look at economic relations between men and women across the life course and gauge their cumulative effects on older women. It also points to inequalities in the gender-based division of labour and argues for major changes in the way society defines, structures, and rewards "work." Patricia Hill Collins' (2000) work on standpoint in Black feminist theory highlights the intersecting systems of race, class, and gender oppression that operate in and through the state and virtually all other social institutions. This critique has reached age relations as well (Estes, 2003).

2. For example, increasing numbers of grandparents are providing assistance in raising their grandchildren. In the United States, 7.6 percent of grandparents have a grandchild living with them. Predictably, grandmothers play the primary role in such arrangements (Wang and Marcotte, 2007).

3. The explanation for this relative lack of savings is complex and should not be couched in simply moral terms (failure to save). Boomers have lived through a period of dramatically increased housing costs. Other areas of the economy, for example, education-related costs such as tuition, have also grown markedly along with the demand for higher education credentials. Certainly, the remarkable expansion of the consumer society has also played a significant role in creating "needs."

4. Katz (1996) says old men are also subject to ageism. They need to assert their manliness by spending money and remaining active because they have lost their institutional grip on the hegemonic ideals of manhood once out of the labour market, the realm of those considered sexually desirable by the young.

Suggested Readings

Calsanti, T., and K. Slevin. 2006. *Age matters: Realigning feminist thinking*. London: Routledge. This book discusses why feminists ought to be concerned with age relations and explores the ways that feminist thinking is transformed when we centre on age.

Mandell, N., S. Wilson, and A. Duffy. 2008. *Connection, compromise and control: Canadian women discuss midlife*. Toronto: Oxford. This study of Canadian women at midlife examines the ways in which growing up with the Women's Movement has shaped their decisions in the areas of intimacy, raising their daughters, employment, health, and well-being. It highlights regrets as well as achievements.

National Advisory Council on Aging. 2005. *Seniors from ethnic cultural minorities*. Ottawa: Minister of Public Works and Government Services Canada. This is an important collection of Canadian policy papers presenting NACA opinions and recommendations on the needs and concerns of seniors who are marginalized or at risk of being marginalized in Canadian society.

National Women's Studies Association Journal. 2006. Special Issue: Aging: A feminist issue. 18(1). This is a peer-reviewed scholarly publication of the American-based National Women's Studies Association, which is committed to providing a forum in which the research of feminist scholars, established and new, results in critical dialogue. The special issue on women and aging contains an excellent selection of articles from humanists and social scientists writing in the field of feminism and aging.

Yook, Hyunsook, and Jon Hendricks, eds. 2006. *Handbook of Asian aging.* Amityville, NY: Baywood. This handbook critically assesses the social and economic policies that require improvement in order for aging reforms to take place in Australia, China, Japan, South Korea, India, Malaysia, Singapore, the Philippines, and Taiwan. Chapters are grouped into sections that focus on economic status, work and retirement, living arrangements, family caregiving and social support, health and long-term care, and community social services.

Discussion Questions

1. What are the differences between being an old woman and a young woman? At what point does one become "old"? Does this vary with social class, ethnicity, or gender?

2. Critically examine two films about aging. What images of old women are portrayed? How is age "performed"?

3. An aging population "tsunami" is about to hit Canada. How will this group fare economically?

4. What types of care work do older women perform and why? How does this vary by ethnic group?

5. Why are feminists afraid of aging? How can feminist theories and studies be altered to include age?

Bibliography

Arber, S. 2004. Gender, marital status, and ageing: Linking material, health, and social resources. *Journal of Aging Studies* 18(1): 91–108.

Arber, S., and J. Ginn. 1991. *Gender and later life: A sociological analysis of resources and constraints.* London: Sage.

Arendell, T. 2000. Conceiving and investigating motherhood: The decade's scholarship. *Journal of Marriage and the Family* 62(4): 1192–1209.

Baines, C.T., P.M. Evans, and S.M. Neysmith. 1991. *Women's caring: Feminist perspectives on social welfare.* Toronto: McClelland and Stewart.

Barnett, R.C. 2005. Ageism and sexism in the workplace. *Generations* 29(3): 25–30.

Bernard, J. 1981. *The female world.* New York: Free Press.

Bryceson, D.F., and U. Vuorela, eds. 2002. *The transnational family: New European frontiers and global networks.* New York: Oxford Univ. Press.

Butler, R.N. 1975. *Why survive? Being old in America.* New York: Harper and Row.

Calasanti, T.M. 2003. Theorizing age relations, in *The need for theory: Critical approaches to social gerontology*, eds. S. Biggs, A. Lowenstein, and J. Hendricks, 199–218. Amityville, NY: Barwood.

Calasanti, T.M., and K.F. Slevin. 2001. *Gender, social inequalities and aging*. Walnut Creek, CA: AltaMira.

Calasanti, T.M., and K.F. Slevin, eds. 2006. *Age matters: Realigning feminist thought*. New York and London: Routledge.

Calasanti, T.M., and A.M. Zajicek. 1993. A socialist-feminist approach to aging: Embracing diversity. *Journal of Aging Studies* 7: 117–131.

Canadian Labour Congress. 2007. *Moving forward together or fend for yourself? The future of Canada pensions*. Discussion paper, 3d CLC Pension Conference.

Che-Alford, J., and B. Hamm. 1999. Under one roof: Three generations living together. *Canadian Social Trends*, Statistics Canada, Catalogue no. 11-008, 6–9.

Chisholm, J.F. 1999. The sandwich generation. *Journal of Social Distress and the Homeless* 8(3): 177–180.

Collins, P.H. 1994. Shifting the center: Race, class and feminist theorizing about motherhood, in *Representations of motherhood*, eds. D. Bassin, M. Honey, and M.M. Kaplan, 56–74. New Haven: Yale Univ. Press.

Collins, P.H. 2000. *Black feminist thought: Knowledge, consciousness and the politics of empowerment*, 2d ed. New York and London: Routledge.

Connidis, I. 2006. Intimate relationships: Learning from later life experience, in *Age matters: Realigning feminist thought*, eds. T.M. Calasanti and K.F. Slevin, 123–153. New York and London: Routledge.

Cooke, M. 2006. Policy changes and the labour force participation of older workers: Evidence from six countries. *Canadian Journal of Aging* 25(4): 387–400.

Cooper, S. 2008. *The new retirement*. Toronto: Viking Canada.

Cranswick, K. 1997. Canada's caregivers. *Canadian Social Trends*, Winter, Statistics Canada, Catalogue no. 11-008-XPE, 2–6.

Estes, C.L. 2003. Theoretical perspectives on old age policy: A critique and a proposal, in *The need for theory: Critical approaches to social gerontology*, eds. S. Biggs, A. Lowenstein, and J. Hendricks, 219–233. Amityville, NY: Barwood.

Estes, C.L. 2004. Social Security privitization and older women: A feminist political economy perspective. *Journal of Aging Studies* 18(1): 9–26.

Farrar, A.L., and L. Gyant. 1998. African-American women, family and hospitality work. *Marriage and Family Review* 28: 125–141.

Folbre, N., L.B. Shaw, and A. Stark. 2005. Introduction: Gender and aging. *Feminist Economics* 11(2): 3–5.

Gee, J.P. 2001. Reading as situated language: A sociological perspective. *Journal of Adolescent and Adult Literacy* 44(8): 714–725.

Ghalam, N.Z. 1997. Attitudes toward women, work and family. *Canadian Social Trends,* Statistics Canada, Catalogue no. 11-008-XPE, 13–17.

Gibson, D. 1996. Broken down by age and gender: The "problem" of old women. *Gender and Society* 10(4): 433–448.

Giles, P., et al. 2004. Income replacement among recent widows. *Perspectives on Labour and Income* 5(5). **www.statcan.ca/english/studies/75-001/10504/high-2.htm**. Accessed August 20, 2008.

Ginn, J., and S. Arber. 2005. Longer working: Imposition or opportunity? Midlife attitudes to work across the 1990s. *Quality in Ageing* 6(2): 26–35.

Glenn, E.N. 1994. Social constructions of mothering: A thematic overview, in *Mothering: Ideology, experience and agency*, eds. E.N. Glenn, G. Chang, and L.R. Forcey, 1–29. New York: Routledge.

Gunnarsson, E. 2002. The vulnerable life course: Poverty and social assistance among middle-aged and older women. *Aging and Society* 22: 709–728.

Habtu, R., and A. Popovic. 2006. Informal caregivers: Balancing work and life responsibilities. *Horizons* 6(3): 27–34.

Harding, S. 1991. *Whose science? Whose knowledge? Thinking from women's lives.* Ithaca, NY: Cornell University Press.

Hollows, J. 2000. *Feminism, femininity, and popular culture.* Manchester, UK: Manchester Univ. Press.

Holstein, M.B., and M. Minkler. 2003. Self, subjectivity and the "New Gerontology." *The Gerontologist* 43(6): 787–797.

Hooyman, N.R., and J.G. Gonyea. 1999. A feminist model of family care: Practice and policy directions. *Journal of Women and Aging* 11(2/3): 149–169.

Hunsley, T. 2006. Work-life balance in an aging population. *Horizons* 8(3): 3–13.

Katz, S. 1996. *Discipling old age: The formation of gerontological knowledge.* Charlottesville, VA: Univ. of Virginia Press.

King, N. 2006. The lengthening list of oppressions: Age relations and the feminist study of inequality, in *Age matters: Realigning feminist thought*, eds. T.M. Calasanti and K.F. Slevin, 47–73. New York and London: Routledge.

Kontos, C. 1999. Local biology: Bodies of difference in ageing studies. *Ageing and Society* 19: 677–689.

Luxton, M., and J. Corman. 2002. *Getting by in hard times: Gendered labour at home and on the job.* Toronto: Univ. of Toronto Press.

Macdonald, B., and C. Rich. 1991. *Look me in the eye: Old women, aging and ageism,* 2d ed. Denver, CO: Spinsters Ink Books.

Macdonald, C.L. 1998. Manufacturing motherhood: The shadow work of nannies and au pairs. *Qualitative Sociology* 21(1), 25–48.

Marshall, K. 2006. Converging gender roles. *Perspectives*, Statistics Canada, Catalogue no. 75-001-XIE, 5–17.

Marshall, L. 2006. Aging: A feminist issue. *National Women's Studies Association Journal* 18(1): vii–xiii.

McCall, L. 2005. The complexity of intersectionality. *Signs: Journal of Women in Culture and Society* 30(3): 1771–1800.

McMullin, J. 2000. Diversity and the state of sociological aging theory. *The Gerontologist* 40(5): 517–530.

Milan, A., and B. Hamm. 2003. Across the generations: Grandparents and grandchildren. *Canadian Social Trends* 71 (Winter): 2–8

Moss, P., and I. Dyck. 2003. *Woman, body, illness.* New York: Rowan and Littlefield.

National Council of Welfare. 1994. *Poverty profile.* Ottawa: Ministry of Supplies and Services.

Overall, C. 2006. Old age and ageism, impairment and ableism: Exploring the conceptual and material connections. *National Women's Studies Association Journal* 18(1): 126–137.

Pension Benefits. 2006. Baby boomer women: Secure retirement futures or not? *Pension Benefits* 15(8): 4–6.

Ray, R. 1996. A postmodern perspective on feminist gerontology. *The Gerontologist* 36(5): 674–680.

Ray, R. 2006. The personal is political: The legacy of Betty Friedan, in *Age matters: Realigning feminist thought,* eds. T. Calasanti and K.F. Sleven, 21–45. New York and London: Routledge.

Reinharz, S. 1986. Friends or foes: Gerontological and feminist theory. *Women's Studies International Forum* 9: 503–514.

Reinharz, S. 1997. Friends or foes: Geronotological and feminist theory, in *The other within us: Feminist explorations of women and aging,* ed. M. Pearsall, 73–91. Boulder, CO: Westview Press.

Reyes, A. 2002. I'm not mad, I'm postcolonial, a woman, and a mother: Introduction, in *Mothering across cultures: Postcolonial representations*, ed. Angela Reyes, 1–31. Minneapolis: Univ. of Minnesota Press.

Schellenberg, G., M. Turcotte, and B. Ram. 2005. What makes retirement enjoyable? *Canadian Social Trends* (Autumn): 12–14.

Sontag, S. 1972. The double standard of aging. *Saturday Review of Society,* September 23, 29–38.

Spitze, G., and J.R. Logan. 1992. Helping as a component of parent-adult child relations. *Research on Aging* 14(3): 291–312.

Statistics Canada. 2000. Incomes of younger retired women: The past 30 years. *The Daily,* December 11.

Statistics Canada. 2004. Study: Seniors at work: An update, 2001. *The Daily,* February 25.

Statistics Canada. 2005. Study: Post-retirement employment. *The Daily*, September 23.

Statistics Canada. 2006a. *Women in Canada: A gender-based statistical report.* 5th ed. Ottawa: Minister of Industry.

Statistics Canada. 2006b. The death of a spouse and the impact on income. *The Daily*, July 10.

Statistics Canada. 2006c. General Social Survey: Time use patterns of older Canadians. *The Daily*, July 26.

Stobert, S., and K. Cranswick. 2004. Looking after seniors: Who does what for whom? *Canadian Social Trends*, Statistics Canada, Catalogue no. 11-008, 2–6.

Sussman, D., and S. Bonnell. 2006. Wives as primary breadwinners. *Perspectives,* Statistics Canada, Catalogue no. 75-001-XIE, 10–17.

Townson, M. 2000. *Reducing poverty among older women: The potential of retirement income policies.* Ottawa: Status of Women Canada.

Turcotte, M. 2006. Parents with adult children living at home. *Canadian Social Trends,* Statistics Canada, Catalogue no. 11-008, 80: 2–10.

Tweedie, J. 2005. Age matters: Mandatory retirement's impact on female academic staff. *OCUFA Forum* (Spring): 12–13.

Twigg, J. 2004. The body, gender and age: Feminist insights in social gerontology. *Journal of Aging Studies* 18(1): 59–73.

United States Senate Special Committee on Aging. 2008. **http://aging.senate.gov/**

Wang, Y, and D.E. Marcotte. 2007. Golden years? The labour market effects of caring for grandchildren. *Journal of Marriage and the Family* 69: 1283–1296.

Wannell, T. 2007. Young pensioners. *Perspectives on Labour and Income* 8(2): 5–14.

Wendell, S. 1996. *The rejected body.* London: Routledge.

Williams, C. 2003. Finances in the golden years. *Perspectives on Labour and Income* 4(11): 5–13.

Woodward, K.M. 1991. *Aging and its discontents: Freud and other fictions.* Indianapolis: Indiana Univ. Press.

Woodward, K.M. 1999. *Figuring age: Women, bodies, generations.* Bloomington: Indiana Univ. Press.

Wray, S. 2007. Women making sense of midlife: Ethnic and cultural diversity. *Journal of Aging Studies* 21: 31–42.

Zajicek, A., et al. 2006. Intersectionality and age relations: Unpaid care work and Chicanas, in *Age matters: Realigning feminist thought,* eds. T.M. Calasanti and K.F. Slevin, 175–197. New York and London: Routledge.

CHAPTER 9

Mothers' Maintenance of Families through Market and Family Care Relations

Amber Gazso

INTRODUCTION

From the mid-20th century onward, there have been significant and observable changes in the market and family care relations of Canadian families. Women have entered the labour force in ever-increasing numbers and more women are combining paid work with raising and caring for children, either with a partner or alone. Canadian families are also increasingly racially/ethnically heterogeneous. This diversity is reflected in differences in women's labour market participation and provisions of caregiving across racial/ethnic groups and is linked to changes in immigration policy. In addition, heteronormative assumptions (the taken-for-granted privileging of heterosexuality in family relations) about Canadian families are more likely to be debunked. Ever-growing public awareness of the market and family care relations of lesbian and gay couples has coalesced with the legalization of their marriages in 2005 and recognition of their entitlement to social programs and benefits associated with employment (e.g., pension and health benefits) and maintaining families in the same manner as opposite-sex couples with children. These latter two changes particularly demonstrate the diversity of Canadian families today. Moreover, for all families, there is the pressing need for parents' labour market attachment. Lone mothers with young children increasingly manage paid work alongside their caregiving responsibilities. For many two-parent families, both parents must engage in paid work in order to "make ends meet." Indeed, more families have little choice but to involve all adult earners in some form of labour market attachment.

Intricately related to many of these changes is the weakening of the Canadian welfare state. Since the 1980s, governments have followed a neo-liberal agenda of reform. As both an economic doctrine and a political ideology (Hartman, 2005), a neo-liberal agenda demands governments' increasing openness to national and international market competition and the reduced role of the state in individuals' lives. Governments consequently spend less on social programs and more greatly prioritize individuals' responsibilities for their own and their family's social and economic well-being. For example, core social policies and programs that provide much needed income support to families, such as child benefits, social assistance (or welfare), and Employment Insurance (EI), have undergone significant changes. Families therefore have a much weaker safety net to turn to in times of need.

In the contemporary political economy, the way mothers maintain families with dependent children through their market and family care relations is a challenge. In addition to their paid work participation, mothers who co-parent with male partners continue to perform the bulk of domestic labour and manage their child-care needs with limited state support to do so. Regardless of family structure, mothers' disproportional engagement in gender-segregated employment accompanied by few benefits (e.g., paid leaves, health and dental benefits, employer sponsored pension plans), translates into fewer resources to provide for their own and their children's income security. This is particularly problematic for lone mothers, who must often stretch limited resources to meet food, shelter, transportation, and child-care demands. Bringing all of these trends together, it is apparent that mothers experience a complex state-family-market nexus in the organization of their daily lives. Mothers' maintenance of families by participating in the labour market and providing care—and juggling both—is indeed the stuff of feminist concern.

In this chapter, we take these changes in Canadian families as our starting point. I show how families—in whatever shape or form—are maintained through mothers' engagement in and managing of market and family care relations. I use the term "market relations" to refer to the structure of the labour market and to capture the paid work experiences of mothers within it, including their interactions with other individuals. "Family care relations" encompass the caregiving relationships mothers have with their children and other family members. In this chapter, I specifically outline mothers' contemporary labour market and child-care experiences, the challenges associated with these experiences, and the strategies mothers adopt to manage them. I also show how the state, via federal and provincial social policies and programs, intersects with mothers' market and family care relations. In doing so, I assume a focus on mothers who engage in paid and unpaid work. I resist focusing on only heterosexual mothers who are part of white, middle/upper class, nuclear families with children and instead adopt a much more inclusive definition of the family, drawing attention to mothers of varying sexuality and race/ethnicity and how they engage in similar or different ways of maintaining families. I focus primarily on Canadian mothers, but where national scholarship is limited I draw upon literature from other Western societies (e.g., the United States) which, like Canada, can be grouped as "liberal welfare states." These societies generally share a greater prioritization of individuals and family rather than state responsibility for citizens' social and economic well-being (see also Baker, 2006; Esping-Andersen, 1990) and are also experiencing similar changes in families' market and care relations. This chapter unfolds with a brief review of some of the ways feminists have understood the connections between women's participation in paid and unpaid work, including housework and child care.

SOME BRIEF FEMINIST INSIGHTS

> To be "feminist" in any authentic sense of the term is to want for all people, female and male, liberation from sexist role patterns, domination, and oppression.
>
> bell hooks (1981: 195)

Feminist scholars have long been concerned with women's (and men's) experiences of paid work and family care responsibilities. All femin*isms* at some time have shared a concern with women's experiences of inequality in one or both domains compared to men's (and other women's) and argued that these women's experiences are public and political issues. Although space does not permit a comprehensive analysis of the historical evolution of these feminisms, brief mention is made of the central interests of some perspectives.

Liberal feminists are concerned with achieving women's equality of opportunity compared to men's in various spheres of society. Concerns for women's equal education, employment and wage opportunities, equality before law, choices surrounding their reproduction, and state-endorsed parental leave and child-care provisions have dominated this feminist perspective. Liberal feminists are also dedicated to achieving equality in women's and men's participation in unpaid work within nuclear families formed through heterosexual unions (Garey, Hansen, Hertz, and MacDonald 2002). The liberal feminist goal of improving women's opportunities in paid employment and their wages, as well as action and calls for dramatic improvements of social and state supports for family care provisions, are intended to improve mothers' ability to balance their participation in paid work and family caregiving.

In contrast, some socialist and radical feminists critique the liberal feminist assumption that women can better compete with men in the marketplace if more equal opportunities are available to them. In their view, this feminist approach overlooks the structural conditions of the marketplace, including gendered power dynamics and ideological assumptions and the fact that the marketplace functions on the basis of others' (read women's) provisions of care (Calixte, Johnson, and Maki, 2005; Garey et al., 2002; Hamilton, 2005).

Another perspective is offered by Marxist feminism, which is cognizant of these economic and structural conditions and blends Marxist interests in deconstructing class-based inequalities with feminist interests in deconstructing gender-based inequalities. Of great concern to many Marxist feminists has been the creation of awareness for and among mothers that their caregiving, nurturing, and domestic activities within the home constitutes *work* and has a productive capacity much like any outside market activities. Women's unpaid housework and caregiving activities have been revealed as underpinning capitalist market processes; the unpaid labour women perform within the home produces and reproduces workers capable of participating in the labour market on a daily and generational basis (Fox, 1980; Luxton, 2006; Seccombe, 1980). Marxist feminist scholarship also seeks to explore how the patriarchal character of gender relations "maintain[s] and reproduce[s] the social relations of capitalism" (Weedon, 1999: 143). In her classic treatment of housework, Hartmann (1981) shows how the nuclear family is a site of power struggles between women and men when marital tensions erupt over what appear to be unequal efforts at producing and redistributing. By and large, husbands' greater privilege in the labour market and dominance associated with earning for a family's survival can mean that they can abstain from increasing their participation in housework (Hartmann, 1981). Men's domination and power in working-class households is grounded materially in their possession of a primary wage (Seccombe, 1980). When women contribute to the household income through wage work, this does weaken the patriarchal basis of power in the home. And yet, as Fox (1980) highlights, married women's involvement in wage work is still a product of their primary responsibility for maintaining families. Managing total household income against everyday needs is part of this responsibility.

Intricately connected to the development of Marxist feminism, socialist feminism also critically considers the inequality that characterizes women's market and family care relations in a capitalist society. Like Marxist feminists, socialist feminists have stressed how unpaid work performed by women is necessary for the capitalist mode of production (Luxton, 2006), and have particularly highlighted the exploitative conditions of this work. As part of heterosexual couples, mothers' primary responsibility for managing child care and the workforce attachment of themselves and their partners is of benefit to their families. However, this same primary responsibility is often detrimental to mothers' own careers and incomes. More women than men engage in part-time work to manage these demands, a point we will return to later in this chapter. Socialist feminist approaches also highlight how structures other than class underpin women's oppression, including gender, race/ethnicity, and sexual orientation. The responsibility for managing child care and market attachment disproportionately and negatively affects racialized lone mothers (or "visible minority" mothers in government and policy discourse). In addition, socialist feminists have emphasized how institutionalized heterosexuality is implicated in the power relations of class and patriarchy (Dunne, 2000a; Weedon, 1999); sexuality cannot be divorced from the material world. Acknowledging heterosexuality as a social institution is necessary for any analyses of paid work and family life (Dunne, 2000a). As Dunne (2000a: 137) explains, when we understand men's labour market participation as facilitated by women's unpaid labour in the home, it is important to recognize that heteronormative assumptions about families "provide the logic that translates women's labour into men's material advantage."

Radical feminists, on the other hand, place a greater deal of emphasis on sex oppression as the root of women's and mothers' inequality in the home and labour market (Calixte, Johnson, and Motapanyane, 2005). As Hamilton (2007) explains, they do not dispute patriarchal capitalist relations, but rather argue that this sex oppression is buried far deeper historically and psychically. For some radical feminists, the family has been understood to be a site where men control women's sexuality; women's roles within the home are created and maintained by men for their own purposes.

Since these feminist perspectives were largely articulated by white women for white women, they initially neglected fully to acknowledge their own inherent racism. These perspectives did not accurately match the realities of racialized women and therefore marginalized women's differences (Hamilton, 2007; Harnois, 2005). Arguably, it was the work of predominantly anti-racist and Black feminists who revealed the Eurocentric and white-centred bias of feminist scholarship from these perspectives. For example, the above feminist perspectives overlook how Black women and mothers have been consistently denied fair participation in the labour market (e.g., through practices of slavery in the 19th century) and/or have had a lengthier history of participating in the labour market because of economic necessity (Calliste, 2003; Harnois, 2005; hooks, 1981). Anti-racist feminists therefore attempt to correct for these oversights. They prioritize how overlapping and historically specific power relations, discourses, and processes—such as colonization, imperialism, slavery, and systemic racism—affect non-white and white women's location and thus their historical and contemporary experiences of subjugation and oppression (Bannerji, 2000; Dua, 1999; Hamilton, 2007). As Lerner (1993: 245) observes: "Race, class, and gender oppression are inseparable: they construct, reinforce, and support one another." Some anti-racist scholarship incorporates the emphasis on material relations embedded within socialist feminism. Anti-racist feminists may examine how race and gender intersect in the division of paid and unpaid labour to the advantage of white women and men (Mandell, 2005). Other scholarship critiques the radical feminist emphasis on families as a site of sexual oppression. Anti-racist scholars have also demonstrated that some women of colour have sought the family as a place of refuge from a racist society (Dua, 1999; Mandell, 2005).

One specific example of anti-racist feminism is the significant insights of Black feminist scholarship. As explained by hooks (1981: 124): "The first white women's rights advocates were never seeking social equality for all women; they were seeing social equality for white women." Black feminist standpoint theory assumes that Black women exist within an "intersectionality matrix," which refers to their specific location within multiple systems of oppression (Few, 2007). In any explorations of women's and men's experiences of market and family care relations, Black feminists are concerned with injecting a Black consciousness or standpoint into such studies to represent the unique experiences of Black women (Collins, 1989; Few, 2007).

Finally, feminist scholars have also approached the study of women's market and family care relations by using a feminist political economy lens. As understood by Clement

(2001: 406), the political economy encompasses the state, including government and governance (the political), and the social, political, and cultural constitution of markets, institutions, and actors (the economy). Scholars who use this approach explore society from a materialist perspective; social relations are connected to economic relations of production (Clement, 2001; Luxton, 2006). Feminists who adopt a political economy approach focus their attention on how political, economic, and cultural processes inter-sect to create societal conditions of inequality for women. Recent uses of this perspective draw upon insights from the above femin*isms* to show how capitalist processes of labour, exchange, and production are connected to the changing distribution of power, resources, and rights among citizens (e.g., welfare state restructuring) within nation states. Inequali-ties that women experience within their market and family care relations are also under-stood as being interlocked with their identities and social structures of race/ethnicity, class, gender, and sexuality (Bakker, 1996; Bezanson, 2006; Danby, 2007; Vosko, 2002). For example, the insights of Marxist and socialist feminists are incorporated into analyses of how the state is not gender neutral and is instead embedded with gendered assumptions surrounding women's and men's participation in market and family care relations (Hamilton, 2005). The scholarly insights of anti-racist and Black feminists are implied in analyses that consider how gender interconnects with race/ethnicity and class; feminists using a political economic lens have shown that poor racialized women have the least capacity to make rights-based claims upon the state to achieve economic security and the well-being of their children. Finally, scholarship in queer theory has sensitized feminist political economy to the need to critique heteronormative assumptions about family lives that fil-ter into family, state, and market relationships (Danby, 2007).

With such a myriad of feminisms, it is a challenge for any feminist to articulate the approach they will use in their own explorations of women's material everyday realities. I approach the content of this chapter using a feminist political economy lens. I show how mothers' manage-ment of their market and family experiences are shaped by gender, race/ethnicity, sexuality, and class *in relation to* structural constraints imposed by the political and economic context in which they live. Stated more specifically, I limit my attention to the contemporary labour market and the changing structure of only some federal and provincial social policies and programs. I show how these institutions affect women's structural positions, their entitlement to government income support, and their everyday experiences as informed by both assump-tions about and women's actual sexuality, gender, race/ethnicity, and class.

THE CONTEMPORARY MARKET AND FAMILY CARE RELATIONS OF MOTHERS

> If paid labor and unpaid domestic labor are combined, the average woman works longer hours and receives substantially less income than the average man.
>
> Debra Rhode (1988: 1207)

Families, in whatever shape and form, are increasingly maintained through two key processes—market and family care relations. As lone parents or co-parents or living in extended family households, mothers intricately combine their work for pay with family care responsibilities, which includes provisions for their children's emotional, physical, and mate-rial needs. Depending on the composition of their families, mothers can also provide this care to partners and other adult dependents. However, relations of production (e.g., paid work) and reproduction (e.g., bearing and rearing children, unpaid work, or domestic labour) are not always equally divided among family members. This is particularly the case in nuclear families where mothers co-parent with fathers; mothers are often responsible for the bulk of caregiving demands. In this section, I explore the inequality that characterizes mothers' market and family care relations. I show it is shaped by mothers' and fathers' decisions as well as economic and structural forces. Prior to doing so, it is useful to first explore and compare the employment and income patterns of women and men more generally in order to better contextualize mothers' unequal experiences in paid and unpaid work.

While differences in women's labour force participation have always varied on the basis of their race/ethnicity and class, women on average have steadily increased their labour force participation since the 1950s. Whereas 42 percent of all women over the age of 15 were part of the paid workforce in 1976, 58 percent of all women were employed and earning wages in some capacity in 2004. During this same period, the proportion of men employed slightly decreased, from 73 percent in 1976 to 68 percent in 2004 (Statistics Canada, 2007). Despite these significant gains made by women, their experiences of the labour market are characterized by differences in the types of work performed and inequality in earnings compared to men (Gazso, 2004). Canadian men still occupy employment with higher status and higher pay than do women (Brooks, Jarman, and Blackburn, 2003), such as supervisory or administrative positions in manufacturing or industry sectors. In contrast, women continue to occupy positions in services and sales sectors (Wilson, 2005).

Various reasons are cited for this wage inequity, including hourly commitment to paid labour, education level, and occupations chosen. Women are more likely to work part time, and accounted for seven out of ten part-time workers in 2004 (Statistics Canada, 2007). Their part-time work falls into the category of non-standard jobs, which are characterized by short-term contracts, low skill, low wages, and few benefits (Benoit, 2000). Men, however, are more likely to be employed on a full-time, full-year basis (Baker, 2006; Frenette and Coulombe, 2007). Although the gap between women's and men's earnings has narrowed over time (Heisz, Jackson, and Picot, 2002), Canadian Census data from 2001 demonstrates that even if both women and men worked full-time, full-year, women made just over 70 cents of every dollar earned by full-time, full-year working men (Statistics Canada, 2001).

In light of women's increasing education levels but continuing income inequality, Frenette and Coulombe (2007) examined the linkages between education and occupations chosen by using Census data from 1981, 1991, and 2001. They found that women aged 25–29 with university degrees who worked full-time for a full year still earned less money than men. Although many women received university degrees, which had the potential to ensure their higher income, Frenette and Coulombe considered that their lower earnings were because of their completion of degrees in gendered fields of study (e.g., education, arts, humanities, social sciences, life sciences, and health) associated with lower economic returns. For example, whereas 20.6 percent of women completed a university degree specializing in education in 2001, only 9.4 percent of men did. And whereas 18.4 percent of men completed a university degree in engineering, only 4.3 percent of women did. Women's and men's choices of education and eventual earnings were also linked to labour market demands. Throughout the 1990s, it was the high tech industry—predominantly concentrated by male employees—that experienced considerable growth and increased earnings in occupations such as engineering and mathematics/computer science. In contrast, employment in the public sector—predominantly the purview of women—was affected by general restructuring and downsizing and reduced earnings in associated occupations (Frenette and Coulombe, 2007).

Women's unequal experiences within the Canadian labour market are further contextualized by their immigration status, race/ethnicity, and relationships with state policy. Immigrant women who have been in Canada for some time (i.e., those who immigrated before 1980) and are engaged in the labour market earn far less than immigrant men but have little difference in earnings compared to other women (Statistics Canada, 2007). On the other hand, women who immigrated to Canada between 1991 and 2000 earned roughly 20 percent less than all immigrant and non-immigrant women in the year 2000. Recent immigrant women are more likely to experience low income or have incomes that fall below Statistics Canada's low income cut-offs (LICOs), than Canadian-born women. Even though women who have recently emigrated to Canada are generally more highly educated than Canadian-born women, they are still less likely to be employed; many women who emigrate to Canada do so as dependants of their spouses (Statistics Canada, 2007). Not only are some immigrant women prevented from labour market engagement, they also experience weaker connections with education and training opportunities for future employment and a greater likelihood of being dependent on the state for income support (Statistics Canada, 2007). Like all women, immigrant women who do work for pay are more likely to experience non-standard work conditions (Zeytinoglu and Muteshi, 2000); among all foreign-born women aged 25–64 who were employed in 2001, 47 percent were engaged in non-standard employment in sales and service (Statistics Canada, 2007).

In general, Canadian-born Aboriginal women, who make up 3 percent of the population, are less likely to be employed, earn less from their paid work, and thus are more likely to experience low income than white women. In 2001, 47 percent of Aboriginal women over the age of 15 were employed compared to 56 percent of non-Aboriginal women (Statistics Canada, 2007). Like non-Aboriginal women, Aboriginal women's work is concentrated in non-standard work such as sales and service occupations. Comparing the 1996 labour force participation of Aboriginal women with non-Aboriginal Canadian women, White, Maxim, and Gyimah (2003) found that Aboriginal women's labour force activity varied by their Aboriginal status (e.g., registered versus non-registered Aboriginal women), education, labour force activity, and family structure. White et al. also found that unemployment among registered Aboriginal women was related to their residence on reserves, low education levels, and the presence of young children. Among all Aboriginal women, those with higher education were more likely to be employed whereas lone mothers with dependent young children were less likely to be employed than woman who were married or living alone (White, Maxim, and Gyimah, 2003).

Regardless of their citizenship or immigration status, racialized women also experience income inequality and segregation in the Canadian labour market. They suffer disproportionately from lower pay and unemployment or underemployment compared to white Canadian-born women (Status of Women Canada, 2005). Racialized women are over-represented in low-paying sectors and non-standard occupations and under-represented in high-paying, high-status occupations (Galabuzi, 2006; Status of Women Canada, 2005). Moreover, immigrant racialized women are triply disadvantaged in the labour market (Palameta, 2004; Wilson, 2005); their employment opportunities are inhibited by their gender, citizenship status, and race/ethnicity.

Women's labour force participation experiences are distinctly linked to their mothering and provisions of child care. Women with children are less likely to be employed than women without children (Statistics Canada, 2007). Generally speaking, having children is a deterrent to women's engagement in continuous full-time full-year paid work (Statistics Canada, 2007; Wilson, 2005). Mothers are more likely to exit the workforce when rearing and caring for pre-school children. However, recent information does demonstrate that mothers with very young children and male partners have increased their labour force participation (McDaniel, 2002), a finding that is not surprising considering the increased cost of living and need for dual-earner families. In 2005, 65 percent of all mothers with children under the age of 3 participated in the labour market, whereas in 1976 only 28 percent of these women worked for pay (Statistics Canada, 2007). Whereas 37 percent of women with children ages 3 to 5 engaged in paid work in 1976, 70 percent of mothers with children of these ages did so in 2004. The majority of mothers who engage in the workforce when rearing children do so full-time, full-year; almost three out of four mothers with at least one child under the age of 16 worked 30 hours or more per week (Statistics Canada, 2007). The paid work engagement of mothers also varies by parental status. Lone mothers are less likely to be employed than mothers in two-parent families, although lone mothers' paid work participation has also increased since the mid-1970s.

In nuclear families where mothers work for pay, mothers' experiences of inequality in the labour market comparative to men dovetail with their greater responsibilities for domestic labour, including housework and child care, compared to their partners. Although studies over the last two decades have demonstrated that men have increased their time in domestic or household work and child care (see Marshall, 2006; Sayer, 2005), women still perform a greater amount of this unpaid work, especially when their partners are male (Gazso-Windle and McMullin, 2003; Marshall, 2006; Sayer, 2005). Marshall (2006) conducted a study of Canadians' time spent in paid and unpaid work in 1986 and 2006 using time use data from the 1985 and 2005 General Social Surveys. As shown in Figure 9.1, the average total work day of paid and unpaid work has increased for all Canadians aged 25 to 54. In 2005, the total work day amounted to 8.8 hours on average, up from 8.2 hours in 1986. In 2006 Canadians were working 9 extra days a year compared to 1986.

Men's increase in total work hours is attributed to the increased time spent in daily housework, including activities such as making lunches, vacuuming, or taking out the garbage. Although women's time spent in housework (e.g., meal preparation, cleaning, laundry, sewing, household paperwork) did not change between 1986 and 2006, their increase in total work hours stemmed from their greater time spent in paid work (including activities related to paid work, such as paid coffee breaks and commuting). Figure 9.1 shows an important difference in time spent in "other unpaid work" by women and men. This category includes time spent as a primary provider of care to children and time involved shopping and accessing services. Neither men's nor women's participation as a primary caregiver changed between 1986 and 2005. Thus, while gender inequality appears to be slightly reduced in terms of women's and men's time spent in housework, it has not been reduced for time spent engaged as a primary caregiver. Women still spend more time providing care than do men. In addition, Marshall (2006) found that dual-earner families (married or common-law heterosexual couples) in 2005 were less satisfied with their work–life balance than families with one earner. Women who were part of dual-earner unions felt particularly time-stressed.

Feminist scholars have devoted considerable energy to offering explanations for the unequal amounts of paid and unpaid work performed by women and men in nuclear

FIGURE 9.1	Time Spent on Paid and Unpaid Work among Men and Women 25–54[1]

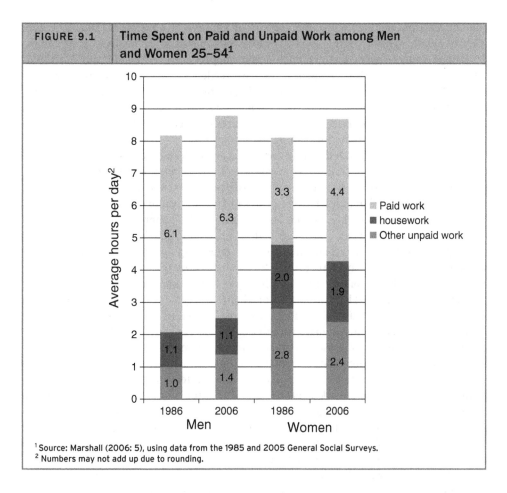

[1] Source: Marshall (2006: 5), using data from the 1985 and 2005 General Social Surveys.
[2] Numbers may not add up due to rounding.

families, especially given women's increased labour force participation. For example, many scholars point to women's greater family responsibilities or gendered workplace structures (e.g., glass ceilings) as contributing to their less than equal experiences compared to men (see, for example, Cotter et al., 2001; Duffy, Mandell, and Pupo, 1989). Other scholars argue that the gendered division of paid and unpaid work is linked to stereotypical distinctions between the types of work women and men perform (Anderson, 2000; Connell, 1985; Nelson, 1994) as well as women's and men's "doing" of gender in everyday workplace and family activity (West and Zimmerman, 1987). Many of these explanations coalesce into a useful distinction between pragmatic strategies and patriarchal dynamics and their role in producing unequal divisions of unpaid work. Pragmatic strategies refer to time availability, time demands, and resources (financial and social) and capture many of the time demands associated with managing one's labour force participation and family care responsibilities. Patriarchal dynamics refer to gender and gender ideology and capture how individuals' behaviours are linked to their internalization and identification with particular constructions of gender behaviour in egalitarian or non-egalitarian ways (McFarlane, Beaujot, and Haddad, 2000). Together, pragmatic strategies and patriarchal dynamics are intricately linked to the unequal amounts of time mothers and fathers spend in paid work, housework, and child care (Gazso-Windle and McMullin, 2003). For example, in a study of the division of domestic labour among married and common-law couples, Gazso-Windle and McMullin (2003) found that men's time spent in paid work decreased their time spent in child care, but the same was not true for women. In addition, women who believed that they are primarily responsible for domestic labour activities in the home spent more time doing housework. In contrast, women who considered paid work to be important to their family's lives spent less time doing housework.

Examining the market and family care relations of lesbian couples reveals unique differences in how responsibilities for market and family relations are divided. Indeed, the experiences of lesbian couples clearly illustrate how assumptions and beliefs about gender-appropriate behaviour have less power in families where partners share genders. When women parent together, gender and parenting roles "appropriate" for heterosexual unions are not applicable (Ben-Ari and Livni, 2006). Scholarship on lesbian relationships suggests that a lesbian lifestyle facilitates employment experiences of both women in interesting ways. According to Dunne (2000a), on the basis of her own research with lesbian women, a lesbian lifestyle "*necessitates* and *facilitates* lifelong financial self-reliance" (138; italics in original). Many of the women Dunne interviewed acknowledged that they self-reflected on how their adult lifestyles would not match a male breadwinning/female caregiving model. These women desired to engage in paid work to support themselves since being economically dependent upon a man was not an option. Whereas heterosexual relations in two-parent families can involve variations in women's dependence on men over time (often linked to women's exits and entrances into the labour market associated with child-bearing and -rearing), Dunne maintains that lesbian relations are based on mutual dependence. Women's relationships with women facilitate their engagement in the labour market because of the more equitable division of domestic labour within their homes. Although it is important to acknowledge Arnup's (1995) caution that not all lesbian mothers share the same view of themselves and their children, the majority of sociological research on lesbian couples with children does suggest that lesbian couples achieve a more equitable division of market and child-rearing tasks than heterosexual couples with children. In particular, several scholars agree that tasks are shared by lesbian couples in terms of quantity and that they are divided in terms of personal characteristics, each partner's capacity and availability to complete them, the material or subjective value attached to them, and the the individual's preference and satisfaction with engaging in them (see for example Ben-Ari and Livni, 2006; Nelson, 2001; Sullivan, 2004).

This review shows that the contemporary market and family care relations of women and men are characterized by differences in occupation and income and by differences in care responsibilities for children. Variations in how mothers participate in these processes must also be understood as contextualized by broader structural forces such as the quality of the labour market, the related availability of family-friendly workplace policy (e.g., benefits), and constraints imposed by the social policy. These variations are also linked to how mothers make choices and take advantage of opportunities as they are informed by their gender, racial/ethnic, and sexual identities. Given the layers of inequality that face mothers' efforts to maintain their families, it is no surprise that conflict and challenges can erupt.

MOTHERS' EXPERIENCES OF WORK–FAMILY CONFLICT

A working mother is a superwoman with the extraordinary flair for balancing her family responsibilities and her responsibilities as an employee.

Mother's Day website, 2008. www.dayformothers.com/motherhood/
working-mothers.html

For many mothers, the challenge is to meet family needs through market and family care relations without their efforts suffering in either of these activities. When this challenge cannot be met, conflict occurs. As a sociological concept, work–family conflict generally characterizes parents' experiences of being unable, or perceiving that they are unable, to meet the challenge of juggling competing and incompatible time demands associated with their market and family relations (Duxbury, Higgins, and Lee, 1994; Tuten and August, 2006; Underhill, 2005). For example, problems can arise in their relationships with their male partners and others as a result of their attempts to juggle their social roles as mothers, partners, and professionals (Guendozi, 2006). Mothers' experiences of work–family conflict dramatically illustrate an important feminist assumption—that the spheres of family and work life are not separate (Hammer, Neal, and Perrin, 2004). Although scholars do define various forms of this conflict, many also tend to agree that there are four major inter-related types: a time crunch, overload, interference, and stress.

Mothers experience a *time crunch* when the time demands associated with paid work reduce their available time for housework and child care, or vice versa. When experiencing a time crunch, mothers feel that they have insufficient time to complete any task well enough and experience stress in undertaking tasks. Using time-use data from the 1998 General Social Survey, Beaujot and Anderson (2007) found that married Canadian women aged 30–59 who were engaged in paid work experienced a greater time crunch if their partners spent more time working for pay than the women did themselves, and if they had greater responsibilities for unpaid work within the home. Alongside their engagement in paid labour, women's greater responsibility for unpaid tasks such as child care contributed to their perceptions of a time crunch. Many women's perceptions of a time crunch are linked to their performance of a "double day" of work—both paid and unpaid—or a "second shift" of unpaid work after the first shift of paid work is complete. In Arlie Hochschild's 1989 study of couples where both mothers and fathers worked for pay, she found that the performance of a second shift was distinctly gendered; more mothers performed a second shift than fathers. Performance of a second shift was also intricately related to class-related tensions in these couples' relations. Among working-class families, tensions erupted that were related to the perceived contradiction between couples' beliefs in stereotypical gender roles (e.g., men's breadwinning, women's caregiving) and their family's economic need for two earners. Among middle- or upper-class families, tensions concerned beliefs in the importance of a family's need for care, but differences between partners in the valuation of the work that is needed to produce this care (Hochschild, 1989).

Sometimes the mental, physical, and emotional work involved in negotiating time spent meeting market and family care demands is so great for mothers that they experience *overload*—juggling too many demands at once (Duxbury, Higgins, and Lee, 1994). Mattingly and Sayer (2006) find that the availability of free time affects women's and men's perceptions of feeling rushed in different and gendered ways. Because women feel more overloaded and pressured in their attempts to combine a high level of paid work engagement with unpaid work responsibilities, Mattingly and Sayer maintain that mothers experience a "family penalty."

Family care demands can hinder mothers' participation in paid work. For example, when a young child is ill and outside care is unavailable, a mother may have to take an unexpected day of leave. For many mothers, meeting the care needs of their children when they are engaged in paid work is a costly and precarious endeavour. High-quality child care spaces are often limited and expensive, and have hours of operation that must be negotiated alongside paid work hours. In fact, since the Royal Commission on the Status of Women in Canada's recommendations for better child-care resources in 1970, the lack of a universal, affordable national system of child care has been credited as a major detriment to women's balancing of market and family care relations (Hamilton, 2005). In a reciprocal manner, mothers' paid work experiences can negatively affect their participation in family care activities. Receiving an unexpected assignment at the end of a work day may interfere with a mother's ability to pick up her child from school on time. Not all workplaces pursue family-friendly policies such as employer-provided child care or flex time to manage child-care needs. Scholars refer to these particular time conflict dynamics as "spillover" or "interference" (Crouter, 1984; Duxbury, Higgins, and Lee, 1994; Skrypnek and Fast, 1996). *Interference* can be characterized more specifically as work-to-family or family-to-work conflict (Hammer, Neal, and Perrin, 2004a). Whereas work-to-family conflict stems from characteristics of the workplace such as a parent's work role, occupation, or work hours, family-to-work conflict is an outcome of characteristics of family life, such as the family or gender role of a parent, and having young children (Roehling, Jarvis, and Swope, 2005). These dynamics of interference are intricately interrelated: "if one's work-related problems begin to interfere with the completion of one's family-related obligations, these unfulfilled family obligations will begin to interfere with one's day-to-day functioning at work and vice versa." (Hammer, Neal, and Perrin, 2004b: 98).

Another related form of work–family conflict is that of work- or family-related *stress* or psychological distress (Rosenberg, 1995). Not surprisingly, mothers experience considerable stress as a result of their awareness that they cannot be in two places at once and when their efforts to negotiate competing demands are not successful. Moreover, all of these types of work–family conflict are distinctly related to a mother's overall experience of satisfaction with her paid work and family life and can have a significant impact on her own mental and physical well-being, as well as her relationship with her partner or children. However, as Guendozi (2006) observes, although stress is a typical outcome of managing market and family care relations, it is also important to recognize that engagement in paid work often provides mothers with an outlet to express their identity in a positive manner.

While sociologists have revealed these types of work–family conflict experienced by mothers, the majority of this scholarship has focused on white professional women who are part of heterosexual, dual-earning unions (Ciabatteri, 2007; Gazso, 2007a; Roehling, Jarvis, and Swope, 2005). Other scholars, however, have recently begun to reveal how mothers' experiences of work–family conflict are distinctly linked to their class, parenthood status, race/ethnicity, and sexuality. Using data collected from a sample of working-class couples transitioning into new parenthood, Goldberg, Pierce, and Sayer (2007) explored the connections among work hours, work schedules, role overload, depressive symptoms, and relationship conflict. For both mothers and fathers, they found that working evening or night shifts correlated with higher levels of depressive symptoms whereas only mothers experienced a greater deal of conflict in their relationships as a result of working rotating shifts. Experiencing role overload, however, was related to both mothers' and fathers' experiences of depressive symptoms and relationship conflict.

Low-income lone mothers who manage paid work and family demands, particularly those who receive income support from the government, face even greater challenges. They have few economic and social resources and more time constraints, and they experience more barriers in the labour market (Albelda, 2001; Baker and Tippin, 1999; McDaniel, 1993; McMullin, Davies, and Cassidy, 2002; Roy, Tubbs, and Burton, 2004). In Canada, lone-mother families constitute the greatest proportion of families on social assistance. Increasingly, social assistance policy and programs (which are managed and administered by each province) assume that mothers will exit assistance and enter into the labour market as soon as possible. Although the ages of children are taken into account, employable mothers must demonstrate that they are seeking employment either by conducting job searches or participating in work and education programs (welfare-to-work programs) in order to maintain their receipt of monthly benefits. Mothers must meet these employment expectations when their children are very young (e.g., 6 months old in Alberta, 3 years old in British Columbia).

Low-income lone mothers on social assistance therefore often experience stress associated with managing their caregiving demands in light of these employment expectations. Most often, lone mothers' limited economic resources (their total welfare benefits fall below LICOs) mean that they have to resort to put their children in inadequate daycare or in the care of other family members. They may have to stay in an unhealthy relationship because of its economic benefits (see also Weigt, 2006). Lone mothers' primary responsibility for caregiving can also prevent their labour market attachment or inhibit their employment stability (Ciabatteri, 2007). Many of the barriers to meeting paid work and family care demands, including lack of transportation and/or mothers' mental and physical health problems, also suggest that their experiences of conflict is inevitable.

In my own past research, I interviewed 16 white and 12 Aboriginal/Métis lone mothers on social assistance in three provinces: British Columbia (BC), Alberta, and Saskatchewan. As part of my research, I was interested in how lone mothers manage policy expectations of their attachment to the workplace with their caregiving responsibilities. I found that lone mothers who were expected to conduct job searches or attend programs in order to prepare for paid work experienced a time crunch, and felt overloaded or overburdened trying to meet the demands of paid work and care for young children, much like that experienced by middle or upper class mothers who engage in paid work (see also Gazso, 2007a). And, like working mothers not on assistance, lone mothers on assistance experienced interference when family care responsibilities hindered their employability efforts and vice versa. Indeed, mothers' experiences of conflict are linked to their receipt of inadequate monthly income benefits. Many mothers cannot afford good quality child care in order to participate in government-endorsed employment readiness programs, as not only do child-care subsidies provided by governments fail to provide the full costs of daycare, but there is also a shortage of licensed daycare spaces (Breitkreuz, 2005). The main difference between the work–family conflict experiences of low-income lone mothers and other working mothers is that lone mothers on social assistance are managing work and family in ways deemed appropriate by social assistance policy.

My research also revealed that compared to white mothers, Aboriginal and Métis lone mothers understood their contemporary experiences of interference as linked to their families' historical experiences of colonization and assimilation, as well as to their family composition. In particular, Aboriginal mothers from a major city in Saskatchewan acknowledged that their opportunities for good jobs were limited due to discrimination and racism in workplaces. They also indicated that many of their extended kin networks that could help with child care were missing in their urban communities; mothers' access to these networks would be greater on reserves.

Scholarly research shows that, for other racialized women, labour market participation can interfere with their satisfaction with their marital unions. In their survey of married Black and white mothers in paid labour, Bridges and Orza (1996) found that Black women's employment in managerial or professional careers was more significantly related to marital conflict with their partners than white women's employment. However, in a study conducted on work-family spillover among diverse families, Grzywacz, Almeida, and McDonald (2002) found that Black families experienced lower forms of negative spillover from work to family compared to white families. Grzywacz et al. state that this difference is likely due to how employed Black family members can rely upon more instrumental assistance, such as caregiving support, from extended families than white families. On the basis of their study of Black, white, and Hispanic families, Roehling, Jarvis, and Swope (2005) argue that differences in perceptions of negative work-family spillover, when conflicts in paid work interfere with individuals' moods and behaviour toward their families, reflect cultural norms and values favouring women's caregiving over their participation in paid work. Roehling et al. found that work-to-family interference was experienced more by Hispanic women than men, particularly when women perceived their paid work activity as inconsistent with gender role expectations of them in the family home.

Recent studies demonstrate that work–family conflict is also experienced by lesbian couples. Like women in relationships with men, the spillover of work life into family life can negatively affect lesbian mothers' family care relations. In their survey of lesbian mothers engaged in paid work (predominantly as managers or professionals) while in long-term relationships, Tuten and August (2006) found that their experiences of work–family conflict were linked to hours worked, job role autonomy, and elements of the workplace culture. In particular, autonomy in a mother's job did not reduce her experience of work–family conflict, leading Tuten and August to argue that a more autonomous job may be accompanied by greater responsibility and more obligations. What is significant about Tuten and August's study is that when coupled with the above findings it can be understood that irrespective of a mother's sexuality, particular dynamics of her workplace are linked to her perceptions of work–family conflict and therefore her subsequent experiences of stress and overall life dissatisfaction.

To summarize, most mothers experience at some time or other feelings of being time crunched or overloaded, or that their family lives are spilling over into their paid work lives and vice versa. Their experiences of work–family conflict are contextualized by broader normative ideological assumptions about gender and caregiving and cultural assumptions specific to their membership in particular racial/ethnic groups. Whether they are lone parents or have male partners, mothers' experiences of work–family conflict are connected to their efforts to reconcile changing but often contradictory gendered and cultural expectations in what are still ideologically separate spheres of work and family. While the rigidity of gender stereotypes and ideologies appear to disappear for lesbian couples with children, they too can experience conflict in trying to manage labour market and family care relations. Mothers' experiences of work–family conflict are also linked to the structure and culture of their workplaces, their income, and their relationships with income support and child-care policies. In response to their experiences of work–family conflict, many mothers rely upon one or more strategies to juggle their competing demands.

STRATEGIES FOR MANAGING AND SUSTAINING MARKET AND FAMILY CARE RELATIONS

> I'm always balancing. It's like there's a little extra here, and I'm losing a little here . . . And I have to watch I don't get behind . . .
>
> Miranda, white lone mother of two children, on social assistance,
> Alberta (Gazso, 2007a: 461)

Existing scholarship shows that mothers who experience work–family conflict in any or all of the above forms adopt a variety of strategies for managing this conflict. Although couple unions may dissolve when mothers and their partners cannot reconcile competing paid work and family demands, this section focuses on some of the strategies mothers use when co-parenting. I also show how low-income, lone-mother families and mothers who are domestic workers and part of transnational families use various strategies to manage their market and family care relations in light of their relationships with state policies.

Some mothers may respond to perceptions of work–family conflict by simply engaging in an "overload" of unpaid work, doing housework and child care on top of paid work hours to the point of experiencing exhaustion or burnout (Luxton, 2001). Other mothers will manage the competing demands of paid and unpaid work by engaging in what Hochschild (1997) identifies as a "third shift": many mothers understood the home as another workplace. In a study of how mothers and fathers manage work and family while employed at a large corporation, Hochschild argues that a cult of efficiency associated with modern workplaces can materialize in the home, creating parents' perceptions of a time bind, which compels parents to schedule quality time with their children or their spouses just as they would schedule meetings at work. The efforts that are required to perform this scheduling—to manage children's resistance and one's own emotions in the process—constitute the third shift.

In nuclear families, mothers also have the option of convincing their partners to share the unpaid labour. As we observed earlier, this is far more difficult than it might seem because of pragmatic factors associated with partners' workplace expectations, as well as ideological assumptions surrounding income earning and caregiving. Moreover, the fact that mothers still do more housework and child care than men, even when both are engaged in paid labour, confirms the difficulty of adopting this strategy. However, as noted earlier, the sharing of unpaid work in an egalitarian manner does seem to be a suitable option for lesbian mothers who co-parent. Lesbian mothers share a need with heterosexual mothers of finding strategies for managing their market and family care relations. However, because creativity, co-operation, and the denial of gendered meanings can shape the lesbian parenting experience, couples with children will often take turns in being the main care provider for children, or the birth mother and her partner may each reduce their hours of work to part time (Dunne, 2000a; Sullivan, 2004).

Lesbian mothers may also use another strategy to manage their perceptions of conflicting time demands. Tuten and August (2006) found that some lesbian mothers could reduce their work–family conflict, including perceptions of time-based and strain-based (e.g., strain in one role affects performance of another role) work–family conflict, by being "out" in their workplace. The act of making one's sexual identity and family care responsibilities visible in the workplace lessened some lesbian mothers' experiences of work–family conflict. As Dunne (2000b) observes, when we focus on women parenting together we gain an alternative sense of how couples can successfully negotiate the competing demands of financing family life and maintaining children's emotional well-being. Women who parent together can extend the boundaries of mothering to a more equal and integrative middle ground.

Another way in which mothers cope with balancing market and family care relations is to change occupations or change from full-time to part-time paid work. Or they may seek a workplace that is more receptive to the challenges mothers' experience. Some work-places endorse "family-friendly" policies, which include not just part-time work but child-care provisions, modified work hours or flex time (shorter or condensed time), and sick days. These family-friendly policies can reduce mothers' levels of stress and therefore prevent loss of their productivity (Glass, 2004). However, as Weedon (2005) observes, family-friendly workplaces may be directly associated with mothers' lower wages and job security, fewer benefits, and fewer opportunities for promotion. Being placed on a "mommy track" can mean that while family care demands are recognized and supported by the workplace, mothers who work there may have to accept lowered employment status and opportunities for advancement (Konrad and Cannings, 1994; Mandel, 2005).

Many mothers rely upon networks of social support to manage their market and family care relations, including formal and informal support (Connidis, 2001). "Formal support" refers to financial or material assistance provided to families by agencies and services on behalf of state programs or community organizations. The general trend toward weakening the welfare state, discussed above, has reduced the formal supports available to families today. Mothers can turn to fewer social policies and programs to support their own and their children's material and emotional needs. Provincial governments increasingly assume that mothers will turn to support provided by community non-government and non-profit organizations, as well as relying on informal support from others (McDaniel, 2002). Indeed, in light of these circumstances, many mothers turn to family, friends, and neighbours for informal support (Connidis, 2001). Informal support can include expressive or emotional support—affection, intimacy, or closeness among family and friends—and/or instrumental support in the form of financial or physical aid (Langer, 1995).

Relationships of informal support among family members often involve reciprocity or exchange within and across generations (Connidis, 2001). As well, the amount, type, and source of informal supports exchanged within mothers' families are linked to their composition. Recent Census data suggest that Canadian families are increasingly characterized by "cluttered nests" (Mitchell, Wister, and Gee, 2004), where more children are living at home with a parent or parents and grandparents (Milan, Vézina, and Wells, 2006). In extended and multi-generational families, mothers draw upon several family members for support in order to meet their labour market and family care relations (Gee and Mitchell, 2003). In my own research, I found that, in addition to income support from the government in the form of social assistance, low-income lone mothers relied on other formal and informal supports. These included formal support from community organizations (e.g., food banks) and exchanges of instrumental and expressive support with parents, siblings, friends, peers, or neighbours in order to meet employment and care-giving needs (Gazso, 2007b). In particular, mothers traded food and child-care services with friends and family as a common coping strategy to meet families's child-care, emotional, and nutritional needs (Gazso, 2007b).

Racially/ethnically diverse families in Canada also involve other family members and friends in social support networks to manage paid work and family demands. Their use of support networks today are particularly contextualized by their historical development and generational transmissions in response to experiences of oppression, racism, and colonization. Fiske and Johnny (2003) illustrate the importance of Aboriginal families' reliance on extended family networks for expressive and instrumental support. Black families also have a rich history of developing and relying upon extended family systems and practices for sharing child care (Calliste, 2003); extended family ties involving multiple generations have played an important role in their lives (Mays et al., 1998; Stack, 1974). Penah-Lopes (2006) argues that the historical and cultural conditions requiring Black mothers to engage in paid work demanded the socialization of children, especially boys, to be competent to perform housework, and this earlier socialization has affected how market and family care relations are managed by these children in later life. Kobayashi's 2000 study of the support relations between generations of Japanese families shows that third-generation adult children conform to "oya koh koh," or filial obligation, to their second-generation parents; they are more likely to provide expressive support to aging parents and more so to mothers than fathers. If adults do provide their parents with financial support, this is related to their parents' actual need for assistance rather than the children's endorsement of oya koh koh. Kobayashi maintains that, when contextualized by the support relations among generations in Japan, support relations and the traditional cultural ideas that have informed them among Japanese-Canadian families have been transformed with each successive generation.

Paying someone else to perform housework, child care, and other family care responsibilities in the home is another strategy that some mothers may use to manage competing work and family demands. In some cases, mothers may hire outside domestic services to visit their home on a weekly or biweekly basis. In other cases, mothers will hire live-in domestic service workers or nannies, many of whom are immigrant women. This strategy particularly highlights how the dynamics of gender, race/ethnicity, and class intersect with a state policy. More than one family is affected by a Canadian mother's purchase of another mother's services to manage her market and family care relations, as we will see.

Transnational Management of Paid Work and Family Care

Many domestic workers migrate to Canada from countries like the Philippines to take on mothering and domestic roles—or women's work—for other Canadian mothers' families. The work of domestic workers permits some Canadian mothers to engage in paid work with less tension and fewer time constraints associated with also meeting family care responsibilities. Arat-Koc (2006) argues that the Live-In Caregiver Program (LCP), the federal social policy that shapes domestic workers' lives in Canada, is based on an implicit assumption that domestic workers are single woman. The majority of migrant domestic workers who enter into Canada, however, are mothers with children. They perform domestic labour for pay in order to provide for their families in their countries of origin; domestic workers usually send at least half of their earnings home. The money that domestic workers earn not only helps meet their families' social and material needs, but also contributes to the economic development of their countries of origin (Arat-Koc, 2006).

Mothers who are domestic workers are thus part of "transnational families" and so engage in transborder management of paid work and family relations. One way that these mothers manage their paid work and their own family care demands from afar is to leave children behind in the care of another female family member. This can create tensions (Salazar Parrenas, 2000), disrupting cultural norms and values about family life in domestic workers' country of origin (Cohen, 2000). Moreover, as recent studies show, transnational mothering invokes mothers' feelings of responsibility and guilt over family separation and deprives mothers of meeting their own needs for intimacy (Arat-Koc, 2006; Cohen, 2000). Women who engage in domestic work must care for someone else's children while being unable to care for their own, as they had before they accepted overseas employment (Salazar Parrenas, 2000). Cohen's 2000 study of Filipina caregivers illustrates that the way mothers manage family income needs and caring from afar is a stressful process. Often, mothers feel that the money they send home is not enough to meet the multiple needs of several family members in addition to their children's needs.

In many ways, the guilt that Canadian mothers can experience when juggling market and family care relations can be decreased by hiring another woman. Domestic workers who are mothers, however, bear a similar guilt, compounded by their desire to meet their children's needs. Moreover, other contradictions emerge along gender, race/ethnicity, and class lines when we critically consider this coping strategy. Reproductive labour is a commodity traditionally bought by class-privileged women (Salazar Parrenas, 2000), as it is predominantly middle- to upper-class white mothers who employ domestic workers (most often racialized women) to perform caregiving services (Cohen, 2000; Hodge, 2006). Although mothers in Canada may be seen as liberated because of their ability to engage in paid work and hire others to facilitate this engagement, their purchase of other women's labour power demonstrates that gendered assumptions about caregiving as a women's domain are still strong (Arat-Koc, 2006; Salazar Parrenas, 2000) and are supported by social policy. At the same time that domestic workers benefit their families through their paid work and Canadian mothers benefit from receiving assistance with juggling multiple demands, the practice of employing domestic workers continues to effectively devalue and feminize domestic work.

Despite these contradictions, Arat-Koc (2006: 87) does make the significant observation that domestic workers and their female employers do share a common condition. Although they may be different in terms of race/ethnicity and class, "they both experience paid work as incompatible with their reproduction roles and responsibilities. For both, the ways they maintain and sustain their families has to be hidden (either at home or in the country of origin) as a condition to secure and keep present employment." For Arat-Koc (2006), this common condition is even more strikingly visible when we see that domestic workers are needed precisely because the Canadian state does not provide enough support, such as accessible and affordable high-quality child care, for mothers to manage their paid work and caregiving needs.

The varieties of strategies mothers use to manage their competing demands reflect several factors and constraints. These include: the particular market and family care relations of families; total household income; family members' values and beliefs; state policies that facilitate the hiring of domestic workers; and structural and economic forces beyond families' control. While space does not permit a comprehensive analysis of how neo-liberal restructuring has affected all programs and policies that support families, the next section does specifically consider whether and how the state, via federal parental leave policy, alleviates the conflict associated with mothers' management of their labour market and family care relations.

THE ROLE OF THE STATE: PARENTAL LEAVE POLICY

> Although feminists disagree about many issues, they do agree that some form of cash benefit at birth is essential for women's employment and their continuing role as mothers.
>
> Maureen Baker (2006b: 126)

Social policies and programs targeted at families with dependent children can be generally characterized as family policies (Mahon, 2001). Table 9.1 outlines some federal and provincial family policies and programs that support provisions of care and children's social and economic well-being. Parental leave falls under the federal government's jurisdiction, specifically Employment Insurance. The Canada Child Tax Benefit is a federal program aimed to help families with the costs of raising children under the age of 18 years; it is targeted at working families with incomes below a particular threshold. As discussed earlier, social assistance programs are provincially administered. Specific health benefits targeted at low-income families also fall under provincial jurisdiction.

Structural/compositional and heteronormative assumptions about families and the way they are maintained have always been deeply embedded in federal and provincial policies and programs for Canadian families. In many ways, current family policies tend to prioritize nuclear family relations, assuming that "family" consists of two cohabiting heterosexual partners and one or more children. In effect, policies for families can obscure and deny the diversity of families as well as the multitude of ways market and family care relations are

TABLE 9-1	Some Family Policies in Canada, 2008[1]
Federal	
Medicare	
Employment Insurance	
Maternity and Parental Leave	
Canada Child Tax Benefit	
National Child Benefit Supplement	
Child Disability Benefit	
Universal Child Care Benefit	
Old Age Security	
Provincial/Territorial[2]	
Adult/child health benefit plans (for low-income families)	
Child benefit and credit programs	
Child-care subsidy programs	
Social assistance programs	
Workers' compensation boards	

[1] This list of examples is not exhaustive but includes the most common policies that families with children can access.

[2] Provincial and territorial offerings of these programs vary in availability, accessibility, structure, benefit amounts, etc.

organized. According to Baker (1990: 170), misconstrued notions of family life that are modelled in social policy "reflect the sociological characteristics of policy makers and their advisors, vested interests, the complex procedures of legislative change, and attempts to minimize state intervention in the family and thereby reduce government expenditures."

In the final section of this chapter, my intent is to show how structural/compositional and heteronormative assumptions are embedded within parental leave policy. In doing so, I also illustrate how mothers' access to parental leave may not necessarily facilitate more equitable divisions of paid and unpaid work in Canadian families.

Some employed mothers in Canada have had access to cash benefits for maternity leave from employment since 1971. Under what was then called the *Unemployment Insurance (UI) Act*, mothers' eligibility for leave was based on the number of weeks worked for pay (Pulkingham, 1998). Mothers were entitled to 15 weeks of leave, whereas both parents were entitled to 10 weeks of unemployment insurance compensation (Baker, 1997). Pregnant women who decided to access both maternity and parental leave benefits could receive a total of 25 weeks of compensation, originally 60 percent of their previous earnings. Provisions of maternity leave (leave for childbirth) were based upon the assumption that it was necessary to compensate for the employment-related hazards, preparation, and recuperation of pregnant mothers. It was not until 1990 that adoptive parents and biological fathers were also entitled to these benefits. The availability of parental leave demonstrated the state's acknowledgement of the participation of both adoptive parents and biological fathers in childbirth and child-care responsibilities.

As part of the general trend of welfare state restructuring, Unemployment Insurance (UI) was replaced with the stricter *Employment Insurance (EI) Act* in 1996. With fewer funds for this program, changes were made to mothers' and fathers' eligibility. When EI was introduced, parents' eligibility for either maternity or parental leave became determined on the basis of their hours of work (as opposed to weeks of work under UI). To be eligible, parents had to work a minimum of 700 hours or 20 weeks of work at 35 hours per week in the past 52 weeks (Benoit, 2000); this change also involved an extension of the work time—35 hours per week (instead of 15) over 20 weeks. Under the *EI Act*, mothers were entitled to 55 percent of their previous earnings for up to 25 weeks if they took both maternity and parental leave.

More recent changes to EI have extended the time parents can access benefits. As of 2001, providing mothers meet 600 hours of insured work, they can access 15 weeks of maternity leave and 35 weeks of parental leave at 55 percent of their earnings, for a total of 50 weeks of paid leave. In addition, new opportunities exist for women to engage in some paid work while on maternity leave. According to then Human Resources Development Canada (2001) (now Human Resources and Social Development Canada, or HRSD) the changes made in 2001 ensured that maternity and parental leave benefits were more accessible, more flexible, and better adapted to families' lives. However, a more critical analysis reveals otherwise.

Expectant mothers who participate in non-standard jobs can be excluded from receiving maternity benefits simply because they may not work the 30 hours of work per week over 20 weeks that makes them eligible (Benoit, 2000; Pulkingham, 1998). Even if mothers are able to access benefits, a 45 percent drop in their monthly income may drive some mothers into poverty (Iyer, 1997). Moreover, race/ethnicity and class intersect and shape women's ability to access parental leave. As observed, recent immigrant women are less likely to be employed and, if they are, they are likely to work in non-standard and insecure occupations. Thus, not all mothers will work the hours needed to be eligible for maternity leave.

Upon introduction of the new policy, HRSD claimed that the new leave duration is more flexible: there is no waiting period for the second claim if parents in a two-parent family decide to share the benefits. And yet, this claim is also misleading. Leave benefits policy did and still does assume nuclear families. Flexibility may exist in terms of access, but not in terms of how leave time is divided among parents. The 55 percent benefit rate tends to assume that pregnant women who qualify for maternity benefits have partners that are primary income earners (Baker, 1997; Iyer, 1997). If the lower-income earner, usually the mother, applies for leave benefits, this thereby ensures that the family income is maintained at a higher level. This also ensures that the mother is primarily responsible for caring for children and is economically dependent on her partner for her own and her children's economic security. If we acknowledge how cultural and ideological beliefs shape mothers' and fathers' gendered identities across race/ethnicity and class, we can see how leave policy can perpetuate inequality in paid and unpaid labour.

Finally, we must question whether the new leave is better adapted to all Canadian families. Parents can now engage in paid work when they take parental leave. They can earn $50 or up to 20 percent of their weekly benefits, whichever is the higher amount. Although parents may benefit from the ability to earn a small income while accessing benefits, it is possible that this capability is limited. For example, it is not clear what type of employment is amenable to this provision and not all employers would agree to a limited employment situation. Moreover, the claim that parental leave is more adaptable is questionable when we consider that the present policy assumes the availability of affordable, accessible, and high-quality child care that will enable parents eventually to return to their paid employment. Some women in two-parent families will choose to stay at home for their children's first few years because it would cost more to put children in daycare than the wage they are earning. As to whether this is an actual "choice" of mothers is a matter of debate—the parameters of leave policy and the inadequate daycare provisions suggest that many women's choices are actually structured and shaped in varying degrees. And yet, it may also be impossible to afford to stay at home. This double bind that women face regarding time and finances is particularly acute for low-income lone mothers (see also Davies, McMullin, Avison, and Cassidy, 2001).

To summarize, the state, via parental leave policy, supports the management of work and family demands for some but not all working mothers. Parental leave policy therefore does not universally alleviate mothers' experiences of conflicting demands associated with earning a living and providing care. This is not to discount the important role that leave policy plays for eligible mothers; it allows them temporarily to negotiate paid work and family care demands associated with having and rearing children. However, considering mothers who co-parent with male partners, the way leave is divided can predict mothers' future experiences of work–family conflict. If mothers in two-parent families access all available leave, their partners may expect them to continue their primary caregiving, and thus, they will be more likely to experience work–family tensions when they re-enter the labour market.

CONCLUSION

This chapter began with a brief overview of how feminist scholars, informed by a variety of perspectives, have devoted considerable attention to how mothers manage their family's economic and social well-being through an intricate juggling of labour market participation and provisions of care to all members. The contemporary labour market experiences of mothers were shown to be unequal compared to those of men, reflecting structural and discriminatory barriers in workplaces and policies that inhibit their labour market participation, as well as mothers' choices about meeting their families' care needs. Mothers' experiences of a time crunch, overload, interference, and stress were strongly linked to their unequal responsibilities for meeting market and family care demands. The challenges mothers face, however, vary with their race/ethnicity or sexuality and can be further exacerbated by low income and ideological expectations of nurturing and caregiving, in addition to available employment, weak state support, and their own choices. Furthermore, some of the coping strategies mothers use to juggle demands and alleviate conflict may have the desired impact of relieving time pressure, while other strategies may have problematic implications, such as perpetuating gender roles in two-parent families or denying mothering to domestic workers who are part of transnational families. Still other policy-endorsed strategies, such as mothers' entitlement to parental leave, reveal how state support is not adequately available to all.

To conclude, I have used a feminist political economy lens in this chapter to highlight how mothers' maintenance of families through their market and family care relations is related to the unequal structural conditions that characterize workplaces in the capitalist labour market and the constraints imposed by social policy subject to a neo-liberal agenda. I also showed how mothers' maintenance of families is linked to their own choices and opportunities in light of these social, political, and economic forces that affect their everyday material realities. Clearly, a state-family-market nexus informs and shapes labour market and family care relations—relations that are predominantly maintained and managed by mothers and thus continue to be of feminist concern.

Suggested Readings

Beaujot, Roderic. 2000. *Earning and caring in Canadian families*. Peterborough, ON: Broadview.

Duffy, A., N. Mandell, and N. Pupo. 1989. *Few choices: Women, work and family*. Toronto: Garamond.

Dunne, Gillian A. 2000. Lesbians as authentic workers? Institutional heterosexuality and the reproduction of gender inequalities. *Sexualities* 3: 133–148.

Gazso, Amber. 2007. Balancing expectations for employability and family responsibilities while on social assistance: Low income mothers' experiences in three Canadian provinces. *Family Relations* 56: 454–466.

Guendozi, Jackie. 2006. "The guilt thing": Balancing domestic and professional roles. *Journal of Marriage and the Family* 68: 901–909.

Roy, K.M., C.Y. Tubbs, and L.M. Burton. 2004. Don't have no time: Daily rhythms and the organization of time for low-income families. *Family Relations* 53(2): 168–178.

Weedon, Chris. 1999. *Feminism, theory, and the politics of difference*. Oxford: Blackwell.

Discussion Questions

1. What is one way in which each feminist perspective reviewed in this chapter has been concerned with women's experiences of inequality in their market and family care relations, compared to men's (and other women's)? Which perspective do you think best explains this inequality?

2. How do gender, race/ethnicity, sexuality, and class intersect to influence women's and men's experiences within the Canadian labour market?

3. What are the four major forms of work–family conflict experienced by Canadian families? Based on your own experience, would you say that any one of these forms of work–family conflict is easier or more difficult to manage?

4. How are the strategies used to balance work and family demands by lesbian mothers different than those adopted by mothers in heterosexual unions? Could the strategies used by lesbian mothers be the basis for a more equitable work–family balance model adopted by mothers in heterosexual unions?

5. In what ways has the Canadian state worsened or facilitated mothers' and fathers' negotiation of their market and family care relations?

Bibliography

Albelda, Randy. 2001. Welfare-to-work, farewell to families? US welfare reform and work/family debates. *Feminist Economics* 7: 119–135.

Anderson, Margaret L. 2000. *Thinking about women: Sociological perspectives on sex and gender.* Boston: Allyn and Bacon.

Arat-Koc, Sedef. 2006. Whose social reproduction? Transnational motherhood and challenges to feminist political economy, in *Social reproduction: Feminist political economy challenges neoliberalism*, eds. K. Bezanson and M. Luxton, 75–92. Montreal: McGill-Queen's Univ. Press.

Arnup, Katherine. 1995. "We are family": Lesbian mothers in Canada, in *Gender in the 1990s: Images, realities, and issues*, eds. E.D. Nelson and B.W. Robinson, 330–345. Toronto: Nelson Canada.

Baker, Maureen. 1990. The perpetuation of misleading family models in social policy: Implications for women. *Canadian Social Work Review* 7(2): 169–182.

Baker, Maureen. 1997. Parental benefit policies and the gendered division of labour. *Social Service Review* 71: 51–71.

Baker, Maureen. 2006. *Choices and constraints in family life.* Don Mills, ON: Oxford Univ. Press.

Baker, Maureen, and David Tippin. 1999. *Poverty, social assistance, and the employability of mothers: Restructuring welfare states.* Toronto: Univ. of Toronto Press.

Bakker, Isabella C. 1996. Introduction: The gendered foundations of restructuring in Canada, in *Rethinking, restructuring*, ed. I.C. Bakker, 2–25. Toronto: Univ. of Toronto Press, Inc.

Bannerji, Himani. 2000. The paradox of diversity: The construction of multicultural Canada and "women of colour." *Women's Studies International Forum* 23: 537–560.

Beaujot, Roderic, and Robert Anderson. 2007. Time crunch: Impact of time spent in paid and unpaid work and its division in families. *Canadian Journal of Sociology* 32: 295–315.

Ben-Ari, Adital, and Tali Livni. 2006. Motherhood is not a given thing: Experiences and constructed meanings of biological and nonbiological lesbian mothers. *Sex Roles* 54: 521–531.

Benoit, Celia M. 2000. *Women, work and social rights: Canada in historical and comparative perspective.* Toronto: Harcourt Brace.

Bezanson, Kate. 2006. *Gender, the state, and social reproduction: Household insecurity in neoliberal times.* Toronto: Univ. of Toronto Press.

Breitkreuz, Rhonda. 2005. Engendering citizenship? A critical-feminist analysis of Canadian welfare-to-work policies and the employment experiences of lone mothers. *Journal of Sociology and Social Welfare* 32: 147–165.

Bridges, Judith S., and Ann Marie Orza. 1996. Black and white employed mothers' role experiences. *Sex Roles* 35: 377–386.

Brooks, Bradley, Jennifer Jarman, and Robert M. Blackburn. 2003. Occupational segregation in Canada: 1981–1996. *Canadian Review of Sociology and Anthropology* 40: 197–213.

Calixte, Shana L., Jennifer L. Johnson, and J. Maki Motapanyane. 2005. Liberal, socialist, and radical feminism: An introduction to three theories about women's oppression and social change, in *Feminist issues: Race, class and sexuality*, ed. N. Mandell, 1–34. Toronto: Prentice Hall.

Calliste, Agnes. 2003. Black families in Canada: Exploring the interconnections of race, class and gender, in *Voices: Essays on Canadian families*, ed. M. Lynn, 199–220. Scarborough: Thomson Nelson.

Ciabatteri, Teresa. 2007. Single mothers, social capital, and work-family conflict. *Journal of Family Issues* 28: 34–40.

Clement, Wallace. 2001. Canadian political economy's legacy for sociology. *Canadian Journal of Sociology* 26: 405–417.

Cohen, R. 2000. "Mom is a stranger": The negative impact of immigration policies on the family life of Filipina domestic workers. *Canadian Ethnic Studies Journal* 32: 76–89.

Collins, Patricia Hill. 1989. The social construction of Black feminist thought. *Journal of Women in Culture and Society* 14: 745–773.

Connell, R.W. 1985. Theorizing gender. *Sociology* 19: 260–272.

Connidis, Ingrid Arnet. 2001. *Family ties and aging*. Thousand Oaks, CA: Sage.

Cotter, David A., et al. 2001. The glass ceiling effect. *Social Forces* 80: 655–682.

Crouter, Ann C. 1984. Spillover from family to work: The neglected side of the work-family interface. *Human Relations* 37: 425–441.

Danby, Colin. 2007. Political economy and the closet: Heternormativity in feminist economics. *Feminist Economics* 13: 29–53.

Davies, Lorraine, Julie Ann McMullin, William R. Avison, and Gayle L. Cassidy. 2001. *Social policy, gender inequality and poverty*. Ottawa: Status of Women Canada.

Dua, Enakshi. 1999. Beyond diversity: Exploring ways in which the discourse of race has shaped the institution of the nuclear family, in *Scratching the surface: Canadian anti-racist thought*, eds. E. Dua and A. Robertson, 237–260. Toronto: Women's Press.

Duffy, A., N. Mandell, and N. Pupo. 1989. *Few choices: Women, work and family*. Toronto: Garamond Press.

Dunne, Gillian A. 2000a. Lesbians as authentic workers? Institutional heterosexuality and the reproduction of gender inequalities. *Sexualities* 3: 133–148.

Dunne, Gillian A. 2000b. Opting into motherhood: Lesbian blurring the boundaries and transforming the meaning of parenthood and kinship. *Gender & Society* 14: 11–35.

Duxbury, Linda, Christopher Higgins, and Catherine Lee. 1994. Work-family conflict: A comparison by gender, family type, and perceived control. *Journal of Family Issues* 15: 449–466.

Esping-Andersen, Gøsta. 1990. *The three worlds of welfare capitalism*. Cambridge: Polity.

Few, April L. 2007. Integrating Black consciousness and critical race feminism into family studies research. *Journal of Family Issues* 28: 452–473.

Fiske, Jo-Anne, and Rose Johnny. 2003. The Lake Babine First Nation family: Yesterday and today, in *Voices: Essays on Canadian families*, ed. M. Lynn, 181–198. Scarborough: Thomson Nelson.

Fox, Bonnie. 1980. Women's double work day: Twentieth-century changes in the reproduction of daily life, in *Hidden in the household: Women's domestic labour under capitalism*, ed. B. Fox, 173–216. Toronto: Women's Press.

Frenette, Marc, and Simon Coulombe. 2007. *Has higher education among young women substantially reduced the gender gap in employment and earnings?* **www.statcan.ca/english/research/ 11F0019MIE/11F0019MIE2007301.pdf**. Retrieved January 12, 2008.

Galabuzi, Grace Edward. 2006. *Canada's economic apartheid: The social exclusion of racialized groups in the new century*. Toronto: Canadian Scholars' Press Inc.

Garey, Anita, Karen V. Hanson, Rosanna Hertz, and Cameron MacDonald. 2002. Care and kinship: An introduction. *Journal of Family Issues* 23: 703–715.

Gazso, Amber. 2004. Women's inequality in the workplace as framed in news discourse: Refracting from gender ideology. *Canadian Review of Sociology and Anthropology* 41: 449–473.

Gazso, Amber. 2007a. Balancing expectations for employability and family responsibilities while on social assistance: Low income mothers' experiences in three Canadian provinces. *Family Relations* 56: 454–466.

Gazso, Amber. 2007b. Staying afloat on social assistance: Parents' strategies of balancing work and family. *Socialist Studies* 3: 31–63.

Gazso-Windle, Amber, and Julie Ann McMullin. 2003. Doing domestic labour: Strategizing in a gendered domain. *Canadian Journal of Sociology* 28: 341–366.

Gee, Ellen, and Barbara Mitchell. 2003. One roof: Exploring multi-generational households in Canada, in *Voices: Essays on Canadian Families*, ed. M. Lynn, 291–311. Scarborough: Thomson Nelson.

Glass, Jennifer. 2004. Blessing or curse? Work-family policies and mothers' wage growth over time. *Work and Occupations* 31: 367–394.

Goldberg, Abbie E., Courtney P. Pierce, and Aline G. Sayer. 2007. Shift work, role overload, and the transition to parenthood. *Journal of Marriage and the Family* 69: 123–138.

Grzywacz, Joseph G., David M. Almeida, and Daniel A. McDonald. 2002. Work-family spillover and daily reports of work and family stress in the adult labor force. *Family Relations* 51: 28–36.

Guendozi, Jackie. 2006. "The guilt thing": Balancing domestic and professional roles. *Journal of Marriage and the Family* 68: 901–909.

Hamilton, Roberta. 2005. *Gendering the vertical mosaic: Feminist perspectives on Canadian society*, 2nd ed. Toronto: Pearson Prentice Hall.

Hamilton, Roberta. 2007. Feminist theories, in *Gender relations in global perspectives: Essential readings*, ed. N. Cook, 49–60. Toronto: Canadian Scholars' Press Inc.

Hammer, Leslie B., Margaret B. Neal, and Nancy A. Perrin. 2004a. The relationship between work-to-family conflict and family-to-work conflict: A longitudinal study. *Journal of Family and Economic Issues* 25: 79–100.

Hammer, Leslie B., Margaret B. Neal, and Nancy A. Perrin. 2004b. The relationship between work-to-family conflict and family-to-work conflict: A longitudinal study. *Journal of Family and Economic Issues* 25: 79–100.

Harnois, Catherine E. 2005. Different paths to different feminisms? Bridging multiracial feminist theory and quantitative sociological gender research. *Gender & Society* 19: 809–828.

Hartman, Yvonne. 2005. In bed with the enemy: Some ideas on the connections between neoliberal-ism and the welfare state. *Current Sociology* 53: 57–73.

Hartmann, H. 1981. The family as a locus of gender, class, and political struggle: The example of housework. *Signs* 6: 366–394.

Heisz, A., A. Jackson, and G. Picot. 2002. *Winners and losers in the labour market of the 1990s.* Ottawa: Statistics Canada, Analytical Studies Branch.

Hochschild, Arlie Russell. 1989. *The second shift: Working parents and the revolution at home.* New York: Viking.

Hochschild, Arlie Russell. 1997. *The time bind: When work becomes home and home becomes work.* New York: Metropolitan Books.

Hodge, Jarrah. 2006. "Un-skilled labour": Canada's live-in caregiver program. *Undercurrents* 3: 60–66.

hooks, bell. 1981. *Aint't I a woman: Black women and feminism.* Boston: South End Press.

Human Resources and Social Development Canada. 2008. Fact sheet: The first year enhanced employment insurance (EI) Maternity/parental benefits. **www.hrsdc.gc.ca/en/cs/comm/news/2002/021106_e.shtml**. Retrieved February 19, 2008.

Human Resources Development Canada. 2001. Changes made to maternity and parental benefits December 31, 2000. **www.hrdc.ca.** Retrieved November 25, 2001.

Iyer, Nitya. 1997. Some mothers are better than others: A re-examination of maternity benefits, in *Challenging the public/private divide: Feminism, law, and public policy,* ed. S.B. Boyd. Toronto: Univ. of Toronto Press.

Kobayashi, K.M. 2000. The nature of support from adult children to older parents in Japanese Canadian families. *Journal of Cross-Cultural Gerontology* 15: 182–205.

Konrad, Alison M., and Kathy Cannings. 1994. Of mommy tracks and glass ceilings: A case study of men's and women's careers in management. *Industrial Relations* 49: 303–322.

Langer, Neil. 1995. Grandparents and adult grandchildren: What do they do for one another?, in *The ties of later life,* ed. J. Hendriks. Amityville, NY: Baywood.

Lerner, Gerda. 1993. Reconceptualizing differences among women, in *Feminist frameworks: Alternative theoretical accounts of the relations between women and men,* eds. A.M. Jaggar and P.S. Rothenberg. New York: McGraw-Hill, Inc.

Luxton, Meg. 2001. Family coping strategies: Balancing paid employment and domestic labour, in *Family patterns, gender relations,* ed. B.J. Fox, 318–338. Toronto: Oxford Univ. Press.

Luxton, Meg. 2006. Feminist political economy in Canada and the politics of social reproduction, in *Social reproduction: Feminist political economy challenges neo-liberalism*, eds. K. Bezanson and M. Luxton, 11–44. Montreal: McGill-Queen's University Press.

Mahon, Rianne. 2001. Welfare state restructuring and changing gender relations: The politics of family policy in Sweden and Canada, in *Family patterns, gender relations,* ed. B.J. Fox, 525–547. Toronto: Oxford Univ. Press.

Mandel, Hadas. 2005. Family policies, wage structures, and gender gaps: Sources of earnings inequality in 20 countries. *American Sociological Review* 70: 949–967.

Mandell, Nancy. 2005. Making families: Gender, economics, sexuality, and race. in *Feminist issues: Race, class, and sexuality,* 4th ed., ed. N. Mandell. Toronto: Pearson Prentice Hall.

Marshall, Katherine. 2006. Converging gender roles. *Perspectives on Labour and Income* 7: 5–17. **www.statcan.ca/english/freepub/75-001-XIE/10706/art-1.htm**. Retrieved January 8, 2008.

Mattingly, Marybeth J., and Liana C. Sayer. 2006. Under pressure: Gender differences in the relationship between free time and feeling rushed. *Journal of Marriage and the Family* 68: 205–221.

Mays, Vicki M., et al. 1998. African American families in diversity: Gay men and lesbians as participants in family networks. *Journal of Comparative Family Studies* 29: 73–87.

McDaniel, Susan. 1993. Single parenthood: Policy apartheid in Canada, in *Single parent families: Perspectives on research and policy,* eds. J. Hudson and B. Galaway, 203–211. Toronto: Thompson Educational Publishing, Inc.

McDaniel, Susan. 2002. Women's changing relations to the state and citizenship: Caring and intergenerational relations in globalizing Western democracies. *Canadian Review of Sociology and Anthropology* 39: 125–150.

McFarlane, Seth, Roderic Beaujot, and Tony Haddad. 2000. Time constraints and relative resources as determinants of the sexual division of domestic work. *Canadian Journal of Sociology* 25: 61–82.

McMullin, Julie Ann, Lorraine Davies, and Gale Cassidy. 2002. Welfare reform in Ontario: Tough times in mothers' lives. *Canadian Public Policy* 28: 297–314.

Milan, Anne, Mireille Vézina, and Carrie Wells. 2006. Family portrait: Continuity and change in Canadian families and households in 2006: Findings. **www12.statcan.ca/english/census06/analysis/famhouse/index.cfm**. Retrieved September 25, 2007.

Mitchell, Barbara, Andrew V. Wister, and Ellen M. Gee. 2004. The ethnic and family nexus of home-leaving and returning among Canadian young adults. *Canadian Journal of Sociology* 29: 543–575.

Nelson, Fiona. 2001. Lesbian families, in *Family patterns, gender relations,* ed. B.J. Fox. 441–457. Toronto: Oxford Univ. Press.

Nelson, Linda. 1994. Interpreting gender. *Signs* 20: 79–105.

Palameta, Boris. 2004. Low income among immigrants and visible minorities. *Perspectives on Labour and Income* 5(4): 12–17. Catalogue no. 75-001-XIE.

Penha-Lopes, Vania. 2006. "To cook, sew, to be a man": The socialization for competence and Black men's involvement in housework. *Sex Roles* 54: 262–274.

Pulkingham, Jane. 1998. Remaking the social divisions of welfare: Gender, "dependency," and UI reform. *Studies in Political Economy* 56: 7–48.

Rhode, Debra. 1988. Occupational inequality. *Duke Law Journal* (December): 1207–1241.

Roehling, Patricia V., Lorna Hernandez Jarvis, and Heather E. Swope. 2005. Variations in negative work-family spillover among white, Black, and Hispanic American men and women: Does ethnicity matter? *Journal of Family Issues* 26: 840–865.

Rosenberg, Harriet. 1995. Motherwork, stress, and depression: The costs of privatized social reproduction, in *Gender in the 1990s: Images, realities, and issues,* eds. E.D. Nelson and B.W. Robinson, 311–329. Toronto: Nelson Canada.

Roy, K.M., C.Y. Tubbs, and L.M. Burton. 2004. Don't have no time: Daily rhythms and the organization of time for low-income families. *Family Relations* 53(2): 168–178.

Salazar Parrenas, R. 2000. Migrant Filipina domestic workers and the international division of reproductive labour. *Gender & Society* 14: 560–580.

Sayer, Liana C. 2005. Gender, time, and inequality: Trends in women's and men's paid work, unpaid work, and free time. *Social Forces* 84: 285–303.

Seccombe, Wally. 1980. Domestic labour and the working-class household, in *Hidden in the household: Women's domestic labour under capitalism,* ed. B. Fox, 25–99. Toronto: Women's Press.

Skrypnek, Berna J., and Janet E. Fast. 1996. Work and family policy in Canada: Family needs, collective solutions. *Journal of Family Issues* 17: 793–812.

Stack, Carol B. 1974. *All our kin: Strategies for survival in a Black community.* New York: Harper Torchbooks, Harper and Row.

Statistics Canada. 2001. *2001 Census: Earnings of Canadians.* **www12.statcan.ca/english/ census01/products/analytic/companion/earn/canada.cfm**. Retrieved January 12, 2007.

Statistics Canada. 2007. *Women in Canada: A gender-based statistical report,* 5th ed. Ottawa: Statistics Canada. **http://dsp-psd.pwgsc.gc.ca/Collection-R/Statcan/89-503-X/0010589-503-XIE.pdf**. Retrieved January 12, 2008.

Status of Women Canada. 2005. *Report on Status of Women Canada's on-line consultation on gender equality.* Ottawa: Status of Women Canada. **www.swc-cfc.gc.ca/resources/consultations/ ges09-2005/finalreport_index_e.html**. Retrieved April 25, 2008.

Sullivan, Maureen. 2004. *The family of woman: Lesbian mothers, their children, and the undoing of gender.* Berkeley: Univ. of California Press.

Tuten, Tracy L., and Rachel A. August. 2006. Work-family conflict: A study of lesbian mothers. *Women in Management Review* 21: 578–597.

Underhill, Elsa. 2005. Winners or losers? Work/life balance and temporary agency workers. *Labour & Industry* 16: 29–59.

Vosko, Leah F. 2002. The pasts (and futures) of feminist political economy in Canada: Reviving the debate. *Studies in Political Economy* 68: 55–83.

Weedon, Chris. 1999. *Feminism, theory, and the politics of difference.* Oxford: Blackwell Publishers.

Weedon, Kim A. 2005. Is there a flexiglass ceiling? Flexible work arrangements and wages in the United States. *Social Science Research* 34: 454–482.

Weigt, J. 2006. Compromises to carework: The social organization of mothers' experiences in the low-wage market after welfare reform. *Social Problems* 53: 332–351.

West, Candace, and Don H. Zimmerman. 1987. Doing gender. *Gender & Society* 1: 125–151.

White, Jerry, Paul Maxim, and Stephen Obeng Gyimah. 2003. Labour force activity of women in Canada: A comparative analysis of Aboriginal and non-Aboriginal women. *Canadian Review of Sociology and Anthropology* 40: 391–415.

Wilson, Suzannah J. 2005. Paid work, jobs, and the illusion of economic security, in *Feminist issues: Race, class and sexuality,* 4th ed., ed. N. Mandell, 226–246. Toronto: Pearson Prentice Hall.

Zeytinoglu, Isik Urla, and Jacinta Khasiala Muteshi. 2000. Gender, race and class dimensions of nonstandard work. *Industrial Relations* 55: 133–167.

CHAPTER 10

Women and Education

Michelle Webber

INTRODUCTION

In this chapter I trouble the prevailing discourse of education as the great equalizer. Despite our best attempts to ensure equity, schooling continues to display gendered, raced, and classed practices that have both material and social effects. Schools, through their organization, interactions, and curricular materials, are engaged in the work of re/producing and regulating particular normative constructions of masculinity and femininity that are associated with middle-class heterosexual white bodies. Both the organization of schooling and people's experiences of schooling demonstrate that the privileging of masculinity, which is generally afforded an advantaged social position over femininity, continues to afford men and boys with social capital, earnings, and so forth. Through a hidden curriculum, girls still learn that they are not as important as boys, which can affect girls' self-esteem and occupational aspirations. Further, women are graduating with university degrees in increasing numbers, yet this does not seem to translate into wide occupational rewards as women still earn less than their male counterparts (with comparable levels of education) and are not well represented in the top positions of power hierarchies. Gender inequality, as it intersects with race, class, and sexuality, persists.

This chapter explores gender, race, and class in relation to both lower and higher education, predominantly focusing on Canada. First, I trace the history of the gender debate in education, beginning with a brief overview of feminist perspectives on education. I show how gender is a persistent concern for educators. Then I turn to the contemporary situation and examine what happens in schools today at both lower and higher education levels. I explore the differential treatment and experiences of girls/women and boys/men as students, teachers, and faculty at the elementary, secondary, and university level. Also examined are contemporary preoccupations and emerging areas in gender education research: the so-called crisis for boys, intersections of race and gender in schools, sexuality and schooling, and the corporatization of higher education. The development of women's studies and feminism in the academy is also considered alongside a brief address of feminist pedagogies.

HISTORICAL BACKGROUND

The preoccupations of researchers in the field of gender research in education have shifted. Early work in the 1970s in this area focused on sex roles. Social relationships were seen as tied to biological differences between men/boys and women/girls. Feminist work critiqued the socializing role of schools as promoting behaviour that conformed to essentialist notions of gender distinctions (Dillabough, 2006). Critiques were launched against patriarchal forms of language used in textbooks and called for the equal representation of girls and women in both curriculum and the education profession itself (Dillabough, 2006). This early work relied on a liberal feminist framework that assumed cognizance of injustices in the educational system was sufficient motivation to engender change (Reynolds, 2001).

Feminist reproduction theory sought to highlight "larger, macro-questions of structure and their role in shaping gender relations as a historically grounded set of gender relations and codes" (Dillabough, 2006: 49). In this approach, schools were understood as sites for both possibilities and limits for the "democratization of gender relations" (Dillabough, 2006: 49). In other words, schools are sites where changes can be enacted and realized.

A more culturally oriented concern emerged in the 1990s when gender education research began to explore how culture, discourse, and identity intersect with macro concerns about men and women's positions in education (Dillabough, 2006). In addition to critiques about the sex/gender distinction, researchers are critical of "singular or binary notions of gender identity as they have been expressed through schooling" (Dillabough, 2006: 53). One strand of this critique aims to disrupt the notion that there are singular categories of "girl" or "boy" (Arnot and Dillabough, 1999); multiple femininities and masculinities exist in our classrooms at any given time. Another critical strand aims to understand how colonialism, culture, race, and gender intersect for youth identity formation (Dillabough, 2006). Someone working in this area might, for example, be concerned with how colonialist and racialized discourses shape students' subjectivities.

Contemporary feminist approaches to theorizing gender and education remain diverse. We continue to see the enduring relevance of feminist reproduction theory as well as the significant increase of studies influenced by post-structuralist and culturalist approaches to the field of gender and education (Dillabough, 2006). This chapter uses a post-structuralist approach in that it deconstructs the prevailing discourse of education as the great equalizer.

LOWER EDUCATION

In this section, I explore the ways in which lower education is gendered, raced, and classed. By examining schooling practices—including teachers' behaviour and expectations, parental behaviour and expectations, and curricular materials—I show how students remain schooled in gendered practices despite widespread acceptance of the importance of gender equality.

Teachers and Principals

Teaching at the elementary and secondary levels in Canada remains a gendered profession. Women have been overrepresented, when compared with the general population, as teachers in Canadian elementary and secondary schools since the late 1880s (Wotherspoon, 2004). Women represented 64 percent of all elementary and secondary school teachers in 1999–2000, up from 59 percent in 1989–1990 (Statistics Canada, 2003). The proportion of women who are both elementary and secondary school teachers has fluctuated between their lowest representation of 55.6 percent in 1980 to their highest proportion of teachers in 1915 (83.4 percent) (Wotherspoon, 2004). Women as teachers are congregated at the elementary level compared with the secondary level, a pattern also found in the United States and Western-European countries (Nelson, 2006; Abbott, Wallace, and Tyler, 2005).

Women account for 47 percent of principals in Canada in 2004-2005 (Statistics Canada, 2006). However, the proportional share of women principals differs between the elementary and secondary levels. At the elementary level, women now account for 53 percent of principals (Statistics Canada, 2006). This is a strong improvement from the 1980s when women made up just under 20 percent of elementary school principals (Cusson, 1990) and the early 1990s when women accounted for only 22 percent of elementary school principals and only 8 percent of secondary school principals (Wotherspoon, 2004). We still see room for progress at the secondary level, as women only represent

42 percent of principals (Statistics Canada, 2006). Overall, though, these statistics represent great improvement for women's representation in the administrative ranks of Canada's elementary and secondary schools.

Women and men's unequal distribution in the educational power hierarchy remains "one of the most salient features of the profession, one that undermines its status" (deMarrais and LeCompte, 1999: 191). Tyack's (1974) classification of schools as "educational harems" remains today where women predominantly teach and men predominantly supervise and administrate. Such feminine teaching and masculine administrative patterns communicate to students "that men hold positions of authority and power in society while women play subordinate roles, having control only over the children in their classrooms" (deMarrais and LeCompte, 1999: 313).

Students

Differential Treatment Historically, Canadian educational institutions were organized to prepare boys and girls for particular societal roles (Davies and Guppy, 2006). In the mid-1800s, citizens were encouraged to commit new tax monies for compulsory schooling for girls and boys. Education leaders lobbied the public on a platform of needing a common moral education. This "common" education was not, however, to be understood as the "same" education (Davies and Guppy, 2006). Even though schooling for students in the early years was similar, by age 10 boys were directed to vocational training and higher education in preparation for the labour market and girls were streamed into domestic science courses (Davies and Guppy, 2006).

Even though boys and girls attended the same schools, they were often segregated within those schools. There were separate entrances and separate playgrounds (often with a wall between the two areas). Girls were seated separately from boys and were even required to perform different recitations (Gaskell, McLaren, and Novogrodsky, 1989; Prentice, 1977). Gendered expectations reinforced teachers', and presumably parents', notions that girls and boys were to be prepared for different occupational and social roles: girls were to be prepared to be housewives or for a limited set of nurturing occupations (nurse, elementary school teacher) while boys were prepared for vocational trades or advanced studies (Davies and Guppy, 2006). Overt gender streaming remained firmly in place until at least the 1950s (Davies and Guppy, 2006).

Contemporary studies continue to document the often unintentional differential treatment afforded to girls and boys by their classroom teachers. The difference now, though, rests in the formal assumption that schools are to educate girls and boys in the same manner. But do boys and girls receive equal classroom treatment? Regardless of whether their teachers are women or men, boys have more interaction with their teachers than do girls (Abbott, Wallace, and Tyler, 2005; deMarrais and LeCompte, 1999; Renzetti and Curran, 1999; Skelton, 1997). Boys are more likely to call out answers in class without raising their hands, and teachers typically accept their answers; however, when girls engage in the same calling out without hand raising, teachers tend to "correct" the girls and tell them their behaviour is inappropriate (Renzetti and Curran, 1999).

Research on teacher/student classroom interactions in Canada, the United States, and the United Kingdom shows how this gendered treatment of students is also racialized (Codjoe, 2001; Dei, 2008; Sadker and Sadker, 2009; Skelton, 1997). White boys are the most likely recipients of teacher attention, followed by boys of colour, white girls, and girls of colour (Sadker and Sadker, 2009). Morris's (2007) research on working-class Black girls and their middle school classroom experiences demonstrates how teachers encourage the girls to conform to a normative model of a docile femininity. Morris argues that the teachers hold racialized perceptions about the undesirability of the Black girls' femininity, seeing the girls as "coarse and overly assertive" (91). Teachers focused on the girls' social etiquette more than their academic development (Morris, 2007). The girls drew the teachers' attention because their actions were seen as "challenging to authority, loud and not ladylike" (Morris, 2007: 501). Black students often report being ignored in their classes, and treated as unimportant by teachers, administrators, and fellow students (Codjoe, 2001).

Teachers' gendered, classed, and racialized notions about appropriate practices and behaviours for girls and boys affect their interactions with students. Boys are often praised by their teachers when they successfully complete a task, while girls may be applauded for their attractive appearance or quiet behaviour (Nelson, 2006). These kinds of gendered interactions may contribute to the promotion of girls' dependence and boys' independence. Girls are praised for being "congenial" and "neat" while boys' work is praised for its intellectual quality (Renzetti and Curran, 1999). A chart of kindergarten awards that was reprinted in the *Wall Street Journal* demonstrates how gender infiltrated a kindergarten classroom: Girls were awarded with "all-around sweetheart," "cutest personality," and "best manners," whereas the boys received awards for "very best thinker," "most eager learner," and "most scientific" (Renzetti and Curran, 1999).

Teachers' differential practices have material effects. Girls learn that boys are more important than themselves, that boys are superior to girls (Bourne, McCoy, and Smith, 1998). Teacher attention is an important contributing factor for both students' academic achievements and for their sense of selves (Sadker and Sadker, 2009). Further, schools (and teachers) reinforce, and thus reproduce, narrow, restrictive normative constructions of what it means to be a girl and what it means to be a boy—what Bob Connell refers to as emphasized femininity and hegemonic masculinity (Connell, 2002).

Curriculum As early as 1970 the Royal Commission on the Status of Women took up the issue of gendered practices within schools. By examining the curricular materials used in Canadian schools to teach reading, mathematics, and social studies, the Commission argued:

> a woman's creative and intellectual potential is either underplayed or ignored in the education of children from their earliest years. The sex roles described in these textbooks provide few challenging models for young girls, and they fail to create a sense of community between men and women as fellow human beings (quoted in Gaskell, McLaren, and Novogrodsky, 1989: 36).

The commission offered a liberal feminist critique of gendered schooling—boys and girls are being treated differently—and a liberal feminist solution—treat them the same. Following the commission's report, numerous studies examined curricular materials and noted the virtual absence of women and girls (Gaskell, McLaren, and Novogrodsky, 1989; Gaskell, 1977). When present, women and girls were constructed traditionally as mothers who baked cookies or girls who played with dolls. Boys were subjected to equally sexist treatment as active and powerful people, playing sports while their fathers worked outside of the home, preferably as educated professionals (Gaskell, McLaren, and Novogrodsky, 1989). Clearly, liberal feminists argued, sexist images prevailed.

As a result of feminist agitation around sexist curricular materials, guidelines were developed around creating non-sexist materials. Has this intervention been successful? More diverse gender images are present in contemporary materials; however, a study 20 years ago by the Ontario federation of women teachers argued that many problematic images remain (Federation of Women Teachers Assocations of Ontario, 1988). The authors of the study argued that school materials need to portray an idealistic world, free from gender segregation, such that children are able to imagine a future for themselves full of possibility (Federation of Women Teachers Assocations of Ontario, 1988; Gaskell, McLaren, and Novogrodsky, 1989). Gaskell, McLaren, and Novogrodsky (1989: 38) argue that textbooks should not go to an extreme where children are only exposed to "androgynous superpeople" but rather there should be a balance of images. An inclusive approach should show women "as secretaries as well as carpenters and girls playing with dolls as well as playing baseball" (Gaskell, McLaren, and Novogrodsky, 1989: 38).

While curricular materials are no longer blatantly sexist, they nevertheless continue subtly to communicate the authority of the status quo—that of white middle-class masculinity (Arnot, 2002). For example, Bourne, McCoy, and Smith's interviews with school girls in Ontario (grades 6–12) reveal accounts of history courses that trivialize, marginalize, or exclude women (Bourne, McCoy, and Smith, 1998). Studies also reveal how First Nations cultures are problematically constructed in curricular materials (Archibald, 1995). Constructions of First Nations cultures are often constructed stereotypically (Archibald, 1995). Both George Dei's (1997, 2008) and Henry Codjoe's (2001) work on race, schooling, and Black Canadian students echoes this; the students cite a desire for courses that are more inclusive of who is in their classrooms, rather than always being exposed to a white Eurocentric curriculum that is dominated by white men with an occasional nod to a white woman or Black man, but never to a Black woman (Codjoe, 2001; Dei, 1997, 2008).

Further, lesbian students speak of an absence of any discussion in their class materials of sexualities other than heterosexuality (Bourne, McCoy, and Smith, 1998). Research on high school textbooks across a range of subject areas reveals that there is virtually no reference made to same-sex sexuality (Macgillivray and Jennings, 2008; Temple, 2005). In these texts, same-sex sexuality, when it appears, is constructed in negative contexts—in discussions of "sexually transmitted diseases, sexual abuse, and prostitution" (Macgillivray and Jennings, 2008: 173). Lesbian, gay, bisexual, and transgendered persons are portrayed as "hapless victims" (Macgillivray and Jennings, 2008: 179). Heterosexuality is a pervasive assumption running through school materials and practices (deMarrais and LeCompte, 1999).

The forms of masculinity and femininity portrayed in curricular materials are ideologically driven. Many forms of masculinity and femininity exist, yet these materials generally show two dominant constructions: hegemonic masculinity and an emphasized femininity (Connell, 2002). These gendered constructions intersect with race (they are white), class (they are middle class), and sexuality (they are heterosexual), and thus alternative masculinities and femininities are rendered inferior and invisible.

Contemporary Research

Crisis for Boys? Are girls outperforming boys? Some critics argue that there is widespread male underachievement in schooling. What do the Canadian statistics tell us? Canadian students recently took part in the Programme for International Student Assessment (PISA) (run by the Organisation for Economic Co-operation and Development, OECD). "PISA is designed to provide policy-oriented international indicators of the skills and knowledge of 15-year old students" (Bussière, Knighton, and Pennock, 2007: 9). Students are tested on their mathematical literacy, reading literacy, and scientific literacy. Whether girls "outperform" boys depends on which levels of data are examined. For example, when looking at the overall science scale, Canadian students showed no gender difference (Bussière, Knighton, and Pennock, 2007). However, when examining the sub-scales within the science category, noticeable gendered differences are apparent. Canadian boys (and those in most other countries) scored higher than girls in "explaining phenomena scientifically," while Canadian girls (and those in most other countries) scored higher than boys in "identifying scientific issues" (Bussière, Knighton, and Pennock, 2007: 37).

The 2006 test scores are consistent with past scores for both mathematics and reading. Canadian boys score higher than girls in mathematics while girls score higher than boys in reading (Bussière, Knighton, and Pennock, 2007). There is a greater difference between boys' and girls' scores in reading than there is in mathematics.

The Canadian data released from the 2006 PISA tests do not analyze performance by race but do provide data based on immigrant status (second-generation immigrants and first-generation immigrants). Non-immigrant Canadian students outperformed both groups of immigrant students in the science category (Bussière, Knighton, and Pennock, 2007). The data also tell us that parental levels of education correspond with student achievement. "Youth with at least one parent who had post-secondary education outperformed their peers whose parents had high school education or less" (Bussière, Knighton, and Pennock, 2007: 40). Further, one's social class influences one's test scores—those students in the top quarter of socio-economic status have higher scores (equal to one proficiency level) than those whose socio-economic status is in the lowest quarter (Bussière, Knighton, and Pennock, 2007).

So what then can we make of what appears to be almost a moral panic about the state of boys in Canada, the United States, and the United Kingdom? In their analysis of literature that takes up the general claim that boys are experiencing a crisis in schooling, Bouchard, Boily, and Proulx (2003) point to three kinds of arguments used in masculinist education discourses. The first argument is one of victimization or the "poor boys discourse" (Bouchard, Boily, and Proulx, 2003). In terms of being able to achieve equality in schools, attention must be turned toward boys as they are "in distress, losing their identity, in crisis, disoriented, guilty, lost ... at the mercy of feminist teachers" and so forth (Bouchard, Boily, and Proulx, 2003: 54–55). Michael Kimmel (2000) argues that these concerns for boys' struggles are really veiled critiques of feminism (Bouchard, Boily, and Proulx, 2003). Women are understood as the source of the boys' problems as schools are feminized spaces that promote feminine practices (Bouchard, Boily, and Proulx, 2003; Lucey, 2001).

The second kind of argument levels attack at the school system itself—that schools themselves are failing boys (Bouchard, Boily, and Proulx, 2003). The logic of this line of work asserts that schools have not adapted to boys and accordingly boys develop both learning and behavioural problems that lead to poor scholastic attainment (Bouchard, Boily, and Proulx, 2003).

The third type of argument uses the essentialist trope of "boys will be boys" (Bouchard, Boily, and Proulx, 2003). In this discourse, boys' troubles in education are reflective of their innate characteristics. Boys are assumed to be "violent, predatory beasts; uncaged, uncivilized animals" (Kimmel, 2000: 8).

All of these anti-feminist arguments used in masculinist discourses about the gendered performance gap generalize to an entire group (boys) an occurrence that affects both boys and girls (Bouchard, Boily, and Proulx, 2003). Further, the rhetoric that circulates about the crisis among boys fails to take an intersectional look at the data. As Skelton (2001) argues, underachievement in schools is both classed and racialized. As we saw from the Canadian data provided above, social class and immigrant status affect school performance. We do not have Canadian data by race, but similar testing in the UK reveals that "the highest achieving group is Chinese girls, followed by Chinese boys, while the lowest-performing are Black Caribbean girls and boys" (Abbott, Wallace, and Tyler, 2005: 95). Bouchard, Boily, and Proulx (2003: 89) conclude:

> The phenomenon of school achievement gaps between boys and girls exists only in industrialized countries, where there are co-educational and democratic public education systems that give girls (and children who do not come from well-to-do families) access to the same education as boys (and the well-to-do). In the past, each gender received differentiated—and hierarchical—training in different venues. For the first time, it is now possible to compare boys and girls enrolled in the same school programs.

Kimmel directs us not to see feminism as the root of boys' "problems"; rather he wants us to see that feminism can help us address male entitlement in such a way that we can "confront racism, sexism and homophobia—both in our communities and in ourselves" (Kimmel, 1999: 90, as cited by Reynolds, 2001: 247). The current debate about boys is really about "restabilizing power and authority that ... has never actually been unseated" (Kehler, 2007: 261).

Intersections of Race and Gender Many scholars are undertaking research that recognizes the simultaneity of race and gender in the area of education. These researchers argue that education continues to be a site for reproducing racialized notions of gender (Codjoe, 2001; Kenny, 2002; Rollock, 2007; Youdell, 2003; Abbott, Wallace, and Tyler, 2005).

In her review essay, Phoenix (2001) presents results from numerous studies documenting educational performance in the UK by ethnicity. Bangladeshi, Pakistani, and Black Carribean students are the most poorly performing groups, although girls from these minoritized groups fare better than the boys (Phoenix, 2001). As stated earlier, Chinese girls and boys are the highest achieving subgroups in the UK (Abbott, Wallace, and Tyler, 2005). In one Canadian study, Jun Li (2004) shows how parental expectations of Chinese immigrants strongly affect their children's school achievements. There is also much evidence documenting "a positive relationship between parental expectations and children's school achievement" among Asian immigrants in North America (Li, 2004: 167).

Several researchers (Codjoe, 2001; Dei, 1997, 2008; Phoenix, 2001) argue that students from racialized groups are treated differentially from white students, and that students themselves actively contribute to reproducing gendered and racialized disadvantage. Phoenix (2001) cites studies demonstrating Black girls' willingness to "forgive" the racist practices at their schools because they need their schooling credentials for future success. Mac an Ghaill (1988) calls this "resistance within accommodation." Young Black men do not appear to engage in such accommodation strategies (Phoenix, 2001).

Mirza and Reay's (2000) research aims to redefine "citizenship" in relation to education and illustrates the possibilities for challenging the white hegemony of schools.

They outline how Black African-Caribbean UK communities (specifically, Black women educators in supplementary schools) developed a "third space"—a space of "strategic engagement." "It is in the 'third space,' a de-essentialised but invisible counter-hegemonic space, where the marginal and the excluded—those situated as such through their gender and radicalized construction—find a voice" (Mirza and Reay, 2000: 70). The work of these women educators destabilizes fixed constructions of citizenship (distinction between private and public spheres) and demonstrates new inclusive forms of citizenship (Mirza and Reay, 2000).

Closer to home, Canadian teacher Alnaaz Kassam reflects on his approach to teaching English and challenging the Eurocentric biased curriculum in light of the multiple and heterogenous identities of his students, and the insistence by many of his students that "there is no racism in Canada" (Kassam, 2007: 356), despite research that shows otherwise in the sphere of education (Codjoe, 2001; Dei, 2008). Through the poem "The Hijabi Girl," written by one of his students outlining the racism she experiences daily as a Muslim girl wearing the hijab in Canada, Kassam explores how students' identities are negotiated through curriculum, media, and global politics and signals the importance of creating classroom spaces that enable students to deconstruct the social relations around them.

Sexuality and Schooling   Researchers are finally turning their attention to how schools work to reproduce gendered sexualities. A main focus in this area examines how schools (through both social and curricular practices) are heterosexualized institutional spaces. Further, schools' assumed heterosexuality often goes unchallenged.

Louisa Allen's 2007 research in New Zealand schools demonstrates how schools both produce and regulate students' sexual identities. Allen points to the "official culture" of schools as a discursive strategy for producing students as "non-sexual." Allen traces how both a discourse of sexual "risk" and an absent discourse of desire in sexual education simultaneously produces students in contradictory ways as both "childlike" and as "sexual decision makers" (Allen, 2007: 231). Allen encourages schools to change their official culture such that student sexuality is understood as "legitimate and positive." Understanding students' sexuality in this way "may open up more spaces for young people to be the kinds of sexual subjects desired by the Health and Physical Education curriculum" (Allen, 2007: 232).

Michael Kehler's research on young men in Canadian high schools demonstrates that male students are expected to perform a "coherent heterosexual masculinity" (Kehler, 2007: 262). Those youth who attempt to resist practices associated with masculine heteronormativity often find themselves cast to the periphery—subject to homophobic taunts. Kehler argues that as a result of such practices, young men avoid developing close friendships with other male youths for fear of being labelled homosexual.

Research on men teachers also reveals the connections between gender and sexuality in educational contexts. Martino and Frank (2006) document how male teachers in a single-sex school negotiate their masculinities. For example, like the students in Kehler's study, the teachers speak of having to establish a "normalized heterosexualized masculinity" (Martino and Frank, 2006: 22). The teachers perceive the male students as policing their masculinities—that as an art teacher, one has to somehow demonstrate strong masculine traits to assure the students of one's heterosexual identity. The art teacher, in this instance, drew on his position as a football coach to reaffirm his heterosexual masculinity (Martino and Frank, 2006).

Lesbian and gay teachers are also subject to regulation in school contexts (Ferfolja, 2008; Jackson, 2006; Khayatt, 1994). Despite harassment, these teachers are hesitant to report abuse for fear of losing their jobs and experiencing further harassment, ostracism, and even violence (Ferfolja, 2008; Jackson, 2006; Khayatt, 1994). By keeping silent about such harassment, teachers contribute to the institutional invisibility of a range of sexualities (Ferforja, 2008).

Rebecca Raby's (2005) Canadian research on student codes of conduct also takes up schools' regulation of students' sexuality. Raby argues that school rules about displays of affection aim to restrict adolescent sexuality while simultaneously developing academic settings that are "separate from the body, rational and self-disciplined" (Raby, 2005: 81). Emma Renold's UK research (2006) similarly explores schools as settings that aim to reproduce compulsory heterosexuality. Renold (2006: 504), drawing on Judith Butler, argues that schools are key spaces for the production of children's gendered identities, which "are performed within a constraining and regulatory hegemonic heterosexual matrix." When sexuality is addressed, it is situated within a heteronormative framework such as passing around condoms (Taylor, 2006). This presumed heterosexuality often goes unchallenged, rendering alternative sexualities problematic.

HIGHER EDUCATION

We now shift our attention to higher education, which also remains gendered, raced, and classed. Women are graduating with university degrees in increasing numbers, yet this has not yet translated into wide occupational rewards as women continue to earn less than men (with comparable education) and are not well represented in the top positions of power hierarchies in their respective fields (Abbott, Wallace, and Tyler, 2005; Hogan, Perucci, and Behringer, 2005; Mandell and Crysdale, 1993). Despite popular sentiment, education does not appear to be the great equalizer.

In this part of the chapter I look at contemporary trends in student enrolment and the professoriate as well as people's experiences of higher education. I then turn to address the development of women's studies and feminist pedagogies in the academy, which both spatially and practically challenge the masculinism of the university. Lastly I examine the rise of the McUniversity and how such corporate challenges are problematic for women and feminism on campus.

Students

Statistical Overview Gendered trends exist in terms of women students' concentration in particular disciplinary areas in higher education. In Canada, the late 1980s marked the shift from men comprising the majority of undergraduate students to women being the majority of undergraduates. By 1988 women and men's enrolment as undergraduates were the same in Canadian universities and 1989 was the first year that women's enrolment exceeded the enrolment of men as undergraduates (Drakich and Stewart, 2007). In undergraduate programmes overall, women now account for 58.2 percent of full-time students (2004–2005) (Canadian Association of University Teachers [hereafter CAUT], 2007a). However, when women's participation as undergraduates exceeded men's, rather than hearing celebration about equal participation we heard concerns "of equity for men and the feminization of universities" (Drakich and Stewart, 2007: 6).

We see the highest proportional representation of undergraduate women in health, parks, recreation, and fitness (72.9 percent) and in education (77.9 percent) while the lowest proportion of women undergraduates are in mathematics and computer and information sciences (25.3 percent) and architecture, engineering, and related technologies (21.2 percent) (CAUT, 2007a). Currently, women represent 50.1 percent of graduate students (CAUT, 2007a). At the graduate level, education again has the highest proportion of women students (73 percent) with social and behavioural sciences and law having the second-highest concentration of women (62 percent). There are fewer graduate women students in personal, protective, and transportation services (22.9 percent) and in architecture, engineering, and related technologies (25.8 percent) (CAUT, 2007a).

When we further subdivide graduate enrolment to differentiate between master's students and doctoral students, we continue to find greater categories of gender divide. While women account for 50.1 percent of all graduate students, they account for only 45.6 percent of doctoral students (CAUT, 2007a). Again, this is a significant improvement from the early 1970s when women accounted for 27 percent of master's students and only 19 percent of PhD students (Drolet, 2007; Human Resources and Social Development Canada, 1999). The 1980s also saw tremendous improvement in women's representation at the graduate level, with women representing 40 percent of master's students and 30 percent of PhD students (Association of Universities and Colleges of Canada [hereafter AUCC], 2007). Education once again has the largest proportion of women doctoral students (70 percent) whereas the field of architecture, engineering, and related technologies has the lowest proportion of women doctoral students (19.2 percent) (CAUT, 2007a).

There are little systematic data on visible minority students in Canada. From survey data, 16 percent of undergraduates self-identified as a member of a visible minority (AUCC, 2007). This percentage representation mirrors the proportion of the general Canadian population who identify as visible minorities. However, for Aboriginals, the picture is not as encouraging. The proportion of Aboriginals aged 25–64 with a university degree is 6 percent, compared to 20 percent of the general Canadian population. Aboriginals are significantly under-represented in terms of their participation as students and as faculty in higher education in Canada (AUCC, 2007).

The continued gendering of particular subject areas leads to differences in career options and salaries for women and men, with men continuing to earn higher annual salaries than women with the same levels of education.

The Professoriate

Statistical Overview In the realm of higher education we can celebrate gradual improvement in women's presence as academics in Canadian universities. Recent Canadian statistics (2004–2005) illustrate that women represent 32.6 percent of all full-time faculty in our universities. This representation is a strong improvement from 11 percent women faculty in 1960–1961 and 20 percent in 1989–1990 (AUCC, 2002; Sussman and Yssaad, 2005). However, women are disproportionately represented in lower academic ranks. In 2004–2005, women accounted for only 18.8 percent of full professors (the highest academic rank in Canada), 34.7 percent of associate professors, 41.4 percent of assistant professors, and 54.8 percent of "other" (including lecturers) (CAUT, 2007a). When compared with other Western, industrialized countries, the United States (public universities) has the largest proportional showing of women at the highest rank (29.9 percent)

(CAUT, 2006). Australia figures slightly ahead of Canada with women making up 19 percent of its highest rank. The United Kingdom fares poorly with only 13.2 percent of its highest rank composed of women (CAUT, 2006).

Figures for academic women's participation change little when we look at other Western countries. In the United States (2003–2004), women represented 33 percent of faculty at doctoral-level institutions and 41 percent of faculty at institutions granting baccalaureates and master's degrees (AAUP, 2004). The United Kingdom (2002–2003) reports that women accounted for 35 percent of full-time faculty (Association of University Teachers, 2004; Higher Education Statistics Agency, 2004). In Australian universities, women represented 39 percent of full-time faculty (this figure includes both full-time faculty and part-time faculty calculated as full-time equivalents) (Department of Education, Science, and Training, 2004).

The numbers above demonstrate a definite accomplishment in terms of women's increasing presence as full-time faculty in the academy. Women's overall representation as faculty is due in part to the increased hiring of women into full-time appointments. For instance, women represented 39.4 percent of all new full-time Canadian university appointments in 2004–2005 (CAUT, 2007a). However, a puzzling scenario comes from the social sciences, where women doctoral graduates have outnumbered men since 1997, yet only 40 percent of new appointments were awarded to women between 1999 and 2004 (Drakich and Stewart, 2007). Another contributing factor to women's increasing presence among university faculty is the retiring of older male faculty (Acker and Webber, 2006; AUCC, 2002).

Despite such appearances of improvement, we still see a persistence of gendered trends. Women in universities continue to be concentrated in the lowest academic ranks, are more likely than men to be employed in part-time (non-secure) academic appointments, are concentrated in particular subject areas (such as the humanities and education), and earn lower salaries than men faculty (Acker and Webber, 2006; CAUT, 2007a). Further, Canadian research demonstrates that women are less likely to be promoted from associate professor to full professor than men, and when they are promoted, they are promoted to the position more slowly than men (spending more time at the rank of associate professor) (Drakich and Stewart, 2007; Dusseault, 2007).

The racial and ethnic representation of women is also not evenly dispersed (Gaskell and Mullen, 2006). It is difficult, though, to provide a statistical profile of the racial and ethnic representation of Canadian university faculty as there is virtually no systematic reporting or collecting of such data (CAUT, 2007b). However, it is clear that the growing diversity of Canadian universities' student population is not yet matched in the professoriate as both people of colour and Aboriginals are under-represented (Henry and Tator, 2007). Only 12.4 percent of all university faculty members identify as visible minorities (2001), which represents a small increase from 11.7 percent in 1996 (CAUT, 2007b). Aboriginal Canadians are significantly under-represented in faculty positions, and account for only 0.7 percent of total faculty appointments, compared with 2.3 percent of positions in the Canadian labour force (CAUT, 2004; Gaskell and Mullen, 2006). In the United States, 89 percent of faculty positions are occupied by whites, yet whites only represent 69 percent of the total US population, leaving Blacks, Hispanics, and American Natives under-represented among faculty ranks (Gaskell and Mullen, 2006; NCES, 2000).

There is also gender segregation in the academy when it comes to disciplinary areas. Overall in Canada 32.6 percent of full-time faculty are women, however only 12.1 percent of engineering and applied sciences faculty and 15.3 percent of mathematics and physical sciences faculty are women. On the other side, there is greater overall representation of women in the health professions and occupations (39.7 percent), fine and applied arts (41 percent), humanities (41.5 percent), and in faculties of education (49.5 percent) (CAUT, 2007a). Nursing represents the area with the highest proportion of faculty appointments, 93.6 percent, given to women (CAUT, 2007a). There are no women faculty in metallurgy, metallurgical engineering, or meteorology (CAUT, 2007a).

A prestigious government initiative, the Canada Research Chairs programme (CRC), awards research faculty positions to outstanding faculty in an effort to both attract and retain exceptional faculty. The strongest criticism against the CRCs is one of gender discrimination. After the first four rounds of CRC appointments, just below 15 percent of the 532 chairs were awarded to women (Kondro, 2002). In 2003, eight women academics filed a complaint against the CRC programme alleging discrimination against women and other minority groups (Birchard, 2004; Tamburri, 2007). In 2004, women accounted for 20 percent of all CRCs (Birchard, 2004), still well below their overall representation in Canadian universities. A "theoretical victory" occurred in 2006 when the CRC programme reached an agreement with the eight women complainants (Tamburri, 2007). Universities are now compelled to develop targets for appointing women, Aboriginals, visible minorities, and people with disabilities to the CRC programme (Tamburri, 2007).

While women are increasingly taking up administrative posts in Canadian universities, they remain a minority in senior positions (Drakich and Stewart, 2007; Grant, 2005). In 2004–2005, 30 percent of senior administrative posts in universities were held by women, a number unchanged since an earlier survey in 2000 (Grant, 2005). The largest concentration of women in administration is at the level of Chair or Head of Department, which is considered a junior administrative position (Drakich and Stewart, 2007). Experiences in these positions tell us that gendered expectations follow women even in these senior administrative posts; women administrators experience expectations to be "wife to the dean and mother to the faculty" (Acker, 2007: 10). Overall, as Drakich and Stewart (2007: 8) argue, there is considerable growth in terms of women's presence in Canadian universities, yet women have "failed to penetrate the still largely male world of academic prestige."

A worrisome trend in the contemporary academy, connected to the growing corporatization of universities, is the increasing reliance on part-time faculty. Hiring part-time faculty (also called contingent or non-permanent faculty) is an effective fiscal strategy for universities (Bauder, 2006). Curtis (2005) argues that the reliance on contingent faculty members symbolizes the most definitive change in the past 20 years in higher education. Part-time women academics proportionately outnumber their full-time counterparts, as almost half (42 percent) of part-timers (1997–1998) are women (Omiecinski, 2003). As Muzzin (2003: 6–7) notes, contingent academic workers are a "feminized (and somewhat racialized, though still mostly white) group supporting the still largely white male academic enterprise." Such a trend raises important questions with respect to the working conditions and career prospects for women employed in these positions in terms of job security, wages, and academic freedom, as well as opportunities for promotion.

Persistent patterns of segregation or lack of representation have profound effects on the academy. When we see an under-representation of groups from the general population (in the case of university faculty, it is members of equity-seeking groups), the academy lacks equity. Lacking equity in our universities may mean that the range of pedagogical approaches may be diminished, particular areas of research may go unexplored, the kinds of questions that should be asked may not be posed, and the range of research methodologies may be narrowed (CAUT, 2007b). The university is still a masculinist, Eurocentric organization (Henry and Tator, 2007). Feminist faculty and faculty of colour both argue that only certain forms of knowledges are legitimized in the contemporary academy (Henry and Tator, 2007; Webber, 2005).

Faculty Experiences Much of our information about the diverse experiences of women academics comes from personal narratives. The narrative approach seems especially suited to highlighting the complexities of the intersection of gender with other processes such as racialization (Carty, 1991; James and Farmer, 1993; Medina and Luna, 2000; Monture-Angus, 2001), generation (Looser and Kaplan, 1997), ableism (Chouinard, 1995/1996), or sexuality (Bensimon, 1997). In some cases (e.g., Bannerji, 1991; Chavez Silverman, 2000) the impact of one's identity on pedagogy as well as career is discussed.

Custom and practice influence what constitutes an academic way of life. A study of Kenyan women academics (Kamau, 1996) explores a range of embedded cultural assumptions about gender that work to limit the possibilities for women's progress. Women's status in this context depends on motherhood rather than on marriage: in order to be accepted, those women academics who were not yet mothers (and therefore had not proved their femininity) needed to take on the role as honorary men. While under Apartheid, academic women in South Africa saw their career mobility curtailed. In the post-Apartheid era, women still struggle against those who seek to maintain the status quo (Moultrie and De La Rey, 2003).

Canadian research on women of colour and Aboriginal women academics outlines the constant inhospitable environment of the white-dominated, male culture of the academy (Henry and Tator, 2007). These faculty members point to the hostility and tension of their white colleagues and students "as a minefield through which they constantly have to navigate" (Henry and Tator, 2007: 25). Students' racist behaviour toward them is not taken up as problematic by their colleagues, department chairs, or deans. The "culture of whiteness" remains dominant in Canadian universities (Henry and Tator, 2007: 25).

There is considerable tension for women academics who combine career and family (Wolf-Wendel and Ward, 2003). Research demonstrates that (heterosexual) women academics in full-time tenured positions in the United States are significantly less likely to be married and have children than full-time tenured men (Mason and Goulden, 2004). Further studies in both Canada and the United States document higher rates of childlessness for younger women academics. For those considering children, women wrestle with how to synchronize progressing in their academic careers (tenure and promotion) with having children (Acker and Armenti, 2004; Ward and Wolf-Wendel, 2004; Williams, 2000; Wolf-Wendel and Ward, 2003). Women academics with young children find it difficult to balance the demands of their careers alongside the demands of their children (Acker and Armenti, 2004; Dillabough, 2007; Raddon, 2002; Wajcman and Martin, 2002). These women speak of high levels of pressure, anxiety, exhaustion, and sleeplessness, and those at research-intensive institutions worry about the effect of taking maternity leaves on their research productivity and colleagues' perceptions about their commitment to their scholarship (Wolf-Wendel and Ward, 2006). As a result of this thinking, many women opt not to take advantage of leaves available to them (Wolf-Wendel and Ward, 2006). As Dillabough (2007: 14) argues, "the traditional model of the independent scholar, autonomous and unencumbered, is a fraught one for any whose goal is to become a learned female in the academy. To embrace this powerful, inherited image is to inflict high levels of guilt upon women academics who are also parents."

Research also examines explicit expectations and implicit assumptions about the kinds of work that women perform in the university. Eveline (2004) uses "glue work" to describe the often unrecognized work performed by women that enables the smooth functioning of the university. Fletcher (1999) says women's relational work "gets disappeared" since it barely registers as a vital contribution to furthering institutional objectives. Women faculty's encouragement and mentoring of women students is documented as a taken-for-granted assumption and expectation (Acker and Feuerverger, 1996; Barnes-Powell and Letherby, 1998). "Institutional housekeeping"—service work—also appears to be unduly allocated to women (Bird, Litt, and Wang, 2004; Park, 1996).

The Chilly Climate In the United States, Roberta Hall and Bernice Sandler (1982) wrote the first report that documented faculty members' often unintentional differential treatment of men and women students in their classes, coining the phrase "the chilly climate" when representing women's experiences on university campuses. Hall and Sandler demonstrate that small instances of inequity exert a cumulative effect when experienced constantly. Some examples of differential interactions between faculty members and women and men students are calling on the men students more than the women (even when women have their hands up), and engaging more with the men in classroom interactions (praising, criticizing, giving feedback). Further, women's issues (such as violence against women) are often downplayed or trivialized. The chilly climate concept illuminates the micro processes of power—the little things that may seem insignificant really do matter.

Canadian research documents that the chilly climate also exists in our universities. A group of faculty members from the University of Western Ontario, calling themselves the Chilly Collective, published a collection called *Breaking Anonymity: The Chilly Climate for Women Faculty* (1995). In the preface to this collection, the Chilly Collective point to Sheila McIntyre's experiences in the Faculty of Law at Queen's University and subsequent publication (1988) of her infamous memorandum ("Gender Bias within a Canadian Law School") as impetus for putting the anthology together. In this memo, McIntyre details "the patterns of stereotyping, sexualization, overt harassment, exclusion, and devaluation" (Chilly Collective, 1995: 1) she experienced in her first year as a faculty member.

Following this publication a group from York University published *York Stories: Women in Higher Education* (York Stories Collective, 2001). The *York Stories* collection includes chapters from undergraduate and graduate students as well as faculty members. The majority of chapters are interviews with women students and faculty and detail horrific experiences of sexism, racism, elitism, heterosexism, and homophobia.

Women's Studies and Feminism in the Academy

Women's studies is heralded as a "site of promise for social and intellectual transformation" (Brathwaite et al., 2004: 10). It became an institutional support for feminism in Canada in the early 1970s (Eichler with Tite, 1990). Individual women's studies courses were first offered in 1970 at the University of British Columbia, University of Toronto, McGill University, University of Waterloo, York University, Université de Montreal, University of Guelph, and Sir George Williams (later renamed Concordia) University (PAR-L, 2008). The first formalized programme in women's studies came in 1973 at the University of British Columbia (PAR-L, 2008). In the United States, California State University at San Diego (1969) housed the first women's studies programme while Cornell University followed suit the following year (Bracken, Allen, and Dean, 2006). The Royal Commission on the Status of Women (1970) "stated that Women's Studies courses indicated the necessity for change, helped show the ways this could be accomplished, and suggested that such courses could improve the conditions for women in future educational systems" (Reynolds, 2001: 248).

Prior to the formal institutionalization of women's studies in universities, some individual faculty members introduced students to the topics of women's liberation and sexism in their classrooms. Women's studies offers a challenge to the masculinist regime that operates in the academy (Smith, 1992) and brings with it the promise of using liberatory pedagogies in its classes. Feminist faculty are supposedly able to "do" academia differently: use feminist perspectives in their research and publications, employ feminist pedagogies in their classrooms, and draw upon feminist principles in their contributions to university governance. The National Women's Studies Association of the United States (NWSA) describes women's studies as

> the educational strategy of a breakthrough in consciousness and knowledge. The uniqueness of Women's Studies has been and remains its refusal to accept sterile divisions between academy and community, between the growth of the mind and the health of the body, between intellect and passion, between the individual and society (NWSA, 2002: xx).

The field of women's studies is now firmly entrenched in Canadian universities, with over 40 institutions across the country offering programmes or housing women's studies institutes. Around the globe, there are over 700 women's studies programmes, departments, institutes, and/or research centres (Korenman, 2007).

Women's studies is not a static monolith; rather, vigorous debate among feminists pushes its boundaries and landscape (HCWSC, 2005). We have seen how women students and faculty of colour, lesbians, bisexuals, and transgenders have criticized feminist theories and projects that only seem to account for white, middle-class, heterosexual women's lives (HCWSC, 2005). We have seen how these debates have changed feminist theories, research agendas, and preoccupying questions.

Women's studies also offers opportunities "to challenge the most egregious effects of a masculinist culture, both within the university and beyond" (Webber, 2006a: 62). Women's studies continues to be a key space for engendering feminist identities and encouraging feminist agency (Webber, 2006a).

Feminist Pedagogies

The impetus for addressing the importance of pedagogical practices came not from theoretical deliberations on feminism (or education or teaching) but from practical concerns of both feminist academics and schoolteachers who wanted strategies to be able to attend to gender, as well as other equity issues, in their classrooms (Weiner, 2006). Interest in feminist pedagogy surfaced from a dissatisfaction with masculinist schools and universities as well as dissatisfaction with non-existent analysis of gender in pedagogic theory (Luke and Gore, 1992; Weiner, 2006).

Building on Paulo Freire's critical pedagogy as developed in his *The Pedagogy of the Oppressed* (1972), feminist pedagogies revolve around intentions to understand and make visible gender relations/gender oppression (also, as connected to race, class, sexuality, and so forth), value the realm of experience, be aware of and attempt to reconstruct power relations in classrooms, interrogate the status quo, and engender social change/social transformation (Bignell, 1996; Briskin, 1994; Fisher, 2001; hooks, 1988; Hornosty, 2004; Morley, 2001; Rinehart, 2002; Welch, 2002). In her work on queer pedagogy, Deborah Britzman calls for pedagogies that go beyond binary constructions of "the tolerant and the tolerated and the oppressed and the oppressor" (Britzman, 1995: 164) in order to have pedagogies that make "all bodies matter" (165). Such an approach requires an engagement with "difference as the grounds of politicality and community" (Britzman, 1995: 152).

Feminist pedagogies are not above criticism. One of the core tenets of feminist approaches to teaching is the inclusion of personal experience in the classroom (of both faculty/teacher and student) (Briskin, 1994; Welch, 1994). Yet in these prescriptive writings, the use of experience is rarely troubled; there is rarely a discussion that takes up how expressions of experience are discursively constructed (Webber, 2006b). Another goal of many feminist pedagogues is to create "safe" and "respectful" classroom spaces (Lewis, 1992; Shrewsbury, 1998). While a laudable goal, classrooms "like all social spaces are imbued with spoken and unspoken assumptions about sexuality, gender and 'race'" (Nairn, 2003: 67). Institutional relations of power make it difficult for feminist faculty to significantly alter power relations in classrooms (Webber, 2006b). Finally, much feminist pedagogical writing is predicated on "modernist and progressivist views of transformative projects" (Weiner, 2006: 87) which assumes that the subjectivity of students in their classes will be one of having a drive for betterment and social change. In reality, numerous subject positions are constantly at work in classrooms (Grant, 1997; Webber, 2006b).

The Rise of the McUniversity

Much contemporary higher education research concerns the corporatization of the academy. One intriguing anthology connects women in the academy to our corporate universities (Reimer, 2004a), and argues that the corporate restructuring of universities can be linked to globalizing processes (Currie and Newson, 1998). Hornosty's chapter explores the links between university corporatization, academic freedom, and gender equity (Hornosty, 2004) and details how feminists successfully used academic freedom as a tool to be able to institutionalize women's studies and incorporate feminist pedagogies and course content in their classrooms. Hornosty is concerned that in a market-based approach to education, where students value skills that prepare them for the marketplace, women's studies' courses will not be seen as marketable. Further, as research priorities become more and more driven by private sector interests, research areas of interest to women academics may come to be seen as irrelevant to the market and business interests. Reimer (2004b) worries that women's studies departments may not survive as university administrators become less willing to provide financial resources to departments with little to no commercial incentive.

When considering the effects of globalization on universities, Ritzer's notion of McUniversity (1998) needs to be addressed. The term "McUniversity" represents an aspect of the *McDonaldization* of society—students are consumers who seek low-cost, accessible education (Rinehart, 2002). Rinehart argues that these student goals are potentially incongruent with feminist educators' goals. Universities as businesses aim to please and satisfy their customers whereas feminist educators explicitly aim to challenge the status quo, to challenge their students. Rather than give up feminist goals in the McUniversity, Rinehart challenges feminists to continue to resist McDonaldization and its accompanying passivity. "The classroom, with all its limitations, remains a location of possibility" (hooks, 1994: 207).

CONCLUSIONS

Education in Canada and elsewhere is gendered, raced, and classed. Through differential experiences (based on interactions with teachers, administrators, and curricular materials), girls still learn that they are not as important as boys. Girls and boys learn to conform to the desired dominant forms of femininity and masculinity or risk marginalization.

Rather than education acting as the great equalizer for girls/boys/women/men, schools (through their organization, interactions, and curricular materials) re/produce and regulate particular normative constructions of masculinity and femininity that are associated with middle-class, heterosexual, white bodies. Despite concern over boys' achievements (or lack thereof), masculinity, which is generally afforded an advantaged social position over femininity, continues to privilege boys and men, affording them social capital, earnings, and so forth. Gender inequality, as it intersects with race, class, and sexuality, persists.

Recent developments in gender education research point to the need for more intersectional and nuanced research. It is difficult to speak of girls/women and boys/men as homogenous, distinct categories. Rather, we need to pay closer attention to the ways that these groups experience schooling and education as differentiated by social class, processes of racialization and ethnicization, sexuality, and physical abilities.

Suggested Readings

Fisher, Berenice Malka. 2001. *No angel in the classroom: Teaching through feminist discourse.* Lanham, MD: Rowman and Littlefield. This monograph weaves together personal reflection as a feminist educator with theoretical writings on feminist pedagogy in university classrooms.

Leonard, D. 2006. Gender, change, and education, in *Handbook of gender and women's studies*, eds. K. Davis, M. Evans, and J. Lorber, 167–182. London: SAGE. A review chapter of theoretical and practical approaches in education.

Luther, R., E. Whitmore, and B. Moreau, eds. 2003. *Seen but not heard: Aboriginal women and women of colour in the academy*, 2d ed. Ottawa: Canadian Research Institute for the Advancement of Women. The collection includes proceedings from a symposium, *Women of Colour and Aboriginal Women: A Dialogue on Equity in the Academy,* that took place in 1999. The papers indicate the need for institutional and personal supports for the integration of faculty members, and demonstrates that the lack of a critical mass of Aboriginal and women of colour faculty results in the marginalization of the few who are in our universities.

Reimer, M., ed. 2004. *Inside Corporate U: Women in the academy speak out.* Toronto: Sumach. A Canadian collection exploring the consequences for women of the increasing corporatization of our universities.

Skelton, C., B. Francis, and L. Smulyan, eds. 2006. *The SAGE handbook of gender and education.* London: SAGE. An important comprehensive international collection on gender and education, covering both lower and higher education.

Discussion Questions

1. For your own institution, find out the gender enrolment breakdown by discipline. Does this breakdown reflect national statistics? How does it vary? What might account for variations?

2. What is the educational history of the women in your family (sister/s, mother, aunt/s, grandmother/s, great grandmother/s? Are their educational experiences likely to be similar or different from your own? In what ways?

3. Does your institution have a women's studies programme? How is it viewed on campus? Do you have a Gender Issues Office or a Diversity Office? What kinds of initiatives does this office undertake? If your campus does not have such an office, how might you go about lobbying for such an office? Why should administrators support such an endeavour on your campus?

4. Think back to your elementary and secondary schooling. Can you name instances where there was overt differential treatment of girls and boys? Can you reflect on subtle ways that gender operated in your schools?

Bibliography

Abbott, P., C. Wallace, and M. Tyler. 2005. *An introduction to sociology: Feminist perspectives*, 3d ed. London: Routledge, 2005.

Acker, S. 2007. Breaking through the ivy ceiling: Sinking or swimming? *Academic Matters*, February: 10–11.

Acker, S., and C. Armenti. 2004. Sleepless in academia. *Gender and Education* 16: 3–24.

Acker, S., and G. Feuerverger. 1996. Doing good and feeling bad: The work of women university teachers. *Cambridge Journal of Education* 26: 401–422.

Acker, S., and M. Webber. 2006. Women working in academe: Approach with care, in *The SAGE handbook of gender and education,* eds. C. Skelton, B. Francis, and L. Smulyan, 483–496. London: SAGE.

Allen, L. 2007. Denying the sexual subject: Schools' regulation of student sexuality. *British Educational Research Journal* 33(2): 221–234.

American Association of University Professors (AAUP). 2004. *Faculty salary and faculty distribution fact sheet 2003–2004.* **www.aaup/org/research/sal&distribution.htm**

Archibald, J. 1995. Locally developed Native studies curriculum: An historical and philosophical rationale, in *First Nations education in Canada: The circle unfolds*, eds. M. Battiste and J. Barman, 288–312. Vancouver: UBC Press.

Arnot, M. 2002. *Reproducing gender? Essays on educational theory and feminist politics*. London: Routledge Falmer.

Arnot, M., and J. Dillabough. 1999. Feminist politics and democratic values in education. *Curriculum Inquiry* 29: 159–189.

Association of Universities and Colleges of Canada (AUCC). 2002. *Trends in higher education.* Ottawa: Publications and Communications Division, Association of Universities and Colleges of Canada.

Association of Universities and Colleges of Canada (AUCC). 2007. *Trends in higher education: Volume 1: Enrolment*. Ottawa: Publications and Communications Division, Association of Universities and Colleges of Canada.

Association of University Teachers (AUT) (UK). 2004. *The unequal academy.* **www.aut.org.uk/ media/pdf/aut_unequalacademy.pdf**

Bannerji, H. 1991. Re: Turning the gaze. *Resources for Feminist Research* 20(3/4): 5–11.

Barnes-Powell, T., and G. Letherby. 1998. All in a day's work: Gendered care work in higher education, in *Surviving the academy: Feminist perspectives*, eds. D. Malina and S. Maslin, 69–77. London: Falmer Press.

Bauder, H. 2006. The segmentation of academic labour: A Canadian example, *ACME* 4(2): 228–239.

Bensimon, E.M. 1997. Lesbian existence and the challenge to normative constructions of the academy, in *Feminist critical policy analysis: A perspective from post-secondary education*, ed. C. Marshall, 141–155. London: Falmer.

Bignell, K. 1996. Building feminist praxis out of feminist pedagogy: The importance of students' perspectives. *Women's Studies International Forum* 19(3): 315–325.

Birchard, K. 2004. Women make gains in getting Canadian research chairs. *Chronicle of Higher Education* 51(14): A38.

Bird, S., J. Litt, and Y. Wang. 2004. Creating status of women reports: Institutional housekeeping as "women's work." *National Women's Studies Association Journal* 16: 194–206.

Bouchard, P., I. Boily, and M. Proulx. 2003. *School success by gender: A catalyst for masculinist discourse*. Ottawa: Status of Women Canada.

Bourne, P., L. McCoy, and D. Smith. 1998. Girls and schooling: Their own critique, *Resources for Feminist Research* 26(1/2): 55–68.

Bracken, S., J. Allen, and D. Dean. 2006. Introduction: The past, present and future—women's studies, higher education and praxis, in *The balancing act: Gendered perspectives in faculty roles and work lives*, eds. S. Bracken, J. Allen, and D. Dean, 1–8. Sterling, VA: Stylus.

Brathwaite, A., et al. 2004. "Passing on": Women's studies, in *Troubling women's studies: Pasts, presents and possibilities*, eds. A. Brathwaite et al., 9–42. Toronto: Sumach.

Briskin, L. 1994. Feminist pedagogy: Teaching and learning liberation, in *Sociology of education in Canada: Critical perspectives theory, research and practice*, eds. L. Erwin and D. MacLennan, 443–470. Toronto: Copp Clark Longman.

Britzman, D. 1995. Is there a queer pedagogy? or, Stop reading straight. *Educational Theory* 45(2): 151–165.

Bussière, P., T. Knighton, and D. Pennock. 2007. *Measuring up: Canadian results of the OECD PISA study, the performance of Canada's youth in science, reading and mathematics*. Statistics Canada, Catalogue no. 81-590-XWE2007001. Ottawa: Minister of Industry.

Canadian Association of University Teachers (CAUT). 2004. Closing the equity gap: A portrait of Canada's university teachers, 1996–2001. *CAUT Education Review* 6: 1–5.

Canadian Association of University Teachers (CAUT). 2006. Women in the academic work force. *CAUT Education Review* 8(1) (March): 1–6.

Canadian Association of University Teachers (CAUT). 2007a. *CAUT almanac of post-secondary education in Canada*. **www.caut.ca/pages.asp?page=442**. Accessed August 26, 2008.

Canadian Association of University Teachers (CAUT). 2007b. A partial picture: The representation of equity-seeking groups in Canada's universities and colleges. *CAUT Equity Review*, November 1.

Carty, L. 1991. Black women in academia: A statement from the periphery, in *Unsettling relations: The university as a site of feminist struggles*, eds. H. Bannerji et al., 13–44. Toronto: Women's Press.

Chavez Silverman, S. 2000. Tropicalizing the liberal arts classroom, in *Power, race and gender in academe: Strangers in the tower?*, eds. S. Geok-Lin Lim, M. Herrera-Sobek, and G.M. Padilla, 132–153. New York: Modern Languages Association.

Chilly Collective, eds. 1995. *Breaking anonymity: The chilly climate for women faculty.* Waterloo, ON: Wilfrid Laurier Univ. Press.

Chouinard, V. 1995/1996. Like Alice through the looking-glass: Accommodations in academia. *Resources for Feminist Research* 24(3/4): 3–11.

Codjoe, H. 2001. Fighting a "public enemy" of black academic achievement—the persistence of racism and the schooling experiences of Black students in Canada. *Race Ethnicity and Education* 4(4): 343–375.

Connell, Bob. 2002. Hegemonic masculinity, in *Gender: A sociological reader*, eds. S. Jackson and S. Scott. New York: Routledge.

Currie, J., and J. Newson, eds. 1998. *Universities and globalization: Critical perspectives.* Thousand Oaks, CA: SAGE.

Curtis, J. 2005. Inequities persist for women and non-tenure-track faculty. *Academe* 91(2): 20–98.

Cusson, S. 1990. Women in school administration. *Canadian Social Trends*, Fall: 18.

Davies, S., and N. Guppy. 2006. *The schooled society: An introduction to the sociology of education.* Don Mills, ON: Oxford Univ. Press.

Dei, G. 1997. Race and the production of identity in the schooling experiences of African-Canadian youth. *Discourse: Studies in the Cultural Politics of Education* 18(2): 241–257.

Dei, G. 2008. Schooling as community: Race, schooling, and the education of African youth. *Journal of Black Studies* 38(3): 346–366.

deMarrais, K., and M. LeCompte. 1999. *The way schools work: A sociological analysis of education*, 3d ed. New York: Longman.

Department of Education, Science, and Training (Australia). 2004. *Staff 2004: Selected higher education statistics.* **www.dest.gov.au/highered/statistics/staff/2004_staff.xls**.

Dillabough, J. 2006. "Education feminism(s)," gender theory and social thought: Illuminating moments and critical impasses, in *The SAGE handbook of gender and education*, eds. C. Skelton, B. Francis, and L. Smulyan, 47–62. London: SAGE.

Dillabough, J. 2007. Parenting and working: A model change needed. *Academic Matters*, February: 14.

Drakich, J., and P. Stewart. 2007. Forty years later, how are university women doing? *Academic Matters*, February: 6–9

Drolet, D. 2007. Minding the gender gap. *University Affairs*, October: 9–12.

Dusseault, C. 2007. UBC confronts gender-related differences in Faculty of Science. *University Affairs*, October: 34–35.

Eichler, M., and R. Tite. 1990. Women's studies professors in Canada: A collective self-portrait. *Atlantis* 16(1): 6–24.

Eveline, J. 2004. *Ivory basement leadership: Power and invisibility in the changing university.* Crawley, AU: Univ. Western Australia Press.

Federation of Women Teachers' Associations of Ontario (FWTAO). 1988. *The more things change ... the more they stay the same.* Toronto: FWTAO.

Ferfolja, T. 2008. Discourses that silence: Teachers and anti-lesbian harassment. *Discourse: Studies in the Cultural Politics of Education* 29(1): 107–119.

Fisher, B. 2001. *No angel in the classroom: Teaching through feminist discourse.* Lanham, MD: Rowman and Littlefield.

Fletcher, J. 1999. *Disappearing acts: Gender, power and relational practice at work.* Cambridge: MIT Press.

Freire, P. 1972. *The pedagogy of the oppressed.* London: Penguin.

Gaskell, J. 1977. Stereotyping and discrimination in the curriculum, in *Precepts, policy and process: Perspectives on contemporary education*, eds. J.D. Wilson and H. Stevenson. Calgary: Detselig.

Gaskell, J., A. McLaren, and M. Novogrodsky. 1989. *Claiming an education: Feminism and Canadian schools.* Toronto: Our Schools, Our Selves.

Gaskell, J., and A. Mullen. 2006. Women in teaching: Participation, power and possibility, in *The SAGE handbook of gender and education*, eds. C. Skelton, B. Francis, and L. Smulyan, 453–468. London: SAGE.

Grant, B. 1997. Disciplining students: The construction of student subjectivities, *British Journal of Sociology of Education* 18(1): 101–114.

Grant, K. 2005. Women in senior university administration in Canada in 2005: Where do we stand? *Senior Women Academic Administrators of Canada E-News*, September: 2–5.

Hall, R., and B. Sandler. 1982. *The classroom climate: A chilly one for women.* Washington: Project on the Status and Education of Women.

HCWSC. 2005. *Women's realities, women's choices: An introduction to women's studies.* New York: Oxford.

Henry, F., and C. Tator. 2007. Through a looking glass: Enduring racism on the university campus, *Academic Matters*, February: 24–25.

Higher Education Statistics Agency (UK). 2004. *Full-time academic staff in all UK institutions by location of institution, gender, principal source of salary and clinical status.* **www.hesa.ac.uk/ holisdocs/pubinfo/staff/staff0203.htm**

Hogan, R., C. Perrucci, and A. Behringer. 2005. Enduring inequality: Gender and employment income in late career, *Sociological Spectrum* 25(1): 53–77.

hooks, b. 1988. *Talking back: Thinking feminist, thinking Black.* Toronto: Between the Lines Press.

hooks, b. 1994. *Teaching to transgress: Education as the practice of freedom.* New York: Routledge.

Hornosty, J. 2004. Corporate challenges to academic freedom and gender equity, in *Inside Corporate U: Women in the academy speak out*, ed. M. Reimer, 43–66. Toronto: Sumach Press.

Human Resources and Social Development Canada (HRSDC). 1999. *Canadian gender trends in education and work.* **www.hrsdc.gc.ca/cgi-bin/hrsdc-rhdsc/print/print.asp?Page_Url=;/en/cs/sp/hrsd/prc/publications/research/1999-002380/page07.shtml**

Hunter College Women's Studies Collective. 2005. *Women's realities, women's choices: An introduction to women's studies,* 3d ed. New York: Oxford Univ. Press.

Jackson, J. 2006. Removing the masks: Considerations by gay and lesbian teachers when negotiating the closet door. *Journal of Poverty* 10(2): 27–52.

James, J., and R. Farmer, eds. 1993. *Spirit, space and survival: African American women in (white) academe.* New York: Routledge.

Kamau, M. 1996. *The experiences of women academics in Kenya.* Unpublished PhD dissertation, University of Toronto.

Kassam, Alnaaz. 2007. Locating identity and gender construction in a post 9/11 world: The case of the hijabi girl. *Intercultural Education* 18(4): 355–359.

Kehler, M. 2007. Hallway fears and high school friendships: The complications of young men (re)negotiating heterosexualized identities. *Discourse: Studies in the Cultural Politics of Education* 28(2): 259–277.

Kenny, C. 2002. *North American Indian, Metis and Inuit women speak about culture, education and work.* Ottawa: Status of Women Canada. **www.swc-cfc.gc.ca/pubs/pubspr/0662318978/200203_0662318978_e.pdf**

Khayatt, D. 1994. Surviving school as a lesbian. *Gender & Education* 6(1): 47–61.

Kimmel, M. 1999. What are little boys made of? *MS Magazine,* October/November: 88–91.

Kimmel, M. 2000. What about the boys? *Women's Educational Equity Act Digest,* November: 1–2, 7–8.

Kondro, W. 2002. Few women win new academic chairs. *Science* 296(5577): 2319.

Korenman, J. 2007. *Women's studies programs, departments and research centers.* **http://research.umbc.edu/~korenman/wmst/programs.html**

Lewis, M. 1992. Interrupting patriarchy: Politics, resistance and transformation, in *Feminisms and critical pedagogy*, eds. C. Luke and J. Gore, 167–191. New York: Routledge.

Li, Jun. 2004. Parental expectations of Chinese immigrants: A folk theory about children's school achievement. *Race Ethnicity and Education* 7(2): 167–183.

Looser, D., and E. Kaplan, eds. 1997. *Generations: Academic feminists in dialogue.* Minneapolis: Univ. of Minnesota Press.

Lucey, H. 2001. Social class, gender and schooling, in *Investigating gender: Contemporary perspectives in education*, eds. B. Francis and C. Skelton, 177–188. Buckingham, UK: Open Univ. Press.

Luke, C., and J. Gore. 1992. Introduction, in *Feminisms and critical pedagogy*, eds. C. Luke and J. Gore, 1–14. London: Routledge.

Mac an Ghaill, M. 1988. *Young, gifted and Black.* Milton Keynes, UK: Open Univ. Press.

Macgillivray, I., and T. Jennings. 2008. A content analysis exploring lesbian, gay, bisexual, and transgender topics in foundations of education textbooks. *Journal of Teacher Education* 59(2): 170–188.

Mandell, N., and S. Crysdale. 1993. Gender tracks: Male-female perceptions of home-school-work transitions, in *Transitions: Schooling and employment in Canada*, eds. P. Anisef and P. Axelrod, 21–41. Toronto: Thompson.

Martino, W., and B. Frank. 2006. The tyranny of surveillance: Male teachers and the policing of masculinities in a single sex school. *Gender & Education* 18(1): 17–33.

Mason, M., and M. Goulden. 2004. Marriage and baby blues: Redefining gender equity in the academy. *Annals of the American Academy of Political and Social Science* 596: 86–103.

McIntyre, S. 1988. Gender bias within the law school: "The memo" and its impact. *Canadian Journal of Women and the Law* 2(1): 362–407.

Medina, C., and G. Luna. 2000. Narratives from Latina professors in higher education. *Anthropology and Education Quarterly* 31(1): 47–66.

Mirza, H.S., and D. Reay. 2000. Redefining citizenship: Black women educators and "the third space," in *Challenging democracy: International perspectives on gender, education and citizenship*, eds. M. Arnot and J. Dillabough, 58–72. London: Routledge.

Monture-Angus, P. 2001. In the way of peace: Confronting whiteness in the university, in *Seen but not heard: Aboriginal women and women of colour in the academy*, eds. R. Luther, E. Whitmore, and B. Moreau, 29–49. Ottawa: CRIAW.

Morley, L. 2001. Mass higher education: Feminist pedagogy in the learning society, in *Identity and difference in higher education: "Outsiders within,"* eds. P. Anderson and J. Williams, 28–37. Aldershot, UK: Ashgate.

Morris, E. 2007. "Ladies" or "loudies"? Perceptions and experiences of Black girls in classrooms. *Youth and Society* 38(4): 490–515.

Moultrie, A., and C. De La Rey. 2003. South African women leaders in higher education: Professional development needs in a changing context. *McGill Journal of Education* 38(3): 407–420.

Muzzin, L. 2003. Report of the professional practice, ethics and policy subcommittee. *The Canadian Sociology and Anthropology Association Annual Report 2002–2003.*

Nairn, K. 2003. What has the geography of sleeping arrangements got to do with the geography of our teaching spaces? *Gender, Place and Culture* 10(1): 67–81.

National Center for Education Statistics (NECS) (US). 2002. *Salary, promotion, and tenure status of minority and women faculty in US colleges and universities* (NCES 2000-173), by M.T. Nettles, et al. Washington, DC: NECS.

National Women's Studies Association (NWSA). 2002. National Women's Studies Association constitution. *NWSA Journal* 14(1): xix–xx.

Nelson, A. 2006. *Gender in Canada*, 3d ed. Toronto: Pearson Prentice Hall.

Omiecinski, T. 2003. Hiring of part-time university faculty on the increase. *Education Quarterly Review* 9(3): 9–15.

PAR-L. 2008. *A chronology of the development of women's studies in Canada: The 1970s.* **www.unb.ca/par-l/chronology1.htm**

Park, S. 1996. Research, teaching and service: Why shouldn't women's work count? *Journal of Higher Education* 67: 46–67.

Phoenix, A. 2001. Racialization and gendering in the (re)production of educational inequalities, in *Investigating gender: Contemporary perspectives in education*, eds. B. Francis and C. Skelton, 126–138. Buckingham, UK: Open Univ. Press.

Prentice, A. 1977. *The school promoters: Education and social class in mid-nineteenth century Upper Canada.* Toronto: McClelland and Stewart.

Raby, R. 2005. Polite, well-dressed and on time: Secondary school conduct codes and the production of docile citizens. *Canadian Review of Sociology and Anthropology* 42(1): 71–91.

Raddon, A. 2002. Mothers in the academy. *Studies in Higher Education* 27(4): 387–403.

Reimer, M., ed. 2004a. *Inside Corporate U: Women in the academy speak out*. Toronto: Sumach.

Reimer, M. 2004b. Will women's studies programs survive the corporate university?, in *Inside Corporate U: Women in the academy speak out*, ed. M. Reimer, 118–137. Toronto: Sumach.

Renold, E. 2006. "They won't let us play ... unless you're going out with one of them": Girls, boys and Butler's "heterosexual matrix" in the primary years. *British Journal of Sociology of Education* 27(4): 489–509.

Renzetti, C., and D. Curran. 1999. *Women, men and society*, 4th ed. Boston: Allyn and Bacon.

Reynolds, C. 2001. The educational system, in *Feminist issues: Race, class and sexuality*, 3d ed., ed. N. Mandell, 242–259. Toronto: Prentice Hall.

Rinehart, J. 2002. Feminist education: Rebellion within McUniversity, in *The McDonaldization of higher education*, eds. D. Hayes and R. Wynyard, 167–179. Westport, CT: Bergin and Garvey.

Ritzer, G. 1998. *The McDonaldization thesis: Explorations and extensions*. London: SAGE.

Rollock, N. 2007. Why Black girls don't matter: Exploring how race and gender shape academic success in an inner city school. *Support for Learning* 22(4): 197–202.

Sadker, M., and D. Sadker. 2009. Missing in interaction, in *Reconstructing gender: A multicultural anthology*, 5th ed., ed. E. Disch, 362–368. New York: McGraw-Hill.

Shrewsbury, C. 1998. What is feminist pedagogy?, in *Contemporary feminist theory*, ed. M. Rogers, 167–171. Boston: McGraw-Hill.

Skelton, C. 1997. Women and education, in *Introducing women's studies: Feminist theory and practice*, 2d ed., eds. D. Richardson and V. Robinson. Basingstoke, UK: Palgrave Macmillan.

Skelton, C. 2001. *Schooling the boys: Masculinities and primary education*. Buckingham/Philadelphia: Open Univ. Press.

Smith, D. 1992. Whistling women: Reflections on rage and rationality, in *Fragile truths: Twenty-five years of sociology and anthropology in Canada*, eds. W. Carroll et al., 207–226. Ottawa: Carleton Univ. Press.

Statistics Canada. 2003. School enrolments and teaching staff. *The Daily*, September 18.

Statistics Canada. 2006. Education matters: Profile of Canada's school principals. *The Daily*, June 26.

Sussman, D., and Yssaad, L. 2005. The rising profile of women academics. *Perspectives on Labour and Income* 6: 6–19.

Tamburri, R. 2007. Mediated agreement reached in CRC dispute. *University Affairs*, January: 40.

Taylor, Y. 2006. Intersections of class and sexuality in the classroom, *Gender and Education* 18(4): 447–452.

Tyack, D. *The one best system*. Cambridge, MA: Harvard Univ. Press, 1974.

Wajcman, J., and B. Martin. 2002. Narratives of identity in modern management: The corrosion of gender difference? *Sociology* 36(4): 985–1102.

Ward, K., and L. Wolf-Wendel. 2004. Academic motherhood: Managing complex roles in research universities. *Review of Higher Education* 27: 233–257.

Webber, M. 2005. "Don't be so feminist": Exploring student resistance to feminist approaches in a Canadian university. *Women's Studies International Forum* 28: 181–194.

Webber, M. 2006a. "I'm not a militant feminist": Exploring feminist identities and feminist hesitations in the contemporary academy. *Atlantis* 31(1): 55–63.

Webber, M. 2006b. Transgressive pedagogies? Exploring the difficult realities of enacting feminist pedagogies in undergraduate classrooms in a Canadian university. *Studies in Higher Education* 31(4): 453–467.

Weiner, G. 2006. Out of the ruins: Feminist pedagogy in recovery, in *The SAGE handbook of gender and education*, eds. C. Skelton, B. Francis, and L. Smulyan, 79–92. London: SAGE.

Welch, Penny. 1994. Is a feminist pedagogy possible? in *Changing the subject: Women in higher education*, eds. S. Davies, C. Lubelska, and J. Quinn, 149–162. London: Taylor and Francis.

Welch, P. 2002. Feminist pedagogy and power in the academy, in *Teaching and research in higher education*, eds. G. Howie and A. Tauchert, 113–124. Aldershot: Ashgate.

Williams, J. 2000. How the tenure track discriminates against women. *Chronicle of Higher Education*, October 27: B10.

Wolf-Wendel, L., and K. Ward. 2003. Future prospects for women faculty: Negotiating work and family, in *Gendered futures in higher education: Critical perspectives for change*, ed. B. Ropers-Huilman, 111–134. Albany: State Univ. of New York Press.

Wolf-Wendel, L., and K. Ward. 2006. Faculty work and family life: Policy perspectives from different institutional types, in *The balancing act: Gendered perspectives in faculty roles and work lives*, eds. S. Bracken, J. Allen, and D. Dean, 51–72. Sterling: Stylus.

Wotherspoon, T. 2004. *The sociology of education in Canada: Critical perspectives,* 2d ed. Don Mills, ON: Oxford Univ. Press.

York Stories Collective, eds. 2001. *York stories: Women in higher education.* Toronto: TSAR Publications.

Youdell, D. 2003. Identity traps or how Black students fail: The interactions between biographical, sub-cultural, and learner identities. *British Journal of Sociology of Education* 24(1): 3–20.

CHAPTER 11

Underpinnings and Understandings of Girls' and Women's Health[1]

Diana L. Gustafson

How do you define health? What implications does this definition have for understanding women's health in particular? Some describe good health as being physically and mentally fit, free of disease, and able to engage in everyday activities of living. Many say that health is a general sense of well-being that results from healthy lifestyle choices, such as eating nutritious meals, getting plenty of rest, participating in regular exercise, getting an annual PAP smear and regular dental care, and learning to cope better with the stress of being a student, a mother, a paid worker or perhaps all three. Others may add that being born with good genes gives some girls and women a healthy advantage.

That some of us reduce health to a functioning of the body that can be measured, monitored, and managed is not surprising. Nor is it surprising that many of us believe that we are personally responsible for our state of health. These understandings of health can be traced, in part, to medical discourse, research and practice that emerge from an often unmarked white, masculinist perspective (Filc, 2004; Weber and Parra-Medina, 2003). Because biomedical knowledge is widely considered authoritative and legitimate in the global north and around the world, it is a key organizer of institutionalized health education, practices, policies, and programs that influence girls' and women's health, re-enforce disparities in health outcomes, and operate as sites of advocacy and resistance (Filc, 2004; Lupton, 2003; Wang and Vijayan, 2001).

This chapter invites you to think first about the underpinnings and understandings of girls' and women's health emerging from two dominant approaches: the biomedical model and the population health model. Then we consider how a critical feminist approach unsettles some taken-for-granted understandings, shifting away from descriptions and measurement of health and illness as objective, abstract concepts toward more integrated and intelligible understandings of the links between subjective, embodied health experiences and the biological, social, and environmental factors that shape girls' and women's health outcomes. A critical feminist perspective also complicates gender as a category of analysis by exposing the health disparities between women and men and among diverse groups of women. These health disparities emerge from differences in social location (race/ethnicity, dis/ability, class, religion, age) and social position in relation to power and pathways to resources that contribute to well-being or ill health. In taking up this critical feminist perspective, we will call attention to girls' and women's health as an equity and social justice issue. To illustrate these points, examples drawn primarily from Canadian sources are organized around the 12 health determinants adopted by the Public Health Agency of Canada (2003). The discussion is decidedly Canada-centric with attention given to historical trends that shape current experience and future action both locally and internationally.

The discussion begins with an overview of the salient features of the biomedical and population health models. Outlining key similarities and differences between the biomedical and population

---

1 My thanks to Margrit Eichler, Janet Bartlett, Nancy Mandell, and Laura Forbes, who shared their comments on an earlier version of this chapter. I am sincerely grateful to Sandra Meadus, Christa McGrath, and Brenda Hillier, whose excellent administrative support contributes enormously to a healthy work environment and my professional well-being.

health models is one way of getting at the factors that contribute to girls' and women's health experiences, the historical underpinnings of knowledge produced about our health, and women's relationships to the health care system as recipients and providers of health care.

UNDERPINNINGS: TWO APPROACHES TO HEALTH

The biomedical and population health models emerged at different historical moments with apparently different orientations toward health and illness. Evolving over time, both models have been taken up, challenged, and accorded value depending on the specific time, place, and issue. Both models reflect and contribute to evolving understandings of health and the factors that contribute to health inequities between women and men, and among diverse groups of women. The following discussion demonstrates a growing convergence of both models grounded in a common scientific discourse.

Biomedical Model

Historians disagree on the precise origins of biomedicine. Some claim a legacy dating back to Ancient Egypt and Imhotep, a healer and author of documents that detailed human anatomy, ailments, and treatments. Others claim biomedicine originated in Ancient Greece with Hippocrates, who is often referred to as the father of medicine. In 1921, Sir William Osler argued that the careful observation of disease and its treatment began in the mid-17th century in Europe and later spread to North America, followed by the emergence of the modern scientific tradition (Osler, 1921).

Many agree that the Flexner Report, commissioned in 1910 by the philanthropic Carnegie Foundation, was a pivotal moment in defining the modern approach to health in North America. Flexner visited over 150 Canadian and American medical schools. He reported that 90 percent of practising doctors lacked a college education and most had attended inadequate medical schools. Medical education was simple because practice was simple, with treatments of choice including bleeding with leeches and ingestion of purgatives to induce vomiting. Many of these schools were commercial rather than public service enterprises that produced, according to Flexner, ill-prepared doctors, some of whom he described as "arrogant and ignorant" (cited in Boelen, 2002). When the recommendations of the Flexner Report were implemented, proprietary schools were closed. Because these schools were the only point of entry into medicine for women and Blacks, this positioned white, middle- and upper-class men as the competitive candidates who were granted entry into university-based schools, and ultimately, a licence to practise medicine (Boelen, 2002).

Whether intended or not, the health promotion and community-based social goals at the core of the Flexner Report were not implemented (Boelen, 2002). Instead, physicians became the primary healers at the centre of a hospital-based care system that focused on illness. Physicians' education was based on knowledge derived from basic and life sciences research. As this research evolved, it focused on the pathophysiology of the body and the identification of internal factors (genes and germs) that cause or protect against disease, the constellation of clinical factors that signal disease or disability, and the appropriate strategies for screening, treating, and managing (but more importantly, curing) disease. Thus, physicians learned to attend to the individual physical body, its function and malfunction, and the diagnosis, treatment, cure, and management of disease, disability, and infirmity rather than on the broader determinants of the health of a population.

This brief overview suggests how the biomedical model and the scientific tradition along with the legacy of colonialism and patriarchy, came to dominate other non-medical health practitioners and the knowledge they produced. For many years, naturopaths, homeopaths, and traditional midwives in Canada were denied professional or legal status. Ayurvedic medicine, traditional Chinese medicine, and other indigenous healing systems were ignored or denigrated as backward, folksy, or primitive when compared with biomedicine that claimed to be scientific, proven, and superior (Dei et al., 2000). In the last two decades, biomedical research and practitioners have begun to acknowledge, study, and in some cases, appropriate these so-called complementary or alternative practices. Feminist historians also point out that women's contribution to the art and science of medicine is largely absent from dominant narratives (Achterberg, 1990; Ehrenreich and English, 1973, 1978), although Clara Barton, Madame Curie, Florence Nightingale, and Margaret Sanger are a few iconic exceptions.

Although biomedical knowledge contributes positively to the treatment and management of pain, some acute diseases, and traumatic injuries, biomedicine as a scientific enterprise and health care system has been seriously questioned by feminists and others (Foucault, 1973; Inhorn and Whittle, 2001; Lupton, 2003; Raphael and Bryant, 2002; Weber and Parra-Medina, 2003).

Population Health Model

The population health model emerged in the 1970s in response to the limitations of the biomedical model and the lack of attention to the social, economic, cultural, and environmental factors that shape health outcomes. Rather than regarding health as a feature of an individual body, the population health model assumes that health is a capacity and a valuable resource that allows human collectives to engage in productive lives (Raphael and Bryant, 2002). The population health model, as the name suggests, focuses on evaluating a broad range of factors that influence the health of a population defined by geography or other common feature. From this perspective, health problems result from inequitable access to the resources that support health, such as adequate nutrition, safe housing, and supportive social networks. Promoting or restoring health is achieved by promoting healthy communities and infrastructure and by redistributing power and social resources more equitably across a population. Whereas the biomedical model intervenes at the level of individuals (e.g., one physician treating one patient with endometriosis), the population health model is oriented toward upstream interventions that affect the conditions that shape a population's chances of being healthy (e.g., promoting safe sex to reduce the risk of pelvic infections). Upstream interventions are based in part on evidence derived from epidemiological studies of the determinants of health.

The Public Health Agency of Canada (2003) (hereafter referred to as PHAC) names 12 health determinants: biology and genetic endowment; gender; culture; personal health practices and coping skills; income and social status; employment and working conditions; education; social environments; physical environments; healthy child development; health services; and social support networks. (We will return to these determinants later.) Although the population health model may appear on the surface to be a values-based approach to health, critics argue that epidemiological studies are, in practice, deeply embedded in the disease model of health, and seek to establish the causal relationships between individual behaviours and decontexualized exposure to risk factors (Inhorn and Whittle, 2001; Raphael and Bryant, 2002).

Limitations of Both Approaches

This brings us to the first of three problems with the production of health knowledge about women and girls. Both the biomedical and population health models advocate evidence-based decision-making, which is expected to reduce uncertainty in health practice, programming, and policy development. The problem is that evidence produced by clinical and epidemiological studies is based on traditional positivist, scientific methods, values, and principles (Inhorn and Whittle, 2001; Raphael, 2000). In the case of biomedical research, randomized double-blind clinical trials are widely considered the gold standard for producing evidence. When health is defined as the absence of disease and disability, the search for evidence leads to finding the most cost-effective way to cure or treat disease. Thus, biomedical research focuses on (for instance) establishing the efficacy of a given intervention such as hormone replacement therapy for the treatment of menopausal symptoms. With population health research, epidemiological studies rely heavily on large data sets to establish causal relationships between (for example) hormone replacement therapy and heart disease. These examples illustrate how the disease model of health drives the production of evidence while according scant attention to issues of power and distribution of resources (Inhorn and Whittle, 2001). Furthermore, the evidence produced by traditional clinical and epidemiological studies does not tell us specifically about women, the communities in which we live, our patterns of interaction, and any context for our experiences or motivations. By stripping the context from the exploration of structural issues, "the population has been taken out of population health" (Raphael and Bryant, 2002: 192). Consider, for example, the powerful message sent to a generation of women that began in 1966 with the publication of Robert Wilson's volume *Feminine Forever* and was later taken up and advanced by many fellow physicians. Menopause was constructed as an "estrogen deficiency disease" brought on by the unnaturalness of women living beyond their reproductive years. Subsequently, thousands of women began taking hormone replacements to treat this dis-ease of female aging.

The second problem with clinical and epidemiological studies is their grounding in a disease model rather than a health model. The goal of research is to produce evidence for making decisions about curing or treating disease in individuals or populations rather than protecting and promoting health. Consider research on breast cancer and the growing public support for fundraisers such as the Pink Ribbon Campaign. Women and families raise research dollars that are directed largely toward improving screening techniques for the early detection of disease (referred to as secondary prevention[2]) and improving the efficacy of chemo-pharmaceutical, surgical, and other high-tech treatments (referred to as tertiary prevention). Although most of us know a woman who has benefited from such research, wouldn't it be preferable if none of us had breast cancer in the first place? Yet far fewer research dollars are directed toward primary prevention—that is, identifying the complex physiological and environmental causes that make some of our daughters, sisters, and mothers more likely to get and/or die of breast cancer.

Consider now the Red Dress Campaign to raise research dollars for women's heart disease. Evidence produced from epidemiological studies justifies media campaigns that

---

2 This example illustrates how the concept of prevention has been subverted in medical discourse. Powerful drugs such as Tamoxifen used in breast cancer treatment are being tested as preventative agents for "high-risk" women (Epstein, 1998). Another example described as prevention is the routine practice of removing normal ovaries in women over 45 years who are undergoing hysterectomy even when cancer is not suspected, a procedure that surgically hurls women into premature menopause.

counsel women to keep our cholesterol within a healthy range by eating right and exercising, and when we fail, to take a cholesterol-reducing drug. These campaigns and similar public health policies implicitly blame individual women for our health status by suggesting that risk of heart disease is confined to lifestyle choices, which ignores the economic forces that shape women's varied experiences of health (Inhorn and Whittle, 2001).

These two examples call attention to the third problem with the biomedical and population health models: They give too little attention to the race, class, ability, and other social hierarchies that limit women's power, agency, and range of choices (Inhorn and Whittle, 2001). The orientation of clinical and epidemiological studies shifts responsibility for women's health from external (collective, systemic) to internal (individual, personal) control. We are expected to monitor our bodies in a variety of ways: knowing the date of our last menstrual period, checking the lumpiness of our breasts, maintaining a body weight within the normal BMI range, and tracking our heart rate during aerobic exercise. Rail and Beausoleil (2003: 3) argue convincingly that "the desire to achieve health has become a new form of corporeal (self) control and guilt has become intimately tied to an individual's failure to achieve it."

To summarize this section, the medical model with clinical trials and the population health model with epidemiological studies give us tools to describe and measure health and determine the causes of disease and injury, one at the body systems level and the other at the population systems level. When a woman gets sick or hurt, biomedicine offers her an organized system of health providers and services for the management of physical expressions of her illness or injury. When women as a collective get sick or hurt because of the poor working conditions in which we live and work, the population health model offers a way of describing and measuring that problem and demonstrating a causal relationship between two or more health determinants.

Feminists argue correctly that description and measurement contribute only one piece to the understanding of women's health. Verifying low blood hemoglobin does not tell us about woman's experiences of being chronically tired and too poor to get enough dietary iron. Nor does statistical information on high rates of obesity and substance use among Aboriginal women help us understand and address the legacy of cultural marginalization, colonialism, poverty, and community hopelessness. Measurement suggests trends without conveying embodied experiences or the local materiality of girls' and women's health lives. Thus, bringing a critical feminist lens to the reframing and interpretation of health research contributes to a richer and more integrated understanding, both of women's health and of the links between lived health experiences and the biological, social, and environmental determinants of health. These improved understandings direct us to think differently about girls' and women's health as an equity and social justice issue.

The next section uses a tool for challenging the production of women's health knowledge and offering in its stead a social justice or rights-based understanding of health.

UNDER THE MICROSCOPE: WOMEN AS OBJECTS OF MEDICAL RESEARCH

Medical research directs our attention to a multitude of genetic, biochemical, physiological, and lifestyle factors linked to women's health problems. We hear about "bad" genes that predispose some women to breast cancer and how HIV crosses the placental barrier from mother to fetus, making women a vector of disease. Public health campaigns tell us to make responsible choices to reduce our risk of contracting sexually transmitted infections. Some women place fetal sonograms on the fridge along with other family photos, demonstrating how public and taken-for-granted the surveillance of women's reproductive function has become. Print and television ads tell us that we need the right products for light days, heavy nights, and mid-cycle leaks to manage the unpredictability of our bodies' menstrual flows and the purported limits placed on our normal activities. What accounts for this?

Women have seldom been in a position to determine what is studied, how it is studied, what constitutes valid evidence, and what is done with the findings. Although women's health issues have received increasing attention over the last 30 years, much of the emphasis has been on women's reproductive functions. Until the early 1990s, women's perspectives and priorities were of little interest in setting medical, academic, and government agendas for women's health (Walters, 1992, 1993).

Increasingly, feminist scholars are partnering with grassroots organizations and feminist bureaucrats in challenging the production of health knowledge about women and girls. One initiative to come out of these partnerships was gender-based analysis (GBA). The goal of GBA in health research and practice was to eliminate gender-bias problems. Rather than simply disaggregating and reporting findings by gender, GBA sought to account for differences in men's and women's health. In 1999, the Canadian federal government, as part of its commitment to gender equality, declared that GBA would be systematically applied to all its substantive work. Responsibility for implementing GBA was decentralized with each federal, provincial, and territorial department and agency (including Health Canada) accountable for incorporating a gender perspective into the development and evaluation of its policies and programs.

A number of frameworks have been proposed for promoting gender equity in research (Canadian Research Institute for the Advancement of Women, 2006; Eichler, Gustafson, and Pompetzki, 1999; Weber and Parra-Medina, 2003). The following discussion uses the BIASFREE[3] Framework (Burke and Eichler, 2006) to illustrate how medical research re-inscribes social hierarchies and the health inequalities that are derived from them. The BIASFREE Framework emerged as a response to the critiques that GBA failed to acknowledge the multiplicity of women's lives and the intersection of the gender hierarchy with other social hierarchies. The framework is based on a rights-based concept of health. First adopted by the World Health Organization (WHO) in 1948, a rights-based concept of health assumes that health and well-being are fundamental human rights.

According to the BIASFREE framework, there are three main types of bias that exist in health research: maintaining a hierarchy, failing to examine differences, and using double standards. Eliminating all bias problems in health research is an essential component of sound practice that produces comprehensive and inclusive knowledge about girls' and women's health.

Maintaining an Existing Hierarchy

The first type of bias occurs when existing hierarchies and power structures are not examined, and therefore are maintained (Burke and Eichler, 2006). The framework advocates unsettling the operation of sexism and racism and other systemic oppressions as key to

---

3   BIASFREE stands for Building an Integrative Analytic System For Recognizing and Eliminating inEquities.

imagining the just redistribution of resources that have an impact on health outcomes. This type of bias takes several forms, two of which we discuss here.

A gendered social hierarchy is maintained through *pathologization* when biological differences between men and women are naturalized and justified. Consider the way that men's (white, heterosexual, able) bodies, minds, and natures have historically represented the standard against which women's were measured and evaluated and, with astounding regularity, found to be "essentially and dangerously inferior to men's" (Morgan, 1998: 102). The female body, with our capacity to bear children, is physiologically different and, through biased extension, medically aberrant. How is this bias reproduced in medical research? Because female bodies share some common primary and secondary sexual characteristics that differ from male bodies, medical research uses these attributes to construct women's and men's health and disease causality differently. For instance, the scope of women's health has historically been reduced to reproductive issues pertaining to menstruation, conception, pregnancy, childbirth, and menopause—what one feminist called a "boobs and tubes" approach to women's health (Morris, 1999).

One striking example of *pathologization* is the medical research on postpartum depression that constructs women's experience as a psychiatric illness rather than as a health problem that is understandable in the context of our lives, relationships, limited social supports, and institutionalized expectations that perpetuate the mother ideal. Natasha Mauthner (1999) calls for a "relational reframing" of postpartum depression based on her qualitative study of 40 women whose experiences she characterizes as a "normal" response to the "public-world losses of identity, autonomy, independence, power, and paid employment."

Gender is just one of the social hierarchies that is pathologized in ways that negatively affect the health of diverse groups of women. Medical research also re-inscribes other categories of social difference as if they were independent biological facts. In keeping with Cartesian dualism, medical discourse constructs dis/ability, and sexual orientation (to name two) as discrete, dichotomous attributes and demographic variables. What results from this reductionist approach is the pathologizing of (for instance) proactive, rational (healthy) male minds in opposition to passive, emotional (weak) female minds; or able (superior, healthy) bodies in opposition to disabled (dysfunctional, unhealthy) bodies; or straight (breeding) bodies in opposition to gay (sexually unnatural) bodies. Consequently, women's bodies and minds that are structured or function differently are pathologized as defective, diseased, or burdensome rather than as reflecting part of the diverse human condition (Burke and Eichler, 2006).

A second way that existing hierarchies are maintained is through victim blaming or faulting the survivor, rather than focusing on the perpetrator or systemic circumstance as a cause of a health problem (Burke and Eichler, 2006). Research on intimate partner violence is an important area of health research that provides many examples of this bias. Violence against women results in physical, emotional, and economic injury, permanent disability, and death and is, therefore, a significant health issue (Campbell, 2002). Statistics Canada (2000) data indicate that 78 percent of female survivors are assaulted by someone they know and 58 percent of female homicide victims are murdered by a family member. More recent data revealed that an estimated 653 000 women aged 15 years and over—approximately 7 percent of Canadian women—reported intimate partner violence between 1999 and 2004. More than half (56 percent) of these women were between 18 and 34 years and of child-bearing years (AuCoin, 2005).

Research on co-dependence put the problem of intimate partner violence squarely with women's problematic psychosocial development, implying that women contribute to their own victimization. Although the theory was widely criticized by feminists and has fallen from academic favour, the concept continues to bubble up in popular discourse. Similarly, research on women's help-seeking behaviour and readiness to change investigates a woman's role in maintaining the pattern of intimate partner violence. Instead of asking, "Why doesn't she leave?" (blaming the victim) unbiased research would ask, "Why don't we have more legal and social interventions that protect women from the perpetrators of violence?" Reframing the research question is one way to challenge rather than maintain social hierarchies in health research.

Failing to Examine Differences

Failing to examine differences is the second type of bias problem and involves ignoring or being insensitive to differences in a context in which they are, in fact, significant (Burke and Eichler, 2006). The solution to this bias problem is to acknowledge the differences between the sexes and accommodate them. This problem is found in everyday medical practice where women with heart disease are inappropriately treated like men and evaluated using a clinical profile developed through empirical studies of men only. Because more recent research has shown that women do not typically present with the same clinical picture as men, women are misdiagnosed, appropriate treatment is delayed, and they have more complications (Cunnius and Kerstein, 2002).

This type of bias also occurs when physicians assume that women patients can and will assert themselves in ways that are similar to men. Focus group interviews with women indicate that women want to participate in making treatment choices but need structural supports to do so (Health Canada, 1999: 16). These findings confirm that power differences exist in the physician–client (traditionally male–female) relationship but do not acknowledge that female physicians tend to have less power within the health care system and in the physician–patient relationship than male physicians (Kilminster et al., 2007). Moreover, dichotomizing this relationship along gender lines ignores differences in education, income, social status, and race/ethnicity that exist in both physician and patient groups. There is significant diversity in the Canadian physician population as increased numbers of women and minoritized groups are entering medicine (Kilminster et al., 2007). Significant diversity is also evident in the patient population with evidence indicating that racialized and newcomer women tend to participate less than white women or men in making decisions about their own health (O'Mahony and Donnelly, 2007; Weber and Parra-Medina, 2003). These examples illustrate the importance of considering the interlocking categories of social difference between women and men and among groups of women. In these contexts, differences among women and between women and men are significant and need to be considered and accommodated.

Double Standard

The third type of bias is the double standard, and the solution to this problem is to acknowledge the similarities between the sexes and treat people equitably. The most common form of expression involves different treatment of a subordinated or non-dominant group where that treatment reinforces a subordinate position (Burke and Eichler, 2006). In other words, an identical or substantially equal situation, trait, or behaviour is evaluated and treated differently based on gender, race, ability, or other social difference. For instance, research on unintended pregnancies and the public education programmes and media messages that emerge from it have traditionally been directed at young women and girls (Greene, 2008). These messages reinforce the social expectation that we are respon-sible for contraception and have the power to negotiate safer sex. In this case, prospective adolescent parents are treated differently in a situation that disadvantages females.

Another expression of this bias is the exclusion or under-representation of females in drug trials (Burke and Eichler, 2006). Levin (2005) describes the consequences of ignoring what he calls the obvious genetic basis for sex differences. The final report of the Physicians Health Study issued in 1989 stated that low-dose aspirin reduced first heart attacks by 44 percent, although these findings were based on an all-male study population. The finding received widespread attention, with physicians prescribing and the general public self-prescribing aspirin as if its preventative value applied to both men and women. However, Levin (2005) reports that the Women's Health Study conducted 15 years later found that aspirin does not, in fact, have a similar protective effect in women. Levin's comments raise concerns about the validity of medical research that excludes women while over-generalizing results to both women and men and indicate that research biases can result in serious negative consequences for women. Although not a direct result of this case, guidelines regulating drug companies have been amended, requiring that women be included in drug trials in the same proportion as that expected to use the drug.

The double standard is also expressed when women are over-identified with issues affecting family, household, or procreation (Burke and Eichler, 2006). This form of bias results in the over-representation of women and under-representation of men in research about (for instance) parenting, contraception, and fertility. This bias is premised on two notions: First, men and women are assumed to operate in separate life spheres and there-fore men are inappropriately excluded from research located in the so-called private sphere. Second, the supposed uniqueness of women's biology is assumed to require "spe-cial types of care and specific kinds of research" (Statistics Canada, 2000: 47). The critical reader who asks, "Unique, special, and specific as compared to whom?" must conclude that such research assumes a masculinist perspective that essentializes and naturalizes women's bodies.

To summarize this section, the BIASFREE Framework is an important tool for unearthing biases and questioning evidence produced by clinical and epidemiological research. The next section looks at various aspects of girls' and women's health. Attention is given to alternative ways of understanding the links between subjective, embodied health experiences and the biological, social, and environmental factors that shape our health.

UNDERSTANDING WOMEN'S HEALTH IN CONTEXT

This section is organized around the 12 health determinants (PHAC, 2003) and draws on qualitative studies of women's health and quantitative data from health information databases.[4] Two cautionary notes are included here for the critical reader. First, many health information databases that claim to measure health actually use indicators of disease (such as mortality and morbidity rates[5]) or indicators of the quality of health care services. Currently, there is no widely accepted set of indicators that combines subjective and objective

4   Unless otherwise noted, all statistics are drawn from a gender-based analysis of Statistics Canada sur-vey data published in 2000.
5   Mortality rates refer to the frequency of deaths in a given population; morbidity rates refer to the inci-dence of disease within a given population.

expressions of health with ideas and practices of health as they are given meaning in structural and historical contexts. Second, the problematic practices associated with the population health model do not necessarily preclude the use of health determinants as a way of organizing a discussion of women's health. We should assume that health determinants are social and political constructs that tend to simplify and compartmentalize factors that, in the living of them, are complex and deeply interconnected. Furthermore, let us continue with an explicit feminist theory of society that assumes there is a dynamic interrelationship among social vulnerabilities that results in disparities in health status and quality of life, and the biological and social processes through which these differences are expressed.

Gender

The first health determinant we examine is gender, which PHAC (2003) defines as "an array of society-determined roles, personality traits, attitudes, behaviours, values, relative power and influence that society ascribes to the two sexes on a differential basis." Gender determines differences in health status and the types of health issues faced by men and women. PHAC also recognizes that there are gendered norms that influence health practices and priorities.

Women make up more than half the Canadian population and have one of the longest life expectancies[6] in the world, an average 81.4 years for females born in 1996 (compared with 76 years for men). This is a significant increase from (for example) 1921, when life expectancy for girls at birth was 61 years. Life expectancy is not, in itself, an indicator of good health. Although Canadian females are living longer than our male counterparts, we are more likely to live with chronic diseases,[7] stress-related illnesses, and injuries relating to intimate partner violence. While significant, these measures do not help us understand the complex differences in health and illness experiences between women and men or among groups of women.

Challenging the gender homogeneity suggested by gender as a demographic variable reveals another picture of health. Life expectancy among Aboriginal peoples is significantly lower than the overall Canadian averages due to higher rates of infant mortality, suicide, and fatal accidents. Women living in poverty, Aboriginal women, women living with disabilities, and women who hold certain jobs have shorter life expectancies and fare less well on quality-of-life indicators than women as a whole. Aboriginal women, especially those living in isolated northern communities, have a higher incidence of preventable disease because of limited access to clean water, adequate sanitation, adequate income, safe housing, and a varied and nutritious diet (Morris, 2001, 2005).

Biology and Genetic Endowment

The combination of biology and genetic endowment is a health determinant that refers to the basic organic body structures and their genetic predisposition to some diseases and illnesses (PHAC, 2003). Both the biomedical and the population health models recognize that biological factors affect women's mortality and morbidity rates. Both agree there are

---

6   Life expectancy is the average length of life predicted for those persons born in any given year.

7   Statistics Canada defines a chronic illness as any disorder that has been diagnosed by a health professional and lasts for at least 6 months.

some physiological differences between men and women, but the extent of these differences, as well as the extent to which these differences account for disparities in health status, is in dispute.

Feminists argue that bodies and bodily processes and experiences cannot be isolated from the social and historical contexts that give them meaning. Feminist literature on embodiment, for example, celebrates the healthy female body as a source of pleasure and satisfaction. In contrast, the intermingling of cultural and medical discourses on body image and body weight represent the female body as an object of male desire, a predictably unpredictable emotional vessel, and an appropriate site for medical intervention. Every day, women and girls are bombarded by conflicting and dangerous messages about our bodies. A multibillion-dollar weight loss industry makes money on misplaced dreams while competing with a multibillion-dollar fast food industry pushing easy meal solutions for busy women. Add to this biomedical research linking obesity in people as young as 3 years old with long-term health problems such as heart disease, stroke, and diabetes that affect life expectancy and quality of life (Canning, Courage, and Frizzell, 2004; Filate et al., 2003).

Obesity is a serious health problem for some women. According to the WHO standards, 24 percent of Canadian women are overweight (cited in Morris, 2001). However, a far greater percentage of women express some level of dissatisfaction with their bodies. Disordered eating, plastic surgery, and skin bleaching and tanning (each associated with negative health outcomes) are a few expressions of this dissatisfaction. The tension between promoting healthy practices and the obsession to attain a flawless, thin, youthful, white body ideal is part of the web of social contradictions that makes women's bodies a site of social control and capitalist enterprise. Critical examination of these issues calls into question medical research that reduces obesity to a body problem linked to genetic predisposition and lifestyle choices.

Income and Social Status

Income and social status are arguably the most sensitive predictor of health and life expectancy. Income levels determine living conditions and access to safe housing and healthy diets. Social status is linked to the degree of control and autonomy in decision-making and the range of options for dealing with stressful life circumstances. The accumulated burden of poverty and low social status is often associated with poorer health status (PHAC, 2003).

How is poverty measured in Canada? The low income cut-off or LICO is the indicator of poverty used most widely by Canadian social policy experts.[8] Individuals and families are classified as low-income if they spend, on average, at least 20 percent more of their pre-tax income than the average Canadian does on food, shelter, and clothing. The indicator takes into account the number of family members and the size of the urban or rural area where the family lives (National Council of Welfare, 2002).

---

8   There is active debate about the use of the LICO. Some policy agencies such as the conservative Fraser Institute argue that the LICO defines poverty too broadly and therefore defines too many people as poor. Others such as the Canadian Council on Social Development lobby for indicators that are even broader than the LICO. Finally, Canadian government documents consistently assert that the LICO is not an official poverty line nor should it be used for that purpose (Statistics Canada, 2000: 140).

Wealthy women live the longest and have greater access to resources to age well. There are many more poor than rich women and more poor women than men in all age groups, and they do not enjoy the same range of options for good health. Women over 65 years, women living with disabilities, Aboriginal women, and lone mothers are among Canada's poorest. First coined by Diana Pearce (1978), the phrase *feminization of poverty* refers to the income inequality and inadequate financial and social support that leaves many single, widowed, and divorced women with dependent children living in poverty.

Although poverty is a predictor of poor health, income inequality—the gap between the haves and the have-nots—is a predictor of poorer health for the whole population. Narrowing the gap between the rich and the poor improves health status across all income groups (Wilkinson, cited in Morris, 2001). With each incremental improvement that reduces the gap in income and social status, population health status improves. Moreover, small improvements in income at the low end of the income scale translate into significant improvements in health for those living in poverty. Despite this evidence, priority is given to changing individual health practices and channelling more dollars into the health care system rather than to healthy public policies that would, for instance, increase the minimum wage. A study published by the National Council of Welfare (2002) reported that welfare benefits in the Atlantic provinces declined in "real dollar" terms by as much as 23 percent between 1991 and 2001 when governments at all levels instituted social security reforms in an effort to reduce deficits and public spending. One Manitoba-wide campaign launched by the Canadian Women's Health Network (2001/2002) announced that "poverty is hazardous to women's health." The message directed at policy-makers and the general public pushed for health policies and programs that take down the structures that sustain poverty rather than dealing with the outcomes arising from them.

Physical Environments

The natural environment (water, air, food, and soil) and the built environment (housing, sanitation and waste disposal, and the design of communities and transportation) influence physical and psychological well-being and constitute another health determinant (PHAC, 2003).

Let's look at the issue of clean water and the differential treatment of a similar crisis in two populations. Data from the 1980s indicated that virtually all Canadians living in urban (100 percent) and rural (99 percent) areas had access to clean water (WHO, cited in Stienstra and Roberts, 1995). The same was not true for Canadian Aboriginal women and their families living on reserves. At the World Conference on Women held in Nairobi in 1985, the Canadian federal government voiced its commitment to women's equality and guaranteed safe water for all Canadian women by pledging to introduce a safe drinking water act in 1990. Ten years passed without meeting that commitment. In 1995, the federal government earmarked $250 million to improve the quality of drinking water delivered to 92 percent of existing on-reserve homes. This amount fell short of meeting a basic need of women and their families living off reserves (Stienstra and Roberts, 1995). Fast forward to May 2000 and the public outrage that ensued when seven people died and 2000 more became ill as a result of *E. coli*–contaminated water in Walkerton, a small rural, predominantly white, southern Ontario community. Within months, the clean water supply was restored. Within 2 years, a public inquiry recommended that the Ontario government spend $280 million to implement a safe drinking water act (CBC News Online, 2002). That promise didn't protect the women

and families living in Kashechewan, a remote northern Ontario Cree First Nation community. In 2005, the federal and provincial governments temporarily evacuated the residents
because the water was contaminated by *E. coli*. Today, women and their families living in
many Aboriginal communities and in rural communities in Newfoundland and Labrador
continue to live without access to safe indoor running water. A health crisis in one community is addressed within a couple of years while marginalized communities remain in crisis
for decades.

The differential impact of decision-making on women's health is also evident when
looking at housing, a feature of the built environment. Women with low incomes face long
waiting lists for co-operative and public housing units (McCracken and Watson, 2004).
Band-aid solutions such as overcrowded homeless shelters are a breeding ground for the
spread of tuberculosis and other communicable diseases. To better meet women's needs,
McCracken and Watson recommend that all levels of government adopt GBA when developing and evaluating all new housing policies and programs.

Consider also the configuration of spaces where women live and work. Few workplaces provide women with safe facilities to regularly engage in physical activities during
or after work hours (Morris, 2001). With the exception of walking and cycling, there are
few inexpensive and safe options for low-income women. Urban neighbourhoods often
lack community centres, public parks, hiking trails, and cycling paths needed for such
activities. Where these are available, many lone mothers do not have dedicated personal
time and child care to engage in regular physical exercise. Here again, we see that some
women, depending on where they live and work, have fewer options for making so-called
healthy lifestyle choices.

Employment and Working Conditions

Employment is another health determinant. Unemployment and underemployment as well
as the physical and psychosocial conditions encountered at paid and unpaid work have a
significant impact on mental, social, and physical health (PHAC, 2003). There are several
factors to consider when looking at how work affects women's health.

Women's occupational health issues are obscured by a research bias that assumes that
women's concerns are captured by studying male workers (Messing and Stellman, 2006).
To have an income, some women (and men) work in unhealthy environments that predispose them to acute and chronic illnesses. Newcomers, racialized women, and those with
little formal education or unrecognized professional credentials are more likely to be
unemployed or underemployed or to be concentrated in "job ghettos." These workplaces
are characterized by repetitive and monotonous tasks and shift work with low wages, little
autonomy, and limited or no health benefits or opportunities for promotion (Ng, 2000;
Reitmanova and Gustafson, 2008a). Consider also that women and men face different hazards because of differences in the kinds of work each do and that women's working conditions can differ from men's even within the same setting.

Women working in female-dominated workplaces can experience a number of negative health outcomes. The most common female-dominated workplace is the home, which
is a common site of accidental poisonings, injuries, and deaths, and (as previously mentioned) abuse, violence, and homicide.

Sweatshops in the Toronto garment district exploit the labour of newcomer women
who work under appalling physical conditions for extended hours doing piecework that

results in income below minimum wage (Ng, 2000). Hairdressers, cashiers, and retail and service workers who stand for long hours experience varicose veins and back, leg, and foot problems that can become chronic health concerns. Flight attendants, health care providers, teachers, and child-care workers are exposed to contagious diseases, stress, and violence in the daily performance of their work. Clerical workers spend long hours in ergonomically poor workspaces where they are subject to repetitive stress injuries, excessive noise, and poor ventilation and lighting. Until the recent ban on smoking in public spaces, women working in restaurants and bars were subject to second-hand smoke and increased risk of lung cancer.

Male-dominated unions and other governing structures tend to address more visible health and safety issues, leaving these normal routes of redress less available to women to take up gendered concerns (Messing and Stellman, 2006). One example of women's effective advocacy for better working conditions is a group of American nurses who, through the collective power of their union, lobbied to implement common-sense solutions to reduce their exposure to hazardous workplace substances linked to cancer, birth defects, asthma, and other diseases (Converso, Martin, and Markle-Elder, 2007).

Education and Literacy

Education and literacy are closely linked to employment and income and social status. Formal education equips women and girls with knowledge, skills (including literacy), and a greater degree of control, mastery, and autonomy, all linked to better health status (PHAC, 2003).

Although women with a university education earn more, on average, than women without post-secondary education, women earn less than their male counterparts at all levels of educational attainment. For example, women with university degrees earn about 74 percent as much as their male colleagues. Newcomer women with formal education in health professions, for instance, are restricted in their access to the labour market because of credential and language requirements and other structural barriers. These barriers negatively affect the physical and mental well-being of women who accept a lower-paying job to support their families while simultaneously providing cheap but competent labour within a restructured health care system (Guruge, Donner, and Morrison, 2000; Lum and Williams, 2000; Murray, Gien, and Solberg, 2003).

Young mothers are more likely than their older counterparts to have lower levels of educational achievement, lower levels of workforce participation, lower income, higher levels of welfare dependence, and (not surprisingly, given their stressful economic and social circumstances) higher levels of mental health disorders (Boden, Fergusson, and Horwood, 2008). International studies recommend building mothers' academic literacy skills as a way to increase their comprehension of health messages and uptake of healthier behaviours, to help them make the transition to employment, and ultimately to improve overall maternal and child health (Rowe et al., 2005; Schnell-Anzola, Rowe, and LeVine, 2005).

Social Environments

The vitality, stability, safety, and cohesiveness of a community contribute to a healthy social environment and influence the health and well-being of individuals and populations (PHAC, 2003). *Social capital* is a term that refers to the relative degree of neighbourhood integration, alienation or safety, political participation, social trust, and trust in institutions available to groups or communities. Women who have positive connections to family and community tend to lead happier, healthier lives. Those who live in a supportive social environment with relatively high levels of social capital tend to have positive disease responses. When ill or injured, a healthy social environment speeds recovery.

The importance of social capital, specifically social trust and trust in institutions, may contribute to differences in the use of health services and morbidity rates between lesbians and straight women. Lesbians are more likely to smoke and use alcohol and to be at greater risk for some cancers. At the same time, lesbians are less likely to seek traditional health care. Individual factors such as physicians' heterosexist practices and women's fear of disclosing sexual identity are barriers to use of health care services. Structural factors that create a hostile social environment, such as exclusionary clinical environments and institutionalized homophobia, are also barriers to use of services. A supportive social environment where lesbians feel safe with disclosure improves health service use and may potentially improve health outcomes and reduce morbidity rates for some diseases (Steele, Tinmouth, and Lu, 2006).

Another example of the impact of social environment on women's health relates to the financial and human costs of a cancer diagnosis. Cancer treatment is covered by provincial health insurance, but other costs associated with a cancer diagnosis are not. Even third-party payers do not cover indirect costs such as lost wages and loss of caregiver income or out-of-pocket expenses for drug dispensing fees, Gravol and other non-prescription drugs, transportation and parking at outpatient clinics, and child care (Mathews and Basky, n.d.). Consequently, Aboriginal women, low-income women, and older women, who live in precarious social environments with less access to health resources, face greater challenges with recovery and are at increased risk of premature death due to breast and gynecological cancers (Gould et al., 2005).

Culture

Culture is another health determinant that refers to the health issues of people who are marginalized, stigmatized, or undervalued by the dominant culture (PHAC, 2003). As a variable in medical research, the term is variously used when referring to race, ethnicity, Aboriginal status, immigrant status, language, country of birth, and the like. Culture is a contested term among feminists because it encompasses such a range of meanings that the term is rendered meaningless while simultaneously serving as a code word for race or "Other" status (Gustafson, 2007, 2008).

Living in a racist society affects all of us but is experienced differently by various groups of women. Racism and social marginalization can lead to feelings of powerlessness and hopelessness among Aboriginal and racialized women. For some women, racism is a chronic stressor that negatively affects health, as Vines and colleagues (2001) found in their study of Black women and disease outcomes. Newcomer women whose first language is not English or French have difficulty gaining access to and negotiating the Canadian health care system, developing a comfortable relationship between themselves and a care provider, understanding treatment regimes, and giving informed consent (Guruge, Donner, and Morrison, 2000; Reitmanova and Gustafson, 2008b).

Feminists propose a number of strategies for improving the health of racialized women and their families: developing culturally and linguistically sensitive health services, facilitating women's participation and representation in decision-making organizations, and forging working alliances among feminist activists, bureaucrats, and specific communities of minoritized women to implement change that begins from women's expressed needs (Guruge and Collins, 2008; Guruge, Donner, and Morrison, 2000).

Healthy Childhood Development

Healthy childhood development refers to the experiences that influence cognitive and physical development, school readiness, and long-term health and well-being (PHAC, 2003). What happens during these formative years from conception to age 6 has long-term impacts. Although healthy childhood development is linked to family income and family status, physical and emotional environment, and access to medical and dental care, it is also a health determinant in its own right.

Research has been used to blame women for our health practices, health status, and the impact of both on our children without considering the circumstances of our lives. Women tend to have less income than men, with lone-mother families among the poorest. Women from households with ongoing issues of food scarcity have significantly less income and less education than women from fully food-secure households (Laraia et al., 2006). In food-insecure households, women before and during pregnancy and breastfeeding may not get sufficient amounts of dietary iron, iodine, folic acid, and vitamin A to support healthy fetal and infant development. Poorly nourished and food-insecure women are more likely to bear stillborn, preterm, low-birth-weight, or neurologically impaired infants. Low birth weight is an important predictor of future poor health. Children living in food-insecure households have less access to adequate amounts of nutritious food. Women, especially low-income women, typically feed their children before themselves, lowering their own resistance to illness (McIntyre et al., 2003; Tarasuk, McIntyre, and Li, 2007).

Kahn and colleagues (2005) argue that disparities in women's income, social status, pre-pregnancy health, and general well-being are dynamically connected to children's short-term and long-term development and behaviour. Public health programs and services that consider the material circumstances of women's lives would address the urgent health needs of women and disadvantaged families, the negative impact on child development, and the reproduction of social disparities across generations.

Personal Health Practices and Coping Skills

This health determinant refers to lifestyle issues or those actions that individuals take to promote health, prevent disease, and cope with problems and challenges (PHAC, 2003). Feminists agree that social and material location influences the range of choices reasonably available to individuals and the range of options for responding to health challenges. The more supportive and inclusive the social and physical environment, the healthier the community and the more options available to women to live healthy lives.

As women age, we are less likely than younger women to describe ourselves as being in good health. This may be due in part to the increased prevalence of chronic illness and degenerative conditions that limit activity, decrease quality of life, and may lead to hospitalization and death. Statistics Canada (2000) reports the most common chronic problems among females 12 years and older are non-food allergies, chronic pain, arthritis or rheumatism, back problems, high blood pressure, migraines, and asthma. Compare this to women's view of their most immediate health concerns: Stress, anxiety, and depression top the list (two of which are not even considered chronic illnesses by the Statistics Canada definition), followed by migraines, arthritis, obesity, back problems, and blood pressure problems. Therefore women's most immediate health concerns are not those receiving medical research attention.

Smoking, alcohol and substance use, obesity, diet, and physical activity are a few of the lifestyle issues that get considerable attention in the media and in public health campaigns. Let's consider the medical research on physical activity. Regular exercise is linked with positive physical and mental health outcomes such as lower rates of heart disease, osteoporosis, and depression. Data from a 1996–1997 National Population Health Survey show that 60 percent of women are sedentary. Activity levels vary across age groups. Older women are generally less active than younger women and women in all age groups are generally less active than their male counterparts. The higher a woman's income the more likely she is to engage in healthy practices such as regular activity and in fewer risky behaviours such as smoking and binge drinking (Health Canada, 2003). How might we explain these differences?

Compared with men, women have less free time available for leisure activities. Married women who are employed full-time spend more time doing unpaid work and have less free time than their male counterparts. Having children affects the way that married women and men allocate their time. Although both groups experience a decrease in the amount of free time and sleep time, as well as changes in patterns of paid and unpaid work, women experience more dramatic changes and assume greater responsibility for unpaid household and caregiver work. Less time for leisure and self care and greater levels of stress are associated with poorer health. One of the factors that can ameliorate this burden and support health is family and social support. We turn to that health determinant next.

Social Support Networks

A social support network is an important health determinant that acts as a "buffer" against health problems (PHAC, 2003). Social participation and an established network of emotional support contribute to mental, physical, spiritual, and social well-being. Caring and respectful relationships with family, friends, and communities are important sources of satisfaction and support for problem solving and dealing with adversity. Let's focus on women and mental health.

Mental health is often measured using indicators of self-esteem or self-worth, sense of mastery and control, and perception of life as meaningful and manageable (Forbes, 2001). These measures locate mental health within the individual and place less emphasis on the systemic factors that structure women's lives and experiences differently from men's. For example, although women and men tend to have the similar levels of self-esteem, women are less likely to have a high sense of mastery. In a society in which social locations are linked to power, women more than men, and marginalized women more than women in general, face greater structural obstacles, leaving many women with good grounds for feeling less masterful.

Women also report higher rates of stress than men. This is connected to the increased *role complexity*, or the number of tasks such as family caregiving, that women are expected to assume (Statistics Canada, 2000: 111). Married mothers with full-time jobs are almost twice as likely as their counterparts without children to be severely time-stressed. By contrast, there is no difference in the incidence of severe time stress for employed married men with or without children. Restructured families and new family forms, as well as the resurgence of the discourse of traditional family values, are adding to women's mother work and may contribute to women's reports of higher rates of stress.

Many women are able to deal successfully with life's challenges most of the time. However, women are twice as likely as men to have a depressive episode (6 percent versus 3 percent). Young women (15–19 years old) are more likely than any other age group to exhibit symptoms of depression. Although a depressive episode may last an average of 5 weeks for women in this age group, women over 75 have symptoms lasting an average of 10 weeks. This latter group also accounts for the largest number of women hospitalized for mental illness. Although women are far less likely than men to complete suicide, suicide rates among Aboriginal women are significantly higher than in the general female population. One possible explanation is that women without an adequate social support network are less able to recover from mental health problems.

Health Services

The last health determinant, health services, refers to the continuum of care from secondary disease prevention (immunizations, breast screening) to disease and injury treatment (medicine for high blood pressure, surgical hip replacement). Access to physicians and other health care professionals and services is considered a cornerstone of biomedicine and a determinant of population health (PHAC, 2003).

Persisting rounds of rationalization and regionalization of health services across Canada have resulted in cuts in local services and longer waiting lines for emergency and specialty services. Women in northern and rural communities are especially hard hit with longer distances to travel for routine health care, childbirth, and cancer treatment, to name a few. One health issue of particular concern is access to safe abortions. The material inequalities under which some women in rural and northern communities negotiate unintended pregnancy contradicts the belief that abortion is available on demand in Canada (Fegan, 2002).

Women are the majority of the users of the health care system. As the numerical majority in the Canadian population, we use the system to access services for ourselves and family members. Women also constitute the majority of unpaid care providers as well as the majority of paid health care workers. Nursing is the single largest health professional group. Composed overwhelmingly (97 percent) of women, the nursing profession holds less institutionalized power, authority, and legitimacy than the traditionally male-dominated medical profession.

Over the last four decades, more women have gained entry into medical education, increasing from 17 percent in 1970 to 59 percent in 2005 (Gradstein, 2008). Women physicians continue to be under-represented in higher levels of the profession (Kilminster et al., 2007) and in authorship of published research (Jagsi et al., 2006). Women tend to perform better and are over-represented in certain specialties that are associated with women's traditional work such as psychiatry, pediatrics, and obstetrics and gynecology (Kilminster et al., 2007).

Gender differences in the practice of medicine and the interpretation of women's health issues play out between individual practitioners and patients. There is some evidence that female physicians are changing the day-to-day practice of medicine, emphasizing collaboration over compliance in decision-making about women's health issues (Kilminster et al., 2007). That said, Canadian physicians operate within a funding structure that ideologically and financially encourages a "magic bullet" approach to disease treatment and accords little value to health promotion and disease prevention strategies. For instance, opportunities for collaborative decision-making are fewer in a fee-for-services structure that makes a physician's income dependent on the quantity rather than the quality of interactions with clients.

Some women express their dissatisfaction with their physicians by opting out of unsatisfactory relationships. A health survey reports that two-thirds of Canadian women who changed doctors did so because they were dissatisfied with their doctor's attitude (cited in Health Canada, 1999: 17). Not all women have that option, such as those living in rural, northern, and isolated communities that face persistent physician shortages.

UNDERTAKING CHANGE: IN CANADA AND GLOBALLY

Canada is an acknowledged world leader in health promotion, producing key documents such as the Lalonde Report (1974) and the Ottawa Charter for Health Promotion (1986). This section examines Canada's role in addressing women's health issues nationally and globally. While at times we make good progress toward equity and social justice, at other times there is retreat and lost ground.

Equality is a core principle in the history of Canadian legislation and the medicare system. In the mid-1990s, the federal government acknowledged the need to invest equality with substantive meaning. In 1996, five Centres for Excellence in Women's Health were established with the mandate "to improve women's health, in part by enhancing the Canadian health system's understanding of and responsiveness to women and women's health issues" (Pederson, 2001: 1). These centres worked with community agencies to ask new questions and generate new knowledge about the realities of women's lives. One such partnership was the Aboriginal Women's Health and Healing Research Group, a national network of First Nations, Métis, and Inuit women researchers who focus on community-based health research about Aboriginal women, their families, and communities. A decade later, federal funding cuts threaten the work of the Centres and consequently support for this and other research groups.

Immigration policies, environmental degradation, and economic agreements such as NAFTA bind together the health of all global citizens. Committed and appropriate government action and increased public awareness are required to address the power inequities that result in global health inequities. Speaking at the 14th Annual International Congress on Women's Health Issues in Victoria, BC, Kathleen Mahoney, co-founder of the Women's Legal Education and Action Fund, called for a rights-based health model to protect and promote the health of women, some of whom are the most vulnerable and at-risk populations around the world (Wang and Pillai, 2001).

Stephen Lewis, the UN Secretary-General's special envoy for HIV/AIDS in Africa and a commissioner of the WHO's Commission on Social Determinants of Health, addressed delegates at the Humanities and Social Sciences Federation of Canada Congress in 2006. Lewis urged Canadians to pay greater attention to health issues faced by women and girls around the globe. Lewis's attention to gender differences stands in stark contrast to the relative neglect of girls' and women's issues at the 15th International AIDS Conference held in Toronto later that year. Women continue to be under-represented in AIDS/HIV research despite evidence that women experience a disproportionately higher HIV burden. Women currently account for half of all HIV infections globally, as we are at higher risk of infection through intercourse and have a lower survival rate than men. Women are more likely than men to drop out of school or lose paid work and income to care for children and relatives with AIDS (Krisberg, 2004; Hawkins, 2006). Add to that the lack of attention at the conference and in the academic literature to women living with HIV during and after pregnancy (Rollins, 2006). The under-representation of women in HIV/AIDS research leaves important knowledge gaps concerning gender-sensitive technologies and treatment, health promotion, disease prevention, and other forms of support appropriate for women's social circumstances.

The United Nations adopted the Millennium Development Goals, advanced during the Millennium Summit in September 2000. The goals recognize that gender equality and women's empowerment are central to achieving sustainable development and combating poverty, hunger, and disease. One of the health goals is to combat the spread of HIV and reduce mortality and morbidity associated with AIDS. A second health goal is to reduce maternal and child mortality levels by two-thirds by 2015. Every year an estimated 500 000 mothers die from pregnancy-related causes. An estimated 4 million fetuses are stillborn and another 4 million die as neonates (within the first 4 weeks of life) from severe infections (26 percent) or asphyxia (23 percent) or because they are preterm (28 percent) (Lawn, Cousens, and Zupan, 2005).

The causes of maternal, neonatal, and child health are complex. Widespread and astonishing levels of poverty, famine, drought, and civil war (with the war crime of sexual violence) are decimating many countries and contributing to the unacceptably high levels of infant and maternal mortality. Almost all (99 percent) neonatal deaths occur in sub-Saharan Africa, south-central Asia and other low-income and middle-income countries of the global south. Yet most of the research on neonatal death focuses on the 1 percent of deaths that occur in rich countries of the global north (Lawn, Cousens, and Zupan, 2005). We do know that low birth weight and maternal complications in labour, both indirect causes of neonatal death, are strongly associated with poverty. Even though these deaths are preventable, little progress has been made in the past 10 to 15 years to reduce neonatal and maternal deaths globally.

There are some examples of feminist participatory action research that aim to improve maternal and child health. Unlike most community health and nutrition programs in countries that focus on women of reproductive age, Aubel and colleagues (2004) included Senegalese grandmothers. The study built on grandmothers' commitment to family well-being and their influential role in the household. Grandmothers integrated new information about decreased workload, improved diet, and breastfeeding practices into discussions they had with their pregnant and breastfeeding daughters. Over a 12-month period, the analysis of qualitative and quantitative data indicated that grandmothers positively influenced their daughters' health behaviours. Findings such as these demonstrate the importance of attending to power relations, gender, cultural context, and social support networks when introducing change.

Missing from the Millennium Development Goals is any mention of universal access to sexual and reproductive health information and services, which Sinding (2005) argues is essential to improving maternal and child health. Sexual and reproductive practices, especially around fertility and contraception, as well as access to information and health services are strongly influenced by religious belief in many countries (Gyimah, Takyi, and Addai, 2006). Again the possible solutions are complex. Some argue that respecting religious beliefs is imperative, while others argue for respecting evidence-based medical science. Some argue for clear and transparent legislation that permits service providers to distribute health information about fertility and contraception. Others argue for a rights-based approach to forming partnerships with and among women to ensure fair access to health services (Shaw, 2006; Wang and Pillai, 2001).

CONCLUSION

Critical feminists bring to the exploration of women and health an explicit theory of society that assumes the dynamic interrelationship among social vulnerabilities. This theoretical approach to women's health makes visible the disparities in health status and quality of life, and the biological and social processes through which these differences are expressed. Healthy public policy reduces social inequalities. This can mean affordable housing and a living wage for women living in poverty, and equitable access to education and employment for women with disabilities. Healthy public policy and programs begin at the local level, are driven by community needs, and are implemented through public participation. This can mean the maintenance of safe public spaces and affordable daycare for children and seniors that fills gaps in material and social needs. Developing linguistically and culturally appropriate services is another way to provide responsive and inclusive health services. Girls' and women's health is an equity and social justice issue in Canada and around the world.

Suggested Readings

Burke, Mary Anne, and Margrit Eichler. 2006. *The BIASFREE Framework: A practical tool for identifying and eliminating social biases in health research*. Geneva: Global Forum for Health Research. This booklet provides an introduction to the BIASFREE Framework with many examples drawn from the health literature. The value to the feminist reader is that it provides a tool for identifying and eliminating biases in all types of research.

Morrow, Marina, Olena Hankivshy, and Colleen Varcoe, eds. 2007. *Women's health in Canada: Critical perspectives on theory and policy*. Toronto: Univ. of Toronto Press. This rich collection of articles offers a feminist critique of health research methods, determinants of health, and other contemporary issues about women's health, our bodies, and our lives.

Poole, Nancy, and Lorraine Greaves, eds. 2007. *Highs & lows: Canadian perspectives on women and substance use*. Toronto: Canadian Association for Mental Health. Substance use is an important health, economic, and social issue in Canada. This book addresses the unique needs and circumstances of women with substance abuse problems from the perspective of health and social service providers, policy-makers, and women themselves.

Discussion Questions

1. What factors contribute to good health? Consider specific groups of women and girls: university students living with a disability; girls growing up in rural Kenyan communities; older lesbians; homeless pregnant teens; mothers living with HIV. What accounts for any differences in the emphasis you place on identified health determinants for each group?

2. How are the healthy body and the body beautiful conflated in the collective imagination? How do the print and visual media contribute to or contest the production of these images? Consider critically the 2008 Dove soap marketing campaign.

3. Compare and contrast the biomedical and the population health models using the example of women's mental health. Use a feminist lens to discuss the factors contributing to differences in mental health between groups of immigrant women and men and among groups of immigrant women.

4. Name and discuss one socio-structural factor that affects the health of women at your university or in your community. Identify a specific, related, and doable action or initiative that you and your peers might organize that would promote, protect, or improve women's health in this context.

Bibilography

Achterberg, Jeanne. 1990. *Woman as healer.* Boston: Shambhala.

Aubel, Judi, Ibrahima Toure, and Mamadou Diagne. 2004. Senegalese grandmothers promote improved maternal and child nutrition practices: The guardians of tradition are not averse to change. *Social Science & Medicine* 59(5): 945–959.

AuCoin, Kathy. 2005. Family violence in Canada: A statistical profile. Ottawa: Canadian Centre for Justice Statistics. **www.statcan.ca/english/freepub/85-224-XIE/85-224-XIE2005000.pdf**

Boden, Joseph M., David M. Fergusson, and L. John Horwood. 2008. Early motherhood and subsequent life outcomes. *Journal of Child Psychology & Psychiatry* 49(2): 151–160.

Boelen, Charles. 2002. A New paradigm for medical schools a century after Flexner's report. *Bulletin of the World Health Organization* 80(7): 592.

Burke, Mary Anne, and Margrit Eichler. 2006. The BIASFREE framework: A practical tool for identifying and eliminating social biases in health research. Geneva: Global Forum for Health Research. **www.globalforumhealth.org/filesupld/Bias%20free/English_BFF_FINAL.pdf**

Campbell, Jacquelyn C. 2002. Health consequences of intimate partner violence. *Lancet* 359(9314): 1331.

Canadian Research Institute for the Advancement of Women (CRIAW). 2006. Intersectional feminist frameworks: An emerging vision. Ottawa: CRIAW-ICREF. **www.criaw-icref.ca**

Canadian Women's Health Network (CWHN). 2001/2002. Poverty is hazardous to women's health—and we can do something about it. *CWHN Newsletter,* Fall/Winter 4/5. **www.cwhn.ca/network-reseau/5-1/5-1pg8.html**

Canning, P.M., M.L. Courage, and L.M. Frizzell. 2004. Prevalence of overweight and obesity in a provincial population of Canadian preschool children. *Canadian Medical Association Journal* 171(3): 243–244.

CBC News Online. 2002. *Inside Walkerton: A water tragedy.* **www.cbc.ca/news/indepth/walkerton/**. Accessed February 16, 2004.

Converso, Ann, Suzanne L. DeMass Martin, and Sara Markle-Elder. 2007. Is your hospital safe? *American Journal of Nursing* 107(2): 37–39.

Cunnius, Peter, and Morris Kerstein. 2002. The silent worker. *Emergency Medical Services* 31(6): 32.

Dei, George, et al., eds. 2000. *Indigenous knowledge in global contexts: Multiple readings of our world.* Toronto: OISE/Univ. of Toronto Press.

Ehrenreich, Barbara, and Deidre English. 1973. *Witches, midwives and nurses: A history of women healers*. New York: Feminist Press at City Univ. of New York.

Ehrenreich, Barbara, and Deidre English. 1978. *For her own good: 150 years of the experts' advice to women*. New York: Doubleday.

Eichler, Margrit, Diana L. Gustafson, and Monika Pompetzki. 1999. *Moving toward equality: Recognizing and eliminating gender bias in health research. A gender-based analysis tool and instructional manual developed for Health Canada*. Ottawa: Health Canada.

Epstein, Samuel S. 1998. *The politics of cancer revisited*. Fremont Centre, NY: East Ridge Press.

Fegan, E. 2002. Recovering women: Intimate images and legal strategy. *Social & Legal Studies* 11(2): 155.

Filate, W.A., et al. 2003. Regional variations in cardiovascular mortality in Canada. *Canadian Journal of Cardiology* 19(11): 1241–1248.

Filc, D. 2004. The medical text: Between biomedicine and hegemony. *Social Science & Medicine* 59(6): 1275–1285.

Forbes, Dorothy A. 2001. Enhancing mastery and sense of coherence: Important determinants of health in older adults. *Geriatric Nurse* 22(1): 29–32.

Foucault, Michel. 1973. *The birth of the clinic: An archaeology of medical perception*, tr. A.M. Sheridan Smith. London: Tavistock.

Gould, Judith, et al. 2005. How gender, poverty, age and Aboriginal identity matter in women's similar experience of breast and gynecological cancer. *Breast Cancer Info Exchange* 9(2): 5–9.

Gradstein, Roetka. 2008. Mothering in medicine: Parenting policies in Canadian medical education. *Atlantis* 32(2): 147–156.

Greene, Saara. 2008. Embodied exclusion: Young mothers' experiences of exclusion from formal and informal sexual health education. *Atlantis* 32(2): 124–135.

Guruge, Sepali, and Enid Collins. 2008. *Working with immigrant women: Issues and strategies for mental health professionals*. Toronto: Centre for Addiction and Mental Health.

Guruge, Sepali, Gail Donner, and Lynn Morrison. 2000. The impact of Canadian health care reform on recent women immigrants and refugees, in *Care and consequences: The impact of health reform,* ed. Diana L Gustafson, 222–242. Halifax: Fernwood.

Gustafson, Diana L. 2007. White on whiteness: Becoming radicalized about race. *Nursing Inquiry* 14(2): 153–161.

Gustafson, Diana L. 2008. Is sensitivity and tolerance enough? Theoretical approaches to caring for newcomer women with mental health problems, in *Working with women and girls in the context of migration and settlement*, eds. Sepali Guruge and Enid Collins, 39–63. Toronto: Centre for Addiction and Mental Health.

Gyimah, Stephen Obeng, Baffour K. Takyi, and Isaac Addai. 2006. Challenges to the reproductive-health needs of African women: On religion and maternal health utilization in Ghana. *Social Science & Medicine* 62(12): 2930–2944.

Hawkins, B. Denise. 2006. The face of AIDS: Overwhelmingly Black and female. *Diverse: Issues in Higher Education* 23(16): 10–11.

Health Canada. 1999. *Health Canada's women's health strategy*. Ottawa: Minister of Public Works and Government Services Canada. **www.hc-sc.gc.ca/pcb/whb**

Health Canada. 2003. *Women's health surveillance report: A multi-dimensional look at the health of Canadian women*. Ottawa: Canadian Institute for Health Information.

Inhorn, Marcia C., and K. Lisa Whittle. 2001. Feminism meets the "new" epidemiologies: Toward an appraisal of antifeminist biases in epidemiological research on women's health. *Social Science & Medicine* 53(5): 553–567.

Jagsi, Reshma, et al. 2006. The "gender gap" in authorship of academic medical literature—A 35-year perspective. *New England Journal of Medicine* 355(3): 281–287.

Kahn, Robert S., Kathryn Wilson, and Paul H. Wise. 2005. Intergenerational health disparities: Socioeconomic status, women's health conditions, and child behavior problems. *Public Health Reports* 120(4): 399–408.

Kilminster, Sue, et al. 2007. Women in medicine—is there a problem? A literature review of the changing gender composition, structures and occupational cultures in medicine. *Medical Education* 41(1): 39–49.

Krisberg, Kim. 2004. HIV/AIDS epidemic a growing threat to world population. *Nation's Health* 34(7): 1–12.

Laraia, Barbara A., et al. 2006. Psychosocial factors and socioeconomic indicators are associated with household food insecurity among pregnant women. *Journal of Nutrition* 136(1): 177–182.

Lawn, Joy E., Simon Cousens, and Jelka Zupan. 2005. 4 million neonatal deaths: When? Where? Why? *Lancet* 365(9462): 891–900.

Levin, Richard I. 2005. The puzzle of aspirin and sex. *New England Journal of Medicine* 352(13): 1366–1368.

Lum, Janet M., and A. Paul Williams. 2000. Professional fault lines: Nursing in Ontario after the Regulated Health Professions Act, in *Care and consequences: The impact of health reform*, ed. Diana L Gustafson, 49–71. Halifax, NS: Fernwood.

Lupton, Deborah. 2003. *Medicine as culture*, 2d ed. London: Sage.

Mathews, Maria, and Greg Basky. n.d. *Closer to home. The burden of out-of-pocket expenses on cancer patients in Newfoundland and Labrador*. Available from Division of Community Health, Health Science Centre, Memorial University of Newfoundland, St. John's, NL, A1B 3V6.

Mauthner, Natasha S. 1999. Women and depression: Qualitative research approaches. *Canadian Psychology* 40(2): 143–161.

McCracken, Molly, and Gail Watson. 2004. Women need safe, stable, affordable housing: A study of social, private and co-op housing in Winnipeg. Prairie Women's Health Centre of Excellence, February. **www.pwhce.ca/safeHousing.htm**

McIntyre, Lynn, et al. 2003. Do low-income lone mothers compromise their nutrition to feed their children? *Canadian Medical Association Journal* 168(6): 686–691.

Messing, Karen, and Jeanne Mager Stellman. 2006. Sex, gender and women's occupational health: The importance of considering mechanism. *Environmental Research*, special issue on *Women's Occupational and Environmental Health* 101(2): 149–162.

Morgan, Kathryn Pauly. 1998. Contested bodies, contested knowledges: Women, health, and the politics of medicalization, in *The politics of women's health*, ed. Susan Sherwin, 83–121. Philadelphia: Temple Univ. Press.

Morris, Marika. 1999. *Shaping women's health research: Scope and methodologies*. Report prepared for the Made to Measure: Designing Research, Policy and Action Approaches to Eliminate Gender Inequity National Symposium, Halifax, NS. **www.acewh.dal.ca/eng/reports/morris.pdf**

Morris, Marika. 2001. *Women, health and action: A fact sheet*. Canadian Research Institute on the Advancement of Women. **www.criaw-icref.ca/indexFrame_e.htm**

Morris, Marika. 2005. *Women and poverty: A fact sheet,* 3d ed. Canadian Research Institute on the Advancement of Women. **www.criaw-icref.ca/indexFrame_e.htm**

Murray, Cynthia L., Lan Gien, and Shirley M. Solberg. 2003. A comparison of the mental health of employed and unemployed women in the context of a massive layoff. *Nurse Educator* 37(2): 55–72.

National Council of Welfare. 2002. *Welfare incomes, 2000 and 2001*. Ottawa: National Council of Welfare. **www.ncwcnbes.net/en/publications/pub-116.html**. Accessed August 28, 2008.

Ng, Roxana. 2000. Restructuring gender, race and class relations: The case of garment workers and labour adjustment, in *Restructuring caring labour: Discourse, state practice and everyday life*, ed. Sheila Neysmith, 226–245. Toronto: Oxford Univ. Press.

O'Mahony, Joyce M., and Tam T. Donnelly. 2007. Health care providers' perspective of the gender influences on immigrant women's mental health care experiences. *Issues in Mental Health Nursing* 28(10): 1171–1188.

Osler, William. 1921. *The evolution of modern medicine*, ed. Fielding H. Garrison. New Haven: Yale Univ. Press. **http://etext.virginia.edu/toc/modeng/public/OslEvol.html**

Pearce, Diana. 1978. The feminization of poverty: Women work and welfare. *The Urban and Social Change Review* 11(1/2): 28–36.

Pederson, Ann. 2001. What's policy got to do with it? *Centres for Excellence in Women's Health Bulletin* 2(1): 1, 3. **www.cewh-cesf.ca/PDF/RB/bulletin-vol2no1EN.pdf**

Public Health Agency of Canada (PHAC). 2003. *Population health—determinants of health*. Public Health Agency of Canada. **www.phac-aspc.gc.ca/ph-sp/phdd/determinants/index.html#determinants**

Rail, Geneviève, and Natalie Beausoleil. 2003. Introduction to "health panic and women's health." *Atlantis* 27(2): 1–5.

Raphael, Dennis. 2000. The question of evidence in health promotion. *Health Promotion International* 15(4): 355–367.

Raphael, Dennis, and Toba Bryant. 2002. The limitations of population health as a model for a new public health. *Health Promotion International* 17(2): 189–199.

Reitmanova, Sylvia, and Diana L. Gustafson. 2008a. Mental health needs of visible minority immigrants in a small urban center: Recommendations for policy makers and service providers. *Journal of Immigrant and Minority Health*. **www.ncbi.nlm.nih.gov/pubmed/18266107**. Accessed August 2, 2008.

Reitmanova, Sylvia, and Diana L. Gustafson. 2008b. "They can't understand it": Maternity health and care needs of immigrant Muslim women in St. John's, Newfoundland. *Maternal and Child Health Journal* 12(1): 101–111.

Rollins, Nigel. 2006. Toronto AIDS conference: Where were the children? *Lancet* 368(9543): 1236–1237.

Rowe, Meredith L., et al. 2005. How does schooling influence maternal health practices? Evidence from Nepal. *Comparative Education Review* 49(4): 512.

Schnell-Anzola, Beatrice, Meredith L. Rowe, and Robert A. LeVine. 2005. Literacy as a pathway between schooling and health-related communication skills: A study of Venezuelan mothers. *International Journal of Educational Development* 25(1): 19–37.

Shaw, Dorothy J. 2006. Women's right to health and the Millennium Development Goals: Promoting partnerships to improve access. *International Journal of Gynecology & Obstetrics* 9: 207–215.

Sinding, Steven W. 2005. Keeping sexual and reproductive health at the forefront of global efforts to reduce poverty. *Studies in Family Planning* 36(2): 140–143.

Statistics Canada. 2000. *Women in Canada: A gender-based statistical report.* Catalogue no. 89-503-XPE. Ottawa: Ministry of Industry.

Steele, Leah S., Jill M. Tinmouth, and Annie Lu. 2006. Regular health care use by lesbians: A path analysis of predictive factors. *Family Practice* 23(6): 631–636.

Stienstra, Deborah, and Barbara Roberts. 1995. *Strategies for the year 2000: A woman's handbook.* Halifax, NS: Fernwood.

Tarasuk, Valerie, Lynn McIntyre, and Jinguang Li. 2007. Low-income women's dietary intakes are sensitive to the depletion of household resources in one month. *Journal of Nutrition* 137(8): 1980–1987.

Vines, A.I., et al. 2001. Development and reliability of a telephone-administered perceived racism scale (TPRS): A tool for epidemiological use. *Ethnicity and Disease* 11(2): 251–262.

Walters, Vivienne. 1992. Women's views of their main health problems. *Canadian Journal of Public Health* 83(5): 371–375.

Walters, Vivienne. 1993. Stress, anxiety and depression: Women's accounts of their health problems. *Social Science and Medicine* 36(4): 393–402.

Wang, Guang-zhen, and Vijayan K. Pillai. 2001. Women's reproductive health: A gender-sensitive human rights approach. *Acta Sociologica* 44(3): 231–242.

Weber, Lynn, and Deborah Parra-Medina. 2003. Intersectionality and women's health: Charting a path to eliminating health disparities. *Advances in Gender Research* 7: 181–230.

World Health Organization (WHO). 2006. *Commission on social determinants of health.* Geneva: World Health Organization.

CHAPTER 12

Women and Religion: Female Spirituality, Feminist Theology, and Feminist Goddess Worship[1]

Johanna H. Stuckey

AIMS AND SCOPE

For the past few decades, religion and spirituality have been areas of increasing feminist concern. This chapter will acquaint readers briefly with the importance of female spirituality and examine how spiritual feminists handle the main issues in three old religious traditions and one new one. I have chosen to focus on the traditions that have had the most impact on Western consciousness: Christianity, Judaism, and Islam. They are, of course, all monotheistic. However, as a scholar of Goddess worship, I could not omit one of the fastest-growing new religions in the West: Feminist Goddess Worship.[2]

THE IMPORTANCE OF SPIRITUALITY FOR FEMINISTS

Many Western feminists and feminist theorists condemn religion as irredeemably patriarchal and think feminist spirituality at best quirky and at worst dangerous (Beattie, 1999; Magee, 2000: 101). So why study female spirituality and women's involvement in religions?

First, feminist commitment to recognizing diversity demands that we honour the myriad forms of women's spirituality and explore in "a positive way" women's spiritual experiences (King, 1989: xii).

Second, what could be more personal than the spiritual? Spiritual orientations and choices shape views of the world and are usually integral to political and social behaviour, yet feminist analysis often ignores them (King, 2000: 219–220).

Third, study of spirituality and religions reveals a major way in which male-dominated political systems have maintained control over women and men. In some societies, religion remains *the* central control mechanism. Gendered religious symbols continue to reflect and influence cultural and political assumptions.

Fourth, Western feminists have to eschew the male habit of separating women's (or people's) lives and selves into compartments. By now we know that mind and body are not unrelated, and spirituality is related to both.

Fifth, until recently, the study of religions, in the West particularly, has meant the study of male religious roles, male understandings of spirituality, and *male* symbols. Half the human population has not existed for most scholars of religious studies.

Sixth, feminist theology examines change in women's lives. Its importance stems from the fact that it facilitates conversion of "mind, heart, and ways of living and judging" (Finson, 1995: 2).

FEMINIST THEOLOGY

Webster's Dictionary defines theology as "the field of study and analysis that treats of God and of God's attributes and relations to the universe; the study of divine things or religious truth" (*Webster's*, 1996: 1967). All theology comes from experience. Both women and men have the transforming and revelatory experiences that give rise to theology. Feminist theologians, within or outside established religions, generally agree that Western religions have devalued and even betrayed women. They also accept that the spiritual/religious is meaningful and valid

298

(Heschel, 2004: 585). Many women need to develop their spirituality in a feminist context and their feminism in a spiritual context (Goldenberg, 2007).

Feminist theology refers mainly to the work of women (and men) who remain inside, and strive to change, male-dominated monotheistic traditions (Reuther, 2001). Feminist theology not only demonstrates that past theological thinking has almost completely ignored female experiences but also uses women's experiences to expose both traditional theology and sacred texts as focused on *male*—not universal—experience (Isherwood and McEwan, 2001: 9; Reuther, 1983: 13). Thus, most Western feminist theologians tend to concentrate on connected issues, for instance, the sexism inherent in both sacred texts and religious organizations, problems caused for women by male God-language and images in sacred books and liturgy, and the paucity of female leadership in religious institutions (Green-McCreight, 2000). Even though they may not deal with them directly, criticisms by feminist theologians have affected most religious traditions (Russell and Clarkson, 1996; Sawyer and Collier, 1999; Juschka, 2001).

Categories of Feminist Theology

Western feminist theology fits into four categories that often overlap: *Revisionist* theology argues that sacred material has been incorrectly interpreted and that correct interpretation makes obvious the liberating message at the religion's core. Many whose work falls into this category insist that using sex-neutral language in (say) liturgy, while keeping the core ideas intact, provides a satisfactory solution to the problem of sexism. Going a step further, *Renovationist*[3] theology seeks to remodel religious traditions to make them hospitable to women: "Revealing a religion's liberating core" is not enough, for we must expose, and refuse to accept, sexism in the tradition. Further, the use of sex-neutral language is not an adequate response to sexism in sacred material. Renovationist theology seeks to amend the language and symbols of deity, as well as liturgical language, to include female imagery. Even more extreme is *Revolutionary* theology, which pushes a tradition to its limits. For instance, it advocates importing from other traditions language, imagery, and occasionally ritual. Those taking a Revolutionary stance often have close connections with feminists who practise Goddess spirituality. Finally, *Rejectionist* theology judges monotheistic religions to be irremediably sexist. Its proponents leave them, usually to create new spiritual traditions, often by employing ancient ideas, symbols, and rituals. Many now practise one of the versions of Feminist Goddess Worship, which they understand as altogether different from other forms of spirituality.

CHRISTIANITY AND FEMINISM

Christianity divides into three basic groups: Eastern or Orthodox, Roman Catholic, and Protestant, the latter having two main streams, liberal and conservative (Bowker, 1997; McManners, 1990).

1. *Eastern or Orthodox*: This Eastern European, North African, and Eastern Mediterranean tradition, a community of self-governing churches, maintains strict hierarchy, usually with females subordinate. It accepts married priests, all male, and permits divorce. It disapproves of contraception, condemns abortion and sexuality outside marriage, and opposes homosexuality (Ware, 1997; Karkala-Zorba, 2006: 36–45; Keller and Reuther, 2006).

2. *Roman Catholicism*: The largest Christian tradition worldwide, Roman Catholicism is hierarchical, its supreme head being the Pope. Its priests, all male, cannot marry. It opposes divorce and sexuality outside marriage, does not permit abortion or artificial means of birth control, and disapproves of homosexuality (Keller and Reuther, 2006; Swidler, 1993: chs. 5 and 6).

3. *Protestantism*: All Protestant churches refuse the authority of the Pope, and almost all Protestant priests can marry. Otherwise, Protestants hold a wide spectrum of views on such topics as divorce, birth control, abortion, sexuality outside marriage, and homosexuality (Swidler, 1993: chs. 5 and 6). Protestantism divides roughly into two groups:

    a. Conservative: Pentecostal churches concentrate on possession by the Holy Spirit. They often allow women to take spiritual leadership roles, although they normally hold traditional views of women's domestic role. Evangelical churches, hierarchical in structure, focus on Jesus and his (male) nature. They see males and females as essentially different, with women subordinate.

    b. Liberal: Mainline churches and sects belong here. Structures vary from hierarchical to increasingly communal, emphasizing female–male equality. Many liberal churches ordain women as priests and even bishops. A number also ordain partnered lesbians and gays.

The Dominant Stream in Christian Feminist Theology

According to Canadian scholar Charlotte Caron, most Christian feminist theologians subscribe to ten principles: First, women's experiences are central. Second, "the personal is political." Third, patriarchy is an evil hierarchical system that oppresses women. Fourth, there is no such thing as objectivity. Fifth, everyone, including gays/lesbians, people of colour, and people with disabilities, must participate freely, fully, and publicly in "the naming and shaping of the common good." None can be saved unless everyone is saved. Sixth, women have a right to control their own lives and especially their own bodies. Seventh, the basis of everything is the community; influential members are accountable to the least powerful. Eighth, exclusively male God-language and imagery are not acceptable; God is both "Creator" and "Mother." Ninth, pluralism is essential—feminism has so far dealt primarily with the concerns of white, middle-class, heterosexual, able-bodied women. Finally, ambiguities and contradictions are expected, and Christian feminists must live with them (Caron, 1993).

Topics in Western Christian Feminist Theology

Feminist theologians deal with such issues as sexism in the churches; the education, ordination, and ministry of women; pastoral care of women and by women; recovering the history of Christian women; Christian ethics; the meaning of Christ (christology); Bible interpretation; and rewriting language, liturgy, and ritual.

Beginning in the second wave, feminist theologians undertook a radical exposure of the sexism of the texts and practices of Christianity. Christian theology at the time was androcentric, neither objective nor universal. Feminist theology demanded that churches and theologians take into account women's experience. Feminist Christians then developed a theology with women's experience at its core. The earliest and perhaps most historically significant of these feminists was Mary Daly, whose books *The Church and the Second*

Sex (1968), *Beyond God the Father* (1973), and *Gyn/Ecology* (1978) reveal religious language and liturgy as androcentric and, finally, affirm the Goddess as the life-loving "being" of women and nature. Also very influential is Rosemary Reuther, whose books *Sexism and God-Talk* (1983), *Gaia and God: An Ecofeminist Theology of Earth Healing* (1992), and *Gender, Ethnicity, and Religion* (2002) restate Christian insights in the context of women's experiences.

The Association of Theological Schools reported that, in 2005, 36 percent of enrolment in all their schools consisted of women (Lindner, 2007: 395). Indeed, in some theological schools, women make up between 50 and 80 percent of the student body. This influx over a 30-year period has had an enormous effect on Christianity, especially upon Protestantism. In the 1980s, women began to enter the Protestant ministry in considerable numbers (Keller and Reuther, 2006). Soon there was a flood of experiential and scholarly studies of women and ministry, to which Canadian scholars have contributed, writing about women in Canadian churches (Anderson, 1990; Muir and Whiteley, 1995), the ordination movement in the Anglican Church (Fletcher-Marsh, 1995), Canadian women in missions to Asia and Africa (Brouwer, 1990, 2002; Rutherdale, 2002), women preachers in Upper Canada (Muir, 1991), and modern women in the ministry, including lesbians and Native and Japanese Canadians (Lebans, 1994).

The consequent discussion of pastoral care of women and by women covers topics such as violence and sexual abuse, poverty, and aging. Perhaps the most controversial book is *Christianity, Patriarchy, and Abuse*, which addresses the possibility that images of Jesus' suffering might recall painful memories to survivors of abuse (Brown and Bohn, 1989).

Since the latter half of the 1980s, an area of burgeoning publication has been Christian ethics, exploring issues such as abortion, homophobia, the function of power in pastoral counselling, power and sexuality, and suffering and evil. Marilyn Legge (1992) examined ethically the concerns of Canadian women in their daily lives.

Christology, or examination of the meaning of Jesus, has produced heated debate (Finson, 1995; Carley, 2002). Rosemary Reuther envisions Christ as "our sister" (1983: 138). Others suggest constructing different visual images. One such attempt, the statue "Crucified Woman," which stands outside Emmanuel College at the University of Toronto, provoked a storm of controversy (Dyke, 1991).

Recovery of religious and church history has also been a very productive area of research (Finson, 1995: 38–41). Historian-theologians have demonstrated that women were instrumental in the establishment and early spread of Christianity (Pagels, 1979; Torjesen, 1993; Kraemer, 1992; Kraemer and D'Angelo, 1999). They have also researched women of the past such as early martyr Perpetua, twelfth-century prophet-mystic Hildegard of Bingen, fourteenth-century mystic Julian of Norwich, Shaker Christ/Messiah Ann Lee, and Roman Catholic social activist Dorothy Day (Setta, Campbell, in Falk and Gross, 1989; King, 1998). Also, a collection of four centuries of American women's religious writing appeared in 1995 (Keller and Reuther, 2000).

Examinations of Biblical texts attempt to develop interpretive methods for uncovering revelatory messages for women (Trible, 1978, 1984; Fiorenza, 1992, 2001; Newsom and Ringe, 1992; Laffey, 2001). In an influential book *In Memory of Her* (1983), Roman Catholic feminist Elizabeth Schüssler Fiorenza discusses the widely used phrase "the hermeneutics of suspicion" (56) and calls for Christian women to form an "*ekklesia* of women," a gathering of equals to decide on spiritual and political matters (344). Today, this "women-church" movement is a worldwide phenomenon (Reuther, 1985; King, 1989: 202–204).

Language, especially that referring to God, continues to be a central focus for feminist theologians (Finson, 1995: 16–17, 42–44). Mary Daly was one of the first to call attention to the problem of the maleness of God and Jesus, as well as androcentric God symbolism (1973, 1985: 180–183). Labelling the use of exclusively male language for God as a kind of idolatry, Rosemary Reuther proposes instead the word *God/ess* (1983: 66, 67).

Since the mid-1970s, women have been rewriting hymns, prayers, and liturgies; collecting women's poetry for use in ritual; and even composing new hymns, complete with music (Finson, 1995: 44–47). They have also been developing liturgies for girls' coming-of-age rituals and lesbians' coming-out ceremonies, as well as rites of passage for divorce and healing rituals, especially for victims of violence and sexual abuse (Reuther, 1985; Procter-Smith and Walton, 1993).

Revisionist solutions include the interpretation of God-language and symbols in ways that are not oppressive. Renovationist ones involve making language neutral or, more extreme, adding female symbols. Revolutionary solutions routinely use female language for God and female symbols. Rejectionists, of course, are already deeply involved with goddesses or other spiritual traditions.

Womanist Theology

Fifteen years after Daly's 1968 pioneering book, *The Church and the Second Sex*, African-American writer Audre Lorde published a devastating critique of Daly's *Gyn/Ecology* (1978). Lorde faults Daly for generalizing about women's experience from white women's experience, which is not the same as African-American women's experience (Kamitsuka, 2003: 46). African-American feminist theorist bell hooks had been making similar criticisms since 1981 (1981, 1984). From these beginnings came womanist or African-American feminist theology (Coleman, 2006). "Womanist" is Alice Walker's term for a feminist woman of colour (Walker, 1983: xi–xii; Williams in King, 1994).

Womanist theologians adhere to four principles. First, putting African-American women's experiences at the centre of their endeavour, they aim to assist African-American women to rely on their own experiences to control the "character" of Christianity in their communities (Williams, 1993b: xiv). Womanist theologians argue that African-American women experience Jesus differently from the way that white people do. Black women see him as co-sufferer, symbol of freedom, equalizer, and liberator (Grant, 1993: 66–69). They identify with him because he identifies with them. For them, Jesus is Black. Since, in their prayers, Black women do not distinguish among the members of the Trinity (Grant, 1989: 211), Jesus is the one to whom they pray. Womanist theologians have also been developing rituals for womanist worship (Powell, 1993; Williams, 1993a).

Second, womanists understand all systems of oppression (gender, race, class, ability, age) as interrelated in "one overarching structure of domination" (Eugene, 1992: 140). They emphasize communal commitment to the survival and wholeness of an entire people, without the sacrifice of any woman's individuality. Effective liberation has to work for all their people and all other oppressed people (Cannon, 1988).

Third, they maintain that "Afrocentric" ideas about family and community, which are quite different from those of the dominant culture, must be a focus of inquiry (Eugene, 1992: 140–143; Williams in King, 1994: 79). Womanist theologians point out that many Black women perceive white feminism, with its attack on family, as a threat to Black family life and to African-American survival (Grant, 1989: 201).

Fourth, with the high value they place on the African-American community, womanists see themselves as linked to the community's folk tradition and consider it important to communicate in the language of ordinary Black people (Eugene, 1992: 146). Most womanists also understand themselves as connected to the traditions of American Black churches (Grant, 1982; Paris, 1993: 120).

The contributions of womanist theologians to feminist theology in general are enormous. Through their criticisms of white feminist theology, they have offered feminism new insights. Not only have they developed a set of theological principles of their own, but they have also spurred other women of colour and women of other ethnicities to follow suit, for instance, Latinas, mujeristas, and Chicanas (Isasi-Díaz, 1996; Aquino, Macado, and Rodriguez, 2002) and Asian-American women (Southard, 1994).

Third-World Feminist Theology

With the proliferation of feminist theology from the "developed" countries, Asian and African feminists began theologizing from their own perspectives; Latin American women were already doing Liberation theology (King, 1994: 3, 63). For some years, *Inheriting Our Mothers' Gardens* was the best-known introduction, though the bulk of its articles discuss American women of colour (Russell et al., 1988). The 1994 appearance of the book *Feminist Theology from the Third World* (King, 1994) provided essays by prominent Asians, Latin Americans, and Africans. Recent studies include Kwok Pui-lan's book on Asian feminist theology (2000) and Mercy Oduyoye's books on African women's theology (2001, 2004). An important article by Nami Kim (2005) reconsidered the global and critical characteristics of Asian feminist theology. Third-world feminist theologians are also deeply concerned with the effect of colonialism on women of different backgrounds and the way in which colonialism intersects with gender and religion in the domination of indigenous populations (Donaldson and Kwok, 2002: 27).

Lesbian Voices

Lesbian issues began to surface in feminist-theological discussion in the late 1980s, concerning such topics as ethics of lesbian choice, friendship, suicide, lesbian priests and ministers, and eroticism. Episcopal (Anglican) priest and feminist theologian Carter Heywood is openly lesbian; topics she addresses include a specifically lesbian view of Christianity (1989a), ethics (1984), and theology and the erotic (1989b), as well as rituals for lesbians (Cherry and Sherwood, 1995). Lesbians raised as Roman Catholics examine their relationship to that faith (Zanotti, 1986), and 50 lesbian nuns present their personal stories (Curb and Monahan, 1985). Other works examine lesbians and gays within organized religions (Comstock, 1996), the Lesbian and Gay Christian Movement (Gill, 1998), lesbian and gay clergy (Hazel, 2000), and lesbians and gays in African-American congregations (Comstock, 2001). The journal *Sinister Wisdom* devoted a special issue to lesbians and religion (Sinister Wisdom, 1994/1995). In the last ten years or so, feminist theologians have been including transgendered and bisexual women in their thinking. Kathy Rudy (1999) published an important book on the effect of such work on Christian ethics. In addition, some lesbians have begun to categorize themselves as "queer," a postmodern term first used primarily by scholars (Stuart 1998; Butler, 2001).

JUDAISM AND FEMINISM

From the 18th century on, many Jews were questioning traditional Judaism, with its numerous, strict rabbinical laws. Some developed what became Reform Judaism, which aimed to remodel Judaism for the modern world. At this time traditional Judaism acquired the name "Orthodox Judaism." The *Hasidim*, "pious ones" (Epstein, 1990: 271), fall into this category (Harris, 1985). Extremely traditional ultra-Orthodox Jews are also called *haredim*, "those who tremble." In Orthodox Judaism, women have traditionally had a very strong, if separate, role in the domestic sphere, but no role in the religion's public life (Schulman, 1996: 312; El-Or, 1994). However, today women can serve as, among others things, "master teachers of rabbinic literature," synagogue presidents, and pleaders in religious courts (Keller and Reuther, 2006).

Well ahead of its time, Reform Judaism's Breslau Conference of 1846 concluded with a call for equality of the sexes in religion, with little response. In the 1890s, feminist foremother Henrietta Szold worked for equality, attended the Jewish Theological Seminary in New York, and ended her days in Palestine, where she founded the network of health care that became modern Israel's Hadassah Medical Organization. The first woman rabbi, Regina Jones, who died in Auschwitz, was ordained in Germany in the 1930s (Nadell, 1998).

In 1875, Reform Rabbi Isaac Mayer Wise founded Hebrew Union College in Cincinnati and encouraged women to study there. Though in 1921 the college's faculty voted to allow women to study for ordination, its board did not approve. Finally, in 1956 the board agreed to ordain women who managed to achieve the requirements (Carmody, 1989: 152).

Other attempts to update the tradition resulted in Conservative Judaism and Reconstructionist Judaism. The goal of Conservative Judaism, the largest denomination in the United States today, is to confront the challenge of integrating tradition with modernity. In 1886 its Jewish Theological Seminary was founded. Today 40 percent of its students are women (Keller and Reuther, 2006). Its ordained rabbis form the Rabbinical Assembly that set up a Committee on Jewish Law and Standards to advise on interpretation of rabbinic law (*halakhah*[4]). Although Conservative Judaism understands *halakhah* as binding, member synagogues can accept or reject committee decisions (Schulman, 1996: 314).

Mordecai Kaplan (1881–1982), founder of Reconstructionist Judaism, was a strong advocate of equality for women (Alpert and Milgram, 1996: 291). A Reconstructionist conference in 1967 set up the Reconstructionist Rabbinical College in Philadelphia. The Reconstructionist Rabbinical Association and the Federation of Reconstructionist Congregations govern the movement, which opposes hierarchy in Judaism. Reconstructionist Jews consider *halakhah* a sacred but non-binding tradition that needs to take into account contemporary ethical standards (Alpert and Milgram, 1996: 291).

Feminism and Feminist Theology

During the past two decades, Jewish feminists, stimulated by and stimulating parallel work in other religions, have been revising basic tenets and premises that have underpinned Judaism in some cases for as much as three millennia. For example, they question male dominance; are involved in forming and naming the tradition (Plaskow, 1990: vii); analyze sacred and legal texts (Levine, 2001); and examine the relationship of feminist theory and Judaism (Plaskow, 2005: 65–80).

Not until recently have feminist theologians dealt with theological issues arising from the Holocaust of World War II (1939–1945). For all Jews the Holocaust was a major occurrence, but for Jewish women it is "the single most important historical event," because the Nazis particularly targeted Jewish women as bearers of "communal and religious continuity" (Stuckey, 1998: 34). Indeed, "Nazism placed women in 'double jeopardy' as object both of anti-semitism and misogyny" (Raphael, 2003: 1). To answer the central question, "Where was God?" Melissa Raphael wrote a Jewish feminist theology of the Holocaust (2003).

With considerable success, Jewish feminists have been taking part in public ritual and filling leadership roles (Nadell, 1998). Today, in the non-Orthodox streams, there are a number of women rabbis, including some 127 in Conservative Judaism (King, 1989: 43; Nadell, 1998; Keller and Reuther, 2006). In Conservative, Reform, and Reconstructionist Judaism, women can publicly read from the Torah, the first five books of the Hebrew Bible. Even in Conservative Judaism, they can usually form part of the *minyan*, the prayer quorum of 10 adults, traditionally all-male (Elwell, 1996).

Feminist theologians also ask what sort of a religion Judaism would be if it incorporated not only the full participation of women, but also their points of view (Plaskow, 2005: 80).

Revisionist Views The earliest Jewish feminist work concentrated on recovering lost women and their contributions (Plaskow, 2005: 66). Today, feminist historians continue to do recovery work, for example, Ellen Umansky and Diana Ashton (1992) and Tikva Frymer-Kensky (1992, 2002). Other studies examined women's place in the synagogue (Brooten, 1982; Goldman, 2000), women and American Judaism (Nadell and Sarna, 2001), women in rabbinic literature (Baskin, 2002), and women's history, 600 BCE to 1900 CE (Taitz, Henry, and Tallan, 2003).

At the First International Conference on Orthodoxy and Feminism in New York in February 1997, most attendees described themselves as "modern or centrist Orthodox." The conference discussed such issues as effecting changes in *halakhah*; the ordination of women; and the *agunot*, women whose husbands refuse to give them religious divorces (*gets*). Participants had already heard that some Orthodox women were performing all rabbinic roles except those involved in public ritual. They had also received a report that a group of Orthodox rabbis had formed a religious court to deal with the *agunot* problem; it had already managed to find ways inside Jewish law to annul the marriages of six women. Speaker after speaker insisted that rabbis could interpret *halakhah* so that Orthodox women could become increasingly active in their own religious lives (Cohen, 1997). Since 1997 numerous small but significant changes have continued to affect the lives of Orthodox women (Ross, 2004; Joseph, 2007: 181–209).

Thus, over the past 30 years, Orthodox women have been expanding their areas of religious expression, for instance, by celebrating women's rites like *Rosh Chodesh*, a monthly new-moon gathering (Feldman, 2003), and by meeting in women's prayer groups, which Joseph (2007: 201) calls "the cutting edge" of the Orthodox women's movement; there are now a few of these in Canada and about 60 worldwide (Joseph, 2007: 201). Often these prayer groups meet to celebrate a *bat mitzvah*, a girl's coming-of-age ceremony. In some synagogues, after the men have read the Torah scroll aloud, they pass it behind the screen separating the women from the men, so that the women may touch it (Cohen, 1997). Orthodox feminists, like most at the 1997 conference, intend to stay "firmly within the bounds of generally accepted halacha [*sic*]" and, from that position, reveal the liberating core of the tradition and the power and influence of women in their families and communities (Frankiel, 1990: xiii, xi).

In the 1990s, a small but vocal feminist group demanded more drastic change in Orthodox Judaism, including Talmud[5] studies for women, the formation of all-women *minyans*, and regular performance by women of the obligations (*mitzvot*) that traditionally only men observe. Such demands, obviously threatening, were "severely criticized from within" (Myers and Litman, 1995: 69). Despite their insistence on remaining Orthodox, we should probably class such women as Renovationist.

Most feminists working inside Conservative Judaism are also revisionist (Schwartz, 2007). Judith Plaskow argues that the educational opportunities now available to women in Conservative Judaism lead only to contradictions. Her example is the *bat mitzvah*, which represents a girl's *final* participation in the congregation, not the beginning, as the *bar mitzvah* does for a boy (Plaskow, 1990: ix).

Feminist pressure, however, has produced alterations even in this stream of Judaism. Starting in 1972, the Conservative Jewish Women's Group began requesting changes that eventually led to women's full involvement in education for the rabbinate. Women were admitted to the Jewish Theological Seminary in 1983. However, the seminary accepted women only if they voluntarily undertook to perform all the obligations enjoined on males. Some female students had problems with this logic, for it implies that women as women are unacceptable, that they must become quasi-males. As one student pointed out, women have to conquer their femaleness to gain equality with males (Schulman, 1996: 315–316). From May 1985 to May 1993, the seminary ordained 52 female rabbis. Most of them stated that, in becoming rabbis, they were seeking not just authority and "equality of obligation," but also "authenticity" in the tradition (Schulman, 1996: 327–328). Normally women do not achieve leadership positions in the largest Conservative synagogues, and they are usually paid at a lower rate than men (Goldman, 2007: 128). In the mid-1970s, the committee of the Rabbinical Assembly that interprets *halakhic* matters pronounced that women could participate in a *minyan* (Schulman, 1996: 314).

Renovationist Views Although Reform Judaism had ordained at least two women before 1940 (Neudel, 1989), American Sally Preisand, ordained in 1972, is usually named as the first woman to become a Reform rabbi (Preisand, 1975). A decade later, there were 61 female Reform rabbis and by 1986 a total of 131 (King, 1989: 43). By 1991, 10 percent of all Reform rabbis were women, and 40 to 50 percent of all applicants to the rabbinic program at Hebrew Union College were female. Recent graduating classes at the College have been close to 50 percent female (Marder, 1996: 287; Goldman, 2007: 128).

Feminist theologians have been quick to attack the sexism in Judaism, the Torah, and especially *halakhah*. Plaskow, raised in the "classical Reform" tradition (Plaskow, 1990: viii), says that Jewish feminist aims must include restructuring the foundations of Jewish life; that entails developing a new way of interpreting the Torah, because the Torah is profoundly unjust (Plaskow, 1995: 230). *Halakhah* change has been central to feminist demands, and some hope to improve the status of women through it. However, to date, feminists have challenged only specific laws, not the law's basic assumptions (Plaskow, 1995: 224; Millen, 2007: 40).

Jewish feminists are committed to challenging male-centred language and God imagery (Spiegel, 1996: 126–127). Rita Gross (1979: 167–168) argued for the necessity of reuniting "the masculine and feminine aspect of God" and of using female language to refer to God. She considered female imagery, however, to be more important than female language. Only a decade later, Gross discussed developing Jewish female God imagery: the use of female language, especially pronouns, and the collection of female images of God from inside and outside the Jewish tradition. She concluded by advocating the addition of "Goddess" to Judaism, a claim that surely pushes the tradition beyond its limits (Gross, in Heschel, 1995).

Feminist theologians have also been examining liturgy, especially the Passover order of service (*Haggadah*) and various prayers and blessing formulas. Women have constructed feminist and women's *Haggadah* texts; they add references to Biblical foremothers, women in legends, and historical women, and they often expand the *Haggadah*'s focus on oppression and liberation to include women's oppression and need for freedom (Cantor, 1979; Elwell, 1996; Goldman, 2007: 124–127). A particularly rich resource is Marcia Falk's collection of feminist prayers and blessings (1996), many of which are now part of ritual in liberal synagogues. In addition, some liberal-synagogue rituals incorporate liturgical/musical prayers by Debbie Friedman (2000).

Renovationists have been instrumental in the creation of women's rituals (Orenstein, 1994; Orenstein and Litman, 1994; Spiegel, 1996: 128ff). They have constructed rituals to mark the female life cycle and other important events, for instance, rites of passage for women in midlife (Adelman, 1990; Fine, 1988) and rituals for the welcoming of daughters into the Jewish community (Plaskow, 1979a).

For Judith Plaskow, remaining Jewish was not just a rational decision, for she felt that "sundering Judaism and feminism would mean sundering [her] being" (Plaskow, 1979b: x–xi). In the introduction to her important book *Standing Again at Sinai*, Plaskow observes that in non-Orthodox Judaism, women's efforts have resulted only in their becoming participants in and teachers/preservers of a male religion. What Plaskow advocates instead seems very Revolutionary: a complete transformation of Jewish religion and society, so that the tradition incorporates women's experiences (Plaskow, 1990: xiv–xv).

For feminist Jews who already belonged to the Reconstructionist stream, it should have been easy to become Revolutionaries. The movement is egalitarian and non-hierarchical and understands God as gender-neutral (Alpert and Milgram, 1996: 292; Moore and Bush, 2007). In fact, although feminist activities inside Reconstructionist Judaism have been quite successful, most feminist theology in this stream remains Renovationist. By the early 1980s, there were 14 female Reconstructionist rabbis, almost 20 percent of all rabbis ordained since the establishment of the Reconstructionist Rabbinical College in 1968; in 1983 the college ordained 47 students, of whom 23 were women (Carmody, 1989: 152–153). Today 105 of the movement's 226 rabbis are female (Keller and Reuther, 2006). Women rabbis have devised "theologies" and rituals that express the experiences of women. They have also worked on text interpretation, inclusive language, and God names (Alpert and Milgram, 1996: 303, 309). In 1983, however, Susannah Heschel could write that, like the Conservative stream, Reconstructionist Judaism was still emphasizing a historical consciousness of Jewish civilization (Heschel, 1995: xlviii).

The Jewish Renewal Movement, the "vision" of which "began over thirty years ago" (Goldberg, 2002: 13), seems Renovationist, though some of its practices are Revolutionary, and some fit "well within a Rejectionist viewpoint, albeit the authors tenuously hold to a Jewish ethos" (Goldberg, 2002: 24). The movement allows "liberal" Jewish women to articulate their "spiritual understandings" (Goldberg, 2002: iv) in a context that welcomes feminist ideas (Weissler, 2007).

Revolutionary Views Very few Jewish feminist theologians take fully Revolutionary stances in their work. In arguing that Judaism needs a goddess, Rita Gross had already moved by 1983 into the Revolutionary category and even beyond it. With the drastic changes that she envisions, Judith Plaskow too may already have one foot in the Revolutionary feminist-theological camp (1990, 2005). The brave women who carried a Torah to the holy West Wall of the Temple in Jerusalem ("Wailing Wall") did a Revolutionary act, though it is unlikely that any would label herself Revolutionary (Zuckerman, 1992; Chesler and Haut, 2003).

In *She Who Dwells Within*, Lynn Gottlieb shows herself to be firmly Revolutionary, and her spiritual history suggests that she has long held such views. Gottlieb focuses on the female "Presence of God," the *Shekinah* (Gottlieb, 1995: 20). She advocates borrowing from other spiritual traditions, like Native American or ancient eastern Mediterranean. Further, she revitalizes and reinterprets elements of the Jewish tradition, and she draws on her own vision for new material from which to construct prayers, rituals, sacred stories, and meditations. What Revolutionary Gottlieb envisions would entail the complete alteration of the Judaism that Judith Plaskow has spoken of (Gottlieb, 1990: xiv–xv).

Judaism, Multiculturalism, and Difference

Most of the feminist theologians discussed above are Ashkenazi (Bowker, 1997: 98–99). Ashkenazic women have been the subjects of most research, as well as being the researchers. However, the voices and theological views of Sephardic women (Bowker, 1997: 875) and those of other origins, while not absent from the record, are not widely available in North America. Special issues of the journals *Bridges* (7[1], 1997/1998) and *Canadian Woman Studies* (16[4], 1996) have begun to improve the situation. Recently, Jewish feminists have been discussing both multiculturalism and difference "without and within" (Plaskow, 2003: 91), as articles by six scholars in the *Journal of Feminist Studies in Religion* demonstrate (Brettschneider and Rose, 2003; Plaskow, 2003; Falk, 2003; Cohler-Esses, 2003; Levine, 2003).

Lesbian Voices

Jewish feminists taking a Revolutionary stance are often lesbians, who usually have difficulty finding acceptance even in liberal streams (Eron, 1993: 103–134; Alpert and Milgram, 1996: 308). Indeed, some lesbians and gays have started their own synagogues (Eron, 1993: 126). In addition, Rebecca Alpert (1997) mentions six openly lesbian Reconstructionist rabbis. The best-known Jewish lesbian publication collects essays, poetry, and stories about women's identity (Beck, 1982). Another contains a number of articles by Jewish lesbians (Balka and Rose, 1989). Lesbians too have devised rituals and liturgy (Butler, 1990; Stein, 1984). A special issue of the journal *Sinister Wisdom* (1994/1995) is devoted to "Lesbians and Religion." In the last ten years or so, feminist theologians have also been including transgendered and bisexual women in their thinking. In addition, some lesbians have begun to categorize themselves as "Queer," a postmodern term first used primarily by scholars (Schneer and Aviv, 2002; Butler, 2001).

ISLAM AND FEMINISM

Unequivocally monotheistic, Islam builds on Judaism and Christianity, but has "original" traits (Buturovic, 1995; Haddad and Esposito, 2001: 1). *Islam* means "surrender" or "submission" to the will of God (Ruthven, 1997: 2–3). Thus, a Muslim is anyone submitting to God and observing His Commandments. Muslims base their faith on the Qur'an, their sacred book that God revealed to the prophet Muhammad (ca. 570–632 CE) over the course of 23 years. In the late 600s, Muslims divided into two main groups, now called Sunnis and Shi'ites. Since then Islam has developed into a highly complex and diverse religion (Haddad, Smith, and Moore, 2006: 4–8). Further divisions produced a number of other groupings, for example, the Druzes and the Ishmailis (Bowker, 1997: 295–296, 480–481).

The Islamic world has also experienced several influential and often fundamentalist[6] reform movements, for instance, Wahhabiya, an ultra-conservative group originating in the 18th century in what is now Saudi Arabia; the latter country today follows the tenets of Wahhabism (Bowker, 1997: 1031). Another example is the Muslim Brotherhood, a religious and political group originating in Egypt in the 1920s, its original aims being first to expel the British and then to establish an Islamic state (Bowker, 1997: 47). Such movements are usually "Islamist," defined by scholars as the use of Islam "as a source of political activism" (Marshall, 2005: 104; Winter, 2001: 9; Cooke, 2002: 145). Another scholar describes these movements as "An Islamist attempts to propagate and purify Islam" which become activist in associations trying to change society "along Islamic lines" (Maumoon, 1999: 269). Most Islamist movements and governments are "highly intolerant and repressive" (Barlow and Akbarzadeh, 2008: 21).

All Muslims accept three basic beliefs: *Tawhid*, the Oneness of God, absolute monotheism; *Nubuwah*, Prophethood; and *Aakhirah*, Life after Death. All Muslims undertake the five duties called "Pillars" (see note 7). All Muslims revere the Qur'an and the Sunna, a collection of sayings and deeds of the Prophet. Together the Qur'an and the Sunna constitute the main source of Islamic law, *Sharia*. Islam is characterized by "indivisibility between the sacred and the secular" (Cleary, 1993: vii). For Muslims, their religion *is* their way of life. Thus, Muslim feminists are often torn in finding that they cannot leave Islam (Khan, 2002: 327).

In most Muslim societies, women manage to express their spirituality despite their involvement in what has developed as a thoroughly male-dominated religion (Shehadeh, 2003). Feminists can be found in Muslim countries and communities worldwide, even though "Islamic feminism" might seem a contradiction to most Western feminists (McGinty, 2007: 474).

In some countries, Muslim feminists are able, more or less freely, to express their views. However, in countries that are experiencing powerful fundamentalist pressures or have fundamentalist governments, an avowed feminist can suffer considerable distress and even face real danger (Alam, 1998; Moghissi, 1999; Jamali, 2007). Not surprisingly, many feminists writing about Islam work in Western societies (Yamani, 1996: ix–xii; Webb, 2000).

Islam and Women

Possibly "more explicitly than any other [monotheistic] sacred text," the Qur'an deals with women both separately and fully (Buturovic, 1995). It states that God made women and men from "one soul" (Koran, 4: 1) and sets out the obligations of the sexes in matters of both social behaviour and faith, expressly understanding female–male equality in the latter (Buturovic, 1997: 53). In principle, the Qur'an expects women to fulfill all religious obligations.

Sura (chapter) 4 of the Qur'an is traditionally called "Women." Since the Qur'an is, for Muslims, the revealed word of God, what it says about women has always been central to Islam's treatment of them. It proclaims that women and men are equal in faith (4: 124–126). As in every other sphere of life, in male–female relationships, the first duty of Muslims is to keep God in the forefront at all times, for God sees and knows everything (4: 1).

The Qur'an permits a man to marry up to four women, provided he can support them economically and treat them equally (4: 3). However, the preference of both the Qur'an and Muslim custom is monogamy, and the ideal relationship is that of Muhammad and his first wife, Khadijah (Carmody, 1989: 191).

The Qur'an states that women can inherit a woman's portion, but men inherit the equivalent of two women's portions (4: 11). Marriage is a contract in Islam, not a sacrament, as in Christianity. A Muslim wife has legal rights, though in many societies, it is often difficult for her to get them. She can insist on the terms of the marriage contract, and she retains her dowry. She also has the right to refuse marriage. If her husband does not support her, she can seek redress from the law. She can also sue for divorce, although traditionally divorce has been easier for men than for women. The Qur'an forbids incest (4: 23), as it does adultery. Four witnesses have to corroborate an accusation of "lewdness" against a woman; if she is guilty, incarceration in the house until death may be her sentence. The law punishes both partners in fornication.

On the other hand, Sura 4: 34 states that men are in charge of women because God has given men superior qualities and because men support women. Good women are obedient and chaste. Men should banish disobedient women from their beds and whip them.

The Qur'an prescribes modesty for both men and women, and it makes clear that a woman's primary role is to be a good wife and mother. If a woman is pregnant or menstruating, she is exempt from the duties of fasting and pilgrimage. Islam does not forbid women to study the Qur'an or to read prayers in mosques (Buturovic, 1995).

Later interpretation of the Qur'an, as well as a body of material relating to the Prophet's life (the Sunna), and the development of Islamic law (Sharia) in the light of local custom often resulted in the subjection of women to very restrictive demands concerning obedience and family honour. Increasingly, Muslim society placed emphasis on woman's role as mother. Certain sayings of the Prophet (*hadiths*), as well as writings by prominent men, have disparaged women; for instance, Muhammad is reported to have said, "Consult [women] and do the opposite" (Carmody, 1989: 195).

Discussing women in Turkey, Julie Marcus examines women's involvement in rituals mainly to do with the life cycle, especially birth and death. She concludes that the female world view is egalitarian (Marcus, 1992: 121ff.). She also demonstrates that, even in extremely male-dominated religions, women make spiritual space for themselves (Wadud, 2006: 255).

Perhaps the most important point to remember about Muslim women is that, as with women of other traditions, there is enormous variation in their social, political, economic, and religious experiences (Mohagheghi, 2006: 63). There can be vast differences between Muslim women even in basically the same religious context. Thus, context is extremely important (Buturovic, personal communication, May 17, 1997).

Feminism and Feminist Theology

A wide variety of feminisms exists in Islam (Buturovic, personal communication, May 17, 1997). Many women who wish to remain Muslims, however, have adopted "Islamist" or "Islamic" feminism (Marshall, 2005). Egyptian feminist Margot Badran opts for the term "Islamist woman," rather than "Islamist feminist" (Buturovic, personal communication, January 1998). Since the adjective "Islamist" has usually described fundamentalist movements that advocate total adherence to Islamic law (Yamani, 1996: 1), the term "Islamic" seems preferable, and so I will use it here.

Islamic feminism is not "a coherent identity." Rather it is "a contingent, contextually determined strategic self-positioning" (Cooke, 2001: 59). It deals with issues that challenge the religious and political establishment of Islam, particularly its scholars (Cooke, 2001: vii). Most Islamic feminists have as their goal female empowerment from inside "a rethought Islam." They plan to achieve their goal mainly through appeal to the rights that Islam grants women (Yamani, 1996: 1–2). Islamic feminists engage in dialogue with tradition and try to bring out the best in it, because they think that women can feel empowered inside Islam without needing to reject values important to them (Buturovic, personal communication, May 17, 1997). Many of them are working on analysis of issues relating to the status of women in their societies (Anwer, 2006: 1–2).

In 1992, this kind of feminism did not go far enough for Yasmin Ali, who insisted that it led only to "a limited extension of opportunity" for a small number of women. Ali saw Islamic feminism as elitist (Ali, 1992: 12). Leila Ahmed also had reservations about it (Ahmed, 1992: 236). However, since the 1990s, Islamic feminists have been increasingly active in most Islamic countries (Fernea, 1998, global; Osman, 2003, Egypt; Marshall, 2005, Turkey; Haddad, Smith, and Moore, 2006, US; Hirsi Ali, 2006, Netherlands; Moghissi, 2006, Diaspora; Ameli and Merali, 2006, UK; McGinty, 2007, Sweden; Barlow and Akbarzadeh, 2008, Iran). Nonetheless, Valentine Moghadam reports that Islamic feminism is still criticized for failing to provide "a liberating alternative to the dominant Islamic discourse and practice of gender and sexuality" (Moghadam, 2002: 1150).

Though she has stayed involved with Islam, long-time feminist activist and Egyptian writer Nawal el Saadawi has declared Islamic tradition sexist (Saadawi, 1980, 1997). Leila Ahmed considers el Saadawi's criticisms to proceed from assumptions and ideas stemming from Western capitalism (Ahmed, 1992: 235–236). Indeed, Islamic feminists describe women like Nawal el Saadawi as Western-style "feminists" (Cooke, 2002: 143; Labidi-Maïza, 2006: 73–74).

In elucidating the attitude of Muslim women to Western feminism, Leila Ahmed argues that, in colonial times, male colonizers appropriated the language of Western feminism—their enemy in their own countries—to attack Muslim men for abuse of women and so to justify the subversion of colonized cultures. In Ahmed's opinion, Western feminists have not been much better, because, "in the name of feminism," they have attacked many practices of Muslim societies, especially the *hijab* (head scarf or veil) (Ahmed, 1992: 243–244).

In modern times, Ahmed maintains, these manipulations are "transparently obvious." She accuses Western media and scholarship, including Western feminist scholarship, of invoking the oppression of women to validate, and "even insidiously" support, antagonism toward Muslims and Arabs (Ahmed, 1992: 246). It is no wonder that, for many women in Muslim countries, identification as a feminist or a women's liberationist connotes giving in to "foreign influences" (Mernissi, 1987: 8).

Other Islamic feminists argue that, in addition, Western feminism has failed in not ensuring "an honoured and recognized space for marriage and motherhood in women's lives and in society." For Islam the family is central. They also fault Western feminists for their emphasis on individualism and for the devaluation of domestic work (Maumoon, 1999: 275, 279).

According to Fatima Mernissi, the Prophet's message, the Qur'an, is egalitarian (1991: ix). However, Amila Buturovic has qualified such a statement by identifying the message's egalitarianism as applying to faith (1997: 53). Furthermore, Muslim women often insist, usually to the incredulity of non-Muslims, that the tradition is non-sexist. Leila Ahmed attributes this sincere belief to the fact that Muslim women respond to "ethical, egalitarian" Islam, rather than the "technical," legalistically focused Islam of the male establishment. It is the latter that is powerful politically (Ahmed, 1992: 239). By making the distinction between what Mernissi has called "political Islam" and "spiritual Islam" (1993: 5), feminists can begin to expose the sexism in their societies. Islamic feminist scholars scrutinize not only political Islam, but also the widely varied religious practices of Islamic communities, most of which practices get their validation, rightly or wrongly, from the sacred texts of Islam, primarily the Qur'an. However, Islam has had, and still has, a long and learned tradition of Qur'an interpretation, and this practice provides a path for some feminists to follow (Stowasser, 1998: 30).

Nonetheless, doing Qur'an interpretation was and is difficult for women not only because, for all Muslims, the Qur'an is the revealed word of God, but also because most Muslim women have not had access to the necessary education. However, the Qur'an is the very centre of Islam. On it rests women's role in Islamic societies. When dealing with the Qur'an, most feminist theologians explicate its message and ignore, or try to explain, its sexism, but they do not question its authority. For instance, an Islamic feminist cannot reject polygamy because the Qur'an expressly permits it (Sura 4: 1–10); she can, however, try to explain it or decide not to deal with it.

A few feminists do study the Qur'an critically. In her early work, Mernissi rejected the Qur'an's sexism, but, in her later work, she accepted the sacred book and attributed women's condition mainly to societal factors (1987: 165–177). For instance, in discussing Sura 4: 34, which states that men have charge of women and may beat them for disobedience, she resigns herself to living with contradictions. Muhammad, she notes, was opposed to violence (1991: 154–155).

Recently, following in this venerable and previously exclusively male tradition, some feminist theologians have begun in earnest the difficult process of Qur'an interpretation (Yamani, 1996: 2). Such scholars include Najla Hamideh (1996) and Riffat Hassan (1997). What seems to be the first thorough examination of the sacred book from a woman's perspective appeared in 1992 (Wadud, 1999).

If the Qur'an is inviolable, the collection of sayings and deeds of the Prophet (the *Sunna*) is another matter. Of course, it is almost as sacred as the Qur'an, but Islam has had a long tradition of study and validation of these texts also. Thus, some feminist scholars question the authenticity of certain of the sayings (*hadiths*). Mernissi addresses one of them: "Those who entrust their affairs to a woman will never know prosperity" (Mernissi, 1991: 1). This *hadith* is widely quoted in Muslim societies. Thus, it is extremely influential when it comes to attitudes to women. A consensus of Islamic scholars holds it authentic, despite the fact that its authenticity was a matter of fierce debate (Mernissi, 1991: 61).

Mernissi points out that Muslim society has had two universes: that of men, which consists of the worldwide religion and all public power, and that of women, focused on the domestic realm, including sexuality (1987: 138). The five obligations or Pillars of Islam[7] connect the two (Marcus, 1992: 65). As to the Five Pillars, women have no problem fulfilling the first, daily witness to the Oneness of God. Though God is understood as male, He is not Father, like the God of Christianity and Judaism, nor does He have feminine characteristics. Thus, since Islam does not emphasize the sex of God, it does not appear to be an issue for women. The second, the giving of alms, causes no problem either (Marcus, 1992: 66).

The other three duties (observation of Ramadan, pilgrimage to Mecca, and daily prayers) are public and require ritual purity. Menstruation and having recently given birth render women impure. Further, no woman who is still menstruating can fast for the full 30 days of Ramadan. The same is true for the time it normally takes a pilgrim to make the journey to Mecca (*hajj*). Most women must postpone both of these obligations until after menopause. Consequently, they have little chance, until they are middle-aged or old, to garner the great respect that comes to a person who has made the *hajj*. Prayer at a mosque on Friday and at dawn on feast days demands total purification beforehand, again impossible for women much of the time. So although Muslims value communal prayer more highly, women usually have to pray in private, as there are no women's mosques (Marcus, 1992: 65–69). In practice, then, few women can (at least while young) fully observe the main obligations. Nonetheless, since God excuses them, they can still remain good Muslims.

Muslim feminist theologians deal with other topics and issues, among them family law and its abuses (Fernea, 1985; Ahmed, 1992: 64ff, 241ff), sexuality (Mernissi, 1987), and the controversy over the veil (Mernissi, 1987; Khanum, 1992; Alvi, Hoodfar, and McDonough, 2003). Some scholarship has been recovering women's history (Tucker, 1985; Mernissi, 1993; Mabro, 1996; Keddie, 2007). One researcher has produced a history of birth control in Islam (Musallam, 1989). Scholars are also making available women's stories and recording their voices (Fernea and Bezirgan, 1977; Sharawi, 1986; Badran and Cooke, 1990). In addition, they have studied women and women's movements both in the Muslim world in general and in various Muslim countries (Beck and Keddie, 1978; Minces, 1982; Tabari and Yeganeh, 1982; Mumtaz and Shaheed, 1987; Musallam, 1989; Lateef, 1990; Wikan, 1991; Sansarian, 1992; Afshar, 1993; Badran, 1995; Osman, 2003; Barlow and Akbarsadeh, 2008).

In the concluding chapter of *Beyond the Veil*, Mernissi maintains that Muslim male writers have insisted that any change in the situation of women necessarily involves religion. Therefore, any attempt to alter the status of women and the conditions they endure would represent a frontal assault on God's ruling and ordering of the world. Mernissi argues, however, that making changes to benefit women in any society is actually primarily a matter of economics (1987: 165). So society needs to be completely reshaped, beginning with economics and finishing with language structure (176). This reshaping is a matter for political Islam, not spiritual Islam (Abu-Lughod, 1998; Moghadam, 2003). Nevertheless, Muslims in general make no such distinction.

Lesbian Voices

Commonly, today's Islamic communities regard heterosexuality as the only acceptable form of sexual expression, appealing to the Qur'an's comment (27: 54) on Lot and Sodom for support (Duran, 1993: 181–197). They generally agree in condemning homosexuality as unnatural, though lesbian scholar Shahnaz Khan observes that there are no suras in the

Qur'an expressly against homosexuality (2002: 329). It's not surprising that, when I first
wrote on Muslim lesbians (Stuckey, 1998), I found very little material, whether about
women in Muslim societies or in the Diaspora, who might have been or are lesbians. However, some Islamic feminists did, even then, discuss the subject (Mernissi, 1987: 27–64;
Ahmed, 1992: 184–87; Imam, 1997).

Today, though, for Muslims living in North America, Europe, and elsewhere, the situation seems somewhat improved. In 2003 there was a conference in Toronto sponsored by
the Muslim homosexual group Salaam Canada and the American Al-Fatihah Foundation;
both groups also have websites (Giese, 2003). Also in 2003, Canadian feminist lesbian
writer and broadcaster Irshad Manji published a controversial book in which she describes
Islam as, among other things, homophobic. In May 2007 a group of lesbian Arabs held a
carefully protected conference in Haifa in Israel. The Gay and Lesbian Arabic Society now
has an internet address, and so does the lesbian magazine *Bint el Nas*.

FEMINIST GODDESS WORSHIP

Today's keen feminist interest in spirituality comes from women's attempts to develop, or
rediscover, language, sacred stories, and myths that speak to their experiences (Christ,
1979a: 228). Emerging alongside feminist spiritualities in the three monotheistic traditions
is a new religion, Feminist Goddess Worship, also called Feminist Spirituality and Spiritual
or Goddess Feminism (Raphael, 1996). Over the past three decades it has become a separate entity with a number of forms, committed to women's spiritual and political issues
while seeking spiritual expression that empowers women and helps them change their lives
(Eller, 1993: ix; Reuther, 2005: 4). Already it has *thealogies* and *thealogians*, studies and
students of the female divine (Christ, 1997, 2003; Raphael, 2000).

In the late 1960s, I was a member of Toronto New Feminists, a radical-feminist group
firmly opposed to religion. I remember intense consciousness-raising (CR) sessions at
which we exchanged significant stories, personal myths, and aspirations. In retrospect, I
realize that they were a combination of therapy session, discussion group, healing circle,
and prayer meeting. One of the reasons many feminists turned to spirituality and goddess-
worship circles in the mid-1970s was to recapture the elation accompanying ritualized
sharing of experiences and communal validation, as well as the comfort, safety, release,
and support that CR groups provided.

Another reason for the growth of Feminist Goddess Worship was the power of Elizabeth
Gould Davis's *The First Sex*, an early statement of the spiritual movement's enabling myth.
Davis's aim was to empower women by demonstrating that women had once ruled. She dismissed received history as "two thousand years of propaganda" about female inferiority, as
she searched myth, literature, findings of archaeology, and patriarchal history for the "Lost
Civilization" of the female-dominated past (Davis, 1972: 18–19). Davis was a prophet for a
new religion that would be many years in the making.

In 1976, Merlin Stone published her enormously influential *The Paradise Papers*
(published in 1978 in the US as *When God Was a Woman*), and Feminist Goddess Worship
had one of its sacred books. Stone's pivotal work inspired women to seek out goddesses.
Since then, myriad books have contributed heavily to the spread of Feminist Goddess
Worship, for example, Riane Eisler's *The Chalice and the Blade* (1987), Elinor Gadon's
The Once and Future Goddess (1989), and Anne Baring and Julie Cashford's *The Myth of
the Goddess* (1991).

The Myth or Sacred Story

Feminist Goddess Worship has a very powerful enabling myth (Raphael, 2000: ch. 3; Reuther, 2005: 13ff.): For millennia, prehistoric peace and harmony prevailed in goddess-worshipping, woman-centred cultures. Then violent conquerors erupted from desert or steppe, devastated the gentle matriarchal societies, and, by force, instituted male dominance or patriarchy (Davis, 1971; Stone, 1976; Gimbutas, 1982, 1989, 1991; Eisler, 1987). The sacred history follows societal development from the arrival of the patriarchal invaders through to the present day, the witch hunts of the early modern period forming a major example of the continuing persecution of goddess worshippers. Donna Read's visually stunning and extremely popular film *Goddess Remembered* (1989) is an evocative testimony to the myth.

Though many devotees no longer insist that events in the "sacred history" actually happened, the myth comes alive in each retelling, made new by each interpretation. A number of women have written it down, but it remains, like all true myth, essentially oral, recounted at parties, celebrations, and, above all, rituals. The myth tells women about ancient goddess worship and matriarchies, patriarchal takeover, women's creativity and wonderful bodily functions, their natural power and strength, and the return of the Goddess and women's re-empowerment in a Goddess-centred religion. Given the tremendous validation women receive from worshipping the Goddess, it is no wonder that Feminist Goddess Worshippers get annoyed at scholars who argue that events may not have happened exactly as the story says (Hurtado, 1990; Frymer-Kensky, 1992; Christ, 1997: 70–88; Eller, 2000; Reuther, 2005).

The Goddess

Carol Christ, feminist thealogian (student of the female divine), explains why women need the Goddess: to help them acknowledge that female power is "beneficent," independent, and legitimate; to validate the female body and "the life cycle expressed in it"; to symbolize "the positive valuation of will" in Goddess rituals; and to permit women to re-assess their connections to one another and to "their heritage" (Christ, 1979b).

Sometimes the Goddess is One, sometimes Many. Her Oneness answers the Oneness of the traditional God (Raphael, 2000: ch. 2). The Goddess chant "Isis, Astarte, Diana, Hecate, Demeter, Kali—Inanna" invokes the Goddess by some of Her myriad names. The Goddess's many aspects relate to women's experiences of their bodies, their cyclical natures, and their intertwining relationships over generations. Whether She is one or many, Feminist Goddess Worshippers often have a special relationship with a particular goddess, who is obviously Herself and not just an aspect of the Goddess.

The Triple Goddess, much-revered in Feminist Goddess Worship, is the epitome of the One and the Many. She is the Moon, whose three phases are represented by specific goddesses. She also corresponds to the phases of womanhood: maiden, mother, and crone. The Triple Goddess seems to be the Feminist Goddess Worship's Holy Trinity (Christ, 1997: 109–112).

Principles

First, the deity is a goddess or goddesses, not just the inclusion of the female in a pair or as an aspect of divinity (Raphael, 1999; Christ, 2003: 227). The religion puts female and feminine at the centre of "its system of symbols, beliefs, and practices" (Eller, 1993: 3). Since it also regards the Goddess as validating the female body, it refuses to accept the body/mind-spirit dualism of Western culture (Christ, 1997: 30, 100; Christ, 2003).

Second, Feminist Goddess Worshippers understand that female empowerment, which often means healing, is the primary aim of their religion. As long as they are not harmful to others, whatever means women employ to achieve that end are valid (Christ, 1997: 165 ff.).

Third, they are almost universally in agreement that Nature is alive and sacred, often personified as a Goddess—Mother Earth, Mother Nature, Gaia. Some see human psychological problems as the result of alienation from Nature (Low and Tremayne, 2001). Others regard the concept of progress with a jaundiced eye and consider the "ascent of man" to be the reason for today's ecological disasters. Thus, ecological activism often attracts them (Christ, 1997: 134).

Fourth, tolerance of other people's differing views and actions or non-actions is, with few exceptions, a given in Feminist Goddess Worship (Christ, 1997: 152–153), as it is generally among Neo-pagans and Wiccans (Adler, 1986: 101).

Fifth, a large number accept "the revisionist version of Western history" (Eller, 1993: 6). Further, many are serious students of ancient cultures and myths, reading widely, attending classes, and passing on their knowledge (Christ, 1997: 50ff.).

Sixth, decentralization is an absolute rule; there can be no central authority and no hierarchy in worship. Feminist Goddess Worship groups are small and independent. In addition, there are no received and inviolate scriptures and no collective liturgy, though much sharing and borrowing goes on (Christ, 1997: 29).

There is also general, if not universal, agreement about the following: Many regard their religion as forcing them into political action, while for others spirituality separates them from politics; for most devotees, the sacred is neither transcendent, nor immanent, but both (Christ, 1997: 101ff.); borrowing from Wiccans, a number of worshippers think that sexuality is sacred, whatever its expression, with, of course, the proviso that it not harm another (Christ, 1997: 147).

There are of course some disagreements among Feminist Goddess Worshippers. One tension concerns men in the movement and the nature of females and males. Are women and men similar or different? Are women superior to men? The nature/culture controversy also produces debate. Some disagree over the structure and organization of ancient matriarchies, the origin and definition of patriarchy, and the form of a truly woman-centred culture. Occasionally there is dispute over the nature of the Goddess. In addition, questions arise about the ethics of appropriation from other traditions and about ideas of good and evil, especially with respect to the practice of "magic."

Practices

Feminist Goddess Worship manifests itself primarily in ritual (Northup, 1997). Ritual connects participants to the Goddess. Ritual also brings worshippers back into harmony with Nature. Thus, many groups meet monthly, or more often, to celebrate the new or full moon (Christ, 1997: 25–30).

Gatherings also contain social and therapeutic elements. Goddess groups provide support for members, validation for changes they may be making in their lives, and, when necessary, group therapy and healing.

Women come together to celebrate with special rituals events in one another's life cycle or the life cycles of relatives and friends: menarche, middle age and menopause; conception and birth, as well as abortion and miscarriage; marriage and divorce. In addition, Feminist Goddess Worshippers celebrate cosmic events like solstices and equinoxes. Sometimes these latter rituals are large, when women gather for a festival (Eller, 1993: 1ff).

Feminist Goddess Worshippers are creative in constructing rituals, borrowing freely from many cultural traditions. Addressing at least four directions, the spirits of west, east, south, and north, seems now to be obligatory, as is "smudging," burning of sage or some other aromatic plant to purify participants with smoke.

In principle, Feminist Goddess Worship groups are leaderless, and all members are priestesses. However, in larger gatherings, those with an aptitude for religious leadership normally take these roles.

A typical ritual starts with the setting up of an altar, the introduction of participants, and the creation of sacred space and time, "casting of the circle." Worshippers do this by "calling in the four directions." When the circle is "closed," the ritual begins. Chanting almost always occurs. One chant, which encapsulates the essence of the religion, goes: "We all come from the Goddess, and unto Her we shall return, like a drop of rain flowing to the ocean." Meditation is another ritual technique, along with role playing and rhythmic dancing. Sometimes a participant will go into trance, sometimes become possessed by a goddess or other spirit. Worshippers bless one another and themselves and listen to the telling of myths or to short homilies.

The core of the ritual is the creation of a "cone of power." Focusing their collective energy through dance, drumming, and chant, the ecstatic participants direct the power they have "raised" to specific ends, often healing (Eller, 1993: 93). Then the group "grounds" the energy through a precise ritual technique. Worshippers conclude the ritual by releasing the spirits of the directions and pronouncing the circle "open, but unbroken." The group then relaxes to enjoy the food and drink that always accompany such occasions. Feminist Goddess Worshippers have borrowed many of these practices piecemeal from Wicca (Starhawk, 1979: 133).

The use of magic in ritual is a controversial topic, magic being understood as the ability to contact the power of the Goddess and focus that power through the will. Starhawk defines magic as changing "consciousness at will," an alteration that can, and does, change the world (Starhawk, 1979: 109). Many Feminist Goddess Worshippers believe that magic exists and that it is very potent.

Feminist Goddess Worship defies categorization. Women are creating, from day to day, an empowering, fulfilling alternative to other religions. Although it is difficult to foresee its future form, most adherents believe, as a lapel button announces, "The Goddess is here, and SHE is ORGANIZING."

Lesbian Voices

According to Cynthia Eller, Feminist Goddess Worshippers in the United States are disproportionately lesbian, the spirituality being "the civil religion of the lesbian feminist community" (1993: 18, 20–21, 35, 41). Unquestionably, there is a "strong lesbian element" in Feminist Goddess Worship (Raphael, 1996: 13, 272). Even more, the new religion has benefited greatly from the strength and energy of lesbian women (Adler, 1986: 340). Lesbian feminist writers, Audre Lorde and Adrienne Rich, for example, have made important contributions to the literature of Feminist Goddess Worship (Lorde, 1989; Rich, 1976).

CONCLUSION

Modern religious-studies scholarship has, until very recently, ignored female spirituality, so that we are only just beginning to find out about it. Nonetheless, women have always expressed their spirituality as fully as their situations have allowed. It is, then, important to listen to what women say about their spiritual experiences and about what those experiences mean. Feminist theologians are correct, therefore, to point to women's experiences as the key. They are the key to our accepting a woman's satisfaction with a fundamentalist religion. Despite our feminist conviction that the religion is generally sexist and demeaning to women, the individual woman's experience tells another story. Women's experiences are also the key to our understanding what it is about religions of complementarity between female and male that makes women inside them insist that they are egalitarian. And it is women's experiences to which we must turn to seek the reason why, despite the obvious appeal of Feminist Goddess Worship, Jewish, Christian, and Muslim feminists stay in their contradictory and ambivalent positions of deep emotional commitment to sexist traditions. Finally, the empowering experiences of feminists who worship the Goddess speak to the power of the new religion to nurture and heal women.

Endnotes

1. To Nancy Mandell goes my deep gratitude for her unstinting help and support. In addition, Aviva Goldberg's knowledge and insights, as well as research assistance, have been invaluable. Further, I owe appreciation to Amila Buturovic, Charlotte Caron, Beth Cutts, Jordan Paper, Jane Robin, and Oana Petrica for their advice and help on this chapter. Needless to say, any errors herein are totally my responsibility.

2. "Feminist Goddess Worship" is my term for the new religion in its various manifestations. I settled on it after considering "Feminist Spirituality," used by many (for example Gross, 1996; Christ, 1997), and "Modern Goddess Worship." I eliminated the latter because it names the worship of goddesses in Hinduism, Chinese religion, and other modern polytheistic traditions. My conviction that many Jewish, Christian, and Muslim feminists are also practising "Feminist Spirituality" forced me to find another term.

3. In the first version of this chapter, I called this category "Reformist," but altered it to avoid confusion with Reform Judaism. Carol Christ's 1983 essay on symbols of deity in feminist theology was my starting point in developing these categories. In that essay Christ distinguishes three feminist-theological positions, equivalent to Revisionist, Renovationist, and Rejectionist. Since 1983, however, a fourth position has emerged, Revolutionary. Though other scholars use different names for these positions, Christ's article has influenced almost all of them (Christ, 1983: 238).

4. Over time, rabbinical interpretation of the Torah, as well as the rest of the Hebrew Bible and the Talmud (see note 5) produced *halakhah*, "the path," rabbinic law. As Plaskow points out, behaviours, not beliefs, are the defining characteristic of Judaism, and *halakhah* elaborates behaviours. *Halakhah* ideally enjoins the observant Jew to fulfill a number of obligations, or *mitzvot*, traditionally 613 in all. However, the rabbis judged that, although adult males who were free, not slaves, were bound by all obligations, women should be exempt from all but three which apply only to women: *challah*, breaking of the bread at Sabbath; *hadlik ner*, lighting of Sabbath candles; and *niddah*, observing laws of family purity (women are to practise sexual abstinence during menstruation and for seven days after, and, before resuming marital relations, to immerse themselves in a purifying ritual bath, *mikveh*) (Frankiel, 1990: 74–85).

5. The Talmud contains the *Mishnah*, the code of Jewish law, and commentaries on it. In 63 volumes it explains and amplifies the Torah.

6. Fundamentalism occurs in many religious traditions, including Christianity, Judaism, Islam, Buddhism, and Hinduism (Ruthven, 2004: 196). The term applies to strict adherence to what followers understand are their religion's basic "truths and practices" (Brink and Mencher 1997: 247). It manifests itself as "a religious way of being" and a strategy adopted to maintain a "distinctive identity" against the assault of "modernity and secularization" (Ruthven, 2004: 8).

7. The "Five Pillars of Islam" are five duties or acts of worship: *shahadah*, daily witness to the Oneness of God; *salah*, prayer five times a day; *zakah*, alms-giving; *sawm*, abstinence in the month of Ramadan; and *hajj*, pilgrimage to Mecca at least once in a lifetime.

Suggested Readings

Christ, Carol P. 1997. *Rebirth of the Goddess: Finding meaning in feminist spirituality*. Reading, MA: Addison-Wesley. Christ's work is the first systematic and theoretical thealogy of Feminist Goddess Worship.

Cooey, Paula M., William R. Eakin, and Jay B. McDaniel, eds. 1997. *After patriarchy: Feminist transformations of the world religions*. Maryknoll, NY: Orbis. This book presents articles by well-known feminist scholars on various traditions, including Judaism, Christianity, and Islam, first published in 1991.

Hampson, Daphne. 1993. *Theology and feminism*. Oxford: Blackwell. This British "post-Christian" feminist theologian presents a full and controversial examination of Christianity.

Plaskow, Judith. 1990. *Standing again at Sinai: Judaism from a feminist perspective*. San Francisco: Harper and Row. The foremost American Jewish feminist theologian analyzes Judaism in detail and concludes that radical change is necessary.

Stuckey, Johanna H. 1998. *Feminist spirituality: An introduction to feminist theology in Judaism, Christianity, Islam, and Feminist Goddess Worship*. Toronto: Centre for Feminist Research, York University. This book presents the background, normative practices, and feminist theology of four religions, with introductory bibliographies on other traditions.

Yamani, Mai, ed. 1996. *Feminism and Islam: Legal and literary perspectives*. New York: New York University. This work presents articles by Islamic feminists on the effect of Islam on women in general and in a number of Muslim countries.

Discussion Questions

1. Into what feminist theological category or categories (Revisionist, Renovationist, Revolutionary) do the suggested readings by Daphne Hampson and Judith Plaskow fit? How does Hampson react to the views of Daly or Reuther, and how would Plaskow react to those of Gottlieb? How would both respond to Christ's *Rebirth of the Goddess*?

2. In what ways is Carol Christ's position in *Rebirth of the Goddess* Rejectionist? Discuss the criticisms implicit in her book of the three monotheistic traditions.

3. Using Plaskow, the articles in Yamani, and the works of Reuther or Fiorenza, discuss critically the reasons why feminists remain inside admittedly sexist religious traditions.

4. What major changes would be necessary in each of Judaism, Christianity, and Islam to satisfy feminist theologians, especially the Revolutionaries?

Bibliography

Abu-Lughod, Lila. 1998. *Remaking women: Feminism and modernity in the Middle East*. Princeton, NJ: Princeton Univ. Press.

Adelman, Penina V. 1990. *Miriam's well: Rituals for Jewish women around the year*, 2d ed. New York: Biblio.

Adler, Margot. 1986. *Drawing down the moon: Witches, Druids, Goddess-worshippers, and other pagans in America today*, Rev ed. Boston: Beacon.

Afshar, Haleh, ed. 1993. *Women in the Middle East*. London: Macmillan.

Ahmed, Leila. 1992. *Women and gender in Islam: Historical roots of a modern debate*. New Haven, CT: Yale Univ. Press.

Alam, S. M. Shamsul. 1998. Women in the era of modernity and Islamic fundamentalism: The case of Taslima Nasrin. *Signs* 23(1): 429–461.

Ali, Yasmin. 1992. Muslim women and the politics of ethnicity and culture in Northern England, in *Refusing holy orders: Women and fundamentalism in Britain*, eds. Gita Saghal and Nira Yuval-Davis, 101–123. London: Virago.

Alpert, Rebecca. 1997. *Like bread on the Seder plate: Jewish lesbians and the transformation of tradition*. New York: Columbia Univ. Press.

Alpert, Rebecca, and Goldie Milgram. 1996. Women in the reconstructionist rabbinate, in *Religious institutions and women's leadership: New roles inside the mainstream*, ed. Catherine Wessenger, 275–288. Columbia, SC: Univ. of South Carolina Press.

Alvi, Sajida S., Homa Hoodfar, and Sheila McDonough, eds. 2003. *The Muslim veil in North America: Issues and debates*. Toronto: Women's Press.

Ameli, Saied R., and Arzu Merali. 2006. *British Muslims' expectations of the government: Hijab, meaning, identity, otherization, and politics: British Muslim women*. Wembley, UK: Islamic Human Rights Commission.

Anderson, Grace M. 1990. *God calls, man chooses: A study of women in ministry*. Burlington, ON: Trinity.

Anwar, Etin. 2006. *Gender and self in Islam*. London: Routledge.

Aquino, Maria Pilar, Daisy L. Macado, and Jeannette Rodriguez, eds. 2002. *A reader in Latina feminist theology: Religion and justice*. Austin: Univ. of Texas Press.

Badran, Margot. 1995. *Islam and nation: Gender and the making of modern Egypt*. Princeton, NJ: Princeton Univ. Press.

Badran, Margot, and Miriam Cooke, eds. 1990. *Opening the gates: A century of Arab feminist writing*. Bloomington: Indiana Univ. Press.

Balka, Christie, and Andy Rose, eds. 1989. *Twice blessed: On being lesbian, gay, and Jewish*. Boston: Beacon.

Baring, Anne, and Jules Cashford. 1991. *The myth of the Goddess: Evolution of an image*. London: Arkana.

Barlow, Rebecca, and Shahram Akbarzadeh. 2008. Prospects for feminism in the Islamic Republic of Iran. *Human Rights Quarterly* 30: 21–40.

Baskin, Judith R. 2002. *Midrashic women: Formations of the feminine in rabbinic literature.* Hanover, NH: Univ. of New England/Brandeis Univ. Press.

Beattie, Tina. 1999. Global sisterhood or wicked stepsisters: Why don't girls with god-mothers get invited to the ball?, in *Is there a future for feminist theology?*, eds. Deborah F. Sawyer and Diane M. Collier, 115–125. Sheffield, UK: Sheffield Academic.

Beck, Evelyn T., ed. 1982. *Nice Jewish girls: A lesbian anthology.* Watertown, MA: Persephone.

Beck, Lois, and Nikki Keddie, eds. 1978. *Women in the Muslim world.* Cambridge, MA: Harvard Univ. Press.

Bowker, John, ed. 1997. *The Oxford dictionary of world religions.* Oxford: Oxford Univ. Press.

Brettschneider, Marla, and Dawn R. Rose. 2003. Meeting at the well: Multiculturalism and Jewish feminism. Introduction. *Journal of Feminist Studies in Religion* 19(1): 85–90.

Bridges. 1997/1998. Special Issue 7(1).

Brink, Judy, and Joan Mencher, eds. 1997. *Mixed blessings: Gender and religious fundamentalism cross culturally.* New York: Routledge.

Brooten, Bernadette. 1982. *Women leaders in the ancient synagogue.* Chico, CA: Scholars.

Brouwer, Ruth. 2002. *Modern women modernizing men: The changing missions of three professional women in Asia and Africa, 1902–69.* Vancouver: Univ. of British Columbia Press.

Brouwer, Ruth C. 1990. *New women for God: Canadian Presbyterian women and India missions.* Toronto: Univ. of Toronto Press.

Brown, Joanne, and Carol Bohn, eds. 1989. *Christianity, patriarchy, and abuse: A feminist critique.* New York: Pilgrim.

Butler, Becky, ed. 1990. *Ceremonies of the heart: Celebrating lesbian unions.* Seattle, WA: Seal.

Butler, Judith. 2001. Contingent foundations: Feminism and the question of "Postmodernism," in *Feminism in the study of religion: A reader*, ed. Darlene M. Juschka, 629–647. New York: Continuum.

Buturovic, Amila. 1995. Islam. Guest lecture, Humanities 2820.06, Female spirituality course, Division of Humanities, Faculty of Arts, York University, Toronto, January 17.

Buturovic, Amila. 1997. Spiritual empowerment through spiritual submission: Sufi women and their quest for God. *Canadian Woman Studies/Les cahiers de la femme* 17(1): 53–56.

Cambell, Debra. 1989. The Catholic earth mother: Dorothy Day and power in the church, in *Unspoken worlds: Women's religious lives*, eds. Nancy A. Falk and Rita M. Gross, 15–24. Belmont, CA: Wadsworth.

Canadian Woman Studies. 1996. *Special issue: Jewish women.* 16(4).

Cannon, Katie G. 1998. *Black womanist ethics.* Atlanta, GA: Scholars.

Cantor, Aviva. 1979. A Jewish woman's Haggadah, in *Womanspirit rising: A feminist reader in religion*, eds. Carol P. Christ and Judith Plaskow, 185–192. New York: Harper and Row.

Carley, Kathleen E. 2002. *Women and the historical Jesus: Feminist myths of Christian origins.* Santa Rosa, CA: Polebridge.

Carmody, Denise L. 1989. *Women and world religions*, 2d ed. Englewood Cliffs, NJ: Prentice Hall.

Caron, Charlotte. 1993. *To make and make again: Feminist ritual thealogy.* New York: Crossroad.

Cherry, Kittredge, and Zalmon Sherwood, eds. 1995. *Equal rites: Lesbian and gay worship, ceremonies, and celebrations.* Louisville, KY: Westminster John Knox.

Chesler, Phyllis, and Rivka Haut, eds. 2003. *Women of the wall: Reclaiming sacred ground at Judaism's holy site.* Woodstock, VT: Jewish Lights.

Christ, Carol P. 1979a. Spiritual quest and women's experience, in *Womanspirit rising: A feminist reader in religion,* eds. Carol P. Christ and Judith Plaskow, 228–245. New York: Harper and Row.

Christ, Carol P. 1979b. Why women need the Goddess: Phenomenological, psychological, and political reflections, in *Womanspirit rising: A feminist reader in religion,* eds. Carol P. Christ and Judith Plaskow, 273–287. New York: Harper and Row.

Christ, Carol P. 1983. Symbols of Goddess and God in feminist theology, in *The book of the Goddess, past and present: An introduction to her religion,* ed. Carl Olson, 231–251. New York: Crossroad.

Christ, Carol P. 1997. *Rebirth of the Goddess: Finding meaning in feminist spirituality.* Reading, MA: Addison-Wesley.

Christ, Carol P. 2003. *She who changes: Re-imagining the divine in the world.* New York: Palgrave Macmillan.

Christ, Carol P., and Judith Plaskow, eds. 1979. *Womanspirit rising: A feminist reader in religion.* New York: Harper and Row.

Cleary, Thomas, ed. 1993. *The essential Koran: The heart of Islam.* San Francisco: HarperSanFrancisco.

Cohen, Debra H. 1997. Chasm between Orthodoxy and feminism closing. *Canadian Jewish News,* February 27: 49.

Cohler-Esses, Dianne, 2003. A common language between East and West. *Journal of Feminist Studies in Religion* 19(1): 111–118.

Coleman, Monica. 2006. Must I be womanist? *Journal of Feminist Studies in Religion* 22(1): 85–134.

Comstock, Gary D. 1996. *Unrepentant, self-affirming, practicing: Lesbian/bi-sexual/gay people within organized religion.* New York: Continuum.

Comstock, Gary D. 2001. *A whosoever church: Welcoming lesbians and gay men into African American congregations.* Louisville, KY: Westminster John Knox.

Cooke, Miriam. 2001. *Women claim Islam: Creating Islamic feminism through literature.* New York: Routledge.

Cooke, Miriam. 2002. Multiple critique: Islamic feminist rhetorical strategies, in *Postcolonialism, feminism and religious discourse,* eds. Laura E. Donaldson and Kowk Pui-lan, 181–198. NY: Routledge.

Curb, Rosemary, and Nancy Monahan, eds. 1985. *Lesbian nuns: Breaking silence.* Tallahassee, FL: Naiad.

Daly, Mary. 1973. *Beyond God the father: Toward a philosophy of women's liberation.* Boston: Beacon.

Daly, Mary. 1978. *Gyn/Ecology: The metaethics of radical feminism.* Boston: Beacon.

Daly, Mary. 1985. The *church and the second sex: With the feminist postchristian introduction and new archaic afterwords by the author.* Boston: Beacon.

Davis, Elizabeth G. 1972. *The first sex.* Baltimore, MD: Penguin.

Donaldson, Laura E., and Kwok Pui-lan, eds. 2002. *Postcolonialism, feminism and religious discourse.* New York: Routledge.

Duran, Khalid. Homosexuality and Islam, in *Homosexuality and world religions*, ed. Arlene Swidler, 181–198. Valley Forge, PA: Trinity.

Dyke, Doris J. *Crucified woman.* Toronto: United Church of Canada.

Eisler, Riane. 1987. *The chalice and the blade: Our history, our future.* San Francisco: Harper and Row.

Eller, Cynthia. 1993. *Living in the lap of the Goddess: The feminist spirituality movement in America.* New York: Crossroad.

Eller, Cynthia. 2000. *The myth of matriarchal prehistory: Why an invented past won't give women a future.* Boston: Beacon.

El-Or, Tamar. 1994. *Educated and ignorant: Ultraorthodox Jewish women and their world.* Boulder, CO: Lynne Rienner.

Elwell, Sue L. 1996. Women's voices: The challenge of feminism to Judaism, in *Religious institutions and women's leadership: New roles inside the mainstream*, ed. Catherine Wessenger, 331–343. Columbia, SC: Univ. of South Carolina Press.

Epstein, Isadore. 1990. *Judaism: A historical presentation.* London: Penguin.

Eron, Lewis. 1993. Homosexuality and Judaism, in *Homosexuality and world religions*, ed. Arlene Swidler, 103–136. Valley Forge, PA: Trinity.

Eugene, Toinette M. 1992. To be of use. *Journal of Feminist Studies in Religion* 8(2): 138–147.

Falk, Marcia. 1996. *The book of blessings: New Jewish prayers for daily life, the Sabbath, and the New Moon Festival.* San Francisco: HarperSanFrancisco.

Falk, Marcia. 2003. My father's riddle, or conflict and reciprocity in the multicultural (Jewish) self. *Journal of Feminist Studies in Religion* 19(1): 97–103.

Falk, Nancy A., and Rita M. Gross, eds. 1989. *Unspoken worlds: Women's religious lives.* Belmont, CA: Wadsworth.

Feldman, Ron H. 2003. "On your new moons": The feminist transformation of the Jewish New Moon Festival. *Journal of women and religion* 19–20: 26–51.

Fernea, Elizabeth W., ed. 1985. *Women and the family in the Middle East: New voices of change.* Austin: Univ. of Texas Press.

Fernea, Elizabeth W. 1998. *In search of Islamic feminism: One woman's global journey.* New York: Doubleday.

Fernea, Elizabeth W., and Basima Q. Bezirgan, eds. 1977. *Middle Eastern Muslim women speak.* Austin: Univ. of Texas Press.

Fine, Irene. 1988. *Midlife—a rite of passage: The wise woman—a celebration.* San Diego, CA: Women's Institute for Continuing Jewish Education.

Finson, Shelley D. 1995. *A historical review of the development of feminist liberation theology.* Ottawa: Canadian Research Institute for the Advancement of Women.

Fiorenza, Elisabeth Schüssler. 1983. *In memory of her: A feminist theological reconstruction of Christian origins*. New York: Crossroad.

Fiorenza, Elisabeth Schüssler. 1992. *But she said: Feminist practices of Biblical interpretation*. Boston: Beacon.

Fiorenza, Elisabeth Schüssler. 2001. *Wisdom ways: Introducing feminist Biblical interpretation*. Maryknoll, NY: Orbis.

Fletcher-Marsh, Wendy. 1995. *Beyond the walled garden: Anglican women and the priesthood*. Dundas, ON: Artemis.

Frankiel, Tamar. 1990. *The voice of Sarah: Feminine spirituality and traditional Judaism*. San Francisco: HarperSanFrancisco.

Friedman, Debbie. 2000. *Timbrels and Torahs: Celebrating women's wisdom* (video). Berkeley, CA: Jot of Wisdom.

Frymer-Kensky, Tikva. 1992. *In the wake of the goddesses: Women, culture, and the Biblical transformation of pagan myth*. New York: Free Press.

Frymer-Kensky, Tikva. 2002. *Reading the women of the Bible*. New York: Schocken.

Gadon, Elinor W. 1989. *The once and future Goddess: A symbol for our time*. San Francisco: Harper and Row.

Giese, Rachel. 2003. Out of the Koran: A conference for queer Muslims is a step toward liberation. *Xtra,* June 12: 15.

Gill, Sean, ed. 1998. *The lesbian and gay Christian movement: Campaigning for justice, truth and love*. London: Cassell.

Gimbutas, Marija. 1982. *The goddesses and gods of old Europe, 6500 to 3500 BC*. Berkeley, CA: Univ. of California Press.

Gimbutas, Marija. 1989. *The language of the Goddess: Unearthing the hidden symbols of Western civilization*. San Francisco: HarperSanFrancisco.

Gimbutas, Marija. 1991. *The civilization of the Goddess: The world of old Europe*. San Francisco: HarperSanFrancisco.

Goldberg, Aviva. 2002. *Re-awakening Deborah: Locating the feminist in the liturgy, ritual, and theology of contemporary Jewish renewal*. Unpublished PhD thesis, York University, Toronto.

Goldenberg, Naomi R. 2007. What's God got to do with it? A call for problematizing basic terms in the feminist analysis of religion. *Feminist Theology* 15(3): 275–288.

Goldman, Karla. 2000. *Beyond the synagogue: Finding a place for women in American Judaism*. Cambridge, MA: Harvard Univ. Press.

Goldman, Karla. 2007. Women in Reform Judaism: Between rhetoric and reality, in *Women remaking American Judaism*, ed. Riv-Ellen Prell. Detroit: Wayne State Univ. Press.

Gottlieb, Lynn. 1995. *She who dwells within: A feminist vision of a renewed Judaism*. San Francisco: HarperSanFrancisco.

Grant, Jacquelyn. 1982. Black women and the church, in *All the women are white, all the Blacks are men, but some of us are brave: Black women's studies*, eds. Gloria T. Hull et al., 141–152. New York: Feminist Press.

Grant, Jacquelyn. 1989. *White women's Christ and Black women's Jesus: Feminist christology and womanist response*. Atlanta, GA: Scholars.

Grant, Jacquelyn. 1993. "Come to my help, Lord, for I'm in trouble": Womanist Jesus and the mutual struggle for liberation, in *Reconstructing the Christ symbol: Essays in feminist christology*, ed. Maryanne Stevens, 54–71. Mahwah, NJ: Paulist Press.

Green-McCreight, Kathryn. 2000. *Feminist reconstructions of Christian doctrines: Narrative analysis and appraisal*. New York: Oxford Univ. Press.

Gross, Rita. 1979. Female God language in a Jewish context, in *Womanspirit rising: A feminist reader in religion*, eds. Carol P. Christ and Judith Plaskow, 167–173. New York: Harper and Row.

Gross, Rita. 1996. *Feminism and religion: An introduction*. Boston: Beacon.

Haddad, Yvonne Y., and John L. Esposito, eds. 1998. *Islam, gender, and social change*. New York: Oxford Univ. Press.

Haddad, Yvonne Y., and John L. Esposito, eds. 2001. *Daughters of Abraham: Feminist thought in Judaism, Christianity, and Islam*. Gainesville, FL: Univ. of Florida Press.

Haddad, Yvonne Y., Jane I. Smith, and Kathleen M. Moore. 2006. *Muslim women in America: The challenge of Islamic identity today*. New York: Oxford Univ. Press.

Haker, Hille, Susan Ross, and Marie-Theres Wacker, eds. 2006. *Women's voices in world religions*. London: SCM.

Hamadeh, Naijla. 1996. Islamic family legislation: The authoritarian discourse of silence, in *Feminism & Islam: Legal and literary perspectives*, ed. Mai Yamani, 331–350. New York: New York Univ. Press.

Harris, Lis. 1985. *Holy days: The world of a Hasidic family*. New York: Summit.

Hassan, Riffat. 1997. Muslim women and post-patriarchal Islam, in *After patriarchy: Feminist transformations of the world religions*, eds. Paula M. Cooey, William R. Eakin, and J. B. McDaniel. Maryknoll, NY: Orbis.

Hazel, Dann. 2000. *Witness: Gay and lesbian clergy report from the front*. Louisville, KY: Westminster John Knox.

Heschel, Susannah, ed. 1995. *On being a Jewish feminist*. New York: Schocken.

Heschel, Susannah. 2004. Gender and agency in the feminist historiography of Jewish identity. *Journal of Religion* 84(4): 580–591.

Heywood, Isabel Carter. 1984. *Our passion for justice: Images of power, sexuality and liberation*. New York: Pilgrim.

Heywood, Isabel Carter. 1989a. *Speaking of Christ: A lesbian feminist voice*, ed. Ellen C. Davis. New York: Pilgrim.

Heywood, Isabel Carter. 1989b. *Touching our strength: The erotic as power and the love of God*. San Francisco: Harper and Row.

Hirsi Ali, Ayaan. 2006. *The caged virgin: An emancipation proclamation for women and Islam*. New York: Free Press.

hooks, bell. 1981. *Ain't I a woman? Black women and feminism*. Boston: South End.

hooks, bell. 1984. *Feminist theory: From margin to center*. Boston: South End.

Hurtado, Larry, ed. 1990. *Goddesses in religions and modern debate*. Atlanta, GA: Scholars.

Imam, Ayesha. 1997. The Muslim religious right ("fundamentalists") and sexuality. *Women Living Under Muslim Laws*, Dossier 17: 7–25 (boite postale 23, 3474, Gravelle, France). **www.wluml.org/english/index.shtml**

Isasi-Díaz, Ada María. 1996. *Mujerista theology: A theology for the twenty-first century.* Maryknoll, NY: Orbis.

Isherwood, Lisa, and Dorothea McEwan, eds. 2001. *Introducing feminist theology*, 2d ed. Sheffield, UK: Sheffield Academic.

Jamali, Umarah. 2007. Muslim groups press India to expel author. *Globe and Mail*, August 28: A13.

Joseph, Norma Baumel. 2007. Women in Orthodoxy: Conventional and contentious, in *Women remaking American Judaism*, ed. Riv-Ellen Prell. Detroit: Wayne State Univ. Press.

Juschka, Darlene M., ed. 2001. *Feminism in the study of religion.* NY: Continuum.

Kamisuka, Margaret D. 2003. Reading the raced and sexed body in *The Color Purple*: Repatterning white feminist and womanist theological hermeneutics. *Journal of Feminist Studies in Religion* 19(2): 45–66.

Karkala-Zorba, Katerina. 2006. Women in the church: A Greek Orthodox view, in *Women's voices in world religions*, eds. Hille Haker, Susan Ross, and Marie-Theres Wacker, 36–45. London: SCM.

Keddie, Nikki R. 2007. *Women in the Middle East, past and present.* Princeton, NJ: Princeton Univ. Press.

Keller, Rosemary S., and Rosemary R. Reuther, eds. 2000. *In our own voices: Four centuries of American women's religious writings.* Louisville, KY: Westminster John Knox.

Keller, Rosemary S., and Rosemary R. Reuther, eds. 2006. *Encyclopedia of women and religion in North America.* Bloomington, IN: Indiana Univ. Press.

Khan, Shahnaz. 2002. Muslim women: Negotiations in the third space, in *Gender and politics in Islam*, eds. Therese Saliba, Carolyn Allen, and Judith A. Howard, 337–346. Chicago: Univ. of Chicago Press.

Khanum, Saeeda. 1992. Education and the Muslim girl, in *Refusing holy orders: Women and fundamentalism in Britain*, eds. Gita Saghal and Nira Yuval-Davis, 124–140. London: Virago.

Kim, Nami. 2002. "My/our" comfort *not* at the expense of "somebody else's": Toward a critical global feminist theology," *Journal of Feminist Studies in Religion* 21(2): 75–94.

King, Ursula. 1989. *Women and spirituality: Voices of protest and promise.* New York: New Amsterdam.

King, Ursula, ed. 1994. *Feminist theology from the Third World: A reader.* Maryknoll, NY: Orbis.

King, Ursula. 1998. *Christian mystics: The spiritual heart of the Christian tradition.* New York: Simon and Schuster.

King, Ursula, ed. 2000. *Religion and gender.* Oxford: Blackwell.

The Koran. 1994. Tr. J.M. Rodwell. London: Dent Everyman.

Kraemer, Ross S. 1992. *Her share of the blessings: Women's religions among pagans, Jews and Christians in the Greco-Roman world.* New York: Oxford Univ. Press.

Kraemer, Ross S., and Mary Rose D'Angelo, eds. 1999. *Women and Christian origins.* New York: Oxford Univ. Press.

Kwok Pui-lan. 2000. *Introducing Asian feminist theology.* Cleveland, OH: Pilgrim.

Labidi-Maiza, Mehrezia. 2006. My father's heir: The journey of a Muslim feminist, in *Women's voices in world religions*, eds. Hille Haker, Susan Ross, and Marie-Theres Wacker, 72–80. London: SCM.

Laffey Alice. 2001. The influence of feminism on Christianity, in *Daughters of Abraham: Feminist thought in Judaism, Christianity, and Islam*, eds. Yvonne Yazbeck Haddad and John L. Esposito. Gainesville, FL: Univ. of Florida Press.

Lateef, Shahida. 1990. *Muslim women in India: Political and private realities*. London: Zed.

Lebans, Gertrude. 1994. *Gathered by the river: Reflections and essays of women doing ministry*. Toronto: United Church of Canada.

Legge, Marilyn J. 1992. *The grace of difference: A Canadian feminist theological ethic*. Atlanta, GA: Scholars.

Levine, Amy-Jill. 2001. Settling at Beer-lahai-roi, in *Daughters of Abraham: Feminist thought in Judaism, Christianity, and Islam*, eds. Yvonne Yazbeck Haddad and John L. Esposito. Gainesville, FL: Univ. of Florida Press.

Levine, Amy-Jill. 2003. Multiculturalism, women's studies, and anti-Judaism. *Journal of Feminist Studies in Religion* 19(1): 119–128.

Lindner, Eileen W., ed. 2007. *Yearbook of American and Canadian churches*. Nashville, TN: Abingdon.

Lorde, Audre. 1989. Uses of the erotic: The erotic as power, in *Weaving the visions: New patterns in feminist spirituality*, eds. Judith Plaskow and Carol P. Christ, 208–213. San Francisco: Harper and Row.

Low, Alaine, and Soraya Tremayne, eds. 2001. *Sacred custodians of the Earth? Women, spirituality, and the environment*. New York: Berghahn.

Mabro, Judy, ed. 1996. *Veiled half-truths: Western travellers' perceptions of Middle Eastern women*. London: Taurus.

Magee, Penelope Margaret. 1995. Disputing the sacred: Some theoretical approaches to gender and religion, in *Religion and gender*, ed. Ursula King. Oxford: Blackwell.

Manji, Irshad. 2003. *The trouble with Islam: A wake-up call for honesty and change*. New York: Random House.

Marcus, Julie. 1992. *A world of difference: Islam and gender hierarchy in Turkey*. London: Zed.

Marder, Janet R. 1996. Are women changing the rabbinate? A Reform perspective, in *Religious institutions and women's leadership: New roles inside the mainstream*, ed. Catherine Wessenger, 271–290. Columbia, SC: Univ. of South Carolina Press.

Marshall, Gül A. 2005. Ideology, progress and dialogue: A comparison of feminist and Islamist women's approaches to the issues of head covering and work in Turkey. *Gender and Society* 19(1): 104–120.

Maumoon, Dunya. 1999. Islamism and gender activism: Muslim women's quest for autonomy. *Journal of Muslim Minority Affairs* 19(2): 269–283.

McGinty, Anna M. 2007. Formation of alternative femininities through Islam: Feminist approaches among Muslim converts in Sweden. *Women's Studies International Forum* 30: 474–485.

McManners, John, ed. 1990. *The Oxford history of Christianity*. Oxford: Oxford Univ. Press.

Mernissi, Fatima. 1987. *Beyond the veil: Male-female dynamics in modern Muslim society*. Bloomington, IN: Indiana Univ. Press.

Mernissi, Fatima. 1991. *Women and Islam: An historical and theological inquiry*. Oxford: Blackwell.

Mernissi, Fatima. 1993. *The forgotten queens of Islam*. Minneapolis: Univ. of Minnesota Press.

Millen, Rochelle L. 2007. "Her mouth is full of wisdom": Reflections on Jewish feminist theology, in *Women remaking American Judaism*, ed. Riv-Ellen Prell. Detroit: Wayne State Univ. Press.

Minces, Juliette. 1982. *The house of obedience: Women in Arab society*. London: Zed.

Moghadam, Valentine M. 2002. Islamic feminism and its discontents: Toward a resolution of the debate. *Signs* 27(4): 1135–1171.

Moghadam, Valentine M. 2003. *Modernizing women: Gender and social change in the Middle East*, 2d ed. Boulder, CO: Lynne Rienner.

Moghissi, Haideh. 1999. *Feminism and Islamic fundamentalism: The limits of postmodern analysis*. London: Zed.

Moghissi, Haideh, ed. 2006. *Muslim diaspora: Gender, culture and identity*. London/New York: Routledge.

Mohagheghi, Hamideh. 2006. Emerging women's movements in Muslim communities, in *Women's voices in world religions*, eds. Hille Haker, Susan Ross, and Marie-Theres Wacker, 63–71. London: SCM.

Moore, Deborah Dash, and Andrew Bush. 2007. Gender, and reconstructionist Judaism, in *Women remaking American Judaism*, ed. Riv-Ellen Prell. Detroit: Wayne State Univ. Press.

Moraga, Cherrie, and Gloria Anzaldua, eds. 1983. *This bridge called my back: Writings by radical women of color*. New York: Kitchen Table.

Muir, Elizabeth G. 1991. *Petticoats in the pulpit: The story of early nineteenth century Methodist women preachers in Upper Canada*. Toronto: United Church of Canada.

Muir, Elizabeth G., and Marilyn F. Whiteley, eds. 1995. *Changing roles of women within the Christian church in Canada*. Toronto: Univ. of Toronto Press.

Mumtaz, Khawar, and Farida Shaheed. 1987. *Women of Pakistan: Two steps forward. One step back?* London: Zed.

Musallam, B.F. 1989. *Sex and society in Islam: Birth control before the 19th century*. Cambridge: Cambridge Univ. Press.

Myers, Jody, and June R. Litman. 1995. The secret of Jewish femininity: Hiddenness, power, and physicality in the theology of Orthodox women in the contemporary world, in *Gender and Judaism: The transformation of tradition*, ed. T.M. Rudavsky, 51–77. New York: New York Univ. Press.

Nadell, Pamela S. 1998. *Women who would be rabbis: A history of women's ordination, 1889–1985*. Boston: Beacon.

Nadell, Pamela S. 2007. Bridges to "a Judaism transformed by women's wisdom": The first generation of women rabbis, in *Women remaking American Judaism*, ed. Riv-Ellen Prell. Detroit: Wayne State Univ. Press.

Nadell, Pamela S., and Jonathan D. Sarna, eds. 2001. *Women and American Judaism: Historical perspectives*. Hanover, NH: Univ. of New England Press/Brandeis Univ. Press.

Neudel, Marian Henriquez. 1989. Innovation and tradition in a contemporary Midwestern Jewish congregation, in *Unspoken worlds: Women's religious lives*, eds. Nancy A. Falk and Rita M. Gross, 221–232. Belmont, CA: Wadsworth.

Newsom, Carol, and Sharon H. Ringe, eds. 1992. *The women's Bible commentary.* Louisville, KY: Westminster John Knox.

Northup, Lesley A. 1997. *Ritualizing women: Patterns of spirituality.* Cleveland, OH: Pilgrim.

Oduyoye, Mercy Amba. 2001. *Introducing African women's theology.* Cleveland, OH: Pilgrim.

Oduyoye, Mercy Amba. 2004. *Beads and strands: Reflections of an African woman on Christianity in Africa.* Maryknoll, NY: Orbis.

Orenstein, Debra, ed. 1994. *Lifecycles: Vol. 1 Jewish women on life passages and personal milestones.* Woodstock, VT: Jewish Lights.

Orenstein, Debra, and Jane R. Litman, eds. 1994. *Lifecycles: Vol. 2. Jewish women on Biblical themes in contemporary life.* Woodstock, VT: Jewish Lights.

Osman, Ghada. 2003. Back to basics: The discourse of Muslim feminism in contemporary Egypt. *Women and Language* 26(1): 73–78.

Pagels, Elaine. 1979. *The Gnostic gospels.* New York: Random House.

Paris, Peter S. 1993. From womanist thought to womanist action. *Journal of Feminist Studies in Religion* 9(1/2): 115–125.

Plaskow, Judith. 1979a. Bringing a daughter into the Covenant, in *Womanspirit rising: A feminist reader in religion*, eds. Carol P. Christ and Judith Plaskow, 179–184. New York: Harper.

Plaskow, Judith. 1979b. Preface, in *Womanspirit rising: A feminist reader in religion*, eds. Carol P. Christ and Judith Plaskow. New York: Harper.

Plaskow, Judith. 1990. *Standing again at Sinai: Judaism from a feminist perspective.* San Francisco: Harper and Row.

Plaskow, Judith. 1995. The right question is theological, in *On being a Jewish feminist*, ed. Susannah Heschel, 23–33. New York: Schocken.

Plaskow, Judith. 2003. Dealing with difference without and within. *Journal of Feminist Studies in Religion* 19(1): 91–95.

Plaskow, Judith, and Donna Berman, eds. 2005. *The coming of Lilith: Essays on feminism, Judaism, and sexual ethics, 1972–2003.* Boston: Beacon.

Powell, Annie Ruth. 1993. Hold on to your dream: African-American Protestant worship, in *Women at worship: Interpretations of North American diversity*, eds. M. Proctor-Smith and J.R. Walton, 43–45. Louisville, KY: Westminster John Knox.

Preisand, Sally. 1975. *Judaism and the new woman.* New York: Behrman.

Prell, Riv-Ellen. 2007. *Women remaking American Judaism.* Detroit, MI: Wayne State Univ. Press.

Procter-Smith, Marjorie, and Janet R. Walton, eds. 1993. *Women at worship: Interpretations of North American diversity.* Louisville, KY: Westminster John Knox.

Raphael, Melissa. 1996. *Thealogy and embodiment: The post-patriarchal reconstruction of female sacrality.* Sheffield, UK: Sheffield Academic.

Raphael, Melissa. 1999. Monotheism in contemporary Goddess religion: A betrayal of early thealogical non-realism, in *Is there a future for feminist theology?*, eds. Deborah F. Sawyer and Diane M. Collier, 139–149. Sheffield, UK: Sheffield Academic.

Raphael, Melissa. 2000. *Introducing thealogy: Discourse on the Goddess.* Cleveland, OH: Pilgrim.

Raphael, Melissa, 2003. *The female face of God in Auschwitz: A Jewish feminist theology of the Holocaust.* London: Routledge.

Read, Donna, dir. 1989. *Goddess remembered.* Studio D, National Film Board of Canada.

Reuther, Rosemary Radford. 1983. *Sexism and God-talk: Toward a feminist theology.* Boston: Beacon.

Reuther, Rosemary Radford. 1985. *Women-church: The theology and practice of feminist liturgical communities.* New York: Harper and Row.

Reuther, Rosemary Radford. 1992. *Gaia and God: An ecofeminist theology of Earth healing.* San Francisco: HarperSanFrancisco.

Reuther, Rosemary Radford. 2001. Christian feminist theology: History and future, in *Daughters of Abraham: Feminist thought in Judaism, Christianity, and Islam,* eds. Yvonne Yazbeck Haddad and John L. Esposito. Gainesville, FL: Univ. of Florida Press.

Reuther, Rosemary Radford, ed. 2002. *Gender, ethnicity, and religion: Views from the other side.* Minneapolis, MN: Fortress.

Reuther, Rosemary Radford. 2005. *Goddesses and the divine feminine: A Western religious history.* Berkeley, CA: Univ. of California Press.

Rich, Adrienne. 1976. *Of woman born: Motherhood as experience and institution.* New York: Norton.

Ross, Tamar. 2004. *Expanding the palace of Torah: Orthodoxy and feminism.* Hanover, NH: Univ. Press of New England/Brandeis Univ. Press.

Rudy, Kathy. 1999. *Her sex and the church: Gender, homosexuality, and the transformation of Christian ethics.* Boston: Beacon.

Russell, Letty M., et al., eds. 1988. *Inheriting our mothers' gardens: Feminist theology in Third World perspective.* Philadelphia: Westminster.

Russell, Letty M., and J. Shannon Clarkson, eds. 1996. *Dictionary of feminist theologies.* Louisville, KY: Westminster John Knox.

Rutherford, Myra. 2002. *Women and the white men's God: Gender and race in the Canadian mission field.* Vancouver: Univ. of British Columbia.

Ruthven, Malise. 1997. *Islam: A short history.* Oxford: Oxford Univ. Press.

Ruthven, Malise. 2004. *Fundamentalism: The search for meaning.* Oxford: Oxford Univ. Press.

el Saadawi, Nawal, ed. 1980. *The hidden face of Eve: Women in the Arab world.* London: Zed.

el Saadawi, Nawal. 1997. *The Nawal El Saadawi reader.* London: Zed.

Saghal, Gita, and Nira Yuval-Davis, eds. 1992. *Refusing holy orders: Women and fundamentalism in Britain.* London: Virago.

Saliba, Therese, Carolyn Allen, and Judith A. Howard, eds. 2002. *Gender and politics in Islam.* Chicago: Univ. of Chicago Press.

Sanasarian, Eliz. 1992. *The women's rights movement in Iran: Mutiny, appeasement, and repression from 1900 to Khomeini.* New York: Praeger.

Sawyer, Deborah F., and Diane M. Collier, eds. 1999. *Is there a future for feminist theology?* Sheffield, UK: Sheffield Academic.

Schneer, David, and Karyn Aviv, eds. 2002. *Queer Jews*. New York: Routledge.

Schulman, Sydell R. 1996. Faithful daughters and ultimate rebels: The first class of Conservative Jewish rabbis, in *Religious institutions and women's leadership: New roles inside the mainstream*, ed. Catherine Wessenger, 311–330. Columbia, SC: Univ. of South Carolina Press.

Schwartz, Shuly Robin. 2007. The tensions that merit our attention: Women in Conservative Judaism, in *Women remaking American Judaism*, ed. Riv-Ellen Prell. Detroit: Wayne State Univ. Press.

Sharawi, Huda. 1986. *Harem years: The memoirs of an Egyptian feminist (1879–1924)*. London: Virago.

Shehadeh, Lamia R. 2003. *The idea of women in fundamentalist Islam*. Gainesville, FL: Univ. of Florida Press.

Sinister Wisdom. 1994/1995. Lesbians and religion issue. 54.

Southard, Naomi P.F. 1994. Recovery and rediscovered images: Spiritual resources for Asian American women, in *Feminist theology from the Third World: A reader*, ed. Ursula King. Maryknoll, NY: Orbis.

Spiegel, Marcia C. 1996. Spirituality for survival: Jewish women healing themselves. *Journal of Feminist Studies in Religion* 12(2): 121–137.

Starhawk [Miriam Simos]. 1979. *The spiral dance: A rebirth of the ancient religion of the great goddess*. San Francisco: Harper and Row.

Stein, Judith. 1984. *A new Haggadah: A Jewish Lesbian seder*. Cambridge, MA: Bebbeh Meiseh.

Stone, Merlin. 1977. *The paradise papers*. London: Virago. (Also published as Stone, Merlin. 1978. *When God was a woman*. New York: Harcourt Brace.)

Stowasser, Barbara. 1998. Gender issues and contemporary Quran interpretation, in *Islam, gender, and social change*, eds. Yvonne Yazbeck Haddad and John L Esposito. New York: Oxford Univ. Press.

Stuart, Elizabeth, ed. 1998. *Religion is a queer thing: A guide to the Christian faith for lesbian, gay, bisexual and transgendered people*. New York: Pilgrim.

Stuckey, Johanna H. 1998. *Feminist spirituality: An introduction to feminist theology in Judaism, Christianity, Islam, and Feminist Goddess Worship*. Toronto: Centre for Feminist Research.

Swidler, Arlene, ed. 1993. *Homosexuality and world religions*. Valley Forge, PA: Trinity International.

Tabari, A., and N. Yeganeh. 1982. *In the shadow of Islam: The women's movement in Iran*. London: Zed.

Taitz, Emily, Sondra Henry, and Cheryl Tallan. 2003. *The JPS guide to Jewish women: 600 BCE–1900 CE*. Philadelphia: Jewish Publication Society.

Torjesen, Karen Jo. 1993. *When women were priests: Women's leadership in the early church and the scandal of their subordination in the rise of Christianity*. San Francisco: HarperSanFrancisco.

Trible, Phyllis. 1978. *God and the rhetoric of sexuality*. Philadelphia: Fortress.

Trible, Phyllis. 1984. *Texts of terror: Literary-feminist readings of Biblical narratives*. Philadelphia: Fortress.

Tucker, Judith E. 1985. *Women in nineteenth-century Egypt*. Cambridge: Cambridge Univ. Press.

Umansky, Ellen, and Diana Ashton, eds. 1992. *Four centuries of Jewish women's spirituality: A sourcebook*. Boston: Beacon.

Wadud, Amina. 1999. *Qur'an and woman: Rereading the sacred text from a woman's perspective*. New York: Oxford Univ. Press.

Wadud, Amina. 2006. *Inside the gender jihad: Women's reform in Islam*. Oxford: Oneworld.

Walker, Alice. 1983. *In search of our mothers' gardens: Womanist prose*. San Diego, CA: Harcourt Brace Jovanovich.

Ware, Timothy. 1997. *The Orthodox church: New edition*. New York: Penguin.

Webb, Gisela, ed. 2000. *Windows of faith: Muslim women scholar-activists in North America*. Syracuse, NY: Syracuse Univ. Press.

Webster's encyclopedic unabridged dictionary of the English language. 1996. New York: Gramercy.

Weissler, Chava. 2007. Meanings of Shekhinah in the "Jewish renewal" movement, in *Women remaking American Judaism*, ed. Riv-Ellen Prell. Detroit: Wayne State Univ. Press.

Wessenger, Catherine, ed. 1996. *Religious institutions and women's leadership: New roles inside the mainstream*. Columbia, SC: Univ. of South Carolina Press.

Wikan, Unni. 1991. *Behind the veil in Arabia: Women in Oman*. Chicago: Univ. of Chicago Press.

Williams, Delores S. 1993a. Rituals of resistance in women's worship, in *Women at worship: Interpretations of North American diversity*, eds. M. Proctor-Smith and J.R. Walton, 215–224. Louisville, KY: Westminster John Knox.

Williams, Delores S. 1993b. *Sisters in the wilderness: The challenge of womanist God-talk*. Maryknoll, NY: Orbis.

Winter, Bronwyn. 2001. Fundamental misunderstandings: Issues in feminist approaches to Islam. *Journal of Women's History* 13(1): 9–41.

Yamani, Mai, ed. 1996. *Feminism and Islam: Legal and literary perspectives*. London: Ithaca.

Zanotti, Barbara, ed. 1986. *A faith of one's own: Explorations by Catholic lesbians*. New York: Crossing.

Zuckerman, Francine, ed. 1992. *Half the kingdom: Seven Jewish feminists*. New York: Crossing.

Weblinks

Chapter 1

Citizenship and Immigration Canada: **www.cic.gc.ca**

National Action Committee on the Status of Women (NAC): **www.nac-cca.ca**

32 Hours: Action for Full Employment: **www. connexions.org/Groups/Subscribers/ cxg14678.htm**

Library and Archives Canada: **www. collectionscanada.gc.ca**

Solidarity: *Against the Current*: **www.solidarity-us. org/atc**

Documents from the Women's Liberation Movement: An Online Archival Collection: **http:// scriptorium.lib.duke.edu/wlm**

VDay: **www.vday.org/main.html**

Always Causing Legal Unrest (ACLU): **www. nostatusquo.com/ACLU/Porn/index.html**

Off Our Backs: **www.offourbacks.org**

HotHead Paisan: **www.hotheadpaisan.com**

Chapter 2

Judith Butler: **www.theory.org.uk/ctr-butl.htm**

Third Space: The Site for Emerging Feminist Scholars: **www.thirdspace.ca**

Challenging Psychiatric Stereotypes of Gender Diversity: **www.transgender.org/gidr/index.html**

Chapter 3

About-Face: **www.about-face.org**

Bitch Magazine: **www.bitchmagazine.org**

Eminism: **http://eminism.org**

Feminist E-Zine: **www.feministezine.com/feminist**

Feministing: **www.feministing.com**

Grrrl Zine Network: **www.grrrlzines.net**

Guerilla Girls: **www.guerillagirls.com**

Strap-on: **www.strap-on.org**

The Miss G Project: **www.themissgproject.org**

Third Space: **www.thirdspace.ca**

Third Wave Foundation: **www.thirdwavefoundation. org**

Chapter 4

The Environmental Justice Resource Center (EJRC): **www.ejrc.cau.edu**

The Canadian Research Institute for the Advancement of Women (CRIAW): **www.criaw-icref.ca**

Association for Women's Rights in Development (AWID): **www.awid.org**

The Native Women's Association of Canada (NWAC): **www.nwac-hq.org/en/index.html**

WomenWatch: **www.un.org/womenwatch**

WomenNet—Canadian Women's Virtual Information Centre/Directory of Women's Resources: **www.womennet.ca**

Chapter 5

Transgender: Definitions and Myths: **www. queensu.ca/humanrights/tgts/tgts_myths.htm**

Definition of "transgender": **www.glbtq. com/ social-sciences/transgender.html**

Description of the lesbian sex wars: **www.glbtq. com/social-sciences/lesbian_sex_ wars. html**

"Lesbian Photography on the U.S. West Coast": **www.cla.purdue.edu/waaw/corinne/index. html#Intro**

Anna Camilleri: **www.annacamilleri.com**

Journal of Canadian Studies on Canada's obscenity laws: **http://findarticles.com/p /articles/ mi_ qa3683/is_199804/ai_n8800218/pg_1**

Chapter 6

About-Face: **www.about-face.org**

Adbusters: **www.adbusters.org**

Ad*Access On-Line Project, Duke University: **http://scriptorium.lib.duke.edu/adaccess**

AdiosBarbie.com: **www.adiosbarbie.com**

Body Modification: **www.upenn.edu/museum/Exhibits/bodmodintro.html**

Gender, Race, Class, Sexuality, and US Cultural Imperialism in Contemporary Popular Culture: **www.wsu.edu/~amerstu/pop/gender.html**

Media Awareness Network: **www.media-awareness.ca/english/tools/site_directory/ index.cfm**

Chapter 7

National Clearinghouse on Family Violence: **www.phac-aspc.gc.ca/ncfv-cnivf/familyviolence/index.html**

End Violence Against Women—United Kingdom: **www.endviolenceagainstwomen.org.uk/pages/resources.html**

White Ribbon Campaign: **www.whiteribbon.ca**

Chapter 8

Canadian Association for the 50Plus: **www.carp.ca**

National Advisory Council on Aging: **www.naca.ca**

Older Women's Network: **www.olderwomensnetwork.org**

The Old Woman's Project: **www.oldwomans project.org**

Chapter 9

Statistics Canada—Census data: **www12.statcan.ca/english/census/index.cfm**

Vanier Institute of the Family: **www.vifamily.ca**

National Council of Welfare: **www.ncwcnbes.net**

Canadian Council on Social Development: **www.ccsd.ca**

Sloan Work and Family Research Network: **http://wfnetwork.bc.edu**

Chapter 10

Status of Women Canada: **www.swc-cfc.gc.ca/pubs/pubssubject_e.html**

United Nations Educational, Scientific and Cultural Organization (UNESCO): **http://portal.unesco.org/education/en/ev.php-URL_ID=48712&URL_DO=DO_TOPIC&URL_SECTION=201.html**

Women's Studies Programmes, Departments and Research Centres: **http: //research.umbc.edu/~korenman/wmst/programs.html**

Chapter 11

Women's Health Strategy: **www.hc-sc.gc.ca/ahc-asc/pubs/strateg-women-femmes/strateg-eng.php**

Aboriginal Women's Health and Healing Network: **www.awhhrg.ca/home.php**

Department of Women, Gender and Health, World Health Organization: **www.who.int/gender/en/**

Chapter 12

Women and Gender Studies Web Sites: **www.libr.org/wss/wsslinks/index.html**

Grace Unfolding/SisterFriends Together: **www.sisterfriends-together.org**

Jewish Orthodox Feminist Alliance: **www.jofa.org**

Women in Islam: **www.womeninislam.org**

Covenant of the Goddess: **www.cog.org**

Index

A

Aboriginal peoples. *See* First Nations (Aboriginal) peoples
Aboriginal Women's Health and Healing Research Group, 290
abortion, 23
ACLU. *See* Always Causing Legal Unrest (ACLU)
African-American feminist theology, 302
Africville, Nova Scotia, 94–95
Against Our Will: Men, Women and Rape, 164
Age of Reason. *See* Enlightenment (Age of Reason)
ageism, 197
  definition, 197
  early retirement and, 203–204
  economic insecurity and, 201–202
  economic perspective of, 199
  employment and, 202
  feminism and, 197–198
  pensions and, 205–206
  pervasiveness of, 197
  political perspective of, 199–200
  poverty and, 200–201
  second-wave feminism and, 198
  single women and, 203
  theories, 198–200
aging,
  bodies and, 211
  care work and, 207–210
  diversity of, 207
  gender and, 210
  sexuality and, 211
Ahmed, Leila, 311
Al-Fatihah Foundation, 314
Ali, Yasmin, 311
Alias (tv series), 126
Alien (movie), 126
alienation, 16

Allen, Charlotte Vale, 164
Allen, Louisa, 254
Almeida, David M., 232
Alpert, Rebecca, 308
Always Causing Legal Unrest (ACLU), 26
America's Next Top Model (tv series), 140
And Still We Rise: Political Mobilizing in Contemporary Canada, 101
Anderson, Doris, 11
Anderson, Robert, 229
anti-racist feminism, 92–94, 222
  whiteness and, 101–102
Anzaldúa, Gloria, 122
Arat-Koc, Sedef, 235, 236
Arden, Elizabeth, 134
Arnup, Katherine, 228
Ashton, Diana, 305
Asian feminist theology, 303
Assembly of First Nations (prev. National Indian Brotherhood), 5
Association of Theological Schools, 301
Astell, Mary, 4
Atkinson, Ti-Grace, 23
Atwood, Margaret, 24
August, Rachel A., 232
Ayurvedic medicine, 274

B

baby boomers, 204
  pensions for, 205
Back to the Drawing Board: African Canadian Feminisms, 101
Badran, Margot, 311
Bagley, Robin, 162
Bailey, Alison, 103
Baker, Maureen, 237
Bannerji, Himani, 19
Baring, Anne, 314
Barry, Kathleen, 28

Bartky, Sandra Lee, 76
Barton, Clara, 274
Basmajian, Silva, 183
bat mitzvah, 305–306
Battered Woman Syndrome, 168–169
BC Human Rights Tribunal, 30
Beaujot, Roderic, 229
Beausoleil, Natalie, 276
beauty culture, 131–132
  history, 132–136
beauty myth, 148
beauty pageants, 141
Bedard, Yvonne, 5, 18
Benston, Margaret, 14
Berger, John, 132
Berlant, Lauren, 54
Bernard, Jessie, 198
Beyond God the Father, 301
Beyond the Veil, 313
BIASFREE framework, 277, 280
biology, 281–282
biomedical model of health, 273–274
  limitations of, 275–276
Bird, Florence, 9
Black Candle, The, 98
black feminism, 69–77, 100–101, 222
  hair and, 150
  women's studies and, 101
Blackstone, Sir William, 170
Blank, Hanne, 79
BMI. *See* Body Mass Index (BMI)
BMI Illustrated Categories Slide Show, 143
bodies, 73–74
  aging and, 211
  beauty of, 131–132
  cosmetic surgery, 151–152
  cosmetics and, 134–135
  empowerment of, 74
  fat activism, 75
  hair and, 150
  ideals, 140–141
  image formation, 136–140
  second-wave feminism and, 110
  weight, 141–143, 145–147
Body Mass Index (BMI), 143

Body Outlaws: Young Women Write About Body Image and Identity, 69, 74
Boe, Roger, 99
Boily, I., 252, 253
Borden, Robert, 8
Bouchard, P., 252, 253
bourgeoisie, 13, 14
Bourne, P., 251
Boys Like Her: Transfictions, 120, 121, 123, 124, 127
Brady, Katherine, 164
Brand, Dionne, 94, 102
Brazen Femme: Queering Femininity, 76
Breaking Anonymity: The Chilly Climate for Women Faculty, 260
Bridges journal, 308
Bridges, Judith S., 12
British North America Act (1867), 8
Britzman, Deborah, 262
Brooks, Ann, 52
Brownmiller, Susan, 164
Brumberg, Joan Jacobs, 74
Buffy (tv series), 126
Bullock, Sandra, 126
Butler v. *the Queen* (1992), 26
Butler, Donald, 26
Butler, Judith, 76, 81, 112, 121
Butler, R. N., 211
Butler, Robert, 197
Buturovic, Amila, 312

C
Calasanti, T. M., 199
Califia, Patrick, 79, 119
California State University, San Diego, 261
Camilleri, Anna, 76, 120, 124, 126, 127
Canada,
  abortion in, 23
  abuse in, 167–169
  colonialism in, 4
  equality in, 10–11
  First Nations peoples in, 5
  obesity rates in, 142
  obscenity laws, 26–27
  old-age poverty in, 200

pension plans in,   205, 206
poverty in,   18
racial and ethnic professors in,
    257–258
racial division of mothering in,   209
racism in,   88–89, 92–94
slavery in,   6
welfare state in,   219
women in prison in,   98–99
women's life expectancy in,   281
Canada Child Tax Benefit,   237
Canada Fitness,   145
Canada Pension Plan (CPP),   18–19, 93,
    201
Canada Research Chairs (CRC) pro-
    gramme,   258
Canadian Auto Workers Union (CAW),
    19
Canadian Bill of Rights,   5
*Canadian Charter of Rights and
    Freedoms* (1982),   27
Canadian Federation of University Women
    (CFUW),   9
Canadian Human Rights Act (1985),   11
Canadian Labour Congress (CLC),   17
Canadian Research Institute for the
    Advancement of Women (CRIAW),
    26
Canadian Violence Against Women
    (CVAW),   165, 171, 178, 179
Canadian Woman Studies journal,   308
Canadian Woman's Suffrage Association,
    7
Canadian Women's Health Network,   283
capitalism,   13, 14–15
care work,   207
    classed,   208
    conditions,   207–208
    dimensions,   207
    gendered,   208
    globalization of,   209
    racial diversity of,   209
    state policies and,   210
Carnegie Foundation,   273
Caron, Charlotte,   300
Carty, Linda,   29

Cashford, Julie,   314
*Catching a Wave: Reclaiming Feminism
    for the 21st Century*,   69
CATW. *See* Coalition Against Trafficking
    in Women (CATW)
CAW. *See* Canadian Auto Workers Union
    (CAW)
censorship,   112
Centres for Excellence in Women's
    Health,   290
CFUW. *See* Canadian Federation of
    University Women (CFUW)
Chalice and the Blade, The,   314
Charlie's Angels (movie),   126
child care,   17–18
    women in labour force and,   225–226
chilly climate (in universities),   260
Chilly Collective,   260
Chinese medicine,   274
Christ, Carol,   315
Christian feminist theology,   299–300
    principles,   300
    topics,   300–302
Christianity, Patriarchy, and Abuse,   301
Christology,   301
Church and the Second Sex, The,
    300–302
Clark, Lorene,   164
class,   1, 19
    care work and,   208
    education and,   252
    inequalities,   13
CLC. *See* Canadian Labour Congress
    (CLC)
Clement, Wallace,   222–223
Coalition Against Trafficking in Women
    (CATW),   28
Coalition to Support Indigenous
    Sovereignty,   101
Codjoe, Henry,   251
Collins, Patricia Hill,   69, 100
colonialism,   3, 19, 88
    First Nations peoples and,   90–91
    health and,   274
    post,   181
    skin whitening,   147–148

Colonize This!: Young Women of Color on Today's Feminism,   69, 83
Communist Manifesto (1848),   13
Concordia (prev. Sir George Williams) University,   260
Connell, Bob,   250
consciousness-raising (CR) sessions, 21–23
Conservative Judaism,   304, 305, 306
Cornell University,   261
Correctional Service of Canada,   99
Cosmopolitan magazine,   135
Coulombe, Simon,   224
Cox, Marie,   77
Coyote, Ivan E.,   120
CPP. *See* Canada Pension Plan (CPP)
CR. *See* consciousness-raising (CR) sessions
CRC. *See* Canada Research Chairs (CRC) programme
CRIAW. *See* Canadian Research Institute for the Advancement of Women (CRIAW)
cultural feminism,   25–26, 71, 73, 125–126
cultural genocide,   90–91
culture,   71–73
    health and,   286–287
Curie, Marie,   274
CVAW. *See* Canadian Violence Against Women (CVAW)
CW Network,   140

D
Da Vinci, Leonardo,   133
Daddy's Girl: A Very Personal Memoir, 164
Dalla Costa, Mariarosa,   15
Daly, Mary,   300, 302
Danica, Elly,   164
date rape drugs,   165
Davis, Angela,   29
Davis, Elizabeth Gould,   314
Day, Dorothy,   301
de Beauvoir, Simone,   132
de Lauretis, Teresa,   121, 122, 132
de Pizan, Christine,   4

Dei, George,   251
Dell, Colleen Anne,   98
Denison, Flora MacDonald,   8
Dent, Gina,   70
Diaz, Angela,   181–182
Differences magazine,   122
Dillabough,   259
disabilities, women with,   178–211
Disabled Women's Network survey (1989),   179
discourse,   47–48
Disney Corporation,   140–141
Diversity magazine,   119
divorce,   203
DIY. *See* Do It Yourself (DIY) feminism
Do It Yourself (DIY) feminism,   71–73
Doe, Jane,   166
Domestic Worker Program,   92–93
domino theory of sexual peril,   113
Don't Ask Don't Tell Coalition,   101
Don't Is a Woman's Word,   164
Dooley, Chantelle,   21
dowry murder,   172
    analyses,   182
Drake, Jennifer,   64
Drakich, J.,   258
Drawing the Line (photography exhibition),   118–119, 140
drug trials,   280
Dunne, Gillian A.,   222, 228
Dworkin, Andrea,   27

E
EA. *See* Employment Authorization (EA) form
Eakle, Zoë,   120
economic perspective,
    ageism and,   201–202
    single women and,   203
education,   6
    codes of conduct,   255
    common,   249
    corporatization of,   262–263
    faculty experiences,   259–260
    feminist pedagogies,   261–262
    gender and,   247
    gendered performance gap,   253

gendered schooling, 250
gendered sexuality, 254–255
gendered teachers in, 248–249
gendered treatment of schoolchildren,
 249–250
higher, 255
immigration and, 252
income inequality and, 224
literacy, 285
lower, 248
masculine discourses, 252
race and gender, 253–254
sexist curriculum, 251
social class and, 252
teacher/student interactions, 250
university corporatization, 258
women in university administration,
 258
women's studies, 260–261
Edut, Ophira, 74
Edwards, Henrietta Muir, 8
EI. *See* Employment Insurance (EI)
Eisler, Riane, 314
el Saadawi, Nawal, 311
Eller, Cynthia, 317
Émile, 4
employment, 202
 post-retirement, 204
Employment Authorization (EA) form,
 19
Employment Insurance (EI), 219, 237,
 238
Employment Insurance Act (1996), 238
Encyclopedia of Feminist Theories, 42
Engels, Friedrich, 13, 14
Enlightenment (Age of Reason), 2, 4, 89
Enough (movie), 126
Ensler, Eve, 24
environment,
 health and, 283–284
environmental racism, 94–96
equal opportunity, 2–3, 4–5
erotic pyramid, 113, 115
essentialism, 29, 252
 against, 181
Eveline, J., 260
Excitable Speech, 81

F
Faith, Karlene, 98
family, 14–22, 93
 changes in, 219–220
 diversity, 219
 ethnically diverse, 235
 government assumptions about,
  237–238
 informal support for, 234–235
 labour force and, 224–234
 role complexity, 288
 social policies for, 237–238
 transnational, 236
 violence, 96–98, 162
 work conflict and, 229, 230
fat activism, 75
Fat Femme Mafia, 75
Father's Days: A True Story of Incest,
 164
Female Refuges Act (1897), 98
femicide, 172
femininity, 75–77
 queer, 124–128
feminism,
 ageism and, 197–198
 anti-racist, 45, 92–94
 beauty culture history and, 132–136
 black, 69–100
 Christianity and, 299–300
 cultural, 25–26
 definition, 1, 220
 DIY, 71–73
 global, 28
 goddess, 314
 health research and, 276
 Islamic, 309–311
 Judaism and, 304
 Latina, 79
 lesbian, 25
 liberal, 13–14
 Marxist, 14–15, 221
 pedagogies, 261–262
 political economic perspective, 223
 pop, 82–83
 poststructural, 44–45
 practice of, 1
 racism and, 89

feminism (*continued*)
  radical, 13–14, 21
  reproduction theory, 247
  second-wave, 90, 110
  socialist, 13–14, 15–16
  spirituality, 298
  theory, 1–2
  third-wave, 63–64
  white-middle-class, 102
feminist goddess worship, 314
  lesbians and, 317
  practices, 316–317
  principles, 315–316
feminist Islam, 309
Feminist Issues, 41
feminist Muslims, 309
Feminist Porn Awards, Toronto, 68
Feminist Practice and Poststructuralist Theory, 42
feminist project, 181
feminist spirituality, 314
feminist theology, 298
  categories, 299
  definition, 298–299
  Judaism and, 304–305
  third-world, 303
Feminist Theology from the Third World, 303
feminization of poverty, 17–19
feminization of work, 20
Feschbach, Seymour, 165
Fiorenza, Elizabeth Schüssler, 301
Fire This Time, The: Young Activists and the New Feminism, 69
First International Conference on Orthodoxy and Feminism (New York, 1997), 305
First Nations (Aboriginal) peoples, 4, 5–9, 90
  clean water, 283–284
  colonialism and, 90–92
  educational curriculum, 251
  life expectancy, 281
  lone mothers, 232
  residential schools and, 91
  violence against women, 96–98, 168, 179
  women in labour market, 225
  women in prison, 98–99
First Sex, The, 314
Fisher, Caitlin, 80
Flesh Mobs, 75
Fletcher, J., 260
Flexner Report (1910), 273
Foster, Jodie, 126
Foucault, Michel, 47, 51, 112, 115, 117
Fox, Bonnie, 221
Frank, B., 254
Frankenberg, Ruth, 103
freedom of choice, 4–5
Freire, Paulo, 261
French Revolution, 3
Frenette, Marc, 224
Freud, Sigmund, 164
Frymer-Kensky, Tikva, 305
Furies, 21
Fuss, Diana, 121

G
Gadon, Elinor, 314
Gaia and God: An Ecofeminist Theology of Earth Healing, 301
Galileo, Galilei, 2
Garner, Jennifer, 126
Gaskell, J., 251
Gay and Lesbian Arabic Society, 314
gay marriage, 54–56
Gazso-Windle, Amber, 228, 233
GBA. *See* gender-based analysis (GBA)
GDP. *See* Gross Domestic Product (GDP)
Gee, James Paul, 211
Gelder, Ken, 64
gender, 19
  age and, 210
  and race in education, 253–254
  care work and, 208
  dichotomy of, 49–50
  education and, 247
  educational expectations, 249
  educational performance, 253
  essentialism, 112, 113
  femininity and, 75–77
  health and, 281

health workers and, 289
inequalities, 13
labour and, 17, 204
pathologization of, 278
professors and, 256–257
roles, 77
schooling, 250
sex and, 13–14
teacher/student interactions, 250
teachers and, 248–249
treatment of school children, 249–250
undergraduates and, 255–256
Gender, Ethnicity, and Religion, 301
gender harassment, 174
*Gender Trouble: Feminism and the
Subversion of Identity*, 112
gender-based analysis (GBA), 277, 284
genetic endowment, 281–282
German Ideology, The (1846), 13
Getting Lost, 42
Girlicious (tv series), 140
GIS. *See* Guaranteed Income Supplement
(GIS)
Glad Day Books, Toronto, 27
Glamour Magazine, 150
globalization, 3, 19
care work and, 209
feminisms and, 181
Globe and Mail, 151
Goddess Remembered (movie), 315
Goldberg, Abbie E., 230
Goldman, Ruth, 122
Good For Her, Toronto, 81
Gosine, Andil, 96
Gossip Girl (tv series), 140
Gottlieb, Lynn, 308
Gray, Kristina, 83
Gross, Rita, 307, 308
Gross Domestic Product (GDP), 17
Grzywacz, Joseph G., 232
Guaranteed Income Supplement (GIS),
201, 205
Guendozi, Jackie, 230
*Guide to Intersex and Trans
Terminologies*, 78
Gyimah, Stephen Obeng, 225
Gyn/Ecology, 301

H
Halberstam, Judith, 77
Hall, Donald, 55
Hall, Roberta, 260
Hamideh, Najla, 312
Hamilton, Lina, 126
Hamilton, Roberta, 222
Handmaid's Tale, The, 24
Hannah Montana (movie), 140
Harber, Scott, 165
Harding, Kate, 143
Hartmann, H., 221
Hassan, Riffat, 312
Hautzinger, Sarah, 181
health, 273
biology and genetic endowment,
281–282
biomedical model of, 273–274
childhood development and, 287
culture and, 286
difference insensitivity, 279
double standard bias in, 279–280
employment and, 284–285
environments and, 283–284
gender and, 281
income and, 282–283
lifestyle and, 287–288
maintaining hierarchies in, 277–279
medical research, 276–277
population model, 274
services, 289–290
social environment and, 286
social status and, 282–283
social support networks and, 288–289
workplace, 284, 285
Henry, Astrid, 122
Heschel, Susannah, 307
heteronormativity, 114–115
vs. heterosexuality, 115–116
heterosexuality, 115–116
Heywood, Carter, 303
Heywood, Leslie, 64
High Crimes (movie), 126
High School Musical (movie), 140
Hildegard of Bingen, 301
Hindustan Lever Limited, 148
historical materialism, 13

History of Sexuality, 112, 117
HIV/AIDS, 112, 169, 276, 290–291
Hochschild, Arlie, 229, 233
Holocaust, 305
homelessness, 178
homophobia, 115
honour killings, 172
hooks, bell (*née* Gloria Watkins), 1, 69, 220, 222
HRSD. *See* Human Resources and Social Development Canada (HRSD)
Human Resources and Social Development Canada (HRSD), 238

I
Iles, Randy, 172
ILO. *See* International Labour Organization (ILO)
immigration, 93
  education and, 252
  labour and, 225
In Memory of Her, 301
incest, 24, 163–164
  power and, 175
Indian Act (1876), 5–9, 12, 18
industrialization, 14
inheritance, 14
Inheriting Our Mother's Gardens, 303
International Criminal Court, 167
International Labour Organization (ILO), 174
International Organization for Migration (IOM), 28
Inuit peoples, 9
IOM. *See* International Organization for Migration (IOM)
Islam, 309
  lesbians and, 313–314
  women and, 310
Islamic feminism, 311–313

J
Jaggar, Alison, 16
James, Selma, 15
Jane Sexes It Up, 80, 110, 112, 122
Jarvis, Lorna Hernandez, 232
Jeffreys, Sheila, 28

Jewish Renewal Movement, 307
Jiwani, Yasmin, 97
Johnson, Freya, 77
Johnson, Lisa, 110, 111, 115
Jolie, Angelina, 126
Joseph, Norma Baumel, 305
Journal of Feminist Studies in Religion, 308
Judaism, 304
  Conservative, 304
  feminist theology and, 304–305
  lesbians and, 308
  multiculturalism and, 308
  Orthodox, 304
  Reconstructionist, 304
  Reform, 304
Judd, Ashley, 126
Julian of Norwich, 301
July, Miranda, 72
Justica for Migrant Workers, 101

K
Kahn, Robert S., 287
Kairos Canada, 101
Kaplan, Mordecai, 304
Kassam, Alnaaz, 254
Katz, S., 211
Kearney, Mary Celeste, 72
Kehler, Michael, 254
Khan, Shahnaz, 313
Khosla, Punam, 95
Kill Bill (movie), 126
Killer's Paradise, A (movie), 183
Kim, Nani, 303
Kimmel, Michael, 252, 253
King, Kathleen, 162–163
Kinsey, Alfred, 164
Kiss & Tell, 119
Kontos, C., 211
Koss, Mary, 165
Koyama, Emi, 63, 78, 79
Kristeva, Julia, 146

L
L Word, The (tv series), 71, 82
laissez-faire markets, 20
Lalonde Report (1974), 290

Lamm, Nomy, 75
Lara Croft (movie), 126
Lather, Patti, 42, 44
Lauzon, Jani, 72
Lavalee v. *R.* (1987), 168
Lavall, Jeanette, 5
Lavell, Jeanette, 18
Lavigne, Avril, 63, 82
Lawrence, Bonita, 91
LCP. *See* Live-In Caregiver Program (LCP)
LEAF. *See* Womens' Legal Education and Action Fund (LEAF)
Lee, Ann, 301
Legally Blonde (movie), 63
Legge, Marilyn, 301
lesbian feminism, 25
    educational curriculum, 251
    feminist goddess worship and, 317
    graffiti, 72
    Islam and, 313–314
    Judaism and, 308
    mothers in workforce and, 233–234
    teachers and, 255
    theology and, 303
    work-family conflict and, 232
    workforce and, 228
Levin, Richard I., 280
Lewis, Debra, 164
Lewis, Stephen, 290
Li, Jun, 253
liberal feminism, 1–2, 89
    access to education, 6
    contemporary, 11
    critiques of, 11\12
    definition, 2–3
    equality of opportunity, 220
    gendered schooling, 250
    global views of, 10–11
    history of, 3–4
    RCSW and, 9–10
    suffrage and, 7–8
liberalism, 3
    history of, 3–4
liberation theology, 303
LICO. *See* Statistics Canada, low income cut-off (LICO)

Listen Up: Voices from the Next Feminist Generation, 69, 75
literacy, 285
Little Sister's Book and Art Emporium, Vancouver, 27, 81
Live-In Caregiver Program (LCP), 18, 235
London Times, 170
Lopez, Jennifer, 126
Lorde, Audre, 67, 303, 317
Lovelace, Sandra, 5, 18

M
Macdonald, Barbara, 197, 198
MacDonald, Eleanor, 79
Macdonald, Sir John A., 8
MacGuff, Juno, 63
MacKinnon, Catherine, 25, 27
MacLeod, Linda, 170
Madonna (*née* Louise Ciccone), 126, 197
Mahoney, Kathleen, 290
Malamuth, Neil, 165
Malik, Kenan, 87
Manet, Claude, 133
Manji, Irshad, 314
Marcus, Julie, 310
Mardorossian, Carine, 180
marital rape, 170–171
    global, 171
marriage, 203
    labour and, 232
Married Women's Property Act (1884), 7
Marshall, Katherine, 226
Martino, W., 254
Marx, Karl, 13, 14–15
Marx Brothers, 73
Marxism, 12, 13–14
    feminist, 14–15
Marxist feminism, 221
masculinities, 182–183
maternity benefits, 238
maternity leave, 238
Mattingly, Marybeth J., 229–230
Mauthner, Natasha, 278
Maxim, Paul, 225
May, Arlene, 172
McClung, Nellie, 8

McCoy, L., 251
McCracken, Molly, 284
McDonald, Daniel A., 232
McGill University, 260
McIntyre, Sheila, 260
McKinney, Louise, 8
McLaren, A., 251
McMullin, Ann, 228
medical research, 276–277
  biases, 277–279, 280
Memmi, Albert, 87
menopause, 275
meritocracy, 2, 3, 4–5, 12
Mernissi, Fatima, 312, 313
metanarratives, 44
Métis peoples, 9
Miles, Robert, 87
Mill, Harriet Taylor, 4
Mill, John Stuart, 4–89
Mills, Sara, 48
Mire, Amina, 147, 148
Mirza, H., 253–254
misogyny, 24
Miss Ability (tv series), 141
Miss G project, 67
Mitchell, Allyson, 65
Mitchell, Juliet, 15
Moghadam, Valentine, 311
Mojica, Monique, 72
monarchy, 3
Montgomery, Lyndell, 120
Monture-Agnes, Patricia, 91, 98
Morgan, Joan, 77
Morimura, Yasumasa, 133
motherhood, 22, 23
  domestic work and, 235–236
  labour force and, 225–226
  lone, 231
  low-income, 231
  overcoming conflict at work, 233
  postcolonial, 209
  racial division of, 209
  social support for, 234
  strategies for, 236
  time crunch and, 229
  work-family conflict and, 229, 230
Mount Allison University, New
  Brunswick, 6

MTV, 126
MUCH MUSIC, 126
Muhammad, 309, 312
multiculturalism, 89–102
  Judaism and, 308
Mulvey, Laura, 124
Murder by Numbers (movie), 126
Murphy, Emily, 8, 98
Muslim Brotherhood, 309
Muzzin, L., 258
Myth of the Goddess, The, 314

N
Namaste, Viviane, 79
Natasha, Nolan, 63
National Action Committee on the Status
  of Women (1973), 11
National Council of Welfare, 17
National Council of Women in Canada
  (NCWC), 7
National Film Board of Canada, 164
National Indian Brotherhood. *See*
  Assembly of First Nations (prev.
  National Indian Brotherhood)
National Womens Studies Association of
  the United States (NWSA), 261
NCWC. *See* National Council of Women
  in Canada (NCWC)
neo-colonialism, 19
New Feminists of Toronto, 21
Newitz, Analee, 77
Newton, Isaac, 2
Nightingale, Florence, 274
Nikita (tv series), 126
Nixon, Kimberly, 30
No One is Illegal, 101
*Not My Mother's Sister: Generational
  Conflict and Third-Wave
  Feminism*, 122
Novogrodsky, M., 251
NWSA. *See* National Womens Studies
  Association of the United States
  (NWSA)

O
O'Connor, Karen, 183
O'Reilly, Andrea, 23
OAS. *See* Old Age Security (OAS)

obesity,   142, 282
  epidemic,   143
Oda, Bev,   11
OECD. *See* Organisation for Economic
  Co-operation and Development
  (OECD)
Off Our Backs journal,   26
Old Age Security (OAS),   201, 205
Once and Future Goddess, The,   314
Organisation for Economic Co-operation
  and Development (OECD),   252
*Origin of the Family, Private Property and
  the State, The* (1884),   13
Oros, Cheryl,   165
Orthodox Judaism,   304, 305
Orza, Ann Marie,   232
Osler, Sir William,   248
Ottawa Charter for Health Promotion
  (1989),   290
Overall, Christine,   115, 116, 123
Owen, Michelle,   55

P
Paglia, Camille,   180
Pande, Rekha,   182
Panic Room (movie),   126
Pankhurst, Christabel,   8
Pankhurst, Emmeline,   8
Pankhurst, Sylvia,   8
Pantin, Emmanuelle,   70
paradigm of domination,   199
Paradise Papers, The,   314
Parlby, Mary Irene,   8
ParticipACTION Campaign,   143, 145
pathologization,   278
patriarchy,   15, 16, 23, 52, 96, 199
  feminist goddess worship and,   316
  health and,   274
  male power,   176
  rape and,   164–165, 175
  second-wave feminism and,   177
  sexual abuse and,   163
  violence against women,   170
Pearce, Diana,   283
Pedagogy of the Oppressed, The,
  261–262
Peiss, Kathy,   134
Penguin Dictionary of Sociology,   42, 46

pensions,   205–206
  see also Canada Pension Plan (CPP);
    Quebec Pension Plan
Perks, Gord,   95
Perpetua,   301
Perry, Adele,   91
Persons Case (1929),   8–9, 90
PHAC. *See* Public Health Agency of
  Canada (PHAC)
Phoenix, A.,   253
Physicians Health Study (1989),   280
Pierce, Courtney P.,   230
Pink Ribbon Campaign,   275
PISA. *See* Programme for International
  Student Assessment (PISA)
Pizzey, Erin,   170
Plaskow, Judith,   306, 307, 308
*Pleasure and Danger: Exploring Female
  Sexuality*,   112, 119
pop feminism,   82–83
population health model,   274
  limitations of,   275–276
pornography,   24, 26–27
  internet,   28
  sexual harassment,   174
  third-wave feminism and,   68
postcolonialism,   181
  mothering and,   209
postmodernism,   42–181
  definition,   42
postpartum depression,   278
poststructuralism,   40, 41–42
  definition,   42
  knowledge critiques,   44–45
  language,   46–47, 48
  power,   50, 51–53
  subject gendering,   48–50
  theorizing difference,   54–56
poverty, feminization of,   17–19, 67, 94,
  283
  ageism and,   200–201
power,   50, 51–53
  rape and,   175
PPPO'd. *See* Pretty Porky and Pissed Off
  (PPPO'd)
Preisand, Sally,   306
Pretty Porky and Pissed Off (PPPO'd),
  75

Programme for International Student Assessment (PISA), 252
proletariat, 13, 14
prostitution, 24, 133–134
    sexual harassment, 174
    tourism, 27–28
Proulx, M., 252, 253
Public Health Agency of Canada (PHAC), 274, 281
Pui-lan, Kwok, 303

Q
Quebec Ministry of Social Welfare, 18
Quebec Pension Plan, 201
Queen's University, 260
queer and lesbian art history, 118, 308
Queer as Folk (tv series), 122
queer femininity, 124–128
queer theory, 114, 121–122

R
race, 1, 29
    and gender in education, 253–254
    care work and, 209
    concept, 87–88
    patriarchy and, 164–165
racism, 19, 80
    concept, 87–88
    education and, 254
    environmental, 94–96
    in Canada, 88–89, 94
    institutionalized, 92–94, 98
    violence against women, 96–98
radical feminism, 13–14
    contemporary, 26
    critiques of, 29–30
    culture and, 25–26
    definitions, 21
    equality of opportunity, 221
    global dimensions of, 27–28
    lesbians and, 25
    obscenity laws and, 26–27
    pornography and, 24
    rape and, 24–25
    reproduction and, 23–24
    sex oppression, 222
    theory of, 22–23

Radicalesbians, 21, 114, 116, 123
Rail, Geneviève, 276
rape, 24–25, 29–30, 52, 164–167
    culture, 167
    global, 166
    marital, 170–171
    myths, 165, 173
    power and, 175
    reporting, 166
    war, 167
Rape Shield Law, 166
Rape: The Price of Coercive Sexuality, 164
rationality, 2, 3, 4
Raymond, Janice, 29
RCSW. *See* Royal Commission on the Status of Women (1970) (RCSW)
Read, Donna, 315
Reay, D., 254
Reconstructionist Judaism, 304, 305
Red Dress Campaign, 275
Red Stockings, 21
Reform Judaism, 304, 305, 306–307
Reimer, M., 262
Reinharz, Shulamit, 198, 212, 213
rejectionist theology, 299
Renold, Emma, 255
renovationist theology, 299
reproduction, 23–24
    theory, 247
retirement, 203–204
    employment after, 204
Returning the Gaze: Essay on Racism, Feminism, and Politic, 101
Reuther, Rosemary, 301, 302
revisionist theology, 299
revolutionary theology, 299
Reyes, Angela, 209
Rhode, Debra, 223
Rich, Adrienne, 25, 80, 115, 116, 123, 317
Riel Rebellions, 7
Rinehart, J., 262, 263
Riot Grrrls, 71, 72, 82
Ritchie, Guy, 126
Ritzer, G., 262
Roehling, Patricia V., 232

Roiphe, Katie, 180
Rooks, Noliwe, 134, 150
Rose, Chloe Brushwood, 76
Rosh Chodesh, 305
Ross, Luana, 98
Rousseau, Jean-Jacques, 4, 89
Rowan, Ruby, 80
Royal Commission on the Status of
    Women (1970) (RCSW), 9–10, 11,
    21, 230, 250, 261
Rubin, Gayle, 111, 112, 113, 114, 115,
    116, 123, 128
Rubinstein, Helena, 134
Rudy, Kathy, 303
Rumack, Leah, 76, 81
Rundle, Bryn, 66
Rush, Florence, 163
Russell, Diana, 162, 171

S

sadomasochism, 119
SAGE. *See* Standing Against Global
    Exploitation (SAGE)
Salaam Canada, 314
same-sex marriage, 121
Sandell, Jillian, 77
Sandler, Bernice, 260
Sanger, Margaret, 274
SAPs. *See* structural adjustment programs
    (SAPs)
Sayer, Aline G., 230
Sayer, Liana C., 229–230
Scott, Joan, 111
Scott, Ridley, 125
Scratching the Surface, 101
*Scream Quietly or the Neighbours Will
    Hear*, 170
Seaboyer case, 166
Search for the Next Pussy Cat Doll (tv
    series), 140
Second World War, 6, 9
second-wave feminism, 90
    ageism and, 198
    feminist project and, 181
    homophobia and, 115
    rape analysis, 164
    sexuality and, 110

violence against women and, 161,
    175
wife battering and, 170
Sedgwick, Eve Kosofsky, 121
sex,
    gender and, 13–14
    labour, 68
    negativity, 112
    oppression, 22
    theories, 112–114
    tourism, 27–28
    trafficking, 28
Sex and the City (tv series), 71
sex wars, 112–115, 117–120
sex/gender system, 120
Sexism and God-Talk, 301
sexual abuse, 162–164
    child, 163–164
    global, 163
    media and, 164
    patriarchy and, 163
sexual harassment, 174
    global, 174
sexuality, 1, 110
    aging and, 211
    as experience, 110–111
    dangers, 117
    definition, 116–117
    empowerment, 80–82
    gendered education and, 254–255
    theories, 112–114
Shaw, Margaret, 99
She Bang!, 73
She Who Dwells Within, 308
Siegel, Deborah, 70
Silenced, 92
Silvera, Makeda, 92
Sinclair, Roberta Lynn, 99
Sinding, Steven W., 291
Sinister Wisdom journal, 303, 308
Skelton, C., 253
skin whitening, 147–149
Smith, D., 251
Smith, Sarah, 80
social capital, 285–286
Social Darwinism, 8
social policies, 237

social status, 282–283
social support,
    for ethnically diverse families, 235
    for families, 234–235
socialist feminism, 13–14, 15–16
    contemporary, 19
    critiques of, 21
    definition, 12–13
    equality of opportunity, 221
    exploitation and, 221–222
    global trends and, 20
    history, 13–14
    labour in home and, 16–17
    poverty and, 17–19
    violence against women and, 175
Sommers, Christina, 180
Sontag, Susan, 210
Spender, Dale, 46
Spice Girls, 71
spousal abuse, 167–168
St. John, Michelle, 72
stalking, 171–172
Standing Again at Sinai, 307
Standing Against Global Exploitation
    (SAGE), 28
Starhawk (*née* Miriam Simos), 317
Stasko, Carly, 71
state, 22
Statistics Canada, 10, 26, 163
    General Social Survey, 167
    low income cut-off (LICO), 94, 201,
        225, 231, 282
Status of Women Canada, 11
Stevenson, Winona, 91
Stewart, P., 258
Stone, Merlin, 314
Stowe, Dr. Emily Howard, 7
Strange, Carolyn, 170
structural adjustment programs (SAPs),
    20
Subcultures Reader, The, 64
Subjection of Women, The, 5
suffrage, women's, 3, 7–8
Super Hero, 124, 127–128
Supreme Court of Canada, 5, 26, 30,
    166, 168, 174
Survivor Project, 78

Swope, Heather E., 232
synthesis, 70
Szold, Henrietta, 304

T
Taste This collective, 120, 123, 126
TEACH. *See* Teens Educating and
    Challenging Homophobia (TEACH)
Teens Educating and Challenging
    Homophobia (TEACH), 67
Tequila, Tila, 63
Terminator (movie), 126
That's So Raven (tv series), 140
Thelma and Louise (movie), 125, 127
*Theorizing Empowerment: Canadian
    Perspectives on Black Feminist
    Thought*, 101
*Thinking Through: Essays on Feminism,
    Marxism, and Anti-Racism*, 101
Third Wave Agenda, 64
third-wave agenda, 77
third-wave feminism, 63
    bodies and, 73–74
    characteristics, 65–66
    critiques of, 180–182
    culture production, 71, 73
    definition, 63–64
    distinctions, 65
    fat activism and, 75
    femininity, 75–77
    gender roles and, 77
    legal strategies, 67
    origins, 64–65
    personal choices, 68
    personal narratives, 68–70
    pornography and, 68
    queer and, 122–123
    racism and, 92–94
    sex work and, 68
    sexual empowerment and, 80–82
    tactics, 66–67
    transgender politics and, 78–79
    violence against women and, 177–180
    whiteness and, 101–102
    zines and, 70
Thistle, Susan, 20
Thomas, Calvin, 123

Thorton, Sarah,   64
Thurman, Uma,   126
To Be Real: Telling the Truth and Changing the Face of Feminism,   69, 70
Tobique Women's Group of New Brunswick,   5
Tomes, Nancy,   170
Toronto Environmental Alliance,   95
Toronto New Feminists,   314
Toronto Street Health Report (1992),   178
Toronto Women's Literary Club,   7
transgender politics,   78–79
transsexuality,   29–30
Trudeau, Pierre Elliott,   143
Tubman, Harriet,   8
Turbo Chicks: Talking Young Feminisms,   66, 69, 71, 76, 80
Turcotte, Shirley,   164
Turtle Gals,   72–73
Tuten, Tracy L.,   232
Two Axe Early, Mary,   5

U
UI. *See* Unemployment Insurance (UI) Act
Umansky, Ellen,   305
Unemployment Insurance (UI) Act,   238
UNESCO. *See* United Nations Educational, Scientific and Cultural Organization (UNESCO)
UNESCO Trafficking Statistics Project,   28
United Nations Educational, Scientific and Cultural Organization (UNESCO),   28
United Nations Human Rights Committee,   5
Université de Montreal,   260
University of British Columbia,   260
University of Guelph,   260
University of Montreal,   183
University of Toronto,   260, 301
University of Waterloo,   260
University of Western Ontario,   260

V
Vagina Monologues, The,   24
Valentine, Gill,   173

Vance, Carol,   112, 117, 119
Vancouver International Burlesque Festival,   68
Vancouver Rape Relief and Women's Shelter,   30
Vanier Correctional Centre for Women,   99
Venus Envy, Halifax,   81
victimization,   29
Vindication of the Rights of Woman, A,   4, 89
violence against women,   22, 96–98, 260, 278–279
  see also femicide; rape; sexual abuse; stalking
  age and,   179
  cycle,   168
  definition,   162
  dimensions of,   161
  family,   162
  in Canada,   167–169
  in public,   173
  lesbians and,   179
  patriarchy and,   170
  second-wave feminism and,   175
  socialist feminists and,   175
  state,   96–98
  symbolic,   124–125
  third-wave feminism and,   177–180
visible minorities,   88
  education and,   256
Vogue magazine,   135

W
wage inequality,   224
Walker, Alice,   302
Walker, Lenore,   168
Walker, Madame C. J.,   134–135
Wall Street Journal,   250
Warner, Michael,   54, 121
Warner, Tom,   54
WCTU. *See* Women's Christian Temperance Union (WCTU)
We Don't Need Another Wave: Dispatches from the Next Generation of Feminists,   69
Webster's Dictionary,   298

Weedon, Chris,   42, 43, 51, 53
Weedon, Kim A.,   234
Weeks, Jeffrey,   115
Wendell, S.,   211
When Chickenheads Come Home to Roost: A Hip Hop Feminist Breaks It Down,   77
When God Was a Woman,   314
WHISPER. *See* Women Hurt in Systems of Prostitution Engaged in Revolt (WHISPER)
White, Jerry,   225
White Ribbon Campaign,   183
white-middle-class feminism,   102
whiteness,   101–102
   education and,   102–103
WHO. *See* World Health Organization (WHO)
Wickenheiser, Hailey,   63
widowhood,   203
wife battering,   170
Wife Battering in Canada: The Vicious Circle,   170
Wife Beaters Act (1882),   170
Wilchins, Riki Anne,   78
Wilson, Gail,   284
Wilson, Robert,   275
Wise, Isaac Meyer,   304
Wollstonecraft, Mary,   4, 89
womanist theology,   302–303
   principles,   302–303
Women Against Pornography,   26
Women Hurt in Systems of Prostitution Engaged in Revolt (WHISPER),   28
Women in Canada Report,   18
Women's Christian Temperance Union (WCTU),   7, 8

Women's Health Study (2004),   280
Women's Legal Education and Action Fund (LEAF),   27, 290
women's shelters,   169
women's studies,   260–261
Wong, Christina Sheryl,   81
Woodward, Kathleen,   199
workforce,
   strategies for overcoming conflict in,   233
   women in,   226–228
World Conference on Women (Nairobi, 1985),   283
World Health Organization (WHO),   277, 282
World Rio Corporation,   150

X
X-Files (tv series),   126

Y
Yentl's Revenge: Young Jewish Women Write About Today's Feminism,   69
Yllo, Kersti,   176
York Stories: Women in Higher Education,   260
York University,   260
Young, D'bi,   63
Young Women's Christian Association (YWCA),   7
YWCA. *See* Young Women's Christian Association (YWCA)

Z
Zajicek, A. M.,   199
Zalewski, Marysia,   45
zine culture,   70